Handbook of Music Terms

by

Parks Grant

Professor of Music,
University of Mississippi

03899

The Scarecrow Press
Metuchen, N. J.   1967

Table of Contents

Preface

This book is a dictionary of music terms, addressed to the following:

(1) The student of music.

(2) The music teacher.

(3) The musical amateur, including the concert-goer and the high-fidelity enthusiast.

Since those in the third category cannot always be expected to read music, the constant objective has been to make definitions intelligible without the accompanying music quotations (where used). Naturally, with some terms this aim could not be fulfilled, but the number of such exceptions is very small.

The availability of several excellent music dictionaries and encyclopedias intended for the scholar, the music professor, and the musicologist points up the need for a book less advanced (though not too brief), intended for persons who make only a modest claim to musical knowledge.

This is perhaps more a handbook or reference book than a dictionary in the strictest sense. Its tone has been kept informal enough to permit occasional explanations of what a term does not mean (in addition to giving its actual significance), for often to clear up an erroneous concept is to go a long way in presenting the correct one. Here and there, attention is directed to incorrect spellings that sometimes find their way even into print, and to certain usages that, although found, are hardly to be recommended.

The inclusion of a few terms, such as the noun medium and the adjective secular, may strike some readers as superfluous, but thirty years' experience as a teacher of music leads the compiler to the belief that they (and certain other simple terms) ought not to be omitted. In two entries--harmonic series and intervals--there has been deliberate repetitiousness. These terms are not always

5

easy for everyone to understand, and meaningfulness is deemed the paramount purpose of a work of this type.

In nearly every entry, the basic definition appears in the first sentence (or at least the first two sentences). There are however a very few terms (e.g., fugue) in which it is impossible to follow this plan and still be truly informative.

The Guiding Philosophy. The compiler believes that it is more to the point to tell what a thing is than to give a formal capsule "definition" of the type characteristic of most dictionaries; hence one-sentence definitions have been replaced by longer explanations in those cases where the former do little or no good. Anyone curious to learn what a fugue is will not be enlightened in the least by a conventional one-sentence definition, for such a formulation is intelligible only to those who already know the significance of the word--and hence for whom no definition whatever is necessary.

The approach throughout is designed in a practical manner for the reader whose background is typically American. For example, the term a2 is entered at the point where one would find "A two," although a cross-reference entry appears under a due. We may be sure that anyone who knows that a2 stands for a due already knows the meaning of a2, and hence would not be looking it up in the first place. Similarly, 8va is entered where "eight-V-A" would appear, although there is a cross-reference entry under ottava. In addition, the piano and cello are described under those headings; the formal full names pianoforte and violoncello receive only cross-reference listings.

Although a musician once remarked that "If a lawyer were as careless in his terminology as the average musician, he would be disbarred," it is nevertheless clear that to be realistic we must come to grips with the terms that are used, even if only to point out the undesirability of certain ones. No dictionary can honestly ignore a living term simply because of widespread professional dislike for it, or because of its author's personal dislike for the term. Even the chance that listing certain questionable terms may encourage their perpetuation hardly constitutes grounds for exclusion.

Hence, if a term is used, and is reasonably common, it appears herein.

Length of Entries. It should not be assumed that the length of an entry is a direct measure of its importance. Some of the most basic terms can be defined quite briefly (for example, accompanist) and nothing is gained by padding them. On the other hand, some terms (such as figured bass) require considerable discussion if the definitions are to be really informative, and skimping was not deemed preferable to clarity.

With the further intention of being helpful, the author has hazarded the devotion of more space to the little-understood subject of the old natural horn than to the simpler subject of the modern horn, and almost as much space to the old natural trumpet as to the modern trumpet. Thus the uninitiated reader will understand the reason for the limited scope of the horn and trumpet parts in orchestral works of Haydn, Mozart, Beethoven, Schubert, Weber, Mendelssohn, and many others (and some horn parts even in early Wagner). Such meaningful discussions seem far more to the point than trying to imply the relative importance of terms through the number of lines devoted to each.

Cross-References have been made in profusion, for surely no frustration is greater than knowing that certain information is contained in a volume, yet being unable to locate it, simply because of inability to imagine where it occurred to the author to place it.

Synonyms are shown where they exist. The reader should at all times bear in mind that a synonym may have almost (but not quite) the same meaning as the given word, as well as exactly the same meaning.

Antonyms are also shown where appropriate, since the significance of certain terms can be brought into sharper focus by pointing out their opposite.

Variant Spellings and Variant Words are shown where they exist. It is, however, quite impossible to list all the variants that arise from the grammatical peculiarities of various languages, or to enter into detailed discussion of the rules that bring them about (e.g., the circumstances under which molto is contracted to molt',

7

poco to po', etc.).

German ä, ö, and ü are sometimes written as ae, oe, and ue, respectively, and the reader should be prepared to encounter additional variants spelled in this fashion (Floete instead of Flöte, Fluegelhorn instead of Flügelhorn, etc.). For alphabetizing purposes, ä, ö, and ü are here considered simply as a, o, and u.

In English there are a number of music terms that can be written quite correctly as two words, as one word, or hyphenated; for example the following all enjoy good usage:

<pre>
folk song.........folksong.........folk-song
concert master....concertmaster... concert-master
contra bass....... contrabass...... contra-bass
</pre>

The compiler wishes to state specifically that he does not intend his usage to be regarded as the "best" or above all as the one-and-only "correct" form.

Additional Variants. Certain Italian terms that usually appear as past participles are occasionally used in the present participle or infinitive form. For example sostenente (literally "sustaining") or sostenere (literally "to sustain") may appear in place of the more familiar sostenuto ("sustained"). On the other hand, with a few words the present and past participles are by no means synonyms. Clearly, animato ("animated") does not mean the same thing as animando ("becoming animated").

The accompanying table shows the infinitive, present participle, and past participle endings of Italian verbs. The reader should bear in mind that there are three conjugations, the -are, the -ere, and the -ire, and that like most languages, Italian has its share of irregular verbs which may or may not present exceptions to the forms given in the table.

INFINITIVE	PRESENT PARTICIPLE	PAST PARTICIPLE
-are	-ando or -ante	-ato
-ere	-endo or -ente	-uto
-ire	-endo or -ente	-ito

Terms with Several Meanings. A number of music terms have more than one meaning. With a few exceptions, an effort has been made to place the most common meaning first. (It usually is that of the present day.) Surely the adopted plan is preferable to employing historical order, an arrangement that all too often rele-' gates the present usage to last place. The adopted procedure is well exemplified in the entry sonata, where the commonest (and first defined) meaning also happens to be the newest.

There are a few entries, however, in which an exception is made, chiefly to preserve the thread of thought more clearly as one definition follows another. An instance will be found in the entry intermezzo. The meaning used by Brahms, undoubtedly frequent, is placed last, since it is for all practical purposes merely a catch-all title; what little significance it does possess is dependent on the other and more legitimate definitions.

Foreign Plurals are given only when deemed necessary. Hence the plural of Italian and German terms is shown, though not of French and Spanish, since most words in the latter two languages pluralize as do most English words: by adding s. (Exceptions are of course noted.) Italian and German plurals are not however mentioned for words normally used only in the singular.

Pronunciation has been indicated for terms from foreign languages other than Italian, and for those English terms about which there might be some uncertainty. (See page 21 for the key to the symbols employed.) This information always appears at the end of the entry, where it will stand out, since readers will some- times have occasion to look up pronunciation rather than meaning.

The pronunciation of Latin terms is not always given, since even Latin scholars disagree as to the mode of speaking that lan- guage, and since several pronunciations are usually acceptable. (Musicians usually seem to prefer the "Church Latin" style.)

In view of the large number of music terms that are pure Italian words, it has been thought advisable to give virtually- complete rules for the pronunciation of that tongue (pages 17-20). All terms preceded by a dagger (†) are pronounced according

9

to those rules.

The way a musician pronounces Italian music terms is modeled on, but hardly identical to, the diction of a native of Italy. Such words as allegro, concerto, sonata, and timpani are usually spoken "more or less" as in Italian, rather than "exactly" so. One need point only to the pronunciation of the letter R--rarely trilled by the English-speaking musician, but invariably trilled in the speech of Italians. The reader should bear in mind that a few pure Italian words--for example cadenza, piano, piccolo, and sonatina--are always anglicized.

Related English Words (Cognate Words). The learning of certain Italian music terms can be simplified by keeping in mind the English word derived from the same root, even though the meaning itself is different. Thus molto, "much," "very," is quickly learned when one realizes it comes from the same root as English "multitude" and "multiply." The same goes for the relation of meno ("less") to "minus," of crescendo ("gradually getting louder") to "increase." On the other hand, this cognate relationship is not pointed out if there is reason to believe it might not be helpful (e.g., the relation of tessitura to "texture").

Capitalized Words. The word to be defined begins with a capital only if it is incorrect when written as lower-case. Hence proper nouns (e.g., Cremona) and German common nouns (e.g., Augenmusik) will be found capitalized among the entries, but all other terms will use a lower-case initial.

Terms Exclusive to This Dictionary. This book lists between 250 and 260 words which the compiler has been unable to find in any other music dictionary. Only a few are recently coined. None are rare; many are indeed among the commonest expressions used in music, for example balance, block chords, ¢ , concert ending, cross-hand, "cut time," directing, first and second endings, four hands, half voice, mixed quartet, musicianship, octavo, open tones, piano-vocal copy, thumb hole, SAB, SSA, TTBB, theorist, high voice, medium voice, low voice, and innumerable others. The information itself doubtless appears in the fourteen other music dictionaries that were consulted, but not under the heading used here--which seems the most likely place for the reader to look for it.

Invented Terms. Since the fundamental purpose of a dictionary is surely to explain terms in actual use, rather than to manufacture new ones, there are only two entries devoted to invented terms-- irregular groupings and sonata-types (and it is by no means impossible that even these have already been used elsewhere). Their employment saves many words in other entries. In addition the expression "Scandinavian form" in connection with the minor mode, "pseudo opus numbers" as used in the entry opus numbers, "primary," "secondary," and "rare" in referring to orchestral instruments, and the half-jocular "Russian method" in the discussion of bass clarinet notation are also possibly inventions of the compiler. But it is believed that there are no others.

A few terms--beat note, crush notes, dead interval, duetting, false octaves--may be unfamiliar to some musicians, but they are in no sense neologisms; all have been observed in use.

Just as a dictionary should rarely if ever invent new terms, it likewise should not strive for sweeping reforms in terminology, as distinguished from pointing out genuinely incorrect or dubious usages. The futility of trying to force terminological reform by decree is pointed up by a relatively little-known event in American music history which might well be mentioned here. In 1906, the Music Division of the National Education Association took it upon itself to empower a terminology committee to make drastic reforms which it apparently believed could be forced upon all musicians in the country. In 1909 this committee delivered itself of the edict that thenceforth the expression "6-8 time" was to become "two-dotted quarter measure." The fact that the new term (and others recommended by the committee) died then and there, more than a half-century ago, eloquently points up the ridiculousness and utter vanity of such attempts.

The assumption throughout this book is that correct music terminology is that which is used by good musicians in careful speech.

11

Music Quotations and References are usually from familiar, even homely, compositions. A music reference, no matter how beautifully or characteristically it illustrates the effect under discussion, might fail to make the intended point if the source composition is little known. Although this dictionary is the work of one who uncompromisingly believes that the most familiar music is by no means all that is worth acquaintance, he is also confident that the sympathetic reader will understand the reason for the policy adopted.

Ranges of Instruments and Voices. The reader should always understand that the most skillful players can extend the range of every string, woodwind, and brass instrument a bit higher than shown herein, and that in a few cases (for instance the horn, trombone, and tuba) a virtuoso player can also extend it lower. The ranges given are those that can be expected of the typical symphony orchestra member. In addition one should bear in mind that ranges have tended to expand as the instruments themselves were perfected and as their players' technique developed. In older compositions ranges will often be found more restricted than shown here.

Given voice ranges can normally be exceeded on both the low and high sides by artist singers. Voice ranges obviously vary widely from one individual to another.

Organ Stops. With a few exceptions, the names of the various organ stops--clarabella, salicional, Rohr flute, bourdon, etc.--are not placed among the definitions. An extensive list of stops will however be found in the entry organ.

Biographical Material. Since this is a terminological dictionary, rather than biographical, information about the lives of musicians is never given. For an up-to-date and reliable biographical dictionary, the reader can without hesitation be referred to Baker's Biographical Dictionary of Musicians, 1965 edition (compiled by Nicolas Slonimsky), published by G. Schirmer, New York.

Words Not Included. Since the present volume is intended to be compact and practical, rather than exhaustive, certain terms could not be included or were deemed unnecessary for inclusion. Some of the omitted terms have been given room in nearly all the dictionaries of the past, despite the fact that references to them are practically never encountered in living usage and despite the fact that no musician really need be familiar with them. No space is wasted here in discussing nail violin, octo-bass, or certain other terms whose existence is almost completely confined to dictionaries.

In brief, the words included are those whose meaning every musician and serious music student should know or would be likely to want to look up, and those which authors of books assume are familiar to the reader.

Definitions purposely omitted are of:

(1) Terms rarely employed.

(2) Terms used only by advanced scholars.

(3) Terms employed almost exclusively in connection with certain limited branches of music, and which are usually explained in books concerned with them, rather than assumed to be already familiar. Examples are Ars Antiqua, Ars Nova, bariolage, caccia, conductus, coup d'archet, flam, hocket, Nuove Musiche, trope, and of course a number of others.

(4) Titles of specific compositions and books, names of organizations, theaters, musical societies, etc. (Exceptions have been made in the case of Bach-Gesellschaft, Bayreuth, B & H, Carnegie Hall, Covent Garden, Cremona, The "Five," Gewandhaus, La Scala, Liber Usualis, Mannheim Group, The "Met," Prix de Rome, The "Six," "Strad," Tin Pan Alley, Town Hall, and Victrola.)

(5) French and German terms pertaining to tempo and manner of performance. Unlike the standard Italian terms, those used by French- and German-speaking composers seem to embrace virtually each complete language rather than to be drawn from a relatively compact "stockpile." Anyone who has examined a work by Debussy, Richard Strauss, or Mahler will acknowledge the utter impossibility of listing all the expressions these composers used, not to mention their fellow-countrymen. No music dictionary can supplant the need for owning a French-English and a German-English dictionary.

(6) Adverbial forms of Italian adjectives. These have not been listed (with a few exceptions) for reasons of space, nor are they necessary. The Italian adverbial suffix -mente is given; it

13

corresponds to the English suffix -ly. Hence it should be apparent that giocosamente, briosamente, pesantemente, etc., are the adverb forms of the defined adjectives giocoso, brioso, pesante, etc. The reader should remember that in Italian, adjectives are often used where in English we employ adverbs (that is, it is permissible for an Italian adjective to modify a verb or another adjective). Thus it is entirely correct to give such directions as leggiero ("light"), or grazioso ("graceful") where correct English usage would require lightly or gracefully. Nevertheless, the use of adverbs is by no means wrong in Italian. Reference to a grammar of that language shows that most adjectives are converted into adverbs according to the following rules (to which there are of course a few exceptions): (A) If the adjective ends in -o (feminine form in -a), use the feminine (-a) form and add -mente; thus: adjective grazioso, adverb graziosamente. (Bear in mind that when the simple adjective direction is given, the masculine or -o form is usual.) (B) If the adjective ends in -e (but not -le preceded by a vowel or -re preceded by a vowel), simply add -mente; thus: adjective pesante, adverb pesantemente. (C) If the adjective ends in -le preceded by a vowel or -re preceded by a vowel, drop the -e and add -mente to the stem; thus: adjective facile, adverb facilmente. In the adverbial form the stress is invariably on the syllable -men-.

(7) Perhaps it would be well to mention that the word music itself is not defined. If the reader does not already know its meaning--and he does--a thousand pages will not enlighten him. Such definitions as "Music is a fine art in which thought and emotion are expressed by a succession or combination of sounds called tones" strike the compiler as prissy and irrelevant.

14

Acknowledgements

I wish to make grateful acknowledgement to the Harvard University Press, Cambridge, Mass., for permission to quote from the Harvard Dictionary of Music by Willi Apel in the entry development, and to the following organizations to make certain music quotations:

American Composers Alliance (Composers Facsimile Edition), New York, N. Y.
Belmont Music Publishers, Los Angeles, Calif.
Elkan-Vogel Co., of Philadelphia, Pa.

I also want to express gratitude for various pieces of information contributed by the following persons:

Canadian Consulate General, New Orleans, La.
Cecil Effinger, President, Music Print Corporation, Denver, Colo.
Mr. Arthur Fisher, Register of Copyrights, Copyright Office, Library of Congress, Washington, D. C.
Mr. and Mrs. Michael Giamo, Plymouth (Philadelphia), Pa.
Dr. Benjamin I. Harrison, University of Mississippi.
Mr. Richard Hoffman, Oberlin College.
Dr. Archie Jones, Kansas City Conservatory of Music.
Keaton Music Typewriter Co., San Francisco, Calif.
Miss Heidi Kern, Mainz, West Germany.
Mr. Thomas Konok, San Francisco, Calif. (formerly of Budapest, Hungary).
Mr. Albert T. Luper, State University of Iowa.
Dr. William Presser, University of Southern Mississippi.
Secrétariat d'État aux Forces Armées (Terre), République Française, Vincennes, France.
Mr. Maurice Ben Stad, Philadelphia, Pa.
Dr. Burnet C. Tuthill, Memphis, Tenn.
Mr. Philip B. Wattenberg, Music Publishers' Protective Association, New York, N. Y.

William Parks Grant

Rules for the Pronunciation of Italian

Since many music terms are pure Italian words, it is advisable to give nearly-complete rules ιfor the pronunciation of that language.

It must at all times be understood that the comparison of Italian sounds with English is only approximate, the proper "accent" in any language being something which can be learned only through hearing.

For explanation of the diacritical marks in the right-hand column, see Key to Pronunciation on page 21.

LETTER	SOUND	ENGLISH EQUIVALENT
a	Always as in <u>a</u>h<u>a</u> (never as in Florid<u>a</u>).	ă
ai	Theoretically both letters are pronounced separately, but sound tends to approach that heard in English <u>ai</u>sle.	ăē, almost I
au	Theoretically both letters are pronounced separately, but sound tends to approach that heard in sa<u>u</u>erkr<u>au</u>t.	ă͞oo, almost ou
b	As in English.	
c	Before <u>e</u> or <u>i</u>, like <u>ch</u> in chur<u>ch</u>.	ch
c	In all other uses, as in <u>c</u>at.	k
cc	Before <u>e</u> and <u>i</u>, like <u>t-ch</u> in at <u>ch</u>urch. In all other uses, like <u>kk</u> in boo<u>kk</u>eeper.	tch
ch	As in or<u>ch</u>estra and <u>ch</u>orus.	k
ci	When in an unstressed syllable and followed by a vowel, like <u>ch</u> in <u>ch</u>ur<u>ch</u>.	ch
d	As in English.	
e	Sometimes as in caf<u>é</u>, sometimes as in m<u>e</u>t; the ear will usually tell which.	ā, ĕ
f	As in English.	

17

LETTER	SOUND	ENGLISH EQUIVALENT
g	Before e or i, as in gem and giant	j
g	In all other uses, as in go.	
gg	Before e or i, like d-j in mid-journey. In all other uses, as in big game.	dj
gh	As in ghost.	g
gi	When in an unstressed syllable and followed by a vowel, like j in jump.	j
gl	Usually like lli in million. Occasionally, however, it sounds as in glass, the term glissando being an example.	ly
gli	When followed by a vowel, like lli in million.	ly
gn	Like ni in onion and ny in canyon.	ny
gu	When followed by a vowel, as in language.	gw
h	Always silent.	
i	When in an unstressed syllable and followed by a vowel, like y in yard.	y
i	In all other uses, always as in machine and police (never as in bit). The sound of i when found in the combinations ci, gi, gli, and sci is explained above and below.	ē
l	As in English.	
m	As in English.	
n	When followed by c or g, as in uncle and sing.	ng or ŋ
n	In all other uses, as in not.	
o	Sometimes as in old, sometimes as in often; the ear will usually tell which.	ō, ǒ
p	As in English.	
q	Always followed by u, which in turn is always followed by a vowel and sounds as in quality and quick.	k (w)
r	Always trilled.	
s	When occurring as the first letter of a word and followed by a consonant, as in nose.	z

18

LETTER	SOUND	ENGLISH EQUIVALENT
s	When occurring between two vowels, often as in nose; however in certain parts of Italy it would be pronounced as in so.	z or s
s	In all other uses, as in so.	
sc	When followed by e or i, like sh in shall.	sh
sch	As in school.	sk
sci	When followed by a, o, or u, like sh in shall.	sh
t	As in English.	
u	When unaccented and followed by another vowel, as in language and quick.	w
u	In all other uses, as in rule (never as in run, push, or unite).	ōō
v	As in English.	
z	Usually like ts in bets, sometimes like ds in beds.	ts (dz)
zz	Usually like ds in beds, sometimes like ts in bets.	dz (ts)

J is regarded as a variant form of i and is pronounced like y in yard. It has gone out of use in present-day Italian; its employment is regarded as antiquated or affected.

It will be noted that k, w, x, and y are not part of the Italian alphabet; they are used only in a few words taken bodily from other languages.

The presence of an apostrophe never interrupts the sound. Thus d'amore and l'istesso are pronounced exactly as if written damore and listesso.

It is important to mention that all doubled consonants are actually pronounced twice in Italian; thus the proper name Giovanni is pronounced jō-vän⁼nē, not jō-vän⁼ē or jō-vä⁼nē. Italian ll, mm, nn, rr, and ss might well be modeled after English illegal, immodest, unnecessary, irrational, and misspell.

Stress (Accent). The stress in Italian usually falls on the next-to-last syllable, and is to be understood as occurring thus in

19

all Italian terms found in this dictionary, with the following exceptions:

(1) Words ending in -issimo (and -issima)--including the familiar fortissimo and pianissimo--in which case it falls on the third syllable from the end (i. e., on -iss-).

(2) Where otherwise specified. The majority of these cases will be found among three-syllable words, many (but by no means all) of which are stressed on the first syllable.

The only mark regularly placed over letters in Italian is the grave accent (`) which has no effect on the pronunciation of the letter so marked, though it does indicate that the syllable in question is stressed.

It might be well to mention that Italian singular nouns ending in a form the plural by substituting e; and that singulars ending in e or o form the plural by substituting i. (There are of course a few exceptions.) The majority of Italian words end in a vowel, most commonly a, e, i, or o.

The reader will probably not be surprised to learn that the Italian usage of many non-Italian composers, including some of the greatest, is grammatically faulty, or at least questionable or unidiomatic. Hence a direction cannot automatically be assumed correct simply because Mozart or Beethoven used it. In addition, even the youngest contemporary non-Italian composers may take expressions used in compositions written during say the eighteenth century, little realizing that they are at present obsolete. This accounts for the fact that musicians still continue to spell the word for "joyful" as giojoso rather than gioioso, to spell the word for "lightly" as leggiero rather than leggero, and to write the expression for "with the voice" as colla voce rather than con la voce.

On the other hand, just as we comprehend the foreigner who says "Me no have saw he" rather than "I have not seen him," so do musicians comprehend the frequently imperfect Italian of composers. As long as the composer's intentions are clear, grammatical slips are perhaps a secondary consideration.

If a term is preceded by a dagger (†) it is pronounced in accordance with the foregoing rules.

20

Key to Pronunciation

ā as in ale

a̱ as in senate

â as in care

ă as in add

a̱ as in account

ä as in arm

a̒ as in ask

a̱ as in sofa

ē as in eve

e̱ as in event

ĕ as in end

e̱ as in patent

ẽ as in maker

ī as in ice

ĭ as in ill

ō as in old

o̱ as in obey

ô as in orb

ŏ as in odd

ᴕ as in soft

o̱ as in connect

ö as in German schön or eu
in French feu

ū as in use

u̱ as in unite

û as in urn

ŭ as in up

u̱ as in circus

oo as in food

oŏ as in foot

ou as in out

oi as in oil

ŋ as in ink

t̶h̶ as in then

th as in thin

tu̯ as in nature

du̯ as in verdure

ü as in French lune or
German über

k̲ as in German ich

n̲ as in French bon

y as in yet

zh as z in azure

21

To pronounce the vowel-sound heard in French lune and German über, represented here by ü, round the lips as if to pronounce o͞o, but instead say e̅.

To pronounce the vowel-sound heard in German schön and French feu, represented here by ŏ, round the lips as if to pronounce o͞o, but instead say a̅.

The German ch, as heard in ich, represented here by k̲, is best modeled after the sound of h in human or hue when those words are whispered.

In regard to the French nasal sounds, represented here by n̲: There is a widespread myth among Americans--propagated with especial enthusiasm by musicians--to the effect that French nasals sound "almost like 'ng'." This is a long way from the truth. It would be more accurate to describe the French nasals as silent, but to point out that they impart a special quality to the vowel which invariably precedes. In speaking such vowels, let the soft palate hang freely and allow the breath to escape through the nose. Do not actually sound the letter, which is always n̲ or m̲; get ready for an ng sound but do not complete it. Any person who has used the American expression uh-huh has already used the nasal sound; it terminates both syllables. By no means is every French n̲ a nasal sound; often it is pronounced as in English noon.

Another myth in regard to French pronunciation is the notion that all French words are stressed on the last syllable. It is more to the point to imagine that there is no stress on any syllable in French; the attempt to pronounce all syllables evenly will produce the slightest trace of a stress on the final syllable--which is just the right amount. Accent marks in French have no effect on stress; they affect the sound of the e̲ so marked.

Notes

NOTE 1.   The insertion of an asterisk (*) indicates that
the word so marked is defined elsewhere, and if its meaning is
not known, it should be consulted.

NOTE 2.   A numeral after a cross-reference--(1), (2), etc.--
indicates the number of the definition; these are used in the case
of terms that have more than one meaning.

A

● †a. To, at, in, for, by. Thus: a
tempo, in *tempo; poco a poco
cresc., getting louder little by little;
a piacere, at pleasure.

A composition written for six voice-
parts or six instruments is sometimes described as being a 6, one
for four instruments or voice-parts
as a 4, etc.

For explanation of a 2 in orchestra
*scores, see the entry a 2.

Variant forms: à, ad.

● †abbastanza. Enough, sufficiently.

● absolute music. Music that does
not "tell a story" or have any descriptive intent.

Synonyms: pure music, abstract
music.

Antonym: program music.

● absolute pitch. The ability to identify any musical tone merely by hearing it, and without comparison to any
previously sounded pitch.

The subject of absolute pitch has
been surrounded by a halo of nonsense. It is by no means a mystic
"gift"; on the contrary, it is distinctly developed. Doubtless many
more people are capable of acquiring
it than have actually done so.

This skill is not without a few
disadvantages; it can be something
of a handicap in playing a *transposing instrument. However, its advantages greatly outweigh the drawbacks.

Synonyms: perfect pitch, pitch recognition.

Compare relative pitch.

See also ear-training.

● abstract music. See absolute music
and neo-classical.

● †a cappella. Usual significance is
"without instrumental accompaniment" (used in reference to choral
singing). The literal meaning is
"in chapel style."

A great amount of misinformation
is circulated regarding a cappella
singing during the era preceding the
seventeenth century. Many musicians
have assumed that since practically

all the older music was nominally
written only for voices, it was
therefore sung unaccompanied.
Musicologists doubt this, for there
is good reason to believe that it
was customary to *double (1) each
voice-part with an instrument — any
instrument that had the requisite
*range. There is certainly no rea-
son to assume that the singers of
earlier times excelled those of today in ability to stay on pitch. It
is also definitely known that during
earlier times, if any voice happened
to be missing, an instrument was
pressed into service to replace it;
in fact, performances entirely by
instruments were by no means unknown. There are many paintings
from the sixteenth and earlier centuries showing musicians, nearly all
including instrumentalists as well as
singers. Some musicologists have
even gone so far as to assert that
unaccompanied choral singing was
unknown until the early seventeenth
century, when composers began to
write works including both voices
and instruments (separate parts for
each group) and containing some
passages during which the instruments were completely silent.

The purity of a cappella or unaccompanied singing is however undeniably a joy to the ear, and any
choral organization capable of it
will most likely sing unaccompanied
in those works which do not require
instruments. (On the other hand,
to omit the instruments in compositions which do require them, such
as most *oratorios and *cantatas,
is nothing short of a musical crime.)

Choral conductors' assertions that
their a cappella choirs sing in *just
intonation should, however, be taken
with a grain of salt.

Briefly, the definition "without
independent instrumental accompaniment" might be more accurate than
the usual definition.

(The spelling a capella is incorrect.)

● †accelerando. Gradually becoming
faster.

25

This term is properly canceled by *a tempo (which indicates an immediate return to the basic *tempo). However it is occasionally carelessly canceled by *rit. or *rall., which should be used only if the pace actually slows down (gradually) to the point where it becomes slower than the basic tempo. (This effect will of course require a tempo as cancellation.)

Thus:

Basic tempo   *accel.*   *a tempo*   Basic tempo   *accel.*   *rit.*   *a tempo*

the most obvious type and is indicated by *sforzando (sf, sfz, fz) or by the symbols > and ∧

Metric accent is the grouping into "strong" and "weak" that is observed in a steady pulsation of beats. This phenomenon is brought about by the fact that the human mind will not accept infinity; a steady succession of sounds of equal length (such as raindrops falling or the throb of a motor) will appear to the mind to

Abbreviations: accel., acceler., occasionally acc.

Synonyms: stringendo, affrettando.

Antonyms: rallentando, ritardando.

● accent. The effect of some tones seeming to be more stressed than others.

Accent by no means always indicates greater loudness. There are several types of accent: dynamic, metric, agogic, and tonic. Strictly, only the first of these is concerned with loudness; the second may be, though not necessarily.

Dynamic accent is the emphasis observable in a tone or chord played louder than its mates: it is

be occurring in groups (usually of two, three, or four) of which the first seems "stronger" than the others; indeed the first seems to generate the others of the group like rebounds. The metric accent that underlies nearly all music is expressed in the *time-signature placed at the beginning of a composition. (See beat, meter.)

Agogic accent is the emphasis due to the length of a tone; a long tone seems more conspicuous than a short one.

Tonic accent is the emphasis that results from height in pitch; that is, a high tone--especially one approached by a *leap--will seem to be more

M   M   M   T   M   A   M   D   M   A   M
     and A

accented than its neighbors. There is also an opposite of this: a sudden low tone, which seems accented in comparison to those that precede and follow.

The various types of accent are illustrated in the accompanying melody. M indicates metric accent; D, dynamic; A, agogic; and T, tonic.

See also sforzando and fp.

● †accentato. Accented.

● †accentuato. Accentuated, well brought out. Accentuato il canto is the equivalent of la melodia marcato.

● †acciaccatura. The ordinary short *grace-note.

● accidentals. A generic term used to indicate the various characters that temporarily alter the pitch of notes, that is, the *sharp, *flat, *natural, *double-sharp, and *double-flat. The term is not used in referring to the sharps or flats of a *key-signature.

Accidentals are placed in front of the notes they affect.

Theoretically an accidental remains in effect until a bar-line is reached (see A). In practice, however, a cancellation is generally written (perhaps enclosed in parentheses) when the affected note is restored in the following *measure (see B). Within the original measure a cancellation, if desired, must of course be written (see C). In extremely long measures modern composers sensibly re-state accidentals if there is likelihood that the performer may forget that one

still remains in effect (see D).
(Sometimes such a reminder accidental is placed <u>above</u> the note.)
When a note affected by an accidental is *tied over a bar-line, the
accidental may or may not be repeated in front of the second note
(see E).

When two or more notes in a
*chord are affected by the same
accidental, it is necessary to place
the character in front of each (see
F). When the notes in question
form the *interval of a second the
composer or engraver must use
great care, if only one of them is
affected, to place the accidental
squarely in front of the proper note
(see G).

Although certain books have stated
that an accidental in front of one
note will affect the notes of the
same letter name in the octave
above or below, that is absolutely
at variance with living practice (see
H). It is also untrue that in piano
notation an accidental on one staff
affects notes of the same letter
name on the other staff (see I).

In writing for two different voices
or instruments on one staff, repetition of the accidental is necessary,
though not in writing for keyboard
instruments nor in writing *double-
stops for string instruments (see J).

A double-sharp may be changed
to a single sharp either by means
of a sharp or by a natural followed

D and F♯   D♯ and F   D♯ and F♯   G and A♭   G♭ and A
                                                 (Easily confused)

Incorrect   Correct

Piano

This note is F ↑
If F♯ is desired a sharp must be used.

by a sharp, but not by a sharp followed by a natural (see K); a similar practice applies to changing a
note affected by a double-flat to a
single flat.

ilies" in an orchestral *score.
Synonym: brace.

● †accompagnamento. *Accompaniment. Often occurs in such form

For explanation of the sharps and
flats placed above notes (rather
than in front of them) found in old
choral music, see musica ficta.
Synonym: chromatics.

● accolade. A rarely-used but convenient term for the sign
usually employed to group
together the simultaneously-
sounding *staffs in writing for
*chamber-music and choral
*ensembles. It is also used to
group together the staffs of the woodwind, the brass, the string, and
sometimes the percussion "fam-

as melodia mf, accompagnamento p,
meaning "melody rather loud, accompaniment soft. "

● †accompagnando. Accompanying,
with subdued tone.
Abbreviation: accomp.
Synonym (approximate): sotto voce.

● †accompagnato. Accompanied. For
recitativo accompagnato see recitativo.

● accompaniment. Subordinate material that supports a more prominent element of the musical fabric,

← Accolade

such as the *melody.

When a melody is harmonized with purely subsidiary material, such as sustained *chords or quiet *arpeggios, this material might well be termed an accompaniment. The word however is often used carelessly. "Accompaniment," when applied to the orchestral part of a *concerto, the piano part of a *sonata for violin and piano, the orchestral part of certain *operas (notably those of Wagner), or even the piano part of many *art-songs, implies a subsidiary character that is far from accurate.

In general, the word is better avoided than used inadvisedly.

For additional accompaniments, see separate entry.

● accompaniment figure. A characteristic motive or design in notes, which persists through various changes of *harmony without losing its authentic shape, and with the listener conscious of its uninterrupted progress. It may or may not take the form of an *arpeggio. An accompaniment figure often runs through a composition like a mosaic,

● accompanist. An instrumentalist who performs with another artist, and whose mode of performance as to *tempo, *dynamics, *nuances, etc. is (theoretically, at least) dictated by this partner. His role is that of an assistant, indeed quite a willing assistant.

Variant form (rare): accompanyist.

● accord, †accordatura. See tuning (2).

● accordion. A portable instrument consisting of an expandable bellows connecting two flat boards, and usually equipped with a keyboard similar to that of the piano (hence called piano-accordion). The tone is produced by metal *reeds supplied with air from the bellows. Buttons mounted in the boards, not very accurately termed basses, supply complete *chords which can be used to accompany a *melody played on the keyboard.

Although the full resources of the instrument are quite remarkable, there is almost no serious literature for it.

The spellings accordian and accordeon are both incorrect.

Example of an accompaniment figure (in Schubert's song *Gretchen at the Spinning Wheel*).

etc.

giving it unity.

The accompaniment figure should not be confused with the much more intellectual *ostinato.

Synonym: figuration.

See also Alberti bass.

Compare concertina.

● acoustics. (1) The science of sounds, musical and otherwise; it is a branch of physics. H. L. F. von Helmholtz (1821-1894) made numerous important

investigations; see his On the Sensa-
tions of Tone. See also Tuning and
Temperament by J. Murray Barbour,
Acoustics by Wilmer T. Bartholomew,
Musical Acoustics by Charles A.
Culver, The Science of Musical
Sounds by Dayton Clarence Miller,
A Fugue in Cycles and Bels by
John Mills, and Music, a Science
and an Art by John Redfield.
   (2) An auditorium is said to have
"good acoustics" if music sounds
natural and carries well when played
there, "bad acoustics" if sounds
carry poorly (if for instance it is
difficult to hear well from certain
seats), or if the *tone-quality is
*distorted (too harsh or too dull),
or if there is too much echo. The
Academy of Music in Philadelphia,
the Mormon Tabernacle in Salt Lake
City, and Carnegie Hall in New
York are among the American audi-
toriums which are celebrated for
excellent acoustics.
   Pronunciation: ạ-kōo-stĭks, occasionally ạ-kou-stĭks.

● action. Name applied to the *mechanism of the *piano, *organ, *harp,
and *harpsichord.

● †adagietto. Quite slow. (Diminutive of *adagio.) (Rare.)

● †adagio. Very slow. (Literally,
"leisurely.") See tempo marks.

● †adagissimo. Extremely slow, as

slowly as possible. (Superlative
of *adagio.) (Rare.)

● adaptation. A *transcription (1)
(arrangement) in which there has
been a certain amount of liberty in
adjusting the *idiom of the original
*medium to that of the new; that is,
the transcription is not very "literal."
   Bach re-worked some of Vivaldi's
compositions in transcribed form,
but in such a way that the result
is closer to an "adaptation" than a
"transcription"--almost as much
Bach as Vivaldi.

● added lines. Same as leger lines.

● added sixth. A tone added to a
*triad, located a sixth (see inter-
vals) above its *root. Most musicians feel that its presence does
not disturb the identity of the chord
--that it is purely a supplementary
ingredient. Thus, the chords
marked with an asterisk (*) in the
accompanying example seem to
be the triad CEG with an extra and
purely decorative addition, rather
than first inversions of the *seventh-
chord ACEG.

● additional accompaniment. Instrumental material added to works for
chorus and orchestra (especially
*oratorios, *cantatas, and occasion-
ally *operas), supplied by an editor.
   When the added material takes the
form of substituting present-day

Added sixths

instruments for archaic ones (*viols,
*recorders, etc.) or when it gives
to certain instruments the notes that
result from *"realizing" a *figured
bass, the practice can doubtless be
considered legitimate. Unfortunately
the additional accompaniment sometimes turns out to be an attempt to
garb a work from the *Baroque or
*Classical era in the trappings of a
later style, such as grafting onto
it the lushness so characteristic of
(and appropriate to) the *Romantic
period. In other cases it produces
thickening in chords (by *doublings)
where the composer has clearly
wanted a thin, transparent texture;
or it may turn *triads into *seventh-
chords, or indulge in other harmonic
tampering. In these instances the
result is of course an artistic trav-
esty.

The best-known example of an
additional accompaniment is that
which Mozart supplied for Handel's
The Messiah.

For the definition of accompaniment, see that entry.
Compare Aufführungspraxis.

● ad lib., ad libitum (Latin). (1) An
indication that a certain instrument or
voice in a group may be omitted,
or that a certain section of a composition may be omitted.

(2) An instruction indicating that
something is optional, for example
repeat ad libitum, attacca ad libitum.

(3) To be performed in any manner
the performer chooses; a synonym for
*a piacere.

This term is almost always written
and spoken in its abbreviation form:
ad lib.

The use of ad libitum by enter-
tainers (not musicians) as a synonym
for improvise or make up as one
goes along--and mispronounced "add
lib"--is not correct in music.

Compare ossia, oppure.
Pronunciation: ăd lĭb'-ĭ-tōom.

● †a due. See a 2.

*After-beat (1)

*After-beats (2)

● Aeolian harp. See Eolian harp.

● †affetto. Affection, love, passion. Con affetto is a synonym for appassionato or amoroso, but without the agitated stir of the former.

● †affettuoso. Same as espressivo.

● †affrettando. Same as accelerando or stringendo.

● A-440. See 440.

● after-beat. (1) The notes written in grace-note type (usually two in number) at the end of a *trill. Whereas the trill has alternated the printed note with the note above, the after-beat makes use of the one below. The length of the tones in the after-beat is usually the same as that of the many individual tones in the trill.
(2) Weak beats, or weak halves of beats, spoken of in relation to stronger beats. Synonym: off-beat.

● †agilità. Agility, nimbleness. Pronunciation: accent last syllable.

● †agilmente. Nimbly, actively.

● †agitato. Agitated.

● agogic accent. See accent.

● air. (1) Same as *melody.
(2) The English equivalent of *aria. Oddly, it has been almost completely displaced by the foreign word.

● air with variations. Same as theme and variations.

● †al. To the, at the, in the. It is a contraction of a and il.

● Alberti bass. A type of figuration found in early music for the piano, during the *Rococo and (especially) *Classical periods. It is a form of *broken chord in which the notes (usually eighths or sixteenths) appear as a rule in groups of four in the order: lowest, highest, middle, highest. The term is derived, almost in ridicule, from the name of Domenico Alberti (c. 1717-1740), an unimportant composer whose compositions for piano are reputed to use the device to excess. The Alberti bass is often encountered in the piano music of Haydn, Mozart, Clementi, Kuhlau, and their contemporaries, but it is fairly rare in Beethoven, still more so in later composers, for the invention of the *damper pedal put a speedy end to its popularity.
See also accompaniment figure.

● album leaf. A catch-all title sometimes applied to short pieces, especially for piano. See titles. The French and German equivalents, feuille d'album and Albumblatt, respectively, are often used.

● †alcuna licenza. A little license, i.e., the *tempo not rigid or too strict; preceded by con, with.
See also tempo rubato, liberamente, a piacere, senza misura, senza rigore.

● aleatoric music, aleatory music. See chance music.

● aliquot tones. See harmonic series.

● †all', †alla. In the manner of, in the style of; at the, in the.
Alla marcia, in march style; alla

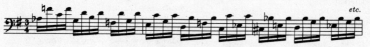

Alberti bass in a Piano Sonata by Mozart

zingarese, in gypsy style.
All' ottava (literally "at the octave") is a synonym for *8va.

● †alla breve. 2-2 time or ¢ Often alla breve also carries the suggestion of a fairly quick *tempo.
Synonym (colloquial): "cut time."

● †allargando. Becoming louder and slower; literally "broadening."
This term is the equivalent of *cresc. e *rit.
Variant forms: largando, slargando.

● †allegramente. Gaily, merrily.

● †allegretto. Slightly fast; the first term quicker than moderato, which signifies a medium *tempo. See tempo marks.
Abbreviation: all^{tto}.

● †allegrezza. Joyousness, cheerfulness. Con allegrezza, cheerfully, joyfully.

● †allegrissimo. Very fast, as fast as possible. (Superlative of *allegro.) (Rare.)

● †allegro. Fast. (The literal meaning is "cheerful," "gay".) This word is probably used with modifiers more often than any other *tempo indication. A list of these, from the least fast to the fastest, follows:
Allegro non troppo, Allegro ma non troppo. Fast, but not too much so.
Allegro moderato. Moderately fast.
Allegro. Fast.
Allegro assai. Fairly fast (literally "cheerful enough").
Allegro vivace, Allegro vivo. Fast and lively.
Allegro molto. Very fast.

The following combinations are also frequently encountered:
Allegro con brio. Fast, with liveliness.
Allegro con fuoco. Fast, with fire.
Allegro energico. Fast and energetically.
Allegro impetuoso. Fast and impetuously.
Allegro tempestoso. Fast and stormy.

It must be borne in mind that this term was originally used in its literal meaning. Hence in older music (up until about the middle of the eighteenth century) it by no means indicates a headlong tempo; when employed by Handel, for example, the term is about the equivalent of the present allegretto.
Abbreviation: all^o.
See also tempo marks.

● allemande. A type of dance in moderate 4-4 time. The allemande is the first of the four basic dances that make up the Baroque *suite (often called "Classic suite"). As a rule the beats are much subdivided, with many eighth-, sixteenth-, and even thirty-second-notes.
The name literally means "German dance."
Variant spellings: allemand, almand, almain.
Pronunciation: ȧl-mȧnd or ȧl-lĕ-mȧnd.

● alphabet. See notation. Letters are also used in describing *form.

● Alphorn. A Swiss folk instrument, made of wood but working on the principle of a *brass instrument. It has neither *valves nor *slide, hence is able to sound only the tones of the *harmonic series. Looking like a Brobdingnagian straight tobacco-pipe, it is so long that the *bell rests on the ground, many feet in front of the player. Its *tone-color is somewhat like that of the *horn (French horn), though less refined.
Brahms imitates the instrument (on the horn) in the slow introduction to the last movement of his First Symphony.

● †alquanto. Somewhat, a little, rather.

● alt. See in alt.

● †alta. High, higher; opposed to bassa or basso ("low," "lower"). 8va alta is a more complete form of *8va, meaning literally "an octave higher (than written)".

Variant form: <u>alto</u>.

● altered chords. In general, chords that cannot be written without the use of one or more *accidentals (provided the correct *key-signature is in effect). However, since the seventh degree of the *minor scale is normally raised a *half-step, the necessary accidental is here regarded as normal rather than exceptional; hence chords in minor employing the seventh degree are not regarded as altered unless of course an additional accidental is needed for some other note in the chord.

When a *modulation occurs without the *key-signature being changed to that of the new key, chords which would not require an accidental if the new signature <u>were</u> put in are never classified as altered. For example, in modulating from C major to G major the *triad D-F#-A or better the *seventh-chord D-F#-A-C is almost certain to appear, but since the key-signature of G major would contain an F-sharp, the foregoing chord would not be considered altered.

One theory about the source of altered chords is that they are temporarily "borrowed" from the closely-*related keys; they are chords which would naturally "belong" in those keys. Thus the presence of the chord D-F#-A in C major is assumed to be the dominant triad of G, "borrowed" in the key of C; the presence of the chord C-E-G-B♭ in C major to be the dominant seventh of F, "borrowed" by the key of C. A more recent theory suggests that altered chords are based on transposed modal scales temporarily in effect; see <u>modes</u> (1). Thus the presence of the chord D-F#-A in C major is assumed to derive from a (transposed) Lydian scale built on C (i.e., C D E F# G A B C); the presence of the chord C-E-G-B♭ in C major to derive from a (transposed)

Mixolydian scale on C (i.e., C D E F G A B♭ C).

The frequent appearance of altered chords is characteristic of *chromaticism.

There is no universal agreement as to which chords are altered and which are not, for some theorists regard a few chords requiring accidentals as perfectly normal to the key.

Some frequently-used altered chords are shown on the next page, indicated for the keys of C major and A minor. Of course the list is by no means exhaustive.

Certain altered chords are further discussed under the entries <u>augmented sixth chords</u>, <u>Neapolitan sixth</u>, and <u>Picardy third</u>.

Synonyms: <u>chromatic chords</u>, <u>borrowed chords</u>.

Antonym: <u>diatonic chords</u>.

● alto. (1) Same as *contralto. The word <u>alto</u> is generally employed as the name of a part, <u>contralto</u> as the name of a type of female voice--one that sings alto.

<u>Alto</u> is the Italian word meaning "high," hence its use to designate the lowest female voice may seem incongruous.

Plural: <u>altos</u> (English) or <u>alti</u> (Italian).

(2) The *alto horn.

(3) French name for the *viola.

(4) See <u>alta</u>.

● alto clarinet. A rather recently-invented *woodwind instrument, common in the concert *band but very rarely used in the orchestra. *Dance bands often use it.

The *tone-color is about midway between that of the ordinary *clarinet and that of the *bass clarinet. It is rather weak in volume and does not always cut through well.

It is notated a major sixth (see <u>intervals</u>) higher than the sounds desired. (See <u>transposing instruments</u>.)

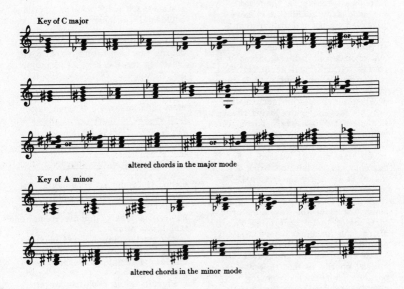

altered chords in the major mode

altered chords in the minor mode

Range:

out of favor there. It has the usual

Range

Written   Sounding
Alto clarinet

It is sometimes equipped with a
low E-flat key, sounding G-flat.

The alto clarinet is often used
to replace the old *basset horn,
though its tone-color differs considerably, being thicker and more
"oily" than that of the basset horn.

● alto clef. See clef.

● alto flute. A woodwind instrument
pitched a perfect fourth (see intervals) lower than the ordinary flute.
It is used chiefly for its lowest
tones, which have a breathy and
somewhat eerie sound. The best-
known compositions employing the
alto flute are probably Ravel's
second Daphnis and Chloe suite
and Stravinsky's The Rite of Spring.

three *valves.

The *tone-color of the alto horn
lacks character and distinction; for
this reason the instrument is tending to disappear (in favor of the
*horn, i. e., French horn). Much
less noble than that of the horn,
but lacking the melodious smooth-
ness of the *baritone (2), the tone-
color seems to have nothing that is
uniquely and peculiarly its own.

Some models of the alto horn are
built in upright form, looking like a
little baritone or miniature *tuba;
others are circular in form (and
often called mellophone), somewhat
resembling a horn (French horn)
but *fingered with the right hand
rather than the left.

Range

Written   Sounding
Alto flute

It is notated a perfect fourth higher
than the sounds desired. (See
transposing instruments.)

Its appearance is that of an over-
sized flute.

Synonyms: bass flute, flute in G.

Italian: flauto in sol, flauto contralto, or flautone. French: flûte
en sol or flûte alto. German:
Altflöte.

● alto horn. A brass instrument used
solely in *bands, and rapidly going

Range: marked <u>solo</u>, that for the others,

It is notated a major sixth (see <u>intervals</u>) higher than the sounds desired; that is, it is normally an E-flat instrument. (See <u>transposing instruments.</u>) However some alto horns also boast an F *crook, with which the notes would be written a perfect fifth above the sounds desired (as if writing for a horn in F), and which would give an actual pitch range a whole-step higher than shown.

Some musicians contemptuously call this instrument the <u>peck horn</u>.

Synonyms: <u>E-flat alto, althorn, alto</u> (2).

● alto oboe. Name occasionally given to the *English horn.

● alto-tenor. A term employed by teachers of music in the public schools to designate the changing voice of an adolescent boy (see <u>change of voice</u>). The term is a euphemistic one, as it is usually applied to those changing voices of the most narrow range, most disagreeable quality, and most unmanageable character.

The term <u>cambiata</u> is sometimes applied to the changing voice, despite the fact that the word actually means "changed" rather than "changing." There is of course no connection (except by derivation) with the *non-harmonic tone of the same name.

● alto trumpet. See <u>contralto trumpet</u>.

● †altri. The others. In an orchestral composition, if a part is written for a solo violin while the rest of the section has other notes to play, the music for the single instrument is

<u>gli altri</u> (sometimes <u>le altre</u>, depending on rules of Italian grammar).

● †amabile. Sweet, tender. Literally, "lovable."

Pronunciation: accent second syllable.

● amateur. One who pursues music (or any other activity) as a hobby or avocation, rather than as a profession. The term comes from the word meaning "to love," and hence denotes a person who is interested in a subject purely out of "love" for it.

Theoretically the word is commendatory, but it is often used in a derogatory manner, to suggest superficiality in approach. The latter usage is regrettable, especially since the word <u>dabbler</u> would convey the intended meaning in an unmistakable way.

The adjective <u>amateurish</u> is always derogatory.

Synonym: <u>dilettante</u>.

Pronunciation: ăm-á-tĕr or ăm-á-tyōōr (ăm-á-chōōr is questionable and ăm-á-chĕr should be avoided).

● Ambrosian chant. One of the four "dialects" or styles of *chant that arose in the Roman (or western) church during the early centuries A.D. It appears to have originated in Milan, Italy, and is still used in the diocese of Milan. The name derives from the fact that it was established by St. Ambrose, the bishop of Milan, who was born about 333 and died in 397; however it is highly unlikely that he composed any of the melodies.

Ambrosian chant should not be confused with <u>Ambrosian hymns</u>, which are one of the earliest forms of metrical music. Ambrosian chants, like *Gregorian, are free in rhythm, that is, non-metrical, and of course make no use of *harmony.

Some authors declare that Ambrosian chant is simpler in style than Gregorian, others that it is more ornate. The fact of the matter seems to be that when Ambrosian chants are simple, they are extremely so; when ornate, they again tend to be very much so.

Synonym: Milanese chant.

● American organ. Same as harmonium.

● †amore. Love. Con amore, lovingly, affectionately.

● †amoroso. Loving, amorous.

● anacrusis. Same as up-beat.

● †anche. Also.

● ancient cymbals. Same as antique cymbals.

● †ancora. Still (literally, "again"). Thus: ancora più mosso, still faster (used to indicate a second increase in *tempo, the first presumably indicated by più mosso).

● †andante. Rather slow, moderately slow. Often described as a "walking tempo," the walk being understood as a leisurely stroll. See tempo marks. (See also andantino.)

Abbreviation: andte.

● †andantino. A trifle slow; the first term slower than moderato, which signifies a medium *tempo. Although at present it is used to indicate a pace slightly quicker than andante, until about 1800 or 1825 it meant slightly slower than andante. See tempo marks.

Abbreviation: andno.

● †-ando. Italian present participle ending, equivalent to English ending -ing.

Variant forms: -endo, -ante, -ente.

● Anglican chanting. A type of liturgical music peculiar to the Anglican (Church of England) and Episcopal churches. It is written in four-part harmony and in general the style suggests a *hymn-tune, except that each chant contains two chords which are held an indefinite length of time, depending on the number of words (or syllables) that are to be sung to them. Although no *time-signature is used, there are always *bar-lines and the music is semi-metrical--a partially free 2-2.

All Anglican chants contain seven measures (a few called double chants contain fourteen). The first chord is printed in whole-notes, but actually is repeated for as long or short a time as is necessary, depending on the number of words to be sung to the chord. (If only a one-syllable word or a single syllable of a longer word is to be sung here, the length will be only that of a half-note. If there are several words or syllables the chord will be repeated once for each, thus dividing the whole-note into notes of short value, the exact rhythmic pattern being supposedly determined by the rhythm of the words.) Two chords of half-notes and one of whole-notes fill the next two measures and bring the chant to the midpoint (double barline); the last three syllables in the line of words are sung to these. The second section begins with another indefinite chord of whole-notes, and the chant concludes with four chords of half-notes and one of whole-notes--the last three measures and the last five syllables of the verse. The chant is then repeated as many times as there are verses; that is, all Anglican chants are *strophic.

There are certain special effects and usages, notably a word (or syllable) that is held for double the normal length, thus producing a *slur or *tie in the notes. (In the accompanying example it is indicated by capital letters.)

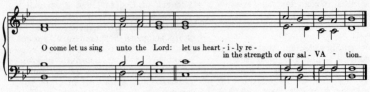

O come let us sing   unto the Lord: let us heart - i - ly re -
in the strength of our sal - VA - tion.

A typical Anglican Chant

There are a number of theories as to how the text should be fitted to the music (or "pointed"), none of which can be proved. Assuredly the widely-used "pointing" advocated in Rev. Charles L. Hutchens's Chant and Service Book (Boston, 1894) cannot fail to be incorrect; indeed it is the highly unmusical effect of this "pointing" which has led to the derogatory name "Anglican thump." On the other hand, like anything else, Anglican chanting can be done well or poorly; when done well it is musical; when done poorly it sounds almost ludicrous.

The term chanting is preferable to chant when applied to this style of music, since there is no relation whatever to true *chant, *Gregorian or otherwise.

The composers of Anglican chants are by no means anonymous; the example quoted above is by a certain Goodson. Most of the chants were composed in the eighteenth or nineteenth century.

● †anima. Life, spirit, animation. Con anima, animated.
Pronunciation: accent first syllable.

● †animando. Becoming animated.

● †animato. Animated, full of life and spirit.

● anthem. A composition in one movement for chorus, usually with organ and sometimes including one or more solo voices, for use at church services. Its function is very largely the same as that of the *motet (1); however it is usually less contrapuntal and its association is with the Protestant churches, rather than Catholic.

It is regrettable that many anthems consist of several short, unrelated sections arbitrarily strung together, their fragmentary and ununified structure leaving the listener with the impression that he has heard many short pieces, rather than a single work. Fortunately not all anthems possess this blemish.

National anthems are discussed under that heading.

A verse anthem employs several solo voices in addition to the full choir (and probably also instruments), the soloists always functioning as a group--like a small choir alternating with the large one. The verse anthem is typical of the late *Renaissance and *Baroque periods. The opposition of a small group of soloists to a larger full choir somewhat recalls (and possibly influenced) the *concerto grosso procedure in orchestral music.

Purcell's Rejoice in the Lord Alway is a fairly familiar example of this form. Naturally the verse anthem *medium has also been applied in larger works, for instance the chorus "The Heavens are Telling" in The Creation by Haydn.

Some verse anthems employ only one solo voice, with chorus.

● anticipation. See non-harmonic tones (4). For free anticipation see non-harmonic tones (7) (escape tones).

● antiphonal. Answering back and
forth; said of two bodies of players
and/or singers. It is usually understood that the two groups are of
about equal power.

Antiphonal singing was apparently
practiced by the ancient Hebrews.
It is still customary, in some
churches, to read psalms antiphonally.

When singing, speaking, or playing alternates between a single person and a group, the proper term
is responsory rather than antiphonal.

The use of two choirs, singing
sometimes antiphonally and sometimes together, was practiced in
St. Mark's Cathedral in Venice,
Italy around the turn of the sixteenth to seventeenth centuries,
and was one of the factors that led
to the *Baroque movement in music.
Pronunciation: ǎn-tǐf́-ŏ-nǎl.

● antique cymbals. A rarely-used
*percussion instrument of definite
pitch. Like the ordinary *cymbals,
a pair of them are usually clashed
together, although sometimes the
player strikes a single plate with a
triangle-beater or a 50-cent piece.

Each pair of antique cymbals can
emit but a single pitch.

Music for antique cymbals is
often played on the *glockenspiel
or the *celesta, both of which have
a somewhat similar *tone-color;
however the antique cymbals give
a wavering, shimmering effect that
the other two instruments lack
completely.

As the name suggests, the instrument is very old, having been known
to the ancient Greeks. This may
well be the "high sounding cymbals"
(sometimes translated "well tuned
cymbals") mentioned in the 150th
Psalm.

Synonyms: ancient cymbals,
crotales.

● †aperto. Open, i.e., not *muted;
used in reference to brass instruments.

● †a piacere. Literally, "at pleasure."
Indicates a certain amount of freedom in performance, leaving the

exact expression to the discretion of
the performer.

Synonyms: ad libitum (3), a
capriccio.

● †appassionato. Impassioned.
Variant form: passionato.

● †appena. Hardly, scarcely.

● †applied music. A term used in college music departments and *conservatories to designate the study of
instruments or of voice, as distinguished from the study of theory,
history of music, music education,
and the like. Chorus, glee club,
orchestra, band, and frequently conducting are also classified as applied
music.

● †appoggiatura. See non-harmonic
tones (6) and grace-notes (2). See
also recitative.

● appreciation. See music appreciation.

● arabesque. A term borrowed from
architecture, where it applies to a
fanciful form of decoration, to refer
to compositions (usually for piano)
characterized by the almost constant
use of certain figures. Some musicians have observed that numerous
arabesques are in *rondo form, though
strictly speaking the word denotes a
device rather than a form.

● arch form. Various form-schemes
(other than ABA) in which the themes
appear during the second half of the
composition in the reverse order to
their appearance in the first half,
for example, ABCBA or ABCDCBA.

Palindrome formations of schematic
letters alone does not produce arch
form; ABACABA, although a palindrome formation, is not arch form,
but a type of *rondo form.

Synonyms: bow form, Bogenform
(German).

● †archi. (1) Bows (plural of arco).
(2) Bowed *string instruments.

● †arco. To be played with the *bow;
used in writing for the bowed *string
instruments to cancel *pizzicato, also

to cancel *col legno. Literally,
"bow." (Related English word:
arch.)
   Plural: archi.

● †ardore. Ardor, fervor.

● †aria. A vocal *solo, comparatively lyrical in style and with
orchestra accompaniment, found in
*operas, *oratorios, and *cantatas.
Some arias are extremely elaborate,
and difficult to perform. The lyrical
character of the aria contrasts sharply with the dramatic and declamatory
style of the *recitative which so
often precedes it.
   During the late *Baroque period
arias were nearly always cast in
three-part or ABA form; indeed
this scheme is sometimes called
aria form to this day (see ternary
form). In more recent works the
aria has no special design; it is a
style rather than a form.
   An aria for two voices is called
a *duet; one for three voices a
*trio (1), etc. (See groups.)
   A composition in aria style, not
part of a larger work, is called a
concert aria.
   Obviously there is a close relationship between the aria and the *song,
although the aria was the first to
develop.
   Synonym (almost obsolete): air
(2).
   Compare arietta, arioso.
   See also recitative, scena.
   Pronunciation: accent first syllable.

● aria form. See ternary form.

● †arietta. A short *aria. It
usually does not have the ABA form-
scheme associated with the older
type of aria.

● †arioso. In vocal music, a style
about halfway between that of the
*aria and that of the *recitative.
Passages in arioso style sometimes
occur at the end of recitatives.
   The first vocal number in Handel's
The Messiah--"Comfort Ye"--is an
example, though actually labeled
"recitative."
   Plural: ariosos or ariosi.

● †armonici. *Harmonics (1, 2).
   Abbreviation: arm., armon.
   Pronunciation: accent second syl-
lable.

● †armonioso. Harmoniously.

● †arpeggiando. Rolled (1). This
word is sometimes used in place
of the symbol
   Abbreviation: arpegg.

● arpeggiate. (1) To *roll (1) a
chord, on the part of the player
of a keyboard instrument.
   (2) To treat a chord in *arpeggio
fashion (break it up into single
tones heard in succession) on the
part of the composer.

● †arpeggio. A *chord whose tones
are heard in succession rather
than simultaneously, that is, a
broken chord.
   It is hardly accurate to think of
an arpeggio as "a chord converted
into a *melody," for it must be
strictly borne in mind that arpeggios
are first and foremost chords, not
melodies. The tones accumulate
in the listener's mind and fuse so
as to make a chordal impression.
   The name is derived from the
Italian arpa, meaning "harp," because of the indisputable fact that
arpeggios are in the *idiom of that
instrument.
   In the accompanying example a
series of chords has been converted
into arpeggios in two different ways.
Many other manners are possible,
of course. See also the entry
Irregular groupings, Exs. 4 and 6,
lower staff. Another arpeggio
appears in the entry bass clarinet.
   The *Alberti bass is a type of
arpeggio, though of a limited range
and with a prescribed shape--hence
not typical.
   Plural: arpeggios or arpeggi.
   See also roll (1), broken, arpeggiando.
   Pronunciation: accent second syllable.

● †arpeggione. An obsolete string instrument shaped like and tuned like the *guitar, but played with a bow, which enjoyed a brief vogue in the early nineteenth century. The fact that Schubert wrote a sonata for arpeggione and piano seems to be the instrument's chief claim to fame. It is sometimes called the guitar violoncello.

● arr. Abbreviation for arranged, arranged by, or arrangement.

● arrangement. A *transcription (1).

● arranging. A synonym for *orchestration, but usually also including *bandstration (band arranging) and *choral orchestration.

● articulation. The exact method of producing tone on a wind instrument, especially as regards use of the tongue, as opposed to use of the breath and lips (see embouchure). Clearness and precision of tone are always implied; it is understood that the playing of anyone who articulates well is free from messiness, indistinctness, and sluggishness.

The term is also used in connection with cleanness and precision in singing.

● artificial soprano, artificial alto. Euphemistic terms for *castrato.

● art-song. A *song of high artistic merit, by a serious composer, and frequently with a text by a serious poet. In the art-song the voice and piano are of about equal importance, that is, the composition often appears

to be a *duo for voice and piano
rather than a mere "vocal *solo"
with piano *"accompaniment. "
     The first composer ever to devote
protracted attention to compositions
of this type was Schubert; however
Haydn, Mozart, and Beethoven (also
Bach in his Geistliche Lieder or
Spiritual Songs) had already produced
excellent examples, although less
numerous. Among other composers
who have written first-class art-songs
are Schumann, Brahms, Hugo Wolf,
Robert Franz, Mahler (most of whose
songs are with orchestra), Debussy,
Fauré, Duparc, Samuel Barber,
Francis Poulenc, etc.
     The term is sometimes used to
indicate any type of song other than
the *folk-song, but this usage is
undesirable, for the term is quite
incongruous if applied to the sentimental *ballad (2).
     Synonym: Lied (plural, Lieder).
     See also song-cycle.

● †aspramente. Harshly.

● †assai. Enough, much, very. In
music it is generally used in the
meaning "very, " but properly it has
less force than molto; hence lento
assai would not be quite as slow as
lento molto. It may often be felici-
tously translated as "quite"; thus:
allegro assai, quite fast.

● †a tempo. Denotes a return to the
original *tempo, canceling the effect
of a ritardando (rallentando) or accelerando (stringendo). It is less
desirably used to denote the end of
a section marked meno mosso or più
mosso.
     It is well to point out that a tempo
signifies an immediate--not gradual--
return to the basic tempo. (On the
rare occasions when a gradual return is wanted, the term *ritornando
al tempo or tornando al tempo is
used.)
     The literal meaning is "in time."
     Variant forms: in tempo, occasional-
ly just tempo.

● †-alto. Italian past participle suffix,
equivalent to English suffix -ed.
     Variant forms: -ito, -uto.

● atonality. Absence of a *tonic
or key-center; not in any *key.
Atonality is the negation of tonality.
     The foregoing definition, simple
as it looks, needs amplification.
In order to clarify the term, it is
necessary first to point out the
meaning of the opposite of atonality,
namely tonality. If a passage of
music is in the key of D major,
the tone D always seems to have a
feeling of being "home"; all of the
tones seem to cluster around D
and to want to progress eventually
to that tone. (See tonic.) Indeed
if the music is suddenly interrupted,
the listener's mind seems to hear
it continuing, in some form or
other, and finally coming to rest on
D. The next tone in importance is
A, while G ranks third. The exact
order of the remaining four tones--
E, F-sharp, B, and C-sharp--may
be debated; however they all precede
in importance any other tones, such
as F-natural, B-flat, G-sharp, etc.,
all of which must be notated by
means of *accidentals (since the
two-sharp *key-signature does not
cover them) and which are regarded
strictly as "visitors, " somewhat
foreign to the key but usable under
certain conditions.
     In atonal music all tones are of
equal importance. No tones are
regarded as foreign; none is first
in importance, second in importance,
etc. Naturally atonal music is
almost invariably written without a
key-signature, since no combination
of sharps or flats would apply.
The number of accidentals encountered is always very great, in fact
the page appears to be littered with
them.
     Some musicians find that atonal
music conveys to them a sense of
great "freedom, " while others find
it confusing and disquieting, and
even assert that only a decadent and
neurotic mind can create or tolerate
it. When the Nazi government in
Germany denounced "cultural
Bolshevism" atonality was among
the techniques included under that
heading; when the Soviet government thunders against "bourgeois
formalism" and music that is

"hostile to the working class," once more atonality finds itself among the condemned devices.

The *twelve tone system is an outgrowth of, and perhaps refinement of, atonality. Nearly all twelve tone music is atonal, but not all atonal music uses the twelve tone technique.

Arnold Schoenberg (1874-1951) is usually credited with being the "inventor" of atonality, his first work in this idiom being the Three Piano Pieces, op. 11, written in 1908; however the American composer Charles Ives (1874-1954) had experimented with it considerably earlier. In addition there are several older devices which might be considered atonal, important among them being the *whole-tone scale, which certainly seems to lack a natural stopping point or center.

The accompanying quotation is from Pierrot Lunaire by Schoenberg. The part for the voice (marked Rezitation) is an example of *Sprechstimme.

Atonality is usually employed all the way through a composition; it seldom alternates with passages of definitely tonal character. (In this respect there is a sharp contrast

with the use of *polytonality, which is rarely employed from beginning to end.)

The terms atonal and atonality have been recklessly used in two meanings which are utterly incorrect, namely (A) As a synonym for *dissonant. Atonal music is normally quite dissonant, but not all dissonant music is atonal. This chord

is extremely dissonant, but it is clearly in the key of A major. (B) To apply to any music lacking a key-signature, where all the accidentals are written in. Here the term is complete nonsense, for music may lack a key-signature and yet be thoroughly--albeit very temporarily-- in some key or other at any given moment. The term atonality is not correctly applied to music which *modulates constantly. Much of Wagner's music contains extremely frequent modulations, but none of it is atonal.

Variant form: atonalism.
Antonym: tonality.
Compare: twelve tone system, polytonality.

● †attacca, attacca subito. Continue with the next *movement at once. This term is used when two movements of a *symphony, *sonata, *string quartet, *concerto, *song-cycle, *suite (or similar work divided into several movements) are to be performed with no stop in between, that is, when one movement is joined directly to the one that follows. Often the work is written in such a way as to make a stop impossible. A familiar instance may be found in the Fifth Symphony by Beethoven, where the third movement leads directly to the fourth.

Synonym: segue (1).

● attack. The element of several instruments or voices being exactly together in playing a chord or beginning a composition. When an orchestra of a hundred men hits a chord "like one man," we say the attack is good; if some are a split second too early or too late, the attack is poor, or ragged. Good attacks are partly the result of the skill of the players or singers, partly of the skill of the *conductor. A clean attack is an important element in good *ensemble.

Antonym: release.

● attendant keys. See related keys.

● a 2. (1) To be played in *unison by the two instruments whose parts appear on the given staff; a direction used in orchestral *scores. On the staff devoted to, say, the part for two *flutes, the writing of two different *parts obviously means that the first flute should play the upper line of notes, the second flute the lower. If the composer wants only the first flute to play a single line of notes, he writes I, 1., or 1º; if he wants only the second flute to play (which is less likely), he writes II, 2., or 2º; if he wants both instruments to play in unison he writes a 2. By supplying every note with two stems, one turned up and one turned down, it would be possible to eliminate the use of a 2, but except for short passages the alternative is laborious to write, difficult to print, and somewhat confusing to the eye. a 3 and a 4 are often encountered where three or four instruments are written on the same staff.

(2) In the *string parts of an orchestral score, this term is sometimes used (undesirably) as a synonym for *divisi.

Variant form: à 2.
German: zu 2.

● aubade (French). A morning piece to be performed out of doors; about the same as serenade (1), except that the word serenade indicates performance in the evening.

Pronunciation: ō-bäd.

● Aufführungspraxis. A German term meaning "practice of performance." Specifically it refers to playing medieval and renaissance music on the archaic instruments for which it was originally written, rather than on modern instruments, and singing or playing it in the exact stylistic manner in vogue at the time the music was written. The object, of course, is to make the music sound exactly as the composer conceived it.

By extension, the principle could be applied to the music of any period.

See also collegium musicum. For a violation of the principle, see additional accompaniments.

Pronunciation: ouf-fü-roongz-präk-sis.

● Augenmusik (German). Literally "eye music." A derisive term applied to musical effects which are impressive in the printed notation, but which cannot be perceived by the ear. The *cancrizans, *inversions (3), and certain types of *canon are examples of Augenmusik, as are extremely subtle, complex, or delicate effects in *orchestration. Highly complicated *counterpoint is an additional example.

Pronunciation: ou-gen-moo-zek.

● augmentation. The presentation of a musical theme or figure with all the time-values doubled, i.e., eighth-, quarter-, and half-notes in the original become respectively quarter-, half-, and whole-notes when presented in augmentation.

Of course it is also possible to multiply original values by 3 or 4, as well as by 2, though these are less common.

A familiar example occurs almost at the end of Wagner's Tristan and Isolde. The example shown below is from the slow movement (second movement) of Dvořák's Fifth (New World) Symphony.

The opposite process is called diminution.

● augmented. See intervals, triad.

● augmented sixth chords. A name given to certain chords, quite conventional in music, which contain the *interval of the augmented sixth. They are not constructed according to the principle which underlies normal chord-building--superimposed thirds--but rather seem to be formed from other intervals.

These chords contain the same tones in both the major keys and their *tonic minors, though the differences between major and minor mode (brought about by the key-signature) cause the scale degrees to appear different in writing.

There are two series of augmented sixth chords. In each series there are three chords, bearing the curious and arbitrary names Italian sixth, French sixth, and German sixth.

The more frequent series is built on the lowered sixth degree

in major and the sixth degree in minor, and consists of the following tones:

In major: Italian sixth--lowered 6, 1, raised 4.

French sixth--lowered 6, 1, 2, raised 4.

German sixth--lowered 6, 1, lowered 3 (or raised 2), raised 4.

In minor: Italian sixth--6, 1, raised 4.

French sixth--6, 1, 2, raised 4.

German sixth--6, 1, 3, raised 4.

They are shown in Example 1. (For an additional example of the German

It will be observed that the German sixth sounds exactly like a dominant *seventh-chord. Its utility as a *pivot chord in *modulation hardly needs to be pointed out.

Naturally these chords may be *inverted; the positions shown in Example 1 are simply the most frequent, as is likewise true in Example 2.

For examples of all three augmented sixth chords (and the Neapolitan sixth in addition), all within a short composition (about four pages) see the song "Der Wegweiser" ("The Sign-Post") in Schubert's song-cycle Die Winter-

Ex. 1

Key of C major   Key of C minor

Italian French German   Italian French German
Augmented sixth chords in major mode.   Augmented sixth chords in minor mode.

sixth in the major mode, see the entry irregular groupings, Ex. 3, lower staff.)

The names "Italian sixth," "French sixth," and "German sixth" are of course quite meaningless, nor do musicians know how they originated. It is important to mention, however, that *Neapolitan sixth is an entirely different type of chord--the first inversion of a *triad, not an augmented sixth chord--and quite possibly was first employed by or at least associated with composers of Naples.

reise (The Winter Journey).

A less frequent series is built on the lowered second degree of both the major and minor scales. These chords are shown in Example 2.

The chord in Example 3--very common in the major mode (it does not exist in minor)--although containing an augmented sixth, is not usually classified among the chords under discussion. It is clearly an altered form of the dominant seventh-chord (see altered

Ex. 2

Key of C major   Key of C minor

Italian French German   Italian French German
Major mode   Minor mode

chords).

Ex. 3

● autographing. A species of music
*manuscript which seeks to duplicate
the exact appearance of engraving. It
has come into wide use during the
past thirty years, often as an economy
measure. It is sometimes difficult
to detect the work of the best auto-
graphers from real engraving.
  See also typewriter (music).

● autoharp. A modified type of
*zither, producing only *chords (but
not *melodies). In recent years it
has come into wide use in music
classes in the public schools, as a
ready means of supplying a simple
*accompaniment for singing.
  The autoharp looks like a shallow
irregular-shaped (trapezoidal) box
with strings stretched across the long
way. At right angles to the strings
are mounted several slim wooden
bars. When one of these is pressed,
felts on the bottom damp out all the
strings except those forming the desired chord, which is identified by a
label on the bar. Using either a
*plectrum or his bare fingers, the
player sweeps his hand over the entire set of strings, but only those
not damped out will sound.
  Some autoharps produce only five
chords. Larger models produce
twelve, the largest size, fifteen.

● auxiliary lines. Leger lines.

● auxiliary tones. Neighboring notes.
See non-harmonic tones (2). The
name auxiliary tones is also given to
the unwritten tones implied by *ornaments; see mordent, turn, trill.

● Ave Maria (Latin). A prayer to the
Virgin Mary, used by Roman Catholics.
There are innumerable musical set-
tings.
  It is ironic that the two best-known
compositions bearing the title Ave
Maria are both highly questionable.
That by Gounod was formed by

grafting a melody of operatic and
saccharine character onto the first
Prelude in Bach's Well-Tempered
Clavier. The result is thoroughly
secular, not to say vulgar.
Schubert's fine song entitled Ave
Maria is a setting of a poem in
Sir Walter Scott's The Lady of the
Lake which happens to contain those
words, and is of course frankly a
non-church composition. The practice of sometimes singing it in
Latin is an affectation; Schubert set
his music to a German translation
of Scott's poem, and it should be
sung either in that language or in
the original English. Needless to
say, Scott's text is not at all liturgical, and bears no relation to the
traditional Latin church text except
perhaps in general spirit. Both of
these compositions have been "black-
listed" for use in Catholic services.
Ave Maria means "hail, Mary."

● †avvivando. Becoming enlivened.
  Synonyms: animando, ravvivando.

● ayre. Type of Elizabethan English
vocal composition, often but not
always for solo voice and lute. It
tends to be *homophonic and is an
important forerunner of the *song.

B

● B & H. The German music-publish-
ing firm of Breitkopf und Härtel, one
of the foremost in the world. Its
edition of the complete set of *parts
for numerous orchestral works is
very extensive and has enjoyed wide
usage.

● †bacchetta. Stick (in the sense of
drum stick). Bacchette di spugna,
sponge sticks; bacchette di legno,
wooden sticks.
  Plural: bacchette.
  Abbreviation: bacch.

● B-A-C-H. See German notation.

●Bach-Gesellschaft. Name of a
society which published an authentic
edition of the complete works of J.
S. Bach (1685-1750), beginning in
1850 and finishing in 1900. A

modern reprint of the Bach-Gesellschaft edition is available.

It is pertinent to note that the *cantatas of Bach are customarily numbered in the order of their publication in this edition. Thus Cantata No. 1 is not the first cantata Bach ever wrote, but the first one published by the Bach-Gesellschaft.

Gesellschaft in German means "company" or "fellowship."

Abbreviation: B. G.

Variant form: Bachgesellschaft.

Pronunciation: bäk̲ᶻge̲-sel-shäft (the s sounds almost like z).

● Bach trumpet. A special, small, high-pitched type of trumpet sometimes used in playing the very high trumpet parts written by Bach; however he actually wrote for a much different (and obsolete) type of instrument.

The name is also sometimes applied to the trumpets designed by Vincent Bach, a well-known authority on brass instruments; here it is a brand name.

● back turn. See turn, sub-head "inverted turn."

● bagatelle. A short piece, usually for piano. A French word meaning trifle.

● bagpipe. A popular instrument, of the *woodwind type, conspicuous for the presence of a bag which serves as bellows for supplying air. Although the bagpipe is usually associated with Scotland and Ireland, the instrument is found in many parts of the world, and is of quite ancient lineage.

The melody is played on a pipe, equipped with finger-holes, called the chanter, while one or more additional pipes, called drones, supply constant sustained tones. It will thus be seen that all music from the bagpipe, like that for the *hurdy-gurdy, of necessity contains a pedal point (see non-harmonic tones (9) and drone bass). Air is supplied partly from the mouth and partly from the bellows-like bag held under and pumped by the player's arm. (In some bagpipes, all air is supplied by the bag.)

The familiar type of bagpipe is played with a double *reed (oboe-type) and has a strong, harsh, slightly shrill, nasal *tone-color. In some countries, however, the instrument uses a single, clarinet-type reed.

The word is often used in plural form. Synonyms such as the Highland pipes, the Irish pipes, or simply the pipes are common. The synonym cornemuse is also occasionally used.

● balalaika. A Russian popular instrument of the *guitar class, with a triangular body. The balalaika is manufactured in several sizes, and "bands" of them frequently play together.

Pronunciation: bäl-a̲-li̲-ka̲.

● balance. The correct proportion in volume among the various instruments and voices that participate in a performance is termed good balance.

A *mixed chorus made up of thirty sopranos, five altos, five tenors, and thirty basses would be very poorly balanced, assuming that all the members possessed voices of approximately equal power.

The proper relation among instruments depends largely on the particular ones under consideration; for example many *string instruments in unison are required to balance one *brass instrument, especially when playing loud. (See orchestra.)

The securing of good balance is one of the problems inherent in the study of *orchestration. Its realization in performance partly depends on the vigilance of the *conductor.

● balken. Same as crossbeam.

● ballad. Strictly speaking, a narrative poem; many ballads are of folk origin. As applied to music, the word is used in two meanings:

(A) A *song which is a setting of a ballad type of poem. Most of these are *folk-songs, Barbara Allen being a familiar example.

(B) A light and often sentimental

type of *song, usually of slight
musical merit. Synonym (contemptuous): "heart" song.
  Compare ballade.

● ballade. An instrumental composition (usually for piano) which is "in
ballad style." It might be imagined
that the ballade would resemble a
brief *symphonic poem; but actually
the word is practically meaningless.
It could be applied to any piano piece
that is not too short; no "story" or
*program is necessary or even implied
in many examples, although naturally
others are distinctly programmatic.
The ballades for piano by Chopin and
Brahms are well known.
  Compare ballad.
  Pronunciation: bă-läd.́

● ballad opera. An *operetta or
*opera wholly or partially pieced
together, patch-work fashion, from
highly successful parts of other operas
and especially from *folk-songs and
popular songs. Naturally it will contain the music of numerous composers.
  Ballad operas were highly successful
during the eighteenth century, the
most famous being The Beggar's Opera.
Their prevalence antedates the enact-
ment of *copyright laws.
  See also Singspiel.

● ballet. A composition for dancers
and orchestra, the graceful dance
motions of which sometimes act out
a sort of pantomime play. Most
ballets are divided into *movements,
some of the longest even into acts,
like an *opera.
  Many operas contain a ballet in
the function of a diversion, between
two of the acts. They are so popular
in France in connection with opera
that a ballet is interpolated between
the acts of any opera which happens
to lack one.
  Naturally there are also many
ballet performances apart from opera.
The music of ballets, minus dancing,
often finds its way into orchestral
concerts.
  The contemporary style of ballet
dancing is usually called modern
dance.
  Pronunciation: bă-lä.́

● ballet, ballett. A short secular
composition, of dancelike character,
for a small group of voices. It
might well be regarded as a species
of *madrigal. The most conspicuous feature is a *refrain or *burden
sung to the nonsense syllables fa
la la. It was at its height in the
late sixteenth and early seventeenth
centuries, being especially popular
in England.
  The word is pronouned exactly as
spelled, with accent on the first
syllable, and has no connection
with the *ballet that is pronounced
bă-lä,́ defined in the preceding
entry.
  Synonym: fala.
  See also canzonetta (2).

● band. (1) A large ensemble of
*woodwind, *brass, and *percus-
sion instruments. Its most conspicuous difference from the *orchestra is the absence of *string
instruments; however many large
bands use one or more *double-
basses, and a few band compositions require the *harp.
  Another important difference is
that in the band most of the parts,
both brass and woodwind, are
played by a group (section) of instruments, whereas in the orchestra
each wind instrument player is a
soloist.
  The band sounds best out-of-
doors, where its extreme brilliance
--even harshness--is diffused and
hence softened.
  Bands are commonly divided into
two types: marching (or military)
bands, and concert (or symphonic)
bands. The latter groups usually
play indoors; they also are frequently
larger and nearly always play
music of a more serious and ambitious character. Naturally many
organizations function sometimes as
marching bands, sometimes as
concert bands.
  The literature written specifically
for band, other than marches, is
almost completely a twentieth century development. The greatest
impetus has occurred in England
and in the United States, in the
latter country partially stimulated

by the proliferation of bands in high schools and colleges. Nevertheless most concert bands still by necessity use many *transcriptions of orchestral compositions.

The group of instruments available in the band, and the proportion among them, is not well standardized. Progress toward this end has been made, but the time has not yet come when a composer can write a band composition with full assurance that the instruments available will be exactly those he has in mind, and in exactly the same proportions. This matter has long been established in the orchestra, and the lack of a parallel development has been one factor in retarding the artistic standing of the band.

Some bands consist exclusively of brass instruments and hence are known as brass bands. The term brass band is, however, often carelessly applied to the ordinary full band.

(2) The word band is often applied to small groups of instruments, always representing much less than a complete *orchestra and usually of the same or closely-related types, playing together; such as *marimba bands, *harmonica bands, *mandolin-and-*banjo bands, etc.

(3) The various sections or "choirs" (4) of the orchestra are sometimes called bands--string band, woodwind band, brass band, and percussion band.

The definition of band as "an incomplete orchestra" fits all three of the foregoing definitions, though in the case of the concert band it gives a misleading impression as to size, for this group often has as many members as the full-sized symphony orchestra. See also dance band, rhythm band.

● band-arranging. See bandstration; see also orchestration.

● bandleader. A person who conducts a *dance band. The word bandleader, however, is not in the vocabulary of serious musicians.

● bandmaster. Band director; the *conductor of a band.

● bandstration. The art of scoring, arranging, or "orchestrating" for the *band (1); band-arranging. This is a portmanteau word derived by telescoping band and orchestration. Although some musicians find this term repugnant, its use is increasing.
Synonym: instrumentation (2).
See also orchestration.

● banjo. A plucked string (*fretted) instrument having a shallow, cylindrical, metal-shelled body, with a tightly-drawn parchment covering the flat side of the cylinder. The *fingerboard is comparatively long.

The *tone-color of the banjo is dry, harsh, and "plunking," in sharp contrast to the mellow and comparatively more sustained "thrumming" sound of the *mandolin, *guitar, and other fretted instruments.

The banjo is made with four, five, or six strings, and consequent variations in tuning. Perhaps the commonest type is the tenor banjo, tuned exactly like the *viola but notated with the treble *clef, usually an *octave higher than the sounds desired though occasionally at actual pitch. Finger-diagrams (see tablature) are often used to replace normal notation.

The plural is usually spelled banjos, but occasionally banjoes is seen.

● bar. (1) A synonym for measure. However, bar is always applied purely to the distance between two *bar-lines, that is, to the visual aspect, while measure suggests in addition the aural aspect of *beats of varying strength (see accent).
(2) A synonym for bar-line.

● barbershop harmony. A colloquial and semi-humorous name for a rather sugary and sentimental type of harmonic style often characterizing pieces used by *male quartets and sometimes men's *glee clubs. A wag has observed that the ambition of such a group appears to be that of singing a diminished-*seventh chord with a *fermata at the climax of every piece.

Typical "barbershop harmony."

Typical "barbershop harmony."

● barcarolle. A boat song, or piece in similar style. It is usually in 6-8 or 12-8 time, in moderate *tempo. It may be either instrumental or vocal. In most examples the gentle rocking of a boat is suggested. By no means the same thing as a *chantey.

    Variant spelling: barcarole.
    Synonym: gondoliera.

● bare fifth. Same as open fifth.

● baritone. (1) The voice midway in *range between the *tenor and the *bass. It is probably the most prevalent male voice. Range:

Easy   For artist

Variant spelling (obsolescent): bary-tone.

Synonym: first bass.

(2) A *brass instrument pitched an octave below the *trumpet in B-flat, having the same range as the tenor *trombone. Its *tone-color is mellow, bland, and more "singing" than that of the trombone, though less so than that of the *horn.

There are two methods of notating it. When written with the treble *clef it is a *tranposing instrument and the composer writes a major ninth higher than the sounds desired; when written with the bass clef it is notated at actual pitch. Range:

In music for the piano, a single long bar-line runs through both staffs. In writing for voice and piano, or for some instrument such as violin with piano, the voice-part or instrument has its own bar-line, the piano part a bar-line through both staffs. For organ music, a long line goes through the two staffs on which the part for the manuals is written, but the pedal part has its own line. With four instruments, such as a *string quartet score, there is a single long line through all four staffs. In writing for chorus, each voice-part has its own bar-line, to avoid

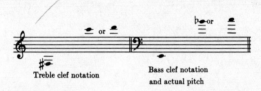

Treble clef notation

Bass clef notation and actual pitch

The baritone differs from the *euphonium in that it has only the usual three *valves rather than four, only the one *bell (the euphonium has a supplementary small bell), a somewhat narrower *range, and a slightly "lighter" tone-quality. Like the euphonium, it is essentially a *band (1) instrument, almost never used in the *orchestra.

Synonyms: baritone horn, military baritone.

● baritone oboe. The heckelphone.

● bar-line. The vertical lines that divide music notation into *measures.

Bar-lines are drawn from the highest line of the staff to the lowest.

Bar-line

interference with the words. In many orchestral *scores a single long bar-line extends through all the staffs, but in better printing there are separate lines for the four sections or "choirs"--woodwind, brass, percussion, strings. If the harp, piano, or celesta is used, it has its own bar-lines.

Dotted bar-lines are sometimes used to subdivide a very long measure so as to facilitate reading; or to indicate the accenting of one of the more unusual *meters (for example, to indicate whether a five-beat measure is to be accented as 3+2 or as 2+3); or to indicate a tentative or suggested bar-line for a passage in very free rhythm.

Synonyms; measure-bar, bar (2).

A double bar-line, as its name suggests, consists of two lines side-by-side. The double bar-line is used (A) when a new *key-signature is to go into effect; (B) when a new *time-signature is to go into effect, unless the composition is of the type in which the time-signature changes quite frequently; (C) when

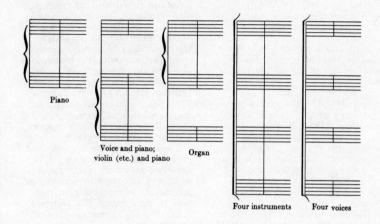

Piano

Voice and piano;
violin (etc.) and piano

Organ

Four instruments   Four voices

a new *tempo is to go into effect;
(D) to mark important divisions within a composition; (E) to precede the
directions *D. C. and *D. S.   It is
often used in *hymns (Hymn-tunes)
to indicate the division into *phrases,
although perhaps more frequently a
single thick line is used.

The double bar-line is sometimes used to mark the end of a
composition, but this usage is not
desirable except perhaps in something very short or in an excerpt
quoted from a composition.

Double bar-line

A double bar-line does not necessarily coincide with the end of a
measure; it may occur during the
course of a measure.

The character which is used to
mark the end of a composition, is

sometimes called a double bar-line,
but observe that the second line is
thick. Actually it has no special
name.

● Baroque Period. The period of
music history extending from about
1600 to about 1750. It was preceded
by the *Renaissance period and
followed by the *Rococo, after having
overlapped with the latter for a number of years. It is often called the
period of *figured bass, due to the
extremely frequent employment of
that device.

The Baroque movement received its
impetus from the polychoral music of
Giovanni Gabrieli and other Venetian
composers and from the founding of
*opera; it culminated in the work of
Bach and Handel. The era may be
subdivided into early, middle, and
late stages.

Baroque music is noted for its
dignity and grandeur. In many compositions the composer sets up a certain
design which is followed through
systematically to the end, or at least
to the end of a clearly-defined section.
This emphasis on mosaic-type designs
has led some musicians to term it,
in all respect, "wall-paper music."

The founding of opera in the early
stages of the Baroque (1600) initiated
a completely *homophonic treble-
dominated style which in those days
was a distinct novelty (see monody).
*Polyphony was however by no means
discarded; rather it remained highly
typical of much Baroque music, including some passages in operas. In
general, however, it may be said that
Baroque thinking took the view that
the highest and lowest *"voices" were
usually more important than those in
the middle of the fabric.

This period witnessed the abandonment of the *modes (1) in favor of the
conventional *major and minor
system of *tonality (2), the gradual
use of all twelve tones of the
*chromatic scale, the appearance
and growth of a type of harmony
that was distinctly *functional, the
advent of practically all types of
*key-signature, the gradual adop-
tion of *equal temperament and
abandonment of *just intonation,
the ascendancy of secular music
over church music, the tremendous
development of instrumental music
(heretofore a rather insignificant
musical sideline) and its eventual
ascendancy over vocal music, and
the appearance of compositions
specially written for both voices
and instruments combined.

The use of *dynamic marks and
*tempo marks was a Baroque in-
novation; previously their employment was entrusted to performers'
judgment. Abrupt changes from
loud to soft, rather than delicate
*nuances, are characteristic of
Baroque style.

Another important development
(in some respects perhaps a retro-
gression) was a gradual tendency
toward regularity and symmetry of
*meter and rhythmic patterns (due
partly to the influence of the meter
of poetry), as contrasted with the
asymmetrical and polyrhythmic
element in the works of the foregoing Renaissance era. This resulted in increased emphasis on
*meter and the introduction of *bar-
lines. Although bar-lines impress
the musician of today as part of the
very substance of musical notation,
they are actually a seventeenth
century innovation.

In addition to the founding and
development of opera, the Baroque
period saw the founding and development of the oratorio, the cantata,
the passion, the concerto, the concerto grosso, the sonata da chiesa,
the sonata da camera, the chorale-
prelude, the suite (1) and chamber
music; it was the heyday of the
fugue, the toccata, and of organ
compositions.

During the early part of this era,
notation made its final evolution
into the form we know today.

The word baroque is sometimes defined as "in corrupt taste," "bizarre," or "contorted," but these meanings do not apply to music of the period. Pronunciation: bȧ-rōk.́

● Baroque sonata. Applied to the *sonata da chiesa and occasionally the *sonata da camera (see sonata, 4) in contradistinction to the classical sonata (1).

● Baryton. An eighteenth-century type of *viol, tuned like the *viola da gamba and equipped with *sympathetic strings like those of the *viola d'amore. Haydn wrote many compositions employing the Baryton which now may be classified as an archaic instrument.

● barytone. Variant spelling of baritone (obsolescent). (The spelling baryton is incorrect in English.)

● bass. (1) The lowest tone in a *chord.
(2) The lowest melodic line of tones in a passage of music; the lowest *"voice."
(3) The lowest male voice, lower than the *baritone (1). The range of course depends on the skill of the individual singer, but is approximately:

(7) The expression "the basses" in orchestral compositions means cellos and double-basses. See bassi.
(8) During the *Baroque period, "bass" indicated cello and a keyboard instrument (harpsichord, organ, or piano), the latter playing from *figured bass; thus a composition described as written for "two violins and bass" was performed by two violins, cello, and a keyboard instrument. See trio sonata (1).
The spelling base, although certainly logical for the first definition and perhaps others, is obsolete.

● †bassa. Low, lower. 8va bassa indicates a passage to be played an octave lower than written. (Opposed to alta, alto, "high," "higher.") Variant form: basso.

● bass clarinet. A *woodwind instrument pitched an octave lower than the ordinary *clarinet and practically identical with it in *mechanism. It is conspicuous for its double-curved mouth-pipe and its upward-curved *bell, both reminiscent of the *saxophone.

In choral music, when there are parts for two bass voices, the upper one ("first bass") is sung by the baritones (1). Synonym: basso. See also Russian bass.
(4) A synonym for the *double-bass (contrabass). This usage is undesirable, though common.
(5) A synonym for the *tuba (undesirable).
(6) That part in a piano composition which is played by the left hand (undesirable; however see Alberti bass).

Its *tone-color is rich, dark, and oily, like that of the lowest (or "chalumeau") register of the ordinary clarinet.
Nowadays the bass clarinet is always built in B-flat. However the bass clarinet in A is often encountered in *scores, though the present-day player must *transpose his music and play it on the B-flat instrument. The bass clarinet in C has been obsolete for many decades.
Orchestration books describe two methods of notating the music for

this instrument, these being given the curious names "French method" and "German method, " neither of which bears any relation to the nationality of the composers who employ them. Actually there are three types of notation, and since the system ignored by treatises may be found in Stravinsky's The Rite of Spring and Liadoff's Kikimora (among others), let us be consistent by calling it the "Russian method."

In "French" notation, all the notes are written with the treble *clef, and sound, on the B-flat bass clarinet, a major ninth (see intervals) lower than written. In "German" notation, the low notes are written with the bass clef, the high ones with the treble, and actual sounds are always a major second (*whole-step) lower than written. The "Russian" method is a hybrid: notes written with the bass clef sound a whole-step lower than written, those with the treble clef a major ninth (octave plus a whole-step) lower. (For the bass clarinet in A the transposition is: "French," minor tenth lower than written, "German," minor third lower.)

To clarify, a passage has been written showing actual pitch, then the equivalent in the three systems of notation.

The now-disused bass clarinet in A was pitched a half step lower than the B-flat instrument. Its lowest tone, written E and sounding C-sharp, was used constantly; hence orchestral players of the B-flat bass clarinet always use an instrument equipped with an extra key providing the written low E-flat (D-sharp), sounding C-sharp. For good measure, some bass clarinets have still an additional key for low D, sounding C.

In Russia the bass clarinet is built to go several steps lower than shown here. These supplementary low tones appear in works of Shostakovich, Khachaturian, and others, sometimes in prominent solos.

As a rule, a bass clarinet player is someone who was originally

Range of the bass clarinet in B-flat:

trained on the ordinary clarinet.
See also transposing instruments.
Italian: clarinetto basso or clarone.
French: clarinette basse. German:
Bassklarinette (often printed
Baßklarinette) or Bassclarinette.
Spanish: clarinete bajo.

● bass clef. See clef.

● bass drum. An indefinite pitch
*percussion instrument. Its shape
is that of a cylinder having a very
large diameter and fairly great depth,
with a parchment head on each flat
side. There are no snares. It is
played while resting on its round shell,
usually in a low stand; that is, the
two heads face to right and left, and
either head may be struck.

or tambora.

● basset horn. An instrument of
the *clarinet type; it might well be
regarded as a "tenor clarinet" or
small *bass clarinet. It was a
favorite instrument with Mozart,
but has become almost obsolete
since his time; however the *alto
clarinet has a comparable *range
though a somewhat different *tone-
color.
The player is of course someone who originally studied the
clarinet.
The basset horn is notated a
perfect fifth higher than the sounds
desired; it is an F instrument.
(See transposing instruments.)
Range:

The bass drum stick has a felt
knob on each end, one knob being
smaller than the other; however the
instrument is also often played with
*timpani sticks.
In the *dance band it is sometimes
played from a pedal attached in such
a way as to activate a small clapper
that strikes the drum. In addition,
pictures are sometimes painted on
the head and a lighted electric bulb
is placed inside. Of course these
practices are scorned in serious
music. Another special implement,
occasionally used in the orchestra,
is mentioned under Rute.
A single tone on a bass drum sounds
like a shot from a cannon--a heavy,
dull thud--while the *roll (2) suggests
distant thunder.
Music for the bass drum is often
written on a one-line *staff.
Synonym: big drum.
Italian: cassa, gran cassa, cassa
grande, or tamburo grande. French:
caisse or grosse caisse. German:
grosse Trommel. Spanish: bombo

Skillful players can go much
higher than indicated here. Sometimes the bass *clef is employed
for the lowest tones, in which case
they are written an octave too low
(i. e., a perfect fourth below the
actual sounds), exactly as in writing for the French *horn in F.
Variant spelling: bassett horn.
Italian: corno di bassetto or
(preferably) corno bassetto; also
(formerly) clarone.

● bass flute. British name for the
*alto flute. The term is some-
what unfortunate, as it invites confusion with the true bass flute, an
extremely rare but quite distinct
instrument which is built an octave
lower than the ordinary flute.

● bass horn. A name sometimes
carelessly applied to the *tuba.
(Undesirable.)

● †bassi. (1) To be played by the
*cellos and *double-basses.

Formerly it was customary, in orchestral *scores, to write the cello and double-bass parts on a single staff. If the composer wanted a certain passage to be played by the cellos only, he used the designation Vlc. or Vc., abbreviations for violoncello. The re-entrance of the double-basses (using the same written notes as the cellos, but sounding so as to produce a series of *octaves with them) was indicated by the word bassi, literally "basses." It is important to mention that this does not mean double-basses only, but double-basses and cellos. On the

● bass oboe.   The heckelphone.

● †basso continuo.   See figured bass and continuo.
Abbreviation: B. C.

● bassoon.   A double reed *woodwind instrument, consisting of a long, round, narrow, wooden body (held diagonally in playing) with a mouth-pipe shaped like a sickle, or a question-mark lying on its side. Most bassoons have a little ring of ivory at the very top of the instrument.
Range:

rare occasions when the double-basses alone were wanted the sign was contrabasso.

When the tenor *clef was used, this alone sufficed to indicate a passage for cellos only, the resumption of the bass clef indicating the re-entrance of the double-basses.

The use of this term can be most readily found in an orchestral score by Haydn or Mozart.

The custom of writing both cello and double-bass on a single staff tended to disappear after about 1830 or 1840.

(2)   Plural of basso.

● †basso.   (1) A male singer with a bass voice.
Plural: bassos or bassi.
Synonym: bass (3).
(2) In orchestral *scores where the cellos and double-basses are written on a single staff, the part is often marked "basso." This does not mean simply double-basses, but rather "the bass part, to be played by cellos and double-basses." See also bassi.
Plural: bassi.
(3) See bassa.

A few bassoons can do down to low A, and some can sound the high E.

The bassoon is notated at actual pitch with the bass *clef, supplemented by the tenor clef for the high notes.

The epithet, "comedian of the orchestra," frequently applied to the instrument by facile books on music appreciation, is of course often appropriate, yet perhaps even oftener it is quite out of character, for the highest tones in particular are eerie and almost blood-curdling. Its hollow *tone-color suggests (to quote Rimsky-Korsakoff's apt description) senile mockery.

Synonym (very rare): fagot.
Italian: fagotto (plural, fagotti). French: basson. German: Fagott (plural, Fagotte). Spanish: bajón (plural, bajones) or fagot (plural, fagotes).

The player is called a bassoonist.

● basso ostinato.   See ostinato.

● bass staff.   A *staff with a bass (or F) *clef. In music for the piano it is the lower of the two staffs bracketed together.

● bass trumpet. A rarely-used *brass instrument built variously in E-flat, C, or B-flat, sounding a perfect fifth, minor seventh, or octave, respectively, below the ordinary B-flat trumpet. It extends trumpet *tone-color down to pitches ordinarily considered in *trombone range.

● bass tuba. A more complete name for the *tuba. However, "tuba" alone indicates the bass tuba; when wishing to indicate the *tenor tuba or the *Wagner tuba the full name must be used.

● bass viol. (1) A rather undesirable name sometimes applied to the *double-bass.
(2) An obsolete instrument, one of the *viol family.

● baton. The short stick or staff, usually made of wood, used by the *conductor of an orchestra, band, or chorus to mark the *beat. He indicates the *tempo and to a certain extent the manner of playing or singing by his use of the baton. (See conducting.)
This is the French word meaning "stick. "
The drum-majors of bands often use a large metal rod or pole, also called a baton, but its purpose is as a rule one of showmanship rather than of conducting.
Many conductors, especially choral conductors, prefer to dispense with the baton.
The writing of this word in French style--bâton--is tending to disappear. The English pronunciation is always used.

● battery. A term sometimes used as a synonym for *percussion instruments, other times to designate all the percussion instruments in an orchestra other than the *timpani, still other times to designate the percussion instruments of indefinite pitch.
Variant spelling: batterie.

● Bayreuth. A town in the Bavarian part of West Germany. northeast of Nuremberg. It is famous as the location of the Festspielhaus designed by Wagner and given over to the performance of his operas.
The town is not a metropolis; it has a population of about 60, 000. Wagner selected it for the very reason that it is both fairly small and remote. He wanted audiences to make a "pilgrimage" to hear his operas, rather than casually dropping by the theater merely to while away an evening.
The Bayreuth festival devoted to Wagner's music is usually held in July and August, but it is not given every year.
Variant spelling: Baireuth.
Pronunciation: bī-roit´or bī⁼roit. (Preferably neither syllable should be accented.)

● Bayreuth tuba. Same as Wagner tuba.

● B. C. Abbreviation for basso continuo. See continuo and figured bass.

● beak flute. See recorder.

● beam. Same as crossbeam.

● beat. (1) One of the individual steady *pulsations or "throbs" that go to make up the *meter of music. These beats tend to group themselves into clusters of two, three, four, or six, occasionally of nine, twelve, five, seven, ten, or eleven, due to the fact that certain ones tend to give the impression of being "strong" ("heavy") or *"accented, " others of being "weak" ("light") or "unaccented. " These clusters of weak and strong beats are called the *meter; each individual cluster is known as a *measure.
The steady succession of beats in a musical composition has often been compared to the steady beating of the heart in the human body, with the further analogy that lack of steadiness denotes a lack of well-being in both.
Tones of various lengths are superimposed on the succession

of beats with the latter furnishing a unit for measuring comparative length (duration); thus we say a certain tone may be two beats in length (or that it "receives" two beats or is "worth" two beats), or four-and-a-half beats, or one-fourth of a beat, or five-and-three-quarter beats, etc.

The beat might well be considered a relative standard of musical time-measurement much as seconds, minutes, and hours are units of ordinary time-measurement, though it must always be remembered that the beat is of no fixed length, for its exact length varies from one composition to another. A beat is essentially a time-measurement, not necessarily a motion made by a *conductor's arm. One beat leads directly to the next, in a continuous flow; there is no separation by moments of "nothing" (vacuums).

For "beating time" see conducting; for down-beat and up-beat see those entries.

Synonyms: pulse (2), count.
Compare rhythm.

(2) A slight throb or oscillation in pitch that is observed when two sounding bodies are not quite perfectly in tune. For instance, if one instrument sounds a tone having 440 vibrations per second, another the tone having 441 vibrations, there will be one beat every second. If the second instrument sounds 442 vibrations, the beats would occur two each second, if 443, three each second, etc. Beats are also observed when octaves, perfect fifths, and other *intervals are not quite perfectly in tune.

● beat note. The note designated by the lower figure in the *time-signature as having the value of one *beat (1); the unit of beat measurement. In time-signatures where the lower figure is 4, the quarter-note is the beat note; where the lower figure is 8, it is the eighth-note; where 2, the half-note.

● beguine. A South American dance somewhat resembling the *bolero.
Pronunciation: bi-gēn.

● †bel canto. Literally, "beautiful singing;" a term used to indicate the smooth, mellifluous, pure *tone-quality admired by the Italian school of singing, which emphasizes it above dramatic expression. When scrutinized, the expression really means almost nothing, for the aim of all singers and all teachers of singing is obviously the production of "beautiful singing."

● bell. (1) The bells required in orchestral and operatic scores are never of the type found in church steeples or the towers of public buildings. Bell or chime effects are usually obtained with *tubular bells, high-pitched tinkling effects with the *glockenspiel.

(2) The outer termination of the tube of a *wind instrument, usually built so as to flare out, is known as the bell. The bells of the brasses flare out very wide, but those of the woodwinds, notably the oboe, do so to a much less pronounced extent. The bassoon can hardly be said to have a bell, while the flute and piccolo have no trace of one. The English horn has a globe-shaped bell.

● bell lyre. A *glockenspiel mounted on a *lyre-shaped frame so that it may be played while marching in a *band.
Variant forms: bell lyra, lyre (3).

● †ben. Well, good. Thus: ben tenuto, well held; ben legato, well connected (both of the foregoing are cautions against any suggestion of *staccato); ben marcato or ben marc., well brought out, prominent, distinctly heard.

● berceuse. A *lullaby. This name is frequently used for instrumental compositions in lullaby style. Although a French word, it is regularly taken into English.
Pronunciation: bâr-sŏŏz´ (English) or bâr-söz (French).

● big drum. The bass drum (rare).

● binary form. A *form-scheme with the pattern: AB. Each section is usually enclosed in *repeat-signs; hence the pattern might better be given as AABB. The B section is sometimes longer than the A.

The B section does not, as a rule, have a distinct theme, but appears more as a highly-modified re-working of the A part. Nevertheless it is distinct enough that the form-scheme cannot be adequately represented as A^1A^2 nor as $A^1A^1A^2A^2$.

Normally the music *modulates to the key of the *dominant near the end of the A section. The B section commences in that key and leads back to the original tonality.

Binary form was in high favor during the *Baroque and *Rococo periods, particularly in the dance movements of *suites (1) and in the so-called keyboard *Sonatas (2) by Domenico Scarlatti.

Synonyms: two-part form, bipartite form.

Pronunciation: bī-nă-rĭ

● binary measure.   Duple meter.

● bind.   Same as tie.

● bipartite form.   Same as binary form.

● bis (French).   Twice. Occasionally this is placed over a measure or a passage intended to be repeated. It is also sometimes used in place of *encore.

See also repeat signs.

Pronunciation: bēs.

● †bisbigliando.   Murmuring, whispering. Used to indicate a very delicate effect, usually in *tremolo.

● bitonality.   Same as polytonality.

● black-and-white process.   A process for reproducing manuscript music which has come into wide usage since the middle 1930's. It is somewhat akin to blue-printing. The copyist or composer writes on a special type of paper known as transparent manuscript paper or thin sheets, which can be obtained in a number of different sizes and with a varying number of staffs already drawn on them. This paper is very thin and translucent, yet not flimsy, being somewhat similar to onion-skin paper. The composer writes on one side only, and with jet-black ink. From his master copy (or original) any blue-printer can reproduce any desired number of copies. These are an exact replica of the original handwriting. The master sheets are stored away after processing and may be re-used at any desired time, for they never deteriorate, nor are they harmed or worn in any way by the reproducing process.

A mistake in the master copy may be corrected by erasing or by cutting the incorrect notes out of the paper with a razor blade; in the latter case a blank spot will appear on the reproduction, which can be filled in with pen and ink. When a text is added with the typewriter, a sheet of carbon paper is placed with the carboned side against the back of the master sheet so that the letters appear on both sides of the latter; this is necessary in order that the copies will turn out clear and dark.

The paper on which the copies are reproduced is often slightly greenish, rather than pure white, and becomes gradually darker with the passing of time, although never so much so as to impair legibility. Copies may be printed on one or both sides of the paper, according to preference.

In preparing the string parts of an orchestral composition, where often as many as nine copies are needed, the great convenience of the black-and-white process is obvious. It is far superior to both stencil- and gelatin-type reproducing methods, and much cheaper than the photostat method.

Since the introduction and perfection of this process, the use of opaque manuscript paper has greatly decreased.

Synonyms: ozalid process, blueprint process, b/w process, blackline print.

● black notes.   Explained under white notes.

● **block chords.** Chords, usually of three simultaneously-sounded tones, devoid of *figuration of any kind (for instance, not handled in *Alberti bass, *broken, or *arpeggio treatment). They are useful in very simple types of accompaniment at the piano, or for reducing a widely-spread arpeggio or *accompaniment-figure to its bare essentials.

Synonym: bongo drums.
Pronunciation: bŏn-gōs (not bŏn-gōz).

● **boogie-woogie.** A type of *jazz characterized by *ostinato bass figures, sometimes repeated almost without change throughout a composition, at other times altered so as to fit the prevailing

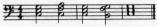

Typical block chords, set
for the piano, left hand.

Typical block chords, set for the piano, left hand.

Antonym: broken chords.

● **block flute.** See recorder.

● **block harmony.** *Parallelisms.

● **blue-print music reproduction.** See black-and-white process.

*harmonies.
Of the following two figures the first is of the former type, the second (in *broken octaves) of the latter type.

● † **bocca chiusa.** Humming. (Literally, "closed mouth.")

● **Bogenform.** German name for *arch form.
Pronunciation: bō-gĕn-fôrm.

● **bolero.** A Spanish dance in moderately fast 3-4 time. Typical bolero rhythms are:

● **bore.** The characteristic diameter of the inside of a wind instrument (either woodwind or brass) is known as the bore. In the flute, clarinet, trumpet, and trombone the bore remains constant from the inner end of the mouthpiece to the beginning of the *bell; this is termed a "cylindrical" bore. In the cornet,

Pronunciation: bō-lä-rō.

● **bombardon.** A brass instrument, practically identical with the *tuba.
This is also the name of an organ stop; see organ.
Pronunciation: bŏm-bär-dǫn or bŏm-bär-dǫn.

● **bongós** (Spanish). An indefinite pitch *percussion instrument consisting of two bucket-shaped drums, each with a single head, played directly with the hands. It is of Cuban origin.

horn, tuba, oboe, bassoon, and saxophone the bore gradually widens, even long before the bell portion is reached; this is termed a "conical" bore.
The nature of the bore (cylindrical or conical) has a great deal to do with the instrument's *tone-color, as has the type of *mouthpiece (cup-shaped or funnel-shaped) in the case of the brass instruments, or the type of *reed (1), (single or double), if any, in the case of the woodwinds. The width of the

bore also produces an effect, wide bores tending toward mellowness, narrow bores toward brilliance.

● borrowed chords.   Same as altered chords.

● borrowed melodies.   Frequently a composer bases a work on some melody not his own. This practice serves as a springboard for setting ideas going in his mind, since getting started--getting something to work with--is sometimes the hardest element in the compositional process. Up through the sixteenth century compositions based on borrowed melodies perhaps outnumbered those that were original from the ground up. The procedure has declined since the seventeenth century, although it is still far from unknown. The amount of quoting is always very slight. Often the borrowed theme is much disguised or varied. The practice is in no way comparable to the puerile and shameless practice of appropriating well-known compositions and turning them into "popular" songs, which is a form of *plagiarism.

The borrowed melody is known under the Latin name cantus firmus (plural, cantus firmi), or by the Italian equivalent canto fermo (plural, canti fermi). Cantus prius factus and tenor (4) are additional synonyms.

Folk music and *Gregorian chants are the reservoirs from which most borrowed melodies are appropriated, although *chorales and *hymn-tunes are also occasionally utilized. A *theme and variations is often built on a melody borrowed from a known composer whose name normally appears as a part of the title. Clearly, only themes in the *public domain may be employed unless permission is specifically granted.

A number of *masses are based on *Gregorian chants, others on secular themes such as *folk songs. Many *cantatas for use in the Lutheran church utilize a *chorale melody--one associated with a text of a spirit similar to that found in the text of the cantata. When such a theme is used systematically in each section (or at least most of them) the effect is one of increased unity; the entire mass or cantata seems truly to "belong together." (See cyclic form.)

The *chorale-prelude is always based on a borrowed melody-- namely that of a chorale.

Musicians have never looked upon the use of borrowed melodies as plagiarism.

● bourrée.   A type of French dance in quick 2-2 time. It usually begins with an *upbeat equivalent to a quarter-note. Bourrées are sometimes found in the Baroque ("Classic") *suite (1).

Pronunciation: bōō-rā.

● bow.   An implement used to play the *violin and related instruments (see string instruments). The player draws the bow across the strings to set them to vibrating.

The lower end, which the player holds, is called the nut, heel, or frog. The opposite end is known as the point or tip.

The bow was originally designed after the archer's bow, but in the course of its evolution the stick has been straightened to the extent where it is almost parallel to the hair; however it curves slightly inward. The wood is very light and a trifle flexible; the tightly-stretched hair has a springy quality.

*Rosin is applied to the hair in order to produce friction with the strings. The hair may be made tighter or looser by turning a little screw located at the frog.

François Tourte (1747-1835), a resident of Paris, is considered the greatest of all bow-manufacturers, and all those of the present day are modeled after the products of his workshop.

Italian: arco (plural, archi). French: archet. German: Bogen (plural, Bögen).

See also bowing, down-bow, up-bow.

● bowed instruments.   *String instruments played with a *bow.

● bow form.   Same as arch form.

●bowing. The manner of using the bow in playing the bowed *string instruments.

The explanation of down-bow and up-bow will be found under those headings.

All notes spanned by a *slur are played with a single movement, up or down, of the bow; the effect is of course *legato. The number of notes that can be slurred together is greater in passages that are soft or fast than in those that are loud or slow.

The absence of a slur denotes the use of alternate down- and up-bows, one for each note. The constant change of bow does not in any way prevent the notes from being played legato when and if desired. Such passages give a delightfully "busy" and "chattering" effect when rapid.

There are a number of bow-strokes, as they are called--special and distinct ways of using the bow--that have acquired special names.

The bowed *tremolo might perhaps also be considered a bow-stroke. Information will be found under that entry.

Other effects possible with string instruments, but not classified as bowing, are *pizzicato, *col legno, sul ponticello, sul tasto (both described under sul), *harmonics (1), *double-stops, and *divisi.

●bow-strokes. See bowing.

●brace. (1) The character used to bracket together a number of *staffs which sound simultaneously. It is almost always used for the two staffs on which music for the piano is written, also for the *harp and for the *manuals (but not *pedals) of the *organ. Synonym: bracket.

(2) A synonym for system.
Compare accolade.
See also great staff.

●brass band. A *band (i. e., military band) consisting entirely of brass instruments, plus a few of the percussion family, but devoid of woodwind instruments. They were once in considerable vogue.

The term brass band is sometimes applied to the *brass instruments of the orchestra, as a synonym for brass family, brass section, or brass choir. It is also sometimes quite incorrectly applied to the full band.

●brass bass. The tuba (undesirable).

●brass instruments. All instruments which work on the principle of a tube which sounds the tones of its *harmonic series, through varying lip tension (with or without the addition of *valves or a *slide) are known as brass instruments.

The use of this generic term is purely a convention; the substance used in their manufacture is not invariably brass, nor are all instruments made of this metal necessarily "brass instruments"; for instance the *saxophone, though always made of brass, is classified as a *woodwind, due to the principle on which it works.

Brass instruments are played with a certain characteristic mouthpiece, which is sometimes cupshaped and sometimes funnelshaped (conical).

These instruments were in a very primitive stage of development until the invention of valves during the early part of the nineteenth century. The *trumpets and *horns for which Bach, Handel, Mozart, Haydn, Gluck, Beethoven, Weber, Schubert, Mendelssohn, and Berlioz were obliged to write were so limited that it is a miracle that these men were able to get any results whatever from them. The resources were scarcely greater than those of the *bugle--the only brass instrument (other than the *post-horn) still not equipped with slide or valves.

The following are classified as brass instruments:

With valves: *trumpet, *horn, *tuba, *euphonium, *baritone (2), *alto horn (mellophone), *cornet, *Wagner tuba (Bayreuth tuba).

With slide: *trombone.

With *keys (3): *keyed bugle, *ophicleide, *serpent (all obsolete).

With finger-holes: *Zink (not actually made of brass; obsolete).

When played fortissimo, the brass instruments are extremely powerful; yet their pianissimo is equally effective. In general, their parts tend to move less rapidly than those of the string and woodwind instruments, due partly to the fact that they are less agile by nature, but mostly to their uncouth, clattering, and alarming effect when played fast.

No brass instrument can play two or more tones simultaneously.

Synonym: brass-wind instruments.

See also orchestra.

● brass quartet. This group usually consists of two *trumpets, a *horn, and a *trombone. The term is, however, by no means as standardized as *string quartet, and is not infrequently used in reference to other combinations of four brass instruments, e. g., two trumpets and two trombones.

See also chamber music.

● brass quintet. Usually two trumpets, horn, trombone, and tuba, although other combinations are occasionally used, for instance two trumpets, euphonium, trombone, and tuba.

See also chamber music.

● Bratsche. German name for the *viola.

Plural: Bratschen.

Pronunciation: brät-shĕ.

● †bravura. Brilliance. Con bravura, brilliantly, boldly.

A bravura passage in a composition is one to be executed in a dashing, seemingly reckless, manner.

(Related English word: bravery.)

● break. (1) An abrupt change in the tone-quality of an instrument or voice as it moves from one *register to another.

In some voices it will be noticed that the quality of the upper tones is much different from that of the lower. In singing down a scale it may be possible to locate the exact two pitches between which the abrupt change occurs. This point is called the break. Its presence is a sign of faulty voice-production. The gradual smoothing over of this break, so that the tone-quality is homogeneous throughout, is the objective of the singer, aided, of course, by his teacher. Some voices are naturally free from this blemish.

A similar abrupt change can be observed in some instruments as they move from one register to another. The clarinet has such a break between the notes

It is conspicuous with a poor player using a cheap instrument, but on a high-quality clarinet in the hands of an experienced player it is impossible to detect the break even with careful listening.

(2) In *jazz, a short passage for a single instrument (commonly saxophone, clarinet, trumpet, or piano) of a bizarre, impertinent, and typically "jazzy" effect, during which the other instruments are silent. Its character is very much that of a short *cadenza.

● breve. (1) Short; often used in connection with the *fermata.

(Related English word: brief.)

Synonyms: corto, corta.

Antonym: lunga.

(2) A note-value tending to disappear from use, written ⊨ ‖o‖ |o| It is twice as long as a whole-note, four times as long as a *half-note, etc.

Handel and others sometimes write a breve in 4-4 time (which theoretically cannot hold it) presumably as an abbreviation for two whole-notes tied, or for a long note of indeterminate length.

Synonym: double whole-note.

See also British terminology, time-values.

Pronunciation (of second meaning): brēv (not brĕv). (Pronunciation of first meaning is according to rules of pronunciation of Italian, shown on page 17 .)

● bridge. A small, thin piece of

wood (often with perforations) over which the strings of a bowed or plucked string instrument pass. There are tiny notches on the upper edge to accommodate the strings. The pitch that the instrument gives off is produced by the vibration of that portion of the string that lies between

Type of note	American name
○	whole-note
♩	half-note
♩	quarter-note
♪	eighth-note
♬	sixteenth-note
♬	thirty-second-note
♬	sixty-fourth-note

the bridge and the point where the finger presses it to the *fingerboard, or in the case wherein an *open string is played, the notch over which the string passes shortly before it winds around the tuning-peg. The tiny segment of string that lies on the other side of the bridge is not used.

The bridge is held in place against the belly of the instrument through pure pressure of the very tense strings.

● bridge passage. A short passage of music that connects two principal sections; an *episode; a transitional passage; a link.

● †brillante. Brilliantly.

● †brindisi. Drinking song.
Plural: brindisi.
Pronunciation: accent first syllable.

● †brio. Vivacity, fire. Musicians often use it (incorrectly) as though it meant "brilliance." Con brio, with fire, with spirit.

● †brioso. Spirited, vivacious, fiery, gay.

● British terminology. There are a few differences between British and American musical terminology, the most conspicuous and only serious one being that involving the name of *time-values (and the corresponding *rests). These are as follows:

	British name
	semibreve
	minim
	crotchet (occasionally, semiminim)
	quaver
	semiquaver
	demisemiquaver
	hemidemisemiquaver

The name for the *breve (2) remains the same in both terminologies, although American usage sometimes terms it a double-whole-note.

The above differences were brought about by the fact that many of the early music teachers in the United States were Germans, who shaped our terminology by translating their German terms into literal English--thereby saving us from such a ludicrous term as hemidemisemiquaver, not to mention the absurdity of minim (literally "least") for one of the longest values and breve (literally "short") for a note of very long value.

There are only a few additional points of variance, such as a tendency to substitute the French term cor anglais for the illogical term English horn, a strong preference for pianoforte and violoncello over piano and cello, a tendency to use note in places where we more correctly use tone or key ("the notes heard from the flute," "the white notes on the pianoforte keyboard," etc.) They also have a slight predilection for fussy spellings like programme and quartette. Of course they always use the characteristic British spelling colour in speaking of tone-color ("tone-colour").

●broken. A *chord is said to be broken if its tones are written in succession rather than simultaneously. Thus all *arpeggios and *Alberti bass figures are examples of broken chords. Antonym: block chords.

*Octaves are said to be broken if the two tones involved are heard in succession (usually rather rapid succession) rather than simultaneously.

Of these the first and last are difficult to play and seldom used, while the second-last is distinctly too low ("flat") in pitch, hence unusable. This leaves just four good tones, and nearly all bugle-calls utilize only these four pitches.

Bugles in F and B-flat are also used. The tones available may be found by transposing the G series down a whole-step or up a minor third, respectively.

●bugle-call. A melody played on a *bugle. In view of the fact that the bugle can play only four tones

Broken chord (C E G)   Broken octaves

●†brusco. Rough, rude.
  (Related English word: brusque.)

●buckwheat notes. See shaped notes.

●†buffo, †buffa. Comical.
  (Related English word: buffoon.)

●bugle. A *brass instrument with neither valves nor slide--a primitive or *"natural"-type *trumpet or *cornet --used almost entirely for signaling purposes by armies, in Boy Scout camps, etc. Its *tone-color most closely resembles that of the cornet; it is considerably less brilliant than the trumpet.

The bugle used in the United States is most frequently built in G, and can sound the following tones:

with ease, bugle-calls are normally composed of only this many tones. (See entry bugle, above.) The melodies might almost as well be described as *arpeggios or *broken chords.

Each bugle-call has a name, and each a certain purpose. Hence in the armed forces the playing of bugle-calls is tantamount to giving the more frequently-used commands.

A *trumpet or *cornet can of course play any bugle-call with excellent effect.

●burden. A *refrain that occurs in the middle of the song, or at both the middle and the end. Many sea *chanteys have burdens.
Variant form (archaic): burthen.

Most useful   Too low

● †burlesco. In the manner of a burlesque or parody.

● †burletta. Comic opera.

● b/w process. See black-and-white process.

● B. W. V. See sub-head "Pseudo-Opus-Numbers" in entry opus-numbers.

● by-tones. Same as non-harmonic tones.

C

● ₵ 4-4 time. Although 4-4 is the commonest of all time-signatures, ₵ does not stand for common, as many persons have imagined. It is really a broken circle, not a C; originally the break could occur at the top, bottom, or left, as well as in the present position. (Its opposite was a circle, used to indicate *meters in 3 or multiples thereof.) Compare ₵

● ₵ . 2-2 time; formerly either 2-2 or 4-2. (Sometimes the character was written twice to indicate 4-2.) Often called alla breve and "cut time." See time-signatures. Compare ₵

● c. Abbreviation for circa (about, around, approximately).

● cabinet organ. Same as harmonium.

● cacophony. Sounds of a discordant, harsh, disorderly character. Pronunciation: kả-kǒf-ổ-nǐ.

● cadence. (1) A close or conclusion, coming naturally in a composition at the ends of the *phrases, *periods, and various sections, and at the end of the entire piece.

Derived from the Latin word meaning "to fall," cadence suggests the many "falls" which constantly occur in music as the counterparts to "rises" which seem to generate them and to balance them. The word cadence should not be confused with *cadenza, to which it is related by etymology but not by function.

Types. Certain frequently-employed cadences have acquired definite names.

A cadence consisting of the dominant *triad or dominant *seventh-chord progressing to the tonic triad (V-I or V_7-I) is called an authentic cadence, full cadence, complete cadence, or perfect cadence.

One consisting of the subdominant triad progressing to the tonic triad (IV-I) is called a plagal cadence; "amen" at the end of a *hymn-tune is customarily set to this progression.

One consisting of some form (not necessarily the root position) of the tonic triad coming to rest on the dominant triad (I-V) is called a half cadence or semi-cadence; as its name suggests, it usually occurs at a point midway in a longer passage.

A cadence in which the dominant triad or dominant seventh-chord moves to the submediant triad (V-VI or V_7-VI) is called a deceptive, surprise, evaded, avoided, broken, or interrupted cadence; it always has an element of surprise due to its failure to move on to the expected, namely the tonic (I) triad. Clearly it cannot close a composition, but it constitutes an excellent device whereby a piece can be kept moving and a premature close avoided.

In the Phrygian cadence the lowest voice descends a *half-step while another voice (usually the highest) moves up a *whole-step. It most frequently occurs in the minor mode through the progression of the first inversion of the subdominant triad to the dominant triad (IV_6-V). The name arises from its frequency in the Phrygian *mode (1). This is often a substitute for the half cadence.

The terms *masculine ending and *feminine ending refer to the *rhythm found at the cadence--not to the harmonic progressions. Synonym: close.

(2) In marching, the number of steps taken per minute is known as the cadence. Thus "a cadence of 120" denotes 120 paces each minute.

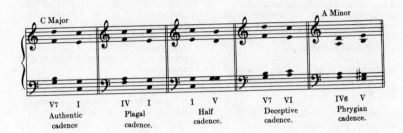

C Major   A Minor

V7   I   IV   I   I   V   V7   VI   IV6   V
Authentic   Plagal   Half   Deceptive   Phrygian
cadence   cadence.   cadence.   cadence.   cadence.

● cadenza. A brilliant display passage for a voice or instrument. Often suggests a bravura *improvisation with the *rhythm rather free.

Short cadenzas are sometimes engraved in fine type--about the size used in printing *grace-notes.

The Cadenza in the Concerto. A prolonged cadenza is normally found in a *concerto. It usually comes in the first movement, very near the end, and is almost invariably for the solo instrument alone, the orchestra being silent. By an established if not justifiable custom, a tonic triad in second inversion (I$^6_4$) very often precedes it, the cadenza normally-- but by no means actually--having the function of a long passage of *dominant harmony which eventually leads to a *cadence on the tonic chord as the orchestra re-enters for the *coda of the movement.

In the concertos of the *Classical period the cadenza was not written by the composer. He merely indicated the place where it should occur, and the soloist was supposed to *improvise it. Naturally no person today would dream of improvising such a passage before an audience, so the soloist interpolates one of the cadenzas that various composers and performers have supplied for practically every concerto. Occasionally the cadenza that is chosen is identified on the program (or, on records and broad-

casts, on the label or in the announcement). Of course one should not always expect to hear the same cadenza (if it is of the type under discussion) with the same concerto; different soloists favor different cadenzas.

Beethoven appears to have been the first composer ever to publish a concerto with a certain prescribed cadenza--that one and no other; more often, however, he contented himself with the interpolated type. Since his time, composers have almost invariably supplied the cadenza themselves; the fact that Brahms called for an interpolated cadenza in his Violin Concerto, written as late as 1878, is definitely an anachronism.

The material of which the cadenza is constructed is supposed to be derived from the *themes of the movement; it should be germane to the work. Naturally some are much better written than others; at their worst they may be a boring display of *virtuosity and nothing more.

There are of course a few concertos without a cadenza, some in which it occurs in a movement other than the first or at some point other than close to the end of the first movement (e. g., Mendelssohn's Violin Concerto), and many in which there is a cadenza in additional movements, even in all three.

Although cadenza is clearly related to the word *cadence, it should not be confused with that term.

See also double sonata-allegro form.

Pronunciation: kä-dĕn⁻zä̱.

● †calando. Gradually becoming softer and slower. It combines the meanings of *diminuendo and *ritardando.

Abbreviation: cal.

● †calmato, calmo. Quiet, peaceful.

Synonyms: quieto, tranquillo, placido.

● †calore. Warmth. Con calore, warmly, with warmth.

● †caloroso. Warmly.

● calypso. A type of popular music of the West Indies, particularly Trinidad, the Bahama Islands, and Jamaica. It is characteristically used by the Negroes of those islands, and displays considerable *jazz influence. The words of calypso songs are often satirical.

● †cambiata. See non-harmonic tones (8); see alto-tenor.

● †Camerata. Collective name for a group of cultured amateurs who met in Florence, Italy during the closing years of the sixteenth and early years of the seventeenth centuries for the purpose of discussing the culture of ancient Greece and Rome, in which interest was then at a high level. Their well-meaning but poorly-informed efforts to revive ancient Greek drama actually led to the invention of a new form--*opera.

Members of the Camerata included Jacopo Peri (1561-1633), composer of the first opera and the first surviving

opera, Giulio Caccini (1546?-1618), Emilio del Cavalieri (1550?-1602), who has incorrectly been credited with the composition of the first *oratorio, Vincenzo Galilei (1520?-1591), father of the great astronomer, and Ottavio Rinuccini (1562-1621), author of the *librettos for several of the earliest operas. Peri, Caccini, and Cavalieri were composers, Galilei a writer on music, and Rinuccini a poet and dramatist.

Camerata is the Italian word meaning "comrade." There is probably also a connection with camera, meaning "chamber" or "salon."

● †campana. Bell; in orchestral scores indicates *tubular bells (chimes).

Plural: campane.

● cancel. Same as natural. (See also accidentals.)

● cancrizans. A device wherein the original notes of a theme or passage are presented in backward order. Since it is impossible to detect the presence of a cancrizans purely by listening (nor is this expected of the listener), it might in all fairness be termed an intellectual artifice.

The word means "crab"; the usage arises from the fact that that animal gives the impression of swimming backward. For an early and celebrated example, see Ma Fin Est Mon Commencement ("My End Is My Beginning") by Guillaume Machaut (1300?-1377).

Synonyms: crab, retrograde, rovescio.

Compare mirror.

Pronunciation: kǎn⁻kri-zǎnz.

● canon. A device in which one *"voice" imitates exactly, note for note, and at a constant *interval and time-lapse, the material that has just been stated in another voice. Children, with their customary directness, have been known to describe the canon as "follow the leader" and "copy cat," both of which are remarkably apt. The two voices involved are called the leader and the follower, or to use Latin terminology, dux and comes. The fabric may also contain additional independent "voices" which do not participate in the canon; indeed this is usually the case.

Sometimes more than two voices participate in the canon, examples of this type being quite a feat of compositional technique.

Inspection of canonic passages will show that the follower voice is sometimes placed higher than the leader, sometimes lower. The *interval-relationship between the participating voices may be any that the composer may see fit to use, though only the canon at the interval of the octave and that at the unison can be readily detected by ear. These are also the most prevalent types, with the canon at the interval of the fifth doubtless next in frequency. Canons at the less usual intervals are seldom detected by the listener, nor are they intended to be obvious.

The time-lapse between the start of the melody in the leader voice and its appearance in the follower is most frequently either half a measure, one measure, or two measures, but any desired time-lapse may be used; examples varying from half a beat to eight or more measures can be found. This element is sometimes called stretto (3).

It is obvious that nearly all canons are feasible at only one certain interval and one certain time-lapse.

Canons in *augmentation, *diminution, *cancrizans, and *inversion are all possible and were frequently used during the fifteenth century. Clearly it is almost never possible to detect the presence of these purely by ear; indeed they are quite inconspicuous even to the eye. Canons of these types are frankly intellectual artifices, though supreme evidence of craftsmanship on the part of the composers who created them.

Few compositions bearing the title canon have been written. The canon is a device or procedure rather than a *form. A canonic passage may occur at any point in a composition and may persist for any convenient length of time.

The distinction between canon

Example A

etc.

and *imitation depends on the length
of time over which the device is
spread; a canon continues for at least
several measures, while imitation
rarely persists for more than eight
or ten notes. The distinction between
the canon and the *round is discussed
under the latter heading.

Example A shows a canon in
Berlioz's Roman Carnival Overture.
Only the participating voices are
shown, the numerous accompanying
parts being omitted. Note that the
follower voice moves in octaves. The
time-lapse is close--only one beat.
Example B shows a canon in inversion; it is from the last (fourth)
movement of Brahms's Trio in A
Minor for clarinet, cello, and piano.
The piano part is omitted here as it
does not participate in the canon.
At the point marked X the imitation
is not exact. (Liberties of this type
are, however, infrequent.) Example
C shows a canon at a rare interval:
the ninth.

● †cantabile. In singing style; song-
like. (Related English word: chant.)
  Abbreviation: cant.
  Pronunciation: accent second syllable.

● †cantando. Singing. About the
equivalent of cantabile.

● †cantante. Same as cantabile and
cantando.

● cantata. A fairly extended composition for *chorus including (usually) solo
voices, with orchestra or possibly
some other instrumental *medium
such as piano or organ. It might well
be described as "a short *oratorio."
Most cantatas are nominally for church
use, hence called church cantatas or
sacred cantatas, although secular
cantatas are by no means rare. However, even church cantatas are probably more often performed at concerts than at religious services.
Cantatas are never staged with scenery,
costumes, or action.

  A cantata normally contains *solos
(both *arias and *recitatives), *duets
and other numbers for several solo
voices, and *choruses, and occasionally an *overture, *prelude, or other
section for orchestra alone. Those

written for use in the Lutheran
church often contain *chorales in
addition, generally at the end.
(For the use of the chorale melody
as a cantus firmus, see borrowed
melodies.) Composers' intentions
normally were that the congregation should join with the choir and
orchestra in the performance of
the chorale sections; hence when
works of this type are presented
in the concert-hall it is not unusual
for the audience to be asked to
sing along with the artists in the
chorales.

  A number of cantatas employ
just a single solo voice, without
chorus, and hence are called solo
cantatas or chamber cantatas. A
solo cantata in one *movement
strongly resembles a *song, while
one in several movements is not
unlike a *song-cycle.

  Pronunciation: kän-tä⁻tä (avoid
kän-tăt⁻a).

● canticle. The portions of church
liturgy which are often sung
rather than spoken. Psalms are
not considered canticles.
  See also Anglican chanting.

● †cantilena. A smoothly-flowing
melody, lyrical in style. The term
is applied to instrumental as well
as vocal music.

● cantillation. Singing or chanting,
particularly in Jewish style.

● †canto. Literally, "song," but
generally used as a synonym for
melodia, melody; thus: il canto ben
marcato, the melody well brought
out.

● †canto fermo. Variant form of
cantus firmus.
  Plural: canti fermi.

● cantor. (1) A church official who
sings the liturgy or leads the singing at services; a precentor.
  (2) Formerly, a choir-director.

● cantus (Latin). Obsolete name
for *soprano.

● cantus firmus (Latin). See bor-

rowed melodies. It is usually understood that this term indicates that the borrowed melody is presented in notes of very long (but not necessarily equal) value.
Plural: cantus firmi (canti firmi is incorrect though frequently seen).
Abbreviation: C. F.
Variant form (Italian): canto fermo (plural, canti fermi).
Synonym: tenor (4) (obsolete).

● †canzona. An early type of instrumental composition, *polyphonic in style. The canzona might be described as the instrumental counterpart of the *madrigal.
Plural: canzone.
Variant form: canzone (plural, canzoni).

● canzonetta. (1) A short composition, usually instrumental, but of song-like character.
(2) A short vocal composition, similar to the *madrigal and *ballett, but simpler. Variant form: canzonet.
Canzonetta literally means "little song."
Pronunciation: usually anglicized.

● Capellmeister. Variant spelling of Kapellmeister.

● †cappella. See a cappella. (Often misspelled capella.)

● †capriccio. Same as caprice. A capriccio, same as capriccioso.
Plural: capriccios (English) or capricci (Italian).
Pronunciation: accent second syllable.

● †capriccioso. In a capricious manner; fancifully, whimsically.

● caprice. A composition in free form containing numerous abrupt and fanciful changes in tempo and mood.
Nevertheless Brahms used the variant form capriccio as title for many piano pieces, some quite uniform in tempo and mood. All however are quite lively; for similar pieces of a quiet nature he employed the title *intermezzo (4).

● carillon. A large set of bells, tuned to the chromatic scale and played from a keyboard or from a mechanism. They are often hung in the towers of churches or other public buildings. A small but growing literature is available for the instrument.
The carillon has been especially popular in Belgium and Holland.
Well-known American carillons are those of the University of Chicago, Riverside Church in New York, and the Bok Tower near Lake Wales, Florida.
Pronunciation: kắr-ĭ-lŏn or (less desirably) kă-rĭl-yŏn.

● Carnegie Hall. A large auditorium in New York City, frequently used for orchestral and other concerts.

● carol. A song, usually joyful in spirit, for use at Christmas or some other festal occasion such as Easter. Many carols are *folk songs.
The carol is normally more folklike and less devotional than the *hymn.
See also noël.

● cassation. Same as divertimento.

● castanets. A *percussion instrument of indefinite pitch. The orchestral instrument consists of two spoon-shaped wooden clappers loosely hinged to a comparatively broad wooden holder, and is played by shaking. It is chiefly associated with Spanish music. The tone is dry, hard, "clacking" and quite penetrating, though not very loud.
Music for the castanets is often written on a one-line *staff.
It is perhaps well to point out that the orchestral form of the castanets is somewhat different from that employed by Spanish gypsies. The latter are not mounted on a stick, but are held around the thumb by a short piece of string.
Metal castanets are sometimes used. These should be considered a distinct instrument.

The word castanets is of course plural; the singular is seldom used. The word is often used as though it were singular.
Variant spelling: castagnettes. Italian: castagnette. French: castagnettes. German: Kastagnetten. Spanish: castañuelas or castañetas.

● †castrato. A man who has been castrated during childhood to prevent his voice from changing (see change of voice); a eunuch singer. A castrato may be either a *soprano or a *contralto, but is usually the former.
The cruel practice necessary to produce a castrato appears to be unknown today. Castrati were in wide vogue, especially in Italy, during the sixteenth, seventeenth, and early eighteenth centuries as choir singers, and, after the introduction of *opera during the seventeenth century, as operatic singers. The latter were extremely popular with audiences, and they commanded very high fees; indeed they may have been the highest paid musicians of all time.
Judging from contemporaneous reports, the male soprano voice possessed an agility and dazzling technique that has never been equaled. Coupled with this it had a *tone-color that was unique; it was neither that of the ordinary female soprano nor that of the boy soprano, much less that of the (male) *tenor voice, but rather a quality all its own, which few living people have ever heard. In addition it was said to possess tremendous power.
The technical problems inherent in compositions intended for this type of voice are so great that such music is rarely performed nowadays, as it is beyond the capabilities of both the normal (female) soprano voice and of the tenor voice (performing an octave lower than intended).
Farinelli (1705-1782) and Caffarelli (1703-1783), whose real names were Carlo Broschi and Gaetano Majorano, respectively, were perhaps the most famous of the castrati.
Plural: castrati.
Synonyms: artificial soprano, evirato (plural, evirati), male soprano.

● catch. A type of *round popular in England during the Restoration period (i. e., late seventeenth century). The text was usually humorous, even bawdy.

● †cavatina. A short *aria, or an instrumental composition of songlike character.

● C clef. See clef.

● †cedendo. Literally "yielding," that is, retarding slightly; may be a caution to allow enough time to prevent hurrying and blurring a passage. (Related English word: cede.)
Abbreviation: ced.
See also senza rigore.

● celesta. A definite pitch *percussion instrument played from a keyboard. It looks like a very small piano. Its *tone-color is delightfully delicate and sugary, like tiny bells; however its volume is quite weak. Tuned metal bars produce the sound.
It is notated an octave below the actual sounds. (However, Tschaikowsky in The Nutcracker--the first composition ever to call for this instrument--writes it at actual pitch.)
Range:

Written   Sounding:

A few celestas have been built to go
an octave lower than shown.
    Variant spelling: celeste.
    Italian: celeste or celesta.   French:
célesta.   German: Celesta. Spanish:
celesta.
    Pronunciation: The word is of
course pronounced sĕ-lĕs-tà, but
some musicians use chà-lĕst, which
is neither the French nor the Italian
pronunciation, much less English.

● cello.   A bowed *string instrument
whose four strings are tuned thus:

The cello is held between the knees
and the player is always seated. The
instrument rests on a rather long peg.
    The lowest tones are heavy and
growling, the middle ones very smooth
and silky, while the highest are intense, and sweet almost to the point
of being cloying. The instrument often
strongly suggests the male voice.
    The range of the cello is:

In *concertos and other solo works
it is not uncommon to find the range
extended a fourth or more higher;
this of course does not include still
higher sounds obtainable with
*harmonics. It will be seen that the
range of the cello is one of the widest
of any instrument. Cello *fingering
(2) technique often employs the thumb,
thus being at variance with violin and
viola technique.
    The cello is basically notated with
the bass *clef; for upper tones the
tenor clef is employed, although this
usage seems to be disappearing in
favor of the treble clef; in any case
the latter is always used for the
highest notes. Formerly it was
customary to write the upper tones

with the treble clef, but an octave
higher than the actual pitches;
however this practice disappeared
early in the present century. (With
this exception the cello is strictly
a non-transposing instrument.)
    Plural: cellos or celli.
    Variant spelling: 'cello.
    Full name: violoncello (not
violincello).
    Italian: violoncello (plural,
violoncelli).   French: violoncelle.
German: Violoncell (plural,
Violoncelle), or Violoncello (plural,
Violoncellos), or Cello (plural,
Cellos or Celli).   Spanish: violoncelo.
    The player is called a cellist
(often spelled 'cellist) or violon-
cellist.
    Pronunciation: chĕl-ō (never
shĕl-ō or sĕl-ō).

● cembalo.   A term used during
the *Baroque period to designate
any keyboard instrument, usually the
harpsichord or the piano, sometimes the organ. (Composers as
well as players were indifferent
as to exactly which of these was
employed.)   The presence of a
keyboard instrument was both
necessary and customary in the
music of this period for *realizing
the *figured bass. (Strictly speaking, the term designates only
harpsichord; it is a shortened form
of clavicembalo and gravicembalo,
both names for the harpsichord.)
    Plural: cembalos (English) or
cembali (Italian).
    Variant forms (rare): cimbalo,
cymbalo.
    Synonym: clavier (2).
    Pronunciation: chĕm-bä-lō.

● C. F.   Abbreviation for cantus
firmus.

●chaconne. See passacaglia and
ostinato.
    Variant forms: ciaconna (Italian);
chaconny (English; obsolete).

●chalumeau (French). (1) A primitive double-reed woodwind instrument,
the ancestor of the present *oboe and,
to some extent, of the *clarinet. The
shepherd's pipe is a type of chalumeau.
It was related to the *shawm. Plural:
chalumeaux.
    (2) The lowest register of the
clarinet, the range being

Some writers restrict it to

The *tone-color of the chalumeau
register is rich, dark, reedy, oily,
and gurgling, and sharply different
from that of any other instrument
except of course the *alto clarinet
and *bass clarinet.
    Pronunciation: shä-lü-mō.

●chamber-music. Music written for
a small group of instruments (usually
three to nine), each of which plays a
separate part.
    Many musicians also consider com-
positions for one or two instruments
as chamber-music, and hence would
include all the literature for piano,
organ, violin and piano, two pianos,
etc. in this category.
    In the opening statement the words
"each of which plays a separate part"
are of decisive importance, for no
ensemble--no matter how small--in
which two or more instruments are
constantly playing in *unison is a true
chamber-music group. For this
reason the frequent classification of
the *string orchestra literature as
"chamber-music" is open to serious
question.
    Often chamber-music is defined as

"music that is played in a small
room." This is nonsense. If a
full *orchestra were to crowd into
a small room, the result would
not suddenly turn into "chamber-
music"; it would remain orchestral
music, but heard under unfavorable
conditions. Conversely, if a
*string quartet (1) should play in
a very large auditorium or even
outdoors, the music itself would
remain chamber-music, but heard
under poor conditions. There can
be no doubt, however, that chamber-
music is heard to best advantage in
an auditorium of moderate dimensions,
for it is probably the most intimate,
most subtle, and least superficial
of all musical *mediums.
    This term should not be applied
to *transcriptions of potpourris
from *operettas and other light
compositions that are played as
*"dinner music." A typical group
used for this far-from-exalted
purpose is violin, cello, and piano
("piano trio"), a combination for
which many true chamber-music
works have been written, but inconsequential music of the type
just described does not automatically
become "chamber-music" simply by
virtue of being performed by a
chamber-music group.
    In all true chamber-music the
instruments tend to be of equal
importance, viewing the composition
as a whole. Team-work is the
primary requisite of the group that
performs it; no member is a "star"
or a "soloist." The instrumentalist
whose concept of music is merely
one of show, or who constantly
feels the need to bask in the
musical spotlight, invariably makes
a poor chamber-music player--
though he seldom is attracted to
it in the first place.
    Most compositions in the chamber-
music category are of major proportions; they are divided into
*movements and normally follow
the same form-plan found in the
*sonata, *concerto, and *symphony
--the form described in this volume
under sonata-types. For a reason
that would be hard to specify, short
one-movement works for chamber-

music combinations are quite rare, though the condensed "sonata-type" form as outlined under one-movement symphony has been occasionally applied in chamber-music works.

Chamber-music is normally performed without a *conductor.

The term vocal chamber-music has been applied to small vocal ensembles, such as groups that sing *madrigals. It has also been applied, though less appropriately, to the art-*song (Lieder) medium.

See chamber-music groups.

● chamber-music groups. Various combinations of instruments which are frequently employed in *chamber-music have acquired certain conventional names that are accepted and understood among all musicians, even though several are hardly to be commended for accuracy or consistency. The most frequent are:

String quartet. 2 violins, viola, cello.

String trio. Violin, viola, cello. Two less frequent combinations are listed under the entry string trio.

String quintet. (A) 2 violins, 2 violas, cello; or (B) 2 violins, viola, 2 cellos. Two less frequent combinations are listed under the entry string quintet.

String sextet. 2 violins, 2 violas, 2 cellos.

String octet and Double quartet. 4 violins, 2 violas, 2 cellos. For distinction see double quartet (2).

Piano trio. Violin, cello, piano. A less frequent combination is given under the entry piano trio.

Piano quartet. Violin, viola, cello, piano.

Piano quintet. 2 violins, viola, cello, piano.

Wind quintet or (less accurately) Woodwind quintet. Flute, oboe, clarinet, horn, bassoon.

Woodwind quartet. Usually flute, oboe, clarinet, bassoon.

Woodwind trio. Usually flute, clarinet, bassoon.

Clarinet quintet. Clarinet, 2 violins, viola, cello.

Brass quartet. 2 trumpets, horn, trombone; less frequently 2 trumpets, 2 trombones, or possibly some other combination of four brass instruments.

Brass quintet. Usually 2 trumpets, horn, trombone, tuba.

Naturally it is neither impossible nor unusual to write for groups other than those just shown; in these cases it is necessary to enumerate the instruments. Some well-known works for less frequent --even unique--combinations include Schubert's Quintet in A ("The Trout") for violin, viola, cello, double-bass, and piano; Brahms's Trio in A Minor for clarinet (or viola), cello, and piano; Brahms's Trio in E-flat for violin, horn, and piano; Bartók's Contrasts for violin, clarinet, and piano; Mozart's Quartet in F for oboe, violin, viola, and cello; Mozart's Quintet in E-flat for horn, violin, 2 violas, and cello; Debussy's Sonata for flute, viola, and harp. Many others might be mentioned.

Most large works for these combinations are cast in the form described under sonata-types; that is, they are divided into *movements, at least one of which is in *sonata-allegro form.

See also groups.

● chamber opera. A type of *opera using a small orchestra, limited scenery and stage-effects, and a fairly small number of singers. Ease of performance and staging are characteristic. Many of them are cast in only one act.

This type of opera has had a remarkable development in the United States during the past twenty years, particularly in colleges, and represents one of the few instances in which American composers have been encouraged to write operas of serious stature.

A chamber opera is not an *operetta.

See also Gebrauchsmusik.

● chamber orchestra. (1) A small orchestra; a sinfonietta (2).

(2) A *string orchestra (undesirable).

(3) One of the larger *chamber-music groups, such as one with nine members (*nonet) or more.

● chamber sonata. Same as sonata da camera.

● chamber symphony. Name applied to a composition in several movements written for a large chamber-music ensemble, or for a very small orchestra.

German: Kammersymphonie.

● chance music. An avant-garde type of music, first appearing around 1950, which leaves some room for the element of chance in performance. The performer may be permitted to play the various sections in any order he chooses, or he may be given some latitude as to what notes to play, or as to the rhythmic pattern to employ, or as to the *tempo. In some ensemble works the performers are required to play certain notes, but permitted to insert them at any time they prefer.

One chance composition requires that twelve AM radios be tuned in to twelve different stations and the chance mixture of sounds becomes the "composition," though the volume-controls are to be manipulated in accordance with directions from a conductor. A "transcription" of this "composition" has been made--probably with tongue in cheek--for eight FM radios!

Chance music has been hailed as a liberation of the performer from domination by the composer and denounced as quackery of the most blatant type.

Synonyms: aleatoric music, aleatory music.

See also improvisation.

● change of voice. The change of both *tone-quality and *range of the singing and speaking voice which occurs in young men during adolescence. In general the voice descends an octave in pitch, due to the fact that the voice-box doubles in size. (It should be borne in mind that the voices of children resemble the *soprano in both quality and range.)

Change of voice usually begins during the thirteenth or fourteenth year. However, no general rule can be given, for it has been known to occur slightly earlier or much later.

In some individuals the change of voice takes place very gradually. The boy loses one high tone after another, but seems to gain a new low tone for each high one lost, almost as compensation, until the process is complete. In these cases the process is long-drawn-out but causes little inconvenience.

In other individuals the voice remains at its original pitch for a long time, then "breaks" abruptly, and there comes a transition period during which the boy can hardly sing at all, or at best his voice has an extremely narrow range and a grotesque quality. (This type of voice is sometimes euphemistically termed *alto-tenor.) In addition the speaking voice may also become unmanageable, often changing suddenly from bass to soprano or vice versa; the ludicrous effect is well known. During this period the singer is advised never to force his voice in either volume or range, as it may cause permanent damage. Formerly teachers of singing even went so far as to forbid all singing until the voice had settled in its new and permanent range.

There is no way of speeding up or slowing down the process; it simply has to run its course.

It is interesting to note that a voice destined to be *tenor usually first descends to *bass, then gradually rises part way back until it settles at tenor range and quality.

Change of voice also occurs in girls, and at about the same age as in boys; however, the change is almost entirely one of quality, little if any of range except in the case of *contraltos, and hence it is neither conspicuous nor troublesome.

Synonym: mutation.

● changing-notes. See non-harmonic tones (5).

● chanson (French). Broadly, the French word for song.

In the fourteenth and fifteenth centuries, chanson was the generic name for several distinct forms, one of which was the *rondeau (1). These compositions were typically performed by one voice (generally on the highest part) and two instruments.

The polyphonic chanson of the sixteenth century was a four- or five-voice vocal work, not very long, that might well be regarded the French equivalent of the *madrigal.
Pronunciation: shän-soṇ.

● chant. The general name given to several distinct varieties of music intended for use in church liturgy. . All types of chant consist of unaccompanied *melodies in free, unmetrical *rhythm, the latter to some extent being an outgrowth of the accent of the words.

True chant should not be confused with *Anglican chanting, used in the Church of England and in the Episcopal Church, which is in four-part harmony and vastly different in style from the type of music under discussion here.

The use of singing at religious services goes back to the dawn of history. The aesthetic purpose appears to be one of enhancing the words, to make the thoughts expressed all the more acceptable to the deity to whom they are addressed. In addition, it is well known that singing "carries" better and penetrates farther than speech; hence there is also a practical reason for employing singing--one which became more and more urgent as larger and larger churches were built.

Chant arose during the musically obscure period in history when the Christian church was still a rather new institution--the early centuries A. D. It was clearly influenced by Greek, Jewish, and near-Eastern music. The Eastern or Byzantine church, centered in Constantinople (now Istanbul, Turkey) developed six styles or "dialects" of chant. The Western or Roman church, centered in Rome, developed four styles: Mozarabic (or Visigothic), Gallican, Ambrosian (or Milanese), and Gregorian (or Roman). Mozarabic, Gallican, and the six types of Eastern chant are of interest only to advanced scholars. Ambrosian chant is con-

siderably more important, and is discussed under that heading. Gregorian chant, historically the last one to make its appearance, is by far the most important of the types, and is discussed at some length under that heading.

The word chant means simply "song."

● chanterelle (French). The highest-pitched string of a bowed *string instrument. The name stems from the supposition that this string (e g., the E-string of the violin) is best suited to music of a "singing" character, the French verb meaning "to sing" being chanter.
Synonym: first string.
Pronunciation: shän-trèl.

● chantey. A *folk-song originating among seamen and sung aboard ship.

Chanteys usually alternate passages for a solo voice with passages for chorus. They are a type of *work-song. One sailor sings the solo passage, the others join in at the choruses, meanwhile working in rhythm so as to lighten the task and obtain synchronized effort. They were especially used in connection with work at the capstans. Chanteys were more frequently used by merchant seamen than by naval sailors.

Modern steamboats have almost put an end to the delightful custom of using chanteys, which belong to the romantic days of the sailing vessel.

A chantey is by no means the same thing as a *barcarolle.
Variant spellings: chanty, shanty.
Pronunciation: shän-tī.

● chanting. See Anglican chanting.

● character piece, characteristic piece. A short piece of a type having some rather definite style but usually not a prescribed form, such as the *nocturne, *pastorale, *barcarolle, *elegy, *caprice, or *berceuse.

The term is not usually applied

to dances, nor to compositions in
which the title describes either the
form or some prominent device, such
as *rondo, *fugue, or *canon; nor is
it applied to pieces whose title merely
describes the function, without implying any special style, such as *prelude, *ballade, or *intermezzo.

● †che. Then, until, that which.
Thus, più mosso che tempo primo
means "faster than the first tempo."

● chest of viols. Name used in
Elizabethan England (late sixteenth
and early seventeenth centuries) for
a group of *viols--six or more. The
inclusion of the word chest arises
from the fact that the instruments
were usually hung in a chest when not
in use; indeed the chest and the
instruments were often bought or sold
as a single transaction.
See also consort.

● chest voice. The lower, thick,
dark, and somewhat rough-toned
*register of the singing voice is known
as the chest voice. The term is
merely a convention and does not
indicate that such tones are actually
produced in the chest.
Compare head voice.

● †chiaro. Clear, bright.

● chimes. (1) Same as tubular bells.
(2) The chimes hung in the towers
of public buildings are similar to the
*carillon, but contain fewer bells
and are usually tuned to the *diatonic
rather than *chromatic scale.

● Chinese blocks. Same as temple
blocks. The singular is also sometimes used as a synonym for wood
block.

● Chinese drum. A shallow, two-
headed drum with short, slightly
convex sides, the latter often painted
red.

● Chinese gong. A more complete
name for the *gong.

● chironomy. Special type of conducting gestures used in directing

*Gregorian chant.
Variant spelling: cheironomy.
Pronunciation: kī-rŏn-ō-mī.

● †chiuso. Stopped, muted. The
use of the equivalent symbol +
is discussed under horn.

● choir. (1) A *chorus, usually
made up of men and women or of
men and boys, which is appointed
to sing at church services. It
performs *anthems, *motets,
*chants, *cantatas, and other
*liturgical music, and augments
and leads the congregation in the
singing of *hymn-tunes and *chorales.
Many choirs wear vestments.
(2) A chorus (usually rather
small) of carefully-selected,
talented singers; used in contradistinction to a large chorus of
less selective membership. This
usage is widely employed in connection with high-school and college
groups.
(3) A certain manual on the
organ. (See organ.)
(4) Any one of the four sections
of the *orchestra--string, woodwind, brass, and percussion; that
is, "string choir," "brass choir,"
etc. are sometimes used instead
of "string section," "brass section,"
etc. Synonym: band (3).
(5) An instrumental *ensemble
comprised usually of instruments
all of the same type. Synonym:
band (2).
(6) The section of a church
where the choir is intended to be
stationed. In Protestant churches
this is usually toward the front,
in Catholic churches on a balcony
in the rear, near the main
entrance. See choir-loft.

● choir-loft. A balcony in a church
from which the choir sings.

● choirmaster. Choir director,
conductor of a choir.

● chorale. (1) A type of *hymn-
tune especially associated with the
Lutheran church.
The chorale is dignified, noble,
stately, solid, masculine. Herein

lies its distinction from ordinary
hymn-tunes. The *tempo is always
rather slow.

The most conspicuous feature in the
printed appearance of a chorale is the
*fermata which appears over the last
chord in each *phrase. However,
there is ample reason for questioning
whether this fermata has its customary
meaning. Many musicologists believe
it was first used in chorales merely
to indicate the ends of the phrases,
and that this idiosyncrasy in printing
has resulted in serious misinterpreta-
tion. Certainly when the chord
consists of a dotted-half-note, prolong-
ing it further is illogical and unmusical. On the other hand there are
some phrases ending with quarter-
notes where a hold--at least a brief
hold--is undoubtedly appropriate.

The chorale melody tends to move
in notes of fairly even length, yet
occasional division of the beat into
two eighth-notes is not uncommon.
Although all four voices theoretically
tend to move in the same rhythm,
the high frequency of such patterns
as two eighths to a beat, of a half-
note for two beats, and of the dotted-
quarter followed by the eighth usually
results in no two voices moving in
the identically same rhythm in any
given measure.

Bach's rich harmonizations of
chorales are models of the style and
of pure four-voice writing as well.

Sometimes in performing a chorale,
the organist improvises a brief passage in organ style between all the
phrases, the choir and congregation
being meanwhile silent.

(2) The term chorale is sometimes
carelessly applied to any passage of
music which resembles the singing of
a *chorus (1). However, to term the
opening of Tschaikowsky's 1812 Overture or the chorus theme in Beethoven's
Ninth Symphony a "chorale" is hardly
accurate.

(3) It has become fashionable of
late to apply the name chorale to a
mixed *chorus (1), especially a small
one of carefully-selected voices. This
usage has all the earmarks of a fad.

(4) In the German language the word
Choral means either chorale or
*Gregorian chant, a circumstance which

has been the source of no little
confusion.

(5) The term is sometimes
carelessly applied to the *chorale-
prelude.

Variant spelling: choral. (This
is not to be confused with the
adjective choral ("pertaining to a
chorus") in such expressions as
choral conducting, choral music,
etc.)

Pronunciation: kō-räl; kō-räl,
kō-räl.

● chorale-prelude. A contrapuntal
composition, usually for organ and
fairly short, based on the melody
of a *chorale (1). Ostensibly a
chorale-prelude is exactly what
its name implies: the prelude to
the singing of a chorale by the
combined choir and congregation.
Nowadays its use for that purpose
is all too infrequent.

Several varieties of chorale-prelude can be distinguished. Probably
the commonest is a type in which
a distinctive *accompaniment-
figure runs all the way through,
like a mosaic, while the chorale
melody appears in fairly long notes,
with or without *ornaments. (The
accompaniment-figure is often derived from the first *phrase of
the chorale melody.) This type
is the chorale-prelude proper.
The chorale fugue employs the first
phrase of the chorale melody as a
*fugue subject; or it may turn each
phrase into a short fugue, resulting in a series of *fughettas, the
latter type sometimes being termed
chorale motet. The chorale variation (or chorale partita) builds a
series of very free variations on
the chorale melody; there are
usually as many variations as the
chorale text has stanzas. Many
compositions of this type employ
only the *manuals of the organ,
hence are playable on the harpsichord or piano, and are as much--
or more--suitable for use in the
home as for use at church. The
chorale fantasia (or chorale fantasy)
is a rather free composition based
on the chorale melody. It sometimes partakes of the style of the

*toccata and may employ virtuoso
effects. (The foregoing types are
subject to further subdivisions, and
naturally some compositions are
hybrids; hence these descriptions are
suggestive rather than comprehensive.)

Chorale-preludes are of highest
importance in the literature of the
organ. They are essentially an innovation of the *Baroque period.
Pachelbel, Buxtehude, and Bach wrote
many of them.

In programing a chorale-prelude,
the title may simply be given as
Chorale-Prelude or the title of the
chorale which serves as base may
appear; or both may be used. When
the second-named practice is observed,
it should not be imagined that the
chorale title describes the mood of
the chorale-prelude. Doubtless the
appearance of such apparently arbitrary
names as "Good Christian Men, Rejoice," "Now All the Woods are Sleep-
ing," or "Now Come, Saviour of the
Heathen" on the program-leaflet at
organ recitals must baffle any uninitiated listeners.

Many chorale-preludes were *improvised without ever being written
down.

Variant spelling: choral-prelude.

Synonyms: organ chorale, Choral
Vorspiel (German).

◉ choral music. Compositions written
for chorus (1)--either men's, women's,
or *mixed--either unaccompanied (*a
cappella), with piano or organ, or
with orchestra.

For further information see anthem,
cantata, glee, madrigal, mass, motet,
oratorio, part-song, passion, requiem,
Stabat Mater, and Te Deum.

The somewhat curious use of the
term octavo music as a synonym for
choral music is explained under octavo.

● choral orchestration. (1) The art
of arranging, or "orchestrating," for
*chorus, either men's, women's, or
mixed. The term is used for want
of a better and more specific expression. (Compare bandstration.)

(2) The art of arranging for chorus
and orchestra in combination.

● chord (1, noun). A combination of
simultaneously-sounding musical
tones. A chord is one unit in
the *harmony of a composition.
Most chords contain either three
or four completely different tones,
any of which may be *doubled.
(See triad, seventh-chord.)

Simultaneous tones all with the
same letter-name--each an *octave
from its closest neighbor--are not
regarded as a chord, but as an
expanded *unison.

A chord of only two tones is
usually called an interval. As to
whether an interval should be considered an incomplete chord, or
a chord considered a combination
of intervals, is a debatable question.

The term chord is normally restricted to those vertical combinations which are of fairly frequent
and well-established occurrence--
enough so as to warrant a particular
name for each distinctive type of
chord, or a *Roman numeral to
describe its function. *Non-
harmonic tones are regarded as
foreign to the chord against which
they appear, rather than as part
of it. However, see sonority (2).

Musicians normally think and
*"spell" chords from the lowest
(or bass) tone toward the highest
(soprano) tone--not from the top
downward.

Various well-recognized types of
chord are discussed under triad,
seventh-chord, ninth-chord, eleventh-chord, thirteenth-chord, inversion (1), altered chords, augmented sixth chords, Neapolitan
sixth, Picardy third, and fourth-
chords. The numbering and naming
system is described under Roman
numerals and triad.

See also harmony, consonant,
dissonant, sonority (2).

(2, verb). To *harmonize a
melody with simple chords, not in
writing, but directly on an instrument, such as the piano. The
process might be called a very
simple form of practical *keyboard
harmony.

This term is a colloquialism.

● chord-member. The opposite of

a *non-harmonic tone, i. e., a tone
which belongs to the harmony prevailing at the moment.
Synonym: chordal tone.
Antonyms: non-harmonic tone; also
unessential tone, by-tone, non-chordal
tone, inharmonic tone.

● chord of nature. Same as harmonic
series.

● choreography. The art of plotting
the action and dancing in a *ballet.
Variant form: choregraphy.

● chorister. A singer in a *choir;
choir-member.

● chôros Portuguese). A term used
in Brazil to apply to any instrumental
combination. One Chôros by Heitor
Villa-Lobos is written for chorus and
orchestra, another for unaccompanied
guitar, still others for various miscellaneous combinations; thus the term
indicates neither *form nor *medium,
though it does connote Brazilian style.
See also titles.
Pronunciation: shō-rōós.

● chorus. (1) A group of singers,
either men, women, or (especially)
men and women (i. e., mixed), sometimes men and boys; a choral society.
A chorus that sings at church services
is called a *choir. A chorus of men
is sometimes called a men's *glee club
(in schools often boys' glee club), one
of women a women's glee club (in
schools often girls' glee club).
Adjective form: choral (not chorale).
See also SATB.
(2) A short composition for chorus;
a choral piece; a *part-song.
(3) A *number in an *opera,
*oratorio, or *cantata, for the chorus,
with or without *soloists, with (occasionally without) the orchestra.
(4) A careless and undesirable
synonym for *refrain. (Nevertheless,
refrains are often performed by a
chorus, with the other portions of the
song allotted to a solo voice.)

● chromatic chords. See altered
chords.

● chromaticism. In harmonic
style, the tendency toward frequent
*modulation and the frequent
employment of *altered chords.
It should not be imagined that
complete or nearly-complete
*chromatic scales will necessarily
occur, though the twelve tones
found in this scale will naturally
be spread through the music.
The opposite of chromaticism is
diatonicism or diatonic style. The
modal system (see modes) is
essentially non-chromatic and even
antipathetic toward chromaticism.
The first all-out tendency toward
chromaticism appeared in the late
sixteenth and early seventeenth
centuries in the *madrigals of
Gesualdo da Venosa (1560?-1613),
an Italian amateur composer, and
to a somewhat less pronounced
degree in the works of his fellow-
countrymen Luca Marenzio (1560?-
1599) and Claudio Monteverdi (1567-
1643) and the Englishman Thomas
Weelkes (1573?-1623). In the
latter part of the nineteenth century
it reappeared in full force in the
music of Wagner, Franck, and
others, and has to some extent
continued to the present day,
especially in the form of *atonality
and the *twelve tone system, which
might be called chromaticism pushed
to the nth degree.
The accompanying typically chromatic passage comes from Wagner's
Tristan and Isolde, act II.
See also the sub-head "enharmonic modulation" in the entry
modulation.

● chromatics. *Accidentals.

● chromatic scale. A scale consisting entirely of *half-steps.
There are twelve different tones,
with a thirteenth--the tone an
*octave from the starting tone--
with which to finish off.
The ordinary *major scale and
*minor scale are termed diatonic
scales in contradistinction to the
chromatic.
The diatonic scale of seven

different tones should be thought of as a framework into which the additional five tones, needed to produce a chromatic scale, have been inserted.

In the chromatic scale below, the basic tones of the diatonic scale are shown in whole-notes, the five additional notes in quarter-note heads. It is a major scale (of the key of C major) which has been converted to chromatic by the addition of five more tones.

as the lowered seventh, sixth, fifth, third, and second degrees. The reason for this practice is largely one of pure convenience; it entails the fewest number of *accidentals. For a reason that would be hard to name, many musicians dislike the sight of the lowered fifth degree and substitute the raised fourth for it in the descending form, even though a natural in front of the normal

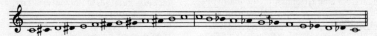

In the ascending form the five additional tones have been written as the raised first, second, fourth, fifth, and sixth degrees, while in the descending form they have been shown

fourth step then becomes necessary; in other words, in the foregoing scale beginning at X there would appear G, F-sharp, F-natural rather than G, G-flat, F.

Of course a minor scale can also be converted to chromatic. Naturally it is impossible to determine, purely by listening, whether the point of departure was the major scale or the minor, unless accompanying chords are present.

● church modes. See modes (1).

● church music. See Ambrosian chant, Anglican chanting, anthem, Ave Maria, cantata, chant, chorale, chorale-prelude, Gregorian chant, hymn-tune, Magnificat, mass, motet, offertory, oratorio, passion, requiem, service, Stabat Mater, and Te-Deum. See also carol, elevation, noël, postlude, sonata da chiesa, spiritual, and voluntary.
Antonym: secular music.

● church sonata. Same as sonata da chiesa.

● cimbalom. Variant spelling of czimbalom.

● C instruments. Explained under transposing instruments.

● cipher. On an organ whose mechanism is slightly out of order, sometimes a pipe will sound continuously and of its own accord at a time when the player is not pressing the key which operates said pipe. This is known as a cipher.
Variant spelling: cypher.

● †circa. Around, about. Thus, M. M. ♩ = circa 108 indicates that the *metronome should be set at approximately 108, increasing or decreasing slightly according to the performer's feeling for the composition. (Related English word: the prefix circum-.)
Abbreviation: c.

● circle of fifths. A table which shows the various *keys (1) that exist, and their inter-relation, placing them in such a fashion that the *tonic or keytone of each is located a perfect fifth (see intervals) distant from the tonic of its nearest neighbor. It is customary to print this in the form of a clock face, because there are twelve keys to be considered. It is normally given in the form of two concentric circles, the outer showing major keys, the inner, minor keys.

Making allowances for *enharmonic keys, it will be observed that moving one degree clockwise causes the key-signature to increase by one sharp or decrease by one flat; moving one degree counterclockwise causes a decrease of one sharp or increase of one flat. It is possible to find all the keys closely related to any given key, with the exception of one relationship, by moving on the circles to the following positions:
(a) on the same circle, one degree clockwise.
(b) on the same circle, one degree counterclockwise.
(c) on the other circle, directly opposite--the closest location to the starting-point.
(d) on the other circle, one degree clockwise.
(e) on the other circle, one degree counterclockwise.
The additional close relation is that of the *tonic minor (or tonic major, when starting from a minor key). For example, the keys closely related to B-flat major are: F major, E-flat major, G minor, D minor, and C minor, as the diagram will show; in addition B-flat minor is also closely related. Similarly the keys closely related to F minor are: C minor, B-flat minor, A-flat major, E-flat major, and D-flat major, plus F major. All the remaining keys are more or less distantly related. The farther one moves from the starting-point, the more remote the relationship grows. The key diametrically opposite is musically the most distant of all.
In the diagram, capital letters denote major keys; lower-case letters denote minor keys.
Synonym: cycle of fifths.
See also key relationships, related keys.

● claque. A group of professional applauders who have been paid to come to a certain concert or (more frequently) opera performance for the specific purpose of applauding the efforts of a certain performer. The employment of a claque is unethical, despicable, and a type of

The Circle of Fifths

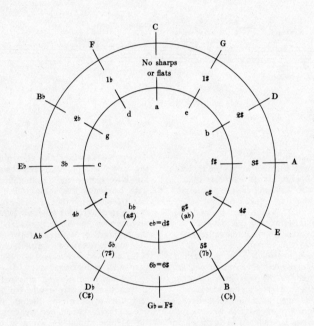

"racket," but the practice is difficult to suppress.

Pronunciation: klăk.

● clarinet. A *woodwind instrument employing a single *reed, which is held in place on the under side of

market.

The mouthpiece is occasionally made of glass.

Two types of clarinet are in general use in the orchestra, that in B-flat and that in A. The range is:

the mouthpiece.

In common with all woodwind instruments, the clarinet is essentially a pipe or tube with six holes (some of them enclosed by rings) drilled in the upper side, which are opened and closed by the fingers. A seventh hole is located on the underside and is known as the thumb-hole, for the left thumb operates it. In addition there are many keys, most of which are operated by the two little fingers. Some of these keys run parallel to the sides of the instrument (several are very long); others run crossways and of course are short, in addition to which they are slightly curved (crescent-shaped). The *octave key (more properly speaker key or register key) is located on the underside adjacent to the thumb-hole; its purpose is to cause the instrument to overblow and enter the upper register. (See overblowing.)

The contrast between loud and soft is probably greater on the clarinet than on any other wind instrument, brass or wood. (See sub-tone.)

Although metal clarinets of good quality have been successfully manufactured for quite a number of years, players tend to prefer the wood instrument--its original material. Ebonite and plastic clarinets are also on the

A few B-flat clarinets also possess the low E-flat a half-step lower than the lowest tone indicated above, with produces the actual pitch D-flat (C-sharp). The B-flat clarinet is notated a major second (whole-step) above the sounds desired, the A clarinet a minor third above the sounds desired. The treble *clef is used exclusively. (See transposing instruments.)

The non-transposing clarinet in C was once widely used, but is now almost obsolete, though still occasionally purchased by those *amateurs whose ambition is to play "popular" music from the piano copy.

The choice between the B-flat and the A clarinet is made by the composer with the object of employing those written pitches which necessitate *key-signatures with as few sharps and flats as possible, for the clarinet's mechanism is of such a nature that it is genuinely more difficult to play in keys with many flats or sharps than in those with few or none. In general, the B-flat instrument is more suitable for keys with flats (actual pitch), the A for keys with sharps.

The clarinet *overblows at the *interval of a twelfth.

Tone-Color. The lower tones are rich, dark, and gurgling, unlike the sound of any other instrument except of course the *bass clarinet and *alto clarinet. This segment of the *range is called the *"chalumeau" register. The name "break register" or "throat tones" is given to the G-sharp, A, and B-flat above *middle C; although these have an inoffensive enough sound, they lack character and distinction. Beginning with the B a major seventh above middle C, the quality is very sweet and almost flute-like for over an octave, but beyond that as the pitch goes higher and higher the tone becomes increasingly squealing and tight, and harder to control. The highest fourth is almost unusable.

As may be gathered from the foregoing, the tone-quality is far from homogeneous, a circumstance which resourceful composers have been known to turn into an advantage rather than merely tolerate as a failing.

In the *band the instrument is of paramount importance. Instead of just two or three clarinets, as in the orchestra, there are entire *sections of the instrument--usually three or four sections, and often named solo, first, second, and third rather than first, second, third, and fourth. Some concert bands employ as many as 32 clarinets. The A clarinet is not used in the band.

It must be borne in mind that the B-flat clarinet cannot be turned into an A clarinet merely by pulling a lever or *crook, in the manner that the B-flat trumpet can be put into A. They are two separate instruments, and the orchestral player must own both of them. Both should be regarded as the "regular" or "ordinary" clarinet. The E-flat clarinet, alto clarinet, bass clarinet, basset horn, and contrabass clarinet should each be regarded as a distinct instrument, not a variant of the ordinary instrument. Each is discussed under its own heading.

Variant spelling: clarionet.

Italian: clarinetto (plural, clarinetti). French: clarinette. German: Klarinette or Clarinette (plural, Klarinetten or Clarinetten). Spanish: clarinete.

The player is called a clarinetist (also spelled clarinettist).

Pronunciation: klȧr-ĭ-nĕt´ or klȧr-ĭ-nĕt.

● clarinet piccolo. The *E-flat clarinet.

● clarinet quintet. Clarinet, two violins, viola, and cello. The best-known compositions for this chamber-music combination are Mozart's Quintet in A (K. 581) and Brahms's Quintet in B Minor (op. 115). Brahms, however, permits the substitution of the viola for the clarinet in his work, although this alternate version is rarely used.

See also chamber-music, chamber-music groups.

● †clarino, clarion. Old names for the *trumpet, still occasionally used to designate the old-style trumpet used in the early eighteenth century.

Synonym: clarin trumpet.

See also trumpet (sub-head ●"the old natural trumpet").

● clarionet. Old spelling of clarinet.

● "classic," "classical." The most uninformed *laymen naively recognize only two types of music: one they call "popular" (1)--meaning largely *jazz; everything else they lump together, seemingly without any discrimination or distinctions, and dub "classical." They appear to imagine that a folk-song, a Gregorian chant, a Palestrina mass, a Bach fugue, a Haydn string quartet, a Schubert song, a Wagner music-drama, a Stravinsky ballet, and a work written in the twelve tone system are all a single kind of music! The correct and exact meaning of this term will be found under Classical Period.

Regrettable though it may be, the use of classical as a synonym for serious music or for everything except jazz is so thoroughly entrenched, at least in the English-speaking world, that eradicating it would be a herculean task; nevertheless the prevalence of such a monstrous notion no more makes it "correct" than the pre-1492 prevalence of the notion about the earth being flat made it "correct" in its day. However any fair-minded person will admit that the application of this term to the music of the late eighteenth and very early nineteenth centuries is an equally curious one, as in strict meaning the word refers to ancient cultures, especially those of Greece and Rome.

● Classical Period. The period of music history extending from about the 1760's to about 1810 or 1815. It followed the *Rococo period (which was the final stage of the *Baroque) and preceded the *Romantic.

Transparency of texture is possibly the most conspicuous element in Classical style. Usually every note can be heard--the fabric has an "X-rayed" quality--and to quote performers, there is no "cover-up" in this music, for the slightest mistake or dynamic indiscretion is readily detected by the hearer.

*Homophonic style was perhaps at its height during this era. Harmony was thoroughly *functional. The tonic, subdominant, and dominant (I, IV, and V) triads were acknowledged the fundamental pegs on which the musical foundation was erected. To this day they are often called the principal or primary triads, and the remaining four the subordinate or secondary triads. (See triad, Roman numerals.)

Harmony was often regarded the underpinning and complement of a melody which in itself clearly implied the chords that accompanied it, hence not so much an essential as a clarification. Many composers asserted that every good melody should be able to stand alone, unharmonized, and still be completely intelligible.

Octave doublings were used more frequently in Classical music than in that which had preceded, though still much less commonly than in the succeeding Romantic style. *Double octaves (1, 2) are not unusual in orchestral works.

One element in Classical style that is always prominent in musicians' minds is the great emphasis on *form.

Form was perhaps deemed more important than actual musical content or expressive truth, although in the works of the greatest composers there is an admirable balance between them. *Sonata-allegro form is a typical Classical development, *theme and variation form and *rondo form were popular, and *ternary (ABA) form was not neglected. *Phrases were clearly defined, tending to group themselves pairwise in question-and-answer style ("antecedent and consequent" formation as it is often described by theorists); phrases were almost monotonously of four measures' length. Symmetry is perhaps the paramount Classical ideal as regards form.

The already-mentioned characteristic of transparency, coupled with the emphasis on form, seems entirely congruous in the music of an era which called itself the "Age of Reason."

One Classical innovation of greatest importance is the contrasting of two different *keys (1) in the course of a composition, the contrast between the tonality of the first theme and second theme in *sonata-allegro form being an excellent example. Heretofore composers had used a single tonality as fundamental, from which excursions were made to related keys. In balancing two tonalities, the composer established a second key as a temporary base of operations, from which to explore its own related keys. The interplay of the principal key and its relatives with the subordinate key and its relatives represents a development to which latter-day ears are all but deaf, and the novelty of which we are much too likely to overlook.

The Classical period saw the discarding of *figured bass (except in some works for chorus and orchestra), the triumph of the piano over the harpsichord, the frequent use of *Alberti bass in piano compositions, the establishment of the symphony, sonata, string quartet, and concerto as we know these today, and the establish-

ment of the orchestra in essentially
its present-day proportions, though
not its present-day size.

Long forms were preferred to
short; compositions that divide into
*movements were much favored over
the short one-movement "piece."
Synonyms: Classicism, Viennese
Period, Classic Period.
See also Mannheim group.

● Classicism.   Same as Classical
Period.

● "classics, the." A vague and perhaps undesirable term applied to
compositions which have stood the test
of time and are widely known by all
finished musicians. These compositions are not necessarily from the
*Classical period, but may stem from
an earlier or later epoch.

This term is probably more happily
used in literature than in music. To
musicians it is about equivalent to
the equally questionable expression
"the standard repertory (repertoire)."

● clavecin.   French name for the
*harpsichord.
Pronunciation: klȧ-v'săn̮.

● clavecinist.   (1) A composer of
music for the *clavecin (harpsichord).
(2) One who plays the clavecin.

● claves (Spanish).   An indefinite pitch
*percussion instrument, consisting of
two small hardwood sticks clapped
together. The player rounds his hand
so as to form a resonating cavity to
increase the volume of the tone. The
instrument is of Latin-American origin.
Pronunciation: klȧ̆-vĕ̆s (the v
slightly like b).

● †clavicembalo.   Italian name for the
*harpsichord.
Variant form: gravicembalo.
Pronunciation: accent -cem-.

● clavichord.   A keyboard instrument
which enjoyed great vogue during the
sixteenth, seventeenth, and eighteenth
centuries. It probably has the softest
tone of any musical instrument, being
so faint as to be barely audible across
an average-sized room. The clavi-

chord's nature was intimate--some-
thing on which one would play for
his own pleasure or for that of
someone stationed very close.
The *tone-color somewhat suggests
that of the guitar.

A unique expressive effect was
possible on the clavichord: if the
player caused his finger to tremble
on the key, something resembling
the *vibrato of string instruments
or the voice could be obtained, this
being known as Bebung, the German
word for "trembling."

There were two types of clavichord, the "free" and the "bound."
The free variety had a string for
every key, but in the bound type
a single string was made to do duty
for more than one pitch by blocking
off a small segment when certain
keys were pressed, somewhat in
the way a string instrument player
shortens the vibrating-length of a
string by fingering it. It is thus
apparent that certain harmonic
tone-combinations were impossible
on the bound clavichord, and since
the method of manufacturing was
far from standardized, its owners
must have been subject to no small
amount of frustration in playing
certain compositions.

No one who has ever seen or
heard both the clavichord and the
*harpsichord would ever confuse
them, for the two are utterly dissimilar.

It is a misfortune that Bach's
great series of preludes and *fugues
which he called Das wohltemperierte
Klavier has been mistranslated
"The Well-Tempered Clavichord,"
for there is no evidence that Bach
really intended the work for that
instrument, and much that he
intended it for the harpsichord.
Klavier (or Clavier) is the present
German word meaning piano or keyboard; formerly it also designated
the harpsichord or any keyboard
instrument (see cembalo), but only
rarely the clavichord.

● clavier.   (1) *Keyboard.
(2) Any keyboard instrument; a
synonym for *cembalo.
In German, Clavier or Klavier

now means <u>piano</u>; formerly it also meant harpsichord. For remarks on Bach's <u>The Well-Tempered Clavier,</u> often misnamed <u>The Well-Tempered Clavichord,</u> see <u>clavichord.</u>

Pronunciation: klä-vēr, also, for first meaning only, kläv-ĭ-ĕr. German pronunciation: klä-fēr.

● **clef.** A character used to identify the notes on a *staff. The clef indicates the name of one note; from this all the other notes can be computed. No staff can be read without a clef.

<u>Clef</u> is the French word meaning "key" (in the sense of door-key); it "unlocks" the meaning of the staff, so to speak. Three clefs are in use at present:

the G clef

the F clef

the C clef

The spiral on the G clef is placed so as to curl around the line having the pitch of the G above *middle C. The two dots drawn in connection with the F clef straddle the line having the pitch of the F below middle C. The line on which the C clef centers is always middle C.

When clefs are placed on staffs, they are given names other than the foregoing letter-designations. These are:

Treble clef

(formed with the G clef)

Bass clef

(formed with the F clef)

Alto clef

(formed by placing the C clef on the middle line of the staff)

Tenor clef

(formed by placing the C clef on the fourth line of the staff)

Other clefs, now obsolete, are the following:

Of the foregoing, the soprano was the most recent to go out of use, having disappeared a little over a hundred years ago.

In writing for the *tenor voice it has become customary in recent years to employ either the G clef with an 8 under it 𝄞 or the double G clef though neither symbol as yet enjoys anything approaching universal acceptance. Notes written with these clefs sound an octave lower than when written with the ordinary G clef. Another innovation, frequently used in Italy, is the G clef supplemented by a tiny C clef

the latter located on the third space.

Still another form of notating the tenor voice is a C clef located on the third space

again causing the pitches to sound an octave lower than the same notes written with the G clef; however some musicians object to the latter usage because strictly the C clef should always be located on a line, never a space. (For further information about writing for the tenor voice, see tenor.)

In order to clarify the reading of these various characters, the first six notes of My Country 'Tis of Thee have been written with a number of clefs; it should be borne in mind that all of these represent exactly the same pitches. See example below.

Any line or space of the staff can be any note, if only the proper

clef is applied, as is shown in the following:

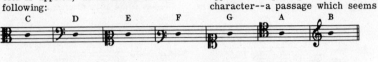

Many musicians accomplish *transposition by mentally substituting a different clef and key-signature for those which are actually printed in the music.

The terms G clef and treble clef are often used interchangeably; the same is true of F clef and bass clef. A more fastidious usage suggests that G clef and F clef, like C clef, are the names of mere symbols, while treble clef and bass clef, like alto clef and tenor clef, designate the character's function.

● climax. A climax in a musical composition is a passage containing a great amount of tension (usually produced by *dissonance), followed by release. Although climaxes are usually loud, not all loud passages

applied to a passage of triumphant character--a passage which seems the culmination of all that has preceded--though peroration might be a more appropriate term.

● close. A synonym for cadence (1).

● close harmony, close position. A chord is said to be in close harmony or close position when the three highest voices are as close together as it is possible to get them; in such cases the soprano and tenor are always less than an *octave apart. The interval between the bass and the tenor (or for that matter, between the bass and any voice) is not taken into consideration.

All of the following chords are in close harmony:

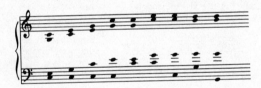

are climaxes; the word is by no means a mere synonym for *fortissimo (ff). As in literature, it denotes a turning-point.

Many compositions contain several climaxes, although one is usually more pronounced than the others. Wagner, Richard Strauss, and Ernest Bloch are masters of creating suspense and tension through deliberated approach to climaxes of tremendous power.

The term climax is also sometimes

Sometimes the three upper voices are written on the same staff, the bass on a staff by itself. However this mode of writing is by no means a requisite for producing close harmony; the term is concerned with the pitch of the notes, not with their place on the staffs.

Compare open harmony.

● cluster chords. Same as tone clusters.

● coda. Conclusion; supplementary concluding portion (literally "tail"). Although all compositions have an end, not all end with a coda, just as all have a beginning but not necessarily an introduction. The function is that of a summing-up so as to bring the composition to a satisfying and logical conclusion. The majority of codas are based on preceding thematic material, somewhat in the manner of *development; indeed the codas of certain movements in *sonata-allegro form are actually second developments. A coda may be very short--perhaps only two chords--or it may be of five minutes' duration. Seldom is it marked coda; its presence can be detected only through musical analysis, not by mechanical means. Sometimes when a *D. C. or *D. S. is used, at one point the performer is directed (by the sign ⊕) to skip to a section marked coda. However, this section may not necessarily be a true coda, as that term is understood in *form and as just defined; it may be no more than the last few measures of an altered version of one of the themes, devoid of supplementary and summing-up nature.

Many compositions conclude with a series of loud alternating *tonic and *dominant chords followed by numerous additional tonic chords. Such a passage is not necessarily a "coda," (though it may well be the concluding portion of one), for the coda has no obvious distinguishing stylistic feature. The feeling of an impending conclusion is, however, quite characteristic; also the presence of a tonic pedal-point (see non-harmonic tones, 9), or of a *modulation to the key of the subdominant and back to the tonic (see key-relationships).

● coda sign. A name sometimes

given to the cross-and-circle ⊕ which is often inserted above the notation to indicate that the player should immediately pass to a concluding section marked coda (although, as stated under the entry coda, the passage may not necessarily be a true coda as that term is understood in *form analysis). For illustration, see repeat signs. This character is also sometimes used to mark the beginning and end of a *cut (see vide).

● †codetta. (1) Literally, "short *coda." The distinction between coda and codetta, however, is as often one of location as of length, for the codetta frequently appears at the end of a theme or section within a composition, while the coda is found only at the end. (2) The *episodes in a *fugue are sometimes called codettas. (3) Many movements in *sonata-allegro form have a codetta in place of the closing theme; it may take the form of a brief reference back to the first theme (principal subject). For familiar examples, see the first movement of Mozart's Symphony in G Minor or of Beethoven's so-called "Pathétique" Sonata (for piano). It is possible for a piece to conclude with both a codetta and a coda (in that order).

● † cogli, †coi, †col. With the; these are contractions, respectively, of con gli, con i, and con il. Other variants for "with the" are coll', colla, and colle. None of these are interchangeable; their correct use depends on the rules of Italian grammar.

● †col canto. Same as colla parte.

● †coll' 8va. Add the notes an

Ex. 1

Written   Played

*octave above to the printed notes; indication for a series of octaves. See Example 1. When it is the composer's desire to duplicate a series of tones with those an octave lower, the indication is coll' 8va bassa, and is usually placed beneath the notes. See Example 2.

of the *Baroque, *Renaissance, and earlier periods on the archaic instruments for which originally written.

Plural: collegia musica.
See also Aufführungspraxis.

●†col legno. A special effect

Ex. 2

coll' 8va bassa

A row of dots is often used to indicate the exact conclusion of the passage to be played in octaves.

This term is most frequently employed in music for the piano. The full form is coll' ottava (not col ottava or col 8va).

●†coll', colla, colle. With the. The first and second are contractions of con la, the third of con le.

●†colla parte. An indication found in piano-parts and other *accompaniments at points where the voice or solo instrument has a passage that is rather free in *rhythm; it is a caution to the accompanist to be ready for anything the soloist may do. At such spots the accompanying instrument or group usually has a *rest or a sustained chord; hence the difficulty of accurate following is seldom great. The literal meaning is "with the part," though "follow the part" is a more helpful concept.

Variant form: con la parte.
Synonyms: col canto, colla voce (used in compositions employing a solo voice).

●†colla voce. Same as colla parte. (Literally, "with the voice.")
Variant form: con la voce.

●collegium musicum (Latin). A musical organization (generally under the sponsorship of a *conservatory or the music department of a college) which specializes in playing compositions

sometimes used in playing the bowed *string instruments. The bow is turned on its side so that both the hair and the stick touch the string. A peculiar, rattling, half-precussive but faint tone results, which can be quite effective with short repeated notes in rhythmic groupings, especially in music of a bizarre or macabre character. The term *arco cancels col legno.

Col legno is often described as "playing with the back of the bow" and indeed the literal meaning is "with the wood;" however the player as a rule does not turn his bow upside down; rather (as stated) the bow is usually turned sideways so that both the hair and the stick contact the string.

Variant form: col ligno.

●coloratura. Term applied to brilliant, *florid material--runs, *trills, *arpeggios, and the like--written for the voice (especially *soprano) for the purpose of *virtuoso display. This style--sometimes rather sarcastically termed "vocal calisthenics"--is normally encountered only in certain *operas; it is not well in place elsewhere.

The peculiar, somewhat birdlike type of light soprano voice which can execute this type of material with comparative ease is known as coloratura soprano. Agility, rather than power or

dramatic expression, is its characteristic.
See also florid, melismatic.

● combination tone. *Resultant tone.

● "combo." A small *dance band.
(Probably a humorous corruption of
combination.)

● †come. Like. Thus: come arpa,
like a harp; come prima, as at first
(i. e., on the first appearance of the
theme); come avanti, as in the preceding section, as before; come
tamburo, like a drum; come sopra,
as above.
For many usages, *alla may be
considered a synonym.
Quasi is sometimes incorrectly used
in place of come.

● comic opera. This term is sometimes substituted for *operetta. The
operetta (or light opera) and the
closely-related *musical comedy contain music of light character (see
light music) and some spoken dialogue.
An opera with a comical plot, yet
serious as to musical content and
sung throughout, is best termed an
*opera buffa. An *opéra comique is
not a comic opera, literal translation
notwithstanding.
For further information, see opera.

● commission. The act of hiring a
composer to write a composition for
a specific purpose or occasion is
termed a commission.

● †commodo. Variant spelling of
comodo.
Pronunciation: accent first syllable.

● common chord. (1) A chord which
exists in two or more *keys, and is
therefore "common" to them. Thus
the chord C-E-G is the *tonic (I) in
C major, the *subdominant (IV) in G
major, the *dominant (V) in F major
and in F minor, the *Neapolitan sixth
in B major and in B minor, the *submediant (VI) in E minor, the *supertonic with raised third ("dominant of
the dominant" or "major supertonic")
in B-flat major; and the foregoing list
is by no means exhaustive. (See triad,

Roman numeral.)
*Modulation is most frequently
made by means of a common
chord, approaching it as if in the
original key, and quitting or *resolving it as if in the new key.
The chord put to this purpose is
often termed a *pivot chord or
hinge chord.
See also key-relationships, related keys, circle of fifths.
(2) A synonym for *triad.

● common keys. See nine common
keys.

● common time. 4-4 time. Although
the symbol C which is often substituted for the time-signature $\frac{4}{4}$
does not actually stand for "common"
(as is widely believed), 4-4 is
undoubtedly the most frequently-
used time-signature.

● †comodo. Comfortably, conveniently. Thus, allegro comodo
means "comfortably fast," rather
than "at a headlong pace"; it is
about equivalent to allegro non
troppo or allegro moderato. (Related English words: commodious,
accommodate.)
Variant spelling: commodo.
Pronunciation: accent first syllable.

● compass. Same as range.

● composed folk-song. See home-
and-community songs and popular
music (3).

● composer. An author of music.
Some sort of professional clarification of this term would be
desirable--the establishment of
some minimum standard that should
be achieved before anyone can term
himself a composer. Just as a
person who has learned to play
Schumann's The Happy Farmer is
not to be called a "pianist" or a
student who writes a theme for a
high-school English class is not
termed an "author," similarly a
person who has finished a required
one-year or one-semester course in
composition at college or a person

who has written a single composition should not be called a "composer."

No composer of any standing has ever devoted his entire efforts to a single *medium, at least not since the perfection of instruments. Hence a "composer of piano music," a "composer of *anthems," or a "song-writer" cannot be seriously regarded as a composer.

● compound meter. This term has unfortunately been used by various theorists with two entirely different meanings, both placed in opposition to simple meter.

In one usage, compound meter denotes all meters except those with 2 or 3 beats; that is meters with 4, 6, 8, 9, or 12 beats. It is based on the theory that a 4-beat meter is a double 2, a 6-beat meter a double 3, a 9-beat meter a triple 3, etc.

In the other usage, compound meter indicates those meters which are divisible by 3, that is, meters with 6, 9, or 12 beats--those based on the "multiple of 3" principle.

A comparision of the two usages follows.

(1) A *symphony which uses two, or more *solo instruments.

A symphonie concertante might well be considered a *concerto grosso which follows the plan and form of the symphony, *sonata, *string quartet, *concerto, etc. (see sonata types), i. e., the form-scheme coincides with *Classical rather than *Baroque practices. See also double concerto, concerto for orchestra.

(2) During the early Baroque period the term concertato was used to designate compositions written for a combination of voices and instruments.

● concerted number, concerted piece. A generic term which includes vocal trios, quartets, quintets, etc.; the term is chiefly used in connection with the *opera, *oratorio, and *cantata.

Synonym: ensemble number.
See groups.

● concert ending. This term is generally encountered in connection with the *music-dramas of Wagner.

	Simple meter	Compound meter	
FIRST USAGE	2, 3	4, 6, 8, 9, 12	Beats per measure
SECOND USAGE	2, 4, 8	3, 6, 9, 12	

See also simple meter.

● †con. With. Thus: con brio, with fire, con espressione, with expression; con fuoco, with fire; con spirito, with spirit.

Variant forms: cogli, coi, col, coll', colla (literally "with the").

Antonym: senza.

● concert. A public performance of music, given either by a single person or by a group. We speak of "hearing" a concert (not "seeing" it).

Many musicians strongly object to the word entertainment when applied to a concert of serious nature.

Synonym: program (1).
See also recital.

● concertant, †concertante, †concertato.

Wagner's music is often so continuous, so closely-knit, that there are no satisfactory points to stop except at the ends of the acts. Hence when excerpts (other than those occurring at the end of acts) are presented at concerts, it is often necessary to use a special ending for the occasion, in order to avoid an abrupt conclusion. Wagner supplied several concert endings for his own works; numerous additional ones have been written by Humperdinck and others. The concert ending is of course always based on thematic material from the opera itself, and is usually quite brief.

● concert flute. (1) A more complete

(and redundant) name for the *flute.
(2) Name of an organ stop; see
organ.

● concert horn. The *mellophone.

● concertina. A portable instrument,
similar to a small *accordion, but
without a keyboard. The bellows
(which is expandable) is mounted
between two hexagonal boards embed-
ded with buttons which give the different tones. The sound is produced
by metal *reeds (2). It is made in
several sizes.

● concertino. (1) A collective name
for the solo instruments (or small
group) in the *concerto grosso.
  (2) A short *concerto; the term
stands in the same relation to concerto that *sonatina and *sinfonietta
(1) stand to *sonata and *symphony,
respectively.
  Pronunciation: kŏn-sĕr-tē-no or
kŏn-chĕr-tē-nō.

● concert mass. See mass.

● concertmaster. The *principal of
the first violins in an orchestra. He
has duties other than those of principals, however; often he is responsible for marking the *bowing of all
the *string instruments and equally
often he serves as assistant *conductor. In addition he very frequently
appears as soloist in violin *concertos.
He is always located at the first
stand (or "desk") of first violins, on
the side nearest the audience. The
player who shares his stand is called
the assistant concertmaster or possibly
second concertmaster.
  Before the custom of using a *conductor was established, the concertmaster served as conductor, gestur-
ing with his bow and his head, and
during *rests possibly waving his bow.
  The German term Konzertmeister is
occasionally used; however the fre-
quently-heard word "concertmeister"
is a polyglot barbarism (and an affectation as well).

● concerto. (1) A composition for a
solo instrument and orchestra (occasionally two solo instruments and

orchestra) in several movements,
usually three. The orchestra is
by no means a mere *accompaniment; hence the definition "for
solo instrument with orchestra
accompaniment" or "...with
orchestra background," which are
frequently heard, suggest a sub-
servience that does not tally with
actuality.
  To save time, the words and
orchestra are often omitted (though
invariably understood) in speaking
of this form; that is, a concerto
for cello and orchestra might be
called simply a "cello concerto"
or "concerto for cello."
  In performing a concerto, the
player of the solo instrument
stands or sits out in front of the
orchestra, as a rule.
  Concertos are often performed
with piano replacing the orchestra.
It should be clearly understood
that these occasions are purely
makeshifts, and are resorted to
simply because no orchestra is
available.
  The concertos written during or
since the *Classical period follow
the plan of the sonata (see sonata
types); those from the *Baroque
period antedate the establishing of
this form, and are distinguished
from the *concerto grosso only by
the *medium. The term solo concerto is sometimes used to
distinguish the concerto from the
concerto grosso.
  See also sonata types, double
sonata-allegro form, concerto
grosso, concerto for orchestra.
  (2) In the Baroque period the
term concerto was sometimes applied to purely orchestral compositions without solo instruments
("orchestra" in this period usually
being *string orchestra). Today
we would probably term such
works *symphonies. The distinction between this orchestral type
of concerto and the symphony
(sinfonia) seems to be merely that
the latter was usually more *contrapuntal. This type of work is
often called the orchestral concerto, though the same term has
also been applied to the concerto

grosso. The orchestral concerto should be distinguished from the more modern *concerto for orchestra. The Baroque orchestral concerto--a "symphony, junior grade"--was of course not really a concerto as that term is understood today. (Nevertheless, Stravinsky and others have revived the term in this meaning in the present era.)

Plural: concertos or concerti.

Pronunciation: kŏn-chĕr⁻tō (not kŏn-shĕr'-tō, kŏn-sĕr'-tō, or kŏn-chĕr⁻tō).

● concerto-allegro form. Same as double sonata-allegro form.

● concerto for orchestra. An orchestral composition, usually divided into *movements, in which each instrument is prominently and perhaps brilliantly featured at some point or other. With this exception, it usually differs from the *symphony only in name.

See also concertant, concerto (2).

● †concerto grosso. A composition in several movements, written for a group of solo instruments and orchestra. The most common solo group is two violins and cello.

All the solo instruments, collectively termed the concertino (1), are usually employed simultaneously, like a tiny orchestra in themselves, then have *rests during the passages allotted to the orchestra (in this usage often called ripieno, concerto grosso, or tutti). Hence it is not inaccurate to define the concerto grosso as "written for two bodies of instruments--one a small group of soloists, the other a large group (or orchestra)." Since these two groups often play alternately it seems almost superfluous to point out that *antiphonal effects are extremely characteristic.

Due to the fact that wind instruments were not well developed during the time concerto grosso was at the height of its popularity, compositions of this type are most frequently written entirely for strings. There are of course exceptions; now and again wind instruments are encountered either in the solo group or in the orchestra, or possibly in both, plus

occasionally timpani in the latter.

The concerto grosso is one of the important forms of the *Baroque period. After the middle of the eighteenth century, composers lost interest in the form, but it has returned to favor during the present century.

Since it was customary during the Baroque period to use a keyboard instrument--harpsichord, piano, or organ--in all instrumental ensembles, the presence of such an instrument is to be expected in any stylistically correct performance of a concerto grosso. It functions in both the solo group and the orchestra.

Although the concerto grosso and the normal *concerto (that is, solo concerto) both arose at about the same time, the uninterrupted development of the ordinary concerto accentuates certain differences between the two forms.

Differences Between the Concerto and the Concerto Grosso.

(A) The concerto is almost always "showy" and brilliant--a display of the soloist's ability; the concerto grosso is rarely brilliant or of a display character.

(B) The concerto is written for one instrument (occasionally two) --string, woodwind, brass, or keyboard--with full orchestra; the concerto grosso (as already stated) is for a group of solo instruments (usually string) with orchestra (usually string orchestra), plus accompanying keyboard instrument. It should be remembered that during the period in question, cellos and double-basses almost invariably had a single part, which actually sounded as octaves, due to the fact that the double-bass is a *transposing instrument sounding an octave lower than written.

(C) The concerto is almost invariably in three movements; the concerto grosso usually in four, while five movement examples are quite common, possibly as much so as those with three movements.

(D) In spite of the fact that the concerto usually has fewer movements, it nevertheless tends to be longer than the concerto grosso; the individual movements in the latter are rarely of protracted length.

(E) Most concertos contain a *cadenza; most concerti grossi do not.

(F) Concertos of the *Classical, *Romantic, and *Modern periods (though not those of the Baroque) normally contain one movement in *sonata-allegro form. Since the concerto grosso was at its height before sonata-allegro form was developed, it of course does not utilize this form and hence cannot be classified among the "sonata types" listed under that heading. (However, see concertant.)

(G) In the concerto, although the solo instrument is often heard alone and the orchestra often alone, most of the time the solo instrument and orchestra play together. As already mentioned, in the concerto grosso there are passages in which the solo group plays by itself, collectively, followed by passages for the orchestra, with the solo instruments either silent or else *doubling the corresponding instruments in the orchestra. It is exceptional for only some of the solo instruments to play, either with or without the orchestra.

(H) The movements in the concerto are less frequently joined together with *attaccas than those in the concerto grosso.

(I) Contrast of *keys is a fundamental concept in the sequence of movements in the concerto; in the concerto grosso sometimes all of the movements are in the same key, although the third movement (in four-movement works) is sometimes in the minor key with the same signature as the basic key (i. e., the *relative minor).

(J) The order of the movements in the concerto grosso as to tempos is most frequently:

first movement: slow
second movement: fast   } often joined together (attacca)

third movement: slow
fourth movement: fast   } often joined together (attacca)

On the rare occasions when a solo concerto has four movements, the order is not that shown above, but that given under *sonata-types (though of course there are a few exceptions).

There is a strong kinship as to form and spirit (but not medium) between the concerto grosso and the *sonata da chiesa (church sonata).

In performing the concerto grosso, the solo instruments as a rule do not stand or sit out in front of the orchestra, but merely play from their usual position.

The most representative concerti grossi are probably those by Handel, Corelli, and Geminiani. The Brandenburg Concertos by Bach, excellent as they are from a musical point of view, are far from typical. The concerti grossi by Vivaldi, though excellent, frequently call for wind instruments and hence are also less typical.

Although concerto grosso literally means "big concerto," it is evident from the preceding discussion that grosso ("big") here denotes a big solo force, not big length.

The classification of the concerto grosso as *chamber music is obviously inaccurate, though regrettably frequent.

It is well to point out that Concerto Grosso does not always appear as the title; often the title is merely Concerto but the form and medium clearly show the work to be a concerto grosso.

Plural: concerti grossi.

● concerto-sonata form. Same as double sonata-allegro form.

● concert overture. See overture (3).

●concert piece. A composition in one movement for solo instrument and orchestra; the *medium and style, if not the organization, suggest the *concerto. Well-known examples include Chausson's Poème for Violin and Orchestra, Gershwin's Rhapsody in Blue, Weber's Konzertstück for Piano and Orchestra, Liszt's Hungarian Fantasy, Fauré's Ballade for Piano and Orchestra, Bloch's Schelomo, Griffes's Poem for Flute and Orchestra, Franck's Symphonic Variations, etc.
   Synonym: Konzertstück (Conzertstück) (German).

●concert pitch. (1) Properly, a standard of tuning in which the A above *middle C

vibrates more than 440 times per second, though the actual frequency seems never to have been determined at a universally-agreed figure. (461.6 is sometimes given.)
   (2) The term is also carelessly used to indicate the actual pitch emitted by *transposing instruments, in contradistinction to the written pitch. The expression actual pitch, which is readily understood, is much to be preferred for this meaning.

●concord. A *consonant *chord. It is always a major or minor *triad, or possibly an *open fifth or *unison.
   Antonym: discord.

●condensed score. See reduction.

●conducting. The art of leading or directing a group of singers, instrumentalists, or both. The conductor's aim is to lead his group through the use of certain gestures which make his wishes clear to the performers. The fundamental gesture is the tracing of the *meter (or "beating time") with the right hand. The accompanying patterns are almost universally employed. It is important to mention that in tracing these patterns the hand never comes to a stop, except possibly in music of a very *staccato character. The hand is constantly in motion; it merely moves much faster between beats than when "on" beats. The use of the word hand may also be misleading, for the gestures are made with the entire arm, swinging from the shoulder.
   It is also important to mention that the number of motions and number of beats per measure do not always coincide. For instance a quick three-beat composition (scherzos, many waltzes) is often conducted with a single gesture each measure, this being of course the first beat; a moderate or fast six-beat composition is treated as two, that is, the conductor indicates beats 1 and 4; and a fast four-beat measure is sometimes handled as two, the baton giving nos. 1 and 3 only. Moderate or quick nine- and twelve-beat measures are treated like three and four, respectively. Conversely, in very slow tempos the conductor may double the number of motions, thus

Two beat
measures

Three beat
measures

Four beat
measures

six beat
measures

indicating each half-beat. This is known as the "divided beat." However, a "divided two" is not traced the same as four, and a "divided three" is certainly not like a six; instead a little rebounding loop is added to the diagram following the point where the first half of each beat is indicated.

The object of the conductor is to induce his performers to play or sing the composition in exactly the manner he believes it should be done--to impose his will upon them. The more completely he succeeds, the better a conductor he is. The best performers are those who carry out his precise wishes the most faithfully and the most willingly. It is obvious that a conductor is a dictator, musically speaking.

The area of the beats is the chief manner of indicating *dynamics; the beats are traced with large motions to indicate loud, with small motions to indicate soft. The *tempo is of course shown by the rapidity with which the beats are traced.

Although the exact expression in performance can be designated to some extent by the right hand, usually the left is also pressed into service, and many facial and even bodily movements added. When the conductor traces the beat in a violent manner, holding his left hand high and his head high, and perhaps showing his teeth, the performers' impulse is to play or sing loud; but when the conductor traces the beats with very small motions, holding his left hand low or perhaps making a "hush" gesture with it, crouching slightly and possibly shaping his lips as in whispering, the performers' impulse is to play or sing very softly. At rehearsals he of course gives many additional directions verbally.

Another duty of the conductor is to *cue (1) or signal his performers for entries after long *rests.

Many conductors use a *baton while others get equally good results without one. Some stand on a *podium, others (particularly tall conductors) do not.

There are some slight differences in the technique of conducting instrumental groups and that of leading choral groups. They are, however, minor details.

Conducting is by far the most recently-developed of the performing arts. The composer Felix Mendelssohn (1809-1847) was probably the first conductor in the modern sense of the word. Before his time the conductor--when there was one--was a mere time-beater, a human metronome. Usually the *concert-master of an orchestra served as an informal sort of conductor, or during the *Baroque period the player of the keyboard instrument (see figured bass) led the performance. The lack of precision in such efforts may well be imagined.

The adulation of the conductor on the part of the public, and his emergence as the equal of other performing artists, is almost entirely a twentieth-century phenomenon.

Conducting is the one musical art in which no woman has as yet achieved real fame; the reason would be difficult to name.

Synonym: directing.
See also attack, release.

● conductor. One who conducts a group of musicians, vocal or instrumental or both; a director.
See conducting.

● Conga drum. A very tall drum, of Latin-American origin, played directly with the hands. If the player stands, he slings the instrument over his shoulder by means of a strap or rope, though he usually sits to play. The sides of the Conga drum taper; the shape is almost that of a cone, the smaller end being on the floor, the larger end (which is the head) being up. It is much larger than the *bongó drum.

● conjoint motion, conjunct motion. *Diatonic motion.

● consecutive. Parallel; explained under contrary, parallel, and oblique motion. Intervals in parallel motion used in a faulty manner are often termed consecutives.

● conservatory. A music school. The earliest conservatories were orphan asylums in Naples, Italy, where parentless children were educated in music. The purpose of these asylums was to save or "conserve" the orphans, hence the name.

Variant forms: conservatorium, conservatoire.

● console. That portion of an *organ which contains the *manuals and *stops (2), but not the pipes. It is a large case.

● consonant. It is difficult to arrive at a definition of consonant or consonance that would satisfy all musicians. Perhaps it would be best to state that any chord is consonant if it contains no *intervals other than the perfect octave, perfect fifth, perfect fourth (but not between the two lowest tones), major or minor third, or major or minor sixth.

The facile statement that "a consonant chord is one that sounds pleasant and a *dissonant chord is one that sounds unpleasant" is a dangerous over-simplification and of course poses the additional question of defining pleasant and unpleasant.

Musicians often point out that a consonant chord sounds "final"-- sounds as if it could stand at the end of a composition, does not want to move on to something else. This is fairly satisfactory provided the chord is considered in complete isolation, for in the rhythmic context it is possible to make any chord seem to "want to move on."

All major and minor *triads in *root position are consonant. First *inversions (1) of the same may possibly be added, but hardly second inversions.

In considering *intervals of two tones the following are consonant: perfect prime, minor third, major third, perfect fifth, minor sixth, major sixth, perfect *octave, and of course the corresponding compound intervals such as tenths. The perfect fourth may possibly be added, at least under certain conditions.

Antonym: dissonant.

See also concord.

● consort. Late sixteenth- and seventeenth-century British term for a *chamber-music ensemble. For example, there are frequent references to "consorts of *viols"; however a consort did not necessarily consist only of viols.

Consort is a corruption of concert.

See also chest of viols.

● contemporary music. See Modern period.

● continued rest. Same as extended rest; explained under rest.

● †continuo. In music of the *Baroque period, the bass line of the music was called continuo or basso continuo. *Figured bass symbols were written under it or over it. These symbols were a type of "musical shorthand" which indicate *chords to be filled in by a keyboard instrument--usually harpsichord, piano, or organ. The printed bass notes themselves were played by a *cello or *viola da gamba if the composition was of the *chamber-music type or for solo voice, by cellos and *double-basses (sounding in *octaves) in orchestral music and in passages for chorus and orchestra (also sometimes in passages for solo voice). The symbols used were chiefly numerals; see the entry figured bass.

It is perhaps apparent that the actual instruments employed will depend partly on which ones are available and partly on the judgment of the conductor or performers. This is entirely congruous with the spirit of the music, and doubtless also represents Baroque practice.

Use of the continuo died out during the *Classical period, except in writing "secco" *recitatives in operas and in works for chorus and orchestra, in which case it persisted even into the early years of the *Romantic era.

Abbreviations: B. C., con., cont.

Pronunciation: accent second syllable.

● contra-. Literally, "against."
When this occurs in compounded
words it means "an octave below,"
e. g., as found in contrabass and
contrabassoon. The prefix counter-
is synonymous in some terms, but
by no means all.

● contrabass. (1) The *double-bass.
(2) Any extremely low tone, voice,
or instrument.

The contrabassoon is built in
a number of different shapes.
Its *tone-color is somewhat like
that of the ordinary bassoon, but
heavier and clumsier, with a
slight suggestion of bass clarinet
quality. Its extremely deep
*range causes it to have a some-
what "inhuman" sound and to
"speak" slowly.

Range:

Variant form: contrabasso.

● contrabass clarinet. A rarely-used
*woodwind instrument, occasionally
found in the *band, but rare in the
*orchestra. There are two types.
(A) The contrabass clarinet in E-flat,
occasionally called the contra-alto
clarinet, is pitched a perfect fourth
(see intervals) below the *bass clarinet, that is, an octave below the
*alto clarinet. (B) The contrabass
clarinet in B-flat, also called the
pedal clarinet, is pitched an octave
below the bass clarinet.

● contrabassoon. A double-reed *woodwind instrument pitched an octave
below the ordinary bassoon, to which
its mechanism is similar. It is the
lowest-pitched instrument in the
orchestra and band.

A few contrabassoons have the
low A, in unison with the lowest
key on the piano.

It will be observed that the
instrument is notated an octave
higher than it sounds; however
Wagner and Debussy wrote for it
at actual pitch. Only the bass
*clef is used.

Bassoonists take up the contrabassoon as a sideline.

Synonym: double-bassoon.

Italian: contrafagotto. French:
contrebasson. German: Kontra-
fagott. Spanish: contrabajón or
contrafagot.

● contrabass trombone. See trombone.

● contralto. The lowest female
voice. Its easy range is shown in
A, the approximate range expected

of an artist in B.

The tone-quality of the contralto is richer, heavier, darker, mellower, more "throaty," and more vibrant than that of the *soprano.

Plural: contraltos or contralti.
Synonym: alto.
See also voices.

●contralto trumpet. A brass instrument designed by the Russian composer Rimsky-Korsakoff. It is built in the key of F and has the same tranposition as the *horn in F (see transposing instruments). Although it can descend lower than the ordinary *trumpet, Rimsky-Korsakoff's desire was not so much to extent trumpet quality downward as to make available the lowest sounds (actual pitch) of the ordinary trumpet in a full, well-rounded tone-quality. On the contralto trumpet these pitches do not lie at the extreme low end of the range. (He was probably dissatisfied with the hoarse, raw quality of the lowest tones of the ordinary trumpet.) Almost every low note he wrote for this instrument could be played on an ordinary B-flat or A trumpet, though with inferior tone-quality.

Only Russian composers seem to have taken any interest in the contralto trumpet.

Synonym: alto trumpet.

●contrapuntal. The adjective form of counterpoint.
Synonym: polyphonic.
Antonym: homophonic.

Pronunciation: kŏn-trȧ-pŭn-tȧl.

●contrary, parallel, and oblique motion. These terms refer to the relationship between the notes given to any two voices or instruments, as they progress. Only three types of motion are possible in any given succession of tones.

(A) If one voice moves up and the other down, the result is called contrary motion (occasionally opposite motion).

Contrary

(B) If both move in the same direction, either up or down, the result is called parallel motion. (However, see similar motion for a fine distinction between "parallel" and "similar" motion.) Consecutive

Parallel

is sometimes substituted for parallel when speaking of a series of *intervals.

(C) If one voice moves either up or down and the other either repeats the tone it had or continues to hold it, the result is termed oblique motion.

When more than two voices or instruments are used, combinations

Oblique

of these types of movement result. In example A the bass moves in contrary motion to the soprano and tenor, which are in parallel motion,

● Conzertstück. *Concert piece (German).
Variant spelling: Konzertstück.
Pronunciation: kŏn-tsĕrt'-shtük.

Ex. A

while all three of these move in oblique motion to the alto. In example B (quoted from the last movement of Beethoven's Sonata in A Minor for violin and piano, op. 23) the right and left hands of the piano-part move in contrary motion during the first two complete measures, in parallel motion during measures 3 and 4; meanwhile everything is in oblique motion to the violin.

● †coperti, coperto. Muffled. This term is used with the *timpani to indicate that a piece of cloth should be laid on the instrument to muffle the tone.

● copyright. A copyright is a patent on a literary, artistic, or musical work. It may be secured by the composer, his agents or heirs, or by his publisher. It

Ex. B

● contredanse. A type of French dance similar to the quadrille and the English country dance.
Variant spelling: contradance.

assigns the right of printing and publishing to certain persons or a certain firm, usually the publisher. No other reproductions, including those made by photographing, by manuscript, or on duplicating machines, may be made without express permission of the copyright-owner. *Transcriptions and arrangements may not be made without permission. A composer cannot even quote from his own music without his publisher's permission. Recording, radio, and television rights are often included with the copyright. Copyrighted music may not be shown through a projection machine except by permission. An infringement on a copyright is punishable by fines.

The right of publicly performing a composition for profit is withheld unless a fee (known as a performance fee) is paid, or express permission obtained. This applies to broadcasts and recordings as well as concerts. Contrary to commonly-held opinion, school and church groups are not exempt from paying performance fees (unless no admission is charged) nor from copyright laws in general.

In the United States a copyright is given for 28 years from the date of issuing; this is renewable for another 28 years, so it may be said that an American copyright is valid for 56 years from the date of issue. In most European countries, copyrights are given for a term of a certain number of years after the death of the composer--usually 50.

Strictly speaking, making a manuscript copy of a copyrighted composition is illegal, although usually there is no complaint provided such copy is used only by the writer for his own personal study, and is not sold or used in a public performance (including a broadcast).

The very writing of the word "copyright" and the composer's name, affixed to the first page of a composition, is termed a common-law copyright, and serves as protection until an ordinary statutory copyright is obtained.

Music on which the copyright has expired is said to be in the *public domain.

● cor anglais. The *English horn. This is the French name of the instrument, but it is also widely used in England and the English-speaking world, possibly because of the complete illogicality of the name English horn.

Pronunciation: kōr-än̯-glĕ́.

● †corda. String. Thus, IV corda indicates the fourth string of a string instrument (e. g., the G string of the violin); una corda ("one string") indicates the *soft pedal of the piano. (Related English word: cord.)

Plural: corde.

See also sul (1), una corda, tre corde, due corde, tutte le corde.

● cornemuse. *Bagpipe (rare).

● cornet. A *brass instrument very similar to the *trumpet--in appearance, in *range, and in *tone-color. Like the trumpet, it has three *valves. The distinction between the two has been confused by manufacturers' fondness for producing instruments which are various stages of hybrids.

Strictly speaking, the cornet is shorter, but its tubing extends lower than that of the trumpet-- the general shape of the tubing is more nearly round. Its tone-color is quieter, less brilliant, and less incisive (although also less distinguished), but is of a nature more suited to quick passages. The frequent charge that the tone is "vulgar" may be due to the trivial type of music with which the cornet has unfortunately become associated, or to poor playing, rather than to any inherent defect in its tone-color.

There are always three or four sections of cornets in the *band, often curiously named solo, first, second, and third, rather than first, second, third, and fourth.

The cornet in use today has the following range:

name sometimes given to the *natural horn.

It will be observed that the notation is a whole-step above the sounds desired. (See transposing instruments.) Most cornets have a portion of tube which can be pulled out (functioning like the *crooks of the *horn) to put the instrument in A, with actual sounds a *half-step lower than those of the B-flat cornet.

Only the treble *clef is used in writing for the cornet.

The E-flat cornet is almost a different instrument, shorter than the ordinary cornet, with a very brilliant tone-quality. It is notated a minor third (see intervals) lower than the sounds desired. It went out of favor very suddenly around 1920.

French composers have been most partial to the cornet, often writing for two cornets and two trumpets in orchestral scores.

Most players believe the cornet is easier to play than the trumpet, though a minority is of the opposite opinion.

Variant form: cornet-à-pistons.

Italian: cornetto (plural cornetti) or cornetta (plural, cornette). French: piston or cornet-à-pistons (plural, cornets-à-pistons). German: Kornett (plural, Kornette) or Piston (plural, Pistons). Spanish: corneta.

The player is called a cornetist (also spelled cornettist).

Pronunciation: kôr-nĕt́, occasionally kôr´-nĕt.

● cornett. Name sometimes given to the *Zink. The term should never be confused with *cornet.

● †corni. *Horns, i. e., French horns (Italian plural).

● †corno da caccia. *Hunting horn;

● corresponding minor, corresponding major. Same as tonic minor, tonic major.

● †corto. Short. Often used in connection with the *fermata. (Related English word: curt.)
    Synonym: breve (1).
    Antonym: lunga.

● cottage organ. Same as harmonium.

● count. Same as beat (1).

● counter-. See contra-.

● countermelody. A *melody of secondary importance, heard simultaneously with another (and presumably more important) melody. It differs from a *descant in that the latter is normally added to an already-existing melody or complete musical fabric, while a countermelody figures in the composition from the moment of its origin.
    Compare obbligato.

● counterpoint. The simultaneous combining of melodic strands; polyphony. (The adjective form is contrapuntal.)
    It is obvious that not just any two or more melodic lines can be combined in a pleasing manner, but rather that all must be planned from the start so as to agree with, and be adjusted to, one another. In music based on counterpoint, all the *voices are considered equally important. There is no predominant *melody--rather everything is a melody--and no subsidiary *accompaniment.

Although the concept of simultaneous melodic lines usually comes to mind first when the word counterpoint is mentioned, the element of rhythmic contrast among them is equally important. Genuine counterpoint cannot be obtained from simultaneous melodies that march yoked together by exactly the same time-values. The principle of rhythmic contrast is basically that of several short moving tones against longer held tones.

The combining of a melodic line with an *arpeggio, even an animated one, is not "counterpoint." Motion alone does not produce counterpoint; it must be melodic movement and rhythmically independent.

It is rather generally believed that primitive music consisted of only an unaccompanied melody. In the Middle Ages, musicians began to combine original melodies with those already in existence, and the phenomena of *harmony and counterpoint made their appearance, the counterpoint aspect developing first. Still later it occurred to composers that it is not necessary to begin with a melody already in existence and then to add others to it, but that works can be fashioned from the ground up entirely from original material.

From the first appearance of harmony, apparently in or about the ninth century, the development of music revolved essentially around counterpoint until the beginning of the seventeenth century, when *homophonic style (melody and *accompaniment) made its appearance with the invention of *opera. Music based on counterpoint then gradually gave way before the newer style, although even as much later a composer as Bach (1685-1750) normally wrote music predominantly contrapuntal in character, while his noted contemporary Handel (1685-1759) wrote in this style with almost equal frequency.

The fact that harmony (or homophonic style) is a later and comparatively recent development, compared to counterpoint (or polyphonic style) is not readily grasped by some persons, for most people are familiar with a much greater amount of homophonic music than polyphonic. Counter-

point reached its nadir during the period from which the average person hears the largest amount of music: late eighteenth and nineteenth centuries, although it did crop up on occasion--in certain works of Mozart, Beethoven, Brahms, and Schumann, in Wagner's Die Meistersinger, and in numerous other (yet distinctly exceptional) instances. As of the present moment, however, homophonic music has become old-fashioned and contrapuntal music is modern, for most contemporary composers think and write much more contrapuntally than their predecessors of a hundred years ago.

Distinction Between Harmony and Counterpoint. Harmony and counterpoint should not be considered two different things, but two phases of the same thing. Both involve simultaneous combinations of tones.

In harmony emphasis is on the appearance of pleasing chords one after another, in a convincing order that seems to be "going somewhere." Naturally each *"voice" that forms one of the tones in the succession of chords must move in some manner from any one chord to that which follows, but whether its movement is melodically interesting or not is a secondary consideration; it is assumed that some "voices" will suffer moments of stagnation, and that if one of them should by chance enjoy a striking melodic twist, this occurs almost accidentally, and at the expense of the other voices. Still more essential is the condition that the chords form a support to a melody which is assumed more important than the chords themselves.

In counterpoint the primary requisite is interesting melodic movement in all voices, coupled with rhythmic contrast. Naturally there is always some sort of harmonic relationship between the simultaneous strands (see sonority, 2) but striving for a feeling of harmonic progression is a secondary consideration; we ask only that the harmonies be reasonably pleasing rather than jarring. They are to a certain extent fortuitous--accidents which occur as the melodic strands go their independent ways. No one of these strands is considered more important than any other.

Briefly, in harmony the emphasis is vertical; in counterpoint it is horizontal.

Linear Counterpoint and Animated Harmony. That type of counterpoint in which harmonic agreement is of so great importance as to have a large role in shaping the melodic strands, tailoring them to fit the chosen chords, is sometimes called-- almost derogatorily--animated harmony. It is more or less associated with some of the music of Handel. That type of counterpoint in which all the emphasis is on the independent and unimpeded movement of the individual "voices," with very slight consideration for harmonious inter-agreement--indeed, permitting considerable *dissonance between them (though minimized in the listener's mind by the strong melodic movement)--is called linear counterpoint (occasionally reckless counterpoint). Much newer than animated harmony, it is especially associated with the music of Richard Strauss, Mahler, Hindemith, and Stravinsky.

Combining Homophonic and Contrapuntal Styles. The question naturally arises: Can homophonic and contrapuntal style be combined? The word combined implies two interpretations: (A) Can a composition be in homophonic style at certain points, and in contrapuntal (polyphonic) style at others? (B) Can a composition contain two or more simultaneous melodies supported by purely subsidiary *accompaniment material? The answer in both cases is yes, but instances are not as plentiful as might be imagined.

Invertible counterpoint (sometimes called double counterpoint) is explained under the former heading.

Synonym: polyphony.

See also harmony, melody, intervals, imitation, canon, fugue, texture, sonority (2), organum.

● countersubject. In a fugue, a theme of secondary importance (really a

continuation of the *subject, or principal theme) which is combined contrapuntally with the subject as it appears successively in each voice. Not all fugues have countersubjects, however.

See fugue.

● countertenor. A very high *tenor voice; the highest male voice. It might well be described as a male alto. The quality is smooth in the extreme, but rather feminine, even effeminate.

● coupler. A mechanical contrivance on the *organ. Through the use of one type of coupler, the player can cause the stops selected for one manual to sound in conjunction with those of the manual on which he is momentarily playing, or to cause the stops for any manual to also sound in the pedals. Couplers of this type are labeled "swell to great," "choir to great," "swell to pedal," and the like.

With another type of coupler the player can cause every tone played on any manual to be duplicated an octave higher or an octave lower, these being called the "4-foot coupler" and the "16-foot coupler," respectively. He can also couple one manual to another in such a way that the coupled stops sound an octave higher or lower ("swell to great 4'," "choir to great 16'," etc.); the stops drawn for the manual on which he plays will continue to sound as usual.

The little tablets or knobs that control the couplers often have the same appearance as those which turn on the various *stops (2). Properly, however, a stop is a set (or "rank") of pipes, while a coupler is a mechanical connecting-device. Couplers emit no sounds of their own; they make an effect only in conjunction with stops.

● courante. A dance in moderate 3-2 time (formerly sometimes in 6-4 time). The courante is the second of the four basic dances that make up the Baroque *suite (sometimes misnamed "Classic

suite"). The beats are much subdivided, with many quarter-, eighth-,
and occasionally sixteenth-notes.

A peculiarity of the courante is that
at the *cadence in the middle and
that at the end (being always in
*binary or AB form, there are always
two prominent cadences), the rhythm
shifts to 6-4, although no new *time-
signature is inserted.   (See hemiola.)

The name literally means "running
dance. "

Variant spelling: courant.
Pronunciation: kōō-ränt.

● court dance. A dance used by the
nobility or the members of the royal
court, as opposed to a peasant dance
or folk dance.

● Covent Garden. A famous theater
and *opera-house in London.

Pronunciation: Covent is pronounced kŭv-ĕnt.

● cow-bells. A *percussion instrument similar to the bell often tied
around a cow's neck. With the
orchestral cow-bell the clapper is
often removed and the instrument
struck with a drumstick.

● crab. Same as cancrizans.

● cracovienne. Same as krakowiak.

● cradle song. A *lullaby.

● †Cremona. A town in northern Italy,
southeast of Milan, once famous for
the manufacture of violins. Stradivarius, Guarnerius, Amati, and
others worked here. Population about
55, 000.

The term "Cremona" is sometimes
applied to any old high-quality, valuable violin, even though not actually
manufactured in that town.

See also "Strad. "

● †crescendo. Gradually becoming
louder. The word is derived from
the same root as "increase. "

It cannot be too strongly emphasized that crescendo does not mean
"loud, " "louder, " or "start softly and get
loud, " but "gradually becoming louder. "
At the conclusion of a crescendo the

music may not necessarily be
genuinely loud; it is possible to
make a crescendo from ppp to
pp (see dynamic marks). The use
of this word by writers of fiction
and magazine articles to mean
"pandemonium, " "crash, " or
"intensive activity" ("the truck and
the car collided with a frightful
crescendo, " "the crime-wave has
reached a crescendo") is absolutely
incorrect and thoroughly illogical.

The symbol ◁
is theoretically equivalent, although
it usually is employed for crescendos of short duration.

Engravers and composers often
denote a long-drawn-out crescendo
by placing a row of hyphens after
the word, or by dividing it into
widely-spaced syllables, thus:
cresc. - - - - - - -
or:
cres - - - - cen - - - - do.
(Compare poco a poco crescendo.)

Although a crescendo normally
culminates in a passage marked
f or ff, it is entirely possible for
it to be followed by a sudden p,
Beethoven being especially fond
of this effect.

When this term is used as a
noun, the plural is spelled
crescendos.

Abbreviation: cresc., cres.,
occasionally cr.

Antonyms: decrescendo, diminuendo. ▷

Pronunciation: krĕ-shen'-dō.

● †crescente. Increasing.

● critic. See music critic.

● crook. An extra piece of tubing
which can be fitted into a *horn
or *trumpet so as to enable it to
play a different set of overtones
(see harmonic series). At one
time crooks were made for the
horn which would pitch it anywhere
from C alto (sounding as written)
to A basso (sounding an octave
and a minor third lower than
written)--sixteen crooks in all.
The trumpet also had a formidable
number.

The application of *valves to the

horn and trumpet during the 1830's
to 1850's rendered the crooks no
longer necessary, and their employment eventually disappeared. A
number of musicians still own an E-
flat crook for the horn, but with
that exception all horn music is now
*transposed when necessary and
played on the horn in F, or occasionally the horn in B-flat alto. Most
trumpets and cornets still have a
slide which can be pulled out to change
the instrument from B-flat to A,
but this slide is not properly a crook,
though essentially it fulfills the same
function. (A crook is detachable;
this contrivance is not.) Other than
the foregoing examples, the system
of crooks belongs mostly to history.
   Synonym: shank.
   See also transposing instruments,
natural horn.

● cross bar. Same as crossbeam.

● crossbeam. The thick, heavy line
that connects groups of eighth-notes.
Two crossbeams are used to connect
sixteenth-notes, three for thirty-
second-notes, etc.

● cross cue. Same as cue (3).

● cross-hand. In playing the
*keyboard instruments it is some-
times advisable to reach with the
left hand over the right, or vice
versa, to touch certain keys.
This device is called crossing the
hands. The left hand is more
frequently crossed over the right
than the other way around, but
both practices are common. Often
only one or two notes are needed
in any single crossing. The keyboard compositions of Domenico
Scarlatti (1685-1757) were the
earliest to use this device frequently.
   For further information, see
the entry r. h.

● cross relation. The appearance
of two different *inflections of a
note, one in one voice, the other
in a different voice, in adjacent
chords. The tones in question
seem to clash and contradict one
another, and a somewhat jarring
effect results. It can be corrected
if both notes are retained in the
same voice. See example at bottom.

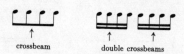

crossbeam   double crossbeams

Synonyms: beam, stroke, cross
bar, occasionally balken.

Most listeners get the impression that the two inflections appear

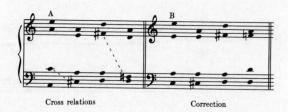

Cross relations   Correction

simultaneously; that is, the second and fourth chords in A above almost sound as follows

and hence give the illusion of being both major and minor at the same time.

Cross relations were very common in English music of the sixteenth and seventeenth centuries. Their piquant effect is, however, of an entirely different order from the bungling results produced by first year students in *harmony (2) classes.

Synonym: false relation.

● cross rhythms. (1) Rhythmic combinations whose subdivisions coincide only at occasional points, such as two against three (A), three against four (B), or three against five (C).

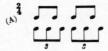

See also irregular groupings.

● crotchet. Quarter-note. See British terminology.

● crush notes. *Grace notes (1) played simultaneously with the principal note and immediately released. They are possible only on keyboard instruments.

● csárdás. Variant spelling of czárdás.

● cue. (1) In *conducting, a signal given to any player or singer just before his entrance after a *rest of considerable length. It reassures him in case he is uncertain whether he has counted out the time of the rest correctly.

(2) In the parts of an orchestral, band, or chamber-music composition, near the conclusion of a long *rest it is customary to print, in small type, a brief passage taken from the part of another of the instruments, so that the player, when he hears the given instrument sound this passage, may re-enter on his own part at the proper moment with complete confidence. Cues serve as a double check against miscounting the number of measures in long rests.

(3) In publications intended for school bands and orchestras, which often do not possess the full required complement of instruments, prominent passages for various instruments are printed in small type in the *parts for other players; for instance an oboe solo may be inserted in fine type in the part for the clarinet or flute. These cues are to be played in case the group lacks the particular instrument for which the passage is really intended. Sometimes the player has to omit his own part in order to perform the cue, which contains material of greater importance.

These are often called cross-cues in contradistinction to the other types of cue.

● cuivré (French). A "brassy," forced type of *tone-quality sometimes required in music for the *horn.
Pronunciation: kwē-vrā.

● †cupo. Obscure, dark, pensive, hollow.

● cut. An excision; a part of a composition that is deliberately omitted.
Cuts are usually made when a performer becomes convinced that the composition is too long. His judgment is of course open to serious reproach. Nevertheless composers themselves have on rare occasion come to the conclusion that certain of their published compositions were too long, and have urged or tolerated certain cuts. Wagner designated them for some of his operas; Rachmaninoff

agreed to them in his Second Symphony. Of course some composers have become convinced that certain works would benefit from pruning, and have issued revised versions or second editions in the light of these convictions; on the other hand, revised versions and second editions have also been known to expand compositions that authors have become convinced were not long enough.
Some performers make cuts to avoid difficult passages. This practice is of course never to be condoned.
The word cut is used both as a noun and as a verb.
See also vide.

● cut time.   2-2 time (colloquial, undesirable). ₵
See also ₵

● cycle of fifths.   Same as circle of fifths.

● cycle of songs.   Same as song-cycle.

● cyclic form, cyclical form. The practice, in a work divided into several *movements, of causing material from one movement to re-appear in another. The purpose is to gain greater unity, to make the separate movements seem to belong together rather than placed side-by-side arbitrarily.
The often-made statement that César Franck (1822-1890) "invented" cyclic form is complete nonsense, though it is quite true that Franck and certain of his pupils, notably Vincent d'Indy (1851-1931) believed in and employed the principle to a thoroughgoing extent. D'Indy himself, in his Cours de Composition Musicale, attributes its invention to Giovanni Battista Vitali (1644?-1692) in a Sonata composed in 1677. Actually the device can be traced back to the fourteenth century, to a Mass written no later than 1364 (possibly earlier) by Guillaume Machaut (1300?-1377?), which also has the distinction of being the oldest known polyphonic

setting of the ordinary of the *mass by a single composer.

Some musicians make distinctions between various types of cyclic form. If there are just casual quotations from one movement to another, the term cyclic is used. If there is a theme which appears systematically in several movements, but with very little change, it is called a motto theme; Tschaikowsky's Fifth Symphony exemplifies this type. If the theme is considerably varied, yet always recognizable, it is called an idée fixe meaning "fixed idea" (a term first used by Berlioz in connection with

former case the direction colle mazzette ("with the mallets") is often appended. Sometimes a suspended cymbal is struck with a small, fan-shaped wire brush; *dance-bands in particular favor this effect.

Cymbals vibrate for a long time after being caused to sound, unless the player *damps them. He does this by bringing them down against his coat. (To damp a suspended cymbal that has been struck with a stick, he clasps it with his hand.) Hence the following have a markedly different effect.

his Fantastic Symphony). If the theme undergoes extensive change--often so much as to be quite unrecognizable by ear--and especially if it leads to the formation of at least one theme in each movement, it is called a generating theme. D'Indy's Symphony on a French Mountain Song (really a piano *concerto rather than a *symphony) is an excellent example.

The employment of a *Gregorian chant or *chorale melody in the various sections of a *mass or *cantata, respectively, is an example of cyclic form.

Many operas and particularly operettas have a cyclic *finale which harks back to certain earlier passages.

Since cyclic form is not really a *"form," the present term is not very accurate. Cyclic principle and cyclic procedure, though less frequent, are both preferable.

● cylinder. See valve.

● cymbalom. Same as czimbalom.

● cymbals. An indefinite-pitch *percussion instrument consisting of a pair of slightly convex brass plates, with a cup-like depression in the center of each, normally played by brushing the two plates together. It is also possible to suspend one plate and play single tones or *rolls with either soft or hard sticks: in the

Observe that, like many indefinite pitch percussion instruments, music for the cymbals is often written on a one-line staff.

Occasionally the music for the cymbals is written with diamond-shaped or cross-shaped notes, rather than round, though there is hardly a good reason for the practice.

Cymbals are tremendously powerful when played fortissimo, but soft tones are possible and of excellent effect.

The word cymbals is of course plural; the singular is used when referring to just one of the plates.

For antique cymbals, see that entry.

Italian: piatti or cinelli. French: cymbales. German: Becken. Spanish: címbalos or platillos.

● cypher. *Cipher.

● czárdás. A Hungarian (actually Hungarian gypsy) dance. It normally has two sections, the first slow and mournful, the second very lively.

Variant spelling: csárdás.
Pronunciation: chär-däsh.

● czimbalom. A Hungarian instrument, trapezoid-shaped and somewhat resembling an old-fashioned square piano minus keyboard and lid. It is a type of *dulcimer; its strings are beaten with two felt- or leather-covered hammers, one held in each hand of the player. *Scales, *arpeggios, and *tremolos (both of one and two tones) can be played with ease. Its *tone-color is very similar to that of the piano, although somewhat more metallic; perhaps it resembles a "Penny Arcade" piano more than anything. The sounds, once struck, tend to linger until they die out of their own accord; hence there is always a pronounced blur, similar to that produced when the piano is played with the damper *pedal depressed.

Liszt imitates the instrument in some of his Hungarian Rhapsodies.

Zoltán Kodály has written a prominent part for the czimbalom in his *opera (and orchestral *suite derived therefrom) Háry János.

The word czimbalom has been confused with *cymbal and *cembalo; of course it bears no relation to either.

Plural: czimbalmok.
Variant spellings: cimbalom, cymbalom.
Italian: cimbalo ongarese.
Pronunciation: tsĭm-bä-lŏm.

D

● †da. At, by, from, to. Dagli, dai, dal, dall', dalla, dalle, dallo. At the, by the, from the, to the. These terms are not interchangeable; their correct usage is determined by the rules of Italian grammar.

● †da capo. See D. C.

● da capo form. See ternary form.

● †dal segno. See D. S.

● damp (verb). To arrest the vibrations of an instrument by touching with the hand or by some other means. When a very short note is to be played, it is sometimes necessary to damp the *harp, the *pizzicato string instruments, the *cymbals, the *gong, the *piano, and occasionally certain drums.

Synonym: secco. Also, for harp only, étouffé or étouffez.

● damper. (1) A device for arresting the vibration of a string or other sounding body. The dampers on the piano are little tufts of felt placed over the strings; their action is described under the entry damper pedal.

(2) Same as mute (1).

● damper pedal. The ordinary right-hand pedal of the piano. It is used to continue the sound produced by keys which the player is no longer touching. Any references to "the pedal," as well as the symbols * Ped. and ⌐_____⌐ or ⌐_____⌐ apply to the damper pedal.

When pressed, it lifts up all the felt dampers which normally lie atop the strings, and hence if any keys are struck, the corresponding strings will keep sounding even though the pianist's hands are elsewhere. Releasing the pedal causes all the dampers to fall back onto the strings and thus to halt the sounding of all tones except any whose keys are being pressed at the moment.

Use of this mechanism increases the *sonority (1) of the instrument, augmented perhaps by *sympathetic vibration. The production of a smooth *legato can be greatly facilitated by skillful employment of the pedal, especially when a series of legato *chords is involved (by using the pedal just long enough to bridge from one to the next).

The introduction of the pedal-equipped piano during the early nineteenth century revolutionized the entire style of writing for the instrument. The new contrivance rendered *arpeggios and widely-spaced chords effective, and put an end to the *Alberti bass as an accompaniment.

Synonyms: loud pedal (undesirable), sustaining pedal.

● dance. It would be impossible to describe the musical characteristics of all the distinct types of dance that are known. This book

lists the following dances, each under
its own heading:

allemande	musette
bolero	paso doble
bourrée	passacaglia
chaconne (ciaconna)	passepied
contredanse (contradance)	pavane
courante	polka
czardas	polo
écossaise	polonaise (polacca)
fandango	quadrille
furiant	reel
gelliard	rumba
gavotte	rigaudon
gigue (jig)	saltarello
habanera	sarabande
hopak (gopak)	schottische
hornpipe	seguidilla
jota	siciliano
krakowiak	tambourin
Ländler	tango
malagueña	tarantella
mazurka	tedesca
minuet (menuetto)	Tyrolienne
Morris dance	waltz (valse)

See also ballet.

● dance band. A small ensemble
specializing in the playing of *jazz.

*Saxophones, particularly the alto
and tenor, have always been conspicuous in the membership of dance
bands, indeed the saxophone has been
termed the chief member of the group.
Other instruments often used include
the clarinet, the alto clarinet, the
trumpet (the muted trumpet is especially favored, and dance-band players
have pioneered in the introduction of
new and unusual types of *mute), the
trombone, the banjo, the piano, the
violin, the double-bass (which is
usually played with a peculiar "slapping" variant on the *pizzicato), not
to mention all manner of percussion
instruments entrusted to a single
musician who sits surrounded by
them, busily engaged in jumping from
one to another or even playing several
simultaneously.

Almost no two dance bands use
exactly the same instruments and in
identical proportions. The best groups
have their music arranged by highly
skillful orchestrators (many of them
gifted composers of serious music
who find this work highly lucrative),
who arrange not only for one
certain combination, but even with
the exact talents of each individual
member in mind, often succeeding
in a way that renders playing of
the arrangement almost an impossibility for any other group. Com-
mercially published arrangements
can however be obtained, though
they are often stereotyped and
insipid in effect.

The frequent presence of the
violin and double-bass has already
been mentioned. This in no way
prevents the organization from being
called a dance band or jazz band,
though the term dance orchestra
is also very commonly encountered.

A small dance band is often
called a "combo."

● dance suite. The Baroque suite.
See suite (1).

● D. C. Go back to the beginning
of the composition and play until
the word *fine (meaning end) is
encountered. Occasionally the
repetition goes only as far as the
sign⊕from which the player
proceeds to an as-yet-unplayed
section marked coda.

In a composition for voices, the words may or may not be the same when the passage repeats.

It is understood that if *repeat signs occur, they are to be observed only in the original playing; when replaying this section (on the D. C.), repeat signs are to be ignored; also if *first and second endings have appeared, only the second ending is to be played when taking the D. C. Often the composer emphasizes this by using the more complete indication D. C. senza replica (or D. C. senza ripetizione)--"from the beginning, without repetition."

The term D. C. is often found in compositions possessing the *form-scheme ABA. The composer writes out only the A and B sections, and the direction D. C. brings about the repetition of A. (See ternary form.)

D. C. is the abbreviation for da capo (literally "from the head").

Compare D. S.

See also repeat signs.

● dead interval. The melodic *interval between the last note of one *phrase and the first note of the following phrase (especially if a *rest intervenes) is known as a dead interval. *Leaps which are ordinarily avoided often occur as dead intervals.

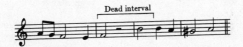

Dead interval

● début. The first public performance given by a musician on a professional basis. In addition to the true début, the term is also used to cover the first appearance in any particular country or city ("American début," "Vienna début," etc.).

Anglicized pronunciation: dā-boo'.

● decibel. A unit adopted by scientists for measuring the loudness of sounds.

● †deciso. Decisively. It is about the equivalent of energico or spiritoso.

Variant form: decisivo.

● †declamando. In a declamatory style.

Variant form: declamato.

● †declamazione. Declamation.

● †decrescendo. Gradually becoming softer. This term is derived from the same root as the English word decrease.

Abbreviations: decresc., occasionally decres., decr.

Synonyms: diminuendo,

(The symbol is generally used to indicate a decrescendo spread over a comparatively short time.)

Antonyms: crescendo,

● degree. (1) One of the tones or "steps" in a *scale.

(2) Any of the locations possible on the *staff, either on a line or on a space.

● †deliberamente. Variant form of liberamente.

● †deliberatamente. Deliberately, unhurried.

● †delicatezza. Delicacy.

● †delicato. Delicately.

● †delirando. Raving, delirious.

● demisemiquaver. Thirty-second-note. See British terminology.

● descant. (1) A melody added, in *contrapuntal combination, to a melody already in existence, in such a way as not to disturb the original harmonization, but to add to it. Most descants appear as the highest part of the fabric. (Compare countermelody, obbligato.)

(2) An old name for the highest voice or part, roughly equivalent to the present word soprano.

Variant spelling: discant.

For English descant see faux bourdon.

● descriptive music. See program
music.

● design. A term occasionally substituted for *form.

● desk. See Pult.

● †desolato. Desolate, distressed,
sorrowful.

● development. A process by which
thematic material is varied in such
a way as to cause it to grow, to
unfold, to expand; the composer's
material is "put through its paces."
    Common devices in development
include:
    (A) Converting material originally
in the *major mode into minor, or
vice versa.
    (B) Extending the theme by re-
iterating and insisting on certain
characteristic rhythms or melodic
twists.
    (C) Very frequent *modulation.
    (D) Using notes from the end of
a *phrase to form the beginning of
a new phrase.
    (E) *Inversion (3).
    (F) *Cancrizans (retrograde motion).
    (G) *Augmentation.
    (H) *Diminution.
    (I) Combining thematic material with
other material, contrapuntally.
    (J) Combining two or more themes
contrapuntally.
    (K) Breaking up a theme into little
fragments.
    (L) Extending the theme by building
a *sequence on it.
    (M) Deriving an *accompaniment-
figure from a few notes of a theme,
then using this to accompany the
theme itself or a different theme.
    The foregoing is of course far from
complete; there are as many types of
development as there are compositions
that use the device.
    The Harvard Dictionary of Music
aptly states: "These devices are used
in a manner designed to bring about
a feeling of evolution and growth, of
increased intensity and higher
'temperature,' of dynamic stress and

climax, of a battlefield where the
musical forces come to grips."
    A certain amount of develop-
ment occurs in nearly all good
music, but its most characteristic
habitat is in *sonata-allegro form,
where the presence of development
is indispensable; otherwise the
form simply is not sonata-allegro.
    Development is also highly
characteristic of the *fugue.
    For a comparison of the develop-
ment process with the variation
process, see theme and variations.
    Synonyms (when used in reference
to sonata-allegro form): development
group, free fantasia, working out.

● †devoto. In a devotional style.
(Related English word: devout.)
    Variant spelling: divoto.

● †devozione. Devotion.

● †di. Of; also from, by, with.
Degli, dei, del, dell', della, delle,
dello, of the. These terms are
not interchangeable; correct usage
depends on the rules of Italian
grammar.
    Variant form: d' (before vowels
and h).

● diamond-shaped notes. See
harmonics (1), cymbals, and
Sprechstimme.

● diapason. (1) Same as octave.
    (2) Same as range.
    (3) One of the four basic types
of *stop on the *organ.
    (4) Standard of tuning, such as
A above middle C having 440
vibrations per second.
    Pronunciation: dī-ă-pā-sŏn or
dī-ă-pā-zŏn.

● diaphony. Same as organum.
    Pronunciation: dī-ăf-ŏ-nĭ.

● diatonic. Stepwise; scalewise;
moving by seconds (see intervals).
If a note progresses to the note
just above or that just below, the
motion is termed diatonic.
    In a diatonic scale a note appears
for every line and space of the
*staff; no line or space is omitted

and none appears in two different *inflections.

Example A is purely diatonic. Example B is not, since there is a *leap at every point except two; that is, it is diatonic at two points only. Example C would probably be classified more as *chromatic than as diatonic.

there are seven different tones, with an eighth tone (located an *octave above the starting sound) to finish off. In writing this type of scale, notes will appear on the various *degrees (locations) of the *staff in order--a note on a line, a note on a space, a note on a line, a note on a space, etc.--

A. (Diatonic style)　　　　　　Beethoven: Symphony No. 9, Fourth movement.

B. (Disjunct or leaping style)
Beethoven: Symphony No. 5, third movement.

C. (Chromatic style)　　　　　　Debussy: The Afternoon of a Faun.

Permission granted by Durand Edition, Paris, France, Copyright Owner, Elkan-Vogel Co., Inc., Philadelphia, Pennsylvania, Agents.

Repeated tones are not considered an interruption in the character of a melody, be it diatonic or full of leaps.

The *major scale, *minor scale, and the *modes are all diatonic, but the *chromatic scale is not.

Synonyms: scalewise, stepwise, conjunct motion, conjoint motion.

Antonyms: leap, skip, disjunct motion.

● diatonic chords. Those conventional chords which can be written without recourse to *accidentals; opposed to *altered chords.

● diatonic scale. The usual, familiar, conventional type of scale in which

no location represented twice and no location omitted.

The conventional *major scale and *minor scale are diatonic, as are the *modes (1, 2); however the *chromatic and *pentatonic scales are not.

● dictation. A musical study taught in *conservatories and the music departments of colleges. In dictation class the student writes down melodies or chord-progressions which the instructor plays. The student who can accomplish this correctly has obviously demonstrated that he knows exactly what tones he has heard.

Dictation is usually combined with *ear-training and *sight-singing, and sometimes also with *harmony (2) and *keyboard harmony. It is an important part of *theory.

● difference tone, differential tone. *Resultant tone.

● dilettante. An *amateur. Like amateur, this word is theoretically a commendatory term, but is frequently used to suggest superficiality--as a synonym for dabbler.
It comes from the Italian word meaning "to delight in" or "to rejoice in."
Plural: dilettantes or dilettanti.
Variant spelling (rare): dilettant.
Pronunciation: dĭl-ĕ-tän̆-tĭ̆ or dĭl-ĕ-tänt.́

● diminished. See intervals, triad, seventh-chords.

● diminuendo. Gradually becoming softer. Its derivation from the same root as diminish is apparent. It must be emphasized that the word does not mean "soft" or "softer," but "gradually becoming softer."
The symbol ══════ is theoretically equivalent, though in practice it is often used to indicate a shorter or less pronounced decrease than diminuendo.
When this term is used as a noun the plural is spelled diminuendos.
Abbreviation: dim., occasionally dimin.
Synonym: decrescendo.
Antonyms: crescendo, ══════

● diminution. The presentation of a musical theme or figure with all the time-values halved, i. e., the half-note of the original becomes a quarter, the quarter becomes an eighth, the eighth a sixteenth, and so on. The E-flat major section of the

Overture to Wagner's Die Meistersinger is a famous example (compare with opening).
Of course it is possible to divide original values by 3 or 4 as well as by 2.
The opposite process is called *augmentation.

● dinner music. Light and inconsequential compositions that are played as "background" music in restaurants are often rather contemptuously called "dinner music." Pieces used for this purpose are not really intended to be heard, but rather overheard. Many musicians object to the utilization of music under such conditions.

● †di nuovo. Again, once more.

● diptych. In painting, a pair of pictures on panels fastened together. This term is sometimes taken into music to indicate a work divided into two movements. The numerous compositions entitled Fastasia and Fugue, Prelude and Toccata, or Prelude and Dance might be cited as examples.
Compare triptych.
Pronunciation: dĭp-tĭk.

● directing. See conducting.

● direct motion. Same as similar motion.

● director. A *conductor. The term also sometimes signifies an *impresario.

● dirge. A vocal or instrumental composition of mournful character; a funeral piece.

● discant. Variant spelling of descant.

● discord. A *dissonant chord.

The layman of course often uses this word as a synonym for wrong note or mistake, but this usage is foreign to the vocabulary of the musician.

Antonym: concord.

● disjunct motion. See leap.

● †disperato. In a despairing manner.

● dispersed position. Same as open harmony.

● displaced accent. See shifted accent.

● dissonant. It is almost impossible to arrive at a definition of dissonant or dissonance which would satisfy all musicians. Perhaps the best definition can be obtained by stating that any chord containg a seventh, second, or an augmented or diminished *interval is dissonant. To this should be added the second *inversion (1) of *triads; at least the second inversion of the tonic triad (I$_4^6$)— theoretically consonant--seems to be more dissonant than the dissonant dominant *seventh-chord which often follows it.

One reasonably satisfactory definition may be obtained by mentioning that dissonant chords seem to want to move on to something else (they are restless), while the opposite--consonant chords--appear to be stable and can easily provide a stopping-point. However, the impression of "seeming to want to move on" can be produced by the *rhythm; hence this

test cannot be applied unless the chord is taken completely out of its context and considered as an isolated phenomenon.

The glib statement that "a dissonant chord sounds unpleasant while a consonant chord sounds pleasant" is highly dangerous and far from true, even if convincing definitions of pleasant and unpleasant could be presupposed.

*Non-harmonic tones almost invariably produce dissonance.

Among conventional chords, all of the following are dissonant: diminished triads, augmented triads, seventh-chords, ninth-chords, eleventh-chords, thirteenth-chords, and fourth-chords. All unusual and unconventional combinations are of course also so classified.

There are distinct degrees of dissonance; some combinations are more dissonant than others, as will be heard in the accompanying three chords.

Dissonant is by no means a synonym for harsh, shrill, strident, raucous, or aggressive. *Tone-quality and *tone-color have nothing to do with consonance and dissonance. A *triad or *unison passage played fortissimo by muted brass instruments is consonant, despite its harsh, noisy, aggressive effect. Consonance and dissonance are in the tones themselves, not in the *dynamics or tone-color.

Synonym: discordant.
Antonym: consonant.
See also discord.

Mildly dissonant   More dissonant   Very dissonant

●†distinto. Distinct, clear.

●distortion. Explained under <u>fidelity</u>.

●ditty. A simple, homely *melody; generally derogatory.

●†diva. A female opera singer who has achieved great popularity and fame; a *prima donna. (Literally "goddess.")
Plural: <u>divas</u> (English) or <u>dive</u> (Italian).

●†divertimento. A composition in several *movements, usually four or more, in any desired order or *form. It is usually written for either a chamber-music combination (often a rather unusual one), or for orchestra, frequently small orchestra. It might well be considered a *suite (2). The literal meaning, <u>divertissement,</u> suggests that it is intended as an interlude between other compositions or activities. In many cases the composer did not intend that all the movements necessarily be played continuously, but that he half-foresaw long interruptions between them, or the complete omission of some of the movements.
The distinctions between the divertimento, the serenade (2), and the cassation are so slight that they may be ignored.
Plural: <u>divertimenti</u> or <u>divertimentos</u>.

●divertissement. Divertimento.

●†divisi. Divided. Used when two different lines of notes appear in the music for the string instruments in orchestral compositions, as an indication that one half of the group should play the upper line, the other half, the lower one.
If the parts cross over one another, it is necessary to put each on a separate *staff.
The direction for all the instruments to resume playing the same part is <u>unis.</u>, abbreviation for <u>unisoni</u> (meaning *unison), or <u>uniti</u> (literally, "united").
Observe that in the accompanying example the second and third notes are to be played as *double-stops, not divisi. Presence of double notes does not automatically indicate divisi. Also observe the momentary unison (indicated by double stems) on the last beat of the fifth measure.
Sometimes the division is made into three or four parts, rather than merely two. In these cases the direction is <u>div. a 3</u> or <u>div. in 3</u>, and <u>div. a 4</u> or <u>div. in 4</u>, respectively.
Divisis are also often encountered in *choral music, and in *band compositions among the parts played by a group of instruments.
Divisis are not always used merely to increase the number of tones in chords or to facilitate certain passages (both of which are makeshifts); they are sometimes intentionally employed to secure a thinner, quieter tone than is possible without them.
Abbreviation: <u>div.</u>
German: <u>geteilt</u>, formerly <u>getheilt</u>.

● divisions. *Variations. This term was once widely used by British composers. It usually occurs in the form "Divisions on a Ground, " meaning variations over an *ostinato bass. Compositions so entitled follow the *passacaglia-chaconne pattern. The word divisions apparently was seldom used in connection with the *theme and variations.

● †divoto. Same as devoto.

● dodecaphony. See twelve tone system.

● dodecuple scale. See twelve tone system.
   Variant spelling: duodecuple scale.

● †dolce. Sweetly. This word is used to caution the performer against any roughness or harshness, and to indicate a smooth, agreeable tone-quality. The implication of softness is obvious, yet the term is often encountered in such a form as f ma dolce--"loud but sweetly, " that is, loud but not blaring, crashing, or banging. It comes from the same root as the English word dulcet.
   Abbreviation (rare): dol.
   Antonyms: feroce, ruvido, stridente.

● †dolcezza. Sweetness. Con dolcezza is a synonym for *dolce.

● †dolcissimo. Very sweetly. (Superlative of dolce.)
   Abbreviation: dolciss.

● †dolente. Same as doloroso.

● †dolore. Grief.

● †doloroso. Doleful, sad, plaintive.
   Variant forms: dolente, dolorosamente.
   Synonyms: con dolore, tristamente, mesto, piangendo.
   Antonyms: giocoso, giojoso, scherzando, con gajezza, gajo.

● dominant. The fifth degree of the *scale, or the *triad built on it. The dominant is considered the second most important tone in the scale, outranked only by the *tonic. Roman numeral for triad: V.
   In the *modes (1) the term dominant is used with a somewhat different meaning; it is by no means always the fifth degree.

● †doppio movimento. Twice as fast as the *tempo which has been in effect; the *time-value of every note is cut in half.
   Pronunciation: in doppio accent first syllable.

● †doppio valore. Twice as slow as the *tempo that has been in effect; the *time-value of every note is doubled. It is just the opposite of *doppio movimento.

● dots. See dotted notes and staccato. For dots and slurs (or ties) see portamento (2) and staccato (3).

● dotted notes, dotted values. Notes which have a dot after them. The dot increases the length of the note by half of its original value. Any *time-value may be dotted.

Dotted whole-note	𝅝· =	𝅝 𝅗𝅥
Dotted half-note	𝅗𝅥· =	𝅗𝅥 𝅘𝅥
Dotted quarter-note	𝅘𝅥· =	𝅘𝅥 𝅘𝅥𝅮
Dotted eighth-note	𝅘𝅥𝅮· =	𝅘𝅥𝅮 𝅘𝅥𝅯
Dotted sixteenth-note	𝅘𝅥𝅯· =	𝅘𝅥𝅯 𝅘𝅥𝅰

When two dots are used, the second adds half the value of the first, i. e., the double dot increases the duration of the note by three-fourths of its original value. It is possible to place

●double. (1, verb) To play or sing in *unison with, or to duplicate at a given *interval. Thus we say that "the piano doubles the voice part," meaning that the

Illustration of the double-dot

three dots, or even more, after a note, though such usages are rare. Each dot adds half the value of its predecessor. It will thus be apparent that no note can be doubled in value by adding dots to it, no matter how many are added.

The dot did not always have its present value, given above. At one time it meant "prolong this note." Although followed by its mathematical complement, the exact values were not necessarily observed. Contrasts in values were more often exaggerated than underdone. The invention of the double dot put an end to this inexact practice.

The expression dotted notes is not normally applied to notes affected by *staccato dots--an effect which of course has no connection with the discussion at hand.

●dotted rhythms. Rhythmic patterns in which *dotted notes are followed by the short notes which complement them. Examples would be: a dotted-quarter-note followed by an eighth (or two sixteenths), a dotted-eighth-note followed by a sixteenth-note (or two thirty-seconds), etc.

piano plays in unison with the voice; or "the melody is doubled a sixth below," meaning that the melody is harmonized as a series of sixths; or "the first violins are doubled in the upper *octave by the flute," meaning that the flute plays an octave higher than the first violins.

(2, verb) Any tone is said to be doubled if it appears twice in a chord. The doubling may be at the unison, at the octave, or at a distance of several octaves. The tone D is doubled in all the chords shown in Example 1. In the chord in Example 2, F-sharp and A are doubled, while D is tripled.

(3, noun) Same as variation (obsolete).

(4, verb) To play two instruments, usually closely-related ones; thus we say that "the second flute-player doubles on piccolo," meaning that the second flute *part alternates with (that is, is *interchangeable with) piccolo.

(5, adjective). Pianists use the terms double thirds and double sixths in referring to series of

Example 1   Example 2

thirds or sixths (see intervals) played
with one hand. Well-developed
technique is demanded in playing
double thirds and double sixths in
rapid *tempos. Thirds or sixths
played between the hands (one note in
the right, one in the left) are considerably easier, and are sometimes
called single thirds and single sixths.

The expression double notes refers
to a series of paired tones played
by one of the hands, but not at a
constant interval, for instance a
mixture of thirds and sixths (and
perhaps of other intervals). This
term is not normally used in speaking
of octaves played by one hand.

For double octave, double-stops,
and other terms beginning with double,
see separate entries.

● double bar-line. See bar-line.

● double-bass. A bowed string instrument, usually with four strings tuned
to the sounds:

It will be apparent that music
for the instrument is always
notated an octave above the sounds
desired.

The bass *clef is basic; however
the tenor clef or occasionally
treble clef is used for the highest
notes.

A few instruments possess a
fifth string tuned in the low C a
major third (see intervals) below
the E-string. (Occasionally low
B is substituted.) Quite a
number of double-basses are
equipped with a mechanical extension which lowers the pitch of the
E-string to low C when desired,
the stopping of the string on the
low C-sharp, D, and E-flat being
effected by means of levers operated
by the player, rather than by the
fingers. (Low C, C-sharp, D,
and E-flat are frequently written
in music for the double-bass.
Musicians whose instrument does

noted thus:

(that is, notated an octave higher). The
player either stands or else sits on a
very high stool. The instrument itself
rests on a rather long, thick peg.

The *tone-color is heavy, gruff, thick,
and somewhat "raw," yet wonderfully
solid, except in the very highest register, where it has a rather strained,
groping quality.

The instrument is occasionally made
of aluminum rather than wood.

The range of the double-bass is:

not have a fifth string or an E-
string extension play these notes
an octave higher than they are
intended to sound.)

The double-bass "speaks" slowly,
especially on its three lower
strings, and although fast passages
are constantly employed, their
effect is one of confusion and
hustle-and-bustle--nearly always of
course intentional on the composer's
part.

*Dance-band double-bass players often use a peculiar "slapping" method of playing the instrument, somewhat akin to the *pizzicato.

The double-bass, unlike the violin, viola, and cello, has sloping shoulders and often a flat back, and hence is a closer descendent of the old *viols. (The synonymous name bass viol is perhaps a vestige of this fact.)

The double-bass seldom has a completely independent part--probably less frequently than any other orchestra instrument except the *contrabassoon; it is nearly always *doubled (1) an octave higher (occasionally in *unison) by the cellos, sometimes bassoon, bass clarinet, trombone, tuba, horn, or violas. This practice is advisable because of its slow "speaking" and indefinite manner of emitting tone. Independent pizzicato passages are, however, considerably commoner and less hazardous as to clarity.

The double-bass is often used in the concert *band--the only bowed string instrument of which this is true, and with the exception of the *harp, the only string instrument of any type to find a place there.

Two quite different types of bow are used with the double-bass. One, known as the "French bow," strongly resembles the bow used in playing the violin, viola, and (particularly) cello; and as with these instruments, the player balances it, holding it at the end of the stick, his relatively straight fingers crossing the stick at a slightly oblique angle. Other double-bass players prefer the "German bow," in which the stick and the hair are comparatively far apart; the player holds the bow not so much by the stick as by the some-what curved piece (called the "frog") that joins the stick and the hair, his fingers being curved around this piece. Although the French bow outranks it in agility, some players maintain that the German type is superior for drawing a powerful tone from the instrument. Its appearance, however, is somewhat unwieldy; its shape has been compared to that of a meat-cleaver, the manner of grasping it to that of holding a saw.

In proportion to the size of the double-bass, its bow is relatively short.

Synonyms: contrabass and (less desirable) bass viol, string bass, bass. The expression bass violin is never used by musicians.

Italian: contrabasso or contrab-basso (plural, contrabassi, contrab-bassi), occasionally violone. French: contrebasse. German: Kontrabass (plural Kontrabässe) or Contrabass (plural Contrabässe). Spanish: contrabajo.

The player is simply called a double-bass player. The term bassist has--perhaps fortunately-- had little acceptance.

● double-bassoon. The contra-bassoon.

● double chorus. Two *mixed choruses, of equal size. *Anti-phonal effects are frequent; herein lies the distinction between two *SATB choruses and a single eight-part SSAATTBB group.

The circumstance that St. Mark's Cathedral in Venice, Italy has two choir-lofts led to the writing of compositions for double chorus, beginning in the late sixteenth century, and was one of the factors that resulted in the *Baroque style in music.

The double chorus should not be confused with the combination of chorus and *semi-chorus.

See also polychoral.

● double concerto. A *concerto for two solo instruments and orchestra. It partakes a bit of the character of the *concerto grosso, but strictly speaking is a concerto. Probably the best-known true example is the Double Concerto in A Minor (op. 102) by Brahms; it is for violin, cello, and orchestra.

A concerto using three solo instruments is called a triple con-certo.

See also concertant.

● double counterpoint. Same as invertible counterpoint.

● double dots. See dotted notes.

●double-flat. A character consisting of two *flats ♭♭ which lowers the pitch of a note a *whole-step. This symbol is used when a note already affected by a flat in the *key-signature is to be lowered an additional *half-step. It always occurs as an *accidental.

The double-flat is canceled back to a single flat either by a flat ♭ or by a natural followed by a flat ♮♭ --not however by a flat followed by a natural. ♭♮ On the rare occasions when a note affected by a double-flat is to be made natural it may be done by either one or two naturals.

See accidental.

●double forte. Spoken form occasionally substituted for *fortissimo.

●double fugue. See fugue.

●double G clef. A 𝄞𝄞 character consisting of two G clefs 𝄞𝄞 It has occasionally been used during recent years in writing for the *tenor voice. The spirals twirl around the second line of the *staff; thus the double G clef denotes the G below *middle C and reads an *octave lower than the ordinary (single) G clef. Sometimes the character 𝄞 is substituted, though it obviously 𝄞 is not called the double G clef.

See also clefs, tenor.

●double octave. This term is used with two entirely different meanings.

(1) Sometimes it indicates the *interval of two *octaves, i.e., the fifteenth.

(2) Sometimes it indicates three appearances of one letter-name, in three different octaves, i.e., one octave stacked on top of another.

●double piano. Spoken term occasionally substituted for *pianissimo.

●double quartet. (1) A group of eight singers who perform music written for four voices or four-part chorus, each voice part being taken by two singers. The normal membership is two sopranos, two altos, two tenors, and two basses. The term double quartet is more accurate than octet, since the latter properly indicates eight independent voice parts.

(2) A *chamber-music composition for two *string quartets, that is, for four violins, two violas, and two cellos. It differs from the string octet for the same instruments in that the two quartets are used *antiphonally, like two separate groups, while in the octet there is comparatively little antiphonal writing and passages for any number of the eight instruments are frequent. Louis Spohr (1784-1859) composed several double quartets.

●double-sharp. A character variously written 𝄪 X and 𝄪 which raises the pitch of a note a *whole-step. This symbol is used when a note already affected by a *sharp in the *key-signature is to be raised an additional *half-step. It always occurs as an *accidental.

The double-sharp is canceled back to a single sharp either by a sharp ♯ or by a natural followed by a sharp ♮♯--not however by a

Double octaves (1)   Double octaves (2)

sharp followed by a natural ♯ ♮
On the rare occasions when a note
affected by a double-sharp is to be
made natural it may be done by
either one or two naturals.

Some textbooks assert that two
sharps 𝄪 may be substituted for the
double-sharp symbol, but this statement is in glaring contradiction to
actual practice.
See accidental.

● double sonata-allegro form. A
variant on *sonata-allegro form often
encountered in the first movement of
*concertos written during the *Clas-
sical and early *Romantic periods.

In this form, the exposition is not
enclosed in *repeat-signs; rather the
music is written out twice, but in
totally different ways. The first
presentation is given to the orchestra
alone, and the two *themes as a
rule are both stated in the same key.
In the second presentation the solo
instrument participates (and remains
active to the end of the movement),
and the two themes are presented in
different keys, the second normally
being in the key of the dominant if
the concerto is in the major mode,
in the relative major key if it is in
the minor mode. (See key-relationships.)

It will be apparent that in a work
possessing this form-scheme the
entrance of the solo instrument is
very late; the composer holds it in
abeyance to make its appearance all
the more welcome.

A typical outline of double sonata-
allegro form, with the *cadenza in its
usual place, would be as follows:

The use of this form, with its
double exposition, tended to
disappear after the time of
Beethoven (1770-1827), in favor
of the more usual *sonata-allegro
form typical of the symphony,
string quartet, sonata and similar
*"sonata types." Its appearance
as late as Brahms's Violin Concerto
(1878) and Dvořák's Cello Concerto
(1896) is distinctly exceptional.

It will be observed that in the
outline above, no provision has
been made for the possibility of
a slow introduction to the movement. For a reason that would
be difficult to name, these are
most unusual in concertos.

Synonyms: concerto-sonata form,
concerto-allegro form.

● double-stop. Two tones played
simultaneously on two strings of a
violin or other bowed string instrument.

A composer must have a
working knowledge of the technique
of these instruments, for some
double-stops are easy, some
difficult, others completely unplayable. Only adjacent strings
can be used.

A chord of three tones is
sometimes called a triple stop,
one of four tones, a quadruple
stop. More frequently, however,
both types are simply termed
chords.

	If in major	In in minor
First theme (orchestra only) ⎫	C	a
Second theme (orchestra only) ⎬ Exposition	C	a
First theme (solo & orch.) ⎪	C	a
Second theme (solo & orch.) ⎭	G	C
Development (solo & orch.)	--	--
First theme (solo & orch.) ⎫ Recapitulation	C	a
Second theme (solo & orch.) ⎭	C	A (or a)
Coda, part one (this section is usually very short, in the nature of a transi-tion, and for orchestra only)	C	a
Cadenza (solo instrument only)	--	--
Coda, part two (orch. only or solo & orch.)	C	a (or A)

(Note: Capital letters indicate major keys; lower-case letters, minor keys.)

● doublet. Same as duplet.

● double-tonguing. A special effect possible on certain woodwind and brass instruments wherein two tones (usually of the same pitch) are made to follow one another as if grouped pairwise. The effect is delightfully light, nimble, fleeting, and fanciful, especially on the *flute and *trumpet. It can be done only in fairly quick *tempos. In producing it the player moves his tongue as if pronouncing T-K.

Triple tonguing is possible on a few instruments, being notably effective on the trumpet. The tongue is moved as if pronouncing T-K-T or T-T-K.

Flutter-tonguing is a special and very peculiar effect possible on some brass and woodwind instruments. Further information will be found under tremolo (3).

● double trio. (1) A group of six singers, usually women, who perform music written in three parts, two singers to each. The term double trio is much more accurate than sextet, since the latter would properly indicate six completely independent voice parts.

(2) A composition with a *trio (2) (middle section) that is repeated is said to have a double trio or repeated trio. The form-scheme is ABABA. (This should not be confused with the expression two trios, which indicates two sections containing entirely different material--B and C in the form-scheme ABACA.) Beethoven was quite fond of the double trio for use in his *scherzo movements. See form.

● double triplet. A name sometimes applied to the *sextuplet which divides into two groups of three notes (as opposed to that dividing into three groups of two notes).

See also irregular groupings.

● double-whole-note. See breve (2) and time-values.

● down-beat. The first *beat in a *measure, so named because in *conducting it is customary to indicate this beat with a downward motion of the hand or *baton.

This term is by no means the antonym of *up-beat.

● down-bow. In playing the bowed string instruments, an action wherein the player draws the bow toward its point (tip). Perhaps it would be simpler merely to say that the player pulls the bow, or that his arm moves from left to right. Compare up-bow.

The symbol for down-bow is ⊓ (sometimes ⊔).

Down-bow is normally used (A) for forceful or accented effects (B) at the beginning of a *measure (C) for *diminuendos.

A single note, or any reasonable number (depending on the length of the bow and the rapidity with which it is drawn) may be played with one down-bow, or for that matter, with one up-bow.

It is possible to play a number of notes with a series of successive down-bows, but these must not follow one another too rapidly; the effect is extremely forceful, even rough. In general, however, players constantly use down-bow and up-bow alternately.

See also bow, bowing.

● †drammatico. Dramatic. Pronunciation: accent second syllable.

● drone bass. A sustained or repeated bass tone, continuing through a long section in a composition or even uninterrupted from beginning to end. Harmonically it is a pedal point. See non-harmonic tones (9).

The *bagpipe plays a continuous drone bass in addition to the *melody; some bagpipes produce two or three simultaneous drone tones. The *hurdy-gurdy also employs a drone bass.

Use of this device is typical of the dance known as the *musette.

● drum. All drums consist of a hollow cylinder with a membrane called the <u>head</u> tightly stretched over one or both ends. In the *timpani (kettle-drums) and *tom-tom the body has the shape of a bowl or hemisphere (approximately) rather than that of a cylinder; in the *conga drum the diameter tapers so that the shape is more or less conical.

Some drums are played with one stick, others with two, while still others are played directly with the hands. The *tambourine is sometimes struck with the hand, sometimes shaken, and sometimes rubbed with the moistened thumb. Only the timpani give definite musical pitches; all other drums are of indefinite pitch.

The term <u>drum</u> is sometimes carelessly used as a synonym for <u>percussion instrument</u>. This of course is incorrect; the triangle, cymbals, and many other percussion instruments are by no means "drums." The term properly includes the following instruments, each of which is discussed under its own entry:

bass drum
bongós
Chinese drum
conga drum
military drum (parade drum, field drum)
snare drum (side drum)
tambourin de Provence (long drum, Provençal drum, tabor)
tambourine
tenor drum
timpani (kettle-drums)
tom-tom (Indian drum)

See also <u>percussion instruments,</u> <u>orchestra</u>.

● D. S. Go back to the sign 𝄋 and play until the word *fine (meaning "end") is encountered. The sign- 𝄋 may occur at any point except the very beginning; when the repeat is to be made from the beginning the term used is *<u>D. C.</u>, not <u>D. S.</u> Occasionally instead of repeating as far as <u>fine</u> the player is directed to play as far as the character ⊕ from which he proceeds to a section marked <u>coda</u>.

It is understood that any *repeat-signs which may have occurred in the opening section are to be ignored in the D. S. Often the composer, to prevent any possibility of misunderstanding, gives the direction in the more complete form: D. S. 𝄋 <u>al fine, senza replica</u> (or ... <u>senza ripetizione</u>), meaning "from the sign- 𝄋 without repetition."

In a composition for voices, the words are sometimes different the second time the passage is performed, sometimes the same.

<u>D. S.</u> is the abbreviation for <u>dal segno</u> (literally "from the sign").

Compare <u>D. C.</u>

See also <u>repeat signs</u>, where an illustration will be found.

●† due corde. (1) With the soft *pedal; used in connection with the piano. The literal meaning is "two strings." In a grand piano three strings tuned in unison are provided for most of the tones. The pressing of the soft pedal shifts the keyboard slightly so that the hammers strike only two of them, thus producing a softer effect.

This term represents the purists' correction of the much more frequent term <u>una corda</u> (literally "one string") which once described accurately the action of this pedal, though in present-day instruments two strings, rather than one, are struck.

It is canceled by <u>tre corde</u> (literally "three strings").

(2) With the string instruments, an indication that the note so indicated is to be played on two strings simultaneously; one of these is an *open string, the other is the string just below, which is fingered. Thus a unison of considerable power is produced.

This effect is normally indicated by placing two *note-heads on the *stem, occasionally (less desirably) by placing two stems on the note-head.

Only three sounds can be so produced on each instrument. A complete list follows: actual pitch of those for the *double-bass is an octave lower than written.

violins, mostly in tenths.
Schubert: Overture to "Rosamunde," near beginning--oboe and clarinet in various intervals.

● dulcimer. Name given to a class of string instruments in which the strings are hit with two little hammers.

For the distinction between the dulcimer and the psaltery, see

Violin   Viola   Cello   Double-Bass

● duet. A composition for two voices or instruments. Literally it means a short duo; however, duo and duet may be considered synonymous with the following two exceptions: (A) In writing for the piano, a composition for one piano four hands (that is, two players at one piano) is usually termed a duet, while a composition for two pianos is termed a duo. (B) The term duo is sometimes used for two instruments not of the same kind, duet for two instruments of the same kind, as "a duo for clarinet and bassoon" but "a duet for two violins."

(The spelling duette is incorrect.)
See also groups.
Pronunciation: dōō-ĕt' or dyōō-ĕt'.

● "duetting." A word occasionally used to express the moving of two instruments or voices (usually in the very same *rhythm) in a series of *intervals such as thirds or sixths. It is not used to indicate the movement of two instruments in *unison, and rarely for *octaves.

Familiar examples of "duetting" effects are:

Brahms: Symphony No. 2, first movement, second subject--cellos and violas in thirds.

Bach: Magnificat, "Esurientes"--two flutes, mostly in sixths.

Mozart: Eine kleine Nachtmusik, second movement--first and second

psaltery.
The piano might well be regarded as a dulcimer operated from a keyboard.

The *czimbalom, a favorite instrument among the Hungarian gypsies, is a type of dulcimer.

● dumka. A type of Slavic *folk-song characterized by abrupt changes from slow melancholy to quick rollicking *tempo. It is most familiar to musicians through its use by Bohemian (Czech) composers. Dvořák wrote several of them; the second movement of his *Piano Quintet in A is in the style of a dumka.
Plural: dumky.
Pronunciation: dōōm'-ka.

● duo. See duet.
Plural: duos (English) or dui (Italian).

● duodecuple scale. See twelve tone system.
Variant spelling: dodecuple scale.

● duple meter. *Meter with two *beats to the *measure. Sometimes multiples of 2, namely 4 and 8, are also included, though usually meter of four beats is called quadruple Six-beat measure, if divided into two groups of three beats (but not three groups of two

beats) is also classed as duple.
Synonym: binary meter.
Compare triple meter.

● duplet. Two notes of equal length
occupying the time of three of the
same kind. It might well be termed
the opposite of the *triplet. Duplets
are possible only in time-signatures
that are divisible by 3.
  There are three methods of notating
duplets. For illustration let us assume that we are in 6-8 time and
want to divide the time-value occupied
by three eighth-notes into two sounds
of exactly the same length. This can
be done by using (A) two eighth-notes
marked with a figure 2, or (B) two
quarter-notes marked with a figure
2, or (C) two dotted-eighth-notes.

suggest four beats, they should
be used.
  The third reasoning is based
on the indisputable fact that two
dotted-eighths divide the combined
value of three normal eighths into
exact mathematical halves. Although
at first this appears logical and
convincing, the objection to it is
that it suggests *syncopation at
a point where the ear detects no
such effect. See bottom diagram.
  Thus it will be seen that all
three methods have points in
their favor.
  Synonyms: doublet, duolet.
  See also triplets, irregular
groupings.

● duration. (1) The length of

The first method is based on the
reasoning that 6-8 time and 2-4 time
are essentially the same thing (also
9-8 and 3-4, 12-8, and 4-4 are in
a like category)--that they are respectively the *compound and *simple
version of *duple meter. Hence if
two normal eighth-notes of simple
meter can be replaced by triplet
eighths, then the three eighth-notes
of compound meter can likewise be
replaced by duplet eighths.

tones; *rhythm.
  (2) The time required to perform
a composition; thus: "Duration, 4
minutes and 45 seconds."

● durchkomponiert (German). Same
as through-composed.
  Pronunciation: doork-kom-po-nert.

● dynamic marks. Markings
(usually abbreviations) used to
indicate the relative loudness or

The second reasoning is based on the
concept that all *irregular groupings
should have the appearance of too
many beats in the measure. Therefore the three eighths that represent
the normal beats should be replaced
by values suggesting more than three
beats; hence, since two quarter-notes

softness with which the music
should be performed. They are
customarily set in Italic type, and
are of Italian origin.
  The following are the commonly-
used abbreviations, the full words,
and the English equivalents,
arranged in order from the softest

ppp	pianississimo	as soft as possible
pp	pianissimo	very soft
p	piano	soft
mp	mezzo piano	rather soft
mf	mezzo forte	rather loud
f	forte	loud
ff	fortissimo	very loud
fff	fortississimo	as loud as possible

The abbreviation m, indicating mezzo (medium), something neither loud nor soft, is almost never used; yet it would be a convenient addition to the foregoing list. It should come between mp and mf.

Occasionally the extremes ffff, fffff, pppp, ppppp, or pppppp (the latter appears in Tschaikowsky's Sixth Symphony) are encountered. Verdi frequently used these in his later works (including ppppppp in Otello), though it is doubtful that he wanted more extreme effects than those usually employed.

The need for dynamic marks (also tempo marks) did not arise until early in the seventeenth century; previous to that time nearly all music had been vocal and naturally the text suggested the manner of performance. The rise of instrumental music independent of voices necessitated explicit directions concerning the manner in which such compositions should be performed. It is generally acknowledged that Giovanni Gabrieli (1557-1612), of Venice, was the first (or one of the first) persons ever to employ dynamic indications, in his Sonata Pian' e Forte published in 1597. The reason that Italian terms are used even to this day stems from the fact that Gabrieli was an Italian, and also that he was a prominent teacher of composition, with a number of foreign pupils who took his methods to other countries. Although later composers of Germany, France, England, and the United States have attempted to substitute their own language in the case of tempo indications, the Italian dynamic terms on the above list have remained unchallenged; they constitute an "international language" for indicating musical effects.

For special dynamic terms see crescendo, decrescendo, diminuendo, rinforzando, and sforzando. For dynamic accent see accent.

See also nuances, tempo marks.

E

● †e. And. Thus accel. e cresc., gradually becoming faster and louder; ff e pesante, very loud and heavily.

Variant form, sometimes used before words beginning with vowels or h: ed.

● ear-training. A subject taught in *conservatories and college music departments, the purpose of which is to train the student's auditory sense to the point where he can immediately identify the exact notes he is hearing--be they *melody, *harmony, or *rhythm, or all these combined. Successfully-taught ear-training in addition includes the ability to hear accurately, in the imagination or "inner ear," the sounds represented in printed music. This skill is known as auditory imagery or tonal imagery, or, as students often express it, "hearing with the eyes."

The reverse process--learning to associate the correct notation for music that is heard--is equally important.

An ear-training course consists of (A) *sight-singing (also called solfeggio or solfège), which attempts to co-ordinate the student's musical awareness with the corresponding notation through singing it; (B) dictation, which consists of writing down the notes for music which the instructor plays on the piano (or some other instrument) or sings; (C) keyboard harmony, which consists of playing certain *chords and chord-progressions on the piano, *harmonizing melodies at sight, etc.

Briefly, the aim is to teach the student "to hear what he sees and see what he hears."

The course in ear-training is often combined with that in *harmony (2). See also relative pitch.

● ecclesiastical modes.   See modes (1).

● †ecco.   Variant spelling of eco.

● échappé, échappée (French).   See non-harmonic tones (7).
   Pronunciation: ā-shä-pā.

● eclogue.   Strictly, a pastoral poem. The name is sometimes applied to musical composition of a similar mood. This term does not imply the stylistic features that are typical of the *pastorale, which superficially might appear to be synonymous.
   Variant spelling: eglogue.

● †eco.   Echo.
   Variant spelling: ecco.

● écossaise.   An English dance in quick 2-4 time.   Oddly, écossaise is

the French word meaning "Scotch."
   Pronunciation: ā-kō-sĕz.

● †ed.   And.   A variant form of

e, it is sometimes used when the following word begins with a vowel or with h; thus: cresc. ed accel.; however cresc. e accel. is also correct.

● editor.   The editor of a musical composition is a person who prepares a composer's manuscript for publication or re-publication. His duties depend on the completeness and exactitude of the notation as the composer supplied it.   As a rule he indicates the *fingering and sometimes the *bowing, *phrasing, and similar technical details.   Many *metronome indications originate with editors.   He may add *slurs or *staccato dots where it is reasonably certain that the composer intended them but did not actually take the pains to write them.   It may be necessary for him to correct certain eccentricities and unconventionalities in the notation--stems turned the wrong way, and the like.   In older works he may have to indicate *tempo marks and *dynamic marks as he imagines they were intended.

In a composition written with *figured bass, he will often write out a suggested *realization.

In the case of music written originally with a now-obsolete type of *clef, the editor substitutes a clef in current use and converts the notation so that it is adjusted to the modern clef.

The work of an editor is obviously much greater with music written several centuries ago than with fairly recent works.

A publication which has not been edited, purposely, is called an *Urtext.

Although the term editor is also used in the world of journalism, a music editor should not be confused with a *music critic.

● E-flat alto.   The *alto horn.

● E-flat clarinet. A short clarinet pitched a perfect fourth (see intervals) above the B-flat clarinet--a diminished fifth above the A instrument. Its thin, biting, hard tone makes it appropriate for music of a parodistic character, but for little else. Range:

on the E-flat clarinet. Another prominent solo for the E-flat instrument appears in the last movement of Berlioz's Fantastic Symphony.

The E-flat clarinet is regularly used in the *band, but its presence

It is notated a minor third lower than the sounds desired; that is, it transposes upward. (See transposing instruments.)

The lowest tones sound much like the lowest of the ordinary clarinet, except that they are a little thinner and less rich. The middle tones are fairly sweet, and compare with the same sounds of the ordinary instrument much the same way the child soprano voice compares with the mature female soprano. The highest tones, which are the most frequently used, have a squealing effect; if badly played they can be downright offensive.

There used to be a similar instrument, pitched a half-step lower and known as the D clarinet. It is for this instrument that Richard Strauss wrote a prominent part in Till Eulenspiegel's Merry Pranks; nowadays this part is played, transposed,

in an orchestral composition is distinctly the exception rather than the rule.

This instrument should not be confused with the *alto clarinet, also in E-flat, but pitched an octave lower than the instrument here under discussion. To prevent such confusion, the E-flat clarinet is occasionally called the E-flat soprano (or sopranino) clarinet.

Synonyms: little clarinet, small clarinet, clarinet piccolo, high clarinet.

Italian: clarinetto piccolo or clarinetto in Mi-♭. French: petite clarinette or clarinette en Mi ♭. German: Es-Klarinette or kleine Klarinette.

● eglogue.   Variant spelling of eclogue.

● †eguale.   Equal, uniform, even. Variant form: uguale.

● 8. The figure 8 sometimes appears under bass notes in compositions for piano. There·is disagreement as to its meaning. According to some musicians, it indicates that the given note is to be played as an *octave, i. e., that the note an octave lower is to be added to the written note; hence it is equivalent to coll' 8va bassa. According to others, it means that the written note is to be played an octave lower than written (as a single note), i. e., that it is equivalent to 8va bassa. All agree that the figure must be repeated for each note so affected.

the exact length of the passage to be so played; it usually concludes with a short downward vertical row of dots to make the termination point clear. The term takes effect beginning with the 8
    Occasionally the more complete form 8va alta is found. See second diagram.
    8va is also placed beneath notes that are to be played an octave lower than written, in which case the horizontal dots conclude with a short upward line. In this case the term is usually given in the form 8va bassa, abbreviation for ottava bassa ("lower octave"). See last diagram.

It is also sometimes used above treble notes to indicate--equally vaguely--the notes an octave higher.
    In general, it would seem that this usage should be avoided.
    The character 8 should not be confused with 8 ‥‥⋮ See 8va.

● eighth-note. See time-values.

● 8va. When this sign is placed above notes, it indicates they are to be played an *octave higher than written. A horizontal row of dots is used to specify

The purpose of the 8va sign is to avoid excessive use of *leger lines, hence to facilitate reading.
    Full form of the term: ottava.
    Variant forms: 8ve, 8 ‥‥⋮
    Synonyms: all' ottava, all' 8va.
    See also 15ma, loco.

● eisteddfod (Welsh). A singing festival for both soloists and choral societies.
    Pronunciation: ā-stĕth-vŏd.
    Plural: eisteddfods (English) or eisteddfodau (Welsh).

● electrical transcription.   A term

used by radio stations to refer to specially-made records produced exclusively for use in broadcasting. They are not for sale to the public; some will not play on ordinary *phonographs. There is of course no connection with the word *transcription as it is normally employed by musicians.

● electronic instruments. Instruments in which the tone is the result of electrical impulses rather than of the vibrating of a string, drum-head, reed, or the player's lips. Their development falls completely within the twentieth century.

Perhaps the most familiar of these instruments is the electronic organ, a number of types of which are on the market, some decidedly better than others. Compared to the ordinary pipe *organ, all offer the advantages of low cost, of taking up very little room, and of never going out of tune. Their disadvantages, however, greatly overbalance these few virtues.

The novachord is familiar to radio owners. It imitates various instruments through synthetically duplicating their characteristic overtone patterns (see harmonic series). A more recent electronic instrument which imitates instruments by artificial means is called the music synthesizer; it can reproduce not only instruments but also the human voice, including the words that are sung!

The electronic piano is portable. If desired, it may be adjusted so that only the player can hear the sounds, through earphones.

The theremin is named after its inventor, the Soviet scientist Leon Theremin. Concertos have been written for it by Joseph Schillinger and Anis Fuleihan. Pitch and volume are controlled by the exact distance the player holds his hands from two rods.

The ondes martenot is an electronic instrument well known in France.

See also stroboscope.

● electronic music. Music composed with the aid of the science of electronics. The movement is in its infancy, but so far has taken two forms. (A) In one, sounds are recorded at one speed and reproduced (usually on a tape recorder) at a different speed. Anyone who has absent-mindedly started a 33-1/3 revolution record at 78 revolutions or vice versa knows that there is not only a difference in pitch, but also a difference in the tone-quality of the sound, and that the tone-quality is often of a type not otherwise produceable. Honestly done, the composer knows by previous experiment the effect he will get in the finished composition; results are not (or should not be) of a hit-or-miss nature. This form is often called tape-recorder music. (B) In the other form, vibration-waves are put directly on the tape without ever having been played or sung. The performer is completely by-passed; the music is created synthetically. The effect achieved may duplicate conventional effects or be of a nature completely new. The latter is the form that would seem to have the brighter and more stimulating future.

See also musique concrète.

● † eleganza. Elegance, grace.

● elegy. A lament. The French spelling Élégie is often used as a title.

● elevation. A composition, usually for organ and fairly short, played during the elevation of the Host in Roman Catholic services.

● eleventh-chord. Theoretically, an eleventh-chord consists of six different tones laid out as a stack of superimposed thirds (see intervals), the members being the root (fundamental), third, fifth, seventh, ninth, and eleventh. In conventional practice the third is usually omitted because of its harsh clash with the eleventh, and in four voice writing it is also necessary to dispense with the fifth.

Only the dominant eleventh-chord

(V_{11}) is used. Since the root almost always appears as bass-tone, the chord will contain the following degrees of the scale: 5, 4, 6, 1. It will look like a *subdominant *triad placed over the fifth or *dominant scale degree. It almost always progresses to the dominant *seventh-chord.

being the French for "again." See also bis.
   Pronunciation (anglicized): än⁻kôr.

● en dehors (French). Prominent, well brought out. (Literally "out-of-doors. ")
   Synonyms: marcato, pronunziato,

Dominant eleventh-chords

See also chord, harmony, triad, seventh-chord, ninth-chord.

● †eloquente. Eloquent.

● embellishing tones, embellishment. See non-harmonic tones (2).

● embouchure. The correct use of the mouth and especially the lips in playing a *woodwind or *brass instrument.
   The term is derived from the French word meaning mouth.
   Pronunciation (anglicized): äm⁻bōo-shŏor.

● encore. (1) A composition performed in addition to those on the printed program, in response to prolonged audience applause. Most compositions used as encores are brilliant, fairly short, and often light or humorous, sometimes even trivial, in character. (2) The repetition of a composition on the announced program, in response to hearty applause. Although the less frequently used, this is actually the correct meaning, encore

accentuato.
   Pronunciation: än dĕ-ōr.

● †-endo. Italian present participle ending, equivalent to English ending -ing.
   Variant forms -ando, -ante, -ente.

● †energia. Energy.
   Pronunciation: accent -gi-.

● †energico. In an energetic manner, full of vigor, forceful.
   Pronunciation: accent second syllable.

● English flute. Old name for the *recorder.

● English horn. A woodwind instrument played with a double reed, pitched a perfect fifth below the *oboe. It might well be regarded as an alto oboe. The English horn is made of wood and has a distinctive small globe-shaped *bell. It is notated with the treble *clef a perfect fifth higher than the sounds desired. (See transposing instruments.)

Its mechanism is similar to that of the oboe; oboists learn it as a secondary instrument. Range:

Dx-E-Fb
E#-F-Gbb
F#-Gb

Written: Sounding:

A few instruments have the low B-flat, sounding E-flat. Skillful players can sound a tone or two higher than the highest indicated above.

Throughout its range the English horn has a very beautiful tone-quality. The lowest tones are a bit thick and dry, but thoroughly pleasant, somewhat reminiscent of the *"chest-voice" tones of the *contralto voice. The middle register has a peculiarly reedy, hollow, lonely sound of tremendous appeal. The highest tones are weak, but agreeable.

The name is something of an etymological mystery; as wits have observed, it is neither English nor a horn. In England it is often called by its French name, cor anglais, perhaps because of the very meaninglessness of the native name.

Italian: corno inglese. French: cor anglais. German: englisches Horn, englisch Horn, or Englischhorn. Spanish: corno inglés or cuerno inglés.

There is no satisfactory term for the player other than English horn player.

● English terminology. See British terminology.

● enharmonic. Tones which sound the same (provided *equal temperament tuning is used) but look different in print, such as C-sharp and D-flat, E-sharp and F, B-flat and A-sharp.

The following is a complete list of all the practical enharmonic equivalents.

B#-C-Dbb
C#-Db
Cx-D-Ebb
D#-Eb

Fx-G-Abb
G#-Ab
Gx-A-Bbb
A#-Bb
Ax-B-Cb

Usages such as Bx, Fbb, etc., are almost entirely theoretical.

The word is used in such expressions as "C-sharp is the enharmonic equivalent of D-flat," "C-sharp is enharmonically equal to D-flat," "C-sharp is enharmonic with D-flat," "C-sharp and D-flat are enharmonic," etc.

Abbreviations: enh., enharm.

● enharmonic modulation. Explained under modulation.

● ensemble. (1) A generic term used for any combination of instruments or voices, or both. The term can be applied to any *medium other than a single instrument or voice, though its use in connection with a solo voice with accompaniment is rare. An "ensemble" may be a *band, *orchestra, *chorus, or *chamber-music combination; however the term is most useful when designating some group not otherwise covered by a familiar term.

(2) The quality of "togetherness" of a group of instruments or voices; used to describe precision in *attacks and *releases, and in carrying out the indications of the *conductor, if any. If the group performs "like one man" we say the ensemble is good; if there is sloppiness and raggedness, we say there is poor ensemble.

This term is the French word

for "together."
See also groups, concerted number,
chamber music groups.
Pronunciation: än-säm-b'l or
än-säm'-b'l.

● entr'acte. Same as intermezzo (1).
Pronounciation: än-träct'.

● entrada (Spanish). Same as intrada.
Pronounciation: en-trä-dä (the d
almost like th).

● Eolian harp. An instrument consisting of a hollow box (resonator) over
which several strings are passed. The
strings are adjusted in tension so as
to produce a *harmonic series. The
Eolian harp is placed in an open
window or hung in a tree so that the
action of the wind will set the strings
to vibrating, thus producing a mysterious and elusive sound of considerable
charm. The volume depends on the
velocity of the breeze.
The Eolian harp was known in
ancient India and China, and has had
a vogue at various times in modern
history.
This is probably the only instrument not played by human beings, yet
not a mechanical instrument; it is
the only non-human source of music
other than bird calls.
Variant spelling: Aeolian harp.
Synonym: Eolian lyre.

● episode. A connecting passage; a
bridge passage. Many episodes
consist of *scales moving up or down.
Episodes often connect the *themes
and sections in a movement in *sonata-
allegro form; they are quite frequent
as connecting links in *fugues.
Synonyms: bridge passage, link,
transition (2).

● equal marks. The equal-sign
familiar in mathematics (=) is often
found in music, placed between two
notes of the same or different
value (thus: ♩ = ♩   ♩ = 𝅝   )
to indicate the time-relationship when
a change of *time-signature or *tempo
occurs.
When the time-value is the same
on both sides of the mark ♩ = ♩
the intention is of course unmistakable;
it is practically a synonym for

*l'istesso tempo. On the other
hand, when the two notes shown
are not equal, two mutually
contradictory usages have found
their way into music. Thus ♩ = ♩
sometimes means that a quarter-
note of the old section becomes
equal to a half-note of the new,
but at other times it means that
a quarter-note of the new section
becomes equal to a half-note of
the old. Ambiguity may be removed if the time-signatures are
added, thus: $\frac{3}{4}$ ♩ = $\frac{4}{4}$ ♩

● equal temperament. A system
of tuning in which all *half-steps
are exactly equal in size and all
*keys (1) equally in tune. *Modula-
tion may be made freely from any
key to any other. Tones such as
F-sharp and G-flat, C-sharp and
D-flat, etc., are accepted as
exactly of the same pitch (see
enharmonic).
In reality, tuning by equal
temperament actually puts the
music slightly out-of-tune,
scientifically speaking, but the
practice is based on the assumption that the deviation is too
minute to be observed by most
ears--so slight as to make no
practical difference. It is a
compromise form of tuning, a
modification. Piano tuners often
express the matter with the words,
"When a piano is 'in tune,' it is
really a bit out-of-tune."
Some musicians maintain that
the adoption of equal temperament
was the most important single event
in the history of music, since it
led to free modulation to all keys,
and thus shaped the course that
the art was to take. It is impossible to single out the exact
year or even decade when this
changeover occurred, for the
transition was a gradual process,
but a comparison of compositions
of the sixteenth century with those
of the eighteenth, examining no
more than the *key-signatures,
will demonstrate the result.
The notion that J. S. Bach
(1685-1750) was the first to suggest equal temperament is complete

nonsense; it was known at least
two hundred years before his time.

To give the full particulars of this
problem would require many pages.
For a detailed explanation, reference
should be made to a treatise on *a-
coustics.

The species of tuning in which all
intervals are scientifically correct is
called just intonation. (For further
information, see that heading.) Other
types of tuning are known as Pythagorean and mean-tone.

● equal voices. A term used to indicate either women's voices or men's
voices, but not a mixture of both.
In most music for such a group the
range is of necessity narrow; the
interval between the lowest and highest
tones sounding at any given moment
will quite often be an *octave or less.

● escape-tone, escaped tone. See
non-harmonic tones (7).
     Synonym: échappée.

● †esitando. Hesitating.

● †espressione. Expression. Thus:
con espressione, with expression;
senza espressione, without expression.
     Abbreviations: espr., espress.

● espressivo. Expressive. To define
this word as "expressive" practically
begs the question, for it is difficult
to put such a meaning into words.
However, anything marked espressivo
is certainly to be performed with
warmth and intensity, certainly not
in a casual or cold manner.
     Synonym: con espressione.
     Abbreviations: espr., espress.,
occasionally espres.

● †estatico. Ecstatic.
     Pronounciation: accent second syl-
lable.

● E-string tuner. A little metal device secured to the tailpiece of the
*violin to help in tuning the E-string
(also called first string), which is

connected to one end of the
tuner-device. When this string is
made of wire--as is usually the
case--accurate tuning with the
pegs is very difficult; hence this
supplementary contrivance, which
gives a finer adjustment, is
well-nigh indispensable. It is
occasionally used for strings other
than the E, and for instruments
other than the violin.

● étouffez, étouffé (French). Arrest
the vibrating of the strings, damp
the strings; used in writing for
the *harp.
     Pronunciation: ā-tōō-fã.

● † -etto, -etta. An Italian diminutive suffix.
     Synonym: -ino, -ina.
     Antonym: -one.

● etude. A composition designed
to strengthen a specific element
in a performer's *technique. This
is the French word meaning "study";
an etude is a study concentrating
on a single technical problem,
such as scales, arpeggios, bowing,
double-tonguing, stressing the
melody and subordinating the accompaniment, etc., etc.

Etudes for the voice are often
called *vocalises and usually have
no words.

Etudes for the piano have been
written by Czerny, Cramer,
Burgmüller, and others, for the
violin by Kreutzer, Fiorillo, and
others, for the trumpet by Arban,
etc.

Originally musical interest was
not the object; the typical etude
was frankly "dry." Chopin introduced a new concept of the term.
His etudes are first and foremost
beautiful music; emphasis on
technical points is purely a by-
product. They are primarily
concert compositions; except for
exploitation of a certain phase of
technique, the term could almost
be considered a catch-all *title.

Liszt, Debussy, Schumann, and others followed in writing this more exalted type of etude.
Variant spelling: étude.
Synonym: study.
See also finger exercise, vocalise.
Anglicized pronounciation: ā-tōōd.

● euphonium. A *brass instrument, regularly used in the *band but very rare in the orchestra. It is similar to the *baritone (2), but has a wider *bore and a slightly fuller and "heavier" tone. Its most conspicuous feature is a second *bell, much smaller than the main bell. A fourth *valve enables it to go lower than the baritone. It is sometimes written with the treble *clef a major ninth (an octave and a whole-step) (see intervals) above the actual sounds, sometimes with the bass clef at actual pitch. Range:

human beings fundamentally learn rhythm by doing it rather than by thinking about it. The founder of the idea was the teacher and composer Émile Jaques-Dalcroze (1865-1950).
Variant spelling: eurythmics.
Synonym: Dalcroze eurhythmics.

● evangelist. Name given to one of the solo roles in a *passion; its function is that of a narrator (presumably the author of one of the four New Testament gospels).

● †evirato. Same as castrato.
Plural: evirati.

● excision. See cut. See also vide.

● exotic music. See Oriental music.

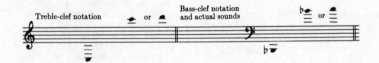

(See transposing instruments.)
The *tone-color is less mellow than that of the *horn, but distinctly more so than that of the *trombone. It has a "singing tone," and has been humorously but appropriately called "the cello of the band."
There seems to be some disagreement among musicians as to whether the euphonium is or is not identical with the tenor tuba; probably it is not.
Plural: euphoniums (not euphonia).

● eurhythmics. A system of teaching *rhythm through bodily movements on the part of the pupil--in other words, gymnastics to correlate movement with music. Eurhythmics is based on the sound principle that

● exposition. (1) A collective name for the first appearance of the first and second theme (principal and subordinate subject)--including their repetition, if indicated--in a composition written in *sonata-allegro form. It does not include the introduction, if there is one.
(2) That portion of a *fugue in which the *subject (theme) makes its initial appearance in each of the participating *voices, one after the other, the number of said voices usually being three or four. It extends from the very beginning to the point where the subject is completed for the first time by the last of the voices that participate. This is the only portion of a fugue which can be said to possess

"form," the balance of the work being more the application of fugal procedure.

(3) Initial statement of a theme, undeveloped and unelaborated.

● expressionism. This term, originally applied to a style of painting, has been borrowed to denote a type of music which seems to reflect the inner workings of the subconscious and unconscious mind (in the Freudian sense). Strictly speaking, expressionism is not a style of music but an aesthetic ideal; however it is largely associated with *atonal and *twelve tone music.

Expressionistic music tends to dwell on the morbid, the neurotic, the overwrought, the perverted, and the gruesome. It seems to reach into the darkest, most hidden, and most nightmarish regions of the mind.

Schoenberg's Pierrot Lunaire, Berg's Wozzeck and Lyric Suite exemplify this trend in music.

● expression marks. See dynamic marks, tempo marks, symbols.

● extemporization. See improvisation.

● extended rest. A rest of two or more measures' duration. See rests,

for forte. It indicates a level of volume louder than *mf, though not as much so as *ff.

See dynamic marks.

● †facile. Easy.
Pronunciation: accent first syllable.

● fagot. A name occasionally applied to the *bassoon.

● †fagotti, Fagotte. Italian and German (respectively) for *bassoons (both plural).

● fala. *Ballett.
Variant form: fal la.

● false fingering. Explained under fingering (3).

● false octaves. A device employed in writing for the piano, in which the effect of *octaves is "faked." Octaves are used alternately with single notes. The object is to simplify the passage, yet at the same time to give the illusion that it contains an uninterrupted series of octaves. The deception is seldom successful, and cannot even be approximated except at a fast *tempo.

False octaves   Intended effect

sub-head "Special Types of Rest."
Synonym: continued rest.

● extra lines. See leger lines.

F

● f. Loud. This is the abbreviation

● false relation. Same as cross relation.

● falsetto. An unnaturally high-pitched effect obtainable in a man's voice, either in speaking or

singing. The effect is like a thin
and grotesque imitation of the voice
of a woman or child. Some musicians
believe that falsetto tones are produced
by what is left of the child voice.
This term is sometimes incorrectly
applied to *mezza voce (half voice).
Falsetto tones find employment in
*yodeling.

● fandango. A type of Spanish dance
in quick 3-4 or 3-8 time.
Pronunciation: fän-däṇ'-gō.

● fanfare. A trumpet call or flourish
played by trumpets (or other brass

harmonizing *Gregorian chant by
singing it largely as *triads in
first *inversion (1), the melody
being in the highest voice. This
custom arose during the fourteenth
century. Normally an *"open
fifth" (that is, a triad consisting
of root, fifth, and root) was used
at the beginning and end of each
phrase, with chords in first inversion on each intervening tone. For
example, the Gregorian Hymn to
St. John the Baptist quoted in the
entry syllables might have begun
somewhat as follows when sung in
faux bourdon:

instruments).

● fantasia. (1) Variant form of
*fantasy.
Compare free fantasia.
(2) The expression con fantasia
means "with imagination" or "with
fancy. "

● fantasy. (1) An instrumental composition in free form. In style it may
resemble an *improvisation. Often
a fantasy is used to precede a *fugue
or other form, in the function of a
*prelude.
(2) A potpourri of the well-known
portions of an *opera, transcribed
for piano or for some instrumental
combination or ensemble, in the
manner of a *medley. The title might
be Fantasy on "Carmen," Rigoletto
Fantasy, etc. Synonym: concert
fantasy.
Variant spellings: fantaisie (French),
phantasy (fantasie is incorrect).
Variant form: fantasia.

● farandole. A lively French dance,
usually in 6-8 time.

● faux bourdon. A special manner of

In common with strict *organum,
faux bourdon was not normally
written out as such, but was more
or less "manufactured" on the spot
from reference to the chant melody.
Faux bourdon is important in
being one of the early employments
of full triads of root, third, and
fifth; it led to the establishment
of such chords, and of chords
based on the *interval of the third,
as a staple in the musical and
harmonic vocabulary. In view of
the frequency of three-voice
writing during the fourteenth and
early fifteenth centuries, and the
adaptability of faux bourdon style
to such resources, it is not
surprising that chords in first
inversion--sometimes several of
them in succession--are frequent
in all music of this period, as a
direct influence of faux bourdon.
There is a legend that faux
bourdon was invented in order to
evade a papal decree issued in
1324, suggesting (and threatening
to require) a return to strict
organum or even to the use of
unaccompanied *chants exclusively;
however faux bourdon is known to

have been already in use before this decree was issued, though its spread and continuance may have been stimulated by a desire to circumvent the pope's wishes.

Faux bourdon literally means "false bass."

English descant was a device superficially resembling faux bourdon, used in the British Isles, but with the chant melody in the lowest or middle voice, not highest.

Variant spellings: faulx bourdon, fauxbourdon.

Variant forms: faburden, falso bordone.

Pronunciation: fō bōōr-dōn or (anglicized) fō-bōōr-dŏn.́

● F-clef. See clef.

●feminine ending. A conclusion on one of the weak *beats of a *measure.

All the following are feminine endings:

that almost invariably the two themes have the same tempo (rate of speed). The greater animation of the "masculine" theme comes through subdivision of the beats and tendency to loudness; the quietness of the "feminime" theme to the predominance of quarter-, half-, and whole-notes and to softer *dynamics.

As a rule the first theme (principal subject) is the "masculine" theme, the second theme (subordinate subject) the "feminine" theme. There are of course many examples in which roles are reversed, for instance the first movement of the Fourth Symphony by Brahms. In other works both themes are of the same general character; thus both themes in the first movement of Brahms's Second Symphony are "feminine."

●†fermata. The symbol ⌢

A conclusion on the first beat of the measure is called a masculine ending. All the following rhythmic patterns, if forming the conclusion, are "masculine" endings.

When placed over (or under) a note, chord, or rest, it indicates prolongation beyond the given time-value. The exact amount of increased length depends on the

References to endings "on" any beat denotes the beat with which the last note begins, not the one with which it ceases.

● "feminine" theme. In the *sonata-allegro form one theme is usually strong and bold, the other quiet and more reserved. The former is often called the "masculine" theme, the latter the "feminine" theme. The terminology is of course popular rather than scientific--a half-truth.

It is of highest importance to mention

judgment of the *conductor or performer; no definite rule can be given. Hence all statements that declare that the fermata means "add half a beat," "add one beat," "add half the given value," or "double the given value" are untrue, although the latter suggestion will most frequently (but by no means always) come closest to coinciding with the actual result.

It is probable that a given performer does not always prolong the same fermata the same number of seconds in various repetitions of any given piece.

A note affected by a fermata is not just a long note; the symbol indicates an effect impossible to secure by any other means. During the course of a fermata the constant beat or meter that underlies the music seems to come to a halt. A *conductor stops beating during a fermata; the players or singers must watch him for the signal to go on.

When this symbol is placed underneath a note, it is written inverted. When the prolongation is very short or optional, the symbol is sometimes put in parentheses.

It should be remembered that this character may affect a *rest as well as a note. When placed over a *barline it indicates a brief halt between the two affected measures. When placed over the space between two notes, it may indicate a brief stop between them, but more often it affects both notes.

When the two notes are *tied together, the symbol may appear over the first note, or over the second, or over both, depending on the activity of other simultaneous instruments or voices; the effects are by no means synonymous.

is discussed under chorale.

Plural: fermatas (English), fermate (Italian).

● †feroce. Fiercely, vehemently, violently, ferociously.

● †fervore. Fervor, ardor.

● †festivo. Festive.

● ff. Very loud. This is the abbreviation for fortissimo. It indicates a level of volume louder than *f, but less so than *fff.
See dynamic marks.

● fff. Extremely loud; louder than *ff. This term is sometimes called fortississimo or triple forte. On occasion such extremes as ffff and fffff are observed.
See dynamic marks.

● fiddle. The violin (humorous or colloquial; however theoretically the word is perfectly respectable. The word fiddler, however, suggests the untrained player.) For medieval fiddle see vielle.

● fidelity. The "faithfulness" or accuracy of a recording or broad-

Fermatas were once placed over bar-lines at the end of sections approached from a *D. C. or *D. S. In modern usage this has been replaced by the term *fine.

The substitution of tenuto or its abbreviation ten. for the fermata is undesirable.

The use of the fermata in chorales

cast. If it is so true as to be impossible to detect from an actual performance, its fidelity is 100 per cent perfect. (This has never been achieved, although some results have come so close as to be startling. It is quite probable that absolutely perfect reproduction will be attained in the not-too-distant future.)

The less a recording or broadcast resembles the actual performance, the lower its fidelity is. The element of difference is called distortion. Strictly speaking, distortion need not be of a disagreeable or raucous nature; emphasis is on the fact that it is inaccurate, and hence a result which might flatter the actual performance is, in strict parlance, distorted. As one commentator has worded it, "A high fidelity reproduction should add nothing of its own personality to the sound as it was recorded or broadcast. "

The world of high fidelity reproduction has developed a patois of its own which contains many terms not known to musicians in general, for example woofer, tweeter, turnover, infinite baffle, and variable reluctance.

The wide adoption of stereophonic reproduction about 1958 added tremendously to an already well-developed fidelity of sound.

See also phonograph.

● field drum. The *military drum.

● fife. A small flute-like instrument, with finger holes but usually without keys. It is rarely used except in a fife and drum corps. The *range is very high, and the tone-quality even shriller and thinner than that of the *piccolo. It is played in transverse position, like the flute.

● 15ma. To be performed two *octaves higher than written. It is sometimes given incorrectly as 15va or 16va. The latter arises from the false reasoning that since *8va denotes an octave higher than written, two octaves higher would be double 8, or 16; however an actual count will demonstrate that the sound two octaves above any given tone is really the fifteenth tone removed, not sixteenth.

15ma is an abbreviation; the full form is quindecima.

● fifteenth. The *interval of two *octaves.

● fifth. This word has several distinct meanings in music, which must not be confused.

(1) It can refer to the fifth degree (or dominant) of a *scale.

(2) It can refer to the fifth of a *triad or *seventh-chord.

(3) It can refer to the *interval of a fifth.

(4) It may possibly be used to refer to the dominant triad or V.

The same plurality of meanings is found with the word third.

● figuration. See accompaniment figure.

● figure. Any pattern of tones that can be easily recognized. See also accompaniment figure.

● figured bass. A system of designating chords by numerals and other symbols placed above or below the bass notes of the composition, rather than writing them out in full. Thus a complete chord can be represented by writing one of its tones--the lowest--and certain numerals.

From the beginning of the *Baroque period (about 1600) through the end of the *Rococo period (around 1775) it was customary to employ some *keyboard instrument in all *chamber-music and orchestral ensembles. No part was written for this instrument; it played from the part for the bass instruments. Over or under the notes appeared a series of numerals; these formed a type of "shorthand" for indicating the chords to be used. Each figure represented a tone at a certain *interval above the written bass part; the conversion of these figures into the tones for which they stood formed the chords. The separate tones might or might not be duplicated in the parts allotted to the other instruments or voices. Figured bass numerals did not indicate the melodic line, however.

In smaller ensembles the bass part in question was that for the *cello (sometimes *viola da gamba), in orchestral groups that for the cellos and *double-basses which had a single part, actually sounding as octaves. (The bassoon sometimes played in unison with the cellos.) This part was named *continuo in recognition of the fact that a keyboard instrument would also play from it continuously throughout the composition.

Formation of Chords. The exact distribution and *doubling (2) in the chords resulting from the figured bass was left to the discretion of the person playing the keyboard instrument; just so he did not inject any intervals that were not indicated or automatically implied, he could distribute and double largely as he saw fit, though certain doublings were (and still are) considered better than others. Probably no two musicians would use exactly the same distributions in playing any given composition, and it is not unlikely that a single player would even make certain slight changes from one performance to another. In no case, however, was the choice of the basic chord itself left to his discretion.

In time the system became conventionalized to the point where a single numeral might stand for a complete chord, the omitted figures being understood without the necessity of writing them. This will be illustrated in the table of abbreviations to follow.

Choice of Instrument. The generic name cembalo was applied to the keyboard instrument, the exact choice of which was largely one of convenience and personal taste. The *harpsichord was most frequently used, but after the invention of the piano, it too found employment in figured bass playing. In church performances the organ often served in this capacity. Although not a keyboard instrument, occasionally the *lute was pressed into service. The *clavichord, however, was never used in playing from figured bass because of its extremely faint tone, which could be drowned out by the gentlest pianissimo of any fellow player or singer.

Realizing the Figured Bass. Players of keyboard instruments referred to the art of converting the numerals into chords as "realizing the figured bass." Thanks to daily practice, they were adept at realizing any passage at sight,

even in music of quick *tempo. Although present-day musicians no longer regularly cultivate this skill, it is utter nonsense to term it a "lost art," for any intelligent person can acquire it through diligent practice.

In modern editions of Baroque music the publisher as a rule employs some composer or editor to furnish the composition with a suggested realization for use by performers who have not cultivated facility with figured bass practices. Where none has been made available, the player normally takes the part home between rehearsals and writes out his realization after careful study and experiment.

The Baroque Attitude. It is obvious that the tones which are added as the result of the indicated figures are to be found in the middle of the fabric. During the Baroque period the highest and lowest lines of tones were considered the most important; hence the exact distribution of the material in the middle was not regarded as of great consequence, except of course in highly polyphonic (contrapuntal) passages.

Slipshod as the figured bass custom may appear nowadays, it nevertheless served its purpose to everyone's satisfaction for about 175 years; indeed the era in question is often referred to as the "figured bass period."

Table of Abbreviations. The table on pages 153-4 shows the usual figured bass abbreviations, the complete figures for which each stood, and the type of chord that resulted. These were extended as new harmonic styles came into existence, hence the table shows several chords that rarely if ever appeared in Baroque and Rococo music.

Decline of Figured Bass. During the *Classical period, the use of figured bass rapidly died out, except in certain works for chorus and orchestra and for use with secco *recitatives in operas and oratorios. The composers known

Table of Figured Bass Abbreviations

Abbreviation	Complete Figures Implied	Result
8 or 5 or 3 or $\frac{8}{3}$ or $\frac{8}{5}$ or $\frac{5}{3}$ or no figure at all	8 5 3	Root position of a triad.
6 or $\frac{6}{3}$ or $\frac{8}{6}$	6 6 8 3 or 6 or 6 3 3 3	First inversion of a triad.
6 4	8 6 4	Second inversion of a triad.
7	7 5 3	Root position of a seventh-chord.
6 5	6 5 3	First inversion of seventh-chord.
4 3	6 4 3	Second inversion of seventh-chord.
$\frac{4}{2}$ or 2	6 4 2	Third inversion of seventh-chord.
4 3	8 8 5 5 4 3	Root position of a triad with a "4-3" suspension.
9 8	9 8 5 5 3 3	Root position of a triad with a "9-8" suspension.
#	$\sharp$ 3 (plus any other figures implied by 3)	An accidental alone affects the third above the given tone.
#6	# 6 (plus any other figures implied by 6)	An accidental in front of a figure indicates the note that interval above is to be affected.

Table of Figured Bass Abbreviations (Continued)

Abbreviation	Complete Figures Implied	Result
8⟍ 4	8 #6 4	Slanting line means raise the pitch a half-step; equivalent to a sharp.
—		Straight line means continue the tones already in use; treat the given note as a *non-harmonic tone.
Tasto solo or T. S.		Play only the given notes; add no chords.
9 or $\frac{9}{7}$	9 7 3	Root position of a ninth-chord.

as the *Mannheim Group made a practice of avoiding it, while Haydn probably dealt the system its death blow by writing most of his symphonies without using it.

Nevertheless the study of figured bass continued as a skill regarded worth cultivating, especially for rapid learning of chords and chord connections. Our present studies of *harmony (2) and *keyboard harmony descend directly from this old custom.

It would be difficult to say who invented figured bass. It is known that it came into existence very late in the *Renaissance period, in a tentative way. The first person to codify and systematize it appears to have been Lodovico da Viadana (1564-1627), but the statement that he "invented" the system is erroneous. It would be equally difficult to name the last figured bass composition ever written; in any event, Weber, who belongs to the early *Romantic period and who died in 1826, used it in one of his masses.

The passage on page 155 shows two possible realizations of a figured bass. The given bass line and the accompanying figures appear on the lower staff, while the upper staff contains tones which fill out the chords as indicated.

Two possible realizations of the bass for the opening measures
of Bach's *Suite in B minor* (flute and string orchestration).

Synonyms: continuo, basso continuo,
general bass, thoroughbass.

● figured bass period. The *Baroque
period of music history, so called
because of the wide use of *figured
bass in chamber, orchestral,

operatic, and choral music.

● figured music. Music by a known
composer, and written for several
voices; used in opposition to
*Gregorian chants, which are
anonymous and *monophonic. Not

connected with the term *figured bass.
Synonym: figurate music.

● final. In the *modes (1), a term
approximately equivalent to *tonic.

● †finale. The last *movement of a
composition that is divided into
movements; this includes the concluding *number of an opera (or act
thereof) or of an oratorio.
   The term is sometimes applied,
less desirably, to the concluding
portion of a movement, or of a
single-movement work.
   This term is by no means a synonym for *coda.

● †fine. End. This term is normally
found somewhere in the course of a
composition containing a *D. C. or
*D. S.; it indicates the point where
the composition concludes.

● finger-diagrams. See tablature·
(2).

● finger exercise. A passage,
long or short, written in such a
manner that playing it repeatedly
tends to strengthen the fingers of
the player of the piano or other
keyboard instrument. Finger
exercises are even more mechanical-
sounding and less musical than
*etudes, but their value in loosen-
ing up the hand, strengthening the
fingers, and promoting completely
independent action by each finger
is hardly open to question.

● fingering. Briefly, the use of
the fingers in playing various instruments.
   (1) Piano. With the piano and
other keyboard instruments it
refers to the finger chosen to

In the above, the performer would
play (sing) from the beginning to
D. C., then return to the beginning
and play to fine. The rewriting of
the material between the beginning
and fine is thus avoided.
   In older music the sign   ⌒   (appearing over the bar-line following
the last measure to be played) was
the equivalent of the term fine.
   The related English word is finish.
   See also D. C., D. S., repeat
signs.
   Pronunciation: according to the rules
for Italian pronunciation, never as in
English. (See page 17   ).

● fingerboard. The long, narrow,
slightly arched piece of black wood
on a string instrument, extending
longitudinally from the nut almost to
the bridge, above which the strings
are stretched, and against which they
are pressed by the player's fingers.
   On the *fretted instruments the
fingerboard is flat and crossed by
latitudinal *frets.

press a certain key in a given
passage. It is apparent that with
a poor choice of fingering any
passage may be rendered very
difficult or even unplayable. The
fingers are numbered as follows:
   thumb -- 1
   index finger -- 2
   long finger -- 3
   ring finger -- 4
   little finger -- 5
These numerals are placed above
or below the notes. In the United
States there was formerly a system
in which the thumb was indicated
by x, the remaining fingers
numbered as shown for the string
instruments below; it was abandoned
before the turn of the century.
   When two figures are connected
by a little curved line, e. g., 2̆3,
this indicates the key is to be
pressed by the second finger, then
without the key being released, the
third finger is to replace the
second. Such substitutions are
often necessary.
   See also pedaling (1).

(2) String Instruments. With the string instruments the term indicates the finger chosen to press the string. The numbers supplied automatically indicate the position (see violin) that is used. The fingers are numbered as follows:

index finger -- 1
long finger -- 2
ring finger -- 3
little finger -- 4

In the fingering of the *cello and *double-bass the thumb is indicated by the symbol ⊕ or ⊙

(3) Wind Instruments. With the *brass and *woodwind instruments the word fingering is used in an entirely different meaning. Instead of indicating the finger chosen to play a certain tone, it refers to the combination of holes, keys, or *valves which the fingers must press in order to cause a particular pitch to emit from the instrument. Many of the tones can be produced by any of several entirely different "fingerings." Two examples will be given.

On the trumpet the tone

can be played with the first and second valves (the usual method), or with the third valve, or with all three valves. On the clarinet the tone

can be played by covering the first, second, third, and fifth holes, plus the *thumb-hole (the usual method), or by covering the first, second, third, and fourth holes, plus the thumb-hole, and pressing the little crescent-shaped trill-key located between the

fifth and sixth holes. The player uses whichever fingering happens to be the easiest in the passage at hand. In general, however, as has been implied, one fingering is regarded as standard; the others are used only when the standard would be awkward. These additional fingerings are termed, by players of brass instruments, false fingerings, or (more desirably) alternate, auxiliary, or secondary fingerings.

Many of the tones on woodwind instruments can be played in more than one way; for instance the highest G on the clarinet has no fewer than seven different fingerings.

"Forked fingerings" are described under woodwind instruments.

● †fioritura. An *ornament or similar effect of embellishment.
    Plural: fioriture.

● fipple flute. Same as recorder.

● first and second endings. Often in a composition containing a repeat (see repeat signs), the conclusion of the second playing differs slightly from the conclusion of the first. In such cases, the composer writes ⌐1   ¬ over the ending to be used the first time, and places ⌐2   ¬ over that for the second. A first or second ending is sometimes only one measure in length. The rewriting of a long section can often be avoided through this expedient.

It is important to emphasize that on the second playing through, the material under ⌐1   ¬ is to be omitted, and only that under 2 ⌐   ¬ used.

The above is an example of the application of first and second endings; another will be found under repeat signs. For a written-out version of this melody, see the entry diatonic, melody A.

● first chair man. In the orchestra, a colloquial name given to the player assigned to the first part among any of the woodwind or brass instruments (such as first flute, first horn, etc.); also the *principal among the various string sections.
  Synonym: first desk man.

● first-movement form. See sonata-allegro form.

● "Five, the." A group of Russian composers devoted to the development of a distinctively Russian type of music. They were especially active during the 1870's. The members were: Nicholas Rimsky-Korsakoff (1844-1908), Modeste Moussorgsky (1839-1881), Alexander Borodin (1834-1887), Mili Balakireff (1837-1910), and César Cui (1835-1918).
  Synonyms: "The Mighty Five," "The Mighty Band."
  See also nationalism.

● five finger position. In piano technique, a passage which is possible to play without having to move the hand either up or down the keyboard is said to be in "five finger position." Each finger operates but a single key, and obviously only five keys are playable in such a position.
  Many very elementary teaching pieces for beginners are written in five finger position throughout.

● fixed do. See syllables.

● flag. The hook attached to the *stem of the eighth-note to distinguish it from the quarter-note. The sixteenth-note has two flags, the thirty-second-note three, the sixty-fourth-note four.
  The flag is always turned toward the right and toward the note-head, regardless of whether the stem turns up or down.

There are two ways of writing the flag: sometimes it appears as a rather heavy straight line, other times as a thin curved line.

● flageolet. A woodwind instrument of the flute type (or more accurately, a species of *recorder), with a thin, *piccolo-like *tone-color. Although a few orchestral scores of the past have included it, the instrument is now obsolete.
  Pronunciation: flăj-ŏ-lĕt́.

● flageolet tones. The *harmonics (1) of the string instruments.

● flamenco. A type of Spanish Gypsy folk music.

● flat. (1) The character ♭ It lowers the pitch of a note one *half-step. It may occur in a *key-signature or as an *accidental.
  A note affected by a flat is said to be "flatted" (not "flattened").
  (2) (Adjective) Slightly too low in pitch. (Verb) In singing, to sink gradually lower and lower in pitch as the performance continues.
  Antonym: sharp (2). See intonation.

● †flautando. Same as sul tasto. See sul (4).

● flautist. Flutist, flute-player.
  Pronunciation: flṓ-tĭst.

● †flauto traverso. Old name for the *flute (to distinguish it from the *recorder).

● †flebile. Plaintive, mournful.
  Pronunciation: accent first syllable.

● florid. Tending to have many notes to the word or syllable of a word; used in connection with music for the voice.

In the following quotation from Handel's The Messiah the word "born" receives an extremely florid treatment, occupying no fewer than 57 notes--quite in contrast to the preceding words "For unto us a child is," which are *syllabic.

range as the trumpet and cornet. See bottom diagram. It is a B-flat *transposing instrument, notated a whole-step higher than the sounds desired.

The flügelhorn is often found in the concert *band, but few orchestral compositions call for

For un-to us a child is born _____

Florid style

See also coloratura.

Synonym (but implying less brilliance): melismatic.

Antonym: syllabic.

● flourish.   *Fanfare.

● flügelhorn.   A brass instrument similar to the *trumpet and *cornet. Just as the cornet has a mellower tone than the trumpet, the flügelhorn is still mellower than the cornet, its *tone-color approaching that of the *horn.   Its lowest tones are fuller and richer than those of the trumpet or cornet, but it does not ascend so easily to its highest tones.

There are several sizes of flügelhorn, the most familiar being that in B-flat, or soprano, which has the same

it.   However, in the stentorian conclusion to The Pines of Rome, Respighi augments an already large orchestra with two soprano, two tenor, and two bass flügelhorns.

Italian: flicorno (plural, flicorni). French: bugle.   German: Flügelhorn (plural, Flügelhörner).

Pronunciation: flü-gel-horn, often anglicized as floo-gel-horn.

● flute.   One of the higher-pitched woodwind instruments.   It is held out to the player's right (transversely), rather than straight out from the mouth.   The flute has no reed, the tone being produced by blowing across a hole.

Written   ♩ or ♩   Sounding ♭♩ or ♩

Range: *recorder.

Many flutes also have the low B, a half-step below the lowest tone here indicated. The highest tone is approximate; skillful players can sound the high C-sharp and D. The flute is notated as it sounds, always with the treble *clef. (There is, however, a D-flat flute, occasionally used in the *band, which is a *transposing instrument. Its range in actual sounds is a half-step higher than shown above and it is notated a half-step lower than the sounds desired. It is tending to go out of use.)

Today the flute is almost invariably made of metal (usually silver); the wooden flute is rarely encountered.

The lowest tones are breathy and "cooing"; they are usually weak in volume. The medium register is limpid, bright, and bird-like. The highest tones are very brilliant and somewhat shrill. The instrument has a pure, cool, refreshing tone.

The flute is extremely agile, and unlike other woodwind instruments, can play in almost all keys with equal ease.

A few composers have written for the soprano flute in E-flat or third flute, (also occasionally coloratura flute) which sounded a minor third higher than written. After many decades of disuse, this instrument is again being manufactured.

The alto flute and piccolo are discussed under separate entries, as is the recorder. The flute stops of the organ are discussed under organ.

Italian: flauto or flauto grande (plural, flauti or flauti grandi). French: flûte or grande flûte. German: Flöte or grosse Flöte (plural, Flöten or grosse Flöten). Spanish: flauta.

The player is called a flutist or flautist; the latter term is something of an affectation.

● flûte à bec. French name for the

Pronunciation: flüt à běk.

● flute in G. The alto flute.

● Flutophone. See simple melody instruments. A trade name.

● flutter-tonguing. See double-tonguing and tremolo (3).

● folk-music, folk-songs. Music which arises spontaneously among the inhabitants of a certain region and is handed down from one generation to another by oral tradition. The words as well as the music are of this type of origin. A true folk-song is a communal composition--the work of several persons, all of whom are unknown. Slight variations in both the melody and text are found in the various localities in which it is sung; all of these must be considered "correct" and legitimate.

In their native habitat, folk-songs are usually sung without *accompaniment, or accompanied with very simple *chords on various popular instruments such as the *guitar or the *accordion.

The folk-song is the musical counterpart of the legend and folk-ballad in literature. It arises out of the need for aesthetic expression in daily life.

The folk-music of any country has a characteristic style peculiar to that one nation, just as does the art music (i. e., the music of known composers). Nevertheless the best examples are of universal appeal and strike a responsive note in both children and adults. Musicians acknowledge that the finest folk-song melodies are equal in beauty to the finest melodies of the great composers, for they become wonderfully refined in their transition from person to person.

Folk-music has had a notable influence in the development of *nationalism.

Use of folk-melodies is open to any composer without being regarded as *plagiarism. (See borrowed melodies.)

A considerable amount of misinformation has arisen in regard to folk-music. One inaccurate concept ascribes its invention exclusively to "peasants" and "the lower classes." Another maintains that it arises among "the people," implying that certain persons evidently are not "people." Commonest of all is the impression that all folk-music is of great antiquity--something which has "come down through the ages." Actually many of these melodies are fairly modern, their style very clearly showing them to date from as recently as 1800; few can be traced back earlier than the sixteenth century, although there is some likelihood that certain melodies are based on older ones.

Folk-songs are still coming into existence, even today, although doubtless in decreased quantities compared to times when communication was less easy.

It is more than likely that many melodies which are considered folk-songs are actually *popular (3) songs by obscure and unimportant composers, rather than the genuine article--songs of the type sometimes called *home- and community songs or composed folk-songs.

● footing. Same as pedaling (1).

● fork. Name sometimes applied to the symbols ————— and ————— for *crescendo and *diminuendo, respectively.

Synonym (humorous): "hairpins."

● form. (1) Orderly design in music; the organization of musical materials into intelligible patterns.

It is impossible for a composition to be utterly without form and still "make sense." The fact that laymen are often not conscious of the form of a work, even unaware of the very existence of such an element, in no way lessens its tremendous importance. Composers' thinking is much more concerned with form than most people imagine.

This term should not be confused with *medium, which is a totally different thing.

The paramount necessity for form in music is due to the fact that the composer works without models in nature. A writer states a thought that is in his mind, a painter draws a picture of something he sees or imagines, but a composer can merely organize musical tones into intelligible designs which have no "meaning" in logic because they are their own meaning.

Although there are quite a few musical forms, some turn up more frequently than others. Among these are:

*Binary or two-part song-form: AB or AABB.

*Ternary or three-part song-form or song-form with trio: ABA.

Variation form: A A^1 A^2 A^3 A^4...(see theme and variations).

*Rondo form: ABA or ABACA or ABACABA or ABACADA. The distinction between the first of these and ternary form is explained under rondo.

Sonata-allegro or first-movement form: See sonata-allegro form.

There are of course other forms which are orderly and convincing but which have been given no special name. It is possible to arrange letters in various logical patterns, and if a long enough search is made, one or more examples of each can eventually be found.

Synonym: design.

See also arch form, passacaglia, ostinato, chorale-prelude, fugue, one-movement symphony, sonatina form, and double sonata-allegro form. Also see rules of music.

(2) The term form is also used to distinguish various styles or types of piece, without regard for the sequence of themes or sections. Such types as the march, the nocturne, all the many varieties of dance, the recitative, the sym-

phonic poem, etc. are sometimes called forms. See character piece for a better term.

●†forte. Loud (literally "strong," "brave"). Normally used in abbreviated form, f.
See dynamic marks.

●†fortepiano. (1) Loud and then immediately soft. Abbreviation fp. It is not synonymous with *sforzando, for it is not relative in value, but absolute; it means the note should be attacked *forte and then sustained *piano.
(2) An old and rare synonym for pianoforte, the full name of the piano.

●†fortissimo. Very loud. Normally used in abbreviated form, ff.
See dynamic marks.

●†forza. Force, power. Con forza, with force, forcefully. Tutta la forza, with all possible power (about the same as fff).

●†forzando, forzato. See sforzando.

●440. It is customary in the United States to tune all instruments to the pitch standard in which the A above *middle C has 440 vibrations per second.

Other standards of tuning are found in other countries or have been used in the United States during the past; for instance formerly the A above middle C often had 435 vibrations per second.
In France the pitch standard was changed in 1955 from 435 to 428.
See also pitch.

●four hands. A composition written for two pianists--both at the same instrument--is said to be written for "piano, four hands."
Synonym: piano duet.
See also primo, secondo.

●four-line staff. Illustrated under neumes, this now-obsolete type of *staff was widely used when notation was developing and is still often used, with neumes, in writing *Gregorian chants. In addition to the four lines there are of course three spaces.

●fourth-chords. Chords which may be reduced to fourths (see intervals).
Fourth-chords (or chords in fourths) are almost exclusively a twentieth century development.
In order to clarify just what a fourth-chord is, it is first necessary to digress long enough to explain what the more ordinary

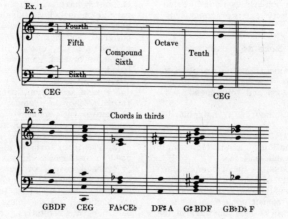

Ex. 1

Fourth / Fifth / Compound Sixth / Octave / Tenth / Sixth

CEG   CEG

Ex. 2   Chords in thirds

GBDF   CEG   FAbCEb   DF#A   G#BDF   GBbDb F

type of chord is.

Conventional chords are those which may be reduced to thirds; that is, in their *spelling position they consist of every other tone, of notes entirely on lines or entirely on spaces of the staff. They are not necessarily made up of thirds piled on top of one another; it is possible for such a chord to possess not a single third (though a tenth may be present). See Example 1. All of the chords in Example 2 are reducible to thirds.

In a like manner, a fourth-chord will not necessarily consist of fourths piled on top of one another. It may have this form, but usually does not; however it must be capable of being rearranged into such a form. All of the chords in Example 3 are aspects of EADG, although only the first consists of a stack of fourths.

term fifth-chords, in which case the existence of fourth-chords is automatically ruled out.)

Some very beautiful effects may be obtained from fourth-chords, when used discreetly. They progress very nicely to ordinary chords (i. e., third-chords) and to *open fifths. It may be argued that fourth-chords and third-chords are not two different things, but two forms of a single thing, for a fourth-chord can be reasoned as an extended form of a third-chord with certain tones omitted, while a third-chord can be reasoned as an extended form of a fourth-chord with certain tones omitted. (It has always been admitted that there are members which can be left out of some chords without destroying their identity; for

A fourth chord in 13 forms

Normally the intervals to which the chord is reduced are perfect fourths. The *"mystic chord" used by Scriabin contains augmented and diminished fourths as well as perfect, and hence is hardly a fourth-chord as that term is generally understood.

Just as there is no such thing as a "chord in sixths" (the first chord in Example 2 is a form of the chord-in-thirds GBDF) there is also no such thing as a "chord in fifths"; it is a chord in fourths in a different distribution. The open strings of the violin, viola, and cello are fourth-chords distributed as perfect fifths. (Some musicians prefer to use the

instance, dropping D from GBDF or G from CEG in no way impairs the effectiveness of these chords.) See Example 4, in which quarter-note heads are employed to represent the tones used, whole-notes to represent the tones that are left out.

Synonym: quartal harmony.

● fourths. See intervals.

● fp. Abbreviation for fortepiano (1). It is not a synonym for sf, fz, and sfz, which are explained under sforzando. The form pf is sometimes substituted, but it is

EADG as an incomplete CEG as an incomplete
chord in thirds   Fourth-chord.

illogical.

● †freddo. Cold, without expression.
(Related English word: frigid.)

● free anticipation. See non-harmonic
tones (7) (escape tones).

● free fantasia. Synonym for development.

● free tone. See non-harmonic tones
(7) (escape tones).

● French harp. The harmonica (undesirable).

● French horn. A more complete
name for the *horn. It is pertinent
to mention that English is the only
language in which this instrument is
designated as "French," thus suggesting
the country from which it was introduced into England; the French, German, and Italian names are simply
cor, Horn, and corno, respectively.
The frequently-seen writing with
the F uncapitalized ("french horn")
cannot be recommended.

● French overture. A type of *overture of considerable importance
during the *Baroque period. It was
used in *operas, *oratorios, and as
the initial movements of orchestral
*suites.
The usual description of the French
overture states that it consists of
three sections in the order: slow, fast,
slow. However, numerous examples
lack the third part completely, while
others finish with only a few measures
in the initial slow *tempo; of course
still others actually do end with a
full-sized slow concluding section--
which may be a repetition or a
varied repetition of the opening part,
or may consist of fresh material.
In the slow sections the rhythmic
patterns ♩. ♪ and ♩.♫

are characteristic. There is
reason to believe that the first of these
patterns was often performed as ♩.. ♪

The fast section is usually fugal in
style.
Jean-Baptiste Lully (or Lulli)
(1632-1687) is usually credited
with establishing the French overture.
Synonym: Lullian overture.
Compare Italian overture.

● French sixth. See augmented
sixth chords.

● †frenetico. Frenetic, frenzied,
as if insane. (Related to English
frantic.)
Pronunciation: accent second
syllable.

● fret. A small piece of wood,
metal, or celluloid imbedded cross-
wise on the *fingerboard of a
string instrument (usually of the
plucked string type). They are
laid out in a series of *half-steps
(semitones). The player, by pressing down on the strings in such a
way that they touch various frets,
causes the vibrating portion of the
strings to be shortened, and thus
produces the tones of which the
instrument is capable.
Since it is unnecessary for the
player to place his fingers at just
one exact point (any spot between
two frets will serve), it is impossible to play a fret-equipped instrument *out of tune, unless the strings
themselves are not correctly on
pitch.
Frets have been applied to the
violin, viola, cello, and double-
bass for use by poor players, but
capable musicians scorn them.
The *vibrato is impossible on an
instrument so equipped.
Frets made of gut were normally
used on the *viols, but in general
they are characteristic only of those
instruments listed below under the
heading fretted instruments.

● fretted instruments. A generic
name for those plucked string instruments which have *fingerboards
equipped with *frets. The most
important are the *mandolin,
*guitar, *Hawaiian guitar, *ukulele,
*banjo, *balalaika, and the more

or less obsolete but formerly important *lute, chitarrone, theorbo, and *vihuela.

Although the *viols and other bowed string instruments have been equipped with frets, the term fretted instruments is normally not applied to them. Synonym: plectral instruments.

● fugal style. Partaking of the style of the *fugue or (more commonly) of the *fugato.

● †fugato. A passage of music corresponding to the material found in the exposition section of a *fugue.

The fugato is not a complete form; it is found as an incidental passage within a single composition. A fugato is most likely to be found at the beginning of a piece or section within it, or in a *development of a movement cast in *sonata-allegro form, or possibly in a *coda.

At the conclusion of the fugato passage the composition may continue with another theme and may even become *homophonic in structure, for such passages are by no means restricted to works that are predominantly *contrapuntal from beginning to end.

The term fugato should not be confused with *fughetta.

● †fughetta. A short *fugue.

● fugue. It would be futile to attempt to formulate a brief definition of the term fugue. The process can be described at length, but it cannot be "defined" in capsule fashion.

The fugue is not so much a *"form" as a style or procedure.

It is essential to point out that the fugue is *contrapuntal (polyphonic) throughout, and that with the exception of the double fugue mentioned below, it is based on a single theme, usually called the "subject" rather than the "theme."

Number of "Voices." Most fugues are written for either three or four contrapuntally-moving parts or *lines (2), which are termed "voices," in spite of the fact that the fugue is with rare exception an instrumental form. A few fugues have only two voices, while others have five or even more.

The difficulty of composition grows in direct proportion to the number of voices used, and it should be borne in mind that the fugue is generally considered the most difficult of all musical forms to compose. It is distinctly of an intellectual nature, but this must by no means be interpreted as suggesting that it is "dry."

In general, the fugue consists of two sections, the exposition and the development, to which is sometimes added a third section, the stretto.

The Exposition. Every fugue begins with an unharmonized statement of the subject (theme) in one of the voices. When the subject proper has concluded, a second voice states it, a fourth or a fifth (see intervals) above or below the first voice. Sometimes it is necessary to make a slight adjustment in the intervals between the first few notes in the subject; the reasons cannot be entered into here. The second entrance of the subject is normally called the answer, and when the afore-mentioned alteration is necessary it is called a tonal answer (otherwise it is called a real answer).

While the second voice is carrying the subject in its "answer" form, the first voice continues with the countersubject. The countersubject should be considered more a continuation of the subject than a separate and distinct theme. Its material is always of a nature that will combine contrapuntally with the subject.

There is usually a very brief *episode (connecting link) before the appearance of the subject in the third voice. This is sometimes termed a *codetta (2).

The third voice takes up the subject in its original form; meanwhile the second voice carries the countersubject and the first voice continues with free material which will combine contrapuntally with the subject and countersubject.

If the fugue is of the four-voice variety, the fourth voice then presents the subject in its "answer" form; meanwhile the third voice has the countersubject and the first and second voices both have free material.

(The counterpoint in the second voice is normally not the same material that the first voice carried when the subject appeared in the third voice.)

The portion thus far described is known as the exposition. It constitutes only about 20 or 25 per cent of the total length of the fugue, but it is the only part whose structure can be described with certainty--the only part that is reasonably predictable. It can be diagrammed as follows, the straight line representing the subject, the wavy line the countersubject, and the dotted line free counterpoint.

rare occasions when there is a complete new exposition (called re-exposition). Some theorists have observed that many fugues go through a certain typical sequence of key-relationships, but exceptions to this probably outnumber the examples. In brief, it is only a slight exaggeration to say that there are as many types of middle section (development) as there are fugues. The richness of the composer's imagination and inventiveness comes into play here.

The Stretto. In many (but by

It should not be imagined that the voices must enter in the order shown here; any feasible order may be used, but normally only one is possible in any given composition. Most composers agree that the effect is best if the subject can always be made to appear in an outside voice.

Development. The exposition, as has been mentioned, is the only part of the fugue that can be described with any degree of assurance. The remaining three-fourths or four-fifths can hardly be said to have "form," but to be more the application of fugal procedure. The *texture (1) is constantly contrapuntal, however.

The middle portion of the fugue is usually called the development, because the process is similar to that found in the development section of other forms. The subject constantly reappears (often with, often without alterations); meanwhile all sorts of other contrapuntal material is combined with it--either countersubject or free material. The subject might be treated in *inversion (3), *cancrizans, *augmentation, or *diminution, or possibly the countersubject may be developed. The voices drop out and return, so that the maximum number do not always appear at any given moment. The texture is not likely, however, to reduce to just a single voice except for the rather

no means all) fugues, near the end there is a passage in which the subject is caused to overlap upon itself; that is, one voice begins the subject and before it has finished with it, another voice takes it up commencing from the first note. This device is called the stretto (1); the subject is made into a short *canon. It hardly seems necessary to mention that not every fugue subject can be treated in stretto, and that this possibility must be "built into" the subject from its very inception. It is the composer's final exultant flaunt of his technique--truly virtuosity in composition. The stretto procedure will usually be shared by all the voices. Its effect is climactic; it seems to "heap Ossa upon Pelion."

As a rule the conclusion of the fugue comes very soon after the stretto, usually with an emphatic appearance of the subject in one of the voices. Often there is a *pedal point as the work concludes.

Additional Remarks. Some fugues do not have a countersubject, in which case it is replaced by free counterpoint. This is especially prevalent in fugues written for the piano. The reason is probably not so much that the composer is unable to invent one as that its inclusion would cause the material to exceed the capabilities of ten fingers.

The *tempo and mood of the fugue may be anything the composer desires. The fact that Bach so often employed a moderate or moderately fast tempo coupled with a mood of masculine sturdiness has misled some musicians into assuming that these qualities are essential attributes of all fugues.

The frequency as to the *medium for which the fugue is written is approximately in this order: piano (harpsichord, clavichord), organ, chamber-music group, orchestra (including string orchestra and band), chorus (probably accompanied). Despite the rarity of fugues for voices, the form is vocal in origin.

Undoubtedly J. S. Bach (1685-1750) was the greatest master of the fugue. His works of that type, for piano and organ, should be consulted. The Well-Tempered Clavier and the unfinished The Art of the Fugue-- a veritable "textbook in examples" on the subject--are of outstanding value.

It will be apparent that *imitation is the most distinctive feature of the fugue. Fugue is distinguished from imitation by reason of being much more thoroughgoing--much more exhaustively worked out.

Many fugues are preceded by a *prelude (1), *fantasy (1), *toccata, or other introductory piece; that is, they appear as the second of a pair (see diptych). Not infrequently the fugue is third in a work divided into three movements. Its appearance in *suites (2) and in the various forms herein called sonata-types, though exceptional, is hardly a matter for surprise.

Double Fugue. The term double fugue has two meanings. (A) It may be a fugue on two subjects, first the one then the other completely subjected to exposition and development, then the two subjects contrapuntally combined with one another.

(B) It may be a fugue which starts with two contrapuntally combined voices rather than with one, the remainder of the exposition and development constantly working with this dual theme.

See also: fughetta, fugato, canon, imitation, fuguing-tune.

● fuguing-tune. A term used by William Billings (1746-1800) and other early American composers to describe compositions containing *imitative entries of the voices, and other devices of *counterpoint. It is more than likely that, due to his imperfect education, Billings had no idea of what a *fugue is.

The term has been revived in recent years by Henry Cowell, Otto Luening, and other American composers. It might well be used as a synonym for a free type of fugue.

● functional harmony. (1) The feeling that chords are progressing in a natural manner toward a *tonic or key-center; the sense that chords are "on the way" to a resting point toward which they are attracted.

When a passage of music is suddenly interrupted, we often have a feeling of hearing it continue in some manner until it comes to rest at a *cadence. For example, the following passage will seem to want to continue to either DFA or FAC, then to GBD(F), then to CEG.

Functional harmony developed largely during the seventeenth century, although there were traces of it long before then. However, the harmonies underlying *Renaissance music were essentially *nonfunctional, due partly to the fact that they were to a certain extent the semi-accidental result of the interweaving of voices in *poly-

phonic music.

Functional harmony is an active element in musical *form. It keeps the composition moving, forms a part of its structure.

Compare non-functional harmony. See also triad, seventh-chord.

(2) The term functional harmony is also applied to a system for explaining harmonic usage which was developed by Hugo Riemann (1849-1919) and Heinrich Schenker (1868-1935).

● fundamental.   (1) Same as root. Fundamental position, same as root position.

(2) The tone which is the generator of a series of overtones (see harmonic series).

● fundamental bass.   The *roots (fundamentals) of a succession of chords, arranged in a line like a melody.   The series of tones that results is purely imaginary.   Only when a chord is in *root position will the tone shown in fundamental bass coincide with the actual bass note of the chord.

(Czech) dance in 3-4 time.   Often its rhythm takes the form

for a few measures (see hemiola). Smetana and Dvořák introduced the furiant into serious literature; the third movement of the latter's *Piano Quintet in A is a furiant, replacing the customary *scherzo.

● †furioso.   Furiously.

● fz.   Same as sforzando.

G

● †gajezza.   Gaiety, merriment. Con gajezza, gaily.
   Variant spelling: gaiezza.

● †gajo.   Gay.
   Variant spelling: gaio.

● Gallant Style.   See Rococo.

● galliard.   A dance in moderately

● †funebre.   Funereal, solemn.
   Pronunciation: accent the first syllable.

● †fuoco.   Fire.   Con fuoco, with fire.

● furiant.   A very fast Bohemian

fast triple meter.   It was popular during the sixteenth century.

The galliard is often preceded by a *pavane.

Variant forms: gaillard, galliarde, gagliard, gagliarda.

● gamba.   A short name for the

*viola da gamba.
Plural: gambas or gambe.
Pronunciation: gäm´-ba or gäm´-bä̱.

● gamelan. Native orchestra of Java.

● gamut. (1) Same as scale (rare).
(2) Same as range.

● gapped scale. Same as pentatonic
scale.

● gavotte. A type of dance in 4-4
time, moderate tempo. The style is
dainty, and most gavottes contain
numerous eighth-notes.
A peculiarity of the gavotte is that
the majority (although not all) begin
on the third beat of the *measure (see
up-beat).
Often the gavotte has a *musette as
middle section, in ABA pattern:
gavotte, musette, gavotte. (See
ternary form.)

● G clef. See clef.

● Gebrauchsmusik (German). Literally
"music for use" or "utility music."
This term refers to compositions which
are of serious purpose and high quality,
yet easy to play, intended for *amateurs,
for the home, for schools, etc., rather
than for *virtuosos. The philosophy
behind Gebrauchsmusik also represents,
to a certain extent, a reaction against
the "art for art's sake" concept. In
many ways it is a return to old ideals--
older than the ideals characteristic of
the age that begot the virtuoso.
The term is especially associated
with Paul Hindemith (1895-1963), who
championed this concept and wrote
numerous examples of Gebrauchsmusik.
See also salon music, chamber opera.
Pronunciation: gĕ-brouks´-mōō-zĕk´.

● Geige (German). *Violin (colloquial,

somewhat analogous to English
fiddle).
Plural: Geigen.
Synonym: Violine.
Pronunciation: gī´-gĕ.

● general bass. See figured bass.

● general pause. See G. P.

● generating theme. See cyclic
form.

● generator. Same as fundamental
(2); see harmonic series.

● German flute. Old name for the
*flute, in contradistinction to the
*recorder, which was often called
the English flute.

● German notation. The most striking
difference between German letter-
names and English is the use of B as
the equivalent of B-flat, and of H for B.
Thus it is possible to spell out Bach's
name with the notes B-flat, A, C, B-
natural. See music diagram below.
However, the foregoing is an irregularity in the German system.
All the remaining natural tones
are as in English. Sharp names
are formed by adding the suffix
-is to the letter; for example Gis
is the German for G-sharp. Flat
names (except B-flat) are formed
by adding the suffix -es, except
with A and E, where -s alone is
added; thus Des is D-flat, As is
A-flat. With double-sharps -isis
is added, with double-flats -eses
(or -ses). Thus Cisis is C-double-
sharp, Deses is D-double flat, and
Ases is A-double-flat.

● German sixth. See augmented
sixth chords.

B   A   C   H

●Gewandhaus (German). A famous concert hall in Leipzig, Germany. The word, curiously, means "clothing house. "
Pronunciation: gĕ-vänt́-hous.

●gigue (French). A lively, rollicking dance in 6-8, 12-8, or 12-16 time. Some gigues are in 4-4 but contain many *triplets, thus giving the impression of 12-8. The Baroque *suite (1) as a rule closes with a gigue, which is the last of the four essential dances that comprise it.
Variant forms: jig, giga.
Pronunciation: zhēg.

●†giocoso. Jocose, mirthful, humorous.

●†giojoso. Joyous, gay.
Variant spelling: gioioso.

●†giusto. Strict, exact. Tempo giusto, in strict time, i. e., without any trace of *tempo rubato.
(Related English word: just.)

●glee. A type of short secular choral composition, originating in England, which had considerable vogue there during the late seventeenth, eighteenth, and early nineteenth centuries, especially from 1750 to 1830. It is written for male voices unaccompanied, usually in three parts but sometimes more, and is intended to be sung by solo voices, rather than sections--a custom probably "more honoured in the breach than in the observance. " It is usually less *contrapuntal than the *madrigal, but more so than the *part song.
The word glee that pertains to music has an entirely different etymology from the word meaning "joy" or "mirth, " being derived from the Anglo-Saxon word meaning "music. " A glee is not necessarily gay in mood.

●glee club. Strictly speaking, a choral organization devoted to the singing of *glees. In the United States, however, the term is generally used--especially in high schools and colleges--to denote choruses entirely of men or entirely of women, or--less frequently--to indicate a small mixed group of selected voices. The term is rarely used as a synonym for large *mixed chorus.
The voice parts found in a men's glee club are normally first tenor, second tenor, first bass, and second bass (TTBB). First bass is a synonym for baritone (1), and that type of voice is assigned to the part; however the terminology first bass is almost invariable. A men's glee club differs from a *male quartet in that it has a section, or group, of voices to each part, rather than a single singer. In high schools the men's glee club is usually called boys' glee club.
The voice parts found in a women's glee club are sometimes first soprano, second soprano, first alto, and second alto (SSAA), and sometimes (especially in high schools and smaller groups) first soprano, second soprano, alto (SSA). Mezzo-sopranos are often assigned to the second soprano part, though perhaps more frequently to the first alto. In high schools the women's glee club is usually called girls' glee club.

●†gli. The (plural).
Variant forms: i, le.

●†glissando. (1) A sliding from one tone to another in such a manner that all intervening pitches--including those of less than a *half-step--are momentarily heard. When accomplished

quickly the effect can be quite artistic, but when done slowly and employed too frequently it is vulgar in the extreme, even ludicrous.

Glissandi can be produced by the voice, the bowed *string instruments, and the trombone; with the former two it is usually termed portamento.

The string glissando is indicated by a straight line between the lowest and highest tones, with perhaps the addition of the abbreviation port. (for portamento) or gliss. (for glissando). The interval in a string glissando (or portamento) may be wide or narrow. The player does not commence the slide as soon as the note begins; rather he holds it nearly its full value; then slides up or down in the brief split-second that remains. See diagram on p. 170.

The vocal glissando (almost always termed portamento) is sometimes indicated like that for the string instruments, though perhaps more frequently with a *grace-note, as follows:

(2) Keyboard Instruments. A sliding over the keys of a keyboard instrument, in such a manner that (if white keys are used) a rapid and brilliant C major scale results without the various tones being fingered separately. It is executed with the back of a finger, usually the thumb or the "second" (index) finger. It is playable on either the white or the black keys (generally the former) but not on a mixture of these. Clearly a glissando is effective in inverse proportion to its frequency.

In notating a glissando for a keyboard instrument the composer may (A) write the first and last notes, and place a straight or wavy line between them; or (B) write out the notes for the first octave and indicate the balance by a straight or wavy line; or (C; not illustrated), write out the glissando complete. In all cases the direction glissando

Vocal glissando

Of course many performers use this device at points where it is not indicated by the composer; however all conscientious artists guard against its overuse.

See also portamento.

or gliss. is added. See diagram below.

(3) Harp. A sliding over the strings of the harp. It may be done with one or both hands. The effect is very easy to play and has doubtless been overused.

Keyboard glissando

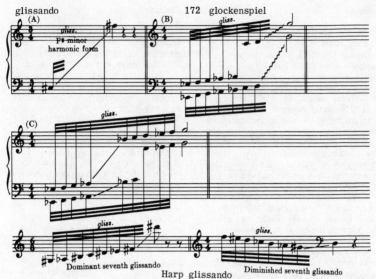

Dominant seventh glissando   Diminished seventh glissando

Harp glissando

In notating a glissando the composer may (A) indicate only the first and last notes, with the addition of a straight or wavy line between them, plus the indication of the name of the scale to be used; (B) write out the notes for the first octave and use a straight or wavy line to indicate the remainder of the notes; (C) write the first few notes of the scale and the last few, with a straight or wavy line to indicate the intervening tones; or (D; not illustrated), write out all the notes. In every case the word <u>glissando</u> or its abbreviation <u>gliss.</u> is added. It is possible to perform any *diatonic scale, the *whole-tone scales, all three diminished *seventh-chords, and certain dominant and other seventh-chords in glissando, due to the peculiar mechanism of the harp and its use of *enharmonic tones. (See <u>harp</u>.)

●glockenspiel. A definite pitch *percussion instrument consisting of little metal bars, graduated in size, laid out like the keys of the piano, played with two little mallets. The tone is very cool, clear, tinkling, and silvery, with much "ping." It differs from the *xylophone in being of smaller size, in having metal rather than wooden bars, and in giving out sounds of slightly longer duration. It is delightful when combined with high woodwind instruments such as flute and piccolo.

Orchestration books differ as to whether it should be notated one octave or two octaves lower than the sounds desired; the former seems to be the practice more widely followed in *scores. Range:

Glissandi may be performed upward or downward, but the former are the more frequent.

Plural: <u>glissandi</u> or <u>glissandos.</u>

Smaller glockenspiels do not descend below **C**.

Glockenspiels played from a keyboard are occasionally found.

Sometimes the instrument is mounted on a metal frame, usually shaped like a *lyre, so that it may be played in a marching *band. In this form it is often called the bell-lyre.
Synonym: orchestra bells.
Italian: campanelli. French: jeu de timbres, carillon, or glockenspiel.
German: Glockenspiel or Glöckchen.
Spanish: timbres, juego de timbres, or órgano de campanas.
Pronunciation: glŏk-ĕn-shpēl.

●† gondoliera. Same as barcarolle.

●gong. An indefinite pitch *percussion instrument. It is a large bronze disk held by two short ropes or suspended in a frame. The edges of the disk are bent backward. The *tone-color is very sinister, especially when struck softly. Its ominous character partly arises from the fact that the sound, instead of commencing immediately to grow softer, at first makes a very short *crescendo, then begins to die away, in which respect it is quite unlike any other percussion instrument.
Music for the gong is sometimes written on a one-line *staff.
Synonyms: tam-tam (however, see that entry for a fine distinction), Chinese gong.
Italian, French, German: tamtam.
Spanish: gongo.

● gopak. Same as hopak.

● Gothic Period. Name given to the period of music history that preceded the *Renaissance period. The approximate dates are 1150-1450.

●gourds. See güiro, maracas.

●G. P. Abbreviation for general pause or grand pause; used to denote a *rest for all the instruments in an orchestra or band (or all the voices in a chorus).
Synonyms: P. G., vuota, vuote.

●grace-notes. Notes printed in small type, and nominally occupying no time in the *measure; the time they consume is subtracted from the following (or sometimes preceding) note.
There are two types: (1) the short grace-note, still used; (2) the long grace-note, no longer used.
(1) The short grace-note or acciaccatura is performed as quickly as possible; it is so infinitesimally short that no ordinary note, not even a sixty-fourth, can represent its value. It is a mere "click" that is heard for a split-second before the sound which follows.
A single short grace-note is written like a tiny eighth-note with a slanting line through the stem. No matter where it appears on the *staff, the stem is turned up. Usually a little *slur joins it to the following note, which is called the principal note in contradistinction. When more than two grace-notes are used, they are usually written as miniature sixteenths, stems nearly always turned up, but without a slanting line, though as a rule a slur joins them to the principal note. See diagram below.
The brevity of the short grace-note can perhaps best be pointed up by mentioning that pianists often play the grace-note and principal note simultaneously, then immediately release the former. It is almost impossible to detect this type of execution from the normal form. When played in this manner the grace-notes are called crush-notes.
Considerable argument has arisen among musicians as to whether the

Short grace-notes (acciaccatura type)

short grace-note should be played with the beat or immediately ahead of the beat. The truth is that nineteen times out of twenty it is quite impossible to tell which way it was played, and even when possible, more often than not the artistic difference is negligible.

(2) Except for the special cases noted further along, the long grace-note or appoggiatura is usually described as having exactly the value which its appearance suggests, its time being subtracted from the following note. Again it is printed in small type and with the stem turned up, but without a slanting line. Seldom does more than one occur at a time. If a chord appears with the principal note, the long grace-note is sounded with the chord before moving on to the principal note.

He who wonders why such a perverse method of notation was ever employed is asking a perfectly reasonable question. One reason that has been given is that the long grace-note is supposed to be slightly accented; at the time it was employed the accent sign > had not yet come into general use. Another reason that has been suggested is that by this mode of writing, the music could be made to look less *dissonant than it really is, the flimsiness of which needs no comment.

When the principal note is dotted, it is believed that the grace-note should take two-thirds of its value (a). In meters with 6, 9, and 12 beats, if a dotted note is tied, the grace-note takes the entire time of the dotted note (b). If the

Long grace-notes (appoggiatura type)

Special uses of the long grace-note

principal note is followed by a *rest, the grace-note takes the time of the principal note, which in turn takes the time of the rest, and the rest is completely eliminated (c).

Some musicians regard it a blessing that the long grace-note dropped out of use early in the nineteenth century. Since then, the word "grace-note" has always indicated the short variety, which provides effects that can be written in no other way.

Due to careless printing and editing, the distinction between the long and short grace-note is not always clear and reliable.

The use of the grace-note to indicate a vocal *glissando (portamento) is explained under glissando (1).

Other Notes in Fine Type. Small notes, about the size of grace-notes, but having a nominally definite rhythmic value, are often used in music engraving for purposes other than those just described. Among these are:

(A) In writing brief passages in which the rhythmic values are to be interpreted a bit freely, for example the fanciful "spills" and filigree-like passages often found in Romantic compositions, particularly those for the piano. (Chopin's works contain many examples.) (See also tempo rubato.)

(B) In writing *recitative-like passages for an instrument, or short *cadenzas where the rhythm is not too strict. In such passages there are often no *bar-lines, or they may be printed as dotted lines, rather than solid.

(C) To indicate that certain notes in chords are optional and hence may be omitted by less skillful players; the notes which are obligatory are engraved in ordinary (large) size. This employment is encountered chiefly in piano music.

(D) To indicate notes which may be substituted for those given; in other words, to indicate an alternate version of a passage. (See oppure and ossia.)

(E) In printing a suggested *realization of a *figured bass. The notes actually written by the composer are given in ordinary (large) size.

(F) To set off a melody from subordinate accompanying material in writing for the piano, using ordinary-sized notes for the former, small notes for the latter. This is a useful method of printing when the melody is located in the middle of the texture.

(G) In indicating the actual pitch of a *harmonic (1) for a bowed string instrument.

(H) In writing cues (2, 3).

(I) In writing the optional *accompaniment for a composition meant to be sung unaccompanied (*a cappella). Usually marked "for rehearsal only," such a piano part is merely a duplication of all the voice parts, arranged on two staffs.

●†gradevole. Pleasing, agreeable. Pronunciation: accent second syllable.

●†gradualmente. Gradually. Synonym: poco a poco.

●gramophone. Phonograph (chiefly British).

●†gran, †grande. Great, much. Con gran espressione, with great expression, with much expression.

●†grandezza. Bigness, greatness.

●†grandioso. In a grandiose, pompous, majestic manner. Passages so marked are nearly always loud. It might well be termed a more forceful synonym for maestoso.

●grand opera. The typical *opera that is sung throughout is a grand opera. The term is used in contrast to *opéra comique and *operetta.

●grand pause. See G. P.

●grand staff. The great staff.

●†grave. Extremely slow. See tempo marks.

●†gravità. Gravity, heaviness, seriousness, dignity. Pronunciation: accent last syllable.

●†grazia. Grace. Con grazia, with grace, gracefully.

Pronunciation: accent first styllable.

● †grazioso. Gracefully.

● great staff. The combined treble and bass staffs.
Its most familiar use is in writing for the piano
Synonym: grand staff, great stave.
See also brace, system.

Great staff
(Grand staff)

● Greek modes. See modes (2).

● Gregorian chant. One of the four "dialects" or styles of *chant that developed in the Western (or Roman) Christian church during the early centuries A. D. Gregorian chant (often called plainsong) is the official liturgical chant for use in the Roman Catholic services.
The name is derived from that of Pope Gregory I (sometimes called "The Great") (c. 540-604) during whose tenure (590-604) the chants were codified and organized. Gregory probably did not compose any of them; in fact, there is no positive evidence that he was especially interested in music.
The period 600-1000 has been called "the golden age of chant," since most of the Gregorian melodies came into existence during that time. However, due to the lack of a satisfactory system of notation--the need for which might not have been felt during earlier days --nothing was written down until about the eighth century. Gregorian chants as of today are a fixed quantity; there are about 3000 of them. No new ones are being composed, nor have any been written for at least 700 years.
Gregorian Modes (Church Modes). The scale basis or tonal organization of Gregorian chant is given under the heading modes (1), but it should be noted that only the first eight modes shown there apply to these melodies; that is, no chants are in the Aeolian or Ionian mode.

B-flat is recognized as an additional tone belonging to every mode. Thus it will be seen that Gregorian chants are built entirely from the tones C, D, E, F, G, A, B-flat, and B.
Authorship. All Gregorian chants are anonymous. It is almost certain that some of them are the work of more than one person-- communal compositions--in which they have a point in common with *folk-songs. Others are based on older melodies, Greek, Jewish, or possibly Byzantine (near-Eastern). Many are doubtless the work of monks and priests who out of piety and modesty refrained from signing their names. (Compare figured music.)
Rhythm. The fact that nearly all of the texts are from the Bible accounts for the wonderfully free and non-metrical rhythm of Gregorian chant, for this element is largely an outgrowth of the rhythm of the words. The absence of mechanical, regularly-recurring metric *accent is due to the circumstance that the Bible is prose; if it were poetry the chant melodies would probably be metrical, and the entire early history of music would be totally different. The student of Gregorian chant must first of all free his mind from the false notion that music must always be divided into *measures of uniform length to which a single *time-signature applies from beginning to end. True, time-signatures and *bar-lines could be inserted into the melody, but not in a symmetrical pattern; only occasionally would any two successive measures contain the same number of beats. This rhythmic irregularity is the ancestor of the frequently-changing time-signatures in so much of the music of our own century, notably that of Stravinsky.
The accompanying example of part

of a Gregorian chant will illustrate its asymmetrical rhythmic character. (A further example will be found in the chant fragment that is quoted in the entry neumes.) This passage could perhaps be supplied with bar-lines and with time-signatures, but the result would be far from regular; the time-signature would change often.

original purity of Gregorian chant. Nevertheless there are competing theories about interpretation that cannot be brushed aside lightly, although the Solesmes version has been accepted as correct and official by the church authorities. Undoubtedly it is the most beautiful and most musical interpretation;

Ky-ri - e e - le - i - son.

Typical Gregorian Chant passage

Expression. It will be noticed that several marks of expression, not found in other music, occur in the foregoing example (as well as in that quoted under neumes). Gregorian chant utilizes certain expressive effects peculiar only to it. These include a note that is softer than its neighbors (about the opposite of a *sforzando), a note that is probably intended to be sung with a slight *vibrato, a special effect called the ictus, and four types of bar-line of varying punctuating effect. Detailed explanation of all these is beyond the scope of an elementary dictionary. The reader should consult the preface to the *Liber Usualis.

The exact expressive style in which Gregorian chant was originally sung is a matter of conjecture rather than positive knowledge. It is, however, definitely known that it became progressively garbled and perverted, especially in rhythm, commencing around the thirteenth century or earlier, and continuing through the nineteenth. This was due in part to the fact that the congregation was once permitted to sing the chants. (At present this practice is discouraged unless the congregation has been given instruction in Gregorian style; otherwise chant-singing is entrusted to the priests and the choir.) The prolonged research made by the Benedictine monks at Solesmes, France is believed by many musicians to have led to the rediscovery of the proper manner of singing these melodies--to the restoration of the

hence whether it is the original manner of performance or not is perhaps beside the point.

The peculiar signs found in the appended chant quotation were developed at Solesmes to indicate those effects for which no sign had existed previously.

Emotion. The purpose of Gregorian chants is of course to enhance the texts that are used in the church services. In order that liturgical music should be strikingly distinct from secular music, the church authorities tried to exclude and avoid any stylistic features that are peculiar to secular melodies. One reason why the Aeolian and Ionian modes were shunned was because of their frequency in folk and secular music, including the melodies of the *troubadours and *minnesingers. Metrical rhythm, so characteristic of poetry, was also avoided due to its association with worldly music.

Since Gregorian chant is essentially church music--the most "churchly" and unworldly of all liturgical music --it is not emotional in an exciting, hectic, or breast-heaving manner; compared with the music of say Tschaikowsky, it does not seem emotional at all. However, it is far from inexpressive or cold. Its emotional expression is a delicate and subtle one, of a type that the listener almost has to learn to detect, but it is present none the

less. The developments in more recent music have all but deafened our
ears to it; hence the listener must
gradually attune himself to Gregorian
chant and learn to hear it on its own
terms.

Absence of Harmony. Gregorian
chants do not contain harmony. In
common with all early music, they
consist of an unharmonized melodic
line. Ideally they should be performed without the aid of any chords
from the organ or other instrument,
and by men's voices only. However,
the Roman Catholic Church realizes
that compromise with ideals is sometimes a practical necessity, and
hence choirs that find themselves unable to stay on pitch are permitted to
use an organ *accompaniment--prefer-
ably a rather well-subdued and subordinate one. Also, although the chants
should ideally be performed only with
men's voices, it is clear that in con-
vents women's voices must be used,
while under other conditions the use of
mixed voices is necessary; here the
women's voices will sound an *octave
above those of the men. In any case,
the voices must not sing in parts; anything in the way of *harmony is supplied entirely by the organ. A number
of different styles and theories of
chant accompaniment have arisen. In
large cathedrals where there is a
pronounced echo, the apparent naked-
ness of the unaccompanied chant melody
is considerably diminished.

Language. Since there is such a
close connection between the words and
the melody, Gregorian chants should
be sung only to the original Latin
words. Translation into English or
any other language destroys the intimate and very delicate relation that
seems to make a chant not a combination of words and music but a single,
indivisible entity.

Importance. Gregorian chant had
a profound influence on the development of music; through the sixteenth
century it was the dominant influence.
Its effect can still be detected; indeed
it has increased during our century.
The borrowing of chant melodies for
use in polyphonic music was once so
common as to be the rule, its
absence the exception. (See borrowed

melodies.) Gregorian chants are
still occasionally utilized by composers of today. (For example,
see the chant melody quoted in
the entry neumes, which is one
of two Gregorian chants that
Respighi employed in The Pines of
Rome.)

Further information can be
obtained from treatises on the
subject by Gregorio Suñol, Willi
Apel, and Peter Wagner, as well
as from books on music history and
musicology.

Although chiefly identified with
the Catholic church, Gregorian
chant is occasionally used in certain
Protestant churches. Several
Lutheran *chorales are based on
Gregorian melodies.

A lengthy chant quotation appears
in the entry syllables.

Synonyms: plain song, plain chant,
Gregorian song, Roman chant.

See also Liber Usualis, chant,
modes (1), Ambrosian chant, neumes.

●Gregorian modes. See modes (1).

●ground bass. See ostinato.
Variant form: ground.
Synonym: basso ostinato.

●groups. The names for different
numbers of performers, from one
through ten, are as follows:

one	solo
two	duet or duo
three	trio (occasionally terzetto)
four	quartet
five	quintet
six	sextet (occasionally sestet)
seven	septet
eight	octet
nine	nonet
ten	dixtuor (French)

The spellings quartette, quintette,
etc. are going out of use. Quartett,
quintett, etc. are incorrect in English;
they are the German spellings. 4^{tet}
(quartet), 5^{tet} (quintet), etc., are
abbreviations.

See also chamber-music groups,
ensemble, concerted number.

●†gruppetto. Name sometimes applied to the *trill, sometimes to the

*turn.

●güiro (Spanish). A Latin-American *percussion instrument of indefinite pitch. It consists of a notched gourd, over which a stick is scraped. Stravinsky writes for it in The Rite of Spring under the French name râpe guero.
    Pronunciation: gwé-rō.

●guitar. A plucked string (fretted) instrument. It is notated an octave higher than the sounds desired and its six strings are tuned as shown:

●"hairpins." Jocular term used among musicians in referring to the symbols for *crescendo and *diminuendo.
    Synonym: forks.

●half-note. See time-values.

●half staccato. See semi-staccato and staccato (3).

●half-step. On the piano, a half-step can be found by starting with any key and going to the first key either up or down, black or white.

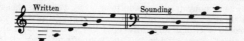

The lowest string is occasionally tuned to D rather than E.
    The instrument has a rather delicate and characteristically "strummed" *tone-color. Some guitarists use a *plectrum while others play with the bare fingers.
    Several *virtuosos have raised the guitar to the level of a serious solo instrument.
    It is sometimes called the Spanish guitar in contradistinction to the *Hawaiian guitar, an instrument of much less importance.
    Italian: chitarra (plural, chitarre). French: guitare. German: Gitarre (plural, Gitarren). Spanish: guitarra.
    Pronunciation: gǐ-tär'.

●†gusto. Taste, enjoyment, zest. Con gusto, tastefully, with zest.
    (Related English word: gustatory.)

H

●habanera (Spanish). A Spanish dance (originally Cuban) similar to (but older than) the *tango, though a little slower. The word is derived from the name of the city of Havana, Cuba.
    The French equivalent, havanaise, is sometimes substituted.
    Pronunciation: ä-bä-nä́-rä (the b somewhat like v).

This is the smallest *interval regularly used in Occidental music.
    The tones in the minor second and its *enharmonic equivalent the augmented prime are a half-step apart. (See intervals.)
    The *chromatic scale consists of nothing but half-steps.
    Synonyms: semitone, half-tone. Compare whole-step.

●half-tone. Same as half-step.

●half voice. See mezza voce.

●Hammerklavier. Old German name for the piano.
    Pronunciation: häm'-mer-klä-fēr'.

●hand horn. The obsolete *horn without *valves. See natural horn.

●harm. To be played as a *harmonic (1, 2, 3).

●harmonica. (1) A small flat instrument, held to the lips, in which the tone results from the player's breath passing over small metallic reeds (2) located inside.
    Although several artist performers on the harmonica have appeared before the public, it has practically no literature and its status is still

that of a musical toy.

Synonyms: mouth harmonica; and (all undesirable) mouth organ, mouth harp, French harp, · and even--among the uninformed--harp.

(2) A now-obsolete instrument invented by Benjamin Franklin which consisted of tuned water-glasses played by finger friction.   No less a person than Mozart wrote two compositions employing it (usually replaced by an organ in present-day performances).

● harmonic rhythm.   The relative frequency of harmonic change within a composition.   In some music a single basic harmony tends to continue through several measures; in other music there is a completely different chord for every *beat or two.   The first is an example of a slow harmonic rhythm even though the *tempo might be actually fast, the latter of a fast harmonic rhythm even though the tempo might be actually slow.

The exact repetition of a chord, no matter how rapid, has no effect on the quickness of harmonic rhythm, nor does the repetition of a single basic harmony in various *inversions or other forms.   Only a new chord, with a different *root, causes a change.

Measured purely in seconds, changes of harmony probably occur at about the same speed in slow pieces as in fast ones.   There will be less material per harmony in the former instance than in the latter.

In typical harmonic rhythm, changes of chord usually occur in a fairly regular pattern.   A passage in which the harmony changes on every beat for eight measures, then stays on a single basic harmony throughout the next eight, is rather exceptional.

● harmonics.   (1) String Instruments.   Tones of thin, ethereal, flute-like quality that are possible on the bowed *string instruments by touching the string lightly (at certain places only) instead of pressing it all the way down to the *fingerboard.   The sounds that result are often of a different pitch from that obtained by pressing down the string all the way, as will be seen from the discussion which follows.

Harmonics are classified as natural and artificial depending on whether one or two fingers must be placed on the string to produce the tone.   Natural harmonics will be explained first.

The following is a table of natural harmonics obtainable on the D string of the violin or viola.

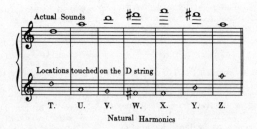

Natural Harmonics

The method of obtaining natural harmonics can also be expressed as follows.

In artificial harmonics, two fingers are placed on the same string, the lower pressing it to

	Spot Where Touched Above the Open String	Actual Sound Above Spot Where Touched	Actual Sound Above Open String
T.	octave	same sound	octave
U.	perfect fifth	octave	octave and perfect fifth
V.	perfect fourth	octave and perfect fifth	two octaves
W.	major third	two octaves	two octaves and major third
X.	minor third	two octaves and major third	two octaves and perfect fifth
Y.	major sixth	octave and perfect fifth	two octaves and major third
Z.	octave and perfect fifth	same sound	octave and perfect fifth

It will be seen that T and Z give the same tone that would be heard if the string were pressed all the way down; the only difference then is purely one of *tone-color. Method Y is an alternate for W, while Z is an alternate for U. Method X is unreliable, hence seldom used.

Natural harmonics are indicated (A) by showing the point where touched with a diamond-shaped note, or (B) by indicating the actual pitch with a little 0 above, or (C) by combining these two methods, though omitting the 0. The abbreviation harm. is often added.

the fingerboard, the upper touching it lightly. The lower finger has the effect of a temporary end-of-the-string. The sounds that result depend on the interval formed between the fingers; they are the same as those obtained with like intervals in natural harmonics. However, it is not possible to touch an interval larger than the perfect fifth, and even that is possible only on the violin and perhaps viola, for the fingers are unable to stretch far enough to span the larger intervals. Thus the only practicable artificial harmonics are those made with the

      (A)   (B)   (C)

perfect fifth, perfect fourth, and major third, plus possibly the minor third. The second of these is probably the most frequently employed.

Artificial Harmonics

Artificial harmonics are very difficult on the double-bass.

In artificial harmonics, the touched note is written with a diamond head, the pressed note in the ordinary manner. Often the actual pitch is added in small type or in parentheses above --three notes to represent one pitch! It will be apparent that most harmonics are of relatively high pitch. The range of all the bowed string instruments can be extended upward by means of harmonics. However, all ranges shown in the various string instrument entries are those possible without recourse to harmonics, that is, by use of the normal type of tone only.

Both natural and artificial harmonics are difficult to play loud.

(2) Harp. Sounds obtained on the *harp by lightly touching the string at its midpoint, while plucking with the other hand. The tone-color is dreamy, delicate, and other-worldly, but faint. The tones to be so played are usually written an octave below actual pitch, with a small 0 over every note. Some composers, however, have written the actual pitches, plus 0 above, so that the intentions are not always clear to the player.

(3) Flute. Sounds obtained on the *flute by *overblowing it a perfect twelfth rather than the usual octave. The quality is somewhat thinner than that of the normal tones. They are seldom used. A small 0 indicates their employment.

(4) Brass Instruments. The *open tones (or natural tones) of the brass instruments, i. e., those obtained

without the use of the *valves (or of the *slide of the trombone).

(5) The individual tones in the *harmonic series. Synonyms: overtones, partials.

Abbreviation (for usages 1, 2, and 3): harm.

● harmonic series. The various additional sounds which automatically result when any musical *tone (1) is sounded; the overtones; the partials. All are higher in pitch than the sounded tone, which is known as the *fundamental (2) or generator. A musical tone is not a simple sound (as the ear accepts it) but actually a composite of many pitches blended together, which the ear has learned to accept as one tone. The sounding body vibrates in segments as well as for its total length.

Expressed in different words, the matter is this:

When any tone is played or sung, there go with it other sounds of which the ear is not particularly aware, but whose presence can be proved with scientific instruments. These additional tones all lie above the tone that is sung or played and which generates them. They are called overtones, harmonics, aliquot tones, or partials. The intervals between them remain constant, the entire series shifting up and down as the sounded tone (fundamental) is moved up or down. The overtones cannot be altered in any way, nor can they be suppressed or strengthened except by various artificial tricks performed with the aid of microphones and the science of electronics.

The tones found in the harmonic

series will be demonstrated twice. At first the intervals will be enumerated as they occur successively, then their relation to the fundamental will be given.

Successive Relation. Regardless what tone is sounded, the first overtone has the pitch an octave higher. The tone which is played or sung (the fundamental) is given the number 1. The first overtone is an octave above the fundamental and is given the number 2.

No. 3 (the second overtone) is a perfect fifth above 2. (See intervals.)

4 is a perfect fourth above 3.

5 is a major third above 4.

6 is a minor third above 5.

7 is slightly out-of-tune; it is a little less than a minor third above 6 (but much more than a major second above it).

8 is a little more than a major second above 7 (and a perfect fourth above 6).

9 is a major second above 8.

10 is a major second above 9.

11 is more than a minor second, yet less than a major second, above 10; it is about a *quarter-tone between the minor second and the major second.

12 is about a quarter-tone more than a minor second above 11; however it is exactly a minor third above 10.

13 is also out-of-tune; it is a little less than a major second above 12.

14 is a little more than a half-step above 13, but since 13 is a little low in pitch, so is 14.

15 is slightly more than a half-step above 14; it is exactly a major third above 12.

16 is a half-step above 15.

The overtones by no means stop with no. 16, but it is neither practical nor necessary to discuss those that lie beyond. Suffice it to say that theoretically the overtones continue infinitely, though eventually they become too high to be detected by the human ear (that is, they reach the *ultrasonic stage).

It should be observed that they grow closer and closer together as the series continues.

Relation to Fundamental. Let us now state the series in a different way: Instead of listing the pitch-difference between each overtone and its nearest neighbor, let us consider the interval between the fundamental and the various overtones.

1 to 2--octave.

1 to 3--perfect twelfth (that is, octave plus a perfect fifth).

1 to 4--two octaves.

1 to 5--two octaves and a major third.

1 to 6--two octaves and a perfect fifth.

1 to 7--a little less than two octaves and a minor seventh (but much more than two octaves and a major sixth).

1 to 8--three octaves.

1 to 9--three octaves and a major second.

1 to 10--three octaves and a major third.

1 to 11--more than three octaves and a perfect fourth but less than three octaves and an augmented fourth.

1 to 12--three octaves and a perfect fifth.

1 to 13--a little less than three octaves and a major sixth.

1 to 14--a little less than three octaves and a minor seventh.

1 to 15--three octaves and a major seventh.

1 to 16--four octaves.

The following three series will illustrate. (See Example 1.)

The various tones which are out-of-tune have been indicated as whole-notes and a minus sign has been placed over them to show that their pitch is too low rather than too high.

Mathematical Interrelation. Observe that the fundamental is numbered 1, the first overtone 2, etc. The reason for so doing is dictated by convenience. It can be proved with scientific

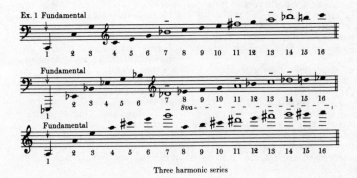

Three harmonic series

instruments that the number of times each overtone vibrates is in the exact mathematical ratio of these figures, provided the numbering is adopted as shown.

It is known, for instance, that if any two tones are an octave apart, the upper vibrates exactly twice as fast at the lower (in other words the lower vibrates exactly half as fast as the upper). For instance, the A above middle C--the tone on which the orchestra "tunes up"--vibrates 440 times per second. From this we can calculate the number of vibrations for all the A's on the piano keyboard. (Example 2.)

The third overtone series shown earlier in Example 1 has as its fundamental a sound that vibrates 220 times per second. Then the vibration-rate of 3 must be 660; of 5, 110; of 9, 1980; of out-of-tune no. 7, 1540, etc. Thus if we know the number of vibrations in one tone in the series, we can compute those for all of the remaining tones.

Note the octave relationship between all tones having the ratio 1:2, that is 2-4, 4-8, 8-16, 3-6, 6-12, 5-10. Even out of-tune no. 7 bears the octave relationship with no. 14, which is equally out-

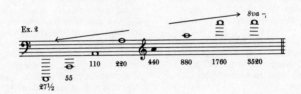

Ex. 2

27½ 55 110 220 440 880 1760 3520

Ex. 3

In C series   In E-flat series   In A series

of-tune. We can determine the identity of some of the overtones above no. 16 by this method, for instance no. 20 in each of the three series in Example 1 will be those shown in Example 3. (The fact that the last of these tones is not playable on the piano is of no importance here; the sound exists in nature, regardless of whether the piano can produce it or not.) Note the similar relationships between all tones possessing the same mathematical ratio; for example take the 1:3 ratio and compare 2-6, 4-12, 5-15, 3-9, etc.-- each pair of tones an octave and a perfect fifth apart.

Demonstration. Now it has already been stated that the ear is rarely conscious of the presence of overtones. However their existence can be demonstrated by a simple experiment at the piano. If the player silently depresses any of the keys in an overtone series (except those which are out-of-tune) and then strikes the fundamental several times quite loud and *staccato, the tones that correspond to the depressed keys will commence to sound of their own accord. This is a species of *sympathetic vibration. The demonstration will not succeed, however, if the piano is not well in tune. (See Example 4.)

Importance of the Overtones. Overtones are the element that makes one instrument or voice sound different from another. If we could equip the human ear with a filter that would obliterate all overtones, allowing only the fundamental to come through, it would be impossible for us to tell the difference between a trumpet, a clarinet, a violin, or any other instruments that can be mentioned.

An experiment with such a filter is of course not practicable for the average person, but there is one familiar device that slightly approaches the effect, namely the tone-control on a radio or phonograph, which suppresses overtones to a certain extent. The further it is turned to the right, the more overtones it lets through, and the more brilliant and sharply-differentiated the sound. But as it is turned to the left, it gradually suppresses more and more overtones, and instruments begin to sound more nearly alike. Now if it were possible to continue turning the tone-control to the left, much farther than it is built to go, there would come a point when all overtones would be eliminated, and the sound would have a "flat," neutral character; it would not only be

Ex. 4 Depress silently and hold   These will sound of their own accord.

impossible to tell one instrument from another, but even to distinguish a voice from an instrument, unless one could hear the words enunciated by the voice; however even the words would be nearly indistinguishable.

The element that causes any instrument to sound different from all others is the fact that the various overtones of a given instrument differ in strength from those of any instrument to which it is compared. Certain overtones are strong, others weak, still others almost completely absent on one instrument, while different ones are strong, weak, and absent on the instrument being compared. Briefly, no two instruments have exactly the same pattern of relative overtone strengths. The oboe has one pattern, the violin a different one, the clarinet differs from both, while the horn (i. e., French horn) is mutually at variance with all of them. And so on, through the entire list of instruments, of voices, of organ *stops. This also accounts for the difference in tone-quality among various instruments of the same kind; for instance a violin made by Stradivarius sounds different from a cheap violin by reason of having a somewhat different inter-relation among the overtones.

On some electronic organs there are draw-bars that control the overtones to a certain extent. It is possible to sound a perfectly "pure" tone--one without overtones--and then to add them in various relative strengths. A tremendous number of *tone-colors can be concocted artificially by this means.

Another respect in which the harmonic series is important is that the tones that can be sounded on a *brass instrument by varying the lip-tension are those made up from it; these are the so-called *open tones or natural tones. For instance, the notes shown in the first harmonic series above are the written open tones of the *horn (French horn); the actual pitches are a perfect fifth lower on the horn in F. However the fundamental is unplayable, so the practical open tones of the horn are represented by the written pitches of nos. 2 through 16.

By transposing this same series of notes down a *whole-step, and venturing no higher than 8 or 9 (10 at the most), one has the open tones of the tenor *trombone (the player would term these notes "in first position").

In the second series, nos. 2 through 6 or possibly 8 happen to be the open tones of the *tuba in E-flat.

The open tones of the bugle in G--the only tones it can play-- are shown in the entry bugle.

It will be observed that the tones playable as the *harmonics (1) on the bowed string instruments, taken in order, are tones of the harmonic series.

Synonyms: overtone series, partials (1), harmonics (5), chord of nature.

See also acoustics, intervals, resultant, sympathetic vibration, tone-color. In addition see harmonics.

●harmonium. A keyboard instrument in which the tone is produced by metal *reeds (2) supplied with air from a foot- or motor-operated bellows; a reed organ.

The "touch" or manner of playing is the same as that for the *organ.

The typical instrument has a single manual and no pedalboard, though some harmoniums are built with two manuals, and a few boast a pedalboard. There are always a number of *stops, although they tend to sound more nearly alike than those of the organ. Some are of 4-foot and 16-foot pitch, but most are 8-foot (see the entry organ for explanation).

The instrument is built in a number of sizes, and the *range depends on the size.

The harmonium has been unfairly ridiculed by musicians as well as laymen who have heard it badly played, probably with piano touch rather than organ touch; when well played the instrument is quite delightful. Others are prejudiced because of an absurd and snobbish notion that it is outdated, due to its immoderate popularity during the Victorian period.

The popular name "old-fashioned organ" is misleading, for the harmoium is actually much newer than the organ.

Synonyms: melodeon, reed organ, American organ, parlor organ, cottage organ, cabinet organ.

● harmonize. To supply a melody with appropriate *harmony (1). The particular chords employed are not fitted in arbitrarily, for a good melody suggests its own harmonies-- certain chords and no others.

● harmony. (1) Musical tones sounded simultaneously; musical sounds in their vertical aspect. The unit of harmony is the *chord.

In the layman's mind, harmony suggests only pleasing combinations, but broadly speaking it embodies all combinations, including the harshest and most *dissonant.

*Octaves of themselves are not considered harmony, no more so than *unisons.

The careful placing of dissonant and *consonant harmonies imparts a forward-moving quality to music because of the effect of tension followed by release, perhaps as much so as does the rhythm, and more so than the melody.

Harmony is one of the three essential components of Occidental music, the other two being melody and rhythm. Nearly all *Oriental music is devoid of it, at least in the sense familiar to Europeans and Americans. It was also absent from ancient music, as far as is known.

The distinction between harmony and *counterpoint is explained under counterpoint.

See also: chord, triad, seventh-chord, homophonic, polyphonic, intervals, texture, sonority (2), Roman numerals.

(2) A subject taught in colleges, *conservatories, and some high-schools, which treats of the building and connecting of chords, the supplying of harmony to a given melody or bass, etc. Musicians often point out that the relationship of this subject to music is very similar to that of grammar to literature.

The expressions close harmony and open harmony are discussed under those headings.

Synonyms: part-writing, thorough-bass (2).

See also keyboard harmony.

● harness bells. Same as sleigh bells.

● harp. The only plucked string instrument regularly used in the orchestra. Its large, light wooden frame (usually painted gold) is of a unique, irregular shape. The diagonal piece of wood which forms its lower end is hollow, and has much to do with the resonance of the instrument. The strings are stretched from this piece upward to the curving top-piece.

The harp has this tremendous range:

Although the volume is quite weak, the *tone-color is so distinct that the harp usually "cuts through" surprisingly well. The sound has an arresting quality that immediately attracts the hearer's attention, plus a calm, classic poise unmatched by any other instrument. The tone is considerably different from that of the bowed string instruments played *pizzicato.

A delightful color-effect can be produced through the use of *harmonics (2), which have a dreamy, otherworldly sound. They are obtainable only in the middle register of the instrument, and are notated (usually) an octave below the sounds desired, with the addition of a little 0 over each note.

The mechanism of the harp is completely different from that of any other instrument. One peculiarity is that certain pairs of notes which are *enharmonic equivalents may actually be played simultaneously on two different strings sounding in *unison, thus giving more volume than is possible with only one. This effect can be obtained on any tones except A, D, and G.

The harp has seven pedals, used to produce chromatic *inflections of the various tones. Each of these controls the pitch of all the strings of a single letter-name--one pedal for all the A's, another for all the B's, a third for all the C's, etc. In addition to its "home" position, any pedal can be pressed downward into one or the other of two notches. When not in either notch, all strings controlled by the pedal in question are flatted; for instance if the C pedal is in "home" position, every C on the harp becomes C-flat. When any pedal is placed in the first notch, all strings of that particular letter-name are raised from flat to natural in every octave; when it is placed in the second notch, they are sharped. It will be apparent that each string does duty for three pitches, according to the way the pedal is set.

Single tones, *chords (either *rolled or with all tones struck simultaneously), diatonic *scales, and *glissandi (3) are all effective, while *arpeggios are so characteristic that the term itself is derived from the Italian word for

harp. *Chromatic scales are unplayable, except in very slow *tempos.

Although the harp is of great antiquity, the instrument as we know it today was not perfected until 1810.

For some odd reason, American orchestras prefer women as harp-players.

The Irish harp should be looked upon almost as a different instrument. It is much simpler and more primitive in development than the orchestral harp.

An instrument called the chromatic harp has been invented in which a separate string is used for each tone. The strings form an X as they pass from the upper to the lower frame.

Italian: arpa (plural, arpe). French: harpe. German: Harfe (plural, Harfen). Spanish: arpa. The player is called a harpist. (The word harper suggest a minstrel who recites poetry to music.)

● harpsichord. A keyboard instrument which was the immediate precursor of the piano. Like the piano, the sound comes from wire strings. It had tremendous vogue from the sixteenth through the middle eighteenth century, and is at present enjoying a vigorous revival for use in performing the keyboard music of that era.

The *tone-color is harsh, brilliant, and twangy, but its salty and slightly nasal sound is ideal for *Baroque and *Rococo music.

When a *key (2) is pressed, it operates a vertical piece of wood known as a jack, near the top of which is located a *plectrum made of leather, quill, or metal, which twangs the strings.

There are several *pedals which function exactly like the couplers of the *organ, and may be regarded as *stops. One coupler automatically will produce all sounds an *octave higher than the keys that are pressed; another produces those an octave lower. Their function is exactly that of the 4-foot and 16-foot couplers of the

organ. By using these two in combination, the pressing of a single key
will sound three tones. Loud effects
are obtained with these coupler-
pedals. Another effect can be obtained
from the so-called lute stop which
gives a more delicate, harp-like
sound.

Most harpsichords have two manuals
(keyboards). By setting a different
pedal combination for each, sudden
alternations of loud and soft are
obtainable which are excellent for
*antiphonal effects.

The harpsichord cannot make
subtle gradations of tone; *crescendos
and *diminuendos are not possible on
it. The amount of force exerted by
the player causes almost no difference
in volume, just as on the organ it
causes no difference whatever. The
only possible variations in volume are
those produced by the afore-mentioned
pedals, and these are sharp, abrupt
changes rather than gradual shadings.
(The full name of the piano--piano-
forte, meaning "soft loud"--arises
from the fact that that instrument,
compared with the harpsichord, can be
played at any *dynamic level, depending on the player's pressure on the
keys. This effect was a novelty when
the piano was in its infancy.)

The harpsichord's sustaining power
is even less than that of the piano.

On the credit side, the instrument
has the advantage of a light, quick
action. The keys "dip" a shorter
distance than those of the piano, and
less muscular effort is required to
play it. Hence music of a nimble,
quick nature is well suited to it, and
can be executed with ease. *Trills
and *mordents for the fourth and
fifth fingers (see fingering (1)),
awkward on the piano, are fairly
easy on the harpsichord.

The virginal and the *spinet might
well be considered "small harpsichords"; in fact the terms harpsichord, spinet, and virginal have
sometimes been carelessly used
interchangeably. On the other hand,
the *clavichord should never be
confused with the harpsichord; except
for being a keyboard instrument, it

in no way resembles the harpsichord in either appearance or
*tone-color.

On some harpsichords, the colors
of the keys are the reverse of the
usual plan.

When no harpsichord is available, sometimes stiff paper is
interwound among the strings of
a piano, under the supposition
that the piano can thus be made
to sound "just like a harpsichord."
The less said about this detestable practice, and its alleged
resemblance to harpsichord tone-
quality, the better.

Italian: clavicembalo or gravicembalo. French: clavecin.
German: Cembalo. Spanish: clave.

● hautbois d'amour. See oboe
d'amore.

Pronunciation: ō-bwä dä-mōōr.

● hautboy. Old name for the
*oboe.

Pronunciation: hō-boi or ō-boi.

● Hawaiian guitar. A form of
guitar, apparently originating in
the Hawaiian Islands, with six
strings usually tuned:

Prominent in the method of playing
the instrument is a small steel
rod, laid across the strings by the
left hand, which takes the place of
fingering the strings. By sliding
this rod along the strings a saccharine *glissando (1) (portamento)
can be obtained.

It comes as something of a shock
that several normally reliable
reference books indicate that the
Hawaiian guitar is the same instrument as the *ukulele. On the
contrary, the size, appearance,
tuning, tone-color, and technique
of the Hawaiian guitar are entirely
different from those of the ukulele.

●head voice. The upper, smooth-toned, clear *register of the singing voice. The term does not indicate that such tones are actually produced in the head; the expression is merely a convention.

●heavy music. Explained under light music.

●heckelphone. A double-reed *wood-wind instrument of the *oboe type, pitched an octave lower than the oboe. It is notated an octave above the sounds desired. Range:

●Heldentenor (German). Heroic tenor. Term applied to the leading tenor role in certain *music dramas by Wagner because of the sweeping, rather bold style. Examples are the role of Tristan in Tristan and Isolde and of Siegfried in Die Walküre, Siegfried, and Götterdämmerung.
     Pronunciation: hĕl-dĕn-tā-nŏr.

●helicon. A *tuba of the *"Sousaphone" type.

●hemidemisemiquaver. Sixty-

Its *tone-color is even drier, darker, and more cheerless than that of the *English horn, which it somewhat resembles.
     Oboists sometimes learn the heckelphone as a side-line instrument.
     Variant spelling: heckelphon.
     Synonyms: bass oboe, baritone oboe.

fourth-note. See British terminology.

●hemiola. A rhythmic relationship characterized by values in the proportion 3:2. *Syncopation is involved. Typical examples are shown below. In the *courante, the apparent change from 3-2 time to 6-4 at

the *cadences is an example of hemiola.

●heterophony. A device wherein one voice (or instrument) presents a simultaneous and varied form of a melody that is being performed by a different voice or instrument; the melody appears in two forms at the same time.

It is well known that heterophony exists in certain types of music which are nominally without harmony, such as Oriental and ancient Greek music. Of course the tones which depart from the strict form of the melody produce harmony of a sort; the Greeks called them "dissenting tones. "

●hi-fi. A colloquialism for high fidelity. See fidelity.

●high fidelity. See fidelity, phonograph.
    Synonym (colloquialism): hi-fi.

●high voice. *Soprano or *tenor. This term is convenient in speaking of *songs printed in various *keys (1). The fact that the tenor voice is approximately an octave lower than the soprano, and that the soprano is the highest female voice and the tenor the highest male voice, makes this a convenient generic term.
    Compare low voice, medium voice.

Heterphony

Pronunciation: hĕt-ẽr-ŏf-ɏ-nĭ.

●hexachord. (1) One of the three scales of six tones recognized by medieval theorists, including Guido of Arezzo. The natural hexachord contains the tones C, D, E, F, G, and A. The soft contains F, G, A, B-flat, C, and D. The hard contains G, A, B, C, D, and E. A hexachord may be considered a *scale which lacks the *leading-tone (seventh degree).
    (2) Half of a twelve tone row. (See twelve tone system.)

●hexatonic scale. A scale of six tones which represents a midway development between the *pentatonic and the ordinary *diatonic scale. Compared to the latter, the hexatonic scale lacks either the fourth or the seventh degree.

●hold. Same as fermata.
    The direction to "hold full value" --a caution against releasing too soon or calling attention to the fact that a note is not to be performed *staccato--is tenuto (abbreviated ten.) or the symbol ⁀ placed over or under the note.

●home-and-community songs. Simple and well-known songs frequently used in the home, at school, at public gatherings, etc., similar in style to *folk-songs. They can quite properly be termed "popular songs, " though this is not the usual connotation of that term; see popular (3). They are sometimes called "composed folk-songs. "
    Stephen Foster is the best-known American writer of this type of music.

Patriotic songs are of this type.
(See national anthems.)

● home tone. Same as tonic. Although
a rather childlike expression, it is
quite apt.

● homophonic. Music which consists
of a predominant *melody with an
entirely subordinate *accompaniment
is termed homophonic. Although
compositions of this type are more
familiar than those based on *counter-
point--which may be termed approximately the "opposite" of homophonic
style--they nevertheless represent a
much later development in the history
of music. Homophonic music did not
make a clear-cut appearance until
the invention of *opera at the beginning
of the seventeenth century.

During the *Classical and *Romantic
periods (that is, the late eighteenth
and nineteenth centuries) homophonic
style predominated. One of the
healthiest trends in music of the
*Modern period is composers' re-
awakening to the value of counterpoint
and their turning their backs on compositions of unrelieved homophonic
character.

The type of homophonic style often
found in early opera is sometimes
called *monody (adjective form,
monodic).

The noun form is homophony (pronounced hō-mŏf-ō̆-nĭ).

Variant form: homophonous.

Synonyms: melody-and-accompaniment style, harmonic style.

Antonyms: polyphonic, contrapuntal,
counterpoint.

Pronunciation: hŏm-ō̆-fŏn-ĭk or
hō-mō̆-fŏn-ĭk.

● hook. See flag.

● hopak. A lively Russian dance of
boisterous character, usually in 2-4
time. It is generally danced by men,
in a squatting position, kicking their
feet forward, and with their arms
folded.

Variant form: gopak.

● horn. (1) A brass instrument,
somewhat circular in shape, with
three *valves and a conical
(funnel-shaped) mouthpiece. It
is often called the French horn.
Some musicians maintain that its
tone-quality suggests that it should
be classified as a *woodwind instrument, rather than brass, but its
mechanism is strictly that of the
brass family, not to mention its
appearance.

Due to its versatility, the horn
is undoubtedly the most useful of
all the *brass instruments. Its
soft tones are wonderfully mellow,
dreamy, and almost melting, its
crisp *staccato sounds suggest the
brisk tang of a frosty morning
(due perhaps to its relation to the
hunting horn), while its loud
sounds are full, resonant, and
"brassy"; yet the instrument has
a dignified, noble character at
all times.

Transposition. Nowadays the
horn is always treated as an F
instrument; that is, it is notated
a perfect fifth (see intervals)
higher than the sounds desired,
and most of the tones are written
with the treble *clef. The lowest
tones, however, are notated with
the bass clef, and are usually
written an octave too low; that is,
the notation appears a perfect
fourth lower than the sounds
desired. Some composers, however,
write all notes--bass and treble
clef alike--a perfect fifth above
the actual sounds.

For reasons that reach far back
into the history of the instrument,
but which are hardly valid today,
it is customary to dispense with
*key-signatures in writing for the
horn; all *accidentals are written
in as needed.

Types of Instrument. Horn-
players in the United States use
three different types of instrument,
depending on personal preference.

The single F horn is the type
having the ideal and typical horn

tone-quality. Its range is: blocking the passage. The pitch

The single B-flat horn produces the highest tones with greater ease than the single F horn, yet it can also reach a few tones below the lowest possible on that instrument. However, its tone-quality is somewhat inferior, being rather reminiscent of that of the trombone. It is always written for as though it were in F; the transposition hence is the same as already described. Some players prefer this type of instrument to the foregoing or to the double horn (see below). The range of the single B-flat horn is:

is automatically raised a half-step; hence the player fingers the instrument a half-step lower than usual in order to obtain the correct note. Called stopped tones, these sounds when played loud are wiry, eerie, and sinister, suggestive of something menacing in the distance. The terms chiuso, bouché(s), cuivré, or gestopft may appear in place of +.

Obsolete Types. Mention has already been made that the horn is always treated today as a transposing instrument in F. Formerly

Theoretically it should be able to reach low E actual pitch, but the tones below the lowest shown here are difficult and risky.

The double horn is essentially the F instrument with an additional amount of tubing which can be thrown into operation by pressing a special valve, temporarily making it a B-flat instrument. It has the combined range and resources of the two single type horns, but there is the disadvantage of the increased weight caused by the extra tubing.

Right Hand. The right hand is normally kept part way in the *bell (2) to quiet the tone; it is taken out only for very loud passages.

When a cross + is written over a note, the player puts his hand as far into the bell as he can get it,

it was possible by means of *crooks to place the instrument in any key, but today their use is unknown, except that occasionally the E-flat crook is still seen in the *band. See natural horn; see also transposing instruments, crook, valve.

Italian: corno (plural, corni). French: cor. German: Horn (plural, Hörner). Spanish: corno, cuerno, or trompa (de armonía).

The player is known simply as a horn player. Attempts to introduce the word hornist have (perhaps fortunately) met with little success.

(2) The alto horn—a totally different instrument from the ordinary, or French horn—is described under that heading; the baritone horn under baritone (2); the saxhorn, flügelhorn, and post horn under

those headings. The name bass horn is sometimes undesirably applied to the *tuba. The English horn and basset horn are of course not "horns" at all; each is described under its proper heading.

(3) The word horn is undesirably used by uninformed laymen as a generic term for any *brass instrument. The player of a woodwind as well as brass instrument may often refer to his instrument as a "horn" in a humorous and affectionate way, well aware that strictly speaking his nomenclature is quite inaccurate.

● "horn fifths." A conventional name given to the succession of *intervals: minor sixth, perfect fifth, and major third, the upper voice moving scale-wise. The name arises from the fact that before the invention of *valves,

Beethoven's Fifth ("Emperor") Piano Concerto, first movement, and is written a major sixth higher than here shown, since it is to be played on horns in E-flat (see transposing instruments).

● hornpipe. A type of English dance, fairly lively, in 3-2 or 4-4 time. It was often used by sailors, being danced by an individual with his arms folded.

● humoresque. A humorous composition.
  Variant spelling: humoreske.

● hunting horn. A primitive brass instrument without *valves or *slide. It is the ultimate ancestor of the present-day *horn (French horn) and is quite similar to the

the foregoing intervals were readily playable on the *natural horns and trumpet. The effectiveness of music in this style when played on brass instruments is so great that the advent of valves by no means induced composers to discard the use of "horn fifths."
  The following passage is typical of "horn fifths" style. It occurs in

*natural horn (hand horn) that was in use up through the early nineteenth century.
  As its name suggests, groups of hunters used to play the instrument for signaling purposes when in the woods.

● hurdy-gurdy. A portable instrument in which the sound is produced

by strings set into vibration by
turning a rosined wheel with a crank.
In addition to the melody strings,
the hurdy-gurdy has two or more
strings which supply a *drone bass.

The instrument was known as
early as the tenth century.

It is unfortunate that the name
hurdy-gurdy is sometimes carelessly
given to the grind-organ (hand organ).

● hymn. Strictly speaking, a hymn
is a literary (not musical) work, for
the purpose of praise or devotion,
with a religious or patriotic sentiment. When of a religious character,
the text is the original creation of
some poet rather than an excerpt
from the Bible.

The musical setting of a hymn,
normally for four voice-parts (soprano,
alto, tenor, and bass) is properly
known as a *hymn-tune, though the
term hymn is also widely if rather
carelessly used.

Patriotic hymns are discussed under
national anthems.

● hymnody, hymnology. A systematic
study of *hymns (hymn-tunes), their
classification, history, use, etc.

● hymn-tune. The musical setting of
a *hymn, normally in four parts--
soprano, alto, tenor, and bass--and
without an independent instrumental
accompaniment.

Since totally different texts are
often sung to the same hymn-tune, it
is given an arbitrary name, this
being the title for the music regardless of the words that appear with it.
Well-known hymn-tunes are named
Nicea, Moscow, St. Anne, Old One
Hundredth, Aurelia, and the like.

At the top of each hymn-tune it
is customary to print formulas such
as 8.7.8.7.4.7., 7.6.7.6.D., 6.6.6.
6., S.M., C.M., L.M., or S.M.
D. These refer to the number of
syllables in each line of the text.
Thus, if 8.7.8.7.4.7. appears,

there will be eight syllables in
the first line of the text, seven
in the second, eight in the third,
and so on, and a six-line stanza
is indicated. S.M. is the abbreviation for Short Metre, the
conventional name for the pattern
6.6.8.6. L.M. stands for Long
Metre or 8.8.8.8., while C.M.
stands for Common Metre or
8.6.8.6. At all times the indication D. means double; hence
S.M.D. or Short Metre, Double
is the name for an eight-line
stanza in the pattern 6.6.8.6.6.6.
8.6.

Compare chorale.

See also processional, recessional.

I

● †i. The (plural).
Variant forms: gli, le.

● idée fixe (French). See cyclic
form.
Pronunciation: ē-dā fēks.

● idiom. The things which an
instrument plays well and readily,
and which sound natural and good
on it; the vernacular of an instrument; the material which is
indigenous to it. Thus we say
that *"trills are idiomatic to the
flute," *"arpeggios are in the
idiom of the harp," "repeated tones
are idiomatic for brass instruments," "on the oboe, arpeggios
are not idiomatic," etc.

● †il. The (masculine definite
article).

● imitation. The repetition of a
melodic fragment by a *"voice"
other than the one that initiated it.
The imitative passage usually overlaps on itself.

Imitation may occur at any *interval. It may be exact (strict) or

Imitation in Schumann's *Nachtstück in F,* middle section

free; the former is the more usual.

The distinction between imitation and *canon is one of length; a passage of imitation may continue for only three to ten notes, while a canon persists for quite a number of measures. In addition a canon is nearly always strict while imitation is rather frequently free. Nevertheless imitation may be rather accurately regarded as "a short canon"; indeed the term is sometimes extended so as to include all canons, *fugues, and *inventions.

Imitation may occur at any point during a composition, but is most frequent at the beginning, or at the beginning of a subdivision within the work. Its employment at such places was extremely common during the *Renaissance and *Baroque periods. Many contemporary composers have returned to this procedure.

● †impercettibilmente. Imperceptibly.

● †impetuoso. Impetuously.
Variant form: impetuosamente.

● †impresario. A concert manager, especially the manager of an opera company.
Plural: impresarios or impresari.
Pronunciation: accent third syllable.

● impressionism. A term borrowed from painting to refer to a style of music which arose during the 1890's and continued into the early part of the twentieth century. Impressionism was largely a French innovation and is chiefly associated with Debussy and Ravel.

Impressionistic style is characterized by delicacy, color effects, understatement, and avoidance of the extreme emotionalism typical of much of the *Romantic music which had preceded. It is often delightfully shadowy and vague. Ruggedness and virility are not very typical. It places much emphasis on *harmony, but comparatively little on *rhythm and almost none on *melody, in fact it seems to be almost "tuneless." *Ninth-chords, *seventh-chords other than the dominant and diminished seventh, *parallelisms, *non-functional harmony, augmented *triads, the *whole-tone scale, and occasional touches of *modality are highly characteristic. Compared to the harmonic practice of the preceding era, the seventh-chords, ninth-chords, and augmented triads do not *resolve.

Impressionism perhaps marks

the first appearance of the *Modern movement in music. Some musicians, however, regard Impressionism as a period of its own, falling between the Romantic and Modern periods.

● impromptu. Nominally, a composition made up on the spur of the moment, that is, an *improvisation or extemporization. Actually the term is used (not very honestly) as a blank title when the composer can think of no other name. (See titles.) The term is especially associated with Schubert and Chopin, and is occasionally used in combinations such as Impromptu-*Waltz, *Fantasy-Impromptu, and the like.

Most impromptus are written for the piano.

● †improvisando. As if improvising.

● improvisation. A piece of music made up as one goes along; an extemporaneous composition.

In the course of a church service it is often necessary for the organist to improvise short passages to connect one musical part of the service to another without interruption. *Chorale-preludes were often improvised.

The art of improvisation was once widely cultivated, especially during the eighteenth century (*Baroque and *Classical periods). Bach's, Handel's, Mozart's, and Beethoven's prowess in improvisation was celebrated in their own days as well as since. The ability to improvise probably promoted facility in *realizing *figured basses readily, though of course this function is not improvisation in the strict sense of the word.

Although Chopin and Liszt were excellent improvisers, in general this skill fell into decline during the nineteenth century, possibly because the need for it subsided. French organists, however, continued to cultivate the ability (Franck's improvisations were fabulous) and have continued to do so to the present day, the organist Marcel Dupré (1886-   ) being especially celebrated in this respect.

Doubtless many wonderful improvisa-

tions have escaped into the four winds forever, unrecorded.

The use of improvisation to mean elaborating on or varying a given melodic line is a less strict application of the word.

See also cadenza (sub-head "The Cadenza in the Concerto"), and impromptu.

● improvise. To extemporize; the verb form of *improvisation. One who improvises is called an improviser or improvisator.

The use of this word to denote a make-shift or emergency device ("The broken arm was placed in a sling improvised from a necktie") does not belong in music.

● in alt. Notes in the *octave (2) beginning with the G in the space above the fifth line of the treble staff are said to be in alt.

Notes in the octave beyond are said to be in altissimo or in altiss.

● †incalzando. Pressing onward. (Literally "chasing" or "pursuing hotly.") It is roughly equivalent to *accelerando.

● incidental music. Music, usually for orchestra, intended to be performed in connection with a play. It may include an *overture (3), *intermezzos (1), songs, music to accompany marches or various dances in the action, and even orchestral music played while some of the actors are speaking on the stage (see also melodrama). Beethoven's incidental music for Goethe's Egmont, Mendelssohn's for Shakespeare's Midsummer Night's Dream, Bizet's for Daudet's L'Arlésienne, and Grieg's for Ibsen's Peer Gynt are all well-known.

The "background music" heard in moving-picture films is a modern kind of incidental music, and a number of excellent examples have been written by prominent contemporary composers.

● Indian drum. The tom-tom.

● inflection. An infrequent but very
convenient term used to describe the
various forms a given *letter-name
may take when affected by *accidentals
and *key-signatures. Thus we may
say that all the possible inflections of
D are: D-natural, D-flat, D-sharp,
D-double-flat, and D-double-sharp.
 Variant spelling: inflexion.

● inharmonic. (1) Same as enharmonic.
 (2) Same as non-harmonic tones.

● inner voices. All the voices except
the highest and lowest. In music
written for soprano, alto, tenor, and
bass, the alto and tenor are the inner
voices.
 Antonym: outer voices.

● † -ino, † -ina. An Italian diminutive
suffix.
 Synonym: -etto, -etta.
 Antonym: -one.

● † inquieto. Restless, slightly
agitated. The literal meaning is
"unquiet," "uneasy," "restless."

● instrumentalist. The player of an
instrument.

● instrumentation. (1) For all
practical purposes, a synonym for
orchestration. Often, however,
instrumentation implies study of the
various instruments singly, orchestration their use in combinations.
 (2) A synonym for bandstration.
 (3) The exact group of instruments
required in any given band or
orchestra composition, or the total
number of players available in the
organization. (The desirability of
the latter usage is open to question.)

● instruments of the orchestra. See
orchestra.

● in tempo. Same as a tempo.

● † intensità. Intensity. Con intensità,
intensely.
 Pronunciation: accent last syllable.

● † intenso. Intense, violent.

● interchangeable with. Alternating
with. The expression "second
flute interchangeable with piccolo"
means that the player of the
second flute *part must be prepared to play certain portions of
his music on the *piccolo (and
perhaps resume with the flute at
another designated spot). It does
not mean that the player has the
choice of using whichever of the
two instruments he prefers.

● interlude. General name given
to any passage of music intervening between other passages,
especially others of greater importance.
 See episode, intermezzo.

● † intermezzo. (1) An orchestral
interlude between the acts of an
*opera, or between the acts of a
play (in *incidental music).
 Synonym: entr'acte.
 (2) A movement of interlude
character in a *suite or other
work divided into *movements.
 (3) In the seventeenth and
eighteenth centuries, a short
*opera inserted between the acts
of a longer opera, in the character
of a diversion. It was usually
of a comical nature. La Serva
Padrona (The Servant as Mistress)
by Pergolesi is probably the best-
known example.
 (4) A catch-all title for a short
piece, especially one for the piano,
possessing a quiet, contemplative,
wistful character. Brahms often
used the word in this connotation.
(See titles.)
 Plural: intermezzos or inter-
mezzi.

● interpretation. Those elements
of variance which unavoidably occur
when two different musicians'
performances of the same composition are compared; personal manner
of performing.
 Just as no two people will read
a given passage from a book in
the same manner, so will no two
people perform a given musical
composition in an absolutely

identical way. Each performer studies and practices a piece, and then gives it back in a manner that depends on the sum total of all his experiences, as influenced by his taste. His prowess in *technique may unavoidably produce some additional differences. These differences, of course, are normally very slight, although not so slight as to be unobservable.

Modern performers strive to play or sing a work in what they conscientiously believe would be the exact way that the composer would use if he were the performer. The attempt to concoct a far-fetched manner of performance--to mold the piece, like so much clay, into any shape one's whim might dictate--is a discredited, old-fashioned, and illegitimate approach.

● intervals. The difference in pitch between any two tones is called an interval.

The name of one interval is familiar to anyone who has even a smattering of musical knowledge: *octave (1). The terms *half-step and *whole-step are almost equally well known.

In view of the complexity and difficulty of interval terminology, coupled with its paramount importance, a highly detailed explanation will be undertaken, even at the risk of appearing over-explicit and redundant.

Basic Names. Octave of course

means "eighth." Intervals of one degree (one step) less than an octave are sevenths; those of two steps less, sixths; those of three steps less, fifths, and so on. These are the basic names of the intervals, but as will be presently seen, they are far from exact. See Example 1 below.

Exact Names. The following is a systematic and exact naming of the intervals:

When two tones have the same pitch--that is, are in unison-- (imagine two instruments both playing the same note) the technical name for this relationship is perfect prime. If the two tones are separated to the extent of a half-step, the interval is called an augmented prime when both are of the same basic letter name, a minor second when two basic letter names are represented. (It will be observed that the exact name of intervals depends on their visual appearance.) See Example 2.

If the difference is widened another half-step, the interval becomes a major second, which is the same as a *whole-step.

The increase of another half-step produces a minor third (C and E-flat, computing from the lower note upward).

Another half-step increase produces a major third (C and E). Still another half-step in the

Octave   Seventh   Sixth   Fifth   Fourth   Third   Second   Prime

Ex. 1

Augmented prime   Minor second   Ex. 2

distance results in a perfect fourth (C and F).

The next half-step increase is called an augmented fourth if the interval is notated basically as a fourth, a diminished fifth if notated as a fifth. The word tritone is often used as a non-committal term to designate either the augmented fourth or the diminished fifth. Incidentally this distance is exactly half of an octave. See Example 3.

Widening the distance between the two tones half-step by half-step, the resulting intervals continue in order: perfect fifth, minor sixth, major sixth, minor seventh, major seventh, and perfect octave.

Example 4 illustrates the intervals as they have so far been explained.

It should not be imagined that intervals are named only from

Ex. 3

Augmented fourth   Diminished fifth   Augmented fourths   Diminished fifths

Ex. 4

Perfect prime   Minor second   Major second   Minor third   Major third   Perfect fourth

Augmented fourth (The same sound notated as a diminished fifth)   Perfect fifth

Minor sixth   Major sixth   Minor seventh   Major seventh   Perfect octave

middle C (as the above examples appear), nor that they are always computed from the lower note upward, nor that the designations apply only to a pair of simultaneous tones. The same names apply to the same distances no matter how the tones may happen to occur; any two tones are related to one another by some sort of an interval which can be named.

When two tones are sounded simultaneously, the result is termed a harmonic interval. If they are sounded one after the other, it is termed a melodic interval; whether the tones rise or fall of course makes no difference.

Careful and reflective study of the foregoing examples will show that there is no mechanical way by which an interval can be determined effortlessly. For instance it is quite impossible to state that "If the lower note is flatted and the upper is natural, and the interval is basically a third, it will always be a major third" for there is no such "system"; the identification and construction of intervals is not a casual or facile matter; each pair of tones has to be studied, calculated, preferably by reference to a piano keyboard, real or imaginary.

Passing mention has been made of the fact that the augmented

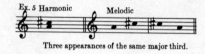

Three appearances of the same major third.

Example 6, on page 203, shows additional specimens of the intervals thus far discussed; some are melodic and some are harmonic. This is a supplement to Example 4.

prime and minor second sound alike (that is, that they are *enharmonic equivalents) and that the same is true of augmented fourths and diminished fifths. There are enharmonic equivalents for all intervals, although some are of

Ex. 6

rare occurrence. A list of these
follows.   As has been stated,

List of Enharmonically Equivalent Intervals

Diminished second	Perfect prime (unison)
Augmented prime	Minor second
Diminished third	Major second
Augmented second	Minor third
Diminished fourth	Major third
Augmented third	Perfect fourth
Augmented fourth	Diminished fifth
Diminished sixth	Perfect fifth
Augmented fifth	Minor sixth
Diminished seventh	Major sixth
Augmented sixth	Minor seventh
Diminished octave	Major seventh
Augmented seventh	Perfect octave

the distinction depends on their
appearance to the eye.   The
foregoing list is arranged so as
to increase half-step by half-
step.

Ex.7—A table of all practical intervals, expanding half-step by half-step, and showing enharmonic equivalents.

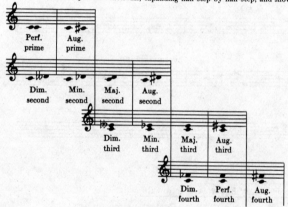

Example 7 (Continued)

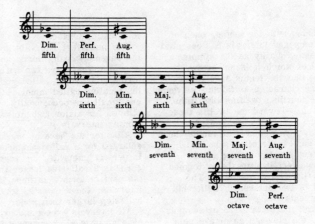

Recapitulation. Example 7 shows in tabular form all the practical intervals and their enharmonic equivalents, half-step by half-step.

Compound Intervals. Intervals greater than an octave are called compound or extended. The ninth is an octave plus a second; the tenth, an octave plus a third, etc.

ferred to "6th," and above all to "6."

Perfect and Imperfect Intervals. It is not easy to explain, briefly and in a logical way, why some intervals are termed perfect and others imperfect. The nomenclature must be accepted, not rationalized, unless an extremely long and not particularly useful explanation is undertaken.

The perfect intervals are the octave, fifth, fourth, and prime. They have one normal form, and

Ex. 8

| Major ninth | Perfect twelfth | Minor tenth | Major tenth | Perfect eleventh | Minor ninth | Augmented ninth |

Beginning with the tenths, each of these compound intervals has essentially the same quality as the simple interval of which it is an octave expansion; that is, tenths have much the same character as thirds, elevenths are like fourths, twelfths like fifths, and so on. Beyond the twelfth these compound names are seldom used; indeed even beginning with tenths the simple names are often substituted, minor tenths being termed minor thirds, perfect twelfths being termed perfect fifths, and the like. The interval of two octaves is a fifteenth (not sixteenth).

Although the tenth is an octave plus a third, the eleventh an octave plus a fourth, etc., one should avoid thinking in terms of "8 plus 3," "8 plus 4," etc., for obvious reasons. It is advisable to regard interval names purely as conventional expressions, never as arithmetical figures. The form "sixth" is always to be pre-

it is called perfect.

The imperfect intervals are the seventh, sixth, third, and second. They have two normal forms, the larger called major, the smaller called minor. (Large and small are occasionally substituted for major and minor in naming intervals.)

All intervals have an unusual, enlarged form called augmented. In perfect intervals, the augmented form is a half-step larger than the perfect form. In imperfect intervals, the augmented form is a half-step larger than major.

All intervals except the prime have an unusual, compressed form called diminished. In perfect intervals, the diminished form is a half-step smaller than the perfect form. In imperfect intervals, the diminished form is a half-step smaller than the minor form.

There is of course so such thing

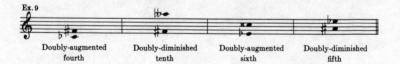

Ex. 9

| Doubly-augmented fourth | Doubly-diminished tenth | Doubly-augmented sixth | Doubly-diminished fifth |

as a "diminished prime."

Unusual Intervals. In addition to all those intervals shown in Example 7 (pages 204-205), it is possible to construct doubly-augmented and doubly-diminished intervals. (Ex. 9) Few of these ever turn up in compositions; the majority can be regarded as purely theoretical. (However see the "German sixth" in major mode under augmented sixth chords, where a doubly-augmented fourth appears.)

Inversion of Intervals. If we raise the lower note in an interval by an octave, or lower the upper one by an octave, the result is termed an *inversion. The quality of the original interval is preserved to a certain degree. (Ex. 10) The ensuing changes can be summarized by a table.

alto, tenor, and bass, the following relationships are present:

B and S--octave and a perfect fifth (perfect twelfth)

B and A--minor seventh

T and S--minor tenth (minor third)

B and T--major third

T and A--diminished fifth

A and S--major sixth

Careless analysis is prone to overlook some of the existing combinations.

Interval names measure distance between two tones just as inches, feet, yards, and miles measure distance between two points.

For dead interval, see that entry. For double sixths, double thirds, etc., see double (5). For wide interval, see leap.

Primes become octaves, and vice versa.
Seconds become sevenths, and vice versa.
Thirds become sixths, and vice versa.
Fourths become fifths, and vice versa.
Major intervals become minor, and vice versa.
Diminished intervals become augmented, and vice versa.
Perfect intervals remain perfect.

Ex. 10

| Major sixth | Minor third | Perfect fifth | Perfect fourth | Major seventh | Minor second | Major third | Minor sixth |

Combinations of Intervals. Any *chord may be conceived as a group of intervals in combination. Every tone in a chord bears some relationship to each of the other tones. If the accompanying chord (Ex. 11) is assumed to be written for soprano,

●†intimo. Intimate, inward.
Pronunciation: accent first syllable.

●intonation. The production of tone in reference to its correct pitch; accuracy in pitch-production.

Ex. 11

If every tone played on a string instrument (or every tone sung) has exactly the precise pitch it ought to have, we say the performer's intonation is perfect. If certain tones are a trifle too high or too low, we say his intonation is faulty, and the further the deviation and the more frequently it occurs, the poorer the intonation.

Keeping intonation correct is a problem with the bowed string instruments, the voice, and the trombone, but a less likely source of trouble with the other brass instruments and woodwinds. With the keyboard and plucked string instruments bad intonation should never occur if they have been tuned properly.

See also out of tune.

●†intrada. (1) Prelude (1, 2); usually a festive character is implied.

(2) Introductory portion.

The literal meaning is "entrance." Variant form (Spanish): entrada.

●†introduzione. Introduction.

●invention. A short piece in free contrapuntal style, in two or three *"voices," written for the piano or other keyboard instrument. It is simpler, less strict, and less exacting than the *fugue.

Bach's fifteen Two-Part Inventions are well known. His fifteen pieces usually called Three-Part Inventions, although very aptly termed, are spurious titles, as Bach originally called them Symphonies, in a now-obsolete usage of that term.

●inversion. (1) A *chord is said to be inverted if any member other than the *root (fundamental) appears as the bass tone. If the third is in the bass, the chord is in first inversion; if the fifth is in the bass, second inversion. With a *seventh-chord, appearance of the seventh in the bass is termed

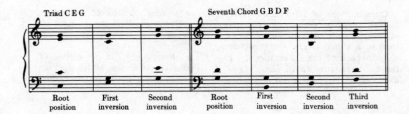

Triad C E G			Seventh Chord G B D F			
Root position	First inversion	Second inversion	Root position	First inversion	Second inversion	Third inversion

third inversion.

Synonymous terms used with *figured bass abbreviations are:

	triads	seventh chords
first inversion	6 or $\frac{6}{3}$ position	$\frac{6}{5}$ position
second inversion	$\frac{6}{4}$ position	$\frac{4}{3}$ position
third inversion	(does not exist)	$\frac{4}{2}$ position

Compare root position.

(2) In an *interval, if the lower tone is raised an *octave, or the upper one dropped an octave, the result is termed inversion. The interval has truly been "turned upside down." A certain amount of the musical character of the original interval remains. This is further discussed under intervals.

(3) A device wherein a theme is restated with all ascending motion converted to descending, and vice versa. The appearance is of course totally changed and the theme cannot be recognized by hearing, but only by eye.

The device, in a skillful composer's hands, is not necessarily an intellectual artifice. A good example may be found at the opening of the third movement of the First Symphony by Brahms, where the second phrase is the inversion of the first. (See Example A.) In the same composer's Second Symphony, the four notes that open the first movement eventually form the beginning of the third movement; Brahms inverts them, repeats two of the notes, and adds two *grace-notes, as well as placing the music in a different key. (See Example B.)

Invertible counterpoint is discussed

Examples of inversion (3)

under that heading.
  See also mirror.

● invertible counterpoint. *Counterpoint written in such a way that one voice or both voices may be raised or lowered an *octave (or some other interval) and still make an agreeable effect, with every interval appearing *inverted (2). This of course has to be determined from the moment of composing the music. See "inversion of intervals" under the entry intervals.

type of note may be considered "irregular" groupings. The *triplet is the most familiar example.
  In dividing (say) a quarter-note into halves, there is a distinct type of note available--the eighth-note; for dividing into fourths there is the sixteenth-note; for its division by 1/8 there is the thirty-second-note. The foregoing fractional portions are quite simple to notate, hence may be considered "regular" groupings.

The mere exchange of two voices does not constitute invertible counterpoint, since no interval is altered. (It is known as voice exchange or Stimmtausch.)

But for dividing values into three, five, six, seven, etc., no distinct type of note is available, so makeshifts must be employed; no note has been invented which is

Original   Voice exchange
                  (not inversion)

Invertible counterpoint is sometimes called double counterpoint.

● I° Abbreviation for primo, "first."

● †ironico. Ironic.
  Pronunciation: accent second syllable.

● irregular groupings, irregular divisions. Notes of equal length which divide a longer time-value into those fractions not provided with a distinct

worth 1/3, 1/5, 1/6, or 1/7 of a beat. Hence in splitting into thirds the type of note proper for division into halves is used, with a figure 3 (often enclosed in a slur or bracket) placed over or under the three notes involved; these three notes are performed in the time of two, the resulting group being collectively called a triplet. The individual notes are not true eighths--they are shorter than true eighths.

In splitting into fifths or sixths of the original value the type of note for division into four is used, with a figure 5 or 6 (as the case may be) placed over (or under) the five or six notes in the group; these are termed quintuplets and sextuplets (or sextolets), respectively.   They represent

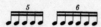

five notes played in the time of four, and six played in the time of four. In neither case are the notes true sixteenths--each is a trifle shorter than a true sixteenth (and "sextuplet sixteenths" are a mite shorter than "quintuplet sixteenths").

With certain fractional divisions two mutually contradictory principles turn up; they might well be termed the "overloaded measure principle" and the "closest approximation principle." (The former is probably the more frequently encountered.) These can be best illustrated when dividing into sevenths. If for example a quarter-note is to be so split, it is apparent that between 1/4 (the sixteenth-note) and 1/8 (the thirty-second-note) no distinctive time-value is available. The "overloaded measure" principle would favor employment of seven sixteenth-notes since it prefers what super-

ficially appears to be too many notes

in the measure (if true sixteenths were involved)--seven notes where there is room for only four.   The "closest approximation principle" would favor seven thirty-second

notes reasoning that 1/7 is closer to 1/8 than to 1/4--seven notes where there should be eight.

The musical result is of course the same in either case.   The "septuplet sixteenths" are considerably shorter than true sixteenths, the "septuplet thirty-seconds" a trifle longer than true thirty-seconds.

Of course two or more notes within these irregular groups may be combined into a longer (and also irregular) value.   One or more of the notes may be replaced by a rest, as will be seen in the accompanying quotation (bottom of page) from Chopin's Etude in F Minor (the first of three supplementary etudes without opus-number).

In meters with three, six, nine, or twelve beats (see compound meter) the division of three beats into two notes of equal length presents a further problem; this is discussed under duplet. Division of three beats into four notes of equal value is made sometimes thus:

and sometimes thus:

etc.

Ex. 1

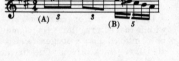

(A)   *3*   *3*   (B)   *5*

(C)   (D)

Ex. 3

(E)   *7*

Ex. 4

(F)   *5*   *5*

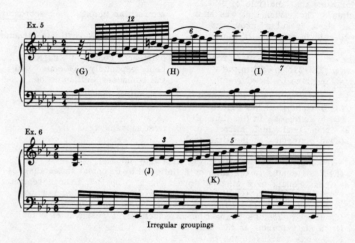

Irregular groupings

In each case these are called <u>quad-ruplets</u>. In addition a mathematically-exact division is sometimes employed, namely:

$$\mathbf{{}^{6}_{8}} \; \flat \, \flat \, \flat \, \flat \, \flat \, \flat \, .$$

Dotted notes can be divided into thirds and sixths very easily, but irregular groupings turn up when dividing them into halves, fourths, eighths, etc., plus other fractions not following the "multiple of 3" principle. Thus much that was said earlier about "regular" groupings fails to hold in the case of dotted notes.

The examples of irregular group-ings on p. 212-213 are from the <u>Sonatas</u> for piano by Beethoven.

it is more important to the musician to be able to play such groups than to explain their mathematical proportions rationally; also that intellectual comprehension of the mathematical values does not guarantee the ability to play the passage involved.

See also <u>triplets, quadruplets, quintuplets, sextuplets,</u> and <u>duplets;</u> in addition see <u>cross rhythms.</u>

● irregular tuning. See <u>scordatura.</u>

● isorhythm. A rhythmic-structural device used in the music of the fourteenth century ("Ars Nova"), being especially associated with the composer Guillaume de

Ex. 1--from <u>Sonata in D</u> ("Pastoral"), op. 28, first movement.
    (A) 3 eighths in the time of 2.
    (B) 5 sixteenths in the time of 4.
Ex. 2--from <u>Sonata in E Minor</u>, op. 90, first movement.
    (C) 6 sixteenths in the time of 4.
    (D) 5 sixteenths in the time of 4.
Ex. 3--from <u>Sonata in E-flat</u>, op. 7, first movement.
    (E) 7 sixteenths in the time of 6 (followed by 6 normal sixteenths).
Ex. 4--from <u>Sonata in F Minor</u> ("Appassionata"), op. 57, first movement.
    (F) 5 sixteenths in the time of 6 (followed by 6 normal sixteenths).
Ex. 5--from <u>Sonata in C Minor</u>, op. 10, no. 1, second movement.
    (G) 12 sixty-fourths in the time of 8 (actually 1 rest and 11 notes).
    (H) 6 sixty-fourths in the time of 4.
    (I) 7 sixty-fourths in the time of 4.
Ex. 6--from <u>Sonatina in G,</u> op. 79, second movement.
    (J) 3 sixteenths in the time of 2.
    (K) 5 thirty-seconds in the time of 4.

It may be said with confidence that   Machaut (1300?-1377?). In iso-

A. Melodic group: D C♯ B A B G

B. Rhythmic group:

The isorhythmic principle

rhythm a pattern of durations is repeated several times, but with a changed melodic line on each occasion.

The most interesting type of isorhythm is one in which a rhythmic pattern of a certain number of notes is coupled with a repeating melodic outline of a different number of notes (usually one more or one less). Hence every time the melody repeats it begins at a different point in the rhythmic scheme, and consequently each note has a different length and a different accent than on the preceding occasion. Numerous repetitions are necessary before the original pattern of both tones and durations will re-appear.

Certain modern composers have revived the use of isorhythm.

Isorhythm literally means "same rhythm" or "equal rhythm."
Pronunciation: ī-sō-rĭth-'m.

● †-issimo, †-issima. Italian superlative suffix; corresponds to English suffix -est, or to modification by very. The accent always falls on the syllable -iss-.

● †istesso. Same. See l'istesso tempo.
Variant form: stesso.

● Italian overture. Type of *opera *overture consisting of three sections in the order: fast, slow, fast. Since the second fast section is normally not a repetition of the first, the form-scheme is ABC, not ABA. This form was of considerable importance during the *Baroque and early *Classical periods.

Alessandro Scarlatti (1659-1725) is usually credited with establishing the Italian overture. Mozart was one of the last composers to use the form, although his best-known overtures are not of this type.

If a complete stop were to be made between the three sections, the result would sound very much like a short *symphony. Musicologists believe that the symphony evolved from the Italian overture.

Synonyms: Scarlatti overture, Neapolitan overture.
Compare French overture.

● Italian sixth. See augmented sixth chords.

● Italian terminology. Many of the common Italian terms used as directions in music are given under dynamic marks and tempo marks. The reason why Italian (rather than some other language) is employed will be found under the former.

● †-ito Italian past participle ending, equivalent to English endings -ed and -en.
Variant forms: -ato, -uto.

J

●jazz. A type of dance music which arose in the United States around 1915, apparently among Negroes employed in the brothels of New Orleans. Perhaps its most outstanding characteristic is the very frequent employment of *syncopation; indeed some laymen have wrongly imagined syncopation to be an effect found only in jazz.

Rhythmic novelty and rhythmic life are its greatest virtues, perhaps even its only virtues. The fact that the rhythm of much twentieth century music has undergone a wholesome emancipation from the deadeningly mathematical subdivision of the beats of measures into halves, fourths, etc., is due in no small degree to the influence of jazz. Few contemporary American composers have escaped the direct influence of jazz rhythms.

The preceding rhythmic patterns are typical.

Frequent use is also made of *polyrhythms and *shifted accents, such as in the following melodic figure:

In addition to its tremendous rhythmic life, jazz has also brought about new effects of orchestral color and combination, due to the peculiar groups of instruments found in the typical *dance band. Against these must be weighed the following weaknesses:

(A) The invariable use of 2-2 time, which underpins the rhythmic diversity of the melody with a deadly metrical monotony. (B) A highly stylized type of melody, which seems hostile to any attempts at originality. (There are of course a few notable exceptions.) (C) A saccharine harmonic style, which although quite distinctive of jazz nevertheless seems to limit it. (D) A palette of moods which appears restricted to three choices only: reckless gaiety, mockery, and insincere sentimentality. (E) Inability to achieve any feeling of earnestness, seriousness, or sincerity. (F) The almost in-

The appearance of jazz was almost immediately followed by the study and use of its novel rhythms by serious composers, although naturally they did not discard all other rhythmic patterns in the process. Many people erroneously imagine that the Rhapsody in Blue by George Gershwin (1898-1937), written in 1924, represents the first use of jazz idioms in a serious composition. This is by no means true; the Harvard Dictionary of Music lists eight pre-1924 compositions of jazz influence, six of them by Europeans.

Jazz players recognize several distinct varieties, which they classify as New Orleans, Dixieland, Chicago, Kansas City, swing, jive, *boogie-woogie, bebop, and so on, though clear explanations of the differences between these are strangely hard to obtain.

variable adoption of a moderately fast tempo; slow tempos and extremely fast ones are rarely encountered. (G) A deadly tendency to uniformity, due to the fact that most of it suffers from the stifling domination of commercialism. Nevertheless, faults or no faults, jazz is a completely American contribution to music; it is in no sense European. (Whether it contains any African influence is unproved--and unlikely.)

The origin of the word jazz is often described as "obscure" or "unknown," perhaps due to ignorance, but more likely to squeamishness. As a matter of fact, it is a smut word (obscene word) which was known many years before the appearance of jazz music, and it is still often employed by foul-mouthed persons in its original meaning. (It is note-worthy that the word contains four letters and that the music originated in disorderly houses.) The term became respectable in referring to music simply for want of any sub-stitute word.

"Rock and roll" is not jazz, and is often disdained by many jazz enthusiasts.

Variant spelling (rare): jass.

See also popular music (1), boogie-woogie.

●jazz band, jazz orchestra. Same as dance band.

●jew's harp. A toy-like instrument of rather ancient origin, consisting of a horseshoe-shaped iron frame to which is attached a short, flexible tongue of metal, the latter twanged with the fingers. The frame is held between the teeth. Resonance is obtained from the cavity within the player's mouth.

The expression jew's harp is an etymological mystery, for the instru-ment is known not to be of Jewish origin. One theory conjectures that the name is a corruption of jaw harp.

●jig. Same as gigue.

●jingles. (1) The little metal disks that are loosely fastened in the slots on the hoop of the *tambourine.

(2) The sleigh bells.

●jodel. Variant spelling of yodel.

●jota (Spanish). A Spanish dance in quick 3-4 time.

Pronunciation: hō-tá (the h roughly pronounced).

●just intonation. A system of tuning in which all intervals are acoustically true. If a piano were to be tuned to C major in just intonation, in that one key the effect would be delightfully smooth and silky, but in any other key a certain degree of out-of-tuneness would be observable; the more sharps and flats in the *key-signature, the more and more progressively out-of-tune it would become, until with six sharps (F-sharp major) or its *enharmonic equivalent six flats (G-flat major) the effect would be intolerably jangling. Hence the normal tuning used for practically every instrument is *equal temper-ament, in which all keys are equally in tune--or more accurately, equally slightly (almost imper-ceptibly) out-of-tune.

The reasons that underlie the matter under discussion would fill many pages; reference should be made to a treatise on *acoustics (1).

It is possible for *a cappella *choruses, bowed *string instru-ments, and *trombones to perform in just intonation. Many a cap-pella choruses and *string quartets (1) strive toward this ideal, though whether they really succeed or not is another matter.

In just intonation, *modulation is impossible, except perhaps to those keys with only one or two flats or sharps in the signature.

With the scientifically-correct pitches employed in just intona-tion, there is no such thing as two notes being *enharmonic. Strictly speaking, F-sharp is

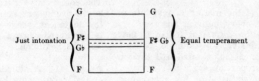

slightly higher in pitch than G-flat, C-sharp slightly higher than D-flat, etc., etc. Theoretically, F-sharp is five-ninths of a *whole-step higher than F (and hence four-ninths of a step lower than G), while G-flat is four-ninths of a step higher than F (hence five-ninths lower than G). It follows that the difference in pitch between the true F-sharp and the true G-flat is one-ninth of a whole-step. *Equal temperament tuning compromises by dividing this ninth-of-a-whole-step in half; consequently the sound F-sharp-G-flat is located exactly a *half-step (that is, half way) between F and G, and hence is one-eighteenth of a whole-step too low in pitch to be a true F-sharp and an equal amount too high to be a true G-flat.

This can be represented graphically in the preceding diagram.

There are many other differences besides those involving the half-step, but they are too numerous and too complicated for discussion here. In brief, it may be said that comparison of just intonation with equal temperament shows that in the latter, the following *intervals are a little too large:

> major third
> augmented fourth
> major sixth
> major seventh

the following a little too small:

> minor second (half-step)
> minor third
> minor sixth

and the following almost scientifically correct:

> major second (whole-step)
> perfect fourth
> perfect fifth
> minor seventh.

The octave is of course exact in both systems.

The gist of the matter in just intonation is that every interval has the same vibration-ratio that it has in the *harmonic series; for example the vibrations in a major third will always be in the proportion 4:5.

The chief justification for abandoning just intonation in favor of equal temperament, which occurred gradually between the sixteenth and eighteenth centuries, was the growing conviction that the difference is too slight to be important or even to be detected by most ears, and that the gains greatly outweighed the disadvantages. Certainly the use of all the possible *key-signatures and the increasing frequency of modulation were both phenomena that bloomed after just intonation was generally discarded.

An interval tuned according to the principles of just intonation is said to be untempered.

See also equal temperament.

K

● **K.** The initial K is used in connection with the music of Mozart in place of opus. See entry opus, sub-head "Pseudo-Opus-Numbers."

● **Kapellmeister** (German). A *conductor, or a musical director; often used derisively. The literal meaning is "chapel-master."
    Plural: Kapellmeister.
    Variant spelling: Capellmeister.
    Pronunciation: kä-pĕl'-mĭs-tĕr.

● **Kapellmeistermusik** (German). A derisive name given to music which is correctly written but devoid of real originality and conviction. The name literally means "chapel-master music," and arises from the fact that the average *Kapellmeister was a mediocrity who could compose nothing really distinguished.
    See also Zopfmusik.
    Pronunciation: kä-pĕl'-mĭs-tĕr-mōō-zĕk.'

● **kettle-drums.** Same as timpani. The comparative rarity of the term kettle-drums presents one of the few instances where a foreign term is preferred when a living English word is available.

● **key.** (1) A *tonality; the perceived relationship between a number of tones and that single tone (called tonic) toward which they all seem to gravitate and around which they seem to cluster.

Key is not synonymous with *scale; the latter is merely a systematic arrangement of the tones that form a key, just as the alphabet is a systematic arrangement of the letters that form words.

The presence or absence of a *key-signature is immaterial, for if necessary all *sharps and *flats could be written in as *accidentals, or a key-signature which does not apply could be canceled by accidentals. The first and last notes of a passage do not always effect its key; this is determined by the tone which has the function of tonic.

Both of the following are in E major; in the first, all necessary sharps are written in, while in the second the four flat key-signature which does not apply is canceled out and the proper sharps that would arise in E are written in as needed.

(2) A key on a piano, organ, harpsichord, etc., is a lever pressed by the finger, connected with the mechanism in such a way as to cause a tone to emit from the instrument. Some keys are white, some black. See keyboard.

(3) A key on a *woodwind instrument is a little finger-operated lever which opens a hole giving the pitch of one tone which the instrument produces, depending also on which other keys are pressed and which finger-holes are covered (or left uncovered) at the moment. Some keys are very short, some are crescent-shaped, and others are very long; the latter are sometimes called levers.

●keyboard. (1) Collective name for all the *keys (2) of the piano and similar instruments--organ, harmonium, harpsichord, spinet (virginal), celesta, clavichord, piano-accordion, etc. The term manual is often substituted in the case of instruments having more than one keyboard, such as the organ, harpsichord, and a few harmoniums.

The pedals of the organ are laid out like a keyboard, but are collectively called the pedalboard.

The fact that the keys employed for playing natural tones are white, those for sharps and flats black, and that the latter are built to lie a bit higher than the former, is so familiar as to make mention almost superfluous; however, it was once customary on the harpsichord keyboard to reverse the colors.

	C# D♭	D# E♭		F# G♭	G# A♭	A# B♭	
C B# D♭♭		D Cx E♭♭	E Dx F♭	F E# G♭♭	G Fx A♭♭	A Gx B♭♭	B Ax C♭

The diagram preceding illustrates the layout of the keyboard. It repeats itself throughout the instrument's *range, all octaves (2) being laid out in the same pattern.

(2) Keyboard instrument. See cembalo.

●keyboard harmony. A subject taught in *conservatories and college music departments consisting of *harmonizing melodies, playing from *figured basses, playing various chord progressions, improvising *modulations, and the like. All of these are done directly at the piano (or possibly organ) rather than in writing, the purpose being to place these skills and this information literally "at the finger-tips" of the students.

See also figured bass, harmony.

●keyboard instruments. Instruments played from a keyboard. Included are the *piano, *harpsichord, *organ, *spinet (virginal), *clavichord, *celesta, *harmonium, and piano-*accordion, the first three being the most important.

●key center. Same as tonic.

●key color. The belief, prevalent among many musicians but stoutly denied by others, that each of the various *keys (1) produces its own distinct effect of mood, brilliance, or mellowness, peculiar only to it, and to no other key. A major and E major are usually described as "brilliant," B-flat minor as "gloomy," A-flat major and D-flat major as "mellow," F major as "plain and colorless," and so on.

Since all keys are made up of *scales that are identical in construction, the concept of key color seems irrational, considered from the point of view of logic. Yet its wide acceptance by some of the finest musicians, and particularly by composers themselves, argues that "logic" notwithstanding, key color is a real thing, apparently rooted in some element of music that is not yet understood.

The very existence of so many different keys argues that composers must have some reason for using each of them, for considerations of *range only occasionally enter the picture. On the other hand, the fact that *songs are published in editions for various voices, and hence in different keys, argues against the supposition.

Key color should not be confused with synesthesia, which associates certain colors of the rainbow with certain keys (E major is "red," F minor "purple," etc.); here the results are purely subjective, and there is little common agreement.

British spelling: key-colour.

●keyed bugle. An obsolete *brass instrument which was equipped with long, flapper-type keys (somewhat like those of the *saxophone) rather than with *valves or a *slide. The perfection of the modern valve *trumpet put a speedy end to its short-lived popularity.

Several types of keyed bugle were invented, of which the bass instrument was the *ophicleide.

Synonym: Kent bugle.

●key-note. Same as tonic.

●key relationship. Just as the exact relationship between members of a family can be expressed by such words as father, grandson, aunt, cousin, sister-in-law, etc., so can the relationship between any two *keys (1) be expressed by equally definite terms. This is accomplished by calling one key by the name which its *tonic (key-note) has when in the other key.

Taking any key at random as a starting-point, the key with one more sharp or one less flat is called the key of the dominant because its tonic or first degree is the dominant or fifth degree of the original key. That with one less sharp or one more flat is called the key of the subdominant because its tonic is the fourth or subdominant degree of the original.

Such expressions as key of the mediant, key of the supertonic, key of the submediant, etc., are self-explaining.

When going from the major mode to the minor (see major and minor) or vice versa, the word major or minor is added to the foregoing expressions. Thus, compared with C major, F minor is the key of the subdominant minor; compared with C-sharp minor, E-flat major is the key of the supertonic major (in *enharmonic equivalent).

Still other relationships can be expressed by adding raised (or sharped) or lowered (or flatted) to the relationship; thus compared to G major, B-flat major is the key of the lowered mediant.

The terms *relative minor and relative major refer to the major and minor keys with the same *key-signature; *tonic (parallel, corresponding) minor and tonic major refer to the major and minor keys with the same *tonic (key-note) or its *enharmonic equivalent.

See also related keys, circle of fifths, common chord, key-signature.

●key-signature. Collective name for the group of sharps or flats which very often appears at the extreme left of the *staff. It indicates the tones that are permanently sharped or flatted.

Key-signatures are purely a convenience. It would be possible to dispense with them and write in every sharp or flat as an *accidental; in fact when frequent modulations occur, this is exactly what is done, for under these conditions a signature is a nuisance because more accidentals are needed to correct and cancel it than are required in dispensing with it completely.

In addition to keys involving signatures up to and including seven sharps and seven flats, there are two keys--C major and A minor--which have no signature. In these cases the very absence of sharps and flats should be considered something of a key-signature in itself, rather than as a blank.

There is no key-signature containing a mixture of sharps and flats; however it is possible, even frequent, for sharps to occur as accidentals in flat key-signatures, and vice versa. Double-sharps and double-flats are never used in signatures; they are always accidentals.

It is necessary to know how to write down only two key-signatures--seven sharps and seven flats--because these contain all

the others; that is, a three sharp signature is the first three of the seven sharps, a four flat signature the first four of the seven flats, etc. The two necessary signatures are shown with treble, bass, alto, and tenor *clefs.

Every key-signature applies to two keys--one major key and one minor key. The following table identifies them.

SIGNATURE	NAME OF MAJOR KEY	NAME OF MINOR KEY
no sharps or flats	C major	A minor
1 sharp	G major	E minor
2 sharps	D major	B minor
3 sharps	A major	F-sharp minor
4 sharps	E major	C-sharp minor
5 sharps	B major	G-sharp minor
6 sharps	F-sharp major	D-sharp minor
7 sharps	C-sharp major	A-sharp minor
1 flat	F major	D minor
2 flats	B-flat major	G minor
3 flats	E-flat major	C minor
4 flats	A-flat major	F minor
5 flats	D-flat major	B-flat minor
6 flats	G-flat major	E-flat minor
7 flats	C-flat major	A-flat minor

Synonym: key-sign.

● key-tone. Same as tonic.

● Konzertmeister. German word for *concertmaster.
Plural: Konzertmeister.
Pronunciation: kōn-tsĕrt-mīs-tĕr.

● Konzertstück (German). *Concert piece.
Plural: Konzertstücke.
Variant spelling: Conzertstück.
Pronunciation: kŏn-tsĕrt-shtük.

● krakowiak. A Polish dance in 2-4 time. Its style is somewhat reminiscent of that of the *polka. The name is derived from that of the city of Krakow (Cracow).
Variant forms: cracovienne, cracoviak.
Pronunciation: krä-kō-vē-äk.

L

● †la. The (feminine definite article.) Before vowels and h it is contracted to l'.
For the syllable la, see syllables.

● †lacrimoso, lagrimoso. Sadly (literally "tearfully").

● laissez vibrer (French). Allow to vibrate. (See lasciare vibrare.)
Pronunciation: lĕs-sā vē-brā.

● †lamentoso. Sadly, in the style of a lament.

● Ländler (German). A type of Austrian slow *waltz.
Variant spelling: Laendler.
Pronunciation: lĕnt-lĕr.

● †languido. Languid.
Pronunciation: accent first syllable.

● †languore. Languor.

● †largamente. In a big, broad manner. Refers to the manner of performance; not normally used as a *tempo indication, although it is usually encountered in slow tempos.

● †largando. Same as allargando.

● †larghetto. Very slow (though not as slow as largo). (Diminutive of largo.)
See tempo marks.

● †larghissimo. Extremely slow,

as slow as possible. (Superlative of largo.) (Rare.)

●†largo. Very slow and broad. (Literally, "large" or "broad.") See tempo marks.

●†La Scala. A famous opera-house in Milan, Italy, noted for excellent *acoustics (2). It is probably the foremost opera-house in the world. The complete name is Teatro alla Scala.

●†lasciare vibrare. Allow to vibrate. This direction is sometimes seen in music written for string instruments *pizzicato, or for the harp, as a direction not to *damp the strings, but to let them continue vibrating until the sound dies away of its own accord. It may also be seen in bowed string passages where there is considerable sweeping back and forth over several strings, and where the composer does not want the player to attempt to silence those strings on which his bow is not playing at the moment. Still another use is with *percussion instruments, especially *cymbals, *gong, *tubular bells, etc.

Sometimes the effect is indicated by a *tie which is not connected to any following note, perhaps with the addition of vibrato or lasciare vibrare.

imply a certain amount of musical training.

●†le. The (plural). Variant forms: gli, i.

●"lead, the." A term sometimes carelessly used to indicate the *melody, or the most prominent part. This usage is undesirable, as the part referred to does not actually "lead" (that is, precede) anything.

●leader. A term sometimes used as a synonym for *conductor or director, sometimes for *principal or *concertmaster.

●leading motive. See Leitmotiv.

●leading-tone. The seventh degree of the *scale--provided it is located a *half-step below the *tonic--or the *triad built on it. The name comes from the fact that the tone a half-step below the tonic has a strong tendency to "lead" on to that degree, which can be powerfully demonstrated by simply playing an ascending scale and stopping short on the leading-tone.

When the seventh degree is situated a *whole-step below the

Harp

vibrato

Synonyms: vibrato (4); also laissez vibrer (French).
Antonyms: étouffé (harp), secco.

●layman. Although a layman, strictly speaking, is anyone not a clergyman, this word is used by extension to denote any person following a vocation other than that of the person who is speaking. Thus musicians use layman when referring to anyone not a musician, sometimes to designate a person untutored in music.

A distinction should be made, however, between a layman and an *amateur or *dilettante, both of which

tonic, the correct term is *subtonic.
Roman numeral for triad: VII.
Synonym (undesirable): leadingnote.

●leaning-note, leaning-tone. Names sometimes given to the appoggiatura; see non-harmonic tones (6).

●leap. When a melodic line does not move *diatonically, it is said to make a leap. Restated in terms of *interval names, any melodic interval other than the second constitutes a leap. It will be apparent that some leaps are wider than others--span a greater distance. The third is sometimes termed a narrow leap, the fourth and all larger intervals, wide leaps.

Synonyms: skip, disjunct motion, jump, wide interval.

Antonyms: diatonic, scalewise, stepwise, conjunct motion.

● ledger lines. Questionable spelling of leger lines.

● †legatissimo. Very legato; the superlative of legato.

In writing for keyboard instruments there are instances in which this term seems actually to indicate a slight overlapping or blurring-together of the tones. Such an effect is certainly possible, especially on the piano when the *damper pedal is

held down.

Abbreviation: legatiss.

● †legato. Bound; connected; to be performed so that each tone leads directly to the following tone, with no space whatever intervening. Indicated either by a *slur or by the use of the direction legato. In general, however, it may be said that legato is understood at all times unless some other specific direction is given.

Abbreviation: leg.

Variant spelling (rare): ligato.
Antonym (which see): staccato.
Compare non legato, marcato (2).

● légende (French). This name has been applied to fairly short instrumental pieces by certain composers of the *Romantic period. The name usually has no more meaning than *ballade when used in similar works.

Pronunciation: lā-zhäñd.

● leger lines. Short lines used for writing notes that lie above and below the *staff, of which leger lines should be considered extensions.

The leger lines accumulate one by one as the notes get farther from the staff.

The use of leger lines is illustrated below. Two incorrect usages are given for purposes of comparison.

The space between two leger lines is sometimes called a leger space.

Variant spelling (questionable): ledger lines.

Synonyms: auxiliary lines, extra lines, added lines.

● †leggerezza. Lightness.

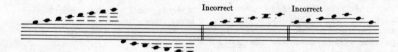

●†leggermente. Same as leggiero.

●†leggero. Variant spelling of leggiero.

●†leggiero. Lightly. The term is usually found in soft passages, frequently *staccato.
Abbreviation: legg.
Variant forms: leggermente, leggero, leggieramente, leggiermente.
Antonyms: pesante, ponderoso.

●†leggio. Music-stand.
Plural: leggii.
Pronunciation: accent -gi-.

● Leitmotiv. A German term, used in connection with the *music dramas of Wagner and subsequent composers, to denote various themes associated with the different characters, emotions, and situations in the action.
Thus in Wagner's The Ring of the Nibelungs (a series of four music dramas) there are Leitmotivs to represent love, world domination, a spear, forgetfulness, a sword, a curse, a rainbow, lightning, paradise, and so on, plus others associated with each character and even groups of characters--gods, giants, dwarfs, etc.
Wagner's purpose was not merely to help the spectator identify the various characters and the situations they sing about, but also to achieve musical unity throughout each work.
The literal meaning is "leading motive."
Plural: Leitmotive (German) or leitmotivs (English).
Variant form: leitmotif (English only).
Pronunciation: līt'-mō-tēf.

●†lentissimo. Very slow, as slow as possible. (Superlative of *lento.) (Rare.)

●†lento. Slow.
See tempo marks.

● letter names. See notation. For explanation of large letters scattered through orchestral and other *scores and *parts, see rehearsal letters.

●l. h. Left hand. The condition under which the need for this term arises is explained under r. h., where synonyms are also supplied.

●†liberamente. Freely; the *tempo should not be too strict, although the suggestion is less forceful than that of *tempo rubato.

●†libertà. Liberty, freedom.
Con libertà, freely, the rhythm not very strict.
' Pronunciation: accent last syllable.

● Liber Usualis (Latin). A collection of the most frequently-used *Gregorian chants (plainsongs).
It is published by the Society of St. John the Evangelist at Tournai, Belgium and may be obtained either in modern notation on a five-line *staff or in *neumes on the obsolete four-line staff.

●†libretto. The text of an *opera.
In some cases the libretto is a completely original piece of work; in others it is an adaptation from a play, novel, narrative poem, or possibly short story. A libretto usually has the size and thickness of a paper-bound pamphlet, and the printed appearance of the text of a play.
At opera performances sung in a foreign language, librettos are normally for sale in the lobby.
Usually both the original words and an English translation are given, in double columns.
The author of a libretto is called a librettist.
By extension, the term is sometimes applied to the words of an *oratorio or *cantata, but it should be avoided when referring to the text of a *song, *hymn, or short choral composition.
The word means "little book" in Italian. (Related English word: library.)
Plural: librettos or libretti.

● Lied (German). Song. This

word is often taken into English (also French) to signify *art-songs, especially German art-songs.

Plural: Lieder.

Pronunciation: (singular) lēt; (plural) lē-dĕr.

● †ligato. Variant spelling of legato.

● light music. Music which is easy to understand and not particularly serious. Light music is not necessarily of poor quality. The waltzes of Johann Strauss and the marches by Sousa, frankly light in character, are excellently written. The same may be said for many *operettas, such as those by Sullivan.

It is pertinent to remark that musicians do not use the term "heavy music" to refer to compositions which are loud, but to those not readily understood on first acquaintance-- those which must be heard several times to be grasped fully.

The terms light and heavy, applied to musical compositions, have exactly the same meanings as when applied to literature.

● light opera. Same as operetta.

● line. (1) See leger lines, phrase, staff, or system.

(2) Same as *"voice."

(3) The general shape or direction of a melody. In some melodies the line tends to ascend, in others to descend, in still others to ascend then descend, etc. (This usage should not be confused with tessitura.) Of course only the predominant tendency is considered; for example the accompanying melody has a rising line.

etc.

(4) This term, especially in the form "long line," is sometimes used to denote the sensation of apparently effortless continuity which is found in all good music.

● link. Same as episode.

● †l'istesso tempo. The same *tempo. Used at the beginning of a new section in a composition, to emphasize that there is to be no change in pace.

Variant form: lo stesso tempo.

See also equal marks.

● little clarinet. The E-flat clarinet.

● liturgical music. Music used in connection with the prescribed form of worship, or liturgy, of any church. See Ambrosian chant, Anglican chanting, Ave Maria, canticle, chant, Gregorian chant, Magnificat, mass, requiem, service, Stabat Mater, and Te Deum.

Other types of religious music, though not of liturgical character, are listed in the entry church music.

● †lo. The. It replaces il under certain conditions required in Italian grammar.

● †loco. A term sometimes used to cancel *8va, in order to preclude misunderstanding. It means "place," in the sense of "at the place where written."

(Related English words: local, location.)

● long drum. The tambourin de Provence.

● †lontano. Far away, distant, remote. Come lontano means "as if heard from afar," "as if coming from a distance."

Lontano and da lontano are some-

times used to mean *off-stage.

● †lo stesso tempo. Variant form of *l'istesso tempo.

● loud and soft. See dynamic marks.

● loud pedal. A careless name for the *damper pedal of the piano.

● low. The word <u>low</u>, as used by musicians, invariably means <u>deep in pitch.</u> It is never used to mean <u>soft.</u>

● low voice. Contralto or bass. Compare <u>high voice, medium voice.</u>

● Luftpause (German). Breath pause. An extremely short stop between notes at a point where no *rest occurs, as if taking breath there.
Pronunciation: lŏŏft'-pou-zĕ.

● †lugubre. Lugubrious, cheerless.
Pronunciation: Accent first syllable.

● lullaby. A *song of soothing, quiet, slightly monotonous character, used to induce a baby to go to sleep. Some are instrumental (and hence not songs); for this type the term *berceuse is often used.
Some lullabies are *folk-songs.
Synonym: <u>cradle song.</u>
French: <u>berceuse.</u> German: <u>Wiegenlied.</u>

● †lungo, †lunga. Long. This term is often used in connection with the *fermata. <u>Lunga pausa,</u> long pause.
Antonyms: <u>breve, corto.</u>

● †lusingando. Caressingly, coaxingly.
Variant form: <u>lusinghiero.</u>

● lute. A plucked string (*fretted) instrument, practically obsolete until revived in recent years. Its body is shaped like a pear that has been sliced in half lengthwise, and often the tuning-pegs are located on an extension bent backward at a sharp angle from the fingerboard. During the sixteenth and seventeenth centuries it was very popular as a solo, accompanying, and *ensemble instrument. It has a fairly large and important literature, some of which is now played on the *guitar. The lute was generally played directly with the fingers, although sometimes a *plectrum was used.
Music for the lute was often written in *tablature.

There were several types of lute (that is, it was a "family" of instruments) among which are the <u>theorbo (theorboe), chitarrone,</u> and <u>mandola.</u> The present-day *mandolin is a descendent of this group.
The tuning of the lute varied according to size, time, and country, and hence is too complex for discussion here. The accompanying tuning, however, was popular, and shows that the instrument usually has six strings.

The player is called a <u>lutist</u> or <u>lutenist</u> (occasionally <u>lutanist</u>).

● luthier. A maker of string instruments.
Pronunciation: lŏŏ-ti-ĕr.

● lyre. (1) An ancient plucked string instrument, conspicuous for its characteristic curving sides. It was rather extensively used by the ancient Greeks. The lyre has become the symbol for music in general.

(2) A clip, shaped like a lyre, which may be attached to a *woodwind or *brass instrument so that the player may fasten his music in it for convenience while marching with a *band.
(3) *Bell lyre.

● lyric, lyrical. (1) A rather vague term often applied to music to denote a smooth, "melodious," and fairly simple style, as contrasted with one of a more dramatic character. Lyrical music places

much emphasis on *melody (especially
melody of a somewhat "vocal" character),
and minimizes *dissonant and violent
effects.

(2) The noun lyric is occasionally
used as a synonym for *song.

● "lyrics." A term used to designate
the words or text of a *song, composition for *chorus (1), *musical comedy,
*operetta, or even *opera. The use
of this word is not very desirable;
words, text, or poem are all preferable.

M

● m. A rarely used *dynamic term
signifying medium or moderate. It
is quite familiar in its coupled forms
*mf and *mp; on the extremely rare
occasions when it is used alone it
occupies a place half way between
those two, indicating a dynamic level
that is neither loud nor soft. It is
the abbreviation for *mezzo or mezza.
The wider use of this term might
be recommended.

● †ma. But.

● madrigal. A secular composition,
comparatively short, usually *polyphonic and usually written for voices
only. It is the secular counterpart
of the *motet. The text is in the
vernacular, not Latin.

The madrigal was at its height
during the sixteenth and early seventeenth centuries, although it arose
during the fourteenth century, in
Italy.

Most madrigals are written for
four, five, or six voice-parts (five
being probably the most frequent),
and are of the highest and most refined type of workmanship. They
are intended to be sung by a group
of solo voices or by a small chorus;
they lose their intimacy when performed by choruses of fifty or a
hundred voices. The madrigal might
be considered "vocal *chamber-
music," although that expression has
also been applied, less appropriately,
to the *art-song.

Although French and German composers did not neglect the madrigal,
its most prolific exponents were

Italians and Englishmen. In
England this form reached its
zenith during the Elizabethan
period which saw an even greater
flowering in literature. It is
quite likely that Shakespeare had
works of this type in mind when
he penned many of his numerous
references to music.

The solo madrigal employed a
single voice with one or more
instruments, often a *lute. It
obviously is a precursor of the
later *art-song.

The *ballet or ballett (not to be
confused with the instrumental
danced *ballet) was in strict
parlance not a madrigal; however,
it is so similar as to *medium
and spirit that it could be termed
a madrigal of a special type.
Its most prominent feature is a
*burden or *refrain with a fa-la-la
text, which may have been danced
during Elizabethan times. The
madrigal (in the narrower meaning) never contained such a refrain. The ballett was always gay
in spirit, but the madrigal could
be either gay or serious, even
tragic.

Monteverdi and Vecchi wrote
*suites of madrigals which can be
regarded as forerunners of the
*opera.

Madrigal is the name of a type
of composition, not of a performing group. A group of people
who sing madrigals should be
called a madrigal group, madrigal
choir, or madrigal ensemble.
See also canzonetta (2).
Compare glee, part-song.
Pronunciation: măd´-rĭ-găl (not
mă-drē-găl´).

● madrigalist. (1) A composer of
*madrigals.
(2) One who sings madrigals.

● †maestoso. Majestic, dignified.
Synonyms: grandioso, pomposo.

● maestro. (1) A teacher of
music, especially one with much
experience in instructing talented
pupils.
(2) An artist performer; a
*virtuoso.

(3) A *conductor.
This is the Italian word meaning
"master."
Plural: maestros (English) or
maestri (Italian).
Pronunciation: mä-ĕs'-trō (not mīs-
trō).

●†maggiore. Major. In a composition written predominantly in a minor
key, a section written in the *tonic
major is sometimes marked (super-
fluously) maggiore. The term is often
seen in a *theme and variations.

● Magnificat. A musical setting of the
song of the Virgin Mary, beginning
with the words "My soul doth magnify
the Lord," found in the Bible (Luke
I: 46-55). There are many musical
settings, those by J. S. Bach and
C. P. E. Bach being especially well-
known, not to mention those by Schütz,
Buxtehude, Palestrina, Lassus, and
many others.
In the Episcopal Church and Church
of England the Magnificat is often
sung in *Anglican chanting (see canticles), while in Catholic services it is
sometimes performed in *Gregorian
chant (plainsong).
Pronunciation: may be anglicized
or pronounced according to "Church
Latin," i. e., măn-yē'-fē-kăt.

● major and minor. In comparing
any *major scale with the ascending
melodic form of the *minor scale
beginning on the same tone (i. e.,
the *tonic minor), it will be observed
that only one of these tones is
different: the third one.

the sixth and perhaps seventh
degrees of the minor scale may
also differ from their counterparts
in the major scale, but this is
not essential. Hence the heart of
the difference between major and
minor modes lies in the location
of the third step. The literal
meanings of major and minor
("larger" and "smaller") really
refer to the location of this all-
important third degree.
Perhaps the best way to distinguish major mode from minor
mode by listening is purely through
intuition; they "sound different."
Description with adjectives is less
desirable, while associating the
major mode with cheerfulness and
the minor with sadness is inaccurate and dangerous.
One can usually tell major from
minor in printed music by glancing
at the last bass note, which is
nearly always the tonic, and hence
the note from which the *key (1)
is named. (These names will be
found under key signatures.) Thus
with a key signature of three sharps
if the last bass note is A, the key
is A major; if F-sharp, it is F-
sharp minor. However, a good
musician should be able to detect
major from minor without resorting to such a device. Comparison
of the predominating notes with
the two scales involved should
disclose the key name at once.
In naming keys, the absence of
either major or minor indicates a
major key; that is "key of D" unmodified signifies key of D major.

In the major mode the third degree
is located a major third (see intervals)
above the *tonic (key-tone); in minor
it is a minor third above. Of course

Often major keys are indicated
by capital letters, minor keys by
lower-case letters.
For major third, minor seventh,

etc., see intervals; for major triad and minor triad see triad.

● major keys. The names of the major keys, and the key-signature for each, will be found in the table in the entry key-signature.

A key is understood to be major unless the designation minor is specifically added, or unless in written form the letter is not capitalized. Thus "key of D" is short for "key of D major;" the capital letter D standing alone indicates D major.

● major scale. A *scale in which the intervals between adjacent steps (degrees) fall in the following order when ascending:

Between 1-2, whole step.
Between 2-3, whole step.
Between 3-4, half step.
Between 4-5, whole step.
Between 5-6, whole step.
Between 6-7, whole-step.
Between 7-8, half step.

All of the following are major scales, in ascending form.

● malagueña. A Spanish dance similar to the *fandango. The word is derived from the name of the city of Málaga.

Pronunciation: mä-lä-gä-nyä.

● male quartet. A group of four men singers--a first tenor, a second tenor, a first bass (or baritone), and a second bass.

Compare men's glee club.
See also TTBB.

● †malincolico, †malinconico. Melancholy, sad.

Synonyms: tristamente, mesto, dolente, piangendo.

Antonyms: giojoso, gajo.
Pronunciation: accent -co-.

● mallet. A rather short, hammer-like implement, usually with a spherical, hard-rubber head, used in playing certain definite-pitch *percussion instruments, including the *glockenspiel, *marimba, *vibraphone, and *xylophone. (These instruments are sometimes

Representative major scales

This formation can also be expressed by pointing out that the major scale consists of two *tetrachords, each formed: whole step, whole step, half step, and that these tetrachords are joined by a whole step.

See also major and minor, minor scale.

called mallet instruments.) The player usually holds one mallet in each hand, but it is possible to hold two of them in one or both hands, thus making three- or four-tone chords a possibility if the *tempo is not too fast.

The mallet should not be confused

with the varied assortment of sticks
used in playing the *snare drum,
*bass drum, *timpani, and the like,
nor with the hammers used to play
various instruments of the *dulcimer
type, including the Hungarian
*czimbalom.

● mandolin.   A plucked string (fretted)
instrument.   There are several types
of mandolin, of which perhaps the
best-known is that having eight wire
strings tuned in pairs to the following
four pitches.

From their dates it is apparent
that the "Mannheim school" is not
entirely a group of contemporaries,
but rather two or three generations.
   The composers of this group
usually dispensed with the use of
*figured bass and at the same time
some of them also avoided the
coquettishness of *Rococo music.
They are credited with founding
orchestral and chamber music as
we know these today, and with
developing *sonata-allegro form.
They did much toward establishing

Briefly, it is tuned to the same
pitches as the *violin.
   The mandolin has a pear-shaped
body. It is always played with a
*plectrum, and reiterated *tremolos
are highly characteristic of it, as a
substitute for sustained tones.
   Variant spelling: mandoline.
   Italian: mandolino (plural, mandolini).
French: mandoline. German: Mandoline (plural, Mandolinen). Spanish:
mandolina.
   Pronunciation: accent first or last
syllable; musicians seem to prefer
the latter.

● Mannheim Group.   The group or
*"school" of composers from whom
the *Classical movement in music
largely stems. They were court
musicians to the elector Karl Theodor,
an accomplished and wealthy *amateur,
who resided at Mannheim, in what is
now Germany.
   The chief members of the "Mannheim school" are:

   Johann Stamitz (1717-1757)
   Karl Stamitz (1746-1801)
   Anton Stamitz (1754-1809)
   Franz Xaver Richter (1709-1789)
   Ignaz Holzbauer (1711-1783)
   Franz Beck (1723-1809)
   Anton Filtz (1730?-1760)
   Christian Cannabich (1731-1798)

the *sonata and the *symphony,
in the present meaning of each
term; for older meanings (now
obsolete) see sonata (2, 3, 4),
sonata da camera, sonata da
chiesa, trio-sonata (1), and symphony (2, 6, 7). Some of these
men were among the first composers
to write for the clarinet in
orchestral works. They introduced
the very nimble, chattering *fina-
les that were later so characteristic of Haydn, Mozart, Dittersdorf,
and other Classicists.
   In their orchestral works they
customarily wrote for string, woodwind, and brass instruments, plus
timpani, in essentially the same
proportion we consider normal
today; in fact they can be credited
with founding the modern orchestra.
It must be rememberd that the
orchestra of the Baroque period
was nearly always entirely a string
orchestra, and on occasions when
wind instruments were used the
number and proportion varied from
one composition to another; hence
no wind grouping was "standard"
or "normal." (The frequently-made
statement that Haydn was the first
composer to divide the orchestra
into strings, woodwinds, brass, and
percussion is inaccurate.)

The "Mannheimers'" compositions are predominantely *homophonic; their avoidance of contrapuntal and fugal style was destined to influence music for fully a century and a half --perhaps to its detriment.

In addition to pointing out the pioneering work of these composers, there should be mention of the orchestra maintained at Mannheim, which was celebrated in its day for its remarkable precision and *ensemble (2). The fact that all of the members could produce a *crescendo or *diminuendo simultaneously was an arresting novelty in the eighteenth century, when the precise and exact art of *conducting was something yet undreamed of. Modern orchestral virtuosity stems largely from the Mannheim orchestra.

● manual. Keyboard. This term is generally used in speaking of instruments which often or usually have two (or more) keyboards, such as the *organ and the *harpsichord, but seldom when referring to one-keyboard instruments such as the *piano, *celesta, *clavichord, *accordion, etc.

● manuscript. Writing by hand as opposed to printing; in this case the calligraphy of music, or the composer's handwritten copy of a composition.

No sensible musician attempts to make manuscript assume the appearance of engraved music, save in the case of *autographing, a highly-specialized type of manuscript sometimes substituted for engraving. With this exception, it is accepted that printed music and handwritten music will not look quite alike, just as printed words and written words do not look alike.

The differences between manuscript and engraved style cannot be enumerated, since handwriting varies among all writers. There is, however, one frequent engraved symbol that no one ever tries to duplicate in writing, due to its complexity: the quarter-rest (see rests).

Some musicians habitually place all note-heads on the "wrong" side of the stem. The advantages of this custom--if there are any--are a mystery.
Abbreviation: MS. (plural, MSS.).

● maracas (Spanish). An indefinite pitch percussion instrument consisting of a hollow gourd filled with seeds which are made to rattle when the instrument is shaken. The gourd is mounted on the end of a holder.

The maracas apparently originated in Cuba. As a rule, a pair of them is used.
Pronunciation: mä-rä́-käs.

● †marcato. (1) Well brought out, marked, prominent; such as melodia ben marcato, melody well brought out.
Abbreviation: marc.
Synonyms; pronunziato, en dehors, accentuato, rilevato.
Antonym: sotto voce.
(2) Played in a detached manner, with the tones well spaced and cleanly separated. The effect is not very *legato, yet not really *staccato.

● march. Any composition with a rhythmic character which makes it suitable for marching, whether it is actually put to such a purpose or not.

A military or quick-step march has two *beats to the measure and the *tempo is fairly lively. A grand march usually has four beats to the measure and the tempo is more moderate. The wedding march and funeral march are special types of grand march. The toy march may be of either of the two types; it is humorous or parodistic and its manner of performance mechanical to the point of exaggeration.

The Italian equivalent, marcia, is often encountered in *tempo indications and other expression marks.

● †marcia. March. Thus: alla marcia, in march style, in the manner of a march; tempo di marcia, in march *tempo.

Pronunciation: accent first syllable.

● marimba. A definite pitch *percussion instrument resembling a large *xylophone. Vertical resonators underneath many of the wooden bars increase the volume and sustaining power of the tone; hence the tone is less hard and dry than that of the xylophone. Large marimbas have a range of six-and-a-half octaves, although the three- or four-octave marimba may be considered the standard type. The instrument proper always rests on a large framework supported by legs often equipped with casters for ease in moving. It is played with two (or more) mallets (hammers). The wooden bars are laid out like a piano keyboard, and are graduated in size, the shortest bars giving the highest pitches.

The marimba has rarely been used in orchestral compositions.

In Mexico and Central America, marimbas are very popular. They are often played by two street musicians in duet fashion, one holding two hammers in each hand, the other holding two hammers in the right hand and one in the left, so that seventone chords are possible. Marimba bands (2) are not uncommon.

● †martellato. Hammered; usually applied to loud *bravura passages for the piano.

● †marziale. Martial, in march style.

● masculine ending. Explained under feminine ending.

● "masculine" theme. Explained under "feminine" theme.

● mass. One of the most important types of service held in the Roman Catholic Church. The text of certain parts of the mass remains the same at every service; these sections are collectively called the Ordinary. The text of certain other parts varies from service to service, a special text being appointed to use for each specific day and service; these are collectively called the Proper.

The mass may be spoken, sung in *Gregorian chant (plainsong), or sung in a setting for several voices (with or without instruments).

The Ordinary is the part normally set to music. Its sections are named as follows:

Kyrie eleison (or simply Kyrie)
Gloria in excelsis (or simply Gloria)
Credo
Sanctus and Benedictus
Agnus Dei

The Ordinary consists of five or six parts, depending on whether the Sanctus and Benedictus are regarded as one section or as two.

When a composer sets the mass to music, there are not necessarily just five or six movements, for he may subdivide several of the above sections. Thus Bach's great Mass in B Minor contains twenty-four movements, some for chorus and orchestra, some for one or more solo voices and orchestra.

Traditionally the mass was of course always sung (or spoken) in Latin at Catholic services. (Nevertheless "Kyrie Eleison" is actually Greek.) Use of the vernacular was authorized in 1964.

Some masses are of a musical character that is quite unchurchly; more than one even contains a florid *aria for *coloratura soprano! Although many of these are excellent from a musical point of view, their secular style renders them unsuitable for use at services. Masses of this type are frequently heard at musical concerts and are termed concert masses; they are frankly regarded (and perhaps intended) as non-liturgical. Bach's B-Minor Mass and Beethoven's Missa Solemnis are in this category; the same can perhaps be said for the masses by Haydn, Mozart, and Schubert. In addition to their unchurchly style, many concert masses are also entirely too long for practical liturgical employment.

Synonym (Latin): missa (plural, missae).

● master singers. See Meistersinger.

● mazurka. A type of Polish dance, lively and rhythmic in character, in 3-4 time. A typical rhythmic pattern is

$$\begin{array}{c}3\\4\end{array}\ \text{♩.}\ \text{♪♩.}\ \ \text{♪}$$

Prominent characteristics of the mazurka are its proclivity for ending on the second beat of the measure, and for notes falling on the second beat to be fairly long--often a dotted-quarter or half- note.

Chopin wrote over fifty mazurkas for the piano. They are of course idealizations of the dance, and not all are of the tempo or rhythmic character suggested above. They also run the gamut of moods.

Pronunciation: mă-zŏŏŕ-kȧ or mă-zĕŕ-kȧ.

● †mazza, mazzetta. Mallet (for use with *cymbals and other *percussion instruments).

● m. d. Right hand; abbreviation for Italian mano destra and French main droite.

For further information see cross-hand and r. h.

● measure. (1) Physically speaking, a measure is the distance between two bar-lines.

● measure-sign, measure-signature. See time-signature.

● mechanism. (1) The way an instrument "works"; the characteristic operation necessary to produce each of the tones which it can sound. This term should not be confused with *technique, which refers to the acquisition of skill by the player.

(2) This term is also used in reference to the mechanical operations inside various instruments, for example, the action of the hammers and dampers within the piano, of the numerous electrical connections within the organ, etc. Synonym: action.

● mediant. The third degree of the *scale, or the *triad built on it. Its name arises from the fact that it is midway between the *tonic and *dominant degrees. Roman numeral for triad: III.

● medieval modes. See modes (1).

● medium. Any musical performing group. Piano is a medium, *orchestra is another, *chorus and orchestra still another, as are *organ, *band, violin and piano, *string quartet (1), voice and

measure   measure   measure

The notes found in any measure are organized by steady *beats which are grouped into a fixed pattern of strong (accented) and weak (unaccented) units. The *time-signature expresses this strong-weak pattern.

Synonym: bar (1).

See also up-beat.

(2) A synonym for meter.

● measure bar. Bar-line.

● measure rest. A name sometimes used for the whole rest. See rests.

piano, unaccompanied chorus, *piano trio, and any other conceivable group.

Composers do not write notes in the abstract; they write definitely for a certain medium, with its possibilities, limitations, and *idiom in mind. (However, see transcriptions.)

Plural: mediums or media.

● medium voice. Mezzo-soprano or baritone.

Compare high voice, low voice.

● medley. Several compositions (or
parts thereof), informally strung
together without interruption, and
thus caused to sound (superficially)
like a single composition. The songs
of Stephen Foster, patriotic pieces
and the like, are often so treated
for use in concerts of a light nature.
    Synonym: potpourri.

● Meistersinger. Amateur German
musicians of the fifteenth and sixteenth centuries. Like the *Minnesinger, *troubadours, and *trouvères,
they wrote both the texts and music
of the songs they used, but unlike
them, the Meistersinger were middle-
class townspeople rather than of
noble descent. Their manner of
composition was mechanical and pe-
dantic, and their work had very little
influence on the history of music as
a whole.
    They should not be confused with
the Minnesinger or even especially
associated with them, for the Meistersinger in general came considerably
later in history and are of far less
importance.
    Hans Sachs was the best-known of
the Meistersinger.
    Wagner satirizes their pendantic
methods (and all musical conserva-
tism in general) in the opera Die
Meistersinger.
    Plural: Meistersinger (German)
or meistersingers (English).
    Variant form: Meistersinger
(singular and plural).
    Synonym (and translation): master
singer(s).
    Pronunciation: mīs-tĕr-sĭng-ĕr
(second s sounds almost like z).

● melisma. In vocal music, a passage in which several notes slurred
together carry one word (or one
syllable of a word) of the text.
    Plural: melismas or melismata.

● melismatic. *Florid. However,
the word melismatic suggests absence
of brilliance or "showiness," qualities
often associated with the word florid.
    See the chant quotation in the entry
Gregorian chant, where the syllable
-e of the word Kyrie receives an
extremely melismatic treatment.

● mellophone. The *alto horn
when manufactured in its circular
shape. It is sometimes built in
E-flat, sometimes in F. It
somewhat resembles the French
*horn in appearance, except that
the player fingers it with his right
hand and keeps his left in the
*bell, rather than the reverse.
    It is occasionally called the
concert horn.

● melodeon. For all practical
purposes, a synonym for harmonium.

● †melodia. Melody. Thus, la
melodia ben marcato, melody well
brought out.
    Pronunciation: accent -di- (not
-lo-).

● melodrama. A composition for
speaking voices with musical *accompaniment, usually orchestra.
Passages of melodrama have sometimes been used in *operas. In
the *incidental music for plays,
any passages during which an actor
speaks his lines while the orchestra
is playing might well be termed
temporary melodramas.
    This term should not be con-
fused with the spoken dialogue in
the *operetta and *opéra comique,
which is done without musical
accompaniment.
    The combination of speaking
and music has never been sufficiently exploited, nor has it
gained much public favor, despite
the fact that two highly successful
modern compositions--Prokofieff's
Peter and the Wolf and Copland's
A Lincoln Portrait--might well be
called melodramas.
    The definition of melodrama that
is used in the theater--a drama
with an extravagant or blood-and-
thunder plot--is not employed in
music, although it well describes
the type of plot found in many
*operas, particularly Italian operas
of the *Verismo school.
    Synonym: monodrama.

● melody. A series of musical
tones; musical tones in their

horizontal aspect; a tune.

A once-popular definition "an orderly succession of tones" is no longer useful, for present-day composers often use melodies that do not answer to the usual connotation of "orderly."

As a rule it is understood that tones which are heard in succession as an *arpeggio are not to be considered a melody but a *chord--that is, considered *harmony--since they undoubtedly fuse together in the hearer's mind to form such an impression.

The word melody is often set in opposition to accompaniment, with the implication that the former is of greater importance. (See homophonic.)

Melody is ordinarily regarded one of the three essential components of music, the other two being *rhythm and *harmony.

Synonyms: tune (1), air (1).

● Melody Flute. See simple melody instruments. A trade name.

●†meno. Less. Thus: meno mosso, slower (literally, "less motion"); meno f, less loud (i. e., a little softer), etc. Al meno, at least. Meno alone is sometimes used for short in place of meno mosso. (Related English word: minus.)

●†-mente. An Italian suffix which converts an adjective into an adverb; corresponds to the English suffix -ly. It should be mentioned, however, that in Italian adjectives are often used, and quite grammatically, where in English strict grammar would call for the adverb.

●†menuetto. Minuet. Some musicians maintain there is a subtle difference between a "minuet" and a "menuetto," but this difference--if it is real--can be dismissed from mind.

●†mesto. Sad, gloomy.

●"Met," the. The Metropolitan Opera Company in New York; a colloquialism.

●†metà. Half. Used in the string parts of orchestral compositions,

indicating a passage to be played by only half of the players in the section.

Pronunciation: accent second syllable.

● metamorphosis of theme. Same as transformation of theme.

● meter. The organization of strong (accented, heavy) and weak (unaccented, light) *beats into recurring patterns.

Just as meter underlies the structure of poetry, so does a like phenomenon underpin the structure of most music. Sounds of various lengths are superimposed on the steady succession or throb of strong and weak beats.

The impression of strength and weakness is largely an illusion. As evidence, it can be pointed out that accenting of this type is utterly impossible on the *organ; yet one can detect the meter of any composition played on it just as readily as with any other instrument. Further comment on this will be found under accent.

In a meter of two beats per measure the accenting is: first beat strong, second beat weak.

$$1\ 2$$

In a meter of three beats it is: first beat strong, second and third both weak.

$$1\ 2\ 3$$

Four beats: first is strong, second weak, third moderately strong, fourth weak.

$$1\ 2\ \overset{3}{}\ 4$$

Six beats: first strong, second and third both weak, fourth moderately strong, fifth and sixth both weak.

$$1\ 2\ 3\ \overset{4}{}\ 5\ 6$$

At a quick *tempo six beats will sound like two, that is, only the first and fourth will be sensed.

For nine beats:

1 2 3 ⁴ 5 6 ⁷ 8 9

For twelve beats:

1 2 3 ⁴ 5 6 ⁷ 8 9 ¹⁰ 11 12

In a quick tempo, a nine-beat meter will sound like three beats and a twelve-beat meter like four.

In a five-beat meter the accenting is sometimes

1 2 3 ⁴ 5

and sometimes

1 2 3 ⁴ 5

*Conductors as a rule indicate the meter in tracing the beats (or "beating time").

The conventional meters used in hymns are discussed under hymn-tune.

Variant spelling: metre.

Synonyms: measure (2), Takt; also (undesirable) time.

Compare rhythm.

See also accent, pulse, duple meter, triple meter, simple meter, compound meter.

● meter-sign, meter-signature. See time-signature.

● metronome. A mechanical device used to indicate the tempo (rate of speed) of a composition. It was introduced (though not invented) in 1816 by Johann Nepomuk Mälzel (1772-1838), who was a well-known inventor of mechanical devices--and incidentally an acquaintance of Beethoven's.

The metronome works on the same principle as the clock, though the frequency of its ticking can be regulated. In general its shape is that of a pyramid. The pendulum is fastened at the bottom rather than the top, and on it there is a little weight which can be slid up or down to decrease or increase the speed of its movement. The composer indicates in the music the exact value of any type of note, and the player adjusts the weight on the inverted pendulum so that it will tick at this same figure; for example, if the composer indicates ♩ = 84, the metronome ticks eighty-four times each minute, and the performer plays one quarter-note while it ticks once, or a half-note to two ticks, or two eighth-notes to one tick, etc. The numerals to which he adjusts the device are given on the pendulum or on the wood immediately behind it.

Some metronomes also have a bell which can be made to ring every second, third, or fourth tick, in order to mark the first beat in each *measure.

In recent years, electrically operated metronomes have come into use; they are superior to the old mechanical type (which are wound like a clock), as they are less likely to get out of adjustment.

The mechanism can be made to tick at any speed from 40 to 208 times per minute. The numerals given on the metronome are as follows: 40, 42, 44, 46, 48, 50, 52, 54, 56, 58, 60, 63, 66, 69, 72, 76, 80, 84, 88, 92, 96, 100, 104, 108, 112, 116, 120, 126, 132, 138, 144, 152, 160, 168, 176, 184, 192, 200, and 208. Of course the

composer may employ any desired figure, but those just indicated are the only ones used regularly.
See also tempo marks.

●†mezza di voce. See mezza voce.

●†mezza voce. (1) Half-voice. It is a form of tone-production used in singing, in which the tones, effort-lessly produced, are quite soft and have a smooth, gentle character. Mezza voce is often carelessly (and incorrectly) termed *falsetto, which is properly an entirely different effect.
Variant form: mezza di voce.
(2) Same as sotto voce.
Abbreviation: m. v.

●†mezzo (1) Half, rather, somewhat, medium, moderately. It is most familiar in such terms as *mezzo forte, *mezzo piano, *mezzo soprano, *mezza voce, etc.
Variant form: mezza.
(2) Colloquial for *mezzo-soprano.

●†mezzo forte. Rather loud, moderately loud. Normally used in its abbreviated form, mf.
See dynamic marks.

●†mezzo piano. Rather soft, moderately soft. Normally used in its abbreviated form, mp.
See dynamic marks.

●mezzo-soprano. A type of female voice midway in range between the *soprano and the *contralto (or alto). The *tone quality is a trifle darker, more "throaty," and less brilliant than that of the soprano, but by no means as much so as that of the contralto.
Range:

Plural: mezzo-sopranos (English) or mezzo-soprani (Italian).
Pronunciation: mĕt-sō sō-prän-ō or mĕd-zō sō-prä-nō.

●mf. Rather loud, moderately loud. This is the abbreviation for mezzo forte, signifying a dynamic level louder than *mp, but not as loud as *f.
Ordinary everyday playing or singing that strives to be neither loud nor soft is at the mf level, which has led some musicians to term it "the most undistinguished musical effect"; nevertheless many musical passages are meant to be so performed.
See dynamic marks.

●m. g. Left hand; abbreviation for French main gauche.
For further information see the entries cross-hand and r. h.

●microtone. Generic name for any interval smaller than a *half-step (semitone), e.g., the *quarter-tone.

●middle C. The note

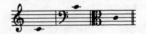

Middle C

It gets its special name from the fact that it is the C nearest to the middle of the piano keyboard and that it must be written with a *leger line no matter whether notated with the treble *clef or the bass clef; also that it is in the middle of the *great staff.

Mezzo-soprano range

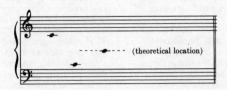

- - - - - - - (theoretical location)

Middle C

● middle pedal. Most grand pianos
and a few uprights possess a middle
pedal. If it is pressed immediately
after a key or group of keys is
struck, those tones, but no others,
will continue vibrating as long as
the middle pedal is held.

This pedal is most frequently used
to sustain low tones through the playing of higher passages without permitting the latter to blur.

On some pianos the middle pedal
operates only for tones of fairly low
pitch; on others it can be used for
any desired tones. Of course it is
possible to press and release the
*damper pedal (also the *soft pedal)
any number of times during the holding of the middle pedal.

Many upright pianos have three
pedals, but the middle one is usually
merely an auxiliary soft pedal.
Synonym: sostenuto pedal.

● military drum. An indefinite pitch
*percussion instrument, similar to
the *snare drum, except that it is
larger, particularly in depth, has a
low pitch, and has a wooden rather
than metal shell.
Synonyms: field drum, parade drum.

● minim. Half-note. See British
terminology.

● Minnesinger. Minstrels active in
Germany and Austria during the
twelfth and thirteenth centuries. They
are the German counterpart of the
*troubadours and *trouvères in
France, and like these, the membership was often drawn from the nobility.
Walther von der Vogelweide (died

1230) is possibly the best-known
Minnesinger.

Like the troubadours and
trouvères, the Minnesinger were
poets as well as musicians, and
composed both the texts and
the melodies of their songs.

The word Minnesinger means
"love singer(s)."
Plural: Minnesinger (German)
or minnesingers (English).
Variant form (both singular
and plural): Minnesänger.
See also troubadours.
Pronunciation: mĭn-nĕ-sĭng-ĕr
(the s almost like z).

● †minore. Minor. In a composition written predominantly in a
major key, a section in the *tonic
minor is sometimes marked (super-
fluously) minore. This is often
seen in a *theme and variations.
See maggiore.

● minor keys. The names of the
minor keys, and the key-signature for each, will be found in
the table in the entry key-signature.

In speaking the name of a minor
key, the word minor must always
be added, for the expression "key
of D," unmodified, would be taken
to indicate the key of D major.

In writing the name of a minor
key, sometimes a lower-case
letter is used, with or without
the word minor. Thus the following
three forms are all seen: "key of
D minor," "key of d," "key of d
minor." The letter D alone indicates
D major. (Refer to the diagram

in the entry circle of fiths.)

A given passage of music either is or is not in a minor key. The commonly-heard expressions "rather minor" and "very minor" are nonsense.

● minor scale. It will be noticed in the description of the *major scale that it has only a single form. The minor scale, however, takes several distinct conventional shapes. As is mentioned in the entry major and minor, the location of the third degree of the scale is the heart of the difference between these two.

One form of the minor scale utilizes exactly the tones that would be expected: those which are in accordance with the *key-signature. This is called the natural, normal, pure, original, primitive or Aeolian form. As some of the foregoing adjectives imply, it is the oldest type, being identical with the Aeolian *mode.

The most commonly used form is called harmonic. In it, the seventh degree is raised a *half-step by means of an *accidental. Consequently the seventh degree is a *leading-tone to the high *tonic; in addition it is located an augmented second (see intervals) above the sixth degree.

In the melodic form the sixth and seventh degrees are raised a *half-step in ascending, but restored to their normal pitch according to the key-signature (that is, canceled) when descending. Thus when descending it is identical with the natural form.

The natural, harmonic, and melodic patterns are all completely conventional.

Three additional species are sometimes mentioned by theorists.

In the mixed form the sixth and seventh degrees are raised in ascending, but only the seventh is raised in descending, the sixth being restored to its pitch according to the key-signature. In other words, it ascends according to the melodic pattern and descends according to the harmonic.

In the Hungarian (or gypsy) form the fourth and seventh degrees are raised a half-step, both ascending and descending. Augmented seconds thus occur between steps 3-4 and steps 6-7.

In the Scandinavian form, the sixth and seventh degrees are raised both ascending and descending. In other words, its pattern

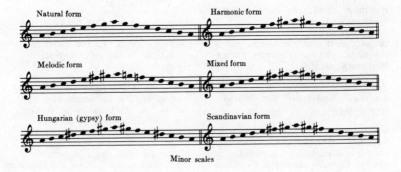

Minor scales

is like that of the ascending melodic (also mixed) form.

The six ways of constructing the minor scale are shown as they occur in the key of A minor.

● minstrels. See troubadours, also trouvères and Minnesinger.

● minstrel show. A type of entertainment which attained great popularity in the Unites States during the middle and late nineteenth century, extending into the early years of the present century. It consisted of various popular songs and dances interspersed with spoken dialogue and jokes. The performers were usually white men blacked up to resemble Negroes.

● minuet. A type of dance, very widely used in the eighteenth century, in moderate or moderately fast 3-4 time.

Minuets mentioned by writers (not musicians) are always described as "very slow" and "stately"; those encountered in actual music are never slow (although seldom very fast) and occasionally far from stately (e. g., that in Mozart's Symphony in G Minor). It is only fair, however, to make a distinction between the minuets of the ballroom and the idealizations found in the works of serious composers.

Through approximately the end of the eighteenth century a minuet was normally employed as the third (occasionally second) movement of a four-movement symphony, chamber-music work, or sonata (see sonata-types). Works with three movements almost always lacked the minuet; hence it was the "extra" movement in those possessing four. In more recent works, the minuet has been displaced by the *scherzo.

The *suites of the *Baroque and *Rococo composers often contained a minuet as one of the optional dances inserted between the sarabande and gigue.

The expression "Minuets I and II" actually means Minuet I, Minuet II, repetition of Minuet I; while "Minuet and Trio" actually means Minuet, Trio, repetition of Minuet (i. e., principal section, middle section, repetition of principal section).

One of the characteristics of the style is a strong tendency to subdivide the *beats; most minuets contain many eighth-notes.

The form-scheme is usually ABA.

Variant forms: menuet, menuetto, minuetto.

● mirror. A device of *contrary motion wherein one voice is the exact *inversion (3) of another, (melodic) interval for interval.

Example 1 is a mirror.

Example 2 is not, since the intervals do not always correspond; it is merely contrary motion.

Example 1 (mirror)

Example 2 (contrary motion)

For "mirroring" a text, see text-painting.

● missa (Latin). Mass.
Plural: missae.

●†misterioso. Mysteriously.

●†misurato. The *time-values to be strictly observed (literally "measured").

● mixed. This word is usually employed to indicate vocal groups consisting of both men and women, such as mixed chorus, mixed quartet.
It is less frequently used in speaking of instruments. When employed here, it may mean instruments not all of the same basic family (string, woodwind, brass, percussion), or not all of the same exact kind, that is, not all violins, not all clarinets, etc.

● mixed chorus. A group of singers, the membership comprising both men and women--normally a section of sopranos, a section of altos, a section of tenors, and a section of basses. The word chorus, unmodified, is understood to mean mixed chorus.
A mixed chorus differs from a *mixed quartet in that there is a section, or group, of voices to a part, instead of just a single singer.
A choir is a mixed chorus that sings at church services.
See also SATB, glee club.

● mixed quartet. A vocal *quartet, consisting of one *soprano, one *alto, one *tenor, and one *bass.
Compare mixed chorus.

● M. M. Abbreviation for "Mälzel's metronome." (See metronome.)

● modal, modality. Pertaining to the *modes (1). These words are generally used in contradistinction to tonality (2).

● mode. For the distinction between major mode and minor mod, see major and minor, major scale, minor scale, and key-signature. For the church modes (Gregorian modes) see modes (1).

●†moderato. Moderately. Used to indicate a *tempo that is neither fast nor slow, i. e., medium. It may be considered the standard in relation to which all other tempos are judged. This word is often used to modify other words, allegro moderato meaning "moderately fast," lento moderato (which is much less common) meaning "moderately slow." Allegretto moderato is occasionally encountered; it could be translated literally as "moderately slightly fast," or more gracefully, "a trifle fast."
It may seem illogical to modify this word, yet the tempo mark molto moderato ("very moderately") is by no means unusual.
See tempo indications.
Abbreviation: modto.

● modern dance. A term used by dancers (rather than musicians) to designate the more modern style of *ballet.

● Modern period. The Modern period in the history of music follows the *Romantic period, thus extending from about 1890 or 1900 to the present. Modern music is often frankly anti-Romantic--the denial and negation of Romanticism--a reaction against it. It is also to a certain extent anti-German, especially anti-nineteenth-century German.

A sharp distinction should be made between modern music and music which is merely recently-written. No composition which still adheres to the style of Romantic music is genuinely "modern," even though written yesterday. Only the most unsophisticated laymen imagine that *jazz and *"popular" (1) music are synonymous with modern music.

Probably the immediate connotation of modern music to most minds is one of *dissonance. Although it is true that works of this period employ dissonance with much greater frequency than any heretofore, still the presence of major and minor *triads and of *"open fifths" is by no means a rarity; there has in fact been a distinct retrenchment from dissonance and cacophony since approximately 1935. (See ultra-modern.)

There is no single style typical of the Modern period; instead there is a frankly confusing multiplicity of trends, some of which are the antithesis of others, or at least contain certain elements which contradict certain elements of other modern styles. For example some composers such as Scriabin have employed the *tritone with excessive frequency, while others shun it completely; some seek the influence of the *folk-song while others avoid it even to the point of seeming to be anti-popular; some such as Vaughan Williams have returned to the *modes (1), while others such as Schoenberg, Webern, and Alban Berg are identified with *atonality and the *twelve tone system, both of which are extreme forms of *chromaticism and hence the very opposite of modality.

There are however a number of elements which unmistakably point to the existence of a common practice during the Modern period, and these tendencies are becoming increasingly conspicuous. The *phrase of four measures which reigned supreme during the *Classical and Romantic eras and the almost mathematical rhythmic symmetry which characterized those periods have both been de-throned. Both these changes are typical of the Modern period's tendency to revive certain features characteristic of *Gregorian chant, the *Renaissance period, and the *Baroque period--characteristics so old as to seem new, many of which should have never gone out of use in the first place. Asymmetrical rhythm is of course also largely influenced by *jazz, and by certain types of folk-music. The tendency toward asymmetrical rhythm brings about the frequent changes of *time-signature so conspicuous in contemporary music. *Sectional style and *phrases in question-and-answer (antecedent and consequent) order are, in general, studiously avoided. The lush, sweeping *arpeggios and the striving for "emotion" and "feeling" so earnestly sought by the Romanticists now seem outdated. The tonic triad in second inversion (I_4^6) and the dominant *seventh chord (V_7) are highly uncharacteristic, the diminished seventh chord equally so. Still another element of older music, conspicuous by its absence today, is the prominence of the *leading-tone. Long passages of exact repetition, and the use of *repeat-signs, *D. C. and *D. S. are notably rare. Melodies are often angular, with unusual or wide *leaps.

Novelty of effect is of course always sought by modern composers, yet sheer inconoclasm and freakish-ness-for-its-own-sake have, with notable exceptions, undergone a recession since the 1930's. Perhaps the most healthy characteristic of Modern music is the return to emphasis on *counterpoint rather than on *homophonic (melody-and-accompaniment) style, the latter having reached its zenith (or rather, nadir) during the Classical and Romantic eras.

The following elements, all of which are typical of certain types of Modern music, are described under the headings indicated: atonality, chance music, electronic music, expresionism, fourth-chords, impressionism, musique concrète, mystic chord, neo-classical, non-functional harmony, pan-diatonic, polychord, polyrhythm, polytonality, quarter-tones, tone-clusters, twelve-tone system, whole-tone scale.

The expression "modern music" is of course purely relative; it is sometimes applied to Classical and Romantic literature, and even Baroque, in contradistinction to Renaissance, *Gothic, and ancient styles. It is also sometimes used to distinguish music written in the major-minor *tonal system form that written in the church *modes (1).

Synonym: contemporary music.

● modes. The tonal resources out of which a given composition is built, systematically arranged (normally in the form of a *scale). Just as words are made out of a repository of 26 letters--the alphabet--compositions are built out of the pitches contained in the modes selected by the composer, though often with the addition of certain other tones.

The difference between major mode and minor mode is discussed under major and minor.

The term under discussion is most frequently employed with reference to the church modes (also called Gregorian, ecclesiastic, or medieval modes) and the much older Greek modes.

(1) Church Modes. Music was based on these scales from the early A. D. centuries through the sixteenth century, after which they were gradually replaced by the system of *tonality (2) and the *major and minor modes which reigned supreme from the eighteenth century onward. Many contemporary composers have, however, revived the use of the Church Modes.

Officially the Church Modes are distinguished by numbers, though names are also used. There were originally eight of them.

The most important tone in any mode is the one called the final. As its name suggests, it is the tone on which the composition concludes. The final is roughly analogous to the *tonic in music built on the major-minor system. Second in importance is the dominant; however, as the following tabulation shows, it is not always the fifth degree in the mode, although often this is the case. (It is sometimes called the reciting tone.)

In the accompanying table of Church Modes the finals have been indicated as quarter-note heads, the dominants as half-notes. Both the numbers and the names are given.

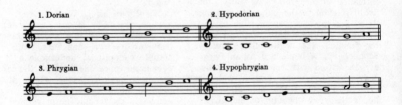

1. Dorian   2. Hypodorian

3. Phrygian   4. Hypophrygian

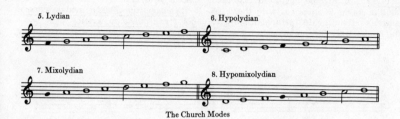

5. Lydian   6. Hypolydian

7. Mixolydian   8. Hypomixolydian

The Church Modes

The odd-numbered modes are called authentic and the even-numbered (those beginning with hypo-), plagal. The difference between the authentic and plagal form of any given mode is purely one of *range; the plagal mode always lies a fourth lower than the authentic; the final is the same for both forms, though the dominant is different. Thus, although the Dorian (first) and Hypomixolydian (eighth) modes consist of exactly the same series of notes, a melody in the former will terminate on D, one in the latter on G; the range of both will tend to run between the two D's shown. (There is of course no connection between the authentic and plagal modes and the authentic and plagal *cadences.)

It will be noticed that no two of the four authentic (odd-numbered) modes have the same structure in regard to the placement of *whole-steps and *half-steps, and that none of these corresponds to the major or minor scale (however see the Aeolian and Ionian modes below).

Use in Gregorian Chants. All *Gregorian chants are based on the foregoing modes. They make use of the tones shown above, plus B-flat, but of no others; however they often exceed the indicated range by a tone or two, especially on the lower side.

Since exactly the same sounds --C, D, E, F, G, A, B, and the supplementary B-flat--make up all the modes, distinction between them centers chiefly on which tone is used as the tonal center, or "home," namely the final. In addition, the Gregorian chant melodies tend to have certain typical figures --certain peculiar melodic twists-- that are characteristic of each individual mode.

Use in Polyphonic Music. As *polyphonic music developed, the four supplementary tones E-flat, F-sharp, C-sharp, and G-sharp were gradually added. These, plus the already-mentioned B-flat, superficially may appear to form a complete *chromatic scale. Really this is not the case, for these tones were never used in their *enharmonic equivalents; C-sharp was not used as D-flat; B-flat does not mean A-sharp. During the era when these modes constituted the raw material of music, the system of *equal temperament had not yet come into general use.

Additional Modes. About the middle of the sixteenth century the following modes were officially added to the eight shown earlier. These had already been characteristic of secular music for centuries; indeed they had been more or less avoided in church music theretofore for that very reason, and the Ionian mode had even been sometimes dubbed modus lascivus. It will be observed that the Aeolian mode is identical with the familiar minor scale (natural form), the Ionian with the major scale.

name diabolus in musica, "the devil in music." Sometimes the numbers 11 and 12 were assigned to the Ionian and Hypoionian modes, sometimes 13 and 14 to the Locrian and Hypolocrian.

Transposition. The modes were not *transposed in writing. In actual performance it was customary

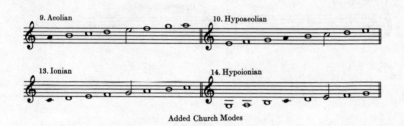

Added Church Modes

The missing modes 11 and 12, called Locrian and Hypolocrian, were entirely theoretical because their final was B, which has a *tritone relationship with the important note F, and the tritone relationship was carefully avoided; in fact it eventually developed the nick-

to transpose a melody either up or down for convenience, to bring it well within the singers' *range, but the music was never written in various "keys"; the present-day system of many *key-signatures was a development that still lay

Two Church Modes transposed

far in the future. (The key-signature of one flat had been in use ever since the thirteenth century, but there were no others.) Hence such things as the preceding were utterly unknown in modal music.

Not until after the advent of tonality (2) were key-signatures (other than that of one flat) ever applied to the modes, transposing them into all possible forms, and by this time the modal system was definitely in eclipse. It is customary to designate a transposed mode as being "on" a certain final (not "in"); for example the Dorian mode on C-sharp and the Phrygian on F have just been shown.

Synonym: tones (4).

See also Gregorian chant.

(2) Greek Modes. The Greek Modes are much older than the foregoing Church Modes. They constitute the basis of the music of ancient Greece, from about the seventh century B. C. to the second century A. D., during most of which time this country was the center of world culture. It will be noticed that they are given in descending form, rather than ascending, because the Greeks conceived scales as going down rather than up. It will also be observed that the scales themselves coincide with several of the Church Modes and that the same group of names is employed, but that the names have been interchanged. Bearing in mind that the Greek system is the older, it is clear that the medieval church musicians were responsible

for the confusion. This was due partly to the later musicians' failure to realize that the Greeks thought the scale in descending form; by the time the misunderstanding had been discovered, it was too late to change. In normal usage, a reference to the "Phrygian mode" is understood to denote the church-system Phrygian, not the Greek Phrygian; the word Greek is prefixed to any reference to these modes for clarity's sake.

Ethos. It is interesting to note that the Greeks attributed various moral qualities to the modes. They believed that melodies in one mode were useful in developing manly character, that those in another were lascivious, even immoral, and so on. Such notions may provoke a smile today, but let it not be forgotten that the people who accepted these tenets numbered among them some of the most brilliant minds the world has ever produced.

There is, perhaps, a slight counterpart in our present controversial concept of *key color.

(3) Major and Minor Modes. From a tentative introduction during the seventeenth century, two modes emerged triumphant during the eighteenth: the major mode and the minor mode (see major and minor, major scale, and minor scale). The major scale is for all practical purposes the same thing as

The Greek Modes

the Ionian church mode, the minor scale about the same as the Aeolian.

The use of the major and minor modes had already been common in secular music for several centuries before all music--church and secular-- became standardized in these two forms.

● †modo. Manner. Modo popolare, popular style, folk-song style.

● modulation. Movement from one *key (1) (tonality) to another. A new *key-signature may or may not go into effect when the new key is established, depending on how long the music is to remain in it; if the stay is brief--which is often the case--there is no change, and all necessary *accidentals are written in.

Modulation is possible only with the conventional tonal system; it did not exist (in the present meaning of the word) in the *modes (1).

A modulation is usually effected by means of a *chord which exists in both of the keys involved (that is, a *common chord); it is approached in a manner that would be typical in the old key, but quit as if it were in the new key. A chord put to this use is known as a pivot chord or hinge chord.

In the accompanying example the music modulates from C major to E minor. The chord marked X is the pivot; it is the submediant or VI of the old key (C major) and the subdominant or IV of the new key (E minor). It is also true that the chord at W is found in both keys--tonic or I in C major, submediant or VI in E minor--thus minimizing any likelihood of abruptness in the modulation. The chord at V, however, clearly does not exist in E minor, while that at Z is equally foreign to C major. The same may also be said of that at Y, for in C major it would be the second inversion of the mediant triad or III_4^6--a chord which can hardly be said to exist--while in E minor it is the second inversion of the tonic triad or I_4^6, which is extremely common.

Enharmonic Modulation. Sometimes the *enharmonic equivalents of the tones found in the pivot chord must be mentally pictured if the relationship of said chord is to

Modulation from C major to E minor.

make sense in the new key, or per- haps in the old. That is, in modulat- ing to a remote key the pivot is ap- proached as if *spelled one way, quit as though the enharmonically-equiv- alent spelling were in force; hence the pivot chord is not ideally spelled in one key or the other.

chord of the old key also appears in the first chord of the new. This is termed a pivot tone or common tone.

Changes of key where neither a pivot chord nor a pivot tone ap- pear can hardly be termed "modula- tions" in the strictest sense of

The accompanying example is taken from the *piano-vocal copy of Wagner's opera Tristan and Isolde. Beginning on the second *inversion of the tonic chord (I_4^6) of A-flat major, the music passes through several keys and with- in four measures comes to rest on the dominant chord (V) of F-sharp minor. The last measure of the quotation is not completely meaningful unless the enharmonic equivalents of the notes in the third measure (added here in letter names) are kept in mind.

In a modulation where the pivot is a diminished *seventh-chord the matter of enharmonic spelling almost always comes up.

In another type of modulation there is no chord common to the two keys involved; instead one tone in the last

the word. They are abrupt; yet their very brusqueness can on occasion be striking and dramatic.

As time has gone on, music has tended to modulate more and more, especially from the age of Wagner onward (that is, since the middle of the nineteenth century).

There are practically no compo- sitions whatever, of even moderate length, written in the conventional tonal system, which are totally devoid of modulations.

Synonym: transition (1).

●†molto. Much, very. Thus: crescendo molto or molto cre- scendo, getting much louder; allegro molto or molto allegro, very fast.

(Related English words: multiply,

multitude.)
Synonyms: di molto, assai.

● moment musical (French). Title
sometimes applied to a short composition, generally for piano and in a
lyrical style. The term comes very
close to being a catch-all title,
except that it suggests brevity. (See
titles.)
Plural: moments musicaux.
Pronunciation: mō-mằn mū-zē-kằl.

● monochord. A device used in
experiments in physics and *acoustics
(1). It consists of a single string
stretched over an oblong wooden box
which acts as a sounding-box or
resonator.
A triangular piece of wood fits in
between the string and the body of the
instrument. By moving this to various
points, the experimenter can determine
which pitches are produced by each
fractional segment of string.
It cannot be considered a musical
instrument as that term is normally
understood.
See also vibration.

● monodrama. Same as melodrama.

● monody. A style of music found in
the first *operas, around 1600. It
employs one voice in a *recitative-
like melodic line with a very subordinate *accompaniment usually in
sustained *chords. This style of
writing represents a reaction against
the involved *polyphonic music of the
preceding century.
The word monody is also sometimes
used as a synonym for *homophonic
style.
The adjective form is monodic.
Pronunciation: mŏn-ŏ-dī.

● monophonic. (1) Music which consists of an unharmonized melodic
line, lacking either *harmony or
*counterpoint, is termed monophonic
(literally "one sound"). It has only
*melody and *rhythm. *Gregorian
chant, in its ideal form, is monophonic. The same is true of the
music of the *troubadours and other
medieval minstrels (as far as is

known), of most *Oriental music,
and of many *folk-songs. Ancient
music is believed to have been
monophonic, though this is somewhat open to doubt.
The noun form is monophony.
Compare harmony, counterpoint,
homophonic, monody, polyphonic.
(2) Since the advent of stereophonic (or binaural) recording, the
older method is sometimes termed
monophonic, but more often monaural, or simply mono.
Pronunciation: mŏn-ŏ-fŏn-ĭc.

● monotone. In general, a single
repeated sound (literally "one
tone").
More specifically, monotone is a
term often applied to a person,
especially a child, who is unable
to "carry a tune." A number of
causes can lead to this condition,
the most frequent probably being
an imperfectly-developed sense of
pitch--lack of a keen musical ear--
usually the result of inadequate
experience in music. The difficulty
can be quite readily cured in
children if the proper efforts toward
that end are made at an early age.
(Reference should be made to a
textbook on the teaching of music
in the elementary school, e.g.,
Grant: Music for Elementary
Teachers.)
The source of this difficulty is
in the ear (or rather the mind)--
not the voice.
In view of the fact that nearly
all persons unable to "carry a tune"
can definitely sing more than one
pitch, albeit not the right pitches
at the right time, the synonyms
defective singer, untuned singer,
out-of-tune singer, etc., are far
more exact than monotone.

● morceau. The French word
meaning "piece." (Related English
word: morsel.)
Plural: morceaux.
Pronunciation: môr-sō.

● mordent. Name of a type of
*ornament, always executed at the
beginning of the time-value of the

note above which it is written. There are four fairly usual types: (1) the mordent ～ (2) the inverted mordent ～ (3) the double mordent ～～ (4) the double inverted mordent. ～～

(1) The mordent consists of the written note, the note just below (going according to the key-signature), both played very fast, followed by the written note, which is then held for the balance of its value. In writing out the effect in ordinary notes, the values used will depend on the tempo, for regardless of whether the pace is slow or fast, the two initial notes are always played as fast as possible. See Example 1.

below the given note.

(2) The inverted mordent or Pralltriller consists of the written note, the note just above (going according to the key-signature), both played very fast, followed by the written note, which is then held for the balance of its value. If an accidental appears over the symbol, it affects the unwritten note that is implied. See Example 3.

It is well to mention that although the inverted mordent is far more frequent that the mordent, and its symbol is simpler, it still bears a designation ("inverted mordent")

If an accidental appears under the mordent, it affects the unwritten note that is implied in the symbol. See Example 2.

that suggests it is the exception rather than the rule, when exactly the opposite is true. Use of the mordent almost disappeared before

It must be emphasized that in the mordent, the unwritten note is the one

the advent of the *Classical period, while the inverted mordent was not

only common during that epoch but was also rather frequently employed by the *Romanticists, and is still occasionally used by contemporary composers.

(3) In the double mordent there are two pairs of quick notes at the beginning rather than one pair. See Example 4.

musicologists have always emphasized that the initial notes are to begin with the beat, not before the beat. See Example 6. However, the matter seems mostly a "tempest in a teapot," for quite often it is impossible to detect whether the mordent began with the beat or before it (so rapid is its execution),

Ex. 4

(4) In the double inverted mordent or double Pralltriller a similar rule holds, except that the unwritten notes impled are the ones just above. See Example 5.

and even when detectable, as often as not the artistic difference is negligible.

Present-day composers have sensibly dispensed with the mordent

Ex. 5

With all forms of the mordent,

symbol in favor of writing out the

Ex. 6

Ex. 7

effect in *grace-notes. Compare the ease with which Example 7 is read with the first four examples of the mordent (appearing in Examples 1 and 2).

When the mordent or inverted mordent appears over a very short note--which is by no means unusual-- the result will usually sound very much like a triplet. Under such conditions the mordent and the *trill become practically synonymous. See Example 8.

Abbreviation: mor.
Synonym: perdendosi.

● †mormorando. Murmuring.

● †mormorio. Murmur.
Pronunciation: accent -ri-.

● Morris dance. A type of dance popular in England for use during May games. Morris dance is probably a corruption of Moorish dance, for at the time of its

Ex. 8 Allegro Written ... Both played

It is perhaps obvious that there is a certain amount of confusion in regard to these symbols. Apparently the character for the double inverted mordent has sometimes been used to indicate the trill without after-beat.

When the mordent appears over a chord or interval it affects only the highest note unless written once for each note. This applies to the parts for two instruments written on the same staff in an orchestral *score. See Example 9.

origin in fifteenth-century France and Spain, it was danced in Moorish costumes. It is usually in 4-4 time.

Variant forms: morrice dance, Moresca, Morisca.

● †mosso. Motion. Thus: più mosso, faster (literally "more motion"); meno mosso, slower (literally "less motion"). The variant form moto is common, preceded by con (with), in such

Ex. 9 Written Performed   Written   Performed

● †morendo. Dying away; a *diminuendo which continues until the sound completely disappears.

In some cases the element of *ritardando (rallentando) would seem to be included, though the word means simply "dying." (Related English word: mortal.)

designations as andante con moto ("rather slow, with motion"). Very often the "motion" might be termed "lilt" or "gentle swing." Con moto alone is about equal to allegretto.

● motet. This term has had several

different meanings during the history
of music.   The only quality common
to all meanings is that it is usually
for use at religious services, particularly in the Catholic church.
(However, secular motets can be
found.)   Latin texts and absence of
instrumental accompaniment are two
other features usually, but not always,
applicable.   The motet might almost
be considered the Catholic equivalent
of the later Protestant *anthem; however motets have been used in
Protestant services, especially the
Lutheran.

(1) The sixteenth century (or
Renaissance) motet was comparatively
short, in one movement, had a Latin
text, and was nominally for voices
only (however, see a cappella).   It
was often--but by no means invariably
--highly contrapuntal; when not contrapuntal it was a series of chords
rather than melody-and-accompaniment
(*homophonic) style.   The number of
parts was usually at least four, and
often more.   Palestrina, Lassus,
Victoria, and other sixteenth century
masters wrote many motets.   Contemporary composers are reviving
this form as a substitute for the less
contrapuntal, less unified, and less
lofty *anthem.

(2) The eighteenth century (or
Baroque) motet sometimes was written
for instruments as well as voices,
and the voice parts occasionally included *solos as well as chorus.   Many
were written in the vernacular, but
others remained in Latin.   They are
often highly contrapuntal, and a
number utilize two choruses.   Some
are in more than one movement, and
hence are practically identical, except
in name, with the *cantata.

(3) The thirteenth century (or Gothic)
motet was usually written for three
voice parts.   There is evidence that
it was often performed with instruments replacing one or even all
voices.   Its most striking feature is
that each part sang a different text,
of which one or two were usually in
the vernacular and extremely secular,
sometimes even bawdy, in spirit.
Another voice (usually the lowest)
was in Latin and its text was from
the liturgy.   It is not certain that

motets were regularly performed
in this polyglot manner, however;
some musicologiests have hazarded
the theory that the various texts
were selected according to the
occasion--one was used when sung
in church, a different one when
sung in a tavern.   If instruments
were substituted for two of the
voices, each text except the one
which was appropriate would have
been automatically suppressed.   In
consequence of the three simultaneous sets of words, most thirteenth
century motets have three titles,
for example Trop Sovent--Brunete--
In Seculum.

It is known that the word motet
in its thirteenth century meaning
is derived from the French mot,
meaning "word."   There is incon-
clusive evidence that later meanings may be related to the Latin
word meaning "move," in token
of the frequently contrapuntal
character of the music.

(The spelling motette, which is
occasionally seen, is incorrect.)

Pronunciation: mō-tĕt.́

● motive.   (1) A group of notes,
forming a distinctive recognizable
pattern of sounds, which makes
up a part of the *theme.   Thus a
theme normally contains several
motives.

(2) A synonym for Leitmotiv.
Variant form: motif.

● †moto.   Variant form of mosso.

● †moto perpetuo.   See perpetual
motion.

● motto theme.   See cyclic form.

● mouth organ.   See harmonica.

● mouth-hole.   The hole near the
left end of the *flute and *piccolo
which is held to the player's lips
and over which he blows to cause
the instrument to sound.   It is
the nearest approach to a *"mouthpiece" that those instruments
possess.

● mouthpiece.   That portion of a

*wind instrument which is held up to
(sometimes inside) the player's mouth.

There are two types of mouthpiece
used with brass instruments: cup-
shaped and funnel- (or cone-) shaped;
the former type is used with the
trumpet, trombone, cornet, baritone
(2) (euphonium), alto horn (mellophone), and tuba, the latter with the
horn and Wagner tubas.

The mouthpiece of woodwind instruments is variously (A) a small section to which the reed is attached,
as in the clarinet and saxophone, or
(B) a hole (more completely, mouth-
hole) over which to blow as in the
flute and piccolo, or (C) a peculiar
notch-like aperture (called a fipple)
which creates vibrations, as in the
recorder and the *simple melody
instruments. With the oboe, English
horn, bassoon, and sarrusophone,
the double reed held directly in the
player's mouth is the nearest approach
to a mouthpiece that these instruments
possess.

Compare mouth-pipe.

● mouth-pipe. The portion of certain
wind instruments that connects the
*mouthpiece to the body of the instru-
ment. The bassoon, saxophone, and
bass clarinet have prominent mouth-
pipes, but certain other instruments
have none at all.

● movable do. See syllables.

● movement. (1) An individual complete piece within a *symphony,
*sonata, *concerto, *string quartet,
*suite, *concerto grosso, etc.

Each of the foregoing terms represents a form that is not a single
composition, but a series or group
of compositions, the individual portions being termed movements rather
than pieces or compositions. When
these are performed, it is preferable
that no interruption, such as applause,
should occur between movements.

The various movements are sometimes
referred to by number ("first movement," etc.), and sometimes by the
Italian *tempo marks ("allegro movement," "adagio movement," etc.),
or by their general character ("slow
movement," "fast movement," etc.),

or by their form or style
("scherzo movement," "variation
movement," etc.). On concert
programs the tempo-marks are
used in listing the various
sections of a work. One can
only speculate on the mystifying
effect these must produce on any
uninitiated persons who happen to
be in the audience.

If there is a change of tempo
within the course of a piece, it
is not desirable to term the various
sections movements, since all of
the whole is an undivided composition. This however is an entirely
different matter from that of joining two movements together without pause, an effect which occasionally is specified (see attacca).

The separate sections within a
*song-cycle, *cantata, or *oratorio
are occasionally termed movements,
although *number is perhaps more
frequent with the latter two types,
and is almost invariable in connection with the *opera.

(2) Rate of speed, tempo.
Abbreviation: movt., mov't.,
mvt.

● †movimento. Movement, motion.

● mp. Rather soft, moderately
soft. This is the abbreviation
for mezzo piano, signifying a
dynamic level softer than *mf, but
not so much so as *p.
See dynamic terms.

● m. s. Left hand; abbreviation
for Italian mano sinistra.
For further information see cross-
hand and r. h.

● musette. A type of dance
featuring a *drone bass or pedal
point; see non-harmonic tones (9).
Musettes are sometimes written
as the middle section of *gavottes,
under the title "Gavotte and
Musette," the order being: gavotte,
musette, gavotte repeated (ABA
form).

The dance is named after a
French folk instrument similar to
the *bagpipe.
Pronunciation: mū-zĕt.

● musica ficta. Additional *accidentals applied to the performance of music although not actually written in the notation; the sharping or flatting of tones not so written in the notation. Musica ficta (Latin for "fictitious music" or "false music") was used from the days of early *polyphony through the sixteenth century. Sharps were more frequently inserted than flats, and the purpose was often that of supplying a *leading-tone, that is, a tone located a *half step below the *tonic (or more properly, *final).

rather than in front of it. Some musicians are of the opinion that a few editors have indicated more accidentals than were really used. However, it is not impossible that various performances during the days of musica ficta might not always have employed accidentals at the same points.

Careless and sloppy though such a practice may seem today, the fact that it was employed for several centuries testifies that it must have been adequate for the needs of its times.

It must be rememberd that during the days when musica ficta was used, nearly all compositions were vocal; to sing the tones in question with chromatic modifications was easy and natural, while to sing them exactly as the notation suggested was rather difficult and hence probably not even thought of. Composers would have considered writing in the omitted accidentals a fussy and quite unnecessary detail--perhaps even an insult to the singers, to whom the raising of the tone by a half step would seem perfectly obvious. (At one time the sharp was called the "fool's sign," implying that insertion was superfluous to an intelligent person.) In the days when musica ficta was used, C-sharp was considered another form of C, B-flat a variety of B, etc., rather than entirely distinct sounds as we think of them today. The employment or non-employment of musica ficta apparently was not an optional matter; the tones to be sung were obvious to the composer and probably to the performers of the day, though hardly so to those of our day.

Present-day *editors indicate a point where they believe musica ficta was employed by placing the sharp or flat above or below the note,

Synonym: musica falsa.

● musical comedy. An *operetta, especially a rather ephemeral one in which the music is distinctly "popular" (1) in style.

Musical comedies are sometimes called musical shows, Broadway shows, or simply musicals.

● music appreciation. A study frequently offered in high schools and colleges to introduce students with little or no musical training to the literature of music. A background of technical knowledge or ability to perform is seldom if ever demanded as a prerequisite to enrollment. The purpose of these courses has often been summarized in the words "to teach students to be intelligent consumers rather than producers."

● music box. A mechanical instrument on which a spring-diven metal cylinder, into which tiny pins are stuck at certain spots, revolves in such a way that the pins contact short, tuned tongues of metal. The exact placing of the pins determines which tongues will be struck and therefore the music that will result. The sound is light, tinkling and charming, and always high-pitched.

● music critic. A music critic is
an employee of a newspaper or magazine, whose business is to attend
*concerts and write reviews of them.
The word critic should be accepted
in its correct meaning--as a synonym
for evaluator or appraiser, not as a
synonym for fault-finder or censurer.
  If any new or fairly new compositions are on the program, he points
out what he believes to be good or
bad about them. In all concerts the
manner of the performance, from the
standpoint of both *technique and
*interpretation, is evaluated for its
good or weak features.
  A music critic must have a comprehensive knowledge of music and a
polished, fluent style of writing. His
profession is far from a sinecure.
Many of these men also write on
drama or art or both.
  A fine discussion of this profession
will be found in Practical Musical
Criticism by Oscar Thompson.
  In addition to Oscar Thompson, well-
known music critics of the past and
present include Olin Downes, Virgil
Thomson, Howard Taubman, Eduard
Hanslick, Ernest Newman, W. J.
Henderson, H. T. Parker, Richard
Aldrich, Henry T. Finck, Lawrence
Gilman, Henry Krehbiel, Deems
Taylor, etc. Debussy, Tschaikowsky,
Cui, Schumann, and Hugo Wolf are
among the famous composers who
were also active as critics.

● music drama. A type of *opera--
probably the highest and most complex development of that form. The
term is especially associated with
the later operas of Wagner and those
of Richard Strauss.
  The following characteristics distinguish the music drama from the
ordinary opera:
  (A) The *overture (1) is usually
replaced by a *prelude (3).
  (B) The orchestra is often more
important than the voices; it carries
forward the action and musical thought
much more than the voices.
  (C) There is no stop in the music
from the beginning of an act until the
curtain falls at its close; the music

drama does not divide into set
*"numbers," such as *recitatives,
*arias, *duets, *choruses, etc.,
in the manner typical of most
operas. Consequently it is often
difficult to take an excerpt from a
music drama (unless it occurs at
the end of the act); for this reason
when an excerpt is presented at
a concert, the beginning and ending
may be unsatisfactory or even
abrupt. (However, see concert
ending.)
  (D) The various characters and
elements in the action are represented by *Leitmotivs, which tend
to give the music drama greater
thematic unity than the average
opera.
  (E) The style of vocal writing
does not classify into two clear-
cut types--aria and recitative--
but instead seems to be a style
half-way between them. (There
are of course many exceptional
passages.)
  (F) Seldom do two or more
characters sing simultaneously.
  (G) Music dramas tend to use a
larger orchestra than the average
opera. (This, however, may be
a coincidence rather than an
essential.)
  (H) There is no attempt to flatter
singers' vanity or to supply
material which will display their
voices.
  (I) The music drama seeks to be
a union of the arts--poetry, acting,
painting (scenery), and music.
  (J) All operatic conventions are
ignored.
  The fact that Wagner's works
were "modern" in style for their
day, that they are difficult to
sing and play, that they are awkward to stage well, that they are
longer than most operas, and that
Wagner in some cases used rare
instruments such as the *bass
trumpet, *Wagner tuba, and contrabass *trombone, are all purely
coincidental rather than true
characteristics of the music drama
in general.

● musicianship. (1) Those qualities

which are a part of the make-up of a musician, other than ability to perform. (It will be seen that this usage, customary in the music profession, is the diametrical opposite of that employed by "the man in the street.")

Musicians often declare that "musicianship is an attitude" or "musicanship is a state of mind"; that is, it does not result from practicing, from "studying hard," or from dazzling technique; it is an adjunct to those skills.

Theoretically it is possible to have musicianship and yet not be able to play any instrument or sing really well. Musicianship designates those qualities of intelligent insight that enable a person to reconstruct the intent of the composer, plus the humility and the willingness to follow these conscientious conclusions.

(2) The term is also used in some college music departments and *conservatories to designate courses in *ear-training, proficiency in which is one of the foremost characteristics of a true musician.

● musicology. The scientific study of music, particularly of its historical and stylistic development.

A genuine musicologist draws his conclusions from the actual study of compositions themselves and from research in source materials, not from books that merely talk about music. The musicological point of view is chiefly an attitude.

In its historical approach, musicology is especially interested in the development of various musical styles--when certain chords and chord-progressions were first employed, when certain instruments came into common use, the times during which certain rhythmic patterns formed music's everyday speech, the appearance, development, and decline of different *forms, and so on.

It is erroneous to assume that musicology is interested solely in music written before 1750, though doubtless certain musicologists have devoted too little attention to recent developments.

Musicologists have evolved a rather extensive lingua franca, much of it

taking the form of mysterious-looking abbreviations such as AdHM, SaHMI, MQ, and SchGMB. These refer to certain books and magazines; for example the foregoing abbreviations designate, respectively, Guido Adler's Handbuch der Musikgeschichte, Curt Sach's History of Musical Instruments, the magazine Musical Quarterly, and Arnold Schering's Geschichte der Musik in Beispielen.

Perhaps the best summary of the term musicology could be given by literally translating its German equivalent, Musikwissenschaft: "music science."

● music typewriter. See typewriter (music).

● musique concrète (French). Modernist movement among certain French composers which introduces noises and non-musical sounds. These noises are sometimes blended together, sometimes mixed with conventional musical tones. They are usually taken down by a *tape-recorder, from which they are reproduced at the concert.

Some musicians have hailed the principle of musique concrète as something which will expand the horizons of the art; others believe its chief appeal will be to charlatans, pointing out that just anybody could be a "composer" by following this procedure.

Pronunciation: mŭ-zĕk kŏn-krĕt.

● †muta. Change, change to. Thus, in the flute part of an orchestral piece, the direction muta in flauto piccolo means "change to piccolo"; in the clarinet part the direction muta in A or muta in la means "change to clarinet in A."

The plural verb form is mutano, used when two or more instruments make the same change. (Mutano is accented on the first syllable.)

● mutation. The *"change of voice" of a young man. There is no connection with the term *mute.

● mute. A device for altering the *tone-color of an instrument.

(1) String Instruments. The mute for the bowed string instruments looks like a tiny wooden or metal comb with three or five prongs. When fastened to the bridge of the instrument it produces a veiled, silky, soft tone ("soft" here being intended to refer not to the volume of the sound but rather to its quality). *Rests must be provided in the music to give the player time to attach it or remove it.

There is a special type of mute, consisting of a small piece of slit rubber, which when not in use is kept on the portion of string lying between the bridge and the tail-piece. It can be put in place and removed more quickly than the ordinary type, and is often called the "Heifetz mute."

A third type, very recently developed, can be put into effect or retired almost instantaneously. It is a little roll of plastic held by wire around two of the strings on the far side of the bridge. With a quick shove of the right hand, the player moves it up to touch the bridge and hence go into effect; another shove throws it back out of use. One beat of rest will suffice to place it or retire it.

The frequently-made statement that "mutes have no effect on tones played *pizzicato" is nonsense.

(2) Brass Instruments. The mutes for the brass instruments are made of metal, wood, or cardboard, and are inserted into the *bell (2) of the instrument. They produce a harsh, pungent, acid, somewhat rasping tone, especially when the instrument is played loud. The soft muted *horn, however, has a really subdued tone.

There are special types of trumpet mute used to produce bizarre effects; these are in vogue in the *dance band. (Even a Derby hat is sometimes used for muting purposes!)

Mutes for both the string instruments and the brass are not intended for reducing the volume; they should not be regarded as a means for muffling the instrument. Their purpose,

as stated above, is to produce a change in tone-color. Muted brass instruments are required to play loud as often as soft; loud muted string passages are not unknown, even though exceptional.

On the trombone and tuba, sufficient time (in the form of rests) must be allowed for the player to put the mute in place and to remove it. On the horn and trumpet, however, insertion and removal can both be accomplished almost instantaneously.

The direction to employ the mute is con sordino, con sordina, or con sordini (normally abbreviated to con sord.), occasionally mettere sordino. The direction for removing it is senza sord., occasionally via sord., alzate sord., or levate sord. The French and German terms for using the mute are avec sourdine(s) and mit Dämpfer(n), respectively (also, for brass instruments, gestopft); for removing it, sans sourdines or ôtez les sourdines and ohne Dämpfer or Dämpfer weg (also, for brass, offen).

Use of the mute is never at the discretion of the string or brass instrument player, and hence is by no means analogous to the use of the *soft pedal of the piano.

● m. v. Abbreviation for mezza voce.

● Mystic Chord. A chord frequently used (even abused) by the Russian composer Alexander Scriabin (1872-1915) in his later compositions. In its normal position it consists (reading upward) of an augmented fourth, a diminished fourth, an augmented fourth, and two perfect fourths. Thus it contains six different tones. However, it is not a *fourth-chord as that term is generally used. (See example on following page.)

Scriabin's "Mystic Chord"

N

● Nachtstück (German).   *Nocturne
(literally, *night piece").
Plural: Nachtstücke.
Pronunciation: näkt-shtük.

● names.   See titles.

● national anthem, national hymn. A
patriotic *song which has received
government recognition for use on official occasions.
   The national anthem of the United
States is The Star-Spangled Banner,
that of France, The Marseillaise, of
England, God Save the King (Queen),
of Canada, O Canada (sometimes God
Save the King), and so on.
   It is only fair to point out that the
composers of these songs are rarely
musicians of first-class standing;
however there is a notable exception
in the case of Austria, whose national anthem was written by Haydn.
   See also home-and-community-songs.

● nationalism.   Stylistic traits peculiar
to the music of one certain country,
distinguishing it from that of other
countries.   One can detect the nationality of many composers merely by
hearing their music; it "sounds"
Russian, or Spanish, or French, etc.
   The emergence of deliberate and
conscious emphasis on nationalism
was one of the phases of *Romanticism.
Nevertheless nationalistic traits, usually
unconscious and unsought rather than
deliberate, can be found in music
written long prior to the nineteenth
century; indeed they may be traced
back to the fifteenth or fourteenth
century.
   The movement is still in progress
today, the music of the United States
being a noteworthy contemporary
example.

   Nationalism has always owed a
conspicuous debt to *folk music.
Folk tunes, imitations of folk
tunes, and various characteristic
melodic and rhythmic patterns
have found their way into the art
music produced in the different
countries--sometimes by design,
other times cropping out spontaneously.
   Nevertheless it is an error to
assume that all typically nationalistic music is folk influenced.
Debussy's works are extremely
"French," Puccini's extremely
"Italian," yet neither composer
exhibits much folk influence. In
addition, many musicians seriously
doubt whether there is such a thing
as music that is not nationalistic
at all.   The literature commonly
assumed to be non-nationalistic
is in reality German or Austrian,
i. e., the works of Bach, Handel,
Haydn, Mozart, Beethoven, Schu-
bert, Mendelssohn, Schumann,
Wagner, Brahms, Richard Strauss,
etc.
   Some composers who were (or
are) avowedly and purposely
nationalistic are:
   Norway: Edvard Grieg (1843-1907).
   Spain: Isaac Albéniz (1860-1909),
Enrique Granados (1867-1916),
Manuel De Falla (1876-1946),
Joaquin Turina (1882-1949).
   England: Ralph Vaughan
Williams (1872-1958), Gustav
Holst (1874-1934).
   Finland: Jan Sibelius (1865-1957).
   Romania: Georges Enesco (1881-
1955).
   Bohemia (Czechoslovakia): Bedrich
Smetana (1824-1884), Antonin
Dvořák (1841-1904), Leos Janáček
(1854-1928).

United States: Aaron Copland
(1900-   ), Roy Harris (1898-   ),
Burrill Phillips (1907-   ), Douglas
Moore (1893-   ), Charles Ives (1876-
1954). (Many others could be added
to this list.)
Brazil: Heitor Villa-Lobos (1887?-
1959).
Mexico: Carlos Chávez (1899-   ),
Silvestre Revueltas (1899-1940).
Hungary: Béla Bartók (1881-1945),
Zoltán Kodály (1882-   ).
Poland: Frederic Chopin (1810-1849).
Russia: Modeste Moussorgsky (1839-
1881), Mili Balakireff (1837-1910),
César Cui (1835-1918), Alexander
Borodin (1833-1887), Nicholas Rimsky-
Korsakoff (1844-1908), Anatole Liadoff
(1855-1914), Sergei Rachmaninoff (1873-
1943), Dmitri Shostakovich (1906-   ).
Nikolai Miaskovsky (1881-1950).
The foregoing list is only suggestive;
it could be extended indefinitely.
See also "Five (The)," folk music.

● natural. The character ♮ It
restores to normal pitch any note which
has been affected by a *sharp, *flat,
*double-sharp, or *double-flat appear-
ing as an accidental, as well as those
notes affected by the flats or sharps
of the *key-signature. It usually occurs
as an *accidental, though it may be
found as a temporary part of a key-
signature at a point where the signature
changes. In the accompanying example,
the three naturals are used to reduce
a five-flat signature to two flats. At
all subsequent points, only the two
flats will appear.
All tones not otherwise affected are
understood to be natural, the word
natural being rarely appended to the
letter-name except for emphasis.
Synonym: cancel. Although rarely
used, this term very aptly describes
the character's function.
See also accidental.

● †naturale. To be played or sung
in the normal manner. This is
often used to cancel sul ponticello
and sul tasto in the music for string
instruments (see sul 3 and 4).
Synonym: ordinario.

● natural horn. The obsolete form
of the *horn (French horn) that was
in use before the invention of
*valves; it was a refined version of
the *hunting horn. This instrument
could play only the tones of the
*harmonic series (which depended
on the *crook in use) and those
tones a *half-step below them. The
latter were called stopped tones and
were obtained by placing the hand
part-way into the *bell (2). Their
*tone-quality was different from
that of the *open tones (i.e., those
of the harmonic series).
The "Waldhorn" required in German scores is a natural horn, the
German for valve horn being Ventil-
horn.
The natural horn (also called hand
horn) was in its heyday during most
of the eighteenth century plus the
early nineteenth. By the use of
*crooks it was possible to put the
instrument in any key from C-alto
(sounding as written) to A-basso
(sounding an octave and a minor
third lower than written--see intervals). A complete list of these will
be found, among other things, in the
entry transposing instruments. However, the most frequently-used horns
were these:
Horn in B-flat alto. Sounded a whole-
step lower than written.
Horn in A. Sounded a minor third
lower than written.
Horn in G. Sounded a perfect fourth
lower than written.
Horn in F. Sounded a perfect fifth
lower than written.

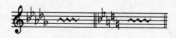

Horn in E. Sounded a minor
sixth lower than written.
Horn in E-flat. Sounded a major
sixth lower than written.
Horn in D. Sounded a minor
seventh lower than written.
Horn in C. Sounded an octave
lower than written.
Horn in B-flat basso. Sounded a
major ninth (an octave and a
whole-step) lower than written.

The written notes available were,
in general, those found in the first
series of tones in the entry harmonic series (the group of notes
built from a fundamental C). The
transposition of the horn will
indicate how these notes should be
transposed to determine the actual
pitches; for instance the second
series shown in said entry (built
from a low E-flat) represents the
actual sounds playable on the horn
in E-flat.

The fact that some of these notes
--7, 11, 13, 14--were out of tune
rendered them useless as open
tones, but the stopped tones available from them (by using the hand)
could be played in tune by employing a slightly different hand-position
from that used with other stopped
tones. Their quality was also
better.

The real ranges differed very
little, for only the highest-pitched
horns could sound the fundamental
(no. 1) but they could not ascend
much above no. 12, while the medi-
um-pitched horns could not sound
the fundamental but could rise to
about no. 16, and the deepest horns
also could not sound the fundamental
but could rise to no. 18 or possibly
20. Thus it will be seen that the
only difference between one crook
and any other was the exact series
of tones that was made available
by the particular crook in use.

The use of this instrument proved
a retarding factor on boldness in
*modulation, for after entering the
new key the set of notes available
on the horn, however useful in the
old key, might now be too few to
be of any real value. (The *natural trumpet was still more limited.)
Off-hand it might seem that resort-

ing to a change of crook would solve
the problem, as tones peculiar to the
new key could thus become available,
if the proper crook were prescribed.
Actually this was usually more of a
hindrance than a help (as rarity of
changing crooks will prove), for while
the player was making the change the
instrument was of course completely
unusable; in addition composers probably
were fearful lest they miscalculate the
amount of time required for the operation. In any case when the music returned to the original key the matter
of changing back to the original crook
posed a second problem.

Perhaps for this reason composers
of the *Classical period were more
conservative in modulating to distant
keys in orchestral compositions than
in those for the piano or for *chamber-
music combinations, for by sticking to
the closely-*related keys and making no
change in crook, the number of tones
at the composer's disposal was practically as many as in the main key.

Early in the nineteenth century the
use of four horns (rather than two)
became common, and it was customary
to crook the first and second horn in
one key, the third and fourth in a
different one, thus providing two series
of tones with which to work. Indeed,
Berlioz and other early *Romanticists
would sometimes prescribe a different
crook for each of the four horns, thus
furnishing themselves four sets of
open tones (i.e., four harmonic series).
An unconventional melody sometimes
would pass from one horn to another.
In chord passages the rules of *voice-
leading often had to be ignored, otherwise the desired chords would not have
been possible at all.

In view of the limitations of the natural horn, still more of the natural
trumpet, it is easy to see why composers
of this period leaned most heavily on the
string and woodwind instruments, which
had no such limitations; and it is difficult to imagine why the *trombones did
not come into common use earlier than
they did (see orchestra), for the trombones were always able to play all the
notes of the *chromatic scale.

The application of *valves to the horn
(also the trumpet), during the 1840's
and 1850's, made it possible to play

any tone within the instrument's range, and proved a great boon to composers. (It may be argued that the tendency of music to modulate more and more frequently made the invention of valves a matter of necessity.) Within 75 years only the horn in F and sometimes that in B-flat alto (also sometimes that in E-flat in the *band) were still in use. The remaining crooks had become obsolete. The present-day horn is described under horn.

Synonym: hand horn.

See also crook, transposing instruments.

● natural tones (brass instruments). Same as open tones.

● natural trumpet. The obsolete *trumpet without *valves, in use through the early part of the nineteenth century. Its resources were not much greater than those of the *bugle. For further description, see trumpet.

● nature's chord. The *harmonic series.

● Neapolitan sixth. An altered form of the *supertonic triad. In the major mode it appears with the root and fifth lowered a half-step, in the minor mode with the root lowered a half-step. The Neapolitan sixth chord is identical in any major key and its *tonic minor; thus in both C major and C minor it consists of D-flat, F, A-flat. It is called "Neapolitan" because of the not-very-accurate belief that it was first used by composers of Naples, Italy; it is called "sixth" because it most frequently appears as a "chord of the sixth" (i.e., in first *inversion (1)--with the third in the bass), and with the third *doubled (2); nevertheless it is occasionally used in *root position though very rarely in second inversion. See example at bottom of page.

The terminology "Neapolitan sixth" is entirely different from, and much more accurate than, the terms "Italian sixth," "French sixth," and "German sixth" (see augmented sixth chords).

See also altered chords.

● neighboring notes. See non-harmonic tones (2).

● †nel, nella. In the, at the.

● neo-classical. A type of twentieth-century music which seeks to avoid being "expressive"; it is a reaction against the tense, breast-heaving, wearing-the-heart-on-the-sleeve emotionalism of some music of the *Roman-

Neapolitan sixth in C major.   Neapolitan sixth in C minor

Mode 5 (Lydian)

The same chant fragment in neumes and in modern notation.

tic period. Neo-classical style avoids the sentimental, the lush, the exciting, the "blood-and-thunder," the "soulful," and the bombastic. Instead it is abstract.

It must be emphasized that neo-classicism is a return to the comparatively cool and unemotional mood and spirit of eighteenth-century *Classical and *Baroque music, but by no means to its melodic, harmonic, or rhythmic style. It is an evocation rather than an emulation. It does, however, frequently revive the *forms of the Baroque and Classical eras.

Neo-classicism stems largely from the ideas of Erik Satie (1866-1925); it flowered in the music of the French composers who were called "The *Six," particularly in that of Milhaud. Many of Stravinsky's works written during or after the First World War are neo-classical in spirit, e.g., L'Histoire du Soldat (The Soldier's Story), the Serenade for Piano, the Octet for Wind Instruments, and the Dumbarton Oaks Concerto.

The styles of Wagner, Tschaikowsky, and Liszt are the antithesis of neo-classicism.

Much neo-classical music displays a studied artlessness; it is often reminiscent of the *folk-song and even of the singing of children. Strictly speaking, however, it is an aesthetic ideal rather than a style.

● neumes. A name given to the characters used in several systems of notation that preceded the appearance of the present system.

(1) The most important (but also most modern) of these is still often used, generally with a staff of four lines (and three spaces) in writing *Gregorian chants (plain-songs). During the approximate period 1200-1450 neumes were the customary form of notation for all music. In the accompanying example modern notation is shown for purposes of comparison.

The illustration shows square neumes with and without stems and those of diamond shape. A third type, used to indicate three tones slurred together, the middle being the lowest in pitch, has this appearance:

N

Still another kind was written small and was to be sung softer than the notes preceding and following it; it might be called the opposite of a *sforzando.

Those who have familiarized themselves with this style of notation declare that Gregorian chants can be read more quickly and easily with neumes than with modern notation. Use of this type of neume is sometimes called Roman choral notation (see chorale (4)).

(2) Another important type, older than the foregoing, is that called staffless, cheironomic (chironomic), or oratorical neumes. As the first of these names suggests, they were used before the invention of the *staff. Their appearance somewhat resembles shorthand. This system of notation was far from satisfactory, for it is doubtful if anyone could read an entirely unfamiliar chant written with it. Staffless neumes were probably adequate only for recalling to mind a melody already somewhat vaguely known to the singer; they were basically a memorandum.

(3) The appearance of still another style of neume, also staffless, may be judged from its amusing German name: Hufnagelschrift--"horseshoe-nail script."

A totally different type of old notation is discussed under tablature.

Variant spelling: neums.

See also Gregorian chant, Liber Usualis.

Pronunciation: nōomz, nyōomz.

● Nibelungen tuba. Same as Wagner tuba.

●† niente. Nothing. Quasi niente, "almost nothing," i.e., extremely soft.

● nine common keys, the. The *key-signatures up to and including four sharps and four flats, plus that of the key of C (i.e., no sharps or flats). Statistics would undoubtedly show that these nine key-signatures are much more frequently used than those of five, six, or seven sharps or flats. Since every key-signature applies to one major and one minor key, actually eighteen keys are involved, and the expression would be more accurate in the form "the nine common key-signatures."

● ninth-chord. A *chord consisting (theoretically) of five different tones laid out as superimposed thirds (see intervals). The five members are the root (fundamental), third, fifth, seventh, and ninth. It may be aptly described as "a *seventh-chord with another third added to the top." In four-part writing the fifth is usually chosen as the member which must of necessity be omitted, since its absence in no way jeopardizes the identity of the chord and even, in some musicians' estimation, improves its sound.

The dominant-ninth chord (V9) is the most frequent chord of this type, although the supertonic (II9) and tonic (I9) ninth-chords are sometimes encountered; the remainder are however extremely rare, some of them having no more than a theoretical existence.

See also: chord, harmony, triad, seventh-chord.

● ninths. *Intervals consisting of an *octave plus a second.

●† nobilmente. Nobly.

● nocturne. A night piece. Nearly all examples are instrumental, the majority being for piano. The style is usually quiet and rather song-like, though a fortissimo climax is by no means a rarity.

The Irish composer John Field (1782-1837) was the first to employ the term regularly, his Nocturnes being for piano; it is clear that the Nocturnes by Chopin were strongly influenced by those of Field.

Debussy's so-called Three Nocturnes for Orchestra ("Clouds," "Festivals," and "Sirens," the latter also utilizing a women's *chorus singing without words) seem almost misnomers.

Variant form (Italian): notturno.

● noël. (1) A Christmas song.
(2) An organ piece for the Christmas season.
Variant spellings: nowel, nowell.
See also carol.

● nomenclature. See notation, dynamic marks, tempo marks, Italian terminology; see also titles.

●† non. Not. Non troppo, not too much; non f, not loud.

● non-chordal tones, non-essential tones. Same as non-harmonic tones.

Dominant ninth-chord in C major.   The same chord with fifth omitted.   Dominant ninth (fifth omitted) in C minor.

● nonet. A composition for nine voices or instruments.

See groups.

Pronunciation: nō-nĕt.

● non-functional harmony. *Chords whose movement to other chords does not seem to be the result of their inherent nature or to occur in response to their natural tendencies; also chords used purely for their effect as chords--sheerly for their sensuous sound. *Functional harmony is "going some place"; non-functional is not.

A close examination of many compositions written during or prior to the sixteenth century (e.g., a work by Palestrina) will show that the vertical *sonorities (2) are not marching toward an inevitable *cadence, but rather that they are pleasing though almost fortuitous combinations resulting from the interweaving of the various strands in the *polyphony.

Non-functional harmony reappears strongly in some twentieth-century music, notably that of the French *impressionists. In the accompanying quotation from The Submerged Cathedral by Debussy, all of the chords are of the dominant-*seventh type of construction, yet none seems to *resolve on toward any particular goal.

● non-harmonic tones. Tones which are not members of the *chords with which they sound--foreign to the harmony prevailing at the given moment. Their character is largely one of ornamenting the skeletal harmonic structure.

Every tone in a composition is either a chord-member (or chordal tone) or else a non-harmonic tone (also called by-tone, unessential tone, non-essential tone, non-chordal tone, inharmonic tone).

Non-harmonic tones are nearly always *dissonant. There are several distinct species, classified according to their behavior.

(1) The passing-tone (or passing-note) is approached and quitted *diatonically (stepwise) or *chromatically, and in the same direction, either up or down. It may be accented or unaccented; the latter type is the more common. Accented passing-tones are sometimes called appoggiaturas, but in a different meaning of the word from that which will be employed later. Passing-tones may occur in any voice. In the example at the top of p. 268, unaccented passing-tones are marked U, accented passing-tones A. The F in the alto of the third measure may at first glance appear to be an unaccented passing-tone; however most *theorists would probably regard it as the seventh of the dominant-*seventh chord.

An example of non-functional harmony in written parallelisms.

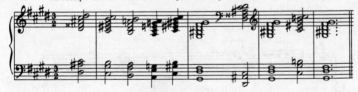

Passing-tones

Passing-tones may progress step-wise to one another before the last one reaches its tone of *resolution; that is, there may be two or more of them in a row (see soprano of second measure and tenor of fourth measure of passing-tone example).

(2) A neighboring-note (also called auxiliary tone, neighbor, or em-bellishing tone) is approached and quitted stepwise, but returns to the identical tone from which it came; that is, it is quitted in the opposite direction from which it is approached. It may be accented or unaccented. There are two types of neighboring-note, the upper and the lower. Lower neighboring-notes are normally just a *half-step below the chordal tone, hence they must often be modified by an accidental. In the example below, U indicates the upper neighboring-notes, L the lower.

(3) A suspension is a tone which holds over (or repeats) as the harmony changes, then resolves stepwise. *Ties are often necessary in notating it. It is invariably accented.

There are always three phases to be kept in mind in handling and analyz-ing the suspension: 1. The preparation, meaning membership in the old chord; 2. the suspension proper, meaning the moment of dissonance; 3. the resolution,

Neighboring-notes

meaning the movement to the chord member to which it progresses naturally. (See first example below.)

Most suspensions resolve downward. Those which resolve upward are sometimes called <u>retardations</u>. Retardations almost invariably occur in the highest voice.

If the dissonant tone has been approached by repeating rather than by holding out, some theorists term it an <u>appoggiatura</u>.

In the second example below, suspensions are marked S; suspensions approached by repetition (appoggiaturas in some terminologies) by SS, and upward-resolving suspensions (retardations in some terminologies) by R.

Suspensions often occur simultaneously in two voices. Note that both the alto and the soprano have suspensions (a retardation in the soprano) in the fourth measure of this example. Mozart often uses three simultaneous suspensions at *cadences.

(4) The <u>anticipation</u> might well be called the opposite of the suspension, since it is a tone belonging to the new chord which is sounded against the old chord. It is usually approached stepwise and always quitted by repetition; here the second tone is a member of the new chord. Most anticipations occur in the highest voice, sometimes in the highest and an inner voice simultaneously, but rarely in an inner voice alone. Anticipations are nearly always

Handling the suspension

Suspensions

very short. The first music diagram below is from Beethoven's Piano Sonata in G (op. 49, no. 2). The anticipations are marked An.

(5) Changing-notes are a pair of tones, one an upper neighboring-note, the other the lower; one moves to its mate, which in turn resolves to the same chord-tone from which the figure originated; however the approach (but not the resolution) is sometimes by leap. Thus the tone of resolution seems to collect two non-harmonic tones and "bring them home" as it were. Again it is normal for the lower neighboring-note to be located a half-step below the chord-tone. Either the upper or the lower neighbor may be the first of the pair. Changing-notes are marked CN in the second example below.

(6) The appoggiatura is approached by a *leap (skip), usually upward, and quitted scalewise, usually in the opposite direction to the leap. (It must be borne in mind, however, that the term appoggiatura has two additional meanings in some terminologies; see passing-tones and suspensions.) The appoggiatura tone is often (but not always) present in the preceding chord. When not present, the appoggiatura is for all practical purposes an *"unprepared suspension."

Appoggiaturas are usually accented and often fairly long, though neither condition is essential. The term is derived from the Italian word meaning "to lean." In the example at the top of the following page the appoggiaturas are marked Ap.

Anticipations

Changing-notes

Appoggiaturas

Further information about the appoggiatura will be found under recitative and grace-note.

The plural is either appoggiaturas or appoggiature.

(7) The escape-tone (also called escaped tone and échappée) is approached stepwise and quitted by a leap, normally of a third but occasionally of a larger interval, usually in the opposite direction. It is always unaccented and as a rule is quite short. If the tone is a member of the chord which follows, some musicians call it a free anticipation; if it is not a member it is sometimes called a free tone. In the example below, the escape-tones are marked ET. The first three are of the "free anticipation" type, the last a "free tone."

(8) The cambiata is approached by a leap of a third and quitted stepwise in the opposite direction. It is unaccented and usually quite short. See the notes marked C in the example at the top of the following page.

Escope-tones (Echappées)

Cambiatas

Many theorists would term the cambiata an unaccented appoggiatura.

(9) The pedal-point (also called pedal and organ-point) is a fairly long tone, generally in the bass, which holds (or repeats) through several changes of harmony. It is (with rare exceptions) a chord-member as it begins and ends, but is foreign to at least one of the chords through which it is sustained. The following example is from the second movement

P.P   Pedal-point   etc.

of Haydn's G Major Symphony (the so-called "Surprise" Symphony). The pedal-point is marked P.P.; it disagrees with the harmony in the third and fourth measures (and perhaps the second also).

The pedal-point tone is usually either the first degree (tonic) of the scale, as in the example shown, or else the fifth (dominant); occasionally the third degree (mediant) is found. A pedal-point on any other degree is extremely exceptional.

When two tones are used simultaneously as pedal-points the result is called double pedal-point; the two tones are usually the first and fifth (tonic and dominant) of the scale. Schubert's song "The Hurdy-Gurdy Man" in the Winterreise (Winter Journey) *song-cycle has a double pedal-point running from beginning to end; but this is quite unusual, almost unique.

A pedal-point in the highest voice, rather than the lowest, is called an inverted pedal-point. One in an inner voice is called an interior pedal-point; these are quite rare.

A *drone-bass always contains a pedal-point.

Summary. The accompanying table summarizes the use of all the non-harmonic tones except the pedal-point.

NAME	APPROACHED	QUITTED	HOW	ACCENTING
passing-tone	by step	by step	same direction	acc. or unacc.
neighboring-note	by step	by step	opp. direction (returns to tone of approach)	acc. or unacc.
suspension	holding out or repetition	by step	usually down	accented
anticipation	by step (usually)	by repetition	same note	unacc., short
changing-notes (always 2 notes that make leap of third)	usually by step, but sometimes by leap	by step	to note that preceded	either note may be acc. or unaccented
appoggiatura	by leap	by step	usually opposite direction	usually acc.
escape-tone	by step	by leap of third	usually opposite direction	unacc., short
cambiata	by leap of third	by step	opposite direction	unacc., short

●† non legato. Not *legato. This term is by no means a synonym for *staccato. It indicates an absence of legato; that is, it denotes a forceful and somewhat "punching" style of playing, but it is not a direction that the notes are to receive less than their written value.

This direction is usually found in music of a vigorous and somewhat loud character.

Compare legato, staccato.
See also marcato (2).

● non-transposing instruments. Instruments which sound the pitches as written; explained under transposing instruments.

●† non troppo. Not too much. (Allegro non troppo or allegro ma non troppo, fast but not too much so.)
Synonym: non tanto.

● non-Western music. See Oriental music.

● "noodles." A slang word used by orchestral musicians to designate moving *accompaniment-figures for the string instruments, requiring a subdued tone, and to be played *legato.

The accompanying examples are taken from the second violin part of Berlioz's Roman Carnival Overture and first violin part of Mendelssohn's Violin Concerto.

● notation. Music consists of sounds of fixed pitches and certain durations. In order for a composer to record the music he hears in his mind or plays on some instrument, and in order for any other musician to be able to reproduce this effect, it is necessary to have symbols which represent these various pitches. The result is called notation. It consists of notes and *rests placed on *staffs, supplemented by *clefs, *accidentals, and other *symbols, with various conventional verbal directions (often given in abbreviated form) to indicate the manner of performance (see dynamic marks and tempo marks).

For convenience in referring to exact pitches during the course of books and magazine articles, many musicians have adopted a scheme of various letter-styles to avoid constant resorting to notes. Unfortunately, several mutually-contradictory systems have been proposed; however the most widely-used is shown on page 275. Note that even this takes several variant forms. Note also that the change always occurs between B and C, rather than between G and A.

"Noodles"

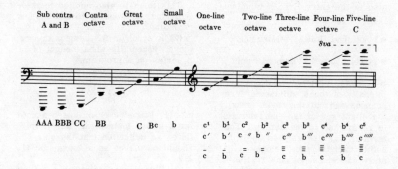

The following shows G♭, a♯², EE, f³, and d♯.

In French-, Italian-, and Spanish-speaking countries, *syllable-names

Because of the phenomenon of the *octave--the fact that every eighth diatonic tone sounds remarkably like the starting tone--only seven different letters are used in naming musical pitches: A, B, C, D, E, F, and G, although sharps and flats are needed in order to name the remaining chromatic tones. The position in which the various letter-names occur on the piano and other *keyboard instruments is shown in the entry keyboard.

(according to the "fixed-do" system) are used instead of letter-names (with ut still used in place of do in France). The familiar use of letters in designating tones is characteristic of German- and English-speaking countries.

The duration of various notes is discussed under time-values. See also dotted notes.

● note-head. The round part of a note, either filled in or open, as distinguished from the *stem. A whole-note has only a note-head.

● note-lengths, note-values. Same as time-values. The appearance of the notes is shown in said entry, also in the entry British terminology.

●† notturno (Italian) *Nocturne.

● nowel, nowell. Same as noël.

● nuances. Subtle variations in the intensity of tones; miniature *crescendos and *diminuendos, usually too slight and of too short duration to be marked in the music. The term is likewise used to apply to subtle variations in *tempo--miniature *accelerandos and *rallentandos that elude exact notation, though necessary if the music is to sound really alive rather than mechanically ground out. In some instances, nuances also applies to slight shadings in *tone-quality.

The artistic use of such shadings, and an intelligent feeling for their correct employment, is part of the equipment of every musician and artist.

An example of the necessity for feeling nuances might be cited by calling attention to the fact that long-held tones nearly always end with a diminuendo, even when none is marked; indeed it is advisable for the composer to use the term sempre f ("always loud") when an exception occurs.

Nuance is the French word meaning "shade," "hue," "tint," or "gradation."

Synonym: shadings.

See also dynamic marks, expression.

Pronunciation: Dictionaries indicate as many as five pronunciations. Among musicians, nōō-än-sĕz seems to be preferred.

● number. (1) In an *opera, each individual *recitative, *aria, *duet, *chorus (3), etc. is often called a number. This usage is especially common in connection with those operas wherein each "number" is fairly independent of all the others, and hence can readily be performed apart from the work as a whole. (This is not true of the *music drama.) The last number of each act is called the *finale.

This term is also applied to the individual sections of *oratorios and *cantatas.

(2) A synonym for composition or piece, especially when thought of in a series on a program.

See also movement, opus.

O

o. (1) Placed over or under a note for a string instrument, harp, or flute--an indication that the note should be played as a *harmonic (1, 2, 3).

(2) Placed over or under a note for a string instrument--to be played as an *open string.

(3) Placed over or under a note for a brass instrument--to be played as an *open tone (natural tone).

(4) Placed over a note for the *horn-- cancels the effect of + (the direction for stopped tones).

● o. Or. (Sometimes printed ò.) Variant form (optional before vowels and h): od.

●† obbligato. A prominent part for a solo instrument (occasionally more than one) in a vocal solo in an *opera, *oratorio, *cantata, or sometimes in a *song. Many examples may be found in Bach's Mass in B Minor: violin in "Laudamus Te," and "Benedictus," flute in the duet "Domine Deus," oboe d'amore in "Qui Sedes," two oboi d'amore in "Et in Spiritum Sanctum," and horn in "Quoniam Tu Solus Sanctus," not to mention the entire section of both first and second violins in the "Agnus Dei."

Originally the term obbligato--literally "obliged" or "obligatory"--was used in its correct meaning--to denote the opposite of *ad libitum (1); that is, it indicated parts that were essential, rather than optional and dispensable. By some odd quirk, it sometimes came to mean exactly the opposite; it became a synonym for ad libitum (optional). A number of sentimental *ballads have "obbligatos" (really ad libitum parts) for violin or cello, occasionally some other instrument. In serious music, however, an obbligato is seldom optional.

Plural: obbligatos or obbligati.
Variant spelling: obligato.
See also descant (1), countermelody.

●† obligato. Variant (and questionable) spelling of obbligato.

● oblique motion. See contrary, parallel, and oblique motion.

● oboe. A double-*reed woodwind instrument which has a comparatively small *bell (2) and no *mouthpiece. It is almost invariably made of wood. The range of the oboe is:

the oboe is essentially a pipe or tube with holes which are opened and closed by the fingers, plus keys. An important matter to the player is the exact condition of the reed; it must be shaped precisely for his lips. For this reason most oboists make their own reeds. The degree of wetness of the reed is also of paramount importance; consequently we often observe the player moistening the reed in his mouth before putting it in place at the end of the instrument. There is a saying among orchestral musicians that "an oboist is as good as his reed."

The instrument requires a notably small amount of breath in playing, as is true of double-reed instruments in general; oboists often comment on the discomfort of having too much air in their lungs. Long passages un-

Some oboes lack the low B-flat. The highest tone is approximate; skillful players can sound two or even three higher tones. It is not a *transposing instrument; in other words, the oboe is notated at actual pitch. Only the treble *clef is used.

The lowest tones tend to be thick, bitter, harsh. The middle register is reedy, nasal, plaintive, and a bit "salty." The highest tones are thin and pinched, yet curiously piercing. This is one of the few instruments in which the lowest tones tend to be louder than the highest. It is said that the oboe's "carrying power" is the greatest of any instrument despite its comparatively soft tone; the sound penetrates well.

The range, it will be observed, is rather narrow. A "vocal" type of melody is perhaps best suited to the oboe.

Like all woodwind instruments,

relieved by *rests are exhausting.

The old wives' tale that playing the oboe will cause insanity is of course utterly without foundation.

Synonym (almost obsolete): hautboy.
Italian: oboè or oboe (plural, oboi).
French: hautbois (plural, hautbois).
German: Hoboe or Oboe (plural, Hoboen or Oboen). Spanish: oboe.

The player is called an oboist. (The spelling oboeist is incorrect.)

Pronunciation: ō-bō; the pronunciation ō-boi seems to have no existence outside of dictionaries.

●† oboe da caccia. A double-reed woodwind instrument, practically obsolete. It is now generally replaced by the *English horn. Strictly, however, the oboe da caccia is more a high *bassoon than a low *oboe.

The name, curiously, means "hunting oboe."

Plural: oboi da caccia.
Pronunciation: in caccia accent first

syllable.

●† oboe d'amore. A mezzo-soprano oboe, pitched a minor third below the ordinary instrument. It has a very beautiful though somewhat frail tone, the quality being about half-way between that of the oboe and that of the English horn, though perhaps not adequately differentiated from either.

The range of the oboe d'amore is:

hollow and sweet. Some of the *simple melody instruments are modeled on the ocarina.

This instrument is humorously called "the musical sweet potato" because of a fancied resemblance to the shape of that vegetable. It is often made of terra cotta.

Pronunciation: ŏk-ă-rē-nà.

● octave. This term is used with two different meanings.

(1) Strictly, an octave is the *interval of eight degrees, either higher or

It is notated a minor third higher than the sounds desired, though Bach wrote for it at actual pitch. (See transposing instruments.)

The oboe d'amore was quite a favored instrument with Bach, but in the late eighteenth century it fell into disuse, remaining neglected until early in the present century, when Richard Strauss wrote for it in his Domestic Symphony, followed by Ravel in his Bolero. The instrument is becoming more accessible, and the custom of replacing it by the oboe or by the English horn is happily falling into discard.

Plural: oboi d'amore or (awkwardly) oboes d'amore.

Synonym (questionable): oboe d'amour.

● oboe d'amour. A garbled (polyglot) name for the *oboe d'amore. It is a mixture of the Italian oboè d'amore and the French hautbois d'amour.

● ocarina. A small, more or less globe-shaped, popular-type instrument, operating on the *woodwind principle of holes opened and covered by the fingers. Its *tone-color is

lower, from any given tone. Only two sounds are required to produce it.

Pitches that are an octave apart sound more nearly alike than those at any other interval, due to the fact that the upper tone vibrates precisely twice as fast as the lower one.

Tones situated an octave apart are particularly easy to detect with the help of the piano keyboard, due to the repetition of patterns of white and black keys; indeed it is even quite possible for a child to locate them, by picking the next key higher or lower that happens to fall in the same relative position as the starting key. See also intervals, acoustics. Compare unison.

(2) The term octave is also used as a collective name for all of the tones occurring between two sounds that are an octave apart. For example the series of notes that intervene between *middle C and the C an octave above it is referred to as "the octave starting on middle C." Several illustrations of the term, used in this meaning, will be found in the entry notation. (See also page 279, top.)

● octave flute. Old name for the *piccolo.

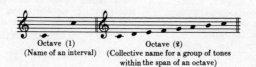

Octave (1)   Octave (2)
(Name of an interval)   (Collective name for a group of tones
                           within the span of an octave)

● octave key. A key on the under-side of a *woodwind instrument, which when pressed causes the in-strument to go into a higher regis-ter, i.e., to *overblow.

Pressing this key does not pro-duce the rise of an octave on every woodwind instrument; on the clarinet the interval is an octave plus a perfect fifth, i.e., a perfect twelfth (see intervals); hence many wood-wind players, especially clarinetists, prefer the terms speaker key or register key.

Some bass clarinets, oboes, and English horns have two octave keys.

● octavo. Properly, a certain size of paper. The prevalence of this size in printing *choral music has caused the word to become practi-cally synonymous with *sheet mu-sic for chorus and even choral compositions in general.

There is an etymological but no musical connection with the word *octave. The name is derived from the fact that this size of paper is obtained by folding larger sheets so as to form eight smaller sheets--sixteen pages, 7-1/2 by 10 inches.

Pronunciation: ŏk-tä̆-vō or ŏk-tä̆-vō.

● octet. A composition for eight voices or instruments. See groups.

Variant spelling: octette.

Pronunciation: ŏk-tĕt́, however some musicians use ŏk-tĕt.

● † od. Or. (Used only--and option-ally--before words beginning with a vowel or h.)

Variant forms: o, ŏ.

● off-beats. The weak (unaccented) beats in the *meter. The off-beats of 2-4, 3-4, 4-4, and 6-8 time follow.

This term is also sometimes applied to the *after-beat (2), i.e., the second half of any beat.

● offertory. (1) A vocal or instrumental composition performed during a church service while the offering is being collected. (2) A certain portion of the "proper" of the *mass. It is not used as an accompaniment to the collection of money. Synonym (Latin): offertorium.

● off-key. See out of tune.

● off-stage. Instruments or voices that perform in back of or at the side of the stage, out of sight of the audience, are said to be "off-stage." The composer's purpose is to give the illusion that the sound, which is of course quite faint, is coming from a tremendous distance. One of the best-known and most effective uses of an off-stage instrument is the trumpet solo that appears twice in Beethoven's Leonora Overture No. 3.

Off-stage passages are often indicated by the Italian word lontano ("distant"), isolato, or interno, by the French lointain ("distant"), or by the German in der Ferne ("in the distance"), entfernt, or sehr weit ("very far away").

● "old masters." A euphemistic term applied by certain persons to composers of the past, particularly to those who antedate the time of those composers with whose music the speakers happen to be most familiar; that is, the term is tantamount to "those old composers whose music I know very little about." Many persons apply this to any composer who lived "before the time of Bach."

The use of "old masters" is hardly desirable; its use is absurd when applied to comparatively recent composers such as Beethoven, Schubert, Wagner, and Brahms.

●† -one. Italian augmentative suffix. Has the effect of adding the adjective big to the noun to which

it is attached. Antonyms: -etto, -ino.

● one-line instrument. Any instrument whose music is written on a single *staff, or which can produce just a single tone at a time, or both. Synonym: single line instrument.

● one-line staff. See staff.

● one-movement symphony. An orchestral composition in a single rather long movement which contains, in condensed form, the nuclei of the three or four movements that make up an orthodox *symphony. It should not be confused with the normal symphony in which various movements are connected by *attaccas, nor does its form coincide with that of just a single movement in the usual symphony. In addition, it should not be confused with the concert *overture (3) or with the *symphonic poem.

The one-movement symphony seems to be the twentieth-century answer to the demand for brevity and condensation, without forsaking continuation and expansion of the symphony form.

A brief description of several typical one-movement symphonies follows.

Symphony No. 21 by Miaskovsky begins with a passage in slow *tempo, similar in style to the introduction to a *sonata-allegro movement or to a slow movement; then there is a quicker part which is a complete sonata-allegro, followed by a return of the slow section in varied form. It is a blend of slow movement and sonata-allegro.

Symphony No. 1 by Samuel Barber contains the seeds of the normal four movements. The portion corresponding to the first movement contains three themes. One of these, in varied form, is later turned into a *scherzo section; the second, also considerably altered, becomes a passage in slow-movement style; while a section corresponding to a *finale is built on a varied form of the third theme, combined with the others.

Symphony No. 7 by Sibelius resembles the slow movement, scherzo, and finale of the ordinary symphony, so skillfully fused that it is impossible to lay one's finger on the exact boundary-line between one division and the next.

Symphony No. 3 by Roy Harris consists of an introduction and five very closely-knit sections following one another almost without transition.

From the foregoing it will be apparent that there is no one "normal" or "conventional" form-scheme. Since the symphony, *sonata, *concerto, and *chamber-music types are all basically the same form (see sonata-types) it will be obvious that a similar procedure may also be applied to these. This practice is less frequent, however, than with the symphony. Nevertheless, and despite the fact that the one-movement symphony is essentially a twentieth-century development, the earliest example appears to be Liszt's Piano Sonata in B Minor. Liszt's two piano concertos also come very close to the form.

● op. The abbreviation for *opus. The abbreviation for the plural is opp., occasionally ops.

● open. Not *muted. Used in speaking of *brass instruments.
See also open string, open tones.

● "open fifth." A *triad consisting of one or more *roots (fundamentals) and one or more *fifths (2), but no *third (2). Since the third determines whether the triad is major or minor, a chord of this type is ambiguous-- its effect is "neuter"; yet it has a certain simple dignity.

Triads without third were widely used from the thirteenth through the seventeenth centuries, after which they became extremely rare (however see the opening of Symphony No. 9 by Beethoven). During the present century composers have re-awakened to their value, and are again utilizing them freely.

Synonyms: open triad, bare fifth.

● open harmony, open position. A chord is said to be in open harmony or open position when it would be possible to insert a chord tone between the soprano and alto, and between the alto and tenor; in such cases the soprano and tenor are always more than an octave apart. However, the bass may be very close to the tenor or even in unison with it; thus it will be seen that the term open harmony essentially refers to the distribution of the three highest voices.

All of the following chords are in open harmony.

Synonyms: dispersed position, extended position.
Compare close harmony.

● **open score.** In general, this term refers to the printing of music with the part for each instrument or voice (or each pair of like instruments) appearing on a staff of its own. As a rule, however, the ability to "read open score" denotes merely facility in reading the music for *mixed chorus, either on the part of the *conductor or on the part of the *accompanist (in playing these four parts--soprano, alto, tenor, and bass--on his instrument).

See also score.

● **open string.** Players of bowed and fretted string instruments use the term open string to denote a string which is not fingered (that is, not "stopped"), hence which vibrates at its full length. Obviously it is very easy to play the open strings.

The use of an open string is sometimes indicated by a small o above or below the note. Unfortunately the same symbol is often used to indicate *harmonics (1).

● **open tones.** (1) The tones that can be produced on a *brass instrument purely by varying the tension of the lips (see embouchure), without the use of the *valves (or in the case of the trombone, without using the *slide). The sounds are those found in the *harmonic series; however the fundamental tone is unplayable on some brass instruments.

The *bugle, which is valveless, has only open tones.

Synonyms: natural tones, harmonics (4), overtones (2), partials (2).

(2) The tones that can be produced on the open strings of the string instruments, bowed or plucked. See open strings.

● **opera.** Perhaps the best definition of opera is the one which is most familiar: "A play set to music." The characters sing their lines instead of speaking them. It is given on a stage, with scenery and costumes, and the singers must act as well as sing. Instrumental support is furnished by an orchestra, which normally is stationed in a "pit" or depressed place located just in front of the stage, and far below it.

The definition "a play set to music" must not be interpreted to mean that every opera was originally a play; on the contrary the story of the great majority of operas was fashioned directly for musical setting. The text is known as the *libretto.

Operas, like plays, are divided into acts, most commonly three or four; however some have only two acts while others have five. Again like plays, at the end of each act of an opera the curtain is lowered, the house-lights are turned on, and there is an intermission before the curtain rises on the following act. Also, just as there are one-act plays, so are there one-act operas, though they are distinctly in the minority. (Mascagni's Cavalleria Rusticana, Puccini's Gianni Schicchi, Wagner's Das Rheingold, Menotti's The Telephone, and Richard Strauss's Salome are perhaps the best-known examples, while Sullivan's Trial by Jury is a well-known one-act *operetta.)

A feature of the opera not normally found in plays is the presence of an *overture (1) or *prelude (3), played by the orchestra before the action has started or the curtain is raised, but after the theater has been darkened. Its purpose is to set the mood for the story which is to unfold.

An opera normally lasts a full evening; only one appears on the program, though most one-act operas are short enough to share the evening with some other work. On the rare occasions when an opera is performed without staging, scenery, costumes, and action (that is, when just the music is performed) the result is called a "concert version" or an "oratorio-style performance." This practice does not of course quite represent the real total effect. Operas heard from radio or records (but not television) give the same effect.

The first opera was Daphne, written partly by Jacopo Peri (1561-1633) and partly by Count Corsi; however most of the music has been lost and the date

TYPE	PLOT	MUSICAL STYLE	AMOUNT OF SINGING
opera (grand opera)	serious (but not necessarily tragic)	serious	sung throughout (though occasionally uses *melodrama)
opera buffa	comical	serious	sung throughout
opéra comique	serious	serious	some spoken dialogue
operetta (light opera)	almost always comical	light	some spoken dialogue
music drama	serious	serious; uses *leitmotivs; voices often subordinate to orchestra	sung throughout
Singspiel	comical	serious	some spoken dialogue
zarzuela	comical or serious	Spanish, serious	some spoken dialogue
ballad opera	usually comical	light; often uses folk-songs or is patch-work	some spoken dialogue
chamber opera	serious or comical	serious; uses small orchestra, modest resources; often fairly easy to perform	with or without spoken dialogue

of first performance is uncertain, being variously given as 1594, 1595, 1596, and 1597. The second opera, and the oldest which has survived, was Euridice by Peri, first performed on October 6, 1600.

Opera may be sub-divided into several types, such as grand opera, opera buffa, opéra comique, Singspiel, music drama, ballad opera, chamber opera, zarzuela, and operetta (see also musical comedy). The accompanying table sums up the distinctions, though each type is further discussed under its own heading. Grand opera is the most typical; the term "opera," unmodified, normally denotes grand opera.

One usually speaks of "hearing" (rather than "seeing") an opera.

● opera (Latin). The plural of *opus.

●† opera buffa. A type of *opera characterized by a farcial plot and the presence of comical characters. It is sung throughout, and has no connection with the *opéra comique or the *operetta. Mozart's Marriage of Figaro and Così Fan Tutte and Rossini's Barber of Seville are well-known examples.

(The word buffa derives from the same source as the English word buffoon.)

Plural: opere buffe.

Pronunciation: in opera accent first syllable.

● opéra comique (French). A type of serious opera that contains spoken dialogue as well as singing. Although the term means, of course, "comic opera," the typical opéra comique is by no means comical; it may even be tragic. Its essential difference from the ordinary grand opera is that it is not sung throughout. Thus it somewhat resembles the *operetta in procedure though by no means in musical style. The dialogue is the counterpart of the *recitatives in grand opera.

Bizet's Carmen was originally an opéra comique, although it is usually given in a version with recitatives composed by the American-born Ernest Guiraud (1837-1892) replacing the dialogue.

Plural: opéras comiques.
Pronunciation: ō-pā-rä́ kō-mēk.
See also Singspiel.

● opera-house. A theater especially intended for the performance of *operas. It has the large stage, curtains, scenery, and other props to be expected in any theater, plus a roomy *orchestra pit. The auditorium portion may have four or more balconies, plus a number of boxes.

An opera-house is also the ideal place in which to give *ballets.

The use of this term, in rural towns, as a synonym for auditorium verges on the ludicrous.

● operetta. A musical play containing both spoken dialogue and singing. The spoken parts correspond to the *recitatives in ordinary *opera, although a few operettas contain both speaking and recitatives.

The operetta differs from the *opéra comique in that its music is distinctly *light rather than of an ambitious character and its plot usually comical, often satirical, rather than serious. It is distinguished from the *opera buffa by the presence of speaking and a lighter musical style.

The operettas by Sir Arthur Sullivan (with *librettos by W. S. Gilbert), Victor Herbert, Kern, Friml, Johann Strauss, Oscar Straus, Romberg, and Offenbach are well-known.

Synonym: light opera. (Comic opera is often also used as a synonym, although theoretically it is possible for an operetta to possess a plot which is serious.)

● ophicleide. An obsolete *brass instrument, being the bass of the *keyed bugle group. It was shaped like a long narrow U, its mouthpipe somewhat suggested that of the *bassoon, and it had the long, flapper-shaped, saxophone-type keys that characterized all keyed bugles.

The perfection of the *tuba put an end to its popularity, and that instrument now replaces the ophicleide in those compositions which were scored for the latter. The *tone-color of the ophicleide was much closer to that of the *euphonium or *baritone (2), however, than that of the tuba.

Pronunciation: ŏf-ĭ-klīd.

● opposite mode. When in the major mode, the minor mode is the "opposite mode," and vice versa. See major and minor, major scale, minor scale.

● opposite motion. Contrary motion; see contrary, parallel, and oblique motion.

● op. post. A work published posthumously (i. e., after the composer's death). See opus.

●† oppure. An indication for an alternate or substitute passage, but usually of the type that is not provided with a staff of its own. See ossia.

Abbreviation: opp.

● opus. Work. Compositions are often assigned numbers (sometimes by the publisher, but preferably by the composer) to distinguish them from one another; thus: Opus 12, Opus 94. Opus-numbers are a convenience, even a necessity, if a composer writes many works bearing the same *title; the main requisite is that no two compositions shall have the same number. Theoretically the numbering is either in the order of writing or in the order of publication, but unfortunately the practice has in some cases been far from systematic. Certain composers have assigned opus-numbers to some of their works but not all.

Several compositions written or published at about the same time, or related in some manner (such as being written as a series), are often assigned the same opus-number, followed by the designation "no. 1," "no. 2," etc.; thus: op. 45, no. 7; op. 19, no. 3. Even compositions that are divided into several *movements may still be designated as a single number within an opus; thus Beethoven's opus 18 consists of six *string quartets, five of them containing four movements, one containing five movements. At other times a very short piece may have a complete number all to itself. Thus it will be seen that various opus-numbers are highly unequal as to the amount of music encompassed.

As a rule, all the compositions in one opus are written for the same *medium, or for closely-related mediums.

The practice of assigning opus-numbers became established around 1790, although the first appearance was early in the seventeenth century, at which time the term was applied to published compositions only, and Roman numerals were usually employed. At present the custom is tending to disappear, though many composers still believe in its usefulness. Others, however, prefer to substitute the year in which the music was written; still others assign an opus-number and indicate the year in addition.

A work published after the composer's death is often marked op. post., i.e., posthumous work.

Opus-numbers are not substitutes for *titles but amplifications of them.

The abbreviation (much commoner than the full word) is op. The plural is opera (not opi); this word however has no connection, except etymologically, with the term *opera. The plural abbreviation is opp., occasionally ops.

Pseudo-Opus-Numbers. Due to the fact that many composers of the past did not use opus-numbers (or at best used them in a far-from-systematic manner), certain persons have felt the advisability of assigning numbers in order that various musical works be properly distinguished one from another.

The best-known set of "pseudo-opus-numbers" (as they might well be called) are those used with the compositions of Mozart, indicated by the letter K, which represents the name of Ludwig von Köchel (1800-1877), an Austrian scholar who compiled a chronological catalogue of Mozart's complete works. The more complete abbreviation K. V. stands for Köchel Verzeichnis which means "Köchel Index" or "Köchel Catalogue." Occasionally a number is preceded by K. Anh. standing for Köchel Anhang, "Köchel Supplement."

Köchel's numbers were revised and corrected by Alfred Einstein (1880-1952), a noted musicologist.

Numbering systems have been formulated for certain other composers' works. Anthony van Hoboken (1887-) has supplied numbers for Haydn's compositions; the Bach Werke Verzeichnis ("Index to Bach's Works"), abbreviated B. W. V., furnishes numbers for J. S. Bach's compositions; Otto Erich Deutsch (1883-) has indexed the music of Schubert, and Marc Pincherle (1888-) has catalogued Vivaldi's compositions. In the case of the so-called "Sonatas" (2) by Domenico Scarlatti, numbers have been assigned by Alessandro Longo (1864-1945) and by Ralph Kirkpatrick (1911-), the latter set being considered the more reliable. In addition, Georg Kinsky (1882-1951) has given numbers to those compositions by Beethoven which the master himself published without opus-numbers.

The practice of assigning pseudo-opus-numbers, where they are needed,

can be expected to continue. To
date, the assignment of such
numbers has been made in a scholarly and careful manner, never
haphazard or arbitrary.

● oratorio. An extended composition for soloists, chorus, and
(usually) orchestra, divided into
many self-complete sections, and
nearly always based on a biblical
subject. A typical oratorio contains *recitatives, *solos, *duets
and other *concerted pieces, and
*choruses (3). Purely instrumental
parts, such as an *overture or
*prelude (3), are by no means un-
known.

The oratorio is performed without scenery, action, or costumes;
that is perhaps its most conspicuous difference from the *opera.

The typical oratorio is divided
into definite sections, each coming
to a full *cadence, thus making
any single part--recitative, solo,
chorus, etc.--capable of being
lifted out of the complete work for
performance by itself.

The story or "action" of which
an oratorio treats usually unfolds
mainly in the recitatives. The
arias, duets, and choruses, although easily the most interesting parts musically, normally have
the function of reflections on or ex-
pansions of the matters mentioned
in the recitatives; in addition they
usually contain a great amount of
text-repetition which is often excessive and occasionally verges on
the tedious.

The only real difference between
the oratorio and the *cantata is the
greater length of the former; indeed
the oratorio might well be described
as "a long cantata. "

For many years musicians were
under the impression that Emilio
del Cavalieri's Representation of
the Soul and Body (1600) was the
first oratorio; actually it is an
*opera on a religious subject, though
it does have a few elements typical
of the oratorio as we know that form
today. The oratorio in its present
sense was inaugurated by Giacomo
Carissimi (1605-1674).

Some of the best-known oratorios
are The Messiah by Handel, The
Creation by Haydn, and Elijah by
Mendelssohn.

A few secular oratorios have been
written, for example, Haydn's The
Seasons.

It may be safely said that oratorios
are as often presented at concerts
as at religious services.

Plural: oratorios.

See also passion.

● orchestra. The orchestra may be
defined loosely as a large ensemble
of *string, *woodwind, *brass, and
(usually) *percussion instruments.
It plays under the direction of a *conductor.

The orchestra's resources are
practically infinite in their richness;
in flexibility and variety of effect it
is unrivaled among all musical *mediums. Some of the greatest compositions are to be found in its
literature.

Instruments. The accompanying
table shows the instruments found in
the orchestra of the present day.

The classifications "primary, "
"secondary, " and "rare, " as applied
to the woodwinds, were invented for
use here. Since the four principal
woodwind instruments are the flute,
oboe, clarinet, and bassoon, they may
aptly be given the designation "primary. " Each of these four has a
"close relation, " as it were, very
similar to it and almost identical in
mechanism; these are here termed
"secondary. " With all except the
bassoon there are one or two supplementary instruments, again similar
in mechanism but even more exceptional, which are here termed "rare. "
(Players take up the "secondary" and
"rare" members as a side-line after
having learned the "primary" instrument.) In addition there are other
woodwind instruments which do not
correspond to any of the primary
four. It should be clearly understood
that "rare" in this usage simply means
rarely used in the orchestra; for example the saxophone is really a very
commonly-encountered instrument, but
its presence in the orchestra is distinctly exceptional. A similar remark

THE INSTRUMENTS OF THE ORCHESTRA

String

Bowed		Plucked
violin		harp
viola		
cello (violoncello)		
double-bass (contrabass)		

Woodwind

Primary	Secondary	Rare
flute	piccolo	alto flute
oboe	English horn	[oboe d'amore]
		[heckelphone]
clarinet	bass clarinet	[E-flat clarinet]
		[basset horn]
bassoon	contrabassoon	
		saxophone family
		sarrusophone

Brass

Primary	Rare
horn (French horn)	cornet
trumpet	euphonium (baritone)
trombone	Wagner tenor tuba
tuba (bass tuba)	Wagner bass tuba
	bass trumpet
	flügelhorn
	contralto trumpet

Percussion

Definite pitch	Indefinite pitch
timpani (kettle-drums)	snare drum (side drum)
glockenspiel	tenor drum
xylophone	bass drum
tubular bells (chines)	tambourin de Provence (tabor)
celesta	tambourine
antique cymbals	gong (tam-tam)
	cymbals
	castanets
	wood block
	triangle
	sleigh-bells (harness-bells)

applies to certain "rare" brass instruments, especially the cornet and the euphonium (baritone). The trombone entry on the list needs further comment in the form of pointing out that two types of trombone are used regularly: the tenor and the bass. The "rare" brass list might be swelled by the addition of the alto and contrabass trombones, even of the obsolete soprano trombone.

Proportionate Numbers. Among the bowed strings there is a group (section) of instruments to a part; thus we expect to find 16 or 18 first violins, 14 or 16 second violins, about 12 violas, 9 to 12 cellos, and 8 to 10 double-basses. Each group normally has a single part. (However, see divisi.) There are invariably two sections of violins--first violins and second violins. The instrument itself is of course the same no matter whether in the first or the second section.

Among the plucked strings, woodwinds, brass, and percussion, there is just one instrument to a part. This does not mean there is only a single representative of each instrument; it signifies there is just one instrument playing each part. Thus if four horns appear in an orchestra, they play four entirely independent parts--first horn, second horn, third horn, and fourth horn. Briefly, each harpist, woodwind player, brass player, and percussion player is a soloist; each string player is a member of a group working in unison.

The reason for the preponderance of string instruments is not because they are more important than the others, but because their tone is so weak that large numbers have to be marshaled to maintain *balance with the essentially louder wind and percussion instruments. However, it is thanks to this circumstance that composers are able to use such effects as divisi and solo violin, the latter explained under solo (3).

Instruments Occasionally Used. The list of percussion instruments in the foregoing table might be ex-

tended almost indefinitely. The *piano, *harpsichord, *marimba, and *vibraphone can be added to the definite pitch group, while the indefinite pitch classification can be augmented by the *tom-tom, *güiro, *claves, *maracas, *bongós, *ratchet, *temple blocks, *cow-bells, *Chinese drum, *flute, *wind machine, thunder machine, metal block, anvil, slap stick (whip), and even such items as chains, cannon, cap pistol, steel plate, policeman's whistle, automobile horn, automobile brake-drums, and so on--all of which have been used in at least one orchestral composition. To the woodwind group can be added the *flageolet, the *recorders, the flute in E-flat, the *oboe da caccia, the *alto clarinet, and the *contrabass clarinet. The *keyed bugle, *Zink, *ophicleide, and *serpent are obsolete members of the brass section, the *post horn, *saxhorn, and *bugle extremely rare members. To the bowed strings can be added the *viola d'amore and *viola da gamba, to the plucked strings the *mandolin, *guitar, *lute, *banjo, and *zither. Otherwise unclassified instruments which have occasionally been used are the *organ, *harmonium, and *czimbalom. And the foregoing lists are by no means exhaustive. Nevertheless the number of compositions which require any of the foregoing is indeed small.

Size of the Orchestra at Various Times. In general, as time has gone along, the orchestra has tended to increase in size, and hence in flexibility. During the *Baroque period, the *string orchestra was the norm, the presence of wind instruments and timpani being the exception rather than the rule. During the *Classical period, the following orchestra is typical:

    two flutes (perhaps only one)
    two oboes
    two bassoons
    two horns
    two trumpets
    timpani
    first violins
    second violins
    violas
    cellos
    double-basses
During the latter part of the period,

two clarinets were standard additions to the above. Three trombones (one alto, one tenor, and one bass) were frequently found in the score of an opera or a work for chorus and orchestra, but for a reason that would be hard to name, they were not employed in symphonies until Beethoven wrote his Fifth Symphony (1805-1807).

It is most important to point out that the number of string instruments was only one-third or one-fourth (one-half at the maximum) the number normally employed today.

(It is well to mention that composers rarely specified the number two. They merely gave the name of the instrument in its plural form (e.g., "flauti," "oboi," etc.) and the presence of two parts, plus the incidental indications *a 2, 1., and 2. automatically indicated the presence of a pair of instruments.)

During the early *Romantic period there was a tendency to have the second flute part *interchange with piccolo, second oboe interchange with English horn, etc. Four horns became standard. A few more percussion instruments frequently appeared, especially triangle, bass drum, and cymbals. The size of the string sections steadily increased. The orchestra grew tremendously during the Romantic period--too much, some musicians believe--and around the turn of the nineteenth to twentieth centuries there were a number of works for gargantuan ensembles. At present the tendency is away from this love of hugeness.

A typical score of the *Modern (also late Romantic) period might call for the following, or a similar array:

    piccolo
    two flutes
    two oboes
    English horn
    two clarinets
    bass clarinet
    two bassoons
    contrabassoon
    four horns
    three trumpets

    three trombones (two tenor,
      one bass)
    tuba
    timpani
    numerous other percussion instruments, both of definite and indefinite pitch
    celesta or piano (possibly both)
    one harp (occasionally two)
    first violins
    second violins
    violas
    cellos
    double-basses

It has become customary in certain catalogues and music magazines to indicate the instruments used in any composition by a series of numerals separated by commas (or dots) and at certain places, dashes. The first four numerals indicate the number of

    flutes (and perhaps piccolo)
    oboes (and perhaps English horn)
    clarinets (and perhaps bass clarinet)
    bassoons (and perhaps contrabassoon)

After a dash, the next four numerals indicate the number of

    horns
    trumpets
    trombones
    tubas

Another dash appears, then the percussion instruments are mentioned (much abbreviated). A large group of percussion instruments may simply be indicated by "perc.," though the presence of timpani is always specifically indicated (abbreviated "timp."). After the next dash piano, celesta, organ, and harp, if used, are mentioned, and after the last dash the string section (which seldom varies) is indicated by "str." If any of the standard woodwind or brass instruments are not used, this fact is represented by a zero at the proper place. Unusual instruments are specifically mentioned, as are solo instruments.

According to this plan, the group described earlier as typical of the Classical period would be indicated thus: 2, 2, 0, 2--2, 2, 0, 0--timp.--str. The zeros denote the absence of clarinets, trombones, and tuba. The group described as typical of the Modern period would be shown thus: 3, 3, 3, 3--4, 3, 3, 1--timp.,perc.--cel., piano--harp--str. Although this

system does not indicate whether
the first 3 stands for three flutes,
three flutes one of which alternates with piccolo, or two flutes
and piccolo, and so forth, it does
have compactness as its chief virtue, and its use may be expected
to increase.

Musicians' reference to "the
orchestra" denotes the group the
layman calls a "symphony orchestra"
or "full orchestra." Small orchestra and incomplete groups such
as the school orchestra are always
specified as such.

The members of an orchestra
always perform seated, except for
the players of the timpani and most
of the percussion instruments, who
stand, and the double-bass players,
who either sit on high stools or
stand.

See also chamber orchestra,
string orchestra, Mannheim group,
and the entries devoted to the individual instruments and to the "families" of instrument (i.e., string,
woodwind, brass, percussion). The
distinction between the band and the
orchestra is given in the entry band.

For the explanation of transposing instruments, see that entry.

● orchestra bells. The glockenspiel.

● orchestral concerto. See concerto for orchestra, concerto (2), and
concerto grosso.

● orchestra pit. A depressed area
in the floor of a theater or *opera-
house, located just in front of the
stage, in which the members of the
orchestra are placed.

● orchestration. The art of writing
for the orchestra, of distributing
the musical materials among the
various instruments in an effective
and pleasing manner. An intimate
knowledge of the *tone-color of
every instrument, both singly and
in all possible combinations, is
needed, plus enough familiarity with
their *technique to recognize when
any given passage is easy, difficult,
barely playable, or unplayable.

Many *laymen are unaware that

the orchestrating of a symphonic
composition is done by the composer,
and not by some other person. Of
course when a composition originally
for some other medium is *transcribed
for orchestra, the arranger is usually
some person other than the composer.

Texts on orchestration have been
written by Berlioz, Richard Strauss,
Gevaert, Widor, Prout, Forsyth,
Rimsky-Korsakoff, Piston, Bernard
Rogers, Kent Kennan, Joseph Wagner,
and others; yet the real skill may be
learned only by studying the *scores
of orchestral compositions, supplemented if at all possible by hearing
them either in actual performance or
via records or broadcasts.

Synonyms: instrumentation, arranging, scoring.

See also bandstration, choral orchestration.

● † ordinario. Ordinary, usual,
customary.

Abbreviation: ord.

Pronunciation: accent third syllable.

● organ. The organ may be defined
as a large instrument played from one
or more keyboards ("manuals") plus
an accompanying pedalboard, the
sounds of which are produced by wind
coursing through wooden or metal
pipes. On large organs, these pipes
may vary in length all the way from
1-1/2 inches to 32 feet. The short
pipes of course produce high pitches,
the long ones low pitches. (One should
mention that the organ pipes that are
visible are nearly always dummies,
the live, speaking pipes being located
behind them and elsewhere, hidden
from sight.)

The organ is without doubt the most
complicated of all musical instruments.
Preliminary study of the piano is
assumed on the part of every organist.

The Manuals. Most organs have two,
three, or four keyboards usually termed
manuals, which are placed one above
the other in stairstep formation, plus
a pedalboard. (Discussion of the pedalboard will be found later on.) There
are a few one-manual organs, but they
are almost too small to be very useful. Five-manual instruments are
occasionally found; however the seven-

manual organ in Atlantic City seems to be a unique affair.

When the instrument possesses only two manuals, the upper one is known as the swell, the lower as the great. In a three-manual organ, the additional one is the lowest, and is called the choir. Originally the choir manual controlled a completely separate organ, and was used in accompanying the singers, as its name suggests; but later builders placed it so to adjoin the other manuals, enclosed in a single *console with them. A four-keyboard instrument adds to the foregoing a solo manual, placed above the swell. Thus the downward order of manuals is: solo, swell, great, choir (the latter three often abbreviated sw., gt., ch.). Roman numerals are sometimes substituted for the names, thus: I--great; II--swell; III--choir; IV--solo.

Of course it is possible to play on one manual with the right hand and on a different one with the left. It is even possible to play on two adjacent manuals with a single hand, the four fingers on the upper one, the thumb on the lower.

All the manuals have the range as shown in the first diagram. The number of pitches produced are actually many more than the written range suggests, due to the presence of 4-foot, 2-foot, and 16-foot stops, which will be explained later.

The Pedals. The pedalboard is for all practical purposes an additional "manual played by the feet." The pedals are located under the manuals and are laid out exactly like a keyboard, with white and black keys in their familiar pattern, except that each key is very large. The best pedalboards are slightly fan-shaped and slightly concave. The range is as shown in the second diagram.

Range of the manuals

Range of the pedals

Again the presence of stops of varying pitch yields a much wider gamut of tones than the foregoing written range might imply. Some older organs lack the high F-sharp and G pedals.

Organists work diligently to acquire a fluent pedal technique, and can execute scales, trills, and some arpeggio-figures at surprisingly quick tempos. It is possible, in moderate tempos, to play two pedals simultaneously, even three or four if they are located in certain positions. It is clear, however, that whereas the organist's two hands supply ten units with which to play, his two feet give only four: two heels and two toes. Just as *editors often indicate *fingering (1) for the hands, they also mark in pedaling for the feet. The conventional signs are: ∧ (occasionally ∨) for the toe, ∪ (occasionally ∩ or ○) for the heel. When written above the notes, these indicate the right foot, when written below, the left foot.

Music for the organ is usually written on three staffs; the notes for the manuals are on the upper two staffs (usually separated according to right and left hand), those for the pedals on the lowest staff.

The Stops. A stop is a group of pipes of different pitches but with a homogeneous tone-color. This tone-color depends on the shape and structure of the pipes in question, as well as on the material from which they are made. A stop is to the organ what an instrument is to the orchestra. To place any stop in action, the organist pulls out a small knob or presses down a small tablet labeled with its name. (This is called "drawing" the stop.) To retire a stop he shoves the knob in or pushes the tablet up. If no stops are drawn the instrument will not sound. Each manual and the pedalboard has its own individual sets of stops.

Two factors arise in discussing the stops: (A) their pitch and (B) their tone-color, including the volume.

(A) Not all stops have the same pitch. A stop which sounds the pitches that are written--the same pitches that the piano would give-- is marked 8-foot; there are more 8-foot stops than those of any other type, except possibly in the pedals. These constitute the standard by which the other stops are judged and are the foundation for all organ-playing. A 4-foot stop sounds an octave higher than written. A 2-foot stop sounds two octaves higher than written; there are usually only one or two of these, except on very large organs. A 16-foot stop sounds an octave lower than written; nearly all of them are found in the pedals, where they equal or even outnumber 8-foot stops in frequency. On the other hand there are few 4-foot stops for the pedals, sometimes none, and often no 2-foot. A few organs have one or two 32-foot pedal stops, sounding two octaves lower than written. (Often these extremely deep sounds are formed synthetically as *resultants.)

From the ranges given above, it will be seen that if a 2-foot stop is drawn, the highest key on the manuals will produce a sound an octave higher than the highest key on the piano. The lowest pedal gives the same pitch as the lowest C on the piano when a 16-foot stop is used, an octave lower than the lowest piano C when a 32-foot stop is available. Tones of the latter type are so deep as to produce more of a rumble than a distinct musical tone.

A 2-2/3-foot stop sounds an octave and a perfect fifth (perfect twelfth) higher than written; one marked 1-3/5 sounds two octaves and a major third higher. The existence of these may puzzle the non-organist. Their purpose is not to produce *transposition, but to reinforce *overtones; they are used only in conjunction with 8-foot plus perhaps 4-foot stops. The purpose of 2-foot and 4-foot stops is also fundamentally that of "brightening" the 8-foot tones. The listener usually does not hear these sounds consciously; like overtones they seem to be absorbed into the principal tone. 2-2/3 and 1-3/5 foot stops are known as mutation stops.

The pitch of the various types of stop, classified in feet, can be summarized thus:

sound of the namesake instruments in the orchestra, but a single line of low-pitched tones suggests a

(B) The various stops differ sharply in volume. The tuba mirabilis emits a stentorian sound; the dulciana, unda maris, and aeoline are so soft as to be nearly inaudible. Of course it is possible to draw more than one stop on any manual and hence to build up the volume by increasing weight of tone, just as orchestral instruments are combined to increase volume. It is also obvious that the composite tone-color of two different stops employed simultaneously differs from that of either one of them when used alone.

Just as all orchestral instruments are classified into four general types (string, woodwind, brass, percussion) so all organ stops can be classified into four types, known as diapason, string, flute, and reed. One or more stops of all types (except perhaps reed) are normally found on each manual and in the pedals. The tone-color combinations of the organ are almost infinite.

Diapason stops have a plain, neutral color, often rather uninteresting, but they are the most typically "organ-like" in their quality, and are the fundamental, everyday stops of the instrument. Despite their lack of strong character, they impart wonderful solidity to the sound, particularly at higher levels of volume. It is nearly impossible to get a really good, sinewy fortissimo without the use of any diapasons.

String stops are not very accurately named. A fairly high-pitched sustained chord, sounded with string stops, does somewhat resemble the

bassoon more than a string instrument. These stops impart clearness and definition to the instrument's tone; they "cut through" well.

Flute stops correspond to the woodwinds of the orchestra. They are subdivided into two types: open flutes, which sound somewhat like the flute, and stopped flutes, which come closer to the clarinet. (It is curious that one common stopped flute bears the incongruous name stopped diapason, for its tone is by no means diapason quality. The more accurate name gedackt is sometimes substituted.) To the orchestral musician the use of the word flute when applied to a sound equal to the lowest C of the piano seems singular indeed; yet 16-foot flute stops include this pitch, and usually pedal stops of 16-foot flute quality outnumber those of the other three types.

Reed stops correspond to the brass instruments and to certain woodwinds. Small organs sometimes do not have a single reed stop, or perhaps only one or two; hence even on large instruments they are usually the least numerous type. Reed stops are much favored in France, and French organists' fondness for their somewhat nasal tone is almost notorious.

There are a few stops that are considered hybrids, but not all organs have them.

A mixture is a special type of stop that sounds a chord, rather than a single tone. The sounds in the chord are some of those in the *harmonic series. Like the mutation stops, they are used to strengthen overtones and thus to "color" and add clarity to the basic stops. Mixtures are found only on large organs.

Some organs have stops labeled chimes, harp, glockenspiel, xylophone, etc.; in the days when the organ was standard equipment in every moving-picture theater, bass drum, cymbals, and other contraptions were also encountered. None of these can be considered a legitimate "stop." Scholarly organists consider them toys.

From the foregoing discussion, it may be already apparent that hardly any two organs have exactly the same stops (or the same "specifications," to use organists' terminology). Familiarizing one's self with the individual instrument and learning its possibilities and idiosyncrasies requires time. Every young organist stands in awe of the virtuoso who travels from one town to another, giving concerts on innumerable organs after only the briefest time to get acquainted with each of them.

The artistic and carefully-considered use of the stops is called registration. It is to the organ what *orchestration is to the orchestra. Obviously a passage that would sound delightful with one registration might be characterless or displeasing with a totally different one.

Couplers. By the use of the *couplers it is possible to combine all the stops selected for two manuals while playing on only one; that is, couplers add manual to manual. Any or all manuals can be coupled to the great and to the pedals; the swell can be coupled to the choir and usually vice versa.

There are also 4-foot and 16-foot couplers on most of the manuals. When the former is drawn, every stop on the manual in question sounds both its normal pitch and the tone an octave higher. The 16-foot coupler gives every stop an octave lower as well as its normal pitch. If the player draws all the stops, then couples swell, choir, and (if it exists) solo to the great--the 4-foot and 16-foot couplers as well as the ordinary ones (swell to great, swell to great 4',

swell to great 16', etc.)--then couples the great to itself 4-foot and 16-foot, his instrument is at maximum volume, and it emits a veritable torrent of sound.

Special Accessories. Crescendos and diminuendos are produced by special appliances known as swell pedals (sometimes called expression pedals). These are located in recesses just over the pedalboard. When the swell pedal is pressed, it gradually closes a row of shutters placed in front of the pipes, and thus causes a reduction in volume. Opening it increases the volume. It is balanced so as to stay in position at any angle to which the player's foot tilts it; hence it can place the shutters just part-way open if the player so desires. In some organs, particularly old ones, the great manual is not controlled by a swell pedal; its volume can be varied only by the number of stops drawn. In the best organs there is a separate swell pedal for each manual, but in cheap ones a single swell pedal affects the entire instrument. Originally the swell pedal was applied only to the swell manual; hence the name.

The crescendo pedal gradually adds one stop after the other, from the softest through the loudest, without the knobs or tablets having to be touched by the hands. This accessory is poorly named, for it is never employed to produce a crescendo. Closing it will gradually remove the stops one by one.

Some organs have a sforzando pedal. It can be pressed into just one position, in which it immediately throws on every stop.

The tremulant, often carelessly called tremolo, is a mechanical device that when engaged produces a steady, pulsating waver in the volume of the tone. It attemps to imitate the *vibrato of string instruments and the voice. In small organs, the tremulant affects every manual, but in larger instruments each manual has its own tremulant. For further information see tremolo (5).

Pistons are little push-buttons located below each manual or placed just above the pedalboard for operation by the toe. When pressed they immediately throw on (or off) any combination of stops which the player has previously selected.

The Touch. The chief difference between organ touch and piano touch is that in the former instrument the keys are pressed; in the latter they are struck. The amount of force exerted by the organist makes absolutely no difference in the volume; this depends entirely on whether the swell pedal is open or closed, plus of course the number of stops that are drawn. Dynamic *accents are impossible on the organ.

List of Stops. As stated, no two organs are alike. The number and identity of the stops is unpredictable. Certain stops are normally located only on certain manuals; certain others are nearly always of 4-foot or 16-foot pitch. The following list classifies commonly-encountered stops into the four basic types, and names a few hybrid stops and mixtures. Of course the typical organ possesses nowhere nearly this many stops. On the other hand, there are many other stops not listed here, but which are sometimes found.

A LIST OF ORGAN STOPS

Diapason

Dulciana
Fifteenth (always 2')
Flautino (usually 2')
Geigen principal or Violin diapason
Octave (always 4')
Open diapason
Stentorphone
Twelfth (always 2-2/3')
Vox angelica

Flute

Blockflöte
Bourdon (usually 16'; often pedal)
Cathedral bourdon (usually 16' pedal)
Chimney flute
Claribel or Claribella
Concert flute
Doppel flute
Flute celeste
Flute d'amour
Gedackt or Stopped diapason
Gross flute
Harmonic flute (usually 4')
Hohlpfeife
Lieblich gedackt (usually 16' pedal)
Melodia
Nachthorn
Nazard (always 2-2/3')
Orchestral flute
Piccolo (always 4' or 2')
Quintadena
Rohr flute or Koppel flute
Sifflöte
Spitz flute
Still gedackt
Suabe flute (usually 4')

String

Aeoline
Celestina (usually 4')
Contra-gamba (always 16')
Dulcet
Gamba celeste
Keraulophone
Salicet
Salicional
Unda maris
Viola
Viola da gamba
Viole d'amour
Viole d'orchestre
Violina (usually 4')
Violoncello
Violone (always 16')
Vox celeste

Reed

Bassoon or Fagotto (usually 16')
Bombarde (usually 16' or 32')
Clarinet
Clarion
Corno di bassetto
Cornopean
English horn
Flügelhorn
French horn
Heckelphone
Krummhorn or Cromorne
Musette
Oboe
Ophicleide (usually 16')
Trombone or Posaune
Trumpet
Tuba

Flute (Cont'd)

Transverse flute
Waldflöte

Hybrids

Erzähler
Gemshorn

Reed (Cont'd)

Tuba mirabilis
Vox humana

Mixtures

Cornet
Cymbel
Fourniture
Sesquialtera

The stops named after various
orchestral instruments usually bear
only a slight resemblance to their
namesakes, but this observation in
no way precludes beauty of tone.
Special Types of Organ. A
Baroque organ is built exactly like
the organs of the *Baroque era,
with the intention of reproducing the
exact tone-colors intended by Bach,
Pachelbel, Frescobaldi, Buxtehude,
Sweelinck, and other composers of
that age. Certain characteristics
of conventional nineteenth and twentieth century organs do not lend themselves well to Baroque music. The
sound of the Baroque organ is
bright, clear, and thin, with a predominance of flute stops.
The theater organ (or movie organ) was found in every well-equipped
moving-picture theater during the
era of silent films. The roster of
stops often included (as has already
been mentioned) such questionable
or freakish items as xylophone,
snare drum, bass drum, and cym-
bals--even a piano stop. (However
the tale that some theater organs
possessed a stop which imitated the
chirping of a cricket may be merely
pleasantry.) The theater organ always had a tremulant of extremely
pronounced effect, and the players
abused this accessory unmercifully.
Often the manuals were equipped
with what is known as "double-
touch," meaning that if the player
exerted extra heavy pressure on a
key, it would press down to a point
lower than the normal stopping-place,
and a different registration, selected
especially for the second touch,
could be brought into play for a
single chord or tone. The usefulness of the double-touch for sudden
effects, with an instrument on which

dynamic accent is impossible, hardly
needs comment.
The invention of the sound film
sounded the death-knell of the theater
organ.
The reed organ is the same thing
as the *harmonium; it should probably
be considered a separate and distinct
instrument rather than a variety of
organ.
In the electric or electronic organ,
electrically-controlled tubes and cir-
cuits replace the pipes of the normal
instrument. See electronic instruments.
The term pipe organ is sometimes
used to distinguish the normal organ
from the reed organ and electronic
organ.
A common mechanical disorder is
described under cipher.
Italian: organo. French: orgue.
German: Orgel. Spanish: órgano.
The player is called an organist.

● organ chorale. See chorale prelude.

● organ-point. See non-harmonic
tones (9).

● organum. Name given to the earliest
types of *harmony or *polyphony (which
may be considered synonymous terms
in the early stages), first described in
the early ninth century. It should be
understood that as far as can be proven,
all ancient music (that is, all pre-
ninth century music) consisted of an
unharmonized melody; at least there is
no documentary evidence that it possessed harmony, so the appearance of
this element is perhaps the most important musical development of medieval
times.
Essentially organum is a method of
adding an additional voice to a *Gregorian chant.
Information on the subject of early

harmony is scanty, for this innovation appeared in northwestern Europe at the time that region was in the darkest of the "Dark Ages."

There are at least four types of organum.

(1) <u>Strict Organum</u>, the earliest known form of harmony, came into existence in the early ninth century, as far as can be determined, and continued at least through the tenth. It consisted of parallel perfect fourths or perfect fifths (see <u>intervals</u>); that is, the melody of a <u>Gre</u>gorian chant (plainsong) was duplicated a fourth or fifth below, both parts moving in exactly the same rhythm. Some musicologists believe that Strict Organum consisted of a completely unrelieved series of fourths (or fifths) from beginning to end; others are of the opinion that both parts started out in unison, but went into fourths after two or three notes, and merged into unison again for the last two or three notes.

It is likely that the application of organum had a detrimental effect on the subtle and flowing rhythm of the original chant; probably all the notes tended toward uniformity in length and it seems assured that the *tempo became too slow and too deliberate, for the singers on both parts, inexperienced in this "new" effect, were probably fearful of getting away from one another.

Organum at the fourth was apparently more commonly used than that at the fifth. In both cases the upper was the principal voice, carrying the chant melody.

Only a few examples of this were ever written down. Notation itself was still in the most primitive stage

and since both parts duplicated a single familiar chant melody, notation was not especially needed. The example shown below is frequently quoted. Only the pitches are indicated, though the tempo is doubtless much more flowing and less regular than whole-notes at first suggest, since music in these days was governed by the rhythm of speech.

Some musicologists believe that organum was applied only to certain passages in the chants, the balance remaining unharmonized (that is, sung in unison). There is reason to believe that the entire choir sang the unison passages, while the portions in organum were entrusted to a single singer (soloist) on each voice.

<u>Parallel Organum</u> is a synonym for <u>Strict Organum</u>. Most references to "organum," unmodified, indicate Strict Organum.

(2) <u>Free Organum,</u> which apparently originated soon after Strict Organum, contained occasional departures from the steady rows of perfect fourth or perfect fifths. Two conditions brought this about. One is that for some reason not clearly understood, the lower voice was not permitted to go below the C an octave lower than *middle C. Hence if the upper voice, carrying the chant melody, moved down toward low C, the lower voice either repeated C or held it out. (The latter expedient produced a slight variety in rhythm, of course.) Thus, if the upper voice were to move down F--E--D--C, the lower part, standing still on C, would produce with it in order: perfect fourth--major third-- major second--unison, relieving the

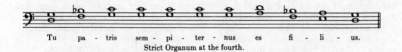

Tu   pa - tris   sem - pi - ter - nus   es   fi - li - us.
Strict Organum at the fourth.

predominant parallel motion by a
little oblique motion. The other
reason is the difficult relation existing between F and B; in organum
at the fourth, an augmented fourth
would have resulted; in organum at
the fifth, a diminished fifth. The
flatting of B does not seem to have
occurred as a solution, nor the
sharping of F. (However, observe
that B-flat does appear in the example of Strict Organum quoted
earlier. It should be borne in mind

the fourth, would be, reading downward: perfect fifth--perfect fourth--
perfect fifth.
  (3) New Organum, appearing in the
eleventh or twelfth century, represented
a noteworthy step forward. Contrary
motion was preferred, and oblique
considered superior to parallel, just
as is true today; but an intermingling
of the three types was regarded best
of all--again a concept that remains
unchallenged to the present day. As
for intervals, the fourth, fifth, and

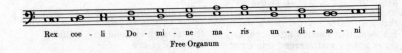

Rex coe - li Do - mi - ne ma - ris un - di - so - ni

Free Organum

that information about this subject
is very scant, and that accounts of
it are not always clear.) In order
to secure a better relationship with
B, some other tone would be substituted, thus providing a different
interval momentarily. (Probably E
or G was used, the result being a
perfect fifth or major third, respectively.) Occasionally the voices
would cross and often at the end the
two voices would come together into
a unison, thus producing *contrary
motion. Hence it will be seen that
in Free Organum parallel motion
predominated, oblique occurred occasionally, but contrary only rarely.
  In both Strict and Free Organum,
each voice was sometimes *doubled
at the octave. The upper (original)
voice was doubled at the octave
below, the lower (added) voice at
the octave above. Under this condition, the intervals between the
four voices, in Strict Organum at

octave were still preferred to the
others, but thirds, sixths, unisons,
and seconds occurred often enough to
provide adequate variety, though
sevenths were rare. Occasionally
one voice had two notes while the
other sang but one. Crossing of
voices was permitted, thus paving
the way toward later polyphonic developments. Due to the influence of
poetry, a more metric type of rhythm
was unfolding simultaneously.
  In New Organum the lower was the
principal voice, carrying the chant
melody in highly modified form. This
is an important feature, as a way was
thus left open for the addition of a
third voice in the developments that
followed organum.
  The example on page 299 is the
opening of Mira Lege, one of the
best-known examples from this period
of musical development. Observe that
the composition tends to fall into
clearly-marked four measure phrases.

New Organum

(4) <u>Melismatic Organum</u> appeared about the same time as New Organum. Here the chant melody again was found in the lower voice; but all respect for its rhythm went completely by the board, for the melody was sung in tremendously long notes, while above it another voice had a quick-moving, elaborate, florid (melismatic) countermelody, thus placing many notes against the long-held tone in the voice below it. The chant text must have been inordinately prolonged by this procedure, though probably it was not treated in such a manner all the way to the end, but rather only in certain chosen sections. Many musicologists believe the florid upper part was sung by a single voice--perhaps *improvised--for the difficulty of keeping a group of singers together on any-

thing so elaborate would have been considerable, since the art of *conducting was a development yet undreamed of. Possibly the solo singer signaled the choir when to go on to the next note in the chant.

Observe that in the brief (and incomplete) accompanying illustration only two syllables of a word (<u>benedicamus</u>) have so far appeared.

Naturally considerable variety of harmonic interval was characteristic of Melismatic Organum.

Synonyms for <u>Melismatic Organum</u> are <u>Organum Purum</u>, <u>Organum Duplum</u>, and <u>St. Martial Organum</u>.

The use of the term <u>organum</u> continued into the thirteenth century with three-part music, by which time the technique of composition had advanced tremendously; however the term is reserved here for the four early va-

Melismatic Organum

rieties of two-voice music.

It is not known whether there is or is not any connection between the terms organum and organ.

Plural: organa.

Synonym: diaphony.

Pronunciation: ŏr´-gă-nŭm or ōr-gä´-nōŏm.

● Oriental music. A detailed discussion of the music of the non-Western (non-Occidental) countries is beyond the scope of an elementary dictionary. Suffice it to say that the music of Oriental, African, and Oceanic lands differs markedly from that of Europe and those countries (such as our own) whose culture is of European origin. The cleavage between Oriental and Occidental music is the supreme argument in support of Kipling's statement that "Oh, East is East, and West is West, and never the twain shall meet. "

Other than such obvious matters as the use of unfamiliar instruments and apparently bizarre vocal techniques, Oriental music differs from Occidental most notably in the following respects:

(A) It does not use *harmony, or at best uses it in a primitive or desultory manner more akin to *heterophony than harmony in the thoroughgoing form characteristic of European and western hemisphere music. What harmony it does contain is often the result of instrumental *ostinatos or pedal-points (see non-harmonic tones, 9).

(B) Its scales sometimes employ pitches not in tune with the *chromatic scale which forms the basis of Western music. Sometimes *quartertones and other minute divisions (*microtones) are used, thus dividing the octave into more than twelve tones; but at other times it employs scales of comparatively few tones, of which some are a trifle higher or lower in pitch than the corresponding tones of our scales (in other words, certain scale-steps seem slightly out-of-tune by our standards). Other types of Oriental music adhere to the *pentatonic scale so characteristic of much primitive music.

(C) The rhythmic patterns are sometimes vastly different from ours, often with no underlying basis of *meter or regularity.

The native music of the various Oriental countries differs as much as do the countries themselves; even a superficial examination makes clear that the musical styles of (for example) China, India, Java, and Persia (Iran) not only differ from that of Europe, but are mutually at variance with one another.

The music of Africa and Polynesia is also strikingly different from that of Europe and the Americas, and is sometimes carelessly termed "Oriental. " Even the music of the American Indians is dissimilar to that of Europe, notably again in its lack of harmony.

Interest in the music of the Orient and other non-Western cultures is distinctly on the increase; that of Bali, Java, and India has influenced several contemporary composers. On the other hand, Occidental music has become tremendously popular in the Orient, especially Japan.

Many European composers have written compositions in what was offered (and possibly even imagined) as an Oriental style--e.g., the "Arabian Dance" and "Chinese Dance" in Tschaikowsky's Nutcracker Suite, Puccini's Madam Butterfly and Turandot, Verdi's Aïda, Cui's Orientale, and so on. Exotic though some of these doubtless sound, they bear little resemblance to real Oriental music. They must be accepted good-naturedly for what they are--pseudo-Oriental, a European's notion of Oriental, but actually unrecognizable to a resident of the Near or Far East. A similar caution is in order in regard to much music which is supposedly "Indian. "

See also "Turkish music. "

● ornaments. Signs used to indicate certain stylized and characteristic patterns which by nature seem more or less superimposed on the skeletal framework of melodic and other strands in the musical fabric. They are chiefly associated with instrumental style rather than vocal. With ornaments, a single note and a symbol can represent several tones; the ornament-symbols might well be thought of as abbreviations.

During the *Baroque period (roughly 1600-1750), especially in its later days, ornaments were generously employed, while during the *Rococo period (roughly 1725-1775) certain composers undoubtedly used them to excess, particularly in compositions for the *keyboard instruments. The *Classical period which followed saw a decrease in their frequency, a trend which continued through the nineteenth century period of *Romanticism. Today it is rare to encounter any ornament other than the trill.

A great many ornaments were invented and used during various periods of musical history. Certain signs employed to indicate them have unfortunately changed during the course of time, creating more than a little confusion. It will suffice here to give only the most frequently-encountered ornaments and in their most usual sign-forms.

Types. The important ornaments are:

The *trill (1), for which the sign is *tr* or *tr* ~~~. It is explained under the entry trill.

The mordent, inverted mordent, double mordent, and double inverted mordent, for which the signs are ~v~ ~v~ ~v~ and ~v~ respectively. All are explained under the entry mordent.

The turn, for which the sign is ~o~ and the inverted turn (or back turn) for which the sign is ~o~ or ~g~ Both are explained under the entry turn.

If an ornament is placed over a chord, it is understood to affect only the highest note. If other notes are affected, the ornament is written a second time, preferably once above and once below the tones in question (or written three times for a three-note chord). If the music for two instruments is written on a single staff, and both parts are affected by an ornament, again it is placed above the note for the upper instrument and below that for the lower instrument. This is illustrated under mordent (Example 9) and trill (Ex-

ample 2).

*Grace-notes undoubtedly have an "ornamental" effect, but since they are not indicated with a conventional sign, but with notes (albeit of a special type), they will not be considered as ornaments for present purposes.

It must be emphasized that a number of other and less common types of ornament have been employed at various times, especially during the sixteenth, seventeenth, and early eighteenth centuries. There is more than a little confusion relative to their exact rendition. There is even uncertainty in connection with some of the commoner ornaments, particularly the turn; in fact the trill seems to be the only one that enjoys even moderate clarity.

The very use of ornaments in the first place may seem an invitation to the confusion which they have brought about; they represent the intrusion of arbitrary hieroglyphics into an otherwise rational and orderly system of notation. It is indeed a blessing that in eight cases out of ten, the artistic difference between various disputed readings is negligible. Even where a pronounced difference in effect occurs, blame for the confusion should be placed squarely on the shoulders of the person who is really responsible for it--the composer, not the performer.

Composers of the twentieth century have wisely discarded all ornament-signs except the trill.

Probably the most authoritative book on ornaments is Putnam Aldrich's Musical Ornamentation in the 17th and 18th Centuries. Russell Lanning has written an important work called Bach Ornamentation.

Synonym: agréments (French).

See also roll (1).

●† ossia. Indication for alternate version of a passage, which may be substituted if desired. The alternate version is often written on a narrower staff than the regular version. In the excerpt (for piano) on p. 302 top, the player may use either of two right-hand parts.

Often the ossia is marked, more completely, "ossia, più facile" (easier);

however, the ossia is not always the easier of the two parts offered.

(but occasionally fround at the top of the texture, or in its middle), which

In vocal music, particularly operatic arias, notes in grace-note size type are often found on the same stem with notes of normal size; they indicate alternative tones and are, in effect, short ossias. Observe that in this case the alternate part does not have a separate staff.

is combined with different material each time it repeats.

The ostinato and the *accompaniment-figure should not be mutually confused. Although an accompaniment-figure has a characteristic shape, the actual notes found in various appearances do not repeat exactly, but undergo changes

*Ad libitum differs from ossia in that the former usually indicates notes which may be omitted (or included) if desired--that is, a choice between certain notes or nothing at all--while ossia normally indicates a choice of one or the other of two readings.

Synonym: oppure.

Pronunciation: the accenting is regular, i.e., on the second syllable (si)--not the first.

●† ostinato. A continually-repeated melodic strand, usually in the bass

which are brought about by the underlying harmony. In an ostinato there is usually no change whatever in the melodic strand as it repeats many times; however in some examples the melody becomes elaborated as the composition progresses. A *pedal-point is not an ostinato (see drone bass), even if trilled; nor is an *Alberti bass.

An ostinato in the bass--the most frequent location--is called a basso ostinato, ground bass, or simply ground. In Italian, the word ostinato means "obstinate" or "stubborn."

A long-repeated rhythmic pattern is

called a rhythmic ostinato.

The Passacaglia and the Chaconne.
The passacaglia and chaconne are
normally built over an ostinato bass
melody. With every statement of
this melody, fresh material appears

been lost.

As a rule the repeating melody is
eight measures in length. The time-
signature is 3-4 (or 3-2) and the mode
is usually minor. The *tempo is
always basically slow, though notes

Ostinato melody

above, harmonically and contrapuntally agreeing with it. Each
repetition of the ostinato melody is
termed a variation, since there is
a change of opposing material every
time. The complexity and grandeur
which can be achieved in this form
are remarkable.

The distinction between passacaglia
and chaconne has provoked no little
musical debating. Among the differences that have been suggested are
these, though they are dubious:

(A) That in the passacaglia, the
repeating melody is invariably in the
bass; that in the chaconne it occasionally changes to the highest
voice, the variation material then
appearing below. Some musicians
insist the distinction is exactly the
other way around.

(B) That in the passacaglia, the
bass melody is first stated unaccompanied, before any other material is heard above it; that in the
chaconne the upper material commences at once, simultaneously
with the ostinato melody.

Neither distinction will hold up
under examination of actual compositions bearing these titles.
Passacaglia and chaconne may therefore be considered synonyms. If
a distinction ever existed, it has

of shorter and shorter value tend to
appear as one variation succeeds
another, thus giving the appearance
of more and more animation.

Musicians have observed that sometimes the ostinato melody in the
passacaglia-chaconne is replaced by a
repeating series of harmonies. However, there are examples containing
neither a repeating melody nor a repeating harmonic succession. These
might quite fairly be considered misnomers; nevertheless their mood and
style are certainly that associated with
the form.

See also boogie-woogie, passacaglia,
theme and variations.

Plural: ostinatos (English) or osti-
nati (Italian).

●† ottava. *Octave. Abbreviated *8va,
occasionally 8ve.

●† ottavino. Italian name for the
*piccolo.

● outer voices. The highest and lowest
voices. In an example written for soprano, alto, tenor, and bass, the soprano and bass are the outer voices.
Antonym: inner voices.

● outline. A melodic fragment constructed out of the tones of a certain

chord, in *broken chord or *arpeggio fashion, is said to "outline" that chord. For example, in The Star-Spangled Banner the words "O say, can you see" and "twlight's last gleaming" outline the tonic (I) chord; in The Old Folks at Home the words "ev'ry where I" outline the subdominant (IV) chord.

● out of tune. Deviating slightly from the correct pitch (either too high or too low, or a mixture or succession of both).

A tone so far astray as to have actually the pitch of the tone higher or lower might better be termed a "wrong note" than "out of tune."

It is possible for an instrument to be out of tune with another instrument, and still be completely in tune with itself.

See also intonation.

● overblowing. On the *woodwind instruments it is possible, by appropriate use of the breath and lips (see embouchure) to cause the instrument to enter a higher segment of its *range while repeating the *fingering (3) used in a lower segment. The use of the upper tones is called overblowing.

All of the woodwind instruments overblow at the interval of the octave except the clarinet, which overblows at the twelfth (i.e., an octave and a perfect fifth; see intervals).

● overtones. (1) The *harmonic series.

(2) The *open tones of the brass instruments.

● overture. (1) The orchestral introduction to an *opera. It is played by the orchestra before the curtain rises on the first act, but after the house lights have been dimmed. Its purpose is to set the mood of the opera that is to follow.

Some overtures (probably a majority) are based on themes occurring later in the opera. Others consist entirely of independent though appropriate music. Still others are based partly on material that occurs later on and partly on independent

material.

Many opera overtures are written in *sonata-allegro form; that is, their form is similar to that of the first movement of a *symphony. Others are hardly more than a potpourri of the tunes that are to occur later; however, those answering to this description can hardly be said to number among the pinnacles of the overture literature.

The tempo of an overture is nearly always basically fast, though very frequently there is a slow introduction.

Overtures normally come to a complete stop before the curtain rises on Act I; one which leads directly into the music of the first act might better be called a prelude. For further remarks on the distinction between overture and prelude, see prelude (3).

A few operas dispense with any semblance of an overture.

(2) A similar orchestral introduction to an *oratorio, *cantata, *ballet, or play, in the last case either with (e.g., Beethoven's Egmont Overture and Mendelssohn's Midsummer Night's Dream Overture) or without (e.g., Beethoven's Coriolan Overture) additional *incidental music.

(3) A purely independent orchestral composition, but similar in style to an opera overture. This type is called concert overture. Many, but by no means all, are in *sonata-allegro form. Familiar concert overtures include Mendelssohn's Hebrides Overture (sometimes called Fingal's Cave Overture), Brahms's Academic Festival Overture and Tragic Overture, Rimsky-Korsakoff's Russian Easter Overture, and Tschaikowsky's 1812 Overture.

The term overture is tending to lose its strict meaning (i.e., introduction)-- to become practically a synonym for any one-movement orchestral composition other than the *symphonic poem. Quite commonly at orchestral concerts an overture forms the closing number on the program!

For French overture and Italian overture, see those entries. An additional, now obsolete meaning will be found under suite (1).

● ozalid process. See black-and-white process.

P

● p.   Soft.   This is the abbreviation for piano. It indicates a dynamic level softer than *mp, but not as much so as *pp.
   See dynamic marks.

● pan-diatonic.   A type of structure found in some *Modern music in which all the tones of the *diatonic scale are treated as of equal importance, and are prone to occur in practically any harmonic combination. Much of Stravinsky's later music is pan-diatonic.

● Pan pipes.   A wind instrument consisting of a series of small pipes, of graduated sizes, fastened together horizontally. It is sounded by blowing over a hole at the top of each pipe.   The appearance suggests miniature organ pipes.
   Synonyms: syrinx, Pandean pipes.

● parade drum.   The military drum.

● parallelisms.   Chords moving entirely in parallel motion (see

● parallel minor, parallel major. Same as tonic minor, tonic major.

● parallel motion.   See contrary, parallel, and oblique motion.

● paraphrase.   This term is used in English grammar and composition to signify a restatement, in one's own words, of the verbal or written thought of another person.
   It has been used in music as a synonym for "free arrangement." Some paraphrases add difficult runs and brilliant passages to a fundamentally simple structure, often in a manner that is far from tasteful. Others are entirely too free, completely forsaking the spirit of the original. The more legitimate type of paraphrase is built on a *borrowed melody which serves as a basis for work which is fundamentally original, the *chorale-prelude being essentially of this nature.
   A paraphrase may or may not also be a *transcription.

●† parlando.   A style of singing that very closely approaches speech.

Parallelism

contrary, parallel, and oblique motion).   The accompanying passage will illustrate.   An additional example will be found under non-functional harmony (the quotation from Debussy's The Submerged Cathedral).
   The French *impressionists were especially fond of this device.
   Synonym: block harmony.

Literally, "talking." The term is sometimes also applied to *recitative-like passages for instruments.

●† parte.   Part.
   Plural: parti.

● partials.   (1) The individual tones in the *harmonic series, or the harmonic series in general.

(2) The *open tones of the brass instruments.

●† partita. (1) Same as suite (1).

(2) An old name for the theme and variations.

Plural: partite.

● parts, the. The music from which each member of an orchestra, chamber-music group, or band reads is known as a part. Normally it contains only the notes to be played by his instrument. The parts are copied out from the composer's *score (1).

When an orchestra purchases a composition with a view to performing it, a score for the *conductor and a set of the parts-- one for each player (in the string section, one for every two players)--is needed.

● part-song. (1) A composition similar to a *song, but written for *chorus (generally *mixed chorus), rather than a single voice, usually with piano. It might well be considered the secular equivalent of the *anthem. Many part-songs can be sung by either a *mixed quartet (a single singer to a part) or a mixed chorus (a section or group of singers to a part). They are normally quite *homophonic in style; herein lies the difference between true part-songs and *madrigals and *glees. Most of them are a product of the *Romantic period, the majority by persons of slight importance, for among important composers, apparently only Brahms, Mendelssohn, and Schumann took the part-song seriously.

(2) Loosely, any short choral composition, including madrigals and glees.

● part-writing. See harmony (2).

● paso doble (Spanish). A type of dance in 6-8 time, gay in spirit, that is popular in Spain and in Spanish-speaking countries.

Plural: pasos dobles.

Pronunciation: pä-sō do-blĕ.

●† passacaglia. A dance in slow 3-4 or 3-2 time, normally based on an eight-measure ground bass (repeating bass melody). New material appears above the bass melody each time it is repeated. It is essentially *contrapuntal.

The passacaglia is further described under ostinato.

For all practical purposes, it may be considered identical with the chaconne.

Most passacaglias are in the minor mode.

The example of passacaglia style on the opposite page is based on a three-measure bass melody.

Variant form (French): passacaille.

Pronunciation: accent third syllable.

Example of passacaglia style, based on a three-measure bass melody.

● passepied. A dance in fairly quick 3-8 or 6-8 time, gay in spirit. It is apparently of French origin.
  Pronunciation: păs-pyā; musicians sometimes anglicize it as păs-ĕ-pēd.

● passing-tones. See non-harmonic tones (1).

● passion. A special type of *oratorio treating of the betrayal, trial, and crucifixion of Christ. The Passion According to St. Matthew and Passion According to St. John by Bach are both well known.

●† passionale. Passional, temper-amental.

●† passionato. Variant form of *appassionato.

●† passione. Passion. Thus, con passione, with passion.

●† pasticcio. Derisive name for a composition that lacks unity; literally, "mess."
  Pronunciation: accent second syllable.

● pastorale. A composition intended to suggest the out-of-doors. Some pastorales feature a *pedal point. Imitation of shepherds' pipes, peasant dances, and bird-calls are not unusual; nevertheless in some examples

(e. g., Franck's Pastorale for organ) there are no characteristic "nature" effects at all.

Pastorales are often written in 6-8 or 12-8 time.

Plural: pastorales or pastorali.

Variant form: pastoral.

See also eclogue.

Pronunciation: päs-tȯ-rä-lĕ.

● † patetico. Pathetic.

Pronunciation: accent second syllable.

● patriotic songs. See home-and-community songs and national anthems.

● patter song. A humorous, breathlessly-rushing song in an *operetta which secures its special effect from coupling a headlong *tempo with employment of many polysyllabic words in the text. The operettas by Sir Arthur Sullivan (to *librettos by W. S. Gilbert) contain a number of patter songs.

● Pauken. The German word for *timpani (kettle-drums).

Pronunciation: poú-kĕn.

● † pausa. Pause.

Plural: pause.

● pause. (1) The *fermata.

(2) An undesirable synonym for *rest.

The general pause or grand pause is explained under G. P.

● pavane. A slow and dignified type of court dance in 2-2 or 4-4 time. It apparently originated during the sixteenth century in Spain, from whence its popularity spread quickly. There is some dispute as to whether the name is derived from the Spanish word for "peacock" or from the name of the city of Padua, in Italy.

It is often coupled with the *galliard in the order: pavane, galliard.

Variant spellings: pavan, pavin.

● pavillon en l'air (French). "Bell in the air"; direction to the player of a wind instrument (usually the

*horn) to raise the *bell of his instrument so as to produce a loud, uninhibited tone.

Pronunciation: pä-vē-yōn än lâr.

● 𝄢. The direction used in piano compositions to indicate that the *damper pedal is to be pressed. This indication is nearly always given in script. The sign to release the pedal is ✳ . These symbols are placed underneath the lower staff.

When 𝄢 appears several times in succession with no ✳ intervening, it indicates that the pedal is to be released and immediately pressed again--that there is to be no time when the pedal is up and hence completely out of use, but only a momentary release to avoid blurring.

Often the symbol └───┐ or └─────┘

is substituted to indicate points where the pedal is pressed and released.

Variant (rare): P.

● pedal. (1) In general, a lever operated by the foot.

The three pedals on a grand piano are:

right--*damper pedal (or sustaining pedal); often incorrectly called loud pedal.

center--*middle pedal (or sostenuto pedal).

left--*soft pedal (or *una corda pedal).

The pedals on the harp are discussed under harp. Their function is to change the pitch of the strings.

Those found on the harpsichord are somewhat analogous to the stops and couplers on the *organ; see harpsichord.

The pedals (or pedalboard) of the organ are discussed under organ; they are like another keyboard or manual, but played with the feet.

Two pedals are used to supply air to the *harmonium and the *player piano. They may also be called treadles.

Modern *timpani (kettle-drums) have pedals to adjust and change the pitch.

The expression "foot pedal" is tautological; all pedals are foot pedals.

(2) A synonym for pedal point (organ point). See non-harmonic tones (9).

For the pedal tones of the trombone, see trombone.

● pedal clarinet. The contrabass clarinet in B-flat.

●† pedale. Pedal, i.e., the right-hand or *damper pedal (sustaining pedal) of the piano. Con pedale or col pedale, with pedal; this does not mean the uninterrupted holding of the pedal but its discreet and careful use where appropriate. Con due pedali, with two pedals, i.e., with the right (damper) and left (soft) pedals.

● pedaling. (1) The use of the feet in playing the *organ. Pedal-ing is the counterpart of *fingering (1) on the keyboard instruments.

The conventional signs used in indicating pedaling are shown under organ and symbols.
Synonym: footing.
(2) The exact manner in which the *damper pedal is used in play-ing the piano. Pedaling is usually indicated by an *editor rather than by the composer, and even then the indication is very general rather than exact, the finer shades of pedaling being left to the player's good judgment.
Variant spelling: pedalling.

● pedal-point. See non-harmonic tones (9).

● peg. One of the wooden pins on a bowed *string or *fretted instru-ment which may be twisted so as to tighten or slacken the string in adjusting it to proper pitch. The end of the string is wound around the peg.
The cavity into which the pegs are inserted is called the peg box.

● pentatonic scale. A scale of five tones, found in much primitive music and folk-music. It contains only whole-steps and minor thirds. Compared to the ordinary diatonic major scale, the fourth and seventh (or third and seventh) degrees are missing.

It will be apparent that this scale lacks half-steps (semitones), probably due to the fact that the simple people whose music employs the pentatonic scale are unable to distinguish this narrow interval.

The black keys of the piano form a pentatonic scale (in F-sharp or G-flat major).
Synonym: gapped scale.

●† per. For.

● percussion instruments. Those instruments played by striking, and in which the tone dies away of its own accord, out of the player's con-trol.

They may be classified into two groups: (A) those of definite (or fixed or determinate) pitch, which are capable of playing *melodies or at least of producing musical tones of fixed pitch, and (B) those of indefinite (or indeterminate) pitch, which produce only a noise (in the scientific rather than derogatory sense of that word).

(A) The definite pitch percussion instruments include the *xylophone, *glockenspiel, *chimes (tubular bells), *timpani (kettle-drums), *antique cymbals, and *celesta, plus such non-orchestral instruments as the *marim-ba, *vibraphone, and *dulcimer.

Many musicians consider the *piano a definite pitch percussion instrument, and with reason. If this classification is accepted, then the *harpsichord, *spinet (virginal), and *clavichord will also find place under it, plus the *czimbalom (a type of *dulcimer). Even the bowed *string instruments when played *pizzicato have a per-cussive effect, and the *plucked string family, including the *harp, could al-most be classified as percussion in-struments. Each one of the foregoing might well be regarded as a hybrid of percussion and string.

(B) The indefinite pitch group in-cludes all drums except the kettle-drums (timpani)-- in other words the *snare drum, *tenor drum, *bass drum, *tom-tom (Indian drum), *tam-bourine, *tambourin de Provence (tabor, Provençal drum), *bongós, plus Oriental and primitive instruments too

numerous to mention--as well as
the *triangle, *castanets, *cymbals,
*cow-bells, *rachet, *gong (tam-
tam), *wood-block, *sleigh bells
(harness bells), *wind machine,
*temple blocks (Chinese blocks),
*güiro, *claves, *maracas, and
slap-stick (whip). Every instrument
found in a *rhythm band is normally of the percussion group.

The music for indefinite pitch
percussion instruments is often
written on a one-line *staff.

Many musicians regard all percussion instruments, except possibly the timpani, as supplementary
rather than basic to the orchestra
and band. Surely these are more
generously supplied with long *rests
than any other instruments, and
their effectiveness is unquestionably
in inverse ratio to the frequency of
their employment. Most of them
pall very quickly. Nevertheless
their felicitous employment can be
tremendously telling when handled
with cunning coupled with restraint.
In addition, compositions written
entirely for ensembles of percussion
instruments have attracted composers' fancy during recent years.

The *dynamic range of these instruments is very great. Every
one of them can produce an all-
but-inaudible whisper; many can
also give forth with a nearly deafen-
ing crash when called upon to do so.

For orchestral purposes, certain
miscellaneous instruments which are
not strictly of the percussion type
are sometimes carelessly classified
with this group because they are
not clearly of the string, woodwind,
or brass type. This usage is of
course open to question.

A percussion instrument player
is expected to be able to handle
every instrument, or almost every
one (except possibly the celesta),
of this group. Versatility must be
a prominent feature of his make-
up.

The term percussionist is sometimes applied to the players of
these instruments. It is far preferable to the vague word drummer.
Synonym: pulsatile instruments.
See also battery, orchestra.

● † perdendosi. Same as morendo,
including the occasional implication
of a concurrent *ritardando. Literally, "losing itself."
Abbreviations: perd., perden.
Variant form: perdendo.
Pronunciation: accent second syllable.

● perfect pitch. Same as absolute
pitch.

● perform. A verb which means
either to sing or to play, as the
case may be, or the two activities
simultaneously. It is also used to
include *conducting.

● performance practice. See
Aufführungspraxis.

● period. A term often used in *form
analysis to designate two *phrases,
the second of which seems to "answer"
the first.
A double period, as its name suggests, consists of two periods, that
is, four phrases in the order: question,
answer, question, answer.
This type of analysis is readily applicable to music of the *Classical
and *Romantic eras, somewhat less
so to the *Baroque and *Rococo, still
less to the *Modern, *Renaissance,
and *Gothic.

● † però. Therefore, thereupon; however, still.
Pronunciation: accent second syllable.

● perpetual motion. A very rapid
composition, with a constantly-moving
figure, is sometimes called a perpetual motion.
Synonyms: moto perpetuo (Italian),
perpetuum mobile (Latin).

● † pesante. Heavily.
Synonym: ponderoso.
Antonym: leggiero.

● † pezzo. Piece.
Plural: pezzi.

● pf. (1) An illogical synonym for
*fp.
(2) Abbreviation for *pianoforte.

● **P. G.**   Same as **G. P.**

● **phantasy.**   Variant spelling of **fantasy.**

● **philharmonic.**   Literally, *harmony-loving"; a high-sounding term often included in the legal corporate name of an *orchestra (and occasionally of a *chorus).

There is of course no difference whatever between a "philharmonic orchestra" and a "symphony orchestra."

     Pronunciation: fĭl-härˌ-mŏnˊ-ĭk or fĭl-ar̆-mŏnˊ-ĭk.

● **phonograph.**   The phonograph was invented in 1877 by Thomas A. Edison. The principle on which it operates is: Sound-vibrations activate a stylus which cuts a somewhat zigzag line (called the sound-track) into tin-foil, zinc, wax, or some other material; when another stylus is run through this soundtrack at the same speed used when the record was made, the original sounds are reproduced.

In the early days, phonograph records were made in cylinder form, like those still in use on certain dictating machines. The disk record was developed by Emile Berliner; it was an improvement over the cylinder record. Manufacturers eventually adopted two standard sizes for disk records-- 10-inch and 12-inch--and settled on 78 revolutions per minute as the turntable speed.

Originally, recording was done by an acoustical (mechanical) process. This gave good reproduction of the voice but was unsatisfactory for instruments because it failed to capture the *overtones correctly and hence did not reproduce proper *tone-color. In addition, very high and very low pitches did not record satisfactorily if at all. Nevertheless the phonograph's popularity grew rapidly.

In 1925, electrical recording, using an electric microphone rather than an acoustical horn, was introduced. With this process, sounds of practically any audible pitch,

with most of their overtones, could be recorded, resulting in a tremendous stride forward in the *fidelity of reproduction. In addition, sounds formerly too soft or too loud to record could now be captured. Improved phonographs, equipped with electric tubes similar to those of the radio, followed, so that records of the new type could be heard and enjoyed properly. The phonograph was now definitely out of the toy class; it had become a musical instrument for the serious study and enjoyment of the tonal art. The number of masterpieces available in recorded form increased rapidly; few important compositions remained unrecorded.

Another great improvement appeared in 1948 in the form of a successful long-playing record, called the microgroove or LP record, revolving at a speed of 33-1/3 turns per minute. Whereas formerly 3 or 3-1/2 minutes for a 10-inch record, 4 or 4-1/2 for a 12-inch, had been the limit of playing time, the duration was now multiplied five- or six-fold. (At the same time, a 7-inch record with a very large center hole, revolving at 45 turns per minute, was introduced, but it has been less frequently utilized with serious music. This type of disk is often called the extended play record.) The number of compositions available in recorded form increased prodigiously with the advent of longplaying records. Meanwhile improvements in the fidelity of recording and of reproduction continued, perhaps even accelerated, and the expression "high fidelity" began to be heard more and more often.

The widespread adoption of "stereophonic sound" around 1958 (sometimes on records, sometimes on tape) provided still another noteworthy stride forward. Also called "binaural recording," the stereophonic method utilizes two microphones in recording the sound, and the record-grooves are formed in parallel pairs, one carrying the sound of one microphone, its mate the sound of the other. With two speakers required to reproduce the music, the effect can be given of sounds coming from various directions, as it does in actual performances. The former method is usually called monophonic (2) or monaural to distinguish it from stereophonic or binaural recording.

It seems to be only a matter of time until recording will be so perfect that music on disks will be indistinguishable from an actual performance.

The real significance of the phonograph seems to have registered much more on the layman than on many musicians. Whereas notation consists merely of symbols and directions for reproducing music, the phonograph and its record produce the sound of the music itself.

Sometimes a phonograph is built into the same cabinet as a radio or television-set, or both.

Synonyms: gramophone, graphophone (rare), Victrola (a trade name), record-player (undesirable -- see that entry), talking machine (obsolescent).

See also tape recorder, wire recorder, player piano, fidelity.

● phrase. A natural division in a *melody, clearly defined as to beginning and end; the shortest meaningful part of a composition. Many musicians have pointed out that the phrase in music roughly corresponds to the sentence in literature.

In vocal music, each phrase coincides with one line of the poem. All music, however--instrumental as well as vocal--divides into phrases. A singer or wind instrument player properly takes breath only between phrases.

Phrases often occur in pairs, like a question and answer, these being known as antecedent phrase and consequent phrase, respectively. This type of phrase-structure was especially prominent in music of the *Classical and *Romantic periods (late eighteenth and nineteenth centuries). See period.

Phrases are probably most frequently of four measures' or two measures' length. During the Classical and Romantic periods they occurred in these sizes with a uniformity that was monotonous--

nearly deadening; at worst this almost took the form of filling up a mold of pre-determined size with the appropriate number of notes. Phrases of three or five measures and of lengths that are not always uniform (i.e., asymmetrical in length)--which were common in *Gregorian chant, during the *Renaissance period, and to some extent during the *Baroque--have been revived by composers of the *Modern period.

The best way to detect the beginnings and ends of phrases is purely by the "feel" of the music--by intuition. Rationalizing and trying to explain are usually of little help.

In printed music, if the phrase structure is not clear, a comma is sometimes placed over the staff to show the proper location. Often a double *bar-line ⌡ or single

thick line ▬ is used in *hymns

(hymn-tunes) to indicate the division into phrases.

● phrasing. The clear and correct observance of the beginnings and endings of the *phrases in the course of a composition, on the part of the performer. Phrasing in music has been likened to punctuation in literature.

With a singer or the player of a wind instrument, correct phrasing is practically synonymous with taking breath at the proper points.

As a rule, correct phrasing is perfectly obvious to a sensitive and intelligent musician and he regards its observance a part of performing itself, not a decorative element superimposed on the performance to render it more palatable. Occasionally the phrase structure is indicated by the *slur, or by placing a comma above the notes at the end of each phrase. Such an expedient becomes advisable when the phrase division does not occur as expected or is unusual in some manner.

● physics of sound. See acoustics (1), harmonic series, vibration.

●† **piacevole.** Agreeable, pleasing, smooth.
Pronunciation: accent -ce-.

●† **piangendo.** Sadly (literally, "weeping.")

●† **pianissimo.** Very soft. Normally used in its abbreviated form, pp.
See dynamic marks.

●† **piano.** Soft. Normally used in its abbreviated form, p. The connection with the musical instrument, the piano, is mentioned in the following entry.
This should be pronounced "pē-ä-nō"; the name of the instrument is pronounced, by English-speaking musicians, "pē-ăn-ō."
See dynamic marks.

● **piano.** In view of the universality of the piano, its modernity comes as a surprise to many. It was invented in 1711 (some accounts give the date as 1709) in Florence, Italy, by Bartolommeo Cristofori (1655-1731). Although musicians at first accepted the instrument with caution, before the eighteenth century had drawn to a close the piano was rapidly sweeping its predecessor the *harpsichord toward oblivion.

The full name of the instrument-- pianoforte, meaning "soft loud"-- arose from the fact that, in contrast to the harpsichord and organ, the volume of tone in the piano can be controlled by the amount of force exerted by the player, which is only slightly true of the harpsichord, and not true at all of the organ. However, the earliest pianos lacked the resonant, full, clanging tone of to-day's instruments; instead it was rather delicate and sometimes wiry in character; the early piano could not produce a thrilling *fortissimo. Neither did it have the *range of the present instrument; the keyboard extended neither as high nor as low. The *damper pedal did not come into common use until early in the nine-teenth century, while the other pedals were added still later. (See soft pedal, middle pedal.)

The piano has the greatest *range of any instrument, except an organ with 2-foot or 32-foot stops, namely:

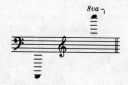

The range has of course not always been this great; pianos which lack the highest A-sharp, B, and C are still occasionally encountered. It is apparent from the ranges found in Beethoven's earlier piano sonatas that they were written for an instrument with these limits:

Mechanism. Three strings tuned in *unison are installed for most of the tones in the piano, but there is only one for the lowest tones, and two for the rather low ones. The striking of a key causes a felt-covered hammer to hit the string and then immediately to fall back in-

Earlier piano compositions display an even more restricted range. The growth of the keyboard during the *Romantic era can be traced by close study of the ranges found in piano works of that time.

The piano is sometimes considered a *string instrument, though perhaps more often *percussion. In reality it is of course a hybrid of the two.

Its value as a solo instrument, in *chamber-music, as an *accompaniment for voices or other instruments, in combination with a second piano, or even in the *orchestra, hardly needs comment. The very colorlessness and neutrality of its *tone-quality is perhaps its greatest asset. It is one of the few instruments which can satisfactorily produce, simultaneously, the three basic elements of music--*rhythm, *melody, and *harmony.

Types and Sizes. The shape of the piano takes three basic forms: grand, upright, and square. The last is no longer manufactured. The largest size of grand piano is called a concert grand, the middle sizes, studio grands, and the smallest, baby grand. The so-called "spinet" type is a variant of the upright; unfortunately its introduction has led to confusion with the true *spinet-- which is by no means a piano--in uninformed persons' minds.

to its original position; but as long as the key continues to be held, a felt damper remains away from the string, allowing it to continue vibrating. Releasing the key allows the damper to fall back onto the string and to stop the sound. Pressing the right-hand or *damper pedal will keep all the dampers away from all the strings and thus will continue the sounds of any keys that are touched during the time it is held. Since the piano is a percussion instrument, the long-held sounds eventually die away of their own accord.

The sustaining power of the lowest tones is very great, that of the highest almost nil.

Many musicians insist that the piano is the basic instrument--that no musician is properly educated unless he has at least a little facility on it, even that piano study should precede study of any other instrument or of voice.

The plural is spelled pianos.

Full name: pianoforte.

Italian: pianoforte (plural, pianoforti); also pianino for upright only. French: piano or piano-forte. German: Klavier (also spelled with a C) (plural, Klaviere), Piano (plural, Pianos), or Pianoforte (plural, Pianoforte); also Flügel (plural, Flügel) for grand piano only. Spanish: piano or pianoforte.

The player is called a pianist (pronunciation: pē-ăn-ĭst or pē-ā-nĭst). The word pianiste, applied to a woman, is something of an affectation.

● **piano-accordion.** See <u>accordion</u>.

● **pianoforte.** The original and complete name of the *piano.
Variant form (obsolete, rare): <u>fortepiano</u>.
Pronunciation: pē-ăn-ō-fôr-tā, pē-ăn-ō-fôr-tĕ, or pē-ăn-ō-fôrt.

● **pianola.** Player-piano.

● **piano quartet.** (1) Violin, viola, cello, and piano. See also <u>chamber-music groups</u>.
(2) The term is occasionally (and quite logically) applied to an ensemble of four pianos.

● **piano quintet.** Two violins, viola, cello, and piano. See also <u>chamber-music groups</u>.
Although Schubert has written a famous quintet for violin, viola, cello, double-bass, and piano-- probably the first ever written for four string instruments and piano-- the term <u>piano quintet</u> is rarely applied to the combination; instead the instruments are enumerated severally.

● **piano trio.** Violin, cello, and piano. (There are a few examples for violin, viola, and piano.) See also <u>chamber-music groups</u>.
The use of this term to indicate three pianos, or three players at one piano (piano six hands) is sometimes encountered, but there is no serious literature for these combinations.

● **piano-vocal copy.** A copy of an *opera, or of an *oratorio, *cantata, or other choral work, in which all the voice parts--both solo and chorus--

are given, but in which the orchestra part has been transcribed ("reduced") for piano. Piano-vocal copies are widely used in rehearsals and in makeshift performances where no orchestra is available.
See also <u>reduction</u>, <u>transcription</u> (1).

● **pibroch.** A type of composition for the *bagpipe, martial or mournful in character, popular in the highlands of Scotland. It has *theme and variations form.
Pronunciation: pē-brŏk.

● **Picardy third.** Many compositions in the minor mode conclude on a tonic *triad which has been made major through raising its third a half-step by means of an *accidental. The name given to the third is <u>Picardy third</u> or <u>tierce de Picardie</u>. The origin of the expression is unknown.
Properly, <u>Picardy third</u> refers only to the third of the chord, not to the chord as a whole; hence it is preferable to say that a composition "ends on a chord with Picardy third" rather than that it "ends on the Picardy third chord."
Synonym: <u>tierce de Picardie</u> (French).

● **piccolo.** A small woodwind instrument of the flute class, sounding an octave higher than the ordinary flute. It is the highest pitched instrument in the orchestra and band. The piccolo today is usually made of metal, though a few wooden ones are still found.
The mechanism is almost identical with that of the flute. Flutists take up the piccolo as a secondary instrument.
The range of the piccolo is:

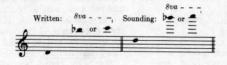

It is notated an octave lower than
the sounds desired. The treble
*clef is of course used exclusively.

The low tones of the piccolo are
thin and whistling, with a "toy
flute" quality. The middle tones
are bright, sparkling, and mechanical. The highest tones are
extremely brilliant and piercing,
almost "fiendish" sounding; their
shrillness is so great that a piccolo
in its highest register can be heard
above a full orchestra playing fortissimo.

A piccolo in D-flat is often used
in the band. Its range is a half-
step higher than shown earlier,
and it is notated a minor ninth (see
intervals) lower than the sounds
desired. It is even more brilliant
than the ordinary (or C) piccolo.

Piccolo is the Italian word meaning "little"--in this case "little
flute, " which in reality the instrument is.

Plural: piccolos or piccoli.

Synonyms (obsolete): octave flute,
piccolo flute.

Italian: flauto piccolo or ottavino.
French: petite flûte or piccolo.
German: kleine Flöte, occasionally
Piccolo. Spanish: flautín.

The player is called simply picco-
lo-player, occasionally piccoloist.

● pick. (1, noun) Same as plectrum.
(2, verb) See pizzicato.

● picked instruments. *Plucked
instruments.

● "pick-up notes." Same as up-
beat.

● piece. A musical composition,
especially one which is short and
not divided into movements.

●† pietoso. Pitiful, unhappy.

● pipe organ. A more complete
name for the *organ, useful to
distinguish it from the reed organ
(*harmonium) or electronic organ.

● piston. (1) Same as valve.
(2) A finger- or toe-operated button
located on the *organ. When pressed,

it throws on (or off) any combination
of stops that the player has selected
in advance.

● pitch. The degree of highness or
lowness of a musical sound, depending on the rapidity of the vibrations.

See also 440.

● pitch names. See notation.

● pitch-pipe. A device used for giving the correct pitch to singers when
no piano is available. Certain pitch-
pipes look like a *harmonica, and
some have a slider which can be
moved in such a way that only the
desired tone will emit. Other types
are circular, with holes around the
edge, each representing a different
pitch. Still others look like tiny
pipes fastened together.

On some pitch-pipes each hole provides two different sounds, one obtained when blowing into it, the other
when drawing or sucking the air.

● pitch recognition. Same as absolute
pitch.

●† più. More. Thus: più mosso,
faster (literally "more motion"); più
animato, more animated; più ritardando, becoming slower, *retarding more.
Il più, the most; thus: il più forte
possibile, as loud as possible. Più
alone is sometimes used for short in
place of più mosso.

(Related English word: plus.)
Pronunciation: accent the u.

●† piuttosto. Rather, rather than,
instead.

● pivot chord. In a *modulation, a
chord which exists in both the old key
and the new one; a *common chord.
Its employment avoids abruptness in
the appearance of the new *key (1).
An example will be found under the
entry modulation.

The pivot chord is used to make the
transfer from one key to the other; it
is the last chord that is natural to the
old key, and at the same time the first
chord natural to the new. The new
key is confirmed by subsequent chords

which are peculiar only to it, and
which establish it.
Synonym: hinge chord.

●† pizzicato. Plucked with the
fingers instead of played with the
*bow; used in connection with the
bowed string instruments.
The direction for employment is
the abbreviation pizz., which remains in effect until contradicted
by arco, meaning "bow."
Single notes and *double-stops
are effective when played pizzicato,
although the tone-quality is poor in
the highest register.
Pizzicato tones are very dry and
snapping on the violin and viola,
more "juicy" on the cello, resonant
and of fairly long duration (unless
*damped) on the double-bass. Natu-
rally only notes of short value can
be used in writing pizzicato; whole-
notes, half-notes, and all dotted
values are rare.
A left-hand pizzicato is also possible, but rather difficult, and
hence seldom met with outside brilliant solo compositions. It has a
spluttering effect.
When used as a noun, the plural
is pizzicati.
Abbreviation: pizz.
Synonyms: picked, plucked.

●† placido. Placid, peaceful, quiet.
Synonyms: tranquillo, calmato,
quieto.
Pronunciation: accent first syllable.

● plagiarism. Passing off the musical, literary, or artistic work of
another person as one's own.
Plagiarism in music was once regarded with extreme tolerance, the
only thing asked being that the composer should improve on the stolen
composition. Handel and Rossini
were notorious plagiarists, even Bach,
Haydn, and Mozart had few scruples
about it, and Wagner readily admitted occasional borrowing from others,
notably Liszt. *Copyright laws have
put a stop to the plagiarizing of any
compositions still subject to copyright, but not of music which is in
the *public domain. Many "popular"
songs have been shamelessly stolen

from well-known compositions.
It is considered entirely proper
to use as one's own a *folk-song,
*Gregorian chant, *chorale melody,
or familiar *hymn-tune. Writing
*variations on a theme by another
composer, when acknowledged in the
title--as is customary--is not regarded as plagiarism.
A direct quotation from another's
music, if acknowledged and if the
composition is in the public domain,
is considered permissible.
Many purported instances of plagiarism, ferreted out by self-appointed
"tune detectives," are of course ridiculous, the resemblances being
superficial and purely accidental. Perhaps the best retort to many allegations
is the answer Brahms gave when
someone fancied a similarity between
a theme in the last movement of his
First Symphony and a theme in the
last movement of Beethoven's Ninth
Symphony: "Every fool notices that."
A sharp distinction must be made
between actual plagiarism and being
influenced by the compositions of
another composer.

● plain chant, plainsong. A synonym
for *Gregorian chant. Broadly speaking, these words could be quite logically used as a generic term that also
includes *Ambrosian and other "dialects" of *chant.

● player-piano. A mechanically operated piano which enjoyed a tremendous
vogue during the 1915-1925 period. In
its usual form, two sliding panels
opened in the upper front, revealing a
horizontal bar with many holes; it
looked like an elongated *harmonica.
Over this was passed a rolled paper,
perforated with slots and holes which
corresponded to the various tones in
the composition recorded. Each hole
or slot fitted exactly over one of the
openings on the afore-mentioned bar,
and tubes led from the latter to the
mechanism of the piano. Operation
was effected by air pressure, the air
usually being supplied by two pedals
pumped by the person using the instrument.
The tempo and dynamics were controlled by the operator, the former

being indicated at the beginning of each "roll" (as the records were called), the latter by indications marked on it.

By shutting off the player mechanism, any player-piano could also be played by hand in the usual manner, although as a rule the *tone-quality was indifferent.

The radio and the perfected *phonograph put a speedy end to the popularity of this instrument, though recent years have seen a small-scale revival of interest in it.

Synonym: pianola.

The *reproducing piano was an improvement on the player-piano, as it duplicated the exact dynamic levels and styles of touch used by the artist in recording the roll; hence it was free of the extreme mechanical effect of the ordinary player-piano. Air was supplied from an electric motor; it did not have to be pumped.

Edwin Welte, a German, invented the reproducing piano in or about 1904.

● plectral instruments. *Fretted instruments. This term arises from the fact that these instruments are often played with a *plectrum; however, since certain players prefer occasionally or always to use the bare fingers, fretted instruments seems the more accurate term.

● plectrum. A small piece of wood, celluloid, metal, ivory, etc. used to pluck the strings of a *fretted instrument. Certain players prefer, however, to pluck the instrument with the bare fingers.

Plural: plectrums or plectra.
Synonym: pick.

● plucked instruments. String instruments played by picking with the fingers or with a *plectrum. This generic term includes the harp, the zither, and all the *fretted instruments. Even the *pizzicato strings could be classified here.

●† pochettino. Double diminutive of *poco.

●† pochetto. Diminutive of *poco.

●† pochino. Diminutive of *poco.

●† pochissimo. Superlative of *poco.

●† poco. A little, rather, somewhat; thus: poco rallentando, becoming gradually a little slower; poco staccato, rather staccato.

The diminutives are pochetto and pochino and may be translated "a very little," thus: pochetto meno mosso, a very little slower. The double diminutive is pochettino and may be translated "extremely little." The superlative is pochissimo which might be translated "the least little bit."

Poco a poco, little by little, by degrees, gradually. Molto poco, very little.

● podium. The little platform on which some *conductors stand so as to be clearly seen by the group they are conducting.

Plural: podia.

●† poi. Then. D. C. al ◆ e poi coda means "play from the beginning to the sign ◆ and then play the *coda."

(See symbols.)

●† polacca. Polonaise.

● polka. A Bohemian (Czech) dance in quick 2-4 time. It contains numerous eighth- and sixteenth-notes and is lively and pert in spirit. Smetana and Dvořák sometimes substituted polkas for the minuet or scherzo in their *sonata-type works.

● polo. A type of Spanish dance in 3-8 time, moderate tempo.

● polonaise. A type of Polish dance in 3-4 time. The tempo is usually moderately fast, the style proud, bold, even haughty. The beats are much subdivided, with numerous eighth- and sixteenth-notes, and perhaps occasional thirty-seconds. This is a common polonaise rhythmic pattern:

$\frac{3}{4}$ ♪♫♫ ♫♪ ♫♫♫|

One of the characteristics is the tendency to end on the last beat of the measure. A typical last measure rhythm is:

$\frac{3}{4}$ ♩. ♫♫. ♫♩ ♪ᵧ|

Chopin wrote a number of idealized polonaises for the piano. The polonaise in Moussorgsky's opera Boris Godounoff is highly representative of the style.
Musicians pronounce this word pō-lô-nāź, not pŏl-ô-nāz.
Variant form (Italian): polacca.

● polychoral. Written for two or more choruses (1), with or without orchestra. Some compositions of the *Renaissance period are polychoral. The frequency of such works among the composers associated with St. Mark's Cathedral in Venice--which has two choir-lofts--was one factor which led to the *Baroque movement in music (around the turn of the sixteenth to seventeenth centuries).

● polychord. A *chord which is in two or more *keys (1); a *polytonal chord.

● polyphony. As a rule, this term is used as a synonym for *counterpoint; the adjective form polyphonic (occasionally polyphonous) is a synonym for contrapuntal.
However, because of its literal meaning--"many sounds" or "many voices"--the word is occasionally employed in its broad sense: to denote either homophonic (melody-and-accompaniment) or polyphonic

(contrapuntal) style; that is, it may denote the opposite of *monophonic.
In addition the term is convenient in referring to musical texture made up of a series of *chords, nominally of contrapuntal basis with all tones of equal importance. Much music of the sixteenth century answers to this description as well as to the description as a complex interweaving of melodic strands; two styles were recognized in those days.
The term Polyphonic Period is sometimes substituted for *Renaissance Period, though hardly with desirability or accuracy.
Pronunciation: pŏ-lĭf-ô-nĭ. (Polyphonic is pronounced pŏl-ĭ-fŏn-ĭk.)

● polyrhythm. (1) Markedly different rhythmic patterns combined simultaneously.
The frequency of this device in modern music should not lead to the supposition that it represents a new development, for actually it is a revival of an old one. Inspection of a *polyphonic composition of the sixteenth century (e.g., one by Palestrina) will show that a number of voices, each with its own distinctive rhythm, have been combined, yet are organized under a single *meter scheme. Polyrhythm can be traced back at least to the fourteenth century.
Many polyrhythmic passages could conceivably be written in more than one way, for instance the passage shown in Example 1.

Polyrhythm

In Example 2, the highest voice appears to be really in 3-4 time, if the opening quarter-rest is considered a silent first beat. The two inner parts moving in eighth-notes seem to be in 5-4 time, moving in combinations of two beats plus three. The lowest part is a true 4-4, but the two parts just above it seem to have no real meter; they are almost arhythmic.

An additional example of polyrhythm will be found in the entry polytonality.

In the ballroom scene *finale to Act I of Don Giovanni, Mozart uses 3-4, 2-4, and 3-8 time simultaneously with *bar-lines occurring at different points, to depict three simultaneous dances.

(2) The term is sometimes used as a synonym for *cross rhythms. See also shifted accent.

Ex. 2
Andante

Polyrhythm

● polytonality. Music that is in two or more *keys simultaneously. Usually only two keys are employed; hence the term bitonality ("two tonalities") is more accurate than the more frequently-used poly-tonality ("many tonalities").

It does not follow that two *key-signatures will appear; usually there is no key-signature and all *accidentals are written in as needed. It should by no means be imagined that the same two keys are used, unchanging, throughout the passage in question, for often *modulations occur in one or both .

Polytonality is rarely used from beginning to end of a composition; it is normally employed only here and there. (In this respect an important contrast with *atonality will be noticed.)

The music on page 322 appears to be in three simultaneous keys. The upper staff is in C major (or possibly A minor, as the last measure suggests). The middle staff might be considered in A major, or a Mixolydian *mode on E, or a Lydian mode on D. The lowest staff suggests G major. (In addition there are *jazz rhythms in the upper line, and the entire texture is in *poly-rhythm, for example the middle line is really in 3-4 time.)

Facile explanations often advise: "Go to the piano and play My Country 'Tis of Thee with the right hand in G and the left hand in F, and that will be polytonality. " Polytonality is not used thus; it is not an arbi-

Allegro Impetuoso

Polytonality

trary distortion of the conventional. Constant references to right and left hand are also misleading, for the device is by no means restricted to piano music, and even when used there, the separation into two keys may not necessarily occur between the hands.

Some musicians stoutly maintain that there is no such thing as polytonality--that the music employs ramifications which have not yet been explained by theorists; that the entire fabric is related to a single key center in some manner not yet fully understood. In support of this is the fact that one key usually appears basic, the other(s), subordinate. Against it may be cited the fact that composers themselves usually declare that they think two keys in composing poly-

tonal passages.

Polytonality is especially associated with the group of French composers called *"The Six," although it is equally characteristic of Igor Stravinsky (1882-   ). However, the American composer Charles Ives (1874-1954) used polytonality as early as 1892. The very earliest instance of its employment was made by Hans Neusiedler (or Newsidler) (1508-1563) in a parodistic lute piece written about 1535 entitled The Jew's Dance. Mozart also employed it in A Musical Joke.

Compare atonality.

●† pomposo.   Pompous, majestic. Synonyms: maestoso, grandioso.

●† ponderoso.   Heavy, ponderous. Synonym: pesante.

Antonym: leggiero.

● † pont., † ponticello. See no. 3 under the heading sul.

● pop concert. A concert at which light music is played. A spirit of informality prevails, and sometimes refreshments are served. During the summer months many pop concerts are given out-of-doors. This term is a colloquialism for "popular concert."

Variant form: pops concert.

● popular music. This term is used in a variety of meanings. Theoretically popular music means "music of the people," but even this is open to objection, since it implies that there are some human beings who are not "people."

(1) The commonest meaning is that used in referring to songs (in the United States of a *jazz character) which enjoy a tremendous but short-lived period of high public favor. It is generally conceded that their ephemeral nature betrays a fatal lack of hardiness, though there are a few rare but notable exceptions. Almost invariably, songs of this type contain two sections, the first called the "verse" (often omitted in performance), the second a *refrain (which is the portion that becomes familiar). Also, with very few exceptions, every song contains 32 *measures, no more, no less. Briefly there are perhaps no compositions in existence more hopelessly stereotyped, more anti-original.

Due to the rather unsatisfactory nature of the above definition, many musicians place the word popular in quotation marks when employing it with this connotation.

(2) The term is sometimes employed, especially in Europe, as a synonym for *folk music, and with entire propriety.

(3) Simple songs of the "home-and-community" type--for example, those by Stephen Foster--are quite properly if infrequently termed popular music.

(4) The term is sometimes used as a synonym for light music.

(5) Since the word popular means "well liked by many people," any composition that answers to such a description could in the broadest sense be termed popular, even though it be a symphony, concerto, or chamber-music work.

See also Calypso, Flamenco.

● † portamento. (1) Same as glissando. Portamento is normally used in connection with the voice and string instruments, occasionally with the trombone, but never in connection with the piano (except in the totally different meaning to follow) or the harp.

Some musicians make this fine distinction between portamento and glissando: in the former case the note is held almost its full value and the slide accomplished just before passing on to the next note (leading directly into it); while in the latter the sliding process commences at once and takes up the entire time allotted.

Thus:

Other musicians maintain that portamento is applied to small intervals, glissando to large ones.

(2) Pianists sometimes apply this word to the very slight detachment between tones that is indicated by both staccato dots and a slur--the very gentle half-staccato (almost a legato) in which tones are held about three-fourths their printed length, the final fourth being an unwritten rest. A better word, however, is portato. See staccato (3).

obtained.

The positions possible on the violin are shown in the account of that instrument.

(2) The positions on the *trombone are discussed under slide (1).

(3) For the positions of various chords, see root position and inversion (1).

●† possibile. Possible; generally used in music in the sense of "as much as possible." Thus il più piano possibile means "as soft as

Written: Played:

(3) Very *legato; a synonym for *legatissimo.

Portamento literally means "carrying" (related to English portable, porter).

Plural: portamenti.
Abbreviation: port.
Synonyms: portando, portato.

●† portando. (1) Same as portamento (1).

(2) Same as legato (rare).

●† portato. (1) The correct term for portamento (2). Synonyms: half staccato, semi-staccato.

(2) A synonym for portamento, all meanings.

● pos. Abbreviation for position (1, 2).

● Posaunen. *Trombones (German, plural).
Pronunciation: pō-sou-nĕn.

● positions. (1) In playing the bowed *string instruments, the left hand is stationed at various points along the *fingerboard in order to get at various pitches. Each of these locations is called a position, and in each position a certain number of tones lie directly under the player's hand and hence can be readily

possible."

Pronunciation: accent second syllable.

● post horn. A simple, high-pitched, *bugle-like brass instrument, without *valves or *slide. It sometimes was built in the form of a crescent, sometimes in the form of a small *horn (i.e., French horn). As the name suggests, it was played by the drivers or attendants on mail-carrying stagecoaches, for signaling purposes.

Schubert imitates the instrument in one part of his *song-cycle Die Winterreise (The Winter Journey).

The post horn has occasionally found its way into serious compositions. Mozart wrote for one in his Serenade No. 9 (in D), K. 320, and for two in his Three German Dances (K. 605), while Mahler includes a prominent post horn solo in the third movement of his Symphony No. 3.

The *tone-color of the post horn, when compared to that of the *trumpet, is more mellow, more "golden," less distinguished, less brilliant; it has a touch of French horn quality.

● postlude. A composition used at the close of some ceremony, especially a church service. Most organ postludes are loud and joyful, but unfortunately their purpose seems to be hardly more

than that of drowning out the noise
made by the departing congregation.

The name is also sometimes applied, not very desirably, to the
instrumental conclusion of a *song,
*aria, or *choral composition.

● pp. Very soft. This is the abbreviation for pianissimo. It indicates a dynamic level softer than
*p, but not as much so as *ppp.
See dynamic marks.

● ppp. Extremely soft; softer than
*pp. This term is sometimes called
pianississimo or triple piano. On
occasion such extremes as pppp,
ppppp, and pppppp are encountered.
See dynamic marks.

● practical music. Name sometimes
substituted for *applied music.

● praeludium (Latin). Prelude.

● Pralltriller (German). The inverted mordent. See, mordent (2).
Pronunciation: präl-trĭl-ĕr.

● pre-band instruments. See simple
melody instruments.

●† precedente. Preceding.

●† precipitando, precipitoso. Pre-
cipitous, overhasty, rash.

●† precisione. Precision, exact-
ness.

●† preciso. Precise.

● pre-Classical. A vague term
used to indicate music written before the *Classical period; thus it
may be a synonym for *Rococo or
*Baroque or both, but it is seldom
applied to periods earlier than
these.

● prelude. In general, a musical
introduction to something that is
to follow. The term is used in
several distinct meanings.
(1) The first number of a work
divided into two or three movements (usually two). The preludes
and fugues comprising Bach's

The Well-Tempered Clavier are examples.
(2) The opening movement of a
*suite (1,2).
(3) An orchestral introduction to
an *opera, fulfilling exactly the same
function as an *overture. The prelude differs from the overture in the
following respects: (A) Its tempo is
usually slow, that of the overture
usually fast, albeit the latter often
has a slow introduction. (B) It
leads directly into the first act without a pause, while the overture comes
to a complete stop. (C) Its form is
less apt to be strict, or at least to
be predictable.
(4) An orchestral introduction to
any act of an opera other than the
first. It is a full-sized piece of music, not just a few introductory measures.
(5) A composition in any form, for
practically any medium. Here the
term is frankly a catch-all title, used
when the composer can think of no
more striking name. The preludes
by Chopin are examples. See titles.
(6) A *voluntary.
The use of the word prelude as a
mere synonym for introduction cannot
be recommended.
For chorale-prelude, see separate
entry.
Synonyms: praeludium (Latin),
Vorspiel (German).
Pronunciation: prĕl-yōōd or prē-lōōd
(but not prä-lōōd).

● première. The first performance
of a composition. The true first performance is called the "world première"
in contradistinction to the first performance in a certain country or city
("American première," "Boston première," etc.).
Pronunciation: prĕ-myĕr or prĕ-mĭr.

● prepared. A *dissonant tone in a
chord is said to be prepared if it
appeared as a *consonant tone (i.e.,
*chord-member) in the preceding
chord (preferably in the same voice).
When this condition is not met, the
dissonance is said to be unprepared,
in which case its effect is considerably
harsher, though often strikingly dramatic.

A prepared dissonance   The same dissonance, unprepared

● près de la table (French). An effect obtainable on the *harp by playing near the sounding board, at the lower end of the string. The sound is dry, metallic, guitar-like.

Pronunciation: prĕ dĕ̆ lă̆ tăbl'.

●† prestissimo. As fast as possible (superlative of *presto). This is usually considered the fastest of all tempo indications.

See tempo marks.

●† presto. Very fast. It is usually understood to be distinctly quicker than either allegro or vivace.

See tempo marks.

●† prima donna. The chief female singer in an opera, or the leading woman member of an opera troupe. By convention, this is nearly always a *soprano. The term * seconda donna is sometimes used to designate a woman having an important secondary role. It is curious that the term primo uomo, indicating the chief male character, is rarely used.

Literally, "first woman."

Plural: prima donnas or prime donne.

Synonym: diva.

●† prima vista. Sight-reading.

● primes. See intervals. See also unison.

●† primo. (1) See tempo primo. Abbreviation: Iº.

(2) The upper part of a composition for piano four hands (two players at one piano). The lower part is termed secondo.

Literally, "first."

● principal. (1) The singer of one of the chief roles in an *opera, as opposed to the singers of minor roles and to members of the chorus; a "star."

(2) In an *orchestra, the leaders of the second violins, the violas, the cellos, and the double-basses are called principals. They are placed at the first stand (or desk) in their group, nearest the audience. The principal in each section is assumed to be the most skillful of the players; any passage marked *solo (3) is entrusted to him. In addition he usually has the responsibility of marking the *bowing.

The principal of the first violins is normally called the *concertmaster.

The term is also used in *bands in reference to the player at the first stand of the various parts that are played by groups of instruments, e.g., the clarinets. In addition it is sometimes used in connection with *choruses (principal *soprano, principal *alto, etc.).

Synonym: first chair man (colloquial).

●† principale. Principal. Often denotes a solo instrument.

●† principio. Beginning. Pronunciation: accent second syllable.

● Prix de Rome. A prize in composition, awarded by the Conservatory in Paris, which gives the recipient the opportunity to live in Rome for four years, on a stipend, devoting his full time to composition. Famous French composers who have received the Prix de Rome include Berlioz, Bizet, Debussy, Gounod, etc.

In 1921 the American Academy in Rome inaugurated an American Prix de Rome, the first recipient being Howard Hanson.

Prix de Rome means "Rome Prize."

Pronunciation: prē dē rōm.

● processional. A *hymn (*hymn-tune) sung while the *choir enters the church, near the beginning of the service.

Compare recessional.

● professional musician. A person who earns his living playing an instrument, singing, or conducting. Often membership in the Musicians' Union is assumed.

The term "professional musician" is not, as a rule, applied to music teachers, composers, writers on music, or critics. (The logic and desirability of this usage is of course open to question.)

●† profondo. Deep, low in pitch. The deepest bass voice (other than the *Russian bass) is called basso profondo (plural, bassi profondi).

(The spelling profundo is incorrect.)

● program. (1) A musical concert of any type.

(2) The printed leaflet, listing the compositions to be performed

at a concert.

(3) The "story" or avowed descriptive intent involved in a piece of *program music is often termed the program, because the listener at a concert must consult that leaflet in order to inform himself of the composer's intentions. The adjective form is programmatic.

Variant spelling: programme.

● program music. Music which is intended to "tell a story" or describe something. To some musicians, all vocal music belongs in this category, since its text of necessity talks about something. In general, however, the term is clearest when restricted to compositions employing only instruments. Since the majority of instrumental works are devoid of any story-telling purpose (that is, they are *absolute or pure music), the program-music literature is thus obviously of comparatively small extent. Most examples of program-music are found in the period 1830-1930, and the predominant *medium is orchestra.

The *symphonic poem (tone poem) is perhaps the acme of this type of music; Richard Strauss's symphonic poems Don Juan, Till Eulenspiegel, and Death and Transfiguration are famous, as are Smetana's The Moldau, Sibelius's The Swan of Tuonela and Finlandia, Dukas's The Sorcerer's Apprentice, and Tschaikowsky's Romeo and Juliet.

Beethoven's Sixth (Pastoral) Symphony and Berlioz's Fantastic Symphony are well-known programmatic symphonies, Rimsky-Korsakoff's Scheherazade, Debussy's La Mer, and Ravel's Mother Goose well-known programmatic suites, Mendelssohn's Hebrides (or Fingal's Cave) Overture and Tschaikowsky's 1812 Overture examples of programmatic concert *overtures. (Many other examples of program music might be cited.)

Naturally a number of compositions are border-line cases not clearly classifiable as program or absolute music, or the distinction depends on the individual's definition. Hard-and-fast boundaries are difficult to set up. A Bach fugue or a Haydn string quartet is clearly absolute music and a Strauss or Liszt symphonic poem is clearly program music, but a Chopin nocturne will be classified according to the individual's interpretation of the term.

The "story" that lies "behind" a programmatic composition is rarely a secret; it is normally stated openly on the fly-leaf of the *score, or is adequately suggested by the title alone. No person can be expected to deduce it purely from listening.

The spirit of program-music is one of "let's pretend that..."

See also symphonic poem, ballade.

● program notes. At certain concerts (especially orchestra concerts), it is customary, in the program book, to give rather detailed information about the compositions to be heard. This material is known as program notes, and is concerned with the background, analysis, or description of the compositions, biographical information about the composers, and the like.

Similar information given on the jackets that hold records is known as jacket notes, sleeve notes, or liner notes.

● prompter. Just as it is advisable, in the performance of plays, to have someone ready to remind the actors of their lines in the event of a memory lapse, a similar person is needed at performances of *opera. He occupies a tiny booth at the front of the stage, its floor being well below the level of the stage floor. A hood at the back conceals the prompter from the audience. The singers on the stage can see only his head and shoulders. A moment before each passage for any singer, the prompter speaks the words to which the opening notes are set.

● † pronunziato. Pronounced, well brought out, promiment.
Synonyms: marcato, en dehors, accentuato.
Antonym: sotto voce.

● Provençal drum. The tambourin de Provence.

● psaltery. A plucked string instrument of great antiquity. Its strings are stretched over a flat sounding-box of triangular, rectangular, or trapezoidal shape. It differs from the *dulcimer in that the strings are plucked by the fingers rather than struck with hammers.

● public domain. Musical, literary, and artistic works on which the *copyright has expired are said to be "in the public domain."

● pulsatile instruments. Percussion instruments.

● pulsation. (1) A steady succession of sounds, thought of without regard to their *meter or *accent.
Compare pulse, beat, rhythm.
(2) Same as vibration.

● pulse. (1) The steady throb, beat, or background that underlies the rhythmic organization of musical compositions; the "go" of the music; the *meter.
Synonyms: Takt (German), meter.
Compare pulsation, rhythm.
See also beat (1), accent.
(2) A synonym for beat (1).

● Pult. The German word for desk. Among the string instruments of an *orchestra, two players usually read from the music on any one music-rack, and each pair is referred to as a "stand" or "desk." If a composer, for the sake of obtaining a thin, soft tone, wants only two players to perform a certain passage, he marks it "1 Pult".
Plural: Pulte.
Pronunciation: poolt.

● † punta, † punto. Point, tip (of the *bow of a *string instrument).

● pure music. Same as absolute music.

Q

● quadrille. A lively dance, of French origin, in 2-4 or 6-8 time.

● quadruplet. Four notes of equal

length, performed in the time of three of the same kind. Quadruplets occur only in *meters divisible by 3.

in the parts for the four string instruments.

Perhaps the best-known quadruplet is that found in Chopin's Waltz in D Flat (often called the Minute Waltz) op. 64, no. 1, in measure 44.
 Synonym: quartolet.
 See also triplet, irregular groupings.

● quality of tone.   See tone-quality, tone-color.

● quartal harmony.   See fourth-chords.

● quarter-note.   See time-values.

● quarter-tones.   Intervals half the size of a *half-step.
 Quarter-tones are regularly found in certain Oriental systems of music, notably that of India, but they are still in the experimental stage in Occidental countries.   They can be played only on the bowed string instruments and the trombone, although they can of course also be sung by anyone possessing a keen ear.   All other instruments must be specially built to play them.   A quarter-tone piano has been manufactured, consisting of two ordinary 88-key keyboards, one tuned a quarter-tone higher than its mate; they are placed one above the other like two manuals on an organ.   Sometimes the extra keyboard is painted red and blue rather than black and white.
 There are several systems for notating quarter-tones, none of which seems to be the "normal" or "accepted" method.
 Perhaps the best-known composition utilizing quarter-tones is Ernest Bloch's Quintet for Piano and String Quartet; however it uses them only occasionally rather than systematically, and of course exclusively

● quartet.   (1) A composition for four voices or instruments.
 (2) Loosely, a *string quartet (1, 2).
 Variant spelling: quartette (however, quartett is incorrect in English).
 See also groups.
 Pronunciation: kwôr-tĕt.

● quartolet.   Same as quadruplet.

●† quasi.   Like, as if (in the sense of "almost").   This word is not synonymous with come (like).   An indication such as andante quasi lento is correct; but quasi tromba, intended to mean "like a trumpet," is not; it should be come tromba.

● quaver.   Eighth-note.   See British terminology.

● quick-step.   See march.

●† quieto.   Quietly.
 Synonyms: tranquillo, calmato, placido.

●† quindecima.   See 15ma.
 Pronunciation: accent second syllable.

● quintet.   A composition for five voices or instruments.
 Variant spelling: quintette.
 See also groups.
 Pronunciation: Dictionaries indicate accent on the second syllable, though musicians often stress the first.

● quintuplet.   Five notes of equal length performed in the time of four of the same kind; also in *meters with 3, 6, 9, or 12 beats, five notes performed in the time of three of the same kind. (Examples on page 330.)
 See also triplet, irregular groupings.

● **quintus.** Second *tenor (obsolete).

R

●† **raddolcendo.** Becoming softer, gentler, and calmer.

● **ragtime.** A type of music (usually instrumental), popular around the turn of the century, which was the predecessor of *jazz. In ragtime, certain prominent melody tones were slightly anticipated or delayed in their entrance by means of *syncopation. Coupled with this was

*trombone, unless we consider the *bugle. However, see natural horn and the sub-head "natural trumpet" in the entry trumpet for instruments of the recent past which were beset with gaps.)

Important Note. Throughout this dictionary, it must always be understood that the ranges indicated are subject to modification depending on the skill of the individual. With woodwind, brass, and bowed string instruments, skillful players can sound several pitches higher than those shown, particularly if the *har-

Written: Played:

always a certain amount of carelessness or even actual sloppiness in performance--doubless often intentional--plus a certain reckless exuberance.

Since the syncopated effects were often interpolated by the player rather than written in the music, ragtime might perhaps better be called "a way of playing music" than "a kind of music."

The term ragtime is probably derived from "ragged time" (i. e., ragged rhythm).

●† **rallentando.** Gradually becoming slower; a synonym for ritardando. Abbreviations: rall., occasionally rallent.

● **range.** All of the pitches any instrument or voice is capable of producing. Ranges are indicated by showing the lowest and highest note possible, every intervening tone being automatically understood as existing unless the presence of a gap is specifically mentioned. (Only one instrument in normal use today has a gap in its range--the tenor

monics (1) of the bowed strings are taken into consideration. (They provide considerable upward extension for the cello and double-bass.) With the horn, trombone, and tuba the downward range may be slightly extended by a good player. On the other hand, the upper limit of the range indicated herein must be modified in the case of less advanced players, and even the lower limit in the case of unskilled brass players. The ranges shown are those which can be expected of typical good performers rather than beginners.

With singers, range is obviously a highly individual matter, and varies considerably even with voices of a single type. (See voices.) Indeed, a given singer's range may vary slightly from day to day. The majority of singers can exceed the given ranges (which are purposely conservative) on at least one end, and usually both.

● **ranz des vaches** (French). A melody played (occasionally sung) by Swiss herdsmen to call the cattle together. (Literally "cows' tune.")
Pronunciation: räns dä väsh.

●† rapidamente. Quickly. This is
not used as a *tempo mark, but as
an indication that the passage so
labeled should be played more quickly than the material that precedes
and follows; that is, it temporarily
supplants the tempo mark in force.
Variant form: rapido.
Synonyms: veloce, volante.

● ratchet. An instrument, more or
less of the percussion type, consisting of a wooden cog-wheel against
which a loosely-held tongue of wood
or metal is caused to strike when
the instrument is whirled around on
its handle. Its harsh sound is
familiar to Hallowe'en and New
Year's Eve merrymakers, who are
perhaps unaware that composers
have occasionally used the instrument
in serious music (e.g., Richard
Strauss in Till Eulenspiegel, where
it is called by its German name,
Ratsche).
Synonym: rattle.
Italian: raganella.

● rattle. Same as ratchet.

●† ravvivando. Becoming enlivened
again (literally "reviving").
Synonyms: avvivando, animando.

● realize, realization. The conversion of the notes and numerals
used in figured bass into full chords
is termed a realization, or realizing the figured bass. It is accomplished at a *keyboard instrument--
harpsichord, piano, or organ. A
realization is not an *improvisation.
See figured bass, Baroque Period.

● recapitulation. A restatement or
repetition of a fairly long section
within a composition. In *sonata-
allegro form this refers to the reappearance, near the close, of the
first and second themes (principal
and subordinate subjects), following
the *development. It does not, however, include the *coda, if there is
one.
Synonyms: reprise, restatement,
re-exposition, return.

● recessional. A *hymn (hymn-tune)
sung near the close of a church service while the choir leaves the auditorium.
Compare processional.

● recit. Abbreviation for *recitando
and *recitative.

● recital. (1) A concert given by a
single performer (with an *accompanist,
if needed), as opposed to a concert
given by a group such as an orchestra,
band, chamber-music ensemble, or
chorus. Piano recitals, vocal recitals,
violin recitals, and organ recitals are
all popular.
(2) A concert given by students, often
called a "student recital" or "pupil recital" for the sake of explicitness.

●† recitando. In declamatory style.
Literally, "reciting."

● recitative. A style of vocal music,
declamatory and dramatic in character,
that approaches the status of a heightened form of speech. A recitative is
never "melodious," "tuneful," or lyric
in character: its melodic lines do not
tempt those who enjoy whistling or
humming; indeed the melody as such
is usually less important than the
rhythm.
In *operas, *oratorios, and *cantatas
most of the "action" takes place in the
recitatives; the *arias and *choruses
(3) seem more to comment on the action
than to forward it. Often a recitative
and aria for the same character or role
are coupled as a pair.
Normally recitatives are for only one
voice. In others, several solo voices
participate alternately, sometimes even
in rapid-fire succession, but it would
be difficult to name more than a handful of recitative passages where two
voices sing simultaneously.
The notation of *rhythm in a recitative is more or less approximate, being
governed by the rhythm of the words;
hence a certain amount of freedom in
performance is always allowable and
intended.
Types. (A) The recitativo secco or
dry recitative comes fairly close to

speech, makes use of very few long tones, and keeps the instrumental *accompaniment limited to a short chord here and there.

In many of the earlier operas and oratorios the accompaniment is supplied by a piano or harpsichord. This custom persisted into the late eighteenth and early nineteenth centuries and may be observed in the operas of Mozart. It represents one of the last employments of the basso continuo (see continuo and figured bass). Later composers used the orchestra in the secco recitative.

(B) The recitativo stromentato, recitativo accompagnato, or accompanied recitative makes a greater use of the orchestra, and the voice part is somewhat more lyrical in character, though it never approaches aria style.

Many recitatives are not clearly of either type, nor is a sharp distinction necessary in the performer's or listener's mind. A number of them contain numerous long-held chords for the orchestra. In the *Baroque period recitatives were often accompanied by a harpsichord reading from *figured bass, with a *cello (occasionally cello and *double-bass, in octaves) sustaining the written bass note.

Peculiarities in Notation. There are three conventions in notating the recitative which may puzzle any musician, nor is there a defensible reason for their existence.

(A) One convention is called the appoggiatura, and employs the *non-harmonic tone of that name. It is sometimes used when the notation shows two short notes of the same

pitch, the first being accented. For the first note the singer may substitute the tone one scale degree higher; see the treatment of the word "desert" in Example 2. Probably the peculiar practice of writing one thing and--perhaps--intending another originated with the aim of causing the underlying harmonic structure to appear clearer to the eyes of the player at the accompanying keyboard instrument, though this theory by no means explains all instances.

Some musicians doubt whether composers intended the appoggiatura to be employed on every possible occasion. It seems to be accepted among singers that its use is left to discretion--the performer has his choice; that it should not always be used, but neither should it never be used.

One might add that its employment is nearly always of excellent effect.

(B) A second peculiarity is that if the recitative concludes on two short notes approached by a leap from above (usually the *interval of a fourth), the first of the two final notes may take the pitch of the note that precedes the downward leap. (See Example 1). Like the appoggiatura custom, this is not always observed; some musicians doubt that it should ever be employed.

(C) The remaining convention cannot be defended in any way. It is frequent, at the conclusion of a recitative, for the final two chords (always for instruments only) to be written one beat earlier than they are intended to be played. That is, in a recitative in 4-4 time, where the final chords are meant to fall on the fourth beat of one measure and the first of the following one, they are actually

Ex. 1
Written: Often performed:

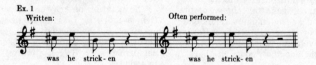

was he strick-en   was he strick-en

placed on the third and fourth beats, and the notation lacks the final measure! (If meant to fall on beats 2 and 3, they are written for beats 1 and 2.) In addition, often the last note of the voice part appears simultaneously with the first of these two final chords, even though it does not agree with the chord harmonically.

The accompanying example, illustrating the first and last of the three arbitrary customs, comes from Handel's Messiah. (Ex. 2).

It is unthinkable that the conclusion could be intended to be performed exactly as shown under "written."

Abbreviation: recit.

Pronunciation: rĕs-ĭ-tȧ-tēv, rĕs-ĭ-tȧ-tēv.

Example 2

Example 2 (Cont'd)

Performed:

Voice

make straight in the des-ert a high-way for our God.

Orchestra

● recorder. (1) An entire family of woodwind instruments of the flute class, but held straight out from the mouth, like a clarinet or oboe, not transversely like a flute. The mouthpiece is fairly thick and has no reed, being of the notched type known as a fipple mouthpiece. Recorders are made of wood or plastic.

The *tone-color may be described as "two-thirds flute and one-third clarinet," with a pleasing, mellow, "piping" quality. The instrument cannot produce a powerful tone; it is soft by nature and rather delicate.

The recorder was in high favor from the sixteenth to the early eighteenth centuries, after which it passed out of use. Recent years have seen a lively revival of interest in the instrument among the better types of *amateur, for whose use it was originally intended. The modern instruments are made in four sizes: soprano or descant, alto or treble,

tenor, and bass.

Synonyms: beak flute, block flute, English flute, fipple flute, flûte à bec, whistle flute.

(2) A machine used for transmitting sounds onto a phonograph record; a recording machine.

● record-player. Strictly speaking, a turntable, usually electrically powered, which is connected into a radio by means of a wire, used so that records may be played through the amplifier and speaker of the radio. The true record-player thus is incapable of emitting sounds; it merely revolves the record.

This term is often carelessly used in place of *phonograph. Some music stores advertise the smaller, cheaper phonographs as "record-players," the larger, expensive, high-fidelity and stereophonic machines as "phonographs."

● reduction. Condensation of the music

for all the instruments in an orchestral *score onto two staffs so
that it has the appearance of piano
music and is playable--not always
very conveniently--on the piano.
Briefly, it is a piano *transcription
of material originally for orchestra.

The most familiar examples are
copies of *operas, *oratorios, and
*cantatas, with the orchestral parts
"reduced" (or condensed) for piano.
All the vocal parts, however--both
solo and chorus--are given just as
in the full *score. Another example is encountered with *concertos, where the orchestra part is
"reduced" for piano, the solo part
remaining exactly as in the original.

Reductions are used constantly at
rehearsals and are also frequently
used in makeshift performances where
no orchestra is available.

Some reductions are printed on
three of four staffs, rather than two,
and are quite unplayable on the piano,
yet superficially resemble the appearance of piano music. The conductor's score of orchestra and band
pieces intended for school use is
often printed in this form.

The reduction principle is also
sometimes applied to *chamber-music and *choral music scores, as
well as to orchestral scores.

In books on music, quotations from
orchestral, operatic, chamber-music, and choral scores are often
given in reduction form.

In creating such a work, the composer of course always first sketches
it in reduction form, and postpones
making the final full-score copy until
he is certain everything is just as
he wants it.

Synonyms: condensed score, short
score.

See also piano-vocal copy, transcription (1).

● reed. (1) A thin piece of cane
used to produce the tones in a *woodwind instrument. By putting the reed
into his mouth and blowing on it
properly, the player sets the reed to
vibrating, which in turn causes the
entire instrument to "speak."

The *clarinet and *saxophone use a
single reed--flat, thin, medium in

width but comparatively long--which
is placed at the bottom of the instrument's mouthpiece, covering a
trough-like slot. An adjustable
metal holder called a ligature keeps
the reed in proper position under the
mouthpiece.

The *oboe (including the *English
horn), *bassoon, *sarrusophone, and
most *bagpipes play with a double
reed, which consists of two very
narrow, thin, and comparatively long
reeds laid one on top of the other,
but leaving a small aperture between
them. Viewed straight from the end,
the two reeds look like a pair of
parentheses turned sideways, thus: ⌒
There is no mouthpiece, strictly
speaking; only the two reeds enter
the player's mouth.

Reeds have to be cut or at least
shaved down to suit the individual
player, this being especially true of
the double variety. There is a saying among oboe players, "The player
is no better than his reed."

(2) A thin tongue of metal, tuned to
a certain pitch, used to produce the
tone in the *harmonium, *harmonica,
*accordion, *concertina, and the reed
stops of the *organ. Each metal reed
can give only a single pitch; hence
there are as many reeds as there are
tones.

● reed instrument. (1) Broadly, any
instrument played with a *reed (1 and
2).

(2) Carelessly, any *woodwind instrument.

(3) Strictly, an instrument played with
a reed (1)--either single reed or double
reed. The oboe, clarinet, saxophone,
and bassoon, and others closely related
(see orchestra)--also the sarrusophone--
are of this type.

● reed organ. Same as harmonium.

● "reeds, the." A term often carelessly substituted for woodwinds. Properly,
the reeds include the *oboe, *English
horn, *clarinet, *bass-clarinet, *bassoon, *contrabassoon, and the *saxophones, but not the *flute and *piccolo,
which use no reed.

● reel. A lively dance in 4-4 time,

used in Ireland, Scotland, and the United States, the Virginia reel being well-known in the latter.

● **refrain.** A passage of music recurring at intervals, usually at the end of each stanza in a *song. Normally the words of the refrain remain unchanged throughout all the stanzas.
The refrain is often carelessly and incorrectly called a *chorus (4).

● **register.** A portion of the *range of a voice or instrument, the tones of which have a fairly uniform quality. Ranges are usually divided into low register, medium (or middle) register, and high (or acute) register. As a rule, tones in the low register sound slack, lack tenseness. They are sometimes dark, thick, "throaty," husky, and occasionally a bit "raw" in character; on certain instruments it is difficult or impossible to play them loud. Tones in the medium register sound natural, effortless, and clear, with a certain amount of brightness. Tones in the high register are of great intensity, force, and brilliance, and in some cases shrill and piercing; on certain instruments they are difficult, especially to play softly.
It is practically impossible to obtain a really brilliant effect from an orchestra, band, or chorus unless nearly all the instruments or voices are playing or singing in their high register, or at least the upper middle register. If all are in their low register, no matter how loudly the passage is performed, the result is merely heavy and dull--not genuinely brilliant.

● **register key.** Same as octave key.

● **registration.** In *organ playing, the use of the various *stops for their expressive and coloristic effect, either as indicated by the composer or as chosen by an editor or by the performer himself. An intimate knowledge of the *tone-color of each stop, both singly and in combinations, is needed.
Registration on the organ is some-

what akin to *orchestration in writing for the orchestra. Nevertheless, since no two organs have exactly the same stops, the choice of registration is left partly to the player's discretion; the composer's or editor's indications are regarded merely as a suggestion. Hence registration is by no means as exact a matter as orchestration; drastic departures from the indications given in the printed copy are permissible and often necessary.

● **rehearsal letters.** Letters placed at strategic points in the copy of orchestral, chamber-music, and possibly choral works, also in operas, to facilitate reference to exact measures during rehearsals. Thus the conductor may ask the performers to repeat the music beginning "at K," or "four measures after T," or "two measures before BB." Sometimes numbers are used instead of letters, although there is always the danger of confusing a request for "four measures after 7" with "seven measures after 4." A few contemporary composers number every measure in a composition, thus obviating any counting forward or backward. The distance between rehearsal letters preferably never exceeds ten or twelve measures.

● **related keys.** Some *keys are considered more closely related than others, depending on the number of tones that the *scales of the two keys have in common. For example, if the scales of C major and G major are compared, six of the seven notes involved are common to both keys--C, D, E, G, A, and B. Only one note is different: in C major we find F; in G major we find F-sharp. On the other hand, a comparison of C major with E-flat major shows only four notes that occur in both keys--C, D, F, and G. Hence C major and G major are more closely related than C major and E-flat major.
The six close relations to any major key are:
The key of the *relative minor (which has the same *key-signature).
The key of the *tonic minor.
The key of the dominant, that is, the

key with one more sharp or one less flat.
The relative minor of the foregoing.
The key of the subdominant, that is, the key with one more flat or one less sharp.
The relative minor of the foregoing.
To find the closely-related keys to any minor key, substitute the word major for minor throughout the above table.
To come down to exact keys, as an example: The keys closely related to C major are, in order according to the above: A minor, C minor, G major, E minor, F major, and D minor. Those closely related to C minor will be, according to the foregoing table modified: E-flat major, C major, G minor, B-flat major, F minor, and A-flat major.
Synonym: attendant keys.
See also circle of fifths, key-relationships, key-signature, modulation.

● relative minor, relative major. Names given to the relationship between the minor key and the major key which have the same *key-signature. Thus A major and F-sharp minor are relative major and minor; D minor is the relative minor of F major, E-flat major is the relative major of C minor, etc. The names of all existing keys appear in the entry key-signature, with each of the various relative major and minor keys shown in double column opposite an indication of the key-signature that applies.
See also related keys, key-relationships.
Compare tonic minor, tonic major.

● relative pitch. The ability to recognize any pitches that are sung or played, provided the identify of a single tone is known in advance, all pitches being judged in their relation to this given sound. It differs from *absolute pitch in that with the latter the pitches are spontaneously identified without necessity for comparison with any sound already known.
Development of relative pitch is

the purpose of courses in *ear-training and *sight-singing and is one of the most valid tests of *musicianship.

● release. The element of several instruments or voices being exactly together in letting go of a chord or in concluding a composition. In general, clean releases are easier to secure than clean *attacks.
Antonym: attack.
See also ensemble (2), conducting.

●† religioso. In religious style.

● religious music. See church music.

● Renaissance Period. The period of music history extending from about 1425 or 1450 to about 1600 or a little later, sometimes less desirably called the Polyphonic or A Cappella Period. The preceding era is usually called Gothic, although the 1400-1450 segment is often termed the Burgundian or Early Renaissance Period, the former term arising from the prominence of Burgundian composers during those years. The *Baroque Period followed the Renaissance.
It will be noticed that the word Renaissance has a much narrower and more specialized application to music history than in general history. In addition, the Renaissance period in music does not represent a "rebirth" of anything; instead it represents pure innovation.
During the era in question nearly all music was vocal; instrumental music enjoyed hardly more than a step-child status. It should be borne in mind however that the *doubling of voices by instruments was an everyday practice; in other words, although compositions were nominally written for voices only, they were usually performed by voices supported by instruments. (See a cappella.) The *madrigal was the most important secular form, though in general it was church music that occupied composers' attention; indeed some of them regarded the writing of secular works as beneath their dignity or even as sinful.
The church music of this period has a "pure," "impersonal," "unworldly" quality, which has led many musicians to term it the finest and most appropriate

of all liturgical literature.

The structure of all Renaissance music is polyphonic, although not necessarily contrapuntal. By this is meant that the fabric consists of voices of equal value, but not necessarily of an intertwining of strongly melodic strands, since many passages are essentially a series of chords. *Homophonic (melody-and-accompaniment) style, however, exists only in embryo form; its development still lay far in the future. The chordal style was known by the special name familiar style or stile famigliare. In music in this style, each voice is independent, but all the voices clearly fit together into a chord and move basically in the same *rhythm.

The equality of all the voices in Renaissance music is quite at variance with the frequent predominance of the highest and lowest tones of the fabric, common in the Baroque Period, and even more with the domination of a single melodic strand (usually the highest) in *Classical and *Romantic styles.

The scale basis of Renaissance music is the church *modes (1). With the exception of one flat, *key-signatures were not regularly employed, although it was recognized that any composition could be *transposed higher or lower when necessary to bring it into comfortable vocal range. The complete roster of tones available to composers was A, B, C, D, E, F, G, B-flat, E-flat (sometimes), F-sharp, C-sharp and G-sharp. The principle of *enharmonic substitution was not used. Occasionally, however, a venturesome composer would slip in a D-sharp, A-sharp, or perhaps some other tone, but the full *chromatic scale was not utilized until the closing years of the sixteenth century, and only rarely then, so may be considered more a Baroque than a Renaissance development. The various flatted and sharped tones sometimes were indicated in the music, sometimes were interpolated by performers as *musica ficta.

Strong *themes are not characteristic of Renaissance music, indeed some musicians find its effect close to athematic. What themes there are do not have a pronounced rhythm in the sense that one might identify a theme merely through tapping out its rhythm, as is often possible with later compositions. Striking or dramatic effects are rare, for conformity rather than originality or individuality seemed to be composers' goal.

The only chord-types used were major and minor triads in root position and first inversion, and diminished and augmented triads in first inversion. (The diminished triad in root position is met with on rare occasion.) Under certain special and restricted conditions there was a sparing and cautious employment of second inversions of major and minor triads, and certain seventh-chord formations in first inversion (but not the diminished seventh and rarely the dominant seventh types). Consequently, real *discords were distinctly unusual. On the other hand, *non-harmonic tones were very common, usually employed in conjunction with basically consonant harmony. The most common were the suspension and passing-tone, although the lower neighboring note, cambiata, and escape-tone were by no means rare. All were always carefully *prepared and *resolved in accordance with certain strict rules.

In the contrapuntal music of the Renaissance Period, agogic *accent was of paramount importance, while the existence of mechanical metric accent was deemed much less important, except in some dances. Since agogic accent is produced by the length of the tones, and since a long tone in one voice was usually placed in opposition to short tones in other voices, the accents thus occur at staggered locations rather than simultaneously in all the voices, in consequence of which the fabric is decidedly *polyrhythmic; there is a veritable "counterpoint of rhythms." The impulse arising from the prominence of long notes is usually called secondary rhythm. Regularity of phrase-length was most uncommon (here Renaissance music is in sharp contrast with Classical and Romantic), and within the course of any voice, phrases tend to be of irregular lengths. This is partially due to the fact that

the *bar-line had not yet come into
use; Renaissance and older music
was not divided into *measures (and
consequently did not employ *ties).
(The bar-lines found in present-day
editions are inserted by *editors.)
The rhythmic (and melodic) style
was still strongly under the influence
of that of *Gregorian chant. The
lack of regular, metric rhythm,
especially as found in church music,
arises from the fact that the texts
were from the Bible and hence prose
rather than poetry. The frequent
repetition of short rhythmic patterns
(duration patterns) in a "driving"
manner is likewise highly uncharacteristic.

From the foregoing facts it will
be apparent that Renaissance music
is highly asymmetrical. The asymmetrical and polyrhythmic elements
found in much Modern music partially
represent a revival from the period
under discussion.

In the music of later periods (especially from the late Baroque onward), harmony is an element used
to keep a composition moving; often
the music will seem to go into a
series of harmonies, the first of
which seems to generate the remainder and even to be a harbinger of
the chord that will conclude the
series. (See functional harmony.)
These elements, so familiar to the
typical lover of music, are quite
foreign to Renaissance style, and
may be one of the factors which
cause it to seem unappealing at first
acquaintance. In addition, in works
of polyphonic structure the harmony
is to a certain extent an "accident"
arising from the intertwining of the
melodic strands. It is casual rather
than a planned part of the structure;
it is *non-functional. Decisive harmonic progressions often appear only
at the most important *cadences.

See the entry counterpoint, especially the sub-head "Distinction Between Harmony and Counterpoint."
Pronunciation: rén-é-sáns, rén-é-
zăns, ré-nă-săns.

● render. This verb, which is a
synonym for *perform (play or sing),
is widely used in the "society"

columns of newspapers, but is
heartily disliked by many musicians.
The noun rendition, however, is more
respectable.

● repeat signs. Repetition is one of
the fundamental characteristics of
music. Since the writing of music
by hand is a laborious process and
the engraving of music an expensive
one, repetition of long sections of
compositions has always been effected
by means of certain conventional symbols.

The sign means to go

back to the point where the same
sign is found turned backward, i. e.

and to perform again the material
that lies between them; in other words,
these signs enclose the passage to be
repeated. If the latter sign is not
found, the repetition is to start from
the beginning of the piece. When
the commencement of one repeated
section coincides with the end of a
preceding one, the sign used is

or

If the composition has words, these
may repeat as the music repeats, or
there may be new words on the
second occasion.

When a *D. C. or a *D. S. is employed, on the second playing through,
repeat signs are to be ignored. (If
*first and second endings have occurred,
only the second ending is performed
in the D. C. or D. S.)

The following miniature composition
illustrates the use of repeat signs,
D. S., first and second endings, and
a jump to a *coda.

Repeat signs are sometimes written with four dots instead of two, thus:

This usage, however, seems to be disappearing.

The location of repeat signs is sometimes reinforced by the addition of the symbol ⸲ at the beginning of the repeated section, and the symbol ⸲ at its end, thus:

Sometimes two thin lines (i. e., a double *bar-line), plus two dots, are substituted for contrasting thin and thick lines, though this usage does not seem to be favored by the best music engravers.

In vocal compositions the material enclosed in repeat signs is sometimes to be performed more than twice. The number of stanzas which appear as text indicates the number of repetitions.

There can be no doubt that repeat signs were written to excess during the late *Classical and early *Romantic periods; Schubert particularly abused them. There is reason to believe that composers often intended these repeats as optional--a means by which the performer could somewhat control the length of the composition. There are some works in which every section is enclosed in repeat signs; to omit all of them will therefore cut the duration exactly in half. *Theme and variations form is especially prone to the excessive employment of repeat signs.

Special Types of Repeat Sign. Although not "repeat signs," strictly speaking, the symbols ⸲ and ⫽ both indicate repetition. The former means to repeat the preceding *measure. When placed across a *bar line, it indicates a repetition of the two preceding measures. The latter symbol denotes a repetition of the preceding beat or preceding half-measure. These signs are the musical counterpart of ditto marks.

See also bis.

● repertoire. Same as repertory.
The word is originally French and
often written in French fashion:
répertoire.
Anglicized pronunciation:
rĕp-ĕr-twär.

● repertory. That body of compositions which an individual or group
has studied and learned, and which
are ready to be performed without
much further practicing. Any composition that has once been played
well in public, and then is kept in
practice, may be termed a composition in one's repertory.
This word is also used to indicate
that body of compositions written
for any given *medium--as a synonym for literature. Thus one might
say that "The repertory for mixed
chorus is extensive," or "The harp
has a small repertory."

●† replica. Same as ripetizione.
Usually occurs in the form *D. C.
senza replica ("from the beginning
without repetition"). The literal
meaning is "reply" or "answer."
See also repeat signs.
Pronunciation: accent first syllable.

● reprise. Same as recapitulation.
Pronunciation: rē-prīz′ or rē-prēz′.

● reproducing piano. An improved
type of *player piano which repro-
duces tones either loud or soft, at
the dynamic level at which the artist
originally played them; its mechanism
is "touch-sensitive." Trade-names
of well-known reproducing pianos
are Ampico, Duo-Art, and Welte-
Mignon. The popularity of the instrument, like that of the player piano,
has vanished since the advent of the
radio and of electrical recording for
the *phonograph.

● requiem. A *mass for the dead.
It is used not only at funerals but
also at services commemorating an
individual or group of deceased persons. Certain parts of the usual
mass are replaced by special sections found only in requiems.
A German Requiem by Brahms is
really not a requiem except in spirit;

instead of using the traditional Latin
text, Brahms substituted favorite
passages from the German version
of the Bible.
Synonym: missa pro defunctis.
Pronunciation: rĕ́-kwĕ-ĕm or
rḗ-kwĕ-ĕm.

● resin. Rosin.

● resolution. (1) The following of
any chord by that chord to which it
appears to want to move. A familiar
example is the moving of the dominant *seventh-chord (V^7) to the tonic
*triad (I). We say that the tonic
triad is the "resolution" of the dominant seventh, or that the dominant
seventh "resolves to" the tonic.
*Dissonant chords seem to clamor
for resolution. In many cases the
chord of resolution is also dissonant,
but it in turn will seem to want to
move on, and so ultimately to terminate (resolve) on a consonant chord,
usually at a *cadence.
A conventional (although infrequent)
succession of chords, each resolving
naturally to that which follows, yet
without reaching complete repose until
arriving at the final tonic triad is:
III^7-VI^7-II^7-V^7-I.
(2) Certain tones in a *melody also
have a restless, unstable quality that
drives them on to other tones for
repose. For example the seventh
degree, or leading-tone, of a *scale
has a strong tendency toward the high
tonic or key-tone above it, while the
fourth or subdominant degree is drawn
toward the third or mediant degree.
This feature is sometimes called tonal
tendencies.
Synonym: quitting.

● resolve. The verb form of resolution. The verb quit is often substituted.

● resonance. Fullness, sonority, and
abundance of tone; reverberating and
amplified sound. Loudness is not a
necessary component, though agree-
ableness is usually implied. A raucous,
shrill, thin, or harsh tone is not resonant.
Any object used to supply resonance
is called a resonator. The wooden body
of the violin and other string instru-

ments and the *sound board of the piano are resonators.

See also acoustics.

● responsory. Explained under antiphonal.

Synonym: responsorial.

● rest. A character that indicates a certain period of silence, just as a note indicates a certain period of sound of a certain pitch.

The rests in common use are:

Quarter-rest. ⌇ or ⌇ In England and France it is sometimes written ⌇ which is undesirable, due to likelihood of confusion with the eighth-rest. The quarter-rest denotes a period of silence equal to a quarter-note. ♩

Eighth-rest. ⌇ Denotes a period of silence equal to an eighth-note. ♪

Sixteenth-rest. ⌇ Equal to a sixteenth-note. ♬

Thirty-second-rest. ⌇ Equal to a thirty-second-note. ♬

Sixty-fourth-rest. ⌇ Equal to a sixty-fourth-note. ♬

Half-rest.   Equal

to a half-note. ♩ It is written on top of the third line of the staff; however when the parts for two instruments or voices appear on the same staff, the half-rest must sometimes be placed on other lines, even a *leger line, but in any case it is always on top of the line.

Whole-rest (occasionally called measure-rest and whole-measure-rest).   Equal to

a whole measure of any kind of time (and strictly speaking, not the equivalent of a whole-note, except by coincidence in 4-4, 2-2, and 8-8 time). It is written below the fourth line of the staff (not the third); however when parts for two instruments

or voices appear on the same staff it sometimes must be placed below other lines, even *leger lines, but in any case it always hangs from the line. Sometimes a figure 1 appears above it, though this is superfluous. Until about the middle of the eighteenth century the whole-rest was used both as the equivalent of a *whole-note and of a whole measure; however the former usage is now obsolete. Occasionally a dotted-whole-rest   fills a whole

measure of 3-2, 6-4, or 12-8 time, but its usage is tending to disappear. Sometimes a breve-rest

is employed to fill a whole measure of 4-2 or 8-4-time, but this usage is also disappearing. The breve-rest--the counterpart of the *breve (2) or double-whole-note--is now generally used only to indicate a rest of two complete measures of any kind of time; a figure 2 is always appended (see below).

The expressions "quarter-note-rest," "half-note-rest," and so on, are sometimes heard, but cannot be recommended.

Dotted rests are sometimes written, especially in 6-8, 6-4, 9-8, and 12-8 time, but more commonly the dot is replaced by the rest to which it is equal--always the rest of the next shorter duration. Thus: instead of

appears   ;

instead of ⌇ appears ⌇ ⌇ ;

instead of ⌇ appears ⌇ ⌇ ,

etc.

It is customary to avoid writing rests in any combination which would produce *syncopation if notes were substituted, presumably under the theory that "silence cannot be syncopated." For example, in 4-4 time, if there is a quarter-note on the first beat followed by three beats of rest, the effect is written thus: ♩ ⌇ ▬ rather than thus:

or thus:

Sometimes in piano music the parts for both hands are temporarily written on a single staff (when both play quite high or quite low). In this case the other staff is not filled with rests, but is left blank. This is again true when the notes pass from one staff to the other, in "interlocking" work between the hands. (See last musical quotation in the entry arpeggio.) However if there is a fairly long passage for only one hand, appropriate rests are written on the other staff.

Special Types of Rest (Extended Rests, Continued Rests).

Indicates a rest of two measures. (An older use, practically obsolete, is explained above.) It is accompanied by a figure 2. Observe that it extends from the fourth line to the third.

Indicates a rest of four measures, and is accompanied by a figure 4. Observe that it extends from the fourth line to the second.

With the two foregoing rests and the whole-rest, it is possible to make up a silence of any practical number of measures, thus:

When still longer rests are needed, the symbol

will serve. See next paragraph.

Indicates a rest of any number of measures except one, the precise number being specified above the symbol; thus a rest of 23 measures would be written

23

This character always surrounds the middle (third) line of the staff.

See also time-values, G. P.

● resultant tone. When two tones are played together fairly loud, a very faint third tone automatically results, its pitch being the difference in vibrations between the two played tones. It is called a resultant. Thus if tones vibrating 660 and 440 times per second are played, a sound vibrating 220 times (the difference between 660 and 440) will result; if the two tones have 550 and 440 vibrations, a sound with 110 vibrations (550 minus 440) results.

Resultants are deeper in pitch than the lower tone played, or of the same pitch, or of a pitch between the two. They are much easier to hear with certain instruments than with others.

The resultant principle is sometimes applied in producing the 32-foot pedal *stops of the *organ.

An illustration of resultant tones appears on the next page.

Synonyms: beat tone, combination tone, difference tone, differential tone, Tartini tone.

Compare harmonic series.

● retard.   A gradual slackening
in *tempo.   See ritardando.
   The spelling ritard is incorrect,
although often used by musicians.
However ritard. (with a period) is
quite correct as an abbreviation for
ritardando.
   The word retard should not be
used to indicate an immediate change
to a slower *tempo; see meno mosso
and ritenuto.

● retardation.   A suspension that
*resolves upward.   See non-harmonic
tones (3) (suspension).

● retrograde.   See cancrizans.

● retransition.   A transition (2)
which leads from the development
section to the recapitulation in a
movement in *sonata-allegro form
is sometimes called a retransition.
Composers are fond of building them
over dominant pedal-points (see non-
harmonic tones, 9).

● rf, rfz.   Abbreviations for rinforzando.

● r. h.   Right hand.   This abbreviation most commonly comes up in
music for the piano when a low-lying
key-- which ordinarily would be expected to be played by the left hand--
may more conveniently be played by
the right, reaching over the left in
*cross-hand fashion.
   R. h. is the abbreviation for German rechte Hand as well as English
right hand.   M. d., abbreviation for
Italian mano destra and French main
droite, is often substituted.
   Passages of a similar type, but

to be played by the left hand crossing
over the right, are marked l. h.
which may be the abbreviation for
either English left hand or German
linke Hand.   M. s., for Italian mano
sinistra, or m. g., for French main
gauche, are often substituted for it.

● rhapsody.   A composition in free
form, sometimes partaking of the
style of an *improvisation.   Virtually
all examples are instrumental.
(Brahms's Alto Rhapsody for contralto,
men's chorus, and orchestra is a
notable exception.)   Some are nationalistic in character.
   For all practical purposes, the
word might be considered a synonym
for fantasy (1).
   The foreign spellings rhapsodie and
rapsodie are sometimes taken into
English.

● rhumba.   Variant spelling of rumba.

● rhythm.   The duration (length) of
tones, thought of either as long sounds
contrasting with short ones or as
sounds of even length succeeding one
another.   If the tone (pitch) element
of music could be removed, rhythm
is what would remain.
   It is obvious that sounds of a non-
musical character, as well as those
of distinct pitch, may posses rhythm.
   In its narrow sense, the word
rhythm refers to the contrast between
the long and short tones of a *melody
or other succession of musical sounds.
More broadly it also includes the steady
succession of *beats that underlies and
underpins the structure of compositions,
and is further discussed under accent
(metric accent) and meter.   This

element is often termed the beat,
Takt (German), or *pulse.

Rhythm is one of the three basic
components of music, the other two
being *harmony and melody. It is
possible for music to lack harmony
or melody or both, but it is impossible for it to be utterly lacking
in rhythm.

The adjective form is rhythmic
or rhythmical; there are no such
words as rhythmatic or rhythmetic.

Secondary rhythm is mentioned
under Renaissance Period.

See also cross rhythms, jazz,
polyrhythm, shifted accent, syncopation, time-values.

● rhythm band. A group of very
simple *percussion instruments--
usually entirely of indefinite pitch--
used in musical instruction for
children. The underlying theory is
the undeniably true one that a person
becomes rhythmic only by doing and
reacting to rhythm--not through
purely intellectual calculation or
abstract thinking about it.

A rhythm band usually plays in
conjunction with a piano or a phonograph record, or occasionally with
singing, either accompanied or unaccompanied.

Legitimate orchestral instruments
such as the snare drum, triangle,
tambourine, wood block, castanets,
cymbals, and sleigh bells are normally found in rhythm bands, although they are often built to a reduced size and unfortunately are also
frequently of inferior tone-quality.
Other typical rhythm band instruments are seldom encountered outside elementary-school classrooms;
among these are:

Rhythm sticks. Two sticks of wood,
struck together. Sometimes they
are painted in bright, attractive
colors.

Jingles or Clogs. Made of wood;
shaped like three-quarters of a
circle on the end of a short, thick,
flat stick. A small tin disk, similar to those found on the hoop of
the tambourine, is loosely attached
to the round section of wood by
means of a nail.

Hand bell. A single sleigh bell,

mounted on the end of a short handle.

Sand blocks. Two blocks of wood,
each covered with sandpaper, which
are struck or rubbed together. Similar blocks, minus the sandpaper, are
also sometimes used.

Hand drum. Resembles a tambourine minus the jingles, and is
mounted on the end of a short stick.

Certain other instruments are occasionally employed, some of which
are of doubtful musical (and hence
educational) value.

Synonyms: toy band, toy orchestra.

● rhythmical signature. Same as
time-signature.

●† ricercar. An early type of instrumental composition (though occasionally vocal), of *polyphonic
structure. One type of ricercar used
considerable *imitation; it developed
from the *motet and was the forerunner of the *fugue. The other type
did not use imitation.

Ricercar is derived from the Italian
word meaning "to seek out," "to
search."

Variant form: ricercare.
Plural: ricercari or ricercars.
Pronunciation: accent last syllable.

● rigaudon. A moderately fast, animated dance, of French origin, in
4-4 or 2-2 time.

The word is French; the related
English word rigadoon is rare among
musicians.

Pronunciation: properly rē-gō-dōn;
rĭg-a-dŏn is suggested as an anglici-
zation.

●† rigore. See senza rigore.

●† rigorosamente. Rigorously, strictly.

●† rilassando. Slackening, relaxing.

●† rilevato. Brought out prominently.
Synonyms: marcato, pronunziato, en
dehors, accentuato.
Antonym: sotto voce.

●† rilievo. Importance, relief. In
rilievo, prominently, "in relief."
Abbreviation: ril.

● rim shot. A special effect used in playing the *snare drum. The player lays a stick so that one end of it rests on the head of the drum and the other end on the rim; then he strikes it with the other stick. The effect is startling, about like a shot from a revolver.

● † rinforzando. Literally, "reinforcing." When applied to a passage of music, it is equivalent to più forte; when applied to a single tone or chord it is equivalent to *sforzando. It would seem that the application to an entire (though brief) passage is the more logical and desirable usage.
 Abbreviations: rf, rfz, rinf., rinfz.

● † ripetizione. Repetition. Usually occurs in the form senza ripetizione, added to *D. C. or *D. S., in a composition involving *repeat signs.
 Synonym: replica.
 See also repeat signs.

● † ripieno. Explained under concerto grosso.

● † ripresa. The sign ※ used with *D. S. to indicate the point to which the player returns, and from which he begins to repeat. See also symbols.
 Synonym: segno.

● † risoluto. In a resolute, firm, energetic manner.

● † risvegliato. Excited, animated, (literally "aroused" or "awakened"). A rarely-used term about equivalent to the more familiar animato.

● † ritardando. Gradually becoming slower; a gradual and progressive slackening or retarding of the *tempo; a retard. It continues in effect until canceled by *a tempo.
 It is well to emphasize that ritardando does not mean "slow" or "slower," but "gradually becoming slower"; it can occur in the quickest tempos.
 Abbreviations: rit., ritard.
 Synonyms: rallentando, trattenuto.
 Antonyms: accelerando, stringendo, affrettando.
 Compare ritenuto.

● † ritenuto. Literally "held back"; used to indicate an immediately slower *tempo, therefore about equivalent to meno mosso. (Related English word: retain.)
 Abbreviation: riten.
 Variant form: ritenente.
 Compare rallentando and ritardando.

● † ritmico. Rhythmic.
 Pronunciation: accent first syllable.

● † ritmo. Rhythm. Il ritmo ben marcato, the rhythm (i.e., rhythmic pattern) well brought out.

● † ritornando al tempo. A rarely-employed term which indicates a gradual (rather than immediate) return to the basic *tempo, following rallentando, ritardando, accelerando, or stringendo; arrival at the normal tempo is to be complete at the point where a tempo appears, rather than to be immediate. Its contrast with the usual employment of a tempo is illustrated below.
 Variant forms: tornando al tempo ritornare al tempo.

| Basic tempo | *rit.* | *a tempo* | | Basic tempo | *rit.* | Riternando al tempo | *a tempo* |

●† ritornello. A passage in an *aria for the orchestra alone. (Related English word: return.)

Plural: ritornellos (English) or ritornelli (Italian).

Variant forms (French): ritornelle, ritournelle.

Synonym (obsolete): symphony (7).

●† robusto. Sturdy, robust.

● Rococo Period. The period of music history extending from about 1725 to about 1775. In France it can be considered as starting about 1700. It was preceded by the *Baroque period, even overlapping with it for perhaps twenty-five years, and followed by the *Classical.

Some historians regard the Rococo movement as the final stage of Baroque rather than a distinct period, but the composers of the time regarded themselves as opponents of Baroque ideals; in fact in contemporaneous eyes the movement was a quite violent reaction against the Baroque.

The Rococo ideal sought to replace the grandeur, severity, dignity, and pompousness (even ponderousness) of Baroque music with a lighter, fanciful, frivolous, witty, polished, coquettish style. It favored *homophonic structure rather than *polyphonic. It regarded music as entertainment. *Ornaments, especially the *mordent and *trill, were used lavishly--even overused in some music for keyboard instruments, where nearly every note of the melody will sometimes have its ornament.

Although *functional harmony had been established before the Rococo period, its position grew during that time; it became entrenched.

There was a sporadic interest in short forms, particularly for harpsichord, as exemplified in the numerous works by François Couperin and the so-called *sonatas (2) by Domenico Scarlatti, these being usually in *binary (AB) form. In the preceding Baroque and the following Classical periods, short forms were not in favor; their lineage to the present day stems from the *Romantic era.

One wholesome trait of Rococo music is the extreme importance of each note; every detail seems to have been carefully weighed and considered in the process of composition; mass general effects were not typical. Any trace of a "faux pas" was abhorrent. On the other hand, the Rococo composers did very little to expand the actual resources of music. The Rococo era essentially was a new aesthetic ideal rather than a striking step forward in musical evolution.

Returning to the positive side, it is well to mention that *orchestration in its modern sense--taking the *tone-color of instruments into consideration--really begins in this era.

The Rococo style was contemporary with the "powdered wig age." It stems from the era of Louis XV and of the petty intrigues, scandals, and artificiality of manners of the French court.

Synonyms: Gallant style, sensitive style.

● roll. (1) In reference to chords, the term roll describes an effect wherein the various tones, instead of being struck absolutely simultaneously, are played in very rapid succession from the lowest note toward the highest, each tone being held out until the *chord is completed. The sign for rolled chords is

or occasionally

(or [

Rolled chords are highly characteristic of the harp and piano; they are also effective on the organ, the bowed string instruments (such as the violin) and the plucked string (or fretted) instruments (such as the guitar).

A piano or harp chord that requires both hands may be rolled either (A) from the lowest finger of the left hand to the highest of the right,

or (B) rolled independently and simultaneously in each hand.

hands, can execute striking all tones simultaneously.

A chord that exceeds the span of the pianist's hand is understood to be rolled even though not specifically so marked. Clearly, a pianist whose hands are small is obliged to roll certain wide chords that another, with larger hands, can execute striking all tones simultaneously.

When a rolled chord for the left hand occurs with an unrolled chord or single tone in the right, it is understood that the right hand plays with the <u>last</u> (highest) of the rolled tones.
    Thus:

On the rare occasions when a chord is to be rolled from the highest note toward the lowest, rather than as usual, the sign used is ↓↕ or sometimes 〰

Synonym: <u>arpeggiando</u> (but not <u>arpeggio</u>).

(2) On the *percussion instruments, a succession of notes played so rapidly that they appear to fuse into a single long sound. A similar effect is produced when a telephone bell or door bell rings. The roll is comparable to the *tremolo of the string instruments.

The roll is highly effective on the *timpani, *snare drum, and *bass drum, and is also rather frequently written for the *triangle and *tambourine. The *cymbal roll is usually produced by attaching one plate to a frame and beating on it with two soft or hard drum sticks.

Rolls are indicated (A) by placing several strokes through the stem of the note, as in writing a tremolo, or (B) by using the sign *tr* as in writing a *trill (1). Thus:

The snare drum roll is sometimes called the <u>paradiddle</u>.

Synonym (undesirable): <u>trill</u> (2).

(3) The type of record used on the *player piano and reproducing piano is called a <u>roll</u>.

● romance, † romanza. Name sometimes given to slow compositions or slow *movements of a song-like, tender character.

● Roman numerals. These are used to indicate the *chords which form the harmonic structure of music. For all practical purposes they are abbreviations for such terms as "tonic *triad" and "submediant triad." Some theorists employ capital Roman numerals for all chords, but others use the capital form with major triads only; for minor triads they employ the lower-case form; for diminished, the lower-case supplemented by a small o placed above (like the mark used to indicate degrees of temperature); and for the augmented triads, the capital form with a small plus-sign added. Thus in the major and minor modes they would indicate the triads as follows:

	Major mode	Minor mode
tonic	I	i
supertonic	ii	ii⁰
mediant	iii	III⁺
subdominant	IV	iv
dominant	V	V (This triad is usually major because as a rule its third--the leading-tone of the scale-- is raised a half-step by means of an accidental.)
submediant	vi	VI
leading-tone	vii⁰	vii⁰

Arabic numerals supplement these to indicate seventh-chords, ninth-chords, etc.; sometimes they are placed higher than the Roman numeral, sometimes lower. Additional Arabic numerals indicate the presence of *inversions; they are also placed either higher or lower than the Roman numerals, but opposite to the placement of those that indicate the seventh-chord forms. Thus the first inversion of a dominant seventh-chord would be written either one of the following ways:

Roman numerals are also used to indicate the various strings on the bowed *string instruments, that is, <u>sul IV</u> in violin music indicates a passage to be played on the fourth (or G) string.

See also <u>triad</u>.

● Romantic Period. The period of music history which extends from about 1815 to about 1890 or 1900. It came between the *Classical and *Modern periods. It had its origin in Germany and Austria, partly as an outgrowth of the Romantic movement in literature, and partly influenced by the new political and social concepts of the French Revolution. Romantic music is subjective.

The Romanticists were chiefly concerned with the emotional and expressive qualities of music, which to them were of greater importance than the *form structure. In the worst examples contempt for form results in a loose, meandering, hodge-podge type of composition; however the wisest and greatest Romanticists realized that cohesion is an absolute musical essential, and further, that this can be integrated with the expressive qualities without the slightest detriment to the latter.

The music of the Romantic period has a warm, rich, colorful, intimate sound, with many octave doublings for the sake of fulness and sonority; thinness and leanness of texture was disdained. The emotional element of Romantic music, at its best, is warm, human, and intimate; at its worst it is saccharine and carries sentiment over into sentimentality.

In general, the four-measure phrase and the balancing of phrases into antecedents and consequents (question-and-answer order) was carried over from the Classical period--perhaps without realizing the important role that these symmetrical patterns played in the Classical form-schemes which many Romanticists pretended to despise.

The predominance of *homophonic structure also continued, though occasional exceptional compositions could be cited.

The invention of the damper *pedal on the piano opened the way for the use of sweeping left-hand *arpeggios on that instrument, and was an important factor in arousing the already-mentioned desire for full, rich texture in all mediums.

The tenet that a melody could if necessary be complete without harmony faded rapidly during this period. Certain Romantic compositions are fundamentally a succession of interesting chords; many Romantic melodies are almost meaningless except in the light of the harmonies that occur with them. These elements continue into present-day compositions.

Melodies of the Romantic period often tend to lie in a lower register than those of the Classical, this being the rather welcome result of the ever-present desire for sonority and warmth.

The Romantic era was the heyday of *program music, including the *symphonic poem; but to imply that all music of this period is programmatic is highly inaccurate, though a frequent error. The movement which was obsessed with program music is called ultra-Romantic or neo-Romantic; Berlioz and Liszt were the leaders. (The term neo-Romantic is also used in *Modern music with a different meaning: the effort to revive certain Romantic tendencies.)

Short forms were highly popular during the period under discussion; indeed they can almost be said to have "come into their own" for the first time during those days. The *song and the short piano piece were especially favored. It may be difficult for us today to realize that these were almost novelties only 125 or 150 years ago.

*Altered chords and the dominant ninth, eleventh, and thirteenth made their appearance or grew in frequency during the era of Romanticism. Modulations occurred more and more often, sometimes going to keys that were not closely related (see related keys); the music of Wagner furnishes a good illustration. As a corollary we find chord-progressions which had hitherto been unknown or of great rarity. The use of the minor mode increased during this age, appearing as frequently as the major mode (see major and minor).

Romantic composers did not hesitate to use the full complement of *key-signatures. It must be borne in mind that the Classicists had rarely used key-signatures of five or six sharps or flats, Baroque composers still less frequently--almost never (Bach's Well-Tempered Clavier being a notable but very rare exception).

The movement known as nationalism flowered during the latter part of the Romantic era; for further information see that entry.

Synonym: Romanticism.

● rondeau. (1) A form commonly used in the music of the early fifteenth century, written for three "voices," the highest performed by a singer (probably *doubled by an instrument), the middle and lowest by instruments only.

There is a peculiar relationship between repetition in the text and repetition in the music which may be shown in the following diagram:

TEXT: A B C A D E A B
MUSIC: A B A A A B A B

This is usually compressed into a single diagram: ABaAabAB. Here repetition of a letter, capitalized or not, indicates music repetition, while the presence of a capital letter means that the text is also the same. Although the rondeau is not the same thing as the later instrumental *rondo, it is obvious that the refrain-like recurrence of text and music has a connection with this form, and that both terms derive from the same root. (However, in French the present word for rondo is rondeau.)

(2) In the latter seventeenth and eighteenth centuries the term rondeau was applied in short instrumental compositions to a form-scheme in which a principal section re-appeared after each contrasting section. A typical (though not the only) form-pattern was ABACADA. With the adoption of a more continuous (rather than *sectional) structure, the rondeau evolved into the modern *rondo.

Plural: rondeaux.
Pronunciation: rŏn-dō′ is an acceptable anglicized pronunciation.

● rondo. A form-scheme in which there is theoretically a return to the principal theme after each appearance of every contrasting theme; that is, in a form-diagram every other letter should be A.

Musicians recognize three distinct types of rondo. In first rondo form there is one digression from the principal theme and one return to it; the form-scheme is ABA. In second rondo form there are two digressions from the principal theme and two

returns to it; the form-scheme is ABABA or ABACA. This is sometimes called the five-part rondo. In third (or big) rondo form--the only true rondo in some musicians' estimation--there are three digressions from the principal theme and three returns to it; the form-scheme is ABACABA or ABACADA. This is sometimes called the seven-part rondo. The frequent returns to the A section give a *refrain-like quality, emphasized by the fact that this section normally is always in the principal *key.

Occasionally a rondo contains a *development section, sometimes replacing theme C.

A rondo may have an introduction or coda or both.

The distinction between first rondo form and *ternary form (often called three-part, song, or aria form), which also has the scheme ABA, rests in the degree of continuity possessed by the music. In first rondo form there is a feeling of continuous motion, even urgency, from beginning to end, while in ternary form each section reaches a complete *cadence, and may even be performable by itself. The same condition distinguishes second rondo form from song form with double trio and song form with two trios. Naturally some compositions are hybrids or borderline examples.

The form scheme in certain compositions, entitled rondo, from the pens of eminent masters, do not actually work out in such a fashion that every other letter is A. Some theorists would probably term these works misnomers, while composers would perhaps maintain that theorists have over-simplified the form diagrams. The term "short-circuited rondo" has been used to describe such a composition.

Rondos are often described as "fast and gay," which beyond doubt is usually true. Strictly speaking, however, the rondo is purely a form, having no necessary connection with *tempo, mood, or style.

Many compositions classified under *"sonata-types" employ a rondo as the final movement.

Plural: rondos.
Pronunciation: rŏn-dō.

● rondo-sonata form. A variant on *sonata-allegro form in which the second theme in the exposition portion is followed by a repetition of the first theme before passing on to the *development section.
Synonym: sonata-rondo form.

● root. That one tone in any *chord out of which the entire chord seems to have grown; the tone which seems to generate the rest of the chord.
When a chord is distributed or *"spelled" as a series of super-imposed thirds (see intervals) the lowest tone is the root, according to conventional textbook theory.
Theorists have proposed a number of rival methods for determining the roots of chords, some of which yield a tone other than that which results when the above method is applied. Although these methods are mutually contradictory, the fact is rather generally accepted that one tone in any chord begets the others--that all are not equally basic.
Synonym: fundamental (1).
See also triad, seventh-chord, harmony.

● root position. A chord whose *root (or fundamental) appears as the bass tone is said to be in root position or fundamental position.
See triad, seventh-chord.
Compare inversion (1).

● rosalia. A derogatory name applied to a *sequence of poor effect.

● rosin. A brittle, somewhat sticky substance obtained from the pine tree as a by-product in the making of turpentine. A highly-refined grade is applied to the hair on the *bows of *string instruments to cause it to grip the strings.
Variant form: resin.

● rote. Anything learned by repetition, by hearing, "by ear," rather than by reading the notation, is said to be learned by rote. The ability to sing by rote is easily acquired, and widely exploited in teaching elementary-school children. To play an instrument by rote is less simple.
Building on an adequate foundation of music learned by rote, it is possible even for young children to be taught music notation in a way that is both meaningful and readily understood.

● roulade. A brilliant scale or *florid passage for the voice.
Pronunciation: rōō-läd.

● round. A special type of vocal *canon, usually for three or four voices. It contains as many phrases as there are voices. The voices enter one by one, a phrase apart, and on reaching the end each returns to the beginning until the round has been sung an agreed number of times. As the round ends the voices drop out one by one. Once all the voices have entered

the music keeps going over the
same ground, but with the various
voices exchanging parts with one
another.

The preceding example represents
the activity in a well-known round,
after all the voices have entered.

Distinction Between Round and
Canon. A round keeps going over
the same ground; it is an infinite
canon and has no natural end. It
is always a short, independent composition for voices. A canon may
be for voices or instruments, may
be combined with other material or
not, and usually occurs as a phase
or section within a longer composition; that is, there are very few
compositions entitled canon, or
with a canon running through from
beginning to end. It does not keep
going over the same material, but
instead goes on to fresh material
which is immediately duplicated in
another "voice." (See canon.)

All rounds are canons, but not
all canons are rounds.

See also catch.

● roundelay. A song in which one
phrase is constantly repeated. This
term is more commonly seen in
literature than in music.

●† rovescio. See cancrizans and
inversion (3).
Pronunciation: accent -ve-.

● row. See twelve tone system.

● r. p. m. Revolutions per minute;
refers to the number of times a
*phonograph turntable revolves each
minute.

●† rubato. See tempo rubato.

● rules of music. Few musical
matters are so thoroughly misunderstood as that of the function of the
rules of music. It would seem that
certain persons imagine that there
are two kinds of music: (a) one kind
(written by persons of meek, sub-
missive disposition) which follows
certain dreaded and exceedingly con-
fining rules, and which avoids in-
fractions with great difficulty and

at the cost of sacrificing every trace
of spontaneity; (b) a second kind,
glorious, free-ranging and untrammeled,
in which the composer "just writes,"
with no irksome restrictions to fetter
him. However, this second type has
no existence outside the imperfect
understanding of certain amateurs and
ill-prepared students, who also have
an entirely wrong conception of the
first type.

Actually, all music is composed according to some set of rules--either
written or understood by observance--
and so thoroughly familiar to the musicians who use them that employment
is a subconscious process rather than a
grudging task, just as speakers and
writers constantly observe the rules
of grammar quite unconsciously. The
misunderstood point is that all music
does not adhere to the same rules.
The rules which guided Dufay, Palestrina, Bach, Mozart, Wagner, Bartók,
and Schoenberg were all mutually at
variance (thinking of the entire set of
rules), but these masters all composed according to some principles,
not haphazardly, at random, or by
guess-work.

Persons with restricted understanding seem unable to detect the operation
of rules in any style of music except
four-voice hymn-tunes. They cannot
discern how the rules of music operate
in a composition written in piano style,
for instance a piano piece with a single
line of notes for each hand (e.g., the
first in the book of Preludes by Chopin,
or the same composer's A-Flat Etude,
op. 25, no. 1), hence they plunge to
the ill-founded conclusion that this is
a type of "free music" written "the
way the composer felt it." The rows
of octaves found in innumerable compositions are not the "parallel octaves"
proscribed in theory texts, but pur-
posely-written strengthenings or thick-
enings of certain "voices."

It is no more possible to write music without some underlying organiza-
tional principle than to write a book
or even a letter without reference to
the rules of sentence-structure and
grammar, admitting that such reference
is almost totally subconscious.

Just as the rules of grammar in any
language are derived from the living

practice of writers and speakers, the rules of music likewise are and always have been derived from the living practice of composers, not arbitrarily concocted by theorists. Practice came first and rules were derived later--not the reverse. The rules of music are not the despotic promulgations of a "ruler." Theorists, it is true, have sometimes recommended certain devices and condemned others, but none has ever had power to enforce his viewpoints or to visit punishment or professional disgrace on those who violated his recommendations. Nothing has ever been officially "forbidden," but there have been many things which composers of certain eras have unanimously shunned or unanimously practiced.

On the rare occasions when composers genuinely have broken the rules that were prevalent, they have done so consciously and purposely, not by accident or through oversight.

See also theorist, theory.

●† rullante. Rolling; refers to the manner of playing various drums.

● rumba. A type of lively Cuban dance. It is often characterized by *jazz-like rhythms such as:

4 (3 + 3 + 2)
4   8

which might also be written:

4
4

In dancing it, the body is moved more than the feet.
Variant spelling: rhumba.
Pronunciation: rŭm̃-bá or rŏŏm-bǎ.

● run. A rapid passage, generally scalewise.

● Russian bass. A type of male voice much cultivated in Russia. The Russian bass can descend considerably lower than the usual bass, even the basso profondo, often at-

taining the tone

or even lower pitches.

● Rute (German). A special implement occasionally used to play the *bass drum. It is a switch made of many pieces of rattan, and looks like a small broom or large clothes-brush.
Rute is the German word meaning "rod."
Variant spelling: Ruthe.
Pronunciation: rōō⁻tē.

●† ruvido. Rough, rude, harsh.
Variant form: ruvidamente.
Antonym: dolce.
Pronunciation: accent first syllable.

S

● SAB. Soprano, alto, and bass. Used in designating the voice parts in choral music.

● sackbut. An obsolete brass instrument played with a *slide. The modern *trombone is a descendent of the sackbut.

● sacred music. See church music, liturgical music.

● salon music. Strictly speaking, salon music denotes compositions of moderate difficulty, intended to be played or sung (usually the former) in the home, for one's self, family, or friends, salon being the French word for parlor. It implies a contrast with difficult works that are performed by *virtuosos at concerts.
Unfortunately the term is almost always applied to music of very slight character, often mawkishly sentimental and of dubious worth, rather than to easy compositions of high quality.
See also Gebrauchsmusik.
Pronunciation: sǎ-lŏn̂.

●† saltando. Bouncing, springing, leaping; refers to a type of *bowing.
Variant form: saltato.

●† saltarello. A quick Italian dance, musically somewhat similar to the *tarantella. Saltarello is derived from the Italian word meaning "to jump."
(Related English word: somersault.)

● sarabande. A dance in slow 3-4 or 3-2 time. As a rule a long note falls on the second beat. The following is a typical sarabande rhythm:

first altos, second altos, tenors, first basses, and second basses, with a solo part for a single soprano.

● saxhorn. An entire family of *brass instruments invented in 1842 by the Belgian instrument-maker Adolphe Sax, who was also the inventor of the *saxophone. Sax constructed them as modified *bugles, with *valves added. There are seven of these instruments, ranging from sopranino to contrabass; the alto saxhorn is similar to the *alto

$$\frac{3}{2}\ \text{♩}\ \text{♩·}\ \text{♩|♩♩♩·}\ \ \text{♩|♩♩♩}\ \text{♩}\ \text{|♩♩♩}\ -\ \|$$

The sarabande is the third of the four basic dances that nominally make up the Baroque *suite (1) (often misnamed the "Classic Suite"). The style is often thoughtful and emotional.
Apparently the sarabande originated in the Near East, from which it was introduced into Spain and other European countries during the sixteenth century, remaining in use until the eighteenth century.
Variant spelling: saraband.
Pronunciation: sär-ä-bänd.

● sarrusophone. An entire family of woodwind instruments, ranging from soprano to contrabass, invented about 1856 by the French military bandmaster Pierre Auguste Sarrus (1817-1873). The sarrusophones are made of metal and play with a double reed, like the *oboe. The only important sarrusophone is the contrabass. It is widely used in France as a substitute for the *contrabassoon, which it closely resembles in both *range and *tonecolor, if not in appearance.
Pronunciation: sär-rŭs-ō-fōn.

● SATB. Soprano, alto, tenor, and bass. Used in designating the voice parts in choral music.
With the four letters S, A, T, and B the voice distribution of any choral composition may be clearly indicated. Thus SAATBB (S solo) indicates a composition for sopranos,

horn, while the tenor saxhorn is for all practical purposes about the same thing as the *baritone (2). In all fairness it may be said that the saxhorns are not sufficiently distinct from such more familiar instruments as the trumpet and tuba to be of practical value. Some musicians also believe they are not sufficiently distinct from the *flügelhorn family.
Sax invented another family of brass instruments called saxotrombas or saxtrombas.

● saxophone. An entire family of *woodwind instruments, played with a single *reed, invented in 1840 (1842 according to some accounts), by Adolphe Sax (1814-1894), an instrument-maker of Brussels, Belgium. Although their mechanism is that of woodwind instruments, saxophones actually are made of glossy, highly-polished brass. They are immediately conspicuous for their curving, sometimes double-curving, mouth-pipes and their upward-turned *bells (though the sopranino and-- usually--the soprano types lack both features), plus the flapper-type keys with metal disks which cover the holes in the instrument's tube. Their shape has been compared to that of a much-enlarged tobacco-pipe.
Each saxophone has the following written range:

(The alto, tenor, and baritone saxophone can also sound the upper E and F.) All saxophones are *transposing instruments; the actual pitches are (with the upper written E and F included for the instruments which can play them):

Hence there are two fundamental types: the sopranino, alto, and baritone are E-flat instruments; the soprano, tenor, and bass, B-flat. However the C melody saxophone, used chiefly by *amateurs, is an exception, falling into neither of the foregoing groups.

The finest players can go considerably higher than the highest notes shown here.

It will be apparent that the various instruments have the following transposition (see intervals):

sopranino--sounds a minor third higher than written

soprano--sounds a *whole-step lower than written

alto--sounds a major sixth lower than written

C melody--sounds an *octave lower than written

tenor--sounds an octave and a whole-step (major ninth) lower than written

baritone--sounds an octave and a major sixth lower than written

bass--sounds two octaves and a whole-step lower than written

In France and other Continental countries, saxophones are sometimes manufactured alternately in F and C rather than E-flat and B-flat. Actual pitches of their ranges are a *whole-step higher than those shown above.

A contrabass saxophone has also been built.

The alto is the type most commonly encountered, followed by the tenor; the baritone is a poor third. The soprano and especially C melody instruments are rapidly losing their once-great popularity. The bass, contrabass, and sopranino types have always been unusual.

The saxophones are always notated with the treble *clef, even the baritone and bass types.

Saxophone *tone-color has the paradoxical quality of being both individual and yet a curious blend of clarinet, horn, viola, bassoon, and cello, with perhaps just a touch of English horn quality. It is regrettable that one seldom hears the saxophone played with a good tone. It has a smooth, singing, "golden," bland tone-color when in the hands of a first-rate player, but is dull and fuzzy when played by a less gifted person.

In orchestral music, the instrument has been utilized most frequently by French composers, not (as one would expect) by Americans. Its presence in the orchestra is distinctly exceptional, although it is firmly established in the band, while in the *dance band it is, of course, perhaps the most characteristic member.

Synonym (colloquial): sax.

Italian: sassofono or saxofono. French: saxophone. German: Saxophon. Spanish: saxofón or saxófono.

●† Scala, La. See La Scala.

● scale. A series of fixed pitches arranged in either ascending or descending order, these pitches being the tonal resources from which compositions are fashioned. Usually one of the pitches is felt as a starting-point or *tonic.

The following types of scale are discussed under their proper headings:

> major scale
> minor scale
> chromatic scale
> diatonic scale
> modes
> pentatonic scale
> whole-tone scale

The various individual tones of the major and minor scales are given names and numbers, these being the same as those used in designating *triads, except that Arabic rather than Roman numerals are generally used. The names of these various tones (or degrees or steps, as they are often called) are:

> 1--tonic
> 2--supertonic
> 3--mediant

> 4--subdominant
> 5--dominant
> 6--submediant
> 7--leading-tone

To finish it is customary to add an eighth tone, located an octave above the starting tone. Also called tonic, it is frequently assigned the number 8 rather than 1. The sixth tone is occasionally called superdominant rather than submediant. The seventh tone is called leading-tone only when it is located a half-step below the upper tonic (as is usual); otherwise the proper name is subtonic.

In naming the tones found in a scale it is customary to give them in ascending order, rather than descending.

Scales are a repository of the tones which exist in various *keys. They are related to music in the way that the alphabet is related to literature, in the way numerals are related to sums, in the way the chemical elements are related to substances, in the way the paints on an artist's palette are related to pictures. They are a storehouse of the ingredients from which compositions are made.

Scales are no magic charm or talisman. Musicians practice them chiefly for two reasons: (A) To become so thoroughly familiar with the tones found in the various keys that playing just these tones, and no others, will become second nature. (B) Because complete scales, both ascending and descending, tend to occur in compositions.

The word scale is derived from the Latin word meaning "ladder" or "stairway."

Synonym (rare): gamut (1).

● scale degree. One of the tones found in a *scale, thought of in its relation to the remaining tones.

Synonym: step (1).

● scalewise. Same as diatonic.

●† scena. A long vocal solo in an opera. It is usually made up of a *recitative and an *aria, sometimes separated by other material in *arioso or *cavatina style.

This term, which can of course be

translated scene, should not be
confused with the word scene that
indicates a subdivision within the
act of an opera.

●† scherzando. Playfully, humorously. (Literally, joking.)
Synonym: scherzoso.

●† scherzo. A movement in very
quick *tempo and of playful, gay,
bantering character, found in four-
movement symphonies, string quartets, sonatas, etc. (see sonata
types). Dance-like rhythms are
typical, as are capricious, fanciful
effects and quick surprises. The
*time-signature is normally 3-4.

The scherzo usually occurs as
the third of the four movements,
though not infrequently as the second.
In all cases its role is largely that
of a counterbalance to the slow
movement.

The earlier symphonies, sonatas,
and chamber-music works contain
a *minuet rather than a scherzo.
During the early nineteenth century,
particularly in the works of Beethoven, the scherzo began to replace
the minuet, and remains in this
function to the present day.

Three-movement examples contain
neither a minuet nor a scherzo,
hence this is the "extra" movement
in those possessing four.

Scherzo is the Italian word meaning joke, raillery, or sport. Most
scherzos are unadulterated joviality,
though some partake of the fiendish,
macabre, or diabolical, others of
good-natured peasant-like gawkiness.

Although Beethoven established the
scherzo as a substitute for the
minuet, he by no means "invented"
it, as facile books on music appreciation have been known to state.

The *form scheme of the scherzo
is usually one of these three: ABA,
ABABA, or ABACA, although strictly
the scherzo is a style rather than
a form.

Chopin, Schubert, Mendelssohn,
Brahms, and others have written
examples which are independent
single-movement compositions rather
than parts of large works.

Plural: scherzos or scherzi.

●† scherzoso.   Same as scherzando.

● "Schmalz". A contemptuous name
for music of over-lush, over-rich,
over-sentimental style. Schmalz is
the German word meaning "lard" or
"grease."
Pronunciation: shmälts.

● school. A group of musicians with
similar aims, styles, practices, or
ideals. Thus we speak of the "French
school of composition," the "Russian
school of violin-playing," the "Italian
school of singing," etc. There is no
implication that all the members of
the group were educated at the same
institution.

The term is also used in the present
meaning in the other arts, e.g., the
Barbizon school in painting, the functional school in architecture, the
Victorian school of literature.

See also: Mannheim group, (the)
Five, (the) Six.

● schottische. A dance in 2-4 time,
musically similar to the *polka and
the *écossaise, but slower than either.
This is the German word meaning
"Scotch."
Pronunciation (anglicized): shŏt-ish.

●† scintillante. Brilliant (literally
"sparkling").

●† sciolto. Fluent, flowing. A
certain amount of rapidity is implied.

●† scordatura. A change in the normal *tuning (2) of a string instrument;
tuning to pitches other than those which
are standard. The change may be
either upward or downward. Many
of Paganini's brilliant violin solos make
use of this expedient.

Examples of scordatura occur in the
following representative works; the list
could of course be expanded.

Saint-Saëns: Danse Macabre.
Solo violin tunes first string from E
down to E-flat.

Stravinsky: Firebird Suite, beginning. First violins tune first string
from E down to D.

Richard Strauss: Ein Heldenleben.
At one point second violins tune fourth
string from G down to G-flat.

Richard Strauss: Don Quixote.
Solo viola tunes fourth string from
C down to B in Variation 3.

Bartók: Contrasts. Violin
tunes first string from E down to
E-flat and fourth string from G up
to A-flat.

Respighi: The Pines of Rome.
At one point half of the cellos tune
fourth string from C down to B.

Kodály: Sonata for Unaccompanied Cello. Third string tuned
from G down to F-sharp, fourth
string from C down to B.

Mahler: Fourth Symphony,
second movement. A solo violin
tunes all four strings a whole-step
up; that is, the instrument is tuned
to F-sharp, B, E, A.

Of course time must be allowed to
make the alteration in pitch, both
into scordatura and back into normal
tuning. Since this must in most
cases be accomplished during the
course of the composition, (occasionally the scordatura holds completely through a composition or at
least a movement), yet silently
enough that the audience is not aware
of it, there is always bound to be
some attendant risk. The device
is never used without extremely
good reason.

● score. (1) A score contains the
music played by all the instruments
or voices (or both) that participate
in a given group, arranged on a
series of *staffs placed one under
another. In a modern orchestral
composition it is not uncommon to
find as many as thirty or more of
these simultaneously-sounding staffs.
The *conductor directs from this
score, and must know its innumerable
details thoroughly.

Each player has only his own music before him; his copy is called
a *part.

The downward order in which the
music for the different instruments
occurs in a score is somewhat variable, but the general tendency is:
woodwinds, brass, percussion,
strings. A typical downward order
would be:

    piccolo (or flutes)
    flutes (or piccolo)

oboes
English horn
clarinets
bass clarinet
bassoons
contrabassoon
horns 1 and 2
horns 3 and 4
trumpets (two staffs are
   advisable if there are more
   than two trumpets)
trombones 1 and 2
trombone 3 and tuba (sometimes there is a separate
   staff for each)
timpani
all the other percussion instruments (usually on a series
   of one-line staffs)
celesta (two staffs)
piano (two staffs)
organ (three staffs)
harp (two staffs)
first violins
second violins
violas
cellos
double-basses

It should not be assumed that the
typical modern composition calls for
as large an ensemble as the foregoing;
the purpose here is to exemplify the
principle governing the downward order
of the instruments. (See orchestra.)

Formerly the cello and double-bass
parts were usually written on a single
staff, but this practice has been rare
during the past hundred years. In a
composition for voices and orchestra,
it is now customary to place the voice-
parts just above the first violins. The
same location is used for the solo
instrument in a *concerto. Formerly
these were often placed between the
violas and the cellos.

In writing a composition for orchestra,
the composer's finished product is the
score. From this the various *parts
are copied out one by one, either by
the composer or by some other person
known as a copyist.

For study purposes, orchestral and
*chamber-music scores are often re-
produced in booklet size. Known as
miniature scores, pocket scores, small
scores, or study scores, they are
widely used by students, *amateurs,
and composers, but they are too small

for the conductor to use with convenience at rehearsals and concerts; here a much larger form, known as a full score, is used.
See also reduction, piano-vocal copy.
Italian: partitura. French: partition. German: Partitur.
(2) A synonym for system.
(3) Musical notation in general (undesirable).
(4) The expression "in score" refers to notating the music for various instruments or voices one above the other on a series of parallel staffs, as opposed to writing their music entirely separately, in a set of *parts.
For the expression open score, see that entry.

● † scorrevole.   Fluent, gliding, flowing.
Pronunciation: accent second syllable.

● scoring.   Same as orchestration.

● Scotch snap.   The rhythmic pattern ♪♫. also ♪♩.
Neither pattern is by any means restricted to Scotch music.

● † secco.   Dry, short. This word is used to call attention to tones or chords that should not be prolonged; for instance as a direction to a harp player to *damp the strings of his instrument immediately after a chord has been struck, rather than allowing them to continue vibrating. It is sometimes used to instruct the player of a harp or other instrument not to *roll a chord--not to play it *arpeggiando.
For secco recitative (recitativo secco) see recitative.
Synonym (French): sec.

See also damp, étouffé.

● secondary seventh-chords.   A generic name sometimes applied to all *seventh-chords other than the dominant seventh and possibly the diminished seventh.

● † secondo.   The lower part in a composition for piano *four hands (two players at one piano).   The upper part is termed primo.
Literally, "second."

● seconds.   See intervals.

● section.   (1) In the orchestra and band, all the instruments of a single kind are sometimes called a section. Thus we speak of the "flute section," "cello section," "trombone section," and the like. At other times the term is used to refer to one of the four main "families" or "choirs" of instrument--string, woodwind, brass, percussion.
(2) In musical *form, a well-defined portion of a composition is called a section, sometimes a strain (2). Some music theorists have arbitrarily used the word section to designate a specified number of *phrases or *periods; the usage depends on the individual's personal definition.

● sectional.   A composition or movement that divides into fairly distinct sections, with clear-cut *cadences, is said to be sectional in formation. This term is used as a contrast to the type of structure in which the beginning of a new *theme overlaps or "dovetails" with the last few notes of the preceding theme, and which is the more subtle and scholarly type of construction.

● secular. Not religous, worldly. All music which is not for church use is called secular music.
Synonym (obsolescent): profane music.
Antonym: church music, sacred music.

●† segno. The sign 𝄋 See D. S.; see also repeat signs.
Synonym (rare): ripresa.

●† segue. (1) A synonym for attacca.
(2) A synonym for simile. Literally, "follows."
(Related English word: sequence.)

● seguidilla. A Spanish dance in triple meter, usually fast.
Pronunciation: sĕ-gĭ-dē-ya̎ or sĕ-gĭ-dē-lya̎.

● selection. This word is often employed as a synonym for piece, work, or composition, but its usage is advisable only when used strictly in its literal sense as something picked out or selected.

● semibreve. Whole-note. See British terminology.

● semi-chorus. As the name suggests, a small body of singers thought of in opposition to a chorus of larger size. Some works are written for chorus and semi-chorus, requiring two choral groups of unequal size. It is understood however that the small unit consists of sections of voices to each part--that it is not merely an ensemble of solo voices (such as a *mixed quartet).
Compare double chorus.

● "semi-classical." A term used by laymen to denote music which is frankly light in nature, but not in "popular" (1) style. The term is rare among musicians, many of whom openly scorn it. Viewed from the strict (musical) meaning of Classical (as applied to the Classical period in music history) the term semi-classical becomes

utter nonsense. We need only to concoct such expressions as "semi-Baroque" and "semi-Romantic" to demonstrate the point.
Common though it is, this term is certainly not desirable.

● semiminim. Old name for the crotchet or quarter-note. (See British terminology).

● semiquaver. Sixteenth-note (British). See time-values and British terminology).

● semi-staccato. The mild form of *staccato indicated by dots and *slurs. Often incorrectly called portamento, its correct name is portato.

● semitone. Same as half-step.

●† semplice. In a simple manner.
Variant spelling: simplice.
Pronunciation: accent first syllable. (However in the variant simplice the accenting is regular, i.e., on the second syllable.)

●† sempre. Always.

●† sensibile. Perceptible, discernible, not "drowned out." Generally occurs in orchestral music to mark a part that might well be "covered up" or for some reason not be sufficiently brought out. The term is by no means as emphatic as *marcato or *pronunziato.
Pronunciation: accent second syllable.

●† sentimento. Sentiment.

●† sentito. Hearty, heartfelt.

●† senza. Without. Thus: senza rall., without slowing down (used to caution the performer to continue the music in strict *tempo); senza espressione, without expression.

●† senza battuta. Same as senza misura.

●† senza misura. Freely; the *time-values not to be strictly observed, following the rhythm suggested by the words. (However, the term is not restricted to vocal music.) This term indicates much greater freedom than *tempo rubato.

Synonyms: senza battuta, liberamente, senza tempo.

Antonyms: misurato, tempo giusto.

● † senza rigore. Literally, "without rigor," that is, not in extremely strict rhythm or in a metronomic manner; to be performed just a trifle free, allowing adequate time to play any short notes without a sense of rushing or crowding. It is sometimes used as a caution against hurrying a passage.

See also cedendo, tempo rubato.

● septet. A composition for seven voices or instruments. See groups.

Variant spelling: septette.

Pronunciation: Dictionaries indicate accent on the second syllable, but musicians often stress the first.

● sequence. The repetition of a pattern of tones commencing from a different pitch, either higher or lower. When this device occurs in a melody it is called a melodic sequence; when in a series of chords, a harmonic sequence.

These two sequential passages are familiar to all Americans:

Both of these have two units, and both are melodic sequences.

Some sequences work down, as do those just quoted, others up.

The six-unit upward-working melodic sequence on the following page comes from the pen of the composer who was perhaps the supreme master of this device-- Handel. It is from the first *aria in The Messiah.

For a three-unit, upward-working harmonic sequence, see the first six chords in the musical quotation found in the entry sforzando.

The best sequences, both melodic and harmonic, do not employ exactly the same *intervals in each unit, but answer the major intervals of one appearance with minor in another, and the like. For example, in the first sequence below, the melody descends first a whole-step, then a half-step (at "fathers died"), but a half-step and then a whole-step in the second unit (at "Pilgrims' pride"). A sequence that preserves all intervals exactly produces a wretched effect as a rule, and is known by the derogatory name *rosalia.

The use of sequences is typical of the process of thematic *development.

Land where my fa - thers died, Land of the Pil - grims' pride.

And the rock - ets' red glare, the bombs burst - ing in air

Shall be - ex - al -

ted.

A six-unit sequence in Handel's Messiah.

● sequentials. Passages, especially technical exercises, which are based on a *sequence pattern.

● serenade. (1) A love-song, performed (strictly, only in the evening) by a man outside the home of his sweetheart, in hopes of attracting her favorable attention. The *accompaniment often suggests a *guitar.

Compare aubade.

(2) Same as divertimento, though with the suggestion that it is intended to be performed out-of-doors and during the evening.

Synonym: serenata.

● serial technique. See twelve tone system. However, the term serial technique may have a broader application than twelve tone system; for example it may also include the serial use of *dynamics, *tone-colors, or *rhythmic patterns.

●† serio † serioso. Serious, earnest, grave.

● serpent. An obsolete deep-pitched wind instrument. Although made of wood, it worked on the principle of a brass instrument, and had the cup-shaped mouthpiece typical of the brass family. It had the peculiar long keys associated with the keyed bugle and ophicleide,

somewhat similar to those of the saxophone.

It was a large instrument, and its curled, snake-like appearance was the source of its fanciful name. The invention of the tuba quickly drove it into limbo. Verdi was one of the last composers ever to employ the serpent, in his opera The Sicilian Vespers (1855).

● service. In the Church of England and Episcopal Church, the musical part of the rites, other than *hymns and *anthems, is collectively known as a service. A number of composers (mostly British) have written complete "services" for the three principal rites, namely Morning Prayer, Evening Prayer, and Communion, the latter being very similar to the Roman Catholic *mass.

● sestet. Variant form of sextet. Pronunciation: accent either syllable.

● seventh-chord. A chord consisting of (or at least implying) four different tones, built in superimposed thirds (see intervals). Just as in *triads it is possible to duplicate any or all of the tones in the *octaves above or below without changing the identity of the chord, the same is again true of seventh-chords. Hence "four different tones" does not necessarily mean only four tones.

For convenience in naming, or "spelling" any type of chord, it is set out as a stack of superimposed thirds, the seventh-chord being no exception to this principle. As in the triad, the lowest tone--when laid out thus--is called the root or fundamental, the next one the third, and the following one the fifth. The new tone, a third above the fifth, is termed the seventh because of its location at the interval of a seventh above the root. It will thus be seen that seventh-chords are really triads with another third added to the top. As in triads, the root, third, fifth, and seventh retain their identity no

structed thus. This species is some-times called dominant seventh type because the seventh-chord built on the fifth (dominant) degree of the *scale (V_7) is formed in this manner.

Another type consists of a minor triad with a minor seventh added. The chord based on the second (supertonic) degree of the major scale is perhaps the most familiar one constructed this way.

Still another form, very familiar, con-sists of a diminished triad with a di-minished seventh above it, and is called the diminished seventh-chord. This chord has become almost disreputable because of its overuse by some com-posers; the frequency of a loud diminished-

matter how the chord tones are distributed.

Types. Just as there are four different types of triad, so are there several different categores of seventh-chord.

One kind consists of a major triad with a minor seventh added. This is the commonest variety; all of the seventh-chords shown above are con-

seventh to coincide with the entrance of the villain in an *opera has attained the status of a joke among musicians.

Remaining species are: major triad with major seventh added; diminished triad with minor seventh added, some-times called the half-diminished seventh; minor triad with major seventh added; augmented triad with major seventh added (these last two forms are very

Minor triads with minor seventh   Diminished triads with diminished seventh ("diminished seventh-chord")   Major triad with major seventh   Diminished triads with minor seventh ("half diminished")   Minor triad with major seventh   Augmented triad with major seventh

harsh). The diminished triad with major seventh added is almost unused; it is also very harsh.

Inversion. Just as triads may be *inverted (that is, any of the tones may appear as bass tone), so seventh-chords may also have either the root, third, fifth, or seventh as the bass tone.

When the root is in the bass, the seventh-chord is said to be in root position (or fundamental position).

When the third is in the bass, it is said to be in first inversion, or

4-3 position (more fully 6-4-3 position).

When the seventh is in the bass, it is called third inversion or 4-2 position (more fully 6-4-2 position).

Omitted Members. In some seventh-chords, especially the dominant seventh type, the omission of the fifth in no way impairs the identity of the chord, and this kind of structure is frequently encountered. The omission of the third is also not unusual. In both cases the root is often *doubled.

First inversions
(6 or 5 position)
5 3

Second inversions
(4 or 4 position)
3 3

Third inversion
(4 or 4 position)
2 2

6-5 position, which might more fully be called 6-5-3 position, since the various tones have those interval-relationships with the bass tone.

When the fifth is in the bass, it is said to be in second inversion or

See also triad, harmony, intervals, figured bass, secondary seventh chords.

Fifth omitted, root doubled   Third omitted, root doubled

● sevenths. See intervals.

● sextet. A composition for six voices or instruments. See groups. Variant spelling: sextette. Variant form: sestet. Pronunciation: sĕks-tĕt; musicians often use sĕks-tĕt.

● sextolet. Same as sextuplet.

● sextuplet. Six notes of equal length performed in the time of four of the same kind.

● sf, sfz. Abbreviation for sforzando.

●† sforzando. A sudden accent, applying only to the tone or *chord under (or over) which this word, or usually its abbreviation sf, sfz, or fz, or ＞ appears. The symbol in common practice usually indicates a slightly lighter accent than sforzando, although theoretically it is equivalent.

It cannot be too strongly emphasized that sforzando not only applies to just a single chord or tone, but also that it is purely relative in intensity; that

It is possible to divide a sextuplet into three groups of two notes or two groups of three. The distribution can be readily shown with sextuplet sixteenth-notes in this manner:

Some musicians maintain that only the former (three groups of two) is the true sextuplet, that the other should be called double triplet. This fine distinction is by no means universally accepted. Variant form: sextolet. See also triplets, irregular groupings.

is, it indicates a sound that is slightly louder than those which precede and follow. The result may not necessarily be genuinely loud; when occurring in a passage marked pp the indicated notes would be only p, or mp at the most. For a sforzando on two or more chords or tones in succession, the sf must be placed under each.

A stronger accent is indicated by sff, sffz, ffz, fffz, sfffz, etc., but even these are still relative.

The circumstance that the term is not permanent (that it does not hold good until contradicted) and also that it is relative is illustrated in this passage from the second movement of Beethoven's Piano Sonata in G (op. 14, no. 2):

Synonyms: <u>forzando</u>, <u>forzato</u>, <u>sforzato</u>, <u>accent</u>, > ∧ (see symbols). There is no antonym in general use, although in the Solesmes interpretation of *Gregorian chant there is an effect indicated by a note in small type (about the size of a *grace-note) which signifies a tone softer than those which precede or follow, the result therefore being about equivalent to the opposite of <u>sforzando</u>.

(Related English word: <u>force</u>.)
Plural: <u>sforzandos</u> or <u>sforzandi</u>.
Compare <u>fp</u>.

● shadings.   See <u>nuances</u>; see also <u>dynamic marks</u>, <u>crescendo</u>, <u>diminuendo</u>.

● shake.   Same as <u>trill</u>.

● shank.   Same as <u>crook</u>.

● shanty.   Variant spelling of <u>chantey</u>.

● shaped notes.   A method of printing vocal music, especially *hymn-tunes, with note-heads of various shapes--triangular, square, diamond, etc.   The notes are printed on an ordinary five-line *staff, with the usual *clefs.   The shape adopted represents the *syllable name of the note; the purpose is increased facility in sight-reading.   This type of notation was devised for persons with little skill or technical knowledge of music.

Shaped notes apparently are purely an American invention, devised in Philadelphia in 1798.   They are still widely used in the South and in Texas, but have long been obsolete elsewhere.
Synonym: <u>buckwheat notes</u>.

● sharp.   (1, noun) The character ♯ It raises the pitch of a note one *half-step.   It may occur in a *key-signature or as an *accidental.

A note affected by a sharp is said to be "sharped" (not "sharpened").

For explanation of the sharps placed above notes (rather than in front of them) that are found in old choral music, see <u>musica ficta</u>.

(2, adjective).   Slightly too high in pitch.   (Verb) To play or sing too high in pitch, especially to become progressively a trifle higher and higher as the performance continues (in singing).   Antonym: <u>flat</u> (2). See also <u>intonation</u>.

● shawm.   A primitive and obsolete woodwind instrument played with a double reed, having a harsh *tone-color. The shawm is the ancestor of the modern oboe and bassoon.

● sheet music.   A piece of sheet music normally consists of a single composition, on as many pages as are necessary, but without stiff covers.   Collections of many compositions, with either stiff or paper covers, are called <u>albums</u>, <u>collections</u>, or <u>volumes</u> in contradistinction.

● shifted accent.   (1) The accenting of a beat that is normally weak, either by performing it louder than the strong beat, or (especially) by means of *syncopation.   The accent seems to be temporarily transferred from the normal beats to others.

(2) Occasionally a *figure will be repeated in such a manner that each appearance causes the *accent to fall at a different point; the term <u>shifted accent</u> is again applied to this phenomenon.   It is frequent in contemporary music, where it appears as a revival of a device that can be traced back to

the fourteenth or even thirteenth century. Musicians often remark that the bar-lines are "concealed" or that the rhythmic pattern "quarrels with the bar-lines."

See also polyrhythm, isorhythm.

● shofar. A wind instrument made from a ram's horn which has been played in Jewish synagogues at the New Year's service since ancient times. It is a primitive type of *bugle (which in turn is a primitive type of *trumpet or *cornet).

It is probably the most ancient of all instruments still used essentially in its original form.

● short score. See reduction.

●† siciliano. An Italian dance, originating in Sicily, in rather slow 6-8 or 12-8 time. The rhythmic figure ♩♫ is very characteristic. The style is graceful, gently lilting.

Plural: sicilianos.
Variant form: siciliana.

● side drum. The snare drum.

● sight-reading. Performance without previous practicing, without previous study of the printed notation, yet with a reasonable degree of accuracy. Emphasis is more on the instantaneous comprehension of the notation than on the avoidance of "mistakes" in manipulating the instrument.

Ability in sight-reading is a severe test of *musicianship.

Sight-reading is, strictly, not a synonym for *sight-singing (solfeggio).

Synonym: prima vista.

● sight-singing. A course taught in *conservatories and the music de-

partments of colleges, consisting of singing various passages and exercises, the purpose being to improve ability in reading music notation and to develop the musical ear. It is well to mention that the singing is usually not actually "at sight" (that is, completely without chance for preparation), for as a rule time is allowed for the student to practice the material outside class.

The reason why this material is sung rather than played on an instrument is that in singing the person is obliged to make the tones himself--he must hear them before he sings them--while in playing an instrument, the tones are automatically made for him; that is, he may have utterly no idea how a passage sounds, but if he resorts to his instrument, it will faithfully produce the correct pitches, every one of which might be a complete surprise to him. Hence the ability to sing at sight is perhaps the surest of all tests of *musicianship.

Sight-singing is by no means a course in "singing" in the sense of voice-development or voice culture.

Synonyms: solfeggio (Italian), solfège (French).

Compare sight-reading.
See also syllables, ear-training.

● signature. The *key-signature, *time-signature, or both.

● signs. See symbols.

●† silenzio. Silence. Sometimes substituted for *G. P.

● similar motion. Movement in the same direction between two voices or instruments, but without the harmonic *interval remaining constant. It differs from parallel motion in that in the latter all the intervals are of the same basic name. However, many musicians and theorists make no distinction between similar and parallel motion, generally

Similar motion   Parallel motion

using the latter term to cover
both types. The distinction verges
on "splitting hairs."
    Synonym: direct motion.
    See contrary, parallel, and
oblique motion.

●† simile. Continue in a similar
manner. Thus in the following

the accented first beat, the rolled
second beat, and the staccato third
beat are to be continued, without
the necessity of marking each appearance.
    Abbreviation: sim.
    Variant form: simili.
    Synonym: segue (2), come sopra.
    Pronunciation: accent first sylla-
ble.

● simple melody instruments. This
name is employed here to denote
the instruments which work on the
principle of the penny whistle--very
simple types of *recorder or *flute--
used in teaching music to young
children in elementary schools. These
instruments are simple enough that
a child of average intelligence, and
with only a modest amount of musical talent, can learn to play them.
They are so easy to blow that any
person can produce a tone on one
immediately, at the first attempt.
Recorders are used in some schools,
but in general they are too complex
for the young and not necessarily
talented children for whom the simple
melody instruments are really intended.
    There are a number of instru-
ments of this type, of varying merit
as to ease of playing, *tone-quality,
and *intonation; they are manufactured under such trade names as
Tonette, Song Flute, Melody Flute,
Flutophone, Symphonet, and others.
    The name pre-band instruments is
often employed, but it must be emphasized that by no means all teachers

regard these as a preparation for
*band (1).

● simple meter. A term which has
unfortunately been used by various
*theorists with two entirely different
meanings, both placed in opposition
to compound meter.
    In one usage, the term indicates
those *meters divisible by 2 and 4
but not by 3, that is, meters with 2,
4, or 8 beats.
    In the other usage, it denotes meters
with 2 or 3 beats, reasoning that 4
beats is nothing but a double 2, 6
beats a double 3, 8 beats a twice-
doubled 2, 9 beats a triple 3, 12
beats a twice-doubled 3, etc.
    See also compound meter.

●† simplice. Same as semplice.

●† sin', † sino. Until. Thus, cresc.
poco a poco sin' al ff means "getting
louder little by little until ff (very
loud) is reached."
    Synonym: fino.

●† sinfonia. The Italian word meaning *symphony. However it was formerly synonymous with *overture.
    Plural: sinfonie.
    Pronunciation: English, stress fo;
Italian, stress ni.

●† sinfonietta. (1) A short *symphony
(1).
    (2) A small *orchestra. Synonym:
chamber orchestra.
    (The spelling "symphonietta" is in-
correct.)

● single line instrument. Same as
one-line instrument.

● Singspiel. A German comic opera
containing some spoken dialogue,
usually less serious than the French
*opéra comique (which it most closely

resembles), but more so than the English *ballad opera. Mozart's Magic Flute, Beethoven's Fidelio, and Weber's Der Freischütz, though hardly true examples, were influenced by the Singspiel.
Plural: singspiels (English) or Singspiele (German).
Pronunciation: sĭng-shpēl (the s almost like z).

● † sino. See sin'.

● sistrum. An ancient instrument of the percussion type, consisting of an oval-shaped metal frame across which a number of parallel horizontal metal rods are loosely mounted (through holes) in such a way that they rattle against the frame when the instrument is shaken by its handle.
Plural: sistrums or sistra.

● "Six, the." A group of French composers who were especially active as a group immediately after the First World War. They represent a reaction against both *Romanticism and *Impressionism. In their strong espousal of *Neo-Classicism, "The Six" both influenced, and were influenced by, Stravinsky. Satire and parody often crop up in their works. Erik Satie (1866-1925) was their artistic mentor, although not officially one of the group.
"The Six" did not function long as a group; they soon went their independent ways. The members are: Darius Milhaud (1892-   ), who has lived partly in Brazil and the United States, Arthur Honegger (1892-1955), who although born in France was a Swiss citizen, Francis Poulenc (1899-1963), Germaine Tailleferre (1892-   ), one of the few women who has ever achieved importance as a composer, Georges Auric (1899-   ), and Louis Durey (1888-   ). The first three of these are by far the most important.

● six-four chord. A *triad in second *inversion, i.e., with the fifth as the lowest tone. The name is derived from the circumstance that the *root of the chord is thus located

a fourth above the *bass (1) tone, while the third is a sixth above the bass tone. The usual *figured bass indication is $\frac{6}{4}$, more completely $\frac{8}{6}$.

● sixteenth-note. See time-values.

● 16va. See 15ma.

● sixth, chord of the. A *triad in first inversion, i.e., with the third in the *bass (1). The name is derived from the circumstance that the *root of the chord is a sixth above the bass tone. The usual *figured bass indication is 6, more completely
$\frac{6}{3}$, $\frac{6}{6}$, $\frac{6}{3}$, or $\frac{8}{6}$.

● sixths. See intervals. For the expression double sixths, see double (5).

● six-tone scale. A synonym sometimes applied to the *whole-tone scale and sometimes to the *hexatonic scale.

● sixty-fourth-note. See time-values.

● skip. Same as leap.

● † slancio. Outburst, impulse, enthusiasm. Con slancio, impulsively.
Pronunciation: accent first syllable.

● † slargando. Same as allargando.

● sleigh bells. An indefinite pitch *percussion instrument consisting of several little hollow but perforated metal spheres, each with a tiny metal ball inside. The individual spheres are usually attached to a piece of leather. The sound is high-pitched, cheery, jingling, and frosty.
It was once customary to mount these on horse-drawn sleighs, or to put them on the horse's harness.
Synonyms: harness bells, jingles.
German: Schellen.

● slentando. Growing slower. (It would seem that this rarely-used term might better be replaced by the more familiar ritardando or rallentando.)

● slide. (1) An elongated U-shaped

metal extension-device used on the
*trombone to secure the results
provided on the other *brass instruments by the *valves. It is
used in seven different positions.
The farther the slide is pushed
forward (away from the player),
the lower becomes the pitch obtained from any given *open tone.
The effect of the use of the slide
is as follows:

first position (or open), the slide
being pulled in as far as it will
go--the "open" tone

second position, the slide being
pushed out a short way--lowers
pitch a half-step

third position--lowers pitch a
whole step

fourth position--lowers pitch a
minor third

fifth position--lowers pitch a
major third

sixth position--lowers pitch a
perfect fourth

seventh position, the slide being
pushed out as far as it will go--
lowers pitch a *tritone

A slide *trumpet and slide *cornet
have also been invented, but they are
not used in the orchestra or band.

(2) A synonym for glissando (1, 2)
or portamento (1).

● slide trombone. The layman's
name for the *trombone.

● slur. A curved line connecting two
or more notes, not all of the same pitch,
indicating that they are to be performed
*legato. (See first music diagram below.)

The physical appearance of the slur
and the *tie is the same: each is a curved
line. Their function, however, is quite
different.

A tie may occur within the course of a
slur. (See second music diagram.)

When more than two notes are slurred
together, a single slur runs from the first
note to the last. (Compare the use of the
tie in this respect.) (See third diagram.)

Deep   riv - er   My

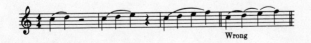

Wrong

When two *chords are to be slurred together, it is unnecessary to connect all the tones with slurs; one will do.

Slurring in vocal music is done to a single syllable of a word or to a one-syllable word.

For slurs and dots, see portamento

Fussy   Satisfactory

When parts for two instruments or voices are written on the same staff, it is, however, safer to indicate each part with its own separate slurs, unless the parts are identical in rhythm (that is, if they are *"duetting").

(2) (which is better termed portato), or staccato (3).

● small clarinet. The E-flat clarinet.

●† smorzando. Theoretically, the same as diminuendo or decrescendo.

Any two voices or instruments

Vague (does the lower instrument slur?)   Unmistakable

In writing for voices (but not for instruments) the joining of eighth-notes and shorter values by a *cross-beam is automatically an indication of legato, and slurs are unnecessary, although their employment is not incorrect. (See both A examples below.) Slurs should be used when eighths or shorter values are mingled with quarter-notes or longer values, or when several groups on crossbeams are all sung to one syllable or word (see the B example).

However, usage in some cases--but by no means all--would seem to indicate a very rapid diminuendo (the equivalent of diminuendo molto); in others it would seem to add the element of retarding (the equivalent of diminuendo e ritardando).

The literal meaning is "extinguishing."
Abbreviation: smorz.
Variant form: smorzato.
Synonyms: morendo, perdendosi.

● snare drum. An indefinite pitch

Com - fort ye   my peo - ple

*percussion instrument, perhaps the most commonly-used of all drums. Its rather shallow cylindrical shell is made of metal. There is a parchment head on both ends of the shell and across the diameter of the lower head are stretched several wire or gut strings called snares which vibrate when the player strikes the upper head (called batter head) with his two light wooden sticks.

The sound of the snare drum is very dry, crisp, crackling, and almost nervous. Single tones are rarely used, but short groups and *rolls (2) are tremendously effective.

Since the instrument is of indefinite pitch, its music is often notated on a one-line staff.

It is possible, through adjusters on the side of the drum, to put the snares out of use, giving a deeper and quite altered *tone-color. Another unusual effect is described under rim shot. Still other effects are obtained by hitting the rim, or by tapping the two sticks together, the drum itself out of use *Dance band players sometimes strike the instrument with a small wire brush.

A variant on this instrument has a wooden shell and is much deeper; this type is usually called the *military drum, field drum, or parade drum.
Synonym: side drum; also (undesirable) trap drum.
Italian: tamburo, tamburo piccolo, or tamburo militare. German: Militärtrommel or kleine Trommel. Spanish: caja clara. French musicians recognize two types of snare drum, the smaller being called caisse claire, the larger, tambour militaire or simply tambour. Ravel, in Daphnis and Chloe, writes for both types.

●† soave. Suave, smooth. Dolce is more or less synonymous.
Variant form: soavemente.

● soft and loud. See dynamic marks.

● soft pedal. The pedal farthest to the left on the piano, sometimes

called una corda pedal. The sign for its employment is *una corda, occasionally *due corde (1); for its release, *tre corde or tutte le corde. (The use of con sordino and senza sordino, respectively, is rare and undesirable.) Pianists often utilize the soft pedal in passages where the printed music does not specifically call for it; that is, its employment is somewhat at the player's discretion, and hence is not quite analogous to the use of *mutes with string and brass instruments.

●† soggetto. Subject.
Plural: soggetti.

●† sognando. Dreamily.

●† solenne. Solemn.

● sol-fa syllables. See syllables.

● solfège (French). Same as sight-singing.
Pronunciation: sōl-fĕzh.

● solfeggio. (1) Same as sight-singing.
(2) A short exercise, without words, used to develop skill in sight-singing. Compare vocalise.
Plural: solfeggios or solfeggi.
Pronunciation: sŏl-fĕj⁻ō or sŏl-fĕj-yō.

● solmization. Singing by *syllables.
Variant spelling: solmisation.
Pronunciation: sŏl-mĭ-zā⁻shŏn.

● solo. (1) A composition for one voice or instrument, with or without accompaniment. See groups.
(2) A prominent passage for one voice or instrument during the course of a composition. The passage may be quite long or may consist of only a few notes. Synonym (undesirable): "the lead."
(3) In music performed with groups (sections) of voices or instruments taking a single part--such as a *chorus or the string section of an *orchestra-- a passage intended to be performed by just a single voice or instrument is marked solo. The re-entrance of the entire section is denoted by *tutti, meaning "all." If the remainder of the section is provided with notes to

perform while the solo is in progress, this part is marked gli
*altri, meaning "the others."

(4) In the *score or *parts of
an orchestral composition, a
direction to bring out a passage
rather prominently; about the equivalent of *marcato. The passage so
marked may not be the chief
melody, but it is definitely something that should not be allowed to
be submerged.
Variant form (for usages 2 and
3): sola, of which the plural is
sole.
Plural: solos or soli.

● solo cantata.   See cantata.

● solo concerto.   A name sometimes
applied to the *concerto to distinguish it from the *concerto grosso.

● soloist.   A person featured in a
*solo; a musician whose part (played
or sung) is not duplicated in any
other voice or instrument.

●† sommo.   Very high, highest,
extreme.

●† sonata.   (1; present meaning)
A composition in several movements
--usually three or four--written for
piano, or for piano with another
instrument (e.g. violin), also occasionally for two pianos, for piano
*four hands, or for organ.   (There
are a few sonatas for an instrument
such as violin without accompaniment.) Sonatas written for piano
and another instrument are often
called by the name of the latter;
that is, a sonata for violin and piano
is often called a "violin sonata" for
short; but since the two instruments
are normally of equal importance,
one should avoid thinking of the
violin-part in this case as a "solo"
or of the piano-part as a mere
"accompaniment."
The present type of sonata has
been a musical form of importance
ever since the middle of the eighteenth century.   The only difference
between the sonata and the *concerto,
*string quartet (and other chamber-
music works), and the *symphony

is the *medium; they are all identical
in *form, the latter being described
under sonata-types.
The following meanings are now
obsolete:
(2) In the early and middle eighteenth century the term sonata was
applied to short one-movement compositions.   Domenico Scarlatti
(1685-1757) wrote many examples for
the harpsichord (or piano), the form
normally being *binary, i.e., two
part form (AB).   (Actually, Scarlatti
used the title Esercizi, meaning
"Exercises.")   For all practical purposes, this meaning of sonata is
almost equivalent to piano piece. The
term "Little Sonata" is occasionally
applied today.
(3) In the early seventeenth century,
when pure instrumental music was
first emerging, the term sonata was
applied to any composition written
entirely for instruments, in contrast
to those for voices, which were termed
cantata (literally, "sung").   There was
no connection with *form.   Sonata
literally means "sounded," though
strictly "sounded with a bow"; however this last-named distinction was
soon lost.   In this sense, sonata
might well be translated "sound
piece."
(4) During the later *Baroque
period the term was used to indicate
compositions in several movements
which are described under sonata da
camera and sonata da chiesa. Synonym: Baroque sonata.
The sonata in music is by no means
the counterpart of the sonnet in literature.
See also trio sonata (1).

● sonata-allegro form.   In the *symphony, *string quartet and other *chamber-music works, *concerto, and
*sonata--that is, those forms classified
in this volume as *sonata-types--at
least one *movement is written in a
form known as sonata-allegro form,
otherwise the work does not live up to
its title.
Many *overtures are also in this
form, though of course they have but
a single movement.   The sonata-
allegro pattern naturally appears now
and again in compositions of other

types, occasionally even in nominally "free forms.

Sonata-allegro form is tremendously flexible. There are two extremes which might be regarded as the minimum and maximum that may occur. However there are quite a few fine compositions which are exceptions to any scheme given below, although the presence of *development (as will be stated later) is indispensable.

Minimum. The very least that a sonata-allegro movement could contain and still fulfill the form by definition is:

first theme) collectively called
second theme) the exposition (usually enclosed in *repeat-signs)

*development
repetition of first theme) collec-
repetition of second theme) tively
    called the recapitulation

Principal subject and subordinate subject (subsidiary subject) are synonyms for first theme and second theme, respectively. Free fantasia, development group, and working-out are synonyms for development. Reprise, restatement, and re-exposition are synonyms for recapitulation. It should not be inferred that the two themes always consist strictly of a single idea apiece; sometimes one or both will be a group if ideas. For this reason some musicians believe that first group and second group are often more accurate designations than first theme (or principal subject) and second theme (or subordinate subject), respectively.

The exposition is normally enclosed in *repeat-signs, especially in *Classical and *Romantic works, though probably more often than not these are ignored in performance. In the very early examples the portion containing the development and recapitulation is also enclosed in repeats, these almost invariably being ignored in present-day performance.

Key-Relationships. In the exposition, the two themes are always in different keys. (Usually the composer does not change the *key-signature; instead he writes in the necessary *accidentals.) The "classic" key-relationship is: if the work is in a major key, the second theme is in the key of the *dominant; if it is in a minor key, the second theme is in the *relative major. In the recapitulation, however, both themes are usually in the principal key; with sonatas in minor mode the second theme as a rule is in the *tonic major key, but it may appear in altered form so as to be in the principal (i.e., minor) key. Beginning with Beethoven, composers often used keys other than the dominant for the first appearance of the second theme; however the key of the *subdominant has always been avoided, since its relaxing effect would be disastrous at the point in question. During the Romantic period, in the recapitulation the second theme often appeared in some key other than the principal key, yet in a different one from that in which it was stated in the exposition. It is perhaps apparent that the recapitulation of the themes is often far from "literal," in fact often decidedly varied.

In a few examples there is only one real theme. At the point where the second theme would be expected, and in the key in which it would be expected, the first theme appears again, in altered form, of course.

An orthodox outline as the keys involved would be as follows:

		If in major	If in minor
first theme) exposition		C	a
second theme)		G	C
development		--	--
first theme) recapitulation		C	a
second theme)		C	A (possibly a)

(In the foregoing, capital letters indicate major keys, lower-case letters, minor keys.)

Optional Elements. Additional elements which may be present are:

(A) An introduction. This is often in a slow *tempo. It may foreshadow a theme to follow; or it may have thematic material of its own, in which case this material may appear in the development section for treatment.

(B) An *episode or connecting passage may link the two themes.

(C) There may be a third theme, usually called the closing theme, which is normally in the same key as the second subject. As a rule it is rather short.

(D) A *codetta may appear in place of the closing theme.

(E) The movement almost invariably ends in a *coda; this may be only two or three chords, or it may be an extended passage of four or five minutes' duration, almost like a second development.

The average sonata-allegro movement naturally falls somewhere between the two extremes. The fact that no two are quite alike has kept the form alive through about two hundred years and notably supports the thesis that "the form of every composition is unique."

Maximum. A summary of the form in its greatest amplitude would be:

	If in major	If in minor
introduction (perhaps slow)	C	a
first theme) exposition	C	a
episode (modulating)) (usually	--	--
second theme) enclosed in	G	C
closing theme or codetta) repeat-signs)	G	C
development	--	--
first theme	C	a
episode (probably will not modulate))	--	--
second theme) recapitulation	C	A (or a)
closing theme or codetta)	C	A (or a)
coda	ending in C	ending in A or a

Where Found. If only one movement is in sonata-allegro form, it is usually the first (hence the synonym first-movement form). Additional movements may also be cast in this pattern, especially the *finale (last movement), but the slow movement is rarely in sonata-allegro form, the *minuet or *scherzo practically never. As the term sonata-allegro suggests, it is a form associated with quick or fairly quick *tempos.

Development. The most important element in sonata-allegro form is by far the development, despite the fact that mention of it in the foregoing tabulation may appear casual. (Ref-

erence should be made to the entry development.) Occasionally new material is introduced during the development section, the first movement of Beethoven's Third ("Eroica") Symphony being a well-known instance of its appearance. The practice is, however, distinctly exceptional.

By definition, the term sonata-allegro form requires the presence of development. There is no such thing as a real sonata-allegro movement without a development section; instead it would be *sonatina form.

Additional Remarks. Perhaps it would be well to point out that the "first theme" is not necessarily the first theme that appears, for if the introduction has its own theme, that will of course be the first theme heard, but the "first theme," as that term applies in form, is the principal subject.

An important variant on sonata-allegro form is found in the first movement of many concertos, and is known as *double sonata-allegro, concerto-allegro, or concerto-sonata form.

Sonata-allegro form was developed during the early *Classical period, especially by those composers known as *"Mannheim Group." Many musicians unhesitatingly term it the greatest of all musical forms.

Synonyms: sonata form, first movement form.

●† sonata da camera. An important type of *Baroque and *Rococo *chamber-music composition, being similar in *form to the Baroque *suite (1). The most frequent medium is two violins, cello, and keyboard instrument (usually harpsichord or piano); the sonata da camera is hence one of the curiously-named *trio sonata (1) forms.

It is advisable to mention that the sonata da camera does not always bear that title; often it is called simply Sonata. The form and medium identify it, not the title. It antedates the sonata in the present meaning of the word. Often all the *movements are in the same key.

Plural: sonate da camera.

Synonym: chamber sonata, Baroque sonata.

Compare sonata da chiesa.

Pronunciation: in camera accent first syllable.

●† sonata da chiesa. One of the important *chamber-music types of the *Baroque period. It was often written for the so-called *trio sonata (1) combination--which actually used four instruments--most frequently two violins, cello, and keyboard instrument (harpsichord, piano, or organ). Other examples are for one instrument, or for a keyboard instrument plus another instrument, e.g. violin.

Although the sonata da chiesa eventually evolved into the present *sonata (1), it is not written in the characteristic form we know today, being a considerably older form. The movements do not fall in the typical *sonata-type sequence; they are often all in the same key, and there is no movement in *sonata-allegro form for the simple reason that that form had not yet appeared at the time the sonata da chiesa was at its height. The movements are usually not very long.

Frequently there are four movements in the order: slow, fast, slow, fast; often movements 1-2 and movements 3-4 are joined together without pause (see attacca) so that there is only one complete stop during the course of the work--at the end of the second movement. The third movement is the only one likely not to be in the basic key, the key of the *relative minor being quite common.

The sonata da chiesa was intended for use at church services. Hence it is usually more dignified than the *sonata da camera, but the occasionally-made statement that it is "always" without movements of a dance-like character is untrue.

The spirit and form of the music often recall those of the *concerto grosso.

It is important to mention that a sonata da chiesa does not of necessity bear that title. Often it is called merely Sonata. Its form, medium, and style, not its title, identify it.

Plural: sonate da chiesa.

Synonym: church sonata, Baroque sonata.

Compare sonata da camera.

● sonata form. See sonata-allegro form.

For the plan or order of movements in the sonata, symphony, concerto, and in chamber-music works, see sonata-types.

● sonata-rondo form. Same as rondo-sonata form.

● sonata-types. The term "sonata-types" is used here to include several important types of composition which are essentially the same as to *form, but which differ in *medium. These are:

(A) The sonata. Written for piano, or for piano and another instrument (e.g. violin and piano). There are also a few sonatas for organ, for two pianos, and for one instrument such as cello or violin without accompaniment.

(B) The concerto. Written for a solo instrument and orchestra, e.g. piano and orchestra, violin and orchestra, etc. There are a few concertos for two solo instruments and orchestra, called double concertos. The concerto and the *concerto grosso should not be associated in mind, since the latter is not one of the types discussed here. (However, see concertante.) (The *concerto for orchestra should be considered a separate form.)

(C) The string quartet and other chamber-music types. Written for a small group of instruments, three to nine (occasionally more) in number, though

most frequently three, four, or five.
(D) The symphony. Written for
orchestra. There are also a few
symphonies for band.

It hardly seems necessary to
point out that rare exceptions to
the foregoing can be found, many of
which might in all fairness be
described as misnomers, for example
the so-called "symphonies" for organ which are of course really
sonatas.

Works falling into the "sonata-
types" classification are not really
one composition, but a group of
compositions, the individual parts
being called *movements; of these
there are generally three or four.
Usually each movement is a complete piece quite performable by
itself. The several movements are
allocated so as to secure variety--
so as to play each one off against
its mates--so as to be mutually
complementary. The conspicuous
point of difference among the movements is their *tempo (rate of
speed).

Plan (Order) of the Movements.
If there are three movements, their
order as to tempo is normally:
    First movement: fast (may have
      a slow introduction)
    Second movement: slow
    Third movement: fast
If there are four movements, their
order as to tempo is most frequently:
    First movement: fast (may have
      a slow introduction)
    Second movement: slow
    Third movement: medium or fast
    Fourth movement: fast
However, quite frequently (about one
example in three) the order of tempos in a four-movement work will
be:
    First movement: fast (may have a
      slow introduction)
    Second movement: medium or fast
    Third movement: slow
    Fourth movement: fast
Here the order of the two middle
movements is reversed, as compared with the preceding outline.

Obviously there are a number of
works whose movements are in an
order that is an exception to any of
the foregoing outlines, modern works

especially.

Examples with only two movements
may be found, particularly among
sonatas, and examples with five movements are not extremely uncommon,
particularly among chamber-music
works and symphonies; however
Beethoven's String Quartet in C-sharp
Minor (op. 131), with its seven connected movements, is distinctly unusual, even unique.

The last movement may always be
called the finale, even when there are
only three movements. On occasion
it may, like the first movement, have
a slow introduction (e. g. Symphony
No. 1 by Brahms).

The concerto almost invariably has
just three movements. Brahms's
Second Piano Concerto (in B-flat major), which has four, is a notable exception; Lalo's Symphonie Espagnole
for violin and orchestra (therefore
actually a violin concerto), with its
five movements, is both a rare exception and a misnomer.

The movement marked "medium or
fast" in the foregoing outlines is
normally either a *minuet or a *scherzo;
if the former, the medium tempo applies; if the latter, the fast tempo.
Since the minuet is always in 3-4 time,
the scherzo usually so, at least one
movement of the types under discussion (usually the third but often the
second) will bear a 3-4 time-signature.
(Naturally others may have the same
time-signature without being minuets
or scherzos.) The use of the minuet
tended to disappear about the time that
dance went out of fashion. Beethoven
is the first composer who frequently
(though not always) replaced it with a
scherzo; however, he by no means
"invented" the scherzo, as superficial
books have sometimes stated. Occasionally the minuet-or-scherzo movement is replaced by some other type
of dance, or (especially in Brahms's
works) by music almost in the character
of an *intermezzo (2, 4).

It will be seen that the minuet-or-
scherzo movement is the "extra" one
which distinguishes the four-movement
works from those with three. It is
usually the shortest movement.

The expressions "fast" and "slow"
in the foregoing outlines must be given

the broadest possible interpretation; a "fast movement" may be anything from slightly fast to extremely fast, and a "slow movement" anything from slightly slow to extremely slow. (See tempo marks.)

Audiences frequently applaud at the end of each movement of a concerto, but with the remaining "sonata-types"--and perhaps even with the concerto--it is preferable if applause occurs only after the last movement is finished.

Title Key. The key which is mentioned in the title of such a work ("Symphony in D Minor," "String Quartet in A Major," etc.) is that of only the first movement; there are examples in which no other movement is basically in this key.

Presence of Sonata-Allegro Form. It is of highest importance to point out that no example can be considered orthodox unless one movement is written in *sonata-allegro form (sometimes called sonata-form or first-movement form). As may be gathered from the last of these synonyms, it is usually the first movement. (It is often also the longest.) Additional movements may be in sonata-allegro form, especially the *finale. The slow movement occasionally is also cast in this pattern, but there seems to be no example wherein it is the only sonata-allegro movement. The minuet or scherzo, however, is rarely if ever in this form.

The sonata-allegro form is described under that heading.

Key-Relationship. The key-relationship of the various movements is important. It is not a matter of chance, but on the contrary is carefully planned.

The first and last movements are normally on the same tonality; that is, if the first movement is in the major mode the last will be in the same key; while if the first is in the minor mode the last will either be in the same key or in the *tonic major (e. g., first movement in A minor, last movement in A major).

The slow movement however is seldom in the basic key. If the composition is fundamentally in the major mode, this movement is most frequently in the key of the *subdominant (see key relationships), sometimes in the key of the *dominant. If the composition is basically in minor, the slow movement is often in the *relative major, often in the key of the *submediant major (i. e., subdominant of the relative major). However, none of these may be considered iron-bound rules; any closely-*related key may be considered normal, although a distant one is distinctly exceptional.

In the earlier examples (such as those by Haydn, Mozart, Beethoven, and their contemporaries) the minuet or scherzo generally occurs in the same key as the first and last movements. With later composers it may be in any closely-related key.

Usual Form of the Movements. As mentioned, the first movement is nearly always in sonata-allegro form. Naturally there are some exceptions, even in the *Classical period. For instance, Beethoven's so-called "Moonlight" Sonata for piano (op. 27, no. 2) opens with a slow movement, while the same composer's Sonata in A-flat (op. 26--with funeral march as the third movement) starts with a *theme and variations, a form which also turns up as the first movement of Mozart's Sonata in A for piano (*K. 331--with the so-called "Turkish March" as the finale). The fact that these three compositions are very well known should in no way obscure their exceptionalness.

Theme and variations form is common for the slow movement, as is ABA form. ABCA, ABABA, and ABACA are not unusual, nor is a monothematic form of long-drawn-out songlike character. Sonata-allegro form, as stated earlier, is rather unusual here. In general, the slow movement is least predictable as to form.

The minuet or scherzo movement nearly always falls into one of three patterns: ABA ("minuet and trio" or "scherzo and trio"), ABABA ("minuet with repeated trio" or "scherzo with repeated trio"), and ABACA ("minuet with two trios" or "scherzo with two trios"); the first is easily the commonest.

With the finale another sonata-allegro or a *rondo may be expected; variation form is a poor third in frequency.

Joining of Movements. Occasionally two or more movements may be joined together without pause. The direction for this, appearing at the close of the first of the affected movements, is attacca or more fully attacca subito, occasionally segue. A readily-accessible example may be found in what is probably the most familiar of all symphonies-- the Fifth Symphony by Beethoven-- where the third movement (scherzo) leads directly into the fourth in such a way as to make a stop utterly impossible--and incidentally with an effect that is almost overwhelmingly thrilling.

It might be well to mention that the term "sonata-types" was coined for use here. It is not a term in general employment, though it is convenient, as it eliminates the necessity for the common practice of giving an elaborate description of the sonata, then of describing the concerto as a "sonata for solo instrument and orchestra," the string quartet as a "sonata for two violins, viola, and cello," and the symphony as a "sonata for orchestra." However, the aptness of the foregoing descriptions is undeniable.

● sonatina. A short *sonata (1).
Variant form: sonatine.

● sonatina form. A *sonata-allegro movement that lacks a *development section, or one in which the development section is very short. Thus the form is:

introduction (optional, rare; may
            be slow)
first theme   )
second theme (in a related) expo-
            key)   ) sition
brief development (optional)
first theme   )
second theme (in main) recapitu-
            key)   ) lation
coda (optional)

The first movement of a *sonatina is normally in this form.

● song. Loosely, any composition that is sung.

More specifically, a song is a composition for one voice (occasionally for two) with piano (occasionally organ, orchestra, or a *chamber-music combination). The text may be sacred or secular, usually the latter; the form may be *strophic or *through-composed.

The application of this term to short compositions for *chorus, and to *arias in *operas, *oratorios, and *cantatas is undesirable; its application to instrumental works, as a synonym for piece or composition, though all to frequent, is a barbarism.

Songs are usually published in at least two editions, one for "high voice," meaning *soprano or *tenor, the other for "low voice," meaning *contralto or *bass; occasionally three or even four editions are available. It is apparent that these versions are in different *keys. Some editors and publishers identify the original key in a foot-note, so that the purchaser may be aware when his edition is a *transposed one. The transposing of songs from one key to another is foreseen and intended by the composer, the only exceptions being those written with a chamber-music group or orchestra, where reasons of various instrumental *ranges preclude this. When the key does not suit the singer, or where only one version is published, it may be necessary for the *accompanist to transpose the piano part.

It will be gathered from the foregoing that, unlike the operatic aria, the song may be sung by either a man or a woman, except when reasons of logic would seem to indicate otherwise; for example it would be absurd for a male singer to program Schubert's Gretchen am Spinnrade (Gretchen at the Spinning-Wheel).

Compare part-song.

See also art-song, folk-song, Lied, song without words.

● song-cycle. A *suite of *songs,

with some continuous thread of thought running through the text. The poems are usually, though not always, taken from the writings of a single author, indeed may even be a connected series of poems.

Beethoven's An die ferne Geliebte (To the Distant Beloved One) is usually considered the first song-cycle, although it more closely resembles a single song of unusual length. Schubert's Die Winterreise and Die schöne Müllerin, and Schumann's Dichterliebe and Frauen-liebe und Leben are well-known song-cycles.

● Song Flute. See simple melody instruments. A trade name.

● song form. A composition with the *form scheme ABA is said to be in song form or song form with trio (2), also known as (and further explained under) ternary form; in addition sometimes called aria form. Song form with double (or repeated) trio has the pattern ABABA; song form with two trios, ABACA. Both of the latter are sometimes called five-part form. Binary or two part song form has the pattern AB or AABB (see binary form).

Song form is by no means typical of *songs.

● song without words. A short in-strumental composition somewhat in the style of a *song. For all practical purposes, the title is almost meaning-less; it could be applied to practically any short instrumental composition of "melodious" character. Mendelssohn wrote 48 compositions for the piano with this title.

The existence of the term song without words complicates the applica-tion of an accurate name to a true song (for voice) that is devoid of words, a number of which have been written; how-ever in this case wordless song or *vocalise (2) is often used.

German: Lied ohne Worte. French: chant sans paroles or chanson sans paroles.

● songwriter. A composer of "popular " songs. The word songwriter is not in the vocabulary of serious musicians.

● sonority. (1) The quality of possessing a full, resonant, rich sound, rather than a weak, thin, or puny sound. Good carry-ing power is implied. See also acoustics (2).

(2) A name sometimes applied to the combination of tones that happen to be sounding as a chord at any given moment, including both those that are new and those that are being sustained. The "sonorities" in the following

B   ABC   C BBB   BAA   AAG F♯ G
G   GGG   G GGF♯ EEE   EDD D   D
D   DDE   D DED   CCC   ABC C   B
G   GGG   G GEE   AAG   F♯F♯DD G

example are shown below with letters.

● † sonoro. Sonorous, resonant; with a full, meaty, "well-nourished" tone. Variant form (French): sonore.

● sopra. Above. This term is sometimes used in *cross-hand passages for the keyboard instruments, indicating which hand should reach over the other.
Come sopra. As above, in the manner in which the passage was played on its first appearance. Sometimes used as a synonym for segue (2) and simile.

● † sopranino. A term applied to certain instruments indicating that they are of a very high range-- higher than soprano. Literally "little soprano."

● soprano. (1) The highest female voice. Its easy range is shown at A, the range expected of an artist at B.

See also treble (3).
(2) The highest tone in a *chord.

● † sordino. The *mute for a string or brass instrument.
Con sord., con sordino, con sordini, with mute(s).
Senza sord., senza sordino, senza sordini (occasionally levate sord., alzate sord., or via sord.), without mute(s).
In piano music, con sordino indicates use of the *soft pedal; for a better and more frequent term, see una corda.
Plural: sordini.
Abbreviation: sord.
Variant form: sordina.

● † sostenuto. Sustained. Properly means "sustaining the tone," but is sometimes used (not very desirably) as a synonym for *ritardando. When used in connection with a *tempo-indication (e.g. andante sostenuto) it suggests moderation.
Abbreviations: sost., sosten.
Variant forms: sostenente, sostenendo.

Soprano voices are of several distinct types. The lyric soprano possesses a light, sweet, "girlish" *tone-quality; the dramatic soprano is darker and much more powerful, suited to *opera; while the coloratura soprano is light in quality and extremely agile, being suited to brilliant music containing much technical display.
The voices of children are normally soprano in range, and somewhat similar to the lyric soprano in quality, though of course thinner and weaker in volume.
(Related English word: supreme.)
Compare mezzo-soprano.
Plural: sopranos or soprani.
Synonyms (obsolete): cantus, superius.

● sostenuto pedal. Same as middle pedal.
The sostenuto pedal is by no means the same thing as the sustaining pedal (see damper pedal).

● † sotto voce. In an undertone, subdued.
Abbreviation: s. v.
Variant form: sottovoce.
Synonym: mezza voce (2).
Antonyms: marcato, accentuato, en dehors, pronunziato, rilevato.

● sound board. In the piano, a large flat piece of wood placed back of the strings to create *resonance. If the sound board cracks, the tone-quality of the instrument is impaired.

● sound post. A small wooden post placed vertically on the inside of the violin, viola, cello, and double-bass, tightly fitted between the back and the belly. The exact location of the sound post has an important effect on the tone of the instrument, and its placement must be entrusted to an expert violin repair-man or violin builder.

● Sousaphone. A style of *tuba designed by the American band-master John Philip Sousa (1854-1932). The tubing surrounds the player and the *bell points forward, not upward. Its tone-quality has less "focus" and less definition than that of the ordinary instrument, but it is also a little less rough. It is easier to carry when marching than the usual type of tuba, since the weight of the instrument rests on the player's shoulders.
Synonym: helicon.

● spaces. See staff.

● Spanish guitar. The *guitar, in contradistinction to the *Hawaiian guitar.

● speaker key. The *octave key of a woodwind instrument.

● specifications. The exact group of stops, couplers, etc. that are found on any given organ are known as its specifications.
See organ.

● spell, spelling. Some musicians, especially teachers, use these words in referring to the notes that make up various *scales and *chords, indeed in speaking of letter-names in general. For example, instead of "The supertonic triad of E major consists of F-sharp, A, and C-sharp," they say "The supertonic triad of E major is spelled F-sharp, A, C-sharp."

●† spianato. Smooth, quiet.

●† spigliato. Prompt, easy.

● spinet. A one-manual keyboard instrument, similar to the harpsichord, but smaller.
This word is also incorrectly employed as the name of a certain style of upright piano--a usage which is misleading and an affectation as well. (Affectation is sometimes compounded by spelling it spinette.)
For all practical purposes, the virginal may be considered the same as the spinet. The virginal, however, was usually a portable instrument, and had a more delicate tone.

●† spirito. Spirit.
Pronunciation: accent first syllable.

●† spiritoso. Spirited (that is, somewhat animanted).
Synonym: con spirito.

● spiritual. A type of American religious folk-song. The majority originated among Negroes during the days of slavery, and may just possibly have been influenced by primitive African music. Others, called white spirituals, originated among white people and seem to have a strong English influence.

● Sprechstimme. A German term literally meaning "speaking voice," used to indicate a special form of singing that is half-way between speaking and ordinary singing. Passages to be performed in Sprechstimme are written on the staff, but as a rule the round *note-heads are replaced by crosses or by diamond-shaped notes, or crosses are placed through the stem, just above the note-head. (An example may be seen in the entry atonality.) Perhaps the best-known (and one of the earliest) instance of its employment is in Schoenberg's Pierrot Lunaire, written in 1912.
Synonym: Sprechgesang.
Pronunciation: shprĕk-shtĭm-mé.

● spurious titles. See sub-head "nicknames" under titles.

● SSA. First soprano, second

soprano, and alto. Used in designating the voice parts in choral music. The meaning of SSAA is apparent.

● Stabat Mater. Originally a thirteenth century Latin poem which is sometimes sung in *Gregorian chant at Catholic services. It is appropriate to Good Friday. The text has often been set to music, well-known examples being from the pens of Palestrina, Pergolesi, Rossini, Verdi, Dvořák, and others.

The opening words of the poem, translated, are: "The sorrowful mother stood at the foot of the cross. "

●† staccatissimo. See staccato. Abbreviation: staccatiss.

●† staccato. Detached, not connected together, separated. Tones performed staccato are not held for their full value; a rest equivalent to the unheld portion intervenes between each note and its successor.

There are three types of staccato.

(1) The ordinary type is indicated by placing a dot over or under each note, or by the indication stacc. or staccato. Each note is held approximately half its written value, the balance being an unwritten rest.

(2) The extreme type is indicated by placing a wedge ▼ over or under the note or by the indication stac-

catiss. or staccatissimo. Each note is held approximately one-fourth its written value, the remaining three-fourths being an unwritten rest. This if often called the wedge staccato or dash staccato.

(3) The mild type is indicated with both dots and slurs. Each note is held approximately three-fourths of its written value, the balance being an unwritten rest (except in the case of *string instruments, where there is no difference in effect between this and the ordinary staccato). This half-staccato effect is sometimes called portato or (incorrectly) portamento (2).

When a single note is to be held for full value during the course of a staccato passage, often a short line — is placed over or under the note, or the term tenuto ("held"), abbreviated ten., is used.

*Time-values longer than the quarter-note are seldom written staccato. *Dotted values (that is, notes followed by dots) are also rarely employed.

Non legato is not a synonym for staccato, despite the fact that it calls for a detached manner of playing. See non legato.

Abbreviation: stacc. Superlative: staccatissimo (abbreviation: staccatiss.). Antonym (which see): legato.

Types of staccato

● staccato dots. The dots placed over or under notes (preferably on the same side as the note-head, rather than on the side with the stem) to indicate staccato; term used in contradistinction to the type of dot placed after notes to increase their length by half. (For explanation of the latter, see dotted notes.)

● staff. The five lines and four spaces on which notes are written.

A staff

It will be observed that the lines are horizontal and equidistant. The spaces should be considered as much a part of the staff as the lines.

The lines and spaces are numbered from the bottom up, that is, the "first line" is the lowest one, the "first space" the space between the first line and the second, and so on. A note is said to be "on" a line or to be a "line note" when half of it extends above the line and half below, the line itself passing through the middle of the note. A note is said to be "on" or "in" a space or to be a "space note" when it occupies the space between two lines, barely touching the line above and the line below.

Notes higher than the space above the fifth line and lower than the space below the first line must be written on *leger lines.

When *Gregorian chants are written with *neumes they are usually notated on a staff with only four lines and three spaces; it is illustrated in the entry neumes.

The parts for *percussion instruments of indefinite pitch are often written on a one-line staff, for example:

Synonym: stave.
Plural: staffs or staves; the latter is the more frequent.

● staff-liner. An implement for drawing a complete *staff on a blackboard with a single motion of the hand. Five sticks of chalk are held in place by stiff wire holders projecting from the edge of a short flat piece of wood. Staff-liners are standard equipment for music classrooms.

Synonym: staff-ruler.

● stage band. (1) A group of instrumentalists who play on the stage (rather than in the *orchestra pit) as part of the action in an *opera. Three stage bands play simultaneously in the amazing *finale of Act I in Mozart's Don Giovanni; another plays in Act II while Don Giovanni eats supper.
   (2) A *dance band.

● stand. See Pult.

● stave. Same as staff.

● stem. The short, straight, vertical line which, together with the round *note-head, forms a note. If the stem is turned up, its lowest point touches the note-head on the right; if turned down, the highest point touches the note-head on the left. A stem turned up is sometimes called an "upstem," one turned down, a "downstem."

The *whole-note lacks a stem, also the *breve (2).

When music for two instruments or voices is written on one staff and both are to play or sing the same pitch at any point (see unison), the effect is indicated by supplying the note-head

A one-line staff

with two stems, one turned up and
one turned down. (See also a 2.)
Double-stemmed notes are also
used in piano compositions, chiefly
in material of accompanying or
subsidiary nature, to indicate certain notes that should be brought
out more prominently than the
surrounding notes, for instance to
indicate a *countermelody buried
in the accompaniment.

● † stentato.   Delayed; occasionally
substituted for ritardando or ritenuto.

● step.   (1) One of the tones in a
*scale; a degree of a scale.
(2) Same as whole-step.

● stepwise.   Same as diatonic.

● stereophonic sound.   An advanced
technique of sound-recording employing two (or more) microphones,
with an equal number of parallel
record-grooves or sound-tracks,
using an equal number of speakers
for reproduction.   Stereophonic
recording gives the effect of sounds
coming from various directions,
and greatly enhances the *fidelity
of the sound.   It is also called
binaural recording; the older method
is termed monaural or monophonic
(2) in contradistinction.
   Synonym (colloquial): stereo.
   See also phonograph.
   Pronunciation: stĕr-ė-ȯ-fŏn-ĭc or
stir-ė-ȯ-fŏn-ĭc.

● † steso.   Spread, relaxed, stretched
out.

● † stesso.   Variant form of istesso;
see l'istesso tempo.

● † stile, † stilo.   Style.

● stop.   (1, verb) Pressing the
fingers into their proper places on
the *fingerboard of a string instrument is known as stopping the
strings.   (Compare open strings.
See also double-stop.)
   (2, noun) The various sets (or
"ranks") of pipes in an organ are
called stops.   Each stop has its own

distinctive *tone-color.   Thus organists speak of the open diapason
stop, the salicional stop, the
melodia stop, etc.   (A list of these
will be found in the entry organ.)
The little tablet which is pressed
down, or the knob which is pulled
out in order to put any of these
ranks of pipes into action, is also
called a stop.   This is the usage
more familiar among laymen.
   The stops on the *harmonium throw
different sets of reeds into action.
   See also registration, specifications.
   (3, verb) The stopped tones of the
horn are discussed under horn.

● "Strad."   A violin made by Antonio
Stradivari (or Stradivarius) (1644-
1737).   See violin.

● strain.   (1) The sound of music;
usually plural (literary).
   (2) A section (usually of medium
length, about 16 or 32 measures)
within a larger composition, especially
a march.   Although no less a person
than Shakespeare uses this word (in
Twelfth Night)--apparently as a synonym for *phrase--its employment is
hardly desirable.

● † strascinando la voce.   Literally,
"dragging the voice"; indicates an
interval to be heavily *slurred.
   Variant form: strascicando la voce.

● street drum.   The military drum.

● † strepito.   Din, noise, uproar.
   Pronunciation: accent first syllable.

● † strepitoso.   Impetuous, boisterous,
noisy.   A certain degree of *accelerando is also implied.

● stress.   See accent.

● † stretto.   (1) The passage often
found near the end of a *fugue in
which the *subject is overlapped on
itself.
   (2) Faster: a synonym for più mosso.
Variant form: stretta.
   (3) With compositions in which the
voices enter successively, stretto is
sometimes used in speaking of the
time-interval between entrances; for

example one might say that "the voices enter in close stretto."
(Related English words: strait, stretch.)
Plural: strettos or stretti.

●† stridente. Strident, harsh. (Literally, "screaming.")

● string bass. The double-bass.

●† stringendo. Gradually becoming faster. It is practically identical with *accelerando, the only difference being that stringendo is sometimes described as denoting an increase in agitation as well as in speed. It is canceled by a tempo which indicates an immediate return to the basic *tempo.
(Related English word: stringent.)
Abbreviation: string.
Synonyms: accelerando, affrettando.
Antonyms: rallentando, ritardando.

● string instruments, stringed instruments. All instruments equipped with either wire or gut strings are termed string (or stringed) instruments. Unlike the wind instruments, they can play two different notes (or more) simultaneously. (See double stop.)
String instruments played with a *bow are known as bowed strings; in this group are found the *violin, *viola, *cello, and *double-bass, plus the old *viols (see viola d'amore and viola da gamba), the *vielles, the rebec, the tromba marina, the crwth (crowd), and innumerable Oriental instruments. All the bowed instruments can also be plucked (picked); see pizzicato.
Those which can only be played by plucking, either with the fingers or with a *plectrum, are called plucked (or picked) strings; among these are the *harp, *guitar, *Hawaiian guitar, *banjo, *mandolin, *balalaika, all *lutes, *ukulele, *psaltery, vihuela, *zither, *autoharp, etc.
Those which are struck with hammers are called dulcimers; only that Hungarian instrument known as the *czimbalom (cymbalom) is even slightly familiar unless we classify

the *piano here.
To all these might be added a type in which the tone is produced by a revolving rosined wheel, the *hurdygurdy being an example.
Of these types the bowed strings are the most important and most versatile. Considered individually, their tone is so faint that entire sections of them must be used in the orchestra in order to preserve *balance with the *woodwind, *brass, and *percussion instruments, but the volume of which these large sections are capable in *fortissimo is formidable; on the other hand their *pianissimo can die away to utter inaudibility.
The resources of the bowed string instruments are much greater than those of the woodwind, brass, or percussion families. In addition to pizzicato, they can produce *harmonics (1), *col legno, *tremolos (1), sul ponticello, sul tasto (both described under sul), *double-stops, and many types of bow-strokes (see bowing); to these should be added the effects obtainable with *mutes (1) and (in the orchestra) by writing *divisi. Still another striking effect--purely orchestral--can be obtained by giving a temporary part to a single string instrument, the remainder of the section either continuing with other music or having *rests; see *solo (3). The difference in *tone-color between a single instrument and that of the full section is remarkable, although considerations of adequate balance are obviously of crucial importance. Parts of this type are indicated solo violin, solo viola, solo cello, etc., while the music for the remainder of the section is marked the others or gli altri. If the others of the section are silent while the solo instrument plays, the resumption of the full group is indicated by tutti (meaning "all").
The bowed string instruments are regarded the heart of the orchestra; their absence is the most prominent (but not the sole) difference between the orchestra and the *band. An orchestra made up entirely of these instruments is an eminently satisfactory *medium for which a very large literature is available (see string orchestra).
Before quitting the discussion of the

bowed string instruments, mention should be made that the customary numbering of the strings is in downward order; that is, the highest-pitched string is known as the "first string," the next highest as the "second," etc. Often the first string is called the *chanterelle.

Among the plucked instruments, only the harp is regularly used in the orchestra. The lute, however, has an important body of literature, while that for the guitar is small but still growing, albeit slowly. Certain plucked string instruments are also generically classed as *fretted instruments or plectral instruments.

The piano, as well as the harpsichord, spinet (virginal), and clavichord are sometimes classified as string instruments, sometimes as percussion, perhaps best of all as hybrids.

See also orchestra.

● string octet. A *chamber-music group consisting (usually) of four violins, two violas, and two cellos.
Compare double quartet (2).

● string orchestra. An orchestra composed entirely of *string instruments; they are usually those found in the string section of the full orchestra, i.e., first violins, second violins, violas, cellos, and double-basses, there always being several instruments (i.e., a section) to a part. The resources of the group are surprisingly rich and varied, its literature very large.

In the *Baroque era, a keyboard instrument (*harpsichord, *piano, or *organ) was normally employed in addition to the string instruments, its duty being to "realize" the *figured bass.

Many examples of the *concerto grosso are written for this medium.

The presence of a *harp or piano nowadays is not considered extraneous to the string orchestra, though this is the exception rather than the rule.

During the Baroque period, "orchestra" usually signified string orchestra, for the wind instruments were not well enough developed to be very useful.

The string orchestra is sometimes classified as a *chamber-music group, but hardly with accuracy, since it always employs a group of instruments (rather than a single player) to a part. The term chamber orchestra, as a synonym for string orchestra, is not very desirable. (See chamber orchestra for more exact meaning.)

● string quartet. (1) A *chamber-music group consisting of two violins, one viola, and one cello. It is by far the most frequently-used of all chamber-music groups.

(2) A composition in three or four movements (occasionally fewer or more) for the foregoing group. It is identical in *form with the *sonata, *concerto, and *symphony, but differs as to *medium. (See sonata-types.)

The use of the term string quartet or string quintet to denote the string section of the full orchestra--which may number sixty or more players, rather than four or five!--is regrettably frequent (especially in foreign usage) but obviously highly undesirable.

The term quartet alone is usually intended to mean string quartet; however due to lack of explicitness this usage can hardly be recommended.

● string quintet. (1) Two violins, two violas, and one cello.

(2) Two violins, one viola, and two cellos.

(3) There are a few examples for two violins, one viola, one cello, and one double-bass.

(4) There is at least one example for three violins, one viola, and one cello.

It will be apparent that the group denoted by string quintet is by no means as definite as that denoted by string quartet.

See also chamber-music.

(5) The term string quintet is sometimes used, particularly in Europe, to denote the string section of an orchestra, especially in connection with printed *scores, probably because these parts have the visual appearance of five instruments--first violin, second violin,

viola, cello, and double-bass. This
usage is thoroughly inaccurate, misleading, and illogical, indeed abomi-
nable.

● string sextet. Two violins, two
violas, and two cellos. Of course
other combinations are possible and
have doubtless been used, but the
foregoing is the most frequent and
best known.
    See also chamber-music.

● string trio. (1) Usually violin,
viola, and cello.
    (2) Occasionally two violins and
viola.
    (3) Occasionally--especially in
connection with the group of solo
instruments (*concertino (1) in the
*concerto grosso)--two violins and
cello.
    See also chamber-music.

● stroboscope. A device used for
determining the speed of a fast-
moving object. One type of stroboscope used in music shows whether
a phonograph turntable is revolving
at exactly 78 or exactly 33-1/3
revolutions per minute, rather than
a bit faster or slower. Another
type, electrically operated, shows
whether an instrument or voice is
sounding its tone exactly on pitch
rather than slightly "sharp" (2) or
"flat" (2).
    Synonym: Stroboconn (a trade
name).
    See also electronic instruments,
440, tuning, tuning-bar.

● stroke. Same as crossbeam.

● strophic. Having the same music
for all stanzas; used in speaking of
*songs, less commonly of *choral
compositions and *arias. *Folk-
songs, *hymns, and that type of
simple popular song commonly called
*"home-and-community song" or
"composed folk-song" (e.g. the songs
of Stephen Foster) are almost invariably strophic.
    Antonym: through-composed.
    Pronunciation: ströf-ĭk or strō-fĭk.

● Stück (German): Piece. (Related

English word: stick.)
    Plural: Stücke.
    Pronunciation: shtük.

●† strumento. Instrument.
    Plural: strumenti.

● study. See etude.

● subdominant. The fourth degree
of the *scale, or the *triad built on
it. Although the name suggests the
meaning "under the *dominant," and
it has such a position, the real significance is "the dominant, or fifth
degree, below the tonic, when descending the scale." It is occasionally called
the under dominant.
    Roman numeral for the triad: IV.

●† subito. Immediately, suddenly.
    Abbreviation: sub.
    Variant form: subitamente.
    Poco a poco might be considered
more or less an antonym.
    Pronunciation: accent first syllable.

● subject. Same as theme. The
theme in a *fugue is normally called
a subject; elsewhere the terms subject
and theme are used interchangeably.

● submediant. The sixth degree of
the *scale, or the *triad built on it.
Many persons are puzzled by this
name, since the location is not "below
the mediant," as the name appears
to indicate. The term arises from
the fact that in going down the scale,
the submediant occurs midway between
the high *tonic and the *subdominant.
    Roman numeral for the triad: VI.
    Synonym (rare): superdominant.

● sub-tone. An extremely soft, almost
whispering effect obtainable on the
saxophone (especially tenor saxophone)
and clarinet (including alto and bass
clarinets). It has been cultivated
chiefly in the *dance band for broadcasting purposes, the instrument being
held very close to the microphone so
that its faint volume may be amplified.

● subtonic. The seventh degree of the
*scale--provided it is located a *whole-
step below the high *tonic--or the
*triad built on it.

When the seventh degree is located a *half-step below the high tonic, the correct term is leading-tone.

● suite. Derived from the French word meaning "to follow," all suites have the common element of being a series of *movements contrasting in mood and *tempo.

(1) The Baroque suite, often carelessly termed "Classic suite," was basically a series of four (or more) dances, most commonly written for a keyboard instrument. Frequently the dances which constitute its essential framework were (in this order): *allemande, *courante, *sarabande, and *gigue, the last-named sometimes replaced by a different dance of lively character. However there are sometimes additional optional movements. Often a *prelude (1) opened the suite, preceding the dance movements. Between the sarabande and gigue the composer might interpolate any other dance or dances that suited his purpose, for example a *minuet, a *gavotte, a *passepied, or a *bourrée. Occasionally additional movements, but not of dance character, also appeared. Thus most Baroque suites contain four, five, or six movements.

The sequence of movements can be tabulated thus:

    prelude (optional)
    allemande (basic)
    courante (basic)
    sarabande (basic)
    one or more additional dances
     (optional)
    gigue (basic)

This order was by no means invariable; exceptions probably outnumber examples.

*Binary form was typical for each dance.

The minuet, gavotte, or bourrée, when used, would usually be marked Minuets I and II, Gavottes I and II, or Bourrées I and II, both the first and second members being cast in binary form. The custom of repeating I after the close of II, brought about by the direction *D. C., would place the dances in the order: I, II, I, thus forming an overall *ternary

or ABA pattern.

Bach's French Suites, English Suites, and Partitas for piano (or harpsichord) are well-known examples of this type of suite.

The *sonata da camera (chamber sonata) was essentially the same form, but written for a *chamber-music combination.

The orchestral works by Bach that are today called suites were originally entitled overtures. Although these contain dance movements, these are not the customary four; hence in strict parlance they are hardly to be classified with works of the type under discussion.

An important characteristic of the Baroque suite is that normally all the movements were in the same *key. The concept of key contrast, as found in the *sonata, *symphony, and other forms herein classified under sonata-types was an innovation of the *Classical period which still lay well in the future. Synonyms: dance suite, partita (1), ordre.

(2) The usual type of suite, often called Modern suite, may be written for any *medium, and places in juxtaposition three or more movements of any desired type. Some Modern suites are *program music, others *absolute music. Some are short; others such as Rimsky-Korsakoff's Scheherazade are very long--even longer than a symphony. A few orchestral suites are symphonies in spirit if not in form.

(3) An orchestral work drawn from various sections of an *opera, *ballet, or *incidental music for a play. Suites of this type are not always organized by the composer; several have been arranged by other musicians, who-- in the case of suites derived from operas--adjust the *orchestration in such a way that instruments take over the parts originally allotted to voices. A few examples are cast in a single long movement, but are still termed suites since this movement is derived from various widely-separated parts of the original work.

●† sul. Upon (the), near (the), over (the). This is a contraction of the preposition su, "upon," "over," "near," and il, "the," often encountered in the following expressions:

(1) Sul G. To be played on the G string (of the violin, viola or cello). Used when the composer wants the peculiar color of the indicated string, yet in a passage that would more usually be played on some higher string. (Such effects are of course impossible if the passage would normally be played on a lower string.) In addition to sul G, one often observes sul D, sul A, etc., each for its own special effect. *Syllable-names may be substituted for the letters ("sul sol," "sul re," "sul la," etc.).

(2) Sul IV. To be played on the fourth string; with the violin this is the equivalent of sul G, with the viola and cello of sul C. Sul III and sul II are also sometimes encountered. The form IVª corda may be substituted.

(3) Sul ponticello (abbreviation: sul pont.), occasionally al ponticello. To be played near the bridge, used in writing for the bowed string instruments. (It is important to understand that normally the player draws his bow over the strings at a point about midway between the bridge and the end of the *fingerboard.) In the effect under discussion the bow is placed close to the bridge and the resulting tone is harsh, thin, nasal, glassy, metallic--ashes of tones rather than full-bodied. This effect can be very striking if not used too long. The bowed *tremolo (1) is almost invariably specified with sul ponticello passages. Sul ponticello is canceled by pos. nat., naturale, or ordinario. French: près du chevalet, sur le pont. German: am Steg.

(4) Sul tasto or sulla tastiera. Here the player draws his bow either above or close to the fingerboard, in exactly the opposite direction from that used for sul ponticello. The effect is soft, veiled, and a bit dull--decidedly different from sul ponticello, though much less conspicuously at variance with conventional tone. Sul tasto is often employed with sustained tones as well as with tremolos. Its color somewhat suggests that obtained with the use of the *mute.

Sul tasto is canceled by the same terms that cancel sul ponticello.
Synonym: flautando.
French: sur la touche. German: am Griffbrett.

Sul is replaced by sulla and sull' under certain conditions required in Italian grammar.

● † sulla tastiera. Same as sul tasto; see sul (4).

● † suono. Sound. Con suono, sonorous.

● superdominant. A term sometimes applied to the *submediant degree of the *scale, or to the submediant *triad (rare).

● supersonic. Same as ultrasonic. This term has the additional meaning of denoting objects (such as airplanes) capable of traveling faster than sound.

● supertonic. The second degree of the *scale, or the *triad built on it. Roman numeral for triad: II.

● suspension. See non-harmonic tones (3).

● sustaining pedal. The *damper pedal (or right pedal) of the piano, often carelessly called the "loud pedal."
The sustaining pedal is by no means the same thing as the sostenuto pedal (see middle pedal).

● s. v. Abbreviation for sotto voce.

● swell. (1) This term is sometimes used as the equivalent of *crescendo.
(2) One of the manuals of the *organ.

● syllabic. Having just one note for each word or syllable of a word; used in reference to music for the voice.
Antonyms: florid, melismatic.

● syllables. Arbitrary monosyllabic words employed for the purpose of helping singers find the correct pitches.

Unlike an instrumentalist, who has an instrument to manufacture the pitches for him, a singer must pick the correct sounds "out of the air"--or rather, out of his mind.

Origin. The monk Guido of Arezzo (995?-1050), who also did much to develop a workable system of notation, probably invented the system of syllables. Guido realized that singers had great difficulty in evoking the correct pitches in sight-reading. He observed that in one of the most widely-known *Gregorian chants--the Hymn to St. John the Baptist--the initial tone of each *phrase happens to be located one step in the scale higher than the initial tone of the preceding phrase,

forming what are known today as the notes C, D, E, F, G, and A. The Latin words which occurred with these tones are: ut, re, mi, fa, sol, and la. By taking these six words and word-fragments and associating them with the corresponding six tones, Guido reasoned that it would be possible to establish a bond deep in the subconscious mind which would suggest the correct pitch to the singer, in any pattern in which the tones might fall. Psychologists today would term the principle that of the "conditioned response." His system met with phenomenal success. Since the theory of music prevalent in his day was based on the *hexachord of six

Hymn to St. John the Baptist

Continued on next page.

fa - mu - li tu - o - rum

sol - ve pol - lu - ti

la - bi - i re - a - tum Sanc - te Jo - an - nes

tones--which could be transposed
to begin on F or G as well as C--
Guido needed only these six syllables.

Expansion. With the advent of
the present theory regarding the
major scale, it occurred to someone to continue Guido's principle
and devise a syllable-name for the
seventh degree. The last two words
of the Hymn to St. John are "sancte
Joannes." In Latin J and I are the
same letter; thus Joannes could also
be written Ioannes. Using the latter
spelling and taking the initials of
the two last words produces si, and
this name was applied to the seventh
degree.

In all countries except France, ut
was changed to do. In the United
States si was changed to ti, and sol

is sometimes shortened to so.

Thus the principle behind Guido's
invention comes down to us to the
present day.

In the United States the raised or
sharped forms of do, re, fa, sol,
and la are: di, ri, fi, si, li. The
lowered or flatted forms of ti, la,
sol, mi, and re are: te, le, se, me,
ra. Thus the complete syllables for
the *chromatic scale are: ascending--
do, di, re, ri, mi, fa, fi, sol, si,
la, li, ti, do; descending--do, ti, te,
la, le, sol, se, fa, mi, me, re, ra,
do.

Systems. There are two principles
under which syllables are used, fixed-
do and movable-do. With the fixed-
do system, C is always do, D is always re, etc. no matter what the key.
With the movable-do system, the first

degree of every major scale is called do, the second degree re, etc. regardless of the letter name of the note. For use in the minor mode (see major and minor) the movable-do system takes two forms. In one, the tonic is called do; this is used in a few colleges and *conservatories. In the other, the tonic is called la; this is always used in public schools and in probably most colleges and conservatories, and hence may be termed the normal method of syllable-singing in the minor mode, at least in the United States.

In France, Italy, and the Spanish-speaking countries there are no letter names for notes, and syllable names (according to the fixed-do system) are used. Thus re maggiore is the Italian equivalent of D major, si bémol mineur the French for B-flat minor, fa mayor the Spanish for F major.

Several systems using other syllables have also been proposed, but the principle remains the same. Although there is certainly no magic in the syllables do re mi fa sol la ti, there is also no advantage in substituting (say) bo ce di ga lo ma ni, or la be ce de me fe ge, or da me ni po tu la be.

Purpose. It is well to repeat that the purpose of syllables is not one of hanging an identification-tag on a tone that has been sung, nor of furnishing euphonious sounds on which to *vocalize, but one of supplying a means by which to find the sound in the first place through subconscious mental association. Their purpose remains exactly that for which Guido employed them 900 years ago.

(There is a possibility that Guido was not the inventor of the syllable principle, but he undoubtedly disseminated the idea.)

Singing by syllables is sometimes called solmization.

A British spelling of the diatonic syllable-names is given under Tonic Sol-fa.

See also sight-singing, ear-training.

● symbolism, musical. A few over-imaginative writers have professed to find some sort of symbolism in "all" music. Undoubtedly a certain amount of symbolism is purposely incorporated into certain compositions, subconsciously into many, but to make sweeping claims for the entire literature is fantastic and ridiculous. Writers who make these statements have no concept of the working of composers' minds; they probably cannot reconcile themselves to the fundamental idea that a composer works in a world of tone-imagery, not of graphic, narrative, philosophical, or idea imagery; they do not realize that music is its own meaning, that most compositions contain no "message" or "meaning" other than the sounds that are heard, that the meaning of music is music.

When genuine symbolism does appear (as it occasionally does), it usually takes the form of a rising melody to emphasize a text that speaks of "upward," a descending melody for "downward," or something equally elementary and naive. (See text-painting.)

Albert Schweitzer believed that Bach's music is full of what he called "tone-symbolism"; that Bach always used melodic figures of certain types to echo certain sentiments of the text.

It is claimed that the music of Mozart's Magic Flute expresses the ideals of the Masonic order.

There are probably other occasional and special cases that could be cited, but the deliberate application of musical symbolism would still remain decidedly the exceptional procedure, not the rule.

● symbols. The essence of written music is notes and *rests which are of course symbols. The following list, however, will be devoted to those symbols other than notes and rests which are commonly used in the writing of music.

1. G-clef or Treble-Clef. See clefs.

2. or : F-clef or Bass clef. See clefs.

3. or or C-clef. See

clefs.

4. *8va - - - - ⌐* To be played an *oc-tave higher than written.

5. *8va_ _ _ _ _ ⌐* or *8va bassa* _ _ _ _ _⌐
To be played an octave lower than written.

6. *15 ma - - - ⌐* or *16 va - - - - ⌐*
To be played two octaves higher than written.

7. · Dot. (A) When placed after a note, a dot means that the number of beats is to be increased by half the original value of the note. See dotted notes. (B) When placed over or under a note, it indicates that it should be performed *staccato.

8. ◄ or ' Wedge staccato. Extremely *staccato.

9. ╱ *Slur; connects notes of
different pitch. Notes covered by the slur are to be played *legato.

10. ⌒ *Tie; connects notes of the same pitch. Notes connected by the tie are joined together into a single tone combining the values shown.

11. ╱⋯⋯ Slur (or Tie) and dots or
Portato. (A) For voices and all instruments except strings--detach slightly; somewhat *staccato. (B) For bowed string instruments-- *staccato, but to be played with the bow continuing in the same direction, either up or down; the bow is stopped for a short time between notes.

12. > Accent. Indicates that the note so marked should be performed a trifle louder than those which precede and follow. Although theoretically the symbol for *sforzando, it is usually understood to have somewhat less force than that designation. This sign is placed over or under the note affected.

13. ∧ Heavy accent. Some theorists maintain that this is the equivalent of > but it is usually

taken to mean a somewhat more decided accent--about the equivalent of s̲f̲z̲ rather than sfz. This symbol is almost invariably placed over the note.

14. – Tenuto. Hold for full value (a precaution against any trace of *staccato); or play the designated notes in a "broad" manner. This is also occasionally used to indicate a very light accent; and although this usage is undesirable, the utility of some symbol for this purpose is apparent to all composers. This symbol may be placed over or under the note affected.

15. ⊤ Tenuto and staccato dot. Hold the note firmly, but make a slight separation before the note to follow. Generally used only with values of fairly long duration.

16. ≧ Tenuto and accent. Accent the note and hold for full value.

17. ♯ *Sharp. Indicates the pitch of the note is raised a *half-step (semitone).

18. ♭ *Flat. Indicates the pitch of the note is lowered a *half-step (semitone).

19. ♮ *Natural (rarely, Cancel). Cancels the effect of a *sharp, or *flat, less frequently of a *double-sharp or *double-flat.

20. ✳ or ✕ or ✕ *Double-sharp. Indicates the pitch of the note is raised a *whole-step.

21. ♭♭ *Double-flat. Indicates the pitch of the note is lowered a *whole-step.

22. ═══ *Staff. Notes are
placed on the lines and spaces of the staff, supplemented where necessary by the addition of *leger lines.

23. ═══ *Bar-line. Indicates
the beginning or end of a *measure.

24. ═══ *Double bar-line. Indicates (A) the beginning of a new

section of the composition; (B) that a change in *tempo occurs at the point indicated; (C) that a change in *time-signature or *key-signature or both occurs at the point indicated; (D) end of an extremely short composition.

25. ▤ Indicates the end

of a composition. Although every piece of music obviously contains this symbol, it has no definite name. Some musicians call it a "double bar-line," but comparison with the true double *bar-line shows that its appearance is conspicuously different. It is also sometimes called (again not very accurately) the "thick double bar-line."

26. ▤ *Repeat sign. Indi-

cates that the passage between

this sign and the sign ▤

(which is the repeat sign turned backward) is to be performed twice, or if the latter if not found, that a repeat is to be made from the beginning of the composition.

27. ▤ (This sign appears

to have no name; it is discussed above under repeat sign.) Marks the beginning of a repeated section. When the symbol :‖ is

encountered, the performer goes back to ‖: and repeats all the material that intervenes. (If ‖:

is not found, the repeat is made from the beginning of the composition.)

28.

▤ or ▤

Indicates the end of one repeated section and beginning of another.

29. ⌢ *Fermata, Hold or Pause. Indicates that the note (or rest) over which this symbol is placed

is to be held longer than its given value suggests. (Sometimes it is placed under the note, and is turned upside down.) The amount of prolongation depends on the performer's judgment.

30. ═══ Same as *crescendo.

31. ═══ Same as *diminuendo (decrescendo).

32. } *Brace or Bracket. Groups

together two (or more) simultaneously-sounding staffs. Used in writing for piano and harp, and for the manuals (but not pedals) of the organ. Also used in orchestral *scores to group together similar instruments: first and second violins, cellos and double-basses, flutes and piccolo, oboe and English horn, trombones and tuba, etc.

33. | *Accolade. Purpose is

similar to that of the brace, though it is seldom if ever used in writing for the piano, organ, or harp. In orchestral *scores, it often groups together the staffs devoted to the four basic "families" of instruments--string, woodwind, brass, and percussion.

34. 𝄴 4-4 time.

35. 𝄵 2-2 time; in older music also 4-2 time.

36. |1. |*First ending. |2. | Second ending. (Both are used only in connection with repeat signs.)

37. ⊓ (bowed string instruments). To be played *down bow (i. e., the player pulls the bow). Occasionally ⊔

38. V (A) For bowed string instruments--To be played *up bow (i. e., the player pushes the bow). (B) For wind instruments or voice--Take breath.

39. ∧ (in organ playing, pedal technique). To be played with the toe. When placed above a note, it indicates the toe of the right foot, when below, the toe of the left foot.

40. ∪ (in organ playing, pedal
technique). To be played with
the heel. When placed above a
note, it indicates the right heel,
when below, the left.

41. ♀ or ♂ (in cello playing). Use the thumb position.

42. ⌣⌣⌣⌣ (horizontal wavy
line). Shows exact duration of
a *trill.

43. ⸽ (vertical wavy line) Symbol
for a *rolled chord.

44. ((vertical slur) A less
desirable symbol for a *rolled
chord, used thus:

45. [(vertical bracket) (A) For
keyboard instruments--Notes so
bracketed are to be played with
the same hand.
Used thus:

46. 𝄢. (in piano technique)--
Press down the *damper pedal.

47. * (in piano technique)--
Release the damper pedal.

48. ⌐————⌐ or ⌐——⌐

(in piano technique)--Shows where
damper pedal is to be pressed
down and released; it is a combination of (and improvement on) the
two symbols immediately preceding.

49. ○ (very small circle) (A) For
the bowed string instruments, harp,
and flute--A symbol for a *harmonic (with the former, especially
a natural harmonic). (B) For the
bowed string instruments-- A symbol indicating the use of an *open
string. (C) In *horn technique--
Often used to cancel + (D) In
brass instrument *fingering (3)--
Indicates an *open tone.

50. + (cross) (A) In *horn tech-
nique--To be played as a harsh
stopped tone. (B) In string tech-
nique--Symbol for left hand *pizzicato.

51. ⊕   Cross-and-circle or Coda

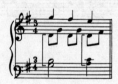

(B) For string instruments--The
two or more notes so marked
should be played as *double-
(triple, - quadruple-) stops, not
*divisi. (C) In piano playing--
Notes so indicated are to be
played with a single finger, usually the thumb. (Both keys must
be white or both black.)

sign. (A) From the point indicated,
go to the section, at the end of the
composition, marked "coda." (The
section so marked may or may not
be a true *coda as that term is
understood in musical *form.) (B)
Beginning and end of an optional
*"cut" (excision). See vide.

52.   ✸   (Sometimes called ripresa, often simply the sign or segno.) After *D. S. is encountered, go back to this sign and play until the word *fine appears.

53.   //   Indication for a short pause or break in the music; a short *rest is to be inserted. This sign is usually placed quite high on the staff, or above it. (Compare with symbol 64.)

54.   tr or tr ⁓⁓⁓   Symbol for the *trill (1); with *percussion instruments, for the *roll (2).

55.   ∿   Symbol for the *mordent.

56.   ⌁   Symbol for the inverted *mordent.

57.   ⌁   Symbol for the double *mordent.

58.   ⌁   Symbol for the double inverted *mordent.

59.   ∾   Symbol for the *turn.

60.   Ƨ   Symbol for the inverted *turn (back turn).

61.   ∾   A less desirable symbol for the inverted *turn.

62.   Indicates that the material in the preceding measure should be repeated. This symbol may recur many times. It might well be called the musical counterpart of ditto marks. See diagram below.

63. 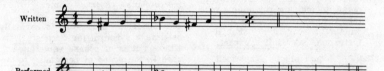   Indicates that
the material in the two measures
preceding should be repeated.
(Some musicians object to this
symbol.)

65. ♪ <u>Comma.</u> Indicates the end
of a *phrase, or the place where
breath should be taken or a breath-
like effect be used. (See also
<u>Luftpause.</u>)

66. Indication for the *tremolo(1).

64. // (A) Indicates that the
material in the preceding half
measure, or the preceding beat,
should be repeated. This symbol
may recur several times and may
be followed by   %   (This symbol is placed in the center of the
staff; compare with symbol 53.)

67. Indication for the *tremolo (2).

68.

(upward slanting line between two
notes) Indication for upward portamento or glissando. A wavy line
is often substituted.

(B) Also used when two or more
instruments play in *unison (or
play a passage having the written
appearance of a unison), to indicate that one of them has the
same notes written for the other.

69.

(downward slanting line between two
notes) Indication for downward portamento or glissando. A wavy line
is often substituted.

N. B. Actual pitch of
the double-bass is an
octave lower than
written; see <u>trans-
posing instruments.</u>

70. ⌒ (short curved line) In piano and organ technique, when connecting two figures (e. g. 45) indicates a change of finger on the key during the course of the note. See fingering (1).

71. ⌐‾‾‾‾¬ or ⌊‾‾‾‾⌋ (bracket). Used in contemporary music to indicate rhythmic groupings that do not coincide with the *meter or *bar-lines. For illustration, see shifted accent.

72. = (equal sign). Explained under equal marks.

73. /or ; (slanting line or row of dots) Shows movement of a *"line" (2) or *"voice" from one staff to another in writing for the piano and other keyboard instruments.

duced by singing or playing the pitch to which one of the strings on a bowed or plucked string instrument is tuned.

An additional experiment using sympathetic vibration is mentioned under harmonic series.

● Symphonet. See simple melody instruments. A trade name.

● symphonic. This word is normally used as a synonym for orchestral, although it is of course sometimes used in the sense of pertaining to the *symphony.

● symphonic poem. A composition for orchestra, usually in one movement, intended to "tell a story" by purely musical means. Often the spirit is more one of characterization than of pure description. Most sym-

● sympathetic vibration. The tendency of a string to sound if some other instrument (or voice) produces the exact pitch to which it is tuned.

Sympathetic vibration can be demonstrated as follows: Silently press a key on the piano, and then sing its pitch into the instrument. (If desired, the *damper pedal may be depressed instead of the key.) If exactly the right sound has been sung or played, the string which the key operates will begin to vibrate of its own accord. This will be most apparent after the sung tone has been released. An instrument, including another piano, could be substituted for the voice.

This same phenomenon can be pro-

phonic poems are of considerable length--seldom less than seven minutes, and in the case of Richard Strauss's Ein Heldenleben (A Hero's Life), nearly 45 minutes.

The symphonic poem is perhaps the clearest-cut type of *program music.

The story to be told is no secret; it is either frankly printed on the flyleaf of the *score or is sufficiently clear from the title alone.

This term appears to have been coined by Franz Liszt (1811-1886), who is also credited--if a single man can be credited--with the "invention" of the symphonic poem, of which he wrote thirteen examples. (It would probably be more accurate to say that Liszt evolved the symphonic poem, clearly influenced by the programmatic symphony and the *overture, especially the concert overture.)

The seven symphonic poems of Richard Strauss (1864-1949) mark the zenith of the form. Other important examples have been written by Smetana, Dvořák, Balakireff, Scriabin, Dukas, Franck, Tschaikowsky, Delius, Elgar, Sibelius, etc. The works which Respighi called symphonic poems are more nearly *suites (2) played without interruption.

The symphonic poem represents a phrase of *Romanticism, and hence is out of favor among composers today. Nevertheless Copland's El Salón México, although not so entitled, comes very close to being a symphonic poem.

It is well to mention that the "story" is told through music alone; Prokofieff's Peter and the Wolf "tells a story," but through a narrator rather than entirely through music, and hence is not a symphonic poem but a *melodrama.

The symphonic poem should not be confused with the programmatic *symphony and *suite.

Synonyms: tone poem, symphonic tone poem.

● symphony. (1) A composition for orchestra, usually in three or four movements, following the plan of the *sonata. It is identical with the sonata, *concerto, and *string quartet in form, the only difference being the *medium. The form is discussed under sonata-types. It is easily the most ambitious form of orchestral music.

A few symphonies for band have been written during recent years. There are also a few symphonies for string orchestra.

(2) In earlier times the word has been used with other meanings, including the following: (A) In its Italian form, sinfonia, as a synonym for *overture. (B) As the name of an orchestral portion within a larger work, such as the "Pastoral Symphony" in Handel's The Messiah which today would probably be called an *intermezzo. (C) As the name applied to the opening, interludes, and conclusion in a *song, i. e., as a synonym for *ritornello.

(3) The word is often carelessly used as a synonym for symphony *orchestra, and even more carelessly used to denote any orchestral composition, including *overtures, *symphonic poems, and the like.

(4) Widor, Vierne, Sowerby, and others have applied the name symphony --not very modestly--to works for organ that are actually *sonatas.

(5) During the twentieth century symphonies in one movement have appeared. They are discussed under the heading one-movement symphony.

(6) The word has occasionally had still other applications; for instance Bach originally gave the name Symphonies to the fifteen compositions now usually called Three-Part *Inventions.

● symphony orchestra, symphonic orchestra. The full-sized orchestra in contradistinction to the incomplete orchestra or school orchestra. The word symphony appears in the corporate name of many such organizations; others prefer "philharmonic orchestra."

Synonym: full orchestra.

● syncopation. (1) The sustaining of a tone through a beat stronger than the beat on which it began. (See "metric accent" in the entry accent.) All of the notes indicated by an asterisk in the following examples are syncopated.

Musicians often mention that in syncopation the accent is shifted, because the normally weak tone seems to absorb the accent belonging to the strong beat through which it is held. (See also shifted accent.)

Syncopation does not occur when a tone is sustained through a beat as strong as that on which it began; thus the following notes are not syncopated:

and piano on six, and so on.

Several systems may appear on each page, depending on the size of the paper and number of staffs per system.

Although system is the best term to use, the expressions line, score (2), and brace are perhaps more frequently heard.

When a tone is sustained through two weak beats, the effect is sometimes termed "soft syncopation." This can appear only in meters divisible by 3.

T

● tablature. An obsolete species of instrumental notation in which the sounds are indicated by diagrams

(2) The stressing, purely by means of loudness, of a normally weak beat, thus:

which show where the fingers should be placed on the instrument, rather than by notes. Tablatures showed

● synesthesia. Explained under key color.
  Variant spelling: synaesthesia.
  Pronunciation: sĭn-ĕs-thē-zhā or sĭn-ĕs-thē-zhĭ-a.

● syrinx. See Pan pipes.
  Pronunciation: sĭr-ĭŋks.

● system. A group of *staffs, placed one under the other and joined by a vertical line on the left. All music written on such a staff-group sounds simultaneously.

  Music for the piano is written on a system of two staffs (see great staff); that for voice and piano, for violin and piano, or for organ on a system of three staffs; that for *string quartet (1) or for unaccompanied *mixed chorus on a four-staff system; that for mixed chorus

sounds in direct application to instruments, whereas the present system of notation shows them in the abstract.

Tablatures were widely used from the fifteenth to the seventeenth centuries, especially in writing for the *lute and the *organ. They were not used in writing for voices. Hence during this era there were two systems of notation: one for voices and one for instruments. It is clear that the present system descends from that used in writing vocal music.

Unfortunately there was little uniformity in tablature style. The system varied from instrument to instrument and from country to country. Thus not only was organ tablature different from that for the lute, but also Italian lute tablature differed from German lute tablature, and so on. The provinciality of the system proved its undoing.

A species of tablature is widely in use at the present time in the form of finger diagrams for the *ukulele, *banjo, and *guitar; these are found in most editions of "popular" songs.

Another type of old notation is described under neumes.

● tabor. The English name for the *tambourin de Provence.

● tacet (Latin). Be silent. This is often used in the *parts for certain instruments on the occurrence of a passage enclosed in *repeat signs, with the direction "tacet first time" or "tacet second time."

Occasionally, in those orchestral compositions that are divided into *movements, a certain instrument may have nothing to play for an entire movement; the indication for this is "second movement tacet."

The plural form, referring to the parts for several instruments, is tacent.

Pronunciation: tă-sĕt or tă-chĕt.

● Takt (German). A synonym for the *beat or *pulse in music.

See also accent, rhythm, pulsation, meter.

Pronunciation: tăkt.

● talon, du talon (French). In music for string instruments, an indication that the passage so marked should be played at the "heel" or "nut" of the *bow--the portion of the bow near the player's hand. A rough, forceful effect may be obtained in this manner. Such a passage is usually played *down-bow.

Pronunciation: (dü) tă-lōn.

● tambourin. A type of French peasant dance, in quick 2-4 or 2-2 time.

This word has of course been confused with the *tambourin de Provence (which is often used to accompany it) and with the *tambourine.

French pronunciation: tăm-bōo-răn.

● tambourin de Provence. A long, narrow, cylindrical drum of indefinite

pitch. Only one of its two heads is beaten, and a single stick is employed; hence *rolls (2) are impossible. It has one snare.

It is almost unnecessary to mention that this instrument is often confused with the *tambourine, which it in no way resembles, neither in appearance nor in sound.

Variant form: tambour de Provence.

Synonyms: tabor, Provençal drum, long drum.

Pronunciation: tăm-bōo-ran dĕ prō-văns.

● tambourine. An indefinite pitch *percussion instrument. It is a small drum with a single head stretched over a small hoop. In the hoop there are slots, inside each of which one or more little metal disks are loosely fastened; the latter are called the jingles.

The instrument may be struck with the hand, or shaken so that only the jingles will sound, or rubbed on the head with the moistened thumb, the last being a technique difficult to acquire.

The tambourine is especially associated with Spanish music. It is suited to passages of a gay or exciting character. Its music is often written on a one-line *staff.

This instrument is not to be confused with the *tambourin de Provence, nor with the dance known as the *tambourin.

Italian: tamburino or tamburo basco. French: tambour de Basque. German: Tambourin, Tamburin, or Schellentrommel. Spanish: pandereta or panderete.

Pronunciation: tăm-bōo-rēn.

● tam-tam. The *gong. Some musicians make a distinction between the tam-tam and the gong, the former being somewhat smaller and hence having a higher pitch; but others use these terms exactly the other way around.

The tam-tam should not be confused with the *tom-tom, which it by no means resembles.

Pronunciation: tăm-tăm.

● tango. A Spanish dance (originally

from Argentina) in moderate 2-4 time. Characteristic tango rhythms (also typical of the *habanera) are:

● Tartini tone. Same as resultant. The name comes from the fact that the composer and violinist Giuseppe

$$\frac{2}{4} \, \sphericalangle \quad || \frac{2}{4} \quad || \frac{2}{4} \quad ||$$

Plural: tangos.

●† tanto. Literally "so much"; for all practical purposes a synonym for troppo.

● tape recorder. A machine for both recording and reproducing sound. In recording, cellophane tape is passed over an electro-magnet; in reproducing, the tape is passed over a receiver device. One great advantage of tape record-ing, compared to recordings made on disks, is that when the material on the tape is no longer wanted, it may be removed ("erased"). Hence if a mistake is made in per-formance, it may be rather easily corrected, while on a disk record-ing the material must be played again and re-recorded from the beginning. Another advantage is that tape containing a mistake may be cut out with scissors and spliced with correctly-played tape.
All commercial recordings are now made on tape and then trans-ferred to disks.
Tape recorders are widely used in homes, schools, offices, police stations, etc., as well as in record-ing and broadcasting studios.
Music composed for, and even on, the tape recorder is discussed under electronic music.
See also phonograph, wire recorder, fidelity.

●† tarantella. A very fast Italian dance, usually in 6-8 or 12-8 time. There is a legend that it originated under the supposition that wild ex-hausting exercise would cure the poisonous bite of the tarantula spider; however there is no real proof that the dance actually originated out of this superstition. Its music some-what resembles that of the *saltarello.
Variant form: tarentelle.

Tartini (1692-1770) was one of the earliest experimenters with this acoustical phenomenon.

●† tasto. See no. 4 under the head-ing sul.

●† tasto solo. Play only the notes written. This direction sometimes appears in a *figured bass; it means that the player of the keyboard instru-ment should not fill in any chords--that he should confine himself to the written notes. Tasto solo is most frequently used with a *unison passage. A familiar instance may be found in the "Hallelujah Chorus" of Handel's The Messiah--provided the original edition with figured bass is consulted --at the words "For the Lord God omnipotent reigneth."
Obviously, the reappearance of figures cancels tasto solo.
Abbreviation: T. S.

● tattoo. A signal played on a drum or bugle.
See also bugle-call.

● t. c. Abbreviation for *tre corde.

● technic, technique. Skill in per-forming; mastery of the instrument (or voice); mechanical facility sufficient to assure a high degree of security in playing or singing.
This term is also applied to the process of composing in the sense of being able to "make the notes do what-ever the composer wants them to do"; that is, as a synonym for workman-ship or craftsmanship.

●† tedesca. A German dance in 3-4 or 3-8 time.

● Te Deum (Latin). A musical setting of a famous Latin hymn used for occasions of rejoicing, festivity, and thanksgiving. A fuller version of the title is Te Deum laudamus ("We Praise Thee, O God"). There are celebrated compositions on this text by Handel, Berlioz, Bruckner, Verdi, and others. The oldest setting is in *Gregorian chant (plain-song), which is still is use. Settings in *Anglican chanting are plentiful.

Pronunciation: tē dē-um or tā dä-ŏom.

● † tema. Theme. Tema con variazioni, *theme and variations.

● temperament. (1) See equal temperament; compare just intonation.

(2) Artistic temperament, in its best sense, refers to that musical sensitivity and spontaneous interest that are necessary in any artist; in its worst (and more usual) sense, it refers to capricious, irresponsible, and unpredictable whims of demeanor and mood that are characteristic of "spoiled" persons, a failing in which musicians are not alone.

● † tempestoso. Stormy.

● temple blocks. An indefinite pitch *percussion instrument, consisting of a set of three or more rounded, hollow blocks of varying sizes. They usually have a shiny, lacquered appearance. Their hollowness produces a "hollow-sounding," brittle tone of fairly high pitch. The fact that the blocks vary in size gives each one a pitch which, although indefinite, is none the less clearly differentiated from that of its mates.

Synonym: Chinese blocks.

● † tempo. (1) Rate of speed, pace. Although the literal meaning is "time," the English word time in connection with music usually has a different connotation; hence the term tempo is much preferable.

Plural: tempos or tempi.

(2) Short for *a tempo.

Abbreviation: T⁰.

● tempo giusto. In strict *tempo;

that is, without any trace of *tempo rubato.

● tempo marks. Terms used in addition to the notation to indicate the approximate rate of speed at which a composition is to be performed. They are usually printed in bold-face type, and are of Italian origin.

The following list shows the most frequently-used tempo marks, arranged as nearly as possible in order from slowest to fastest:

    grave
    largo
    larghetto
    adagio
    lento
    andante
    andantino
    moderato
    allegretto
    allegro
    vivace
    presto
    prestissimo

Moderato, signifying "moderately," "medium," "neither fast nor slow," is the term in relation to which all the others should be gauged.

Order. The exact order of the slowest terms has been the source of much uncertainty and dispute, and it cannot be too strongly stated that the first five entries in the foregoing series are frankly open to challenge. The list is offered as an approximation rather than as assured fact. Some writers do not include grave. Largo, adagio, and lento have each been described as the slowest of the terms, depending on the individual author's concept. Others list largo as the slowest, but reverse the order of adagio and lento. Larghetto clearly is not as slow as largo, but a few musicians regard it as only a trifle slower than andante, rather than falling next in order after largo. There is universal agreement, however, that andante is quicker than grave, largo, larghetto, adagio, and lento, yet slower than moderato. Andantino once indicated a tempo a trifle slower than andante, rather than a trifle faster, as at present; the changeover occurred about 1800 or 1825.

On the fast side, the order is clearer; allegretto is indisputably less fast than allegro; vivace is rather generally considered quicker than allegro, and presto quicker than either allegro or vivace.

The *metronome furnishes a much more precise indication of tempo. Still, Italian terms are far more exact than English, since each represents a reasonably well-understood pace. Although English contains such words as fast, rapid, quick, speedy, swift, etc., all of them suggest an equal degree of speed.

Manner of Performance. Many musicians point out that these terms not only indicate degrees of speed, but also to a certain extent the manner or style in which the composition should be performed. The following literal meanings, taken from an Italian dictionary, might profitably be kept in mind:

Grave--grave, heavy. Largo--broad, large. Adagio--slowly, gently, leisurely. Andante--derived from the word meaning "to go"; literal meaning is "going." (Andante is often described as a "walking tempo," the walk being understood as a leisurely stroll.) Moderato--moderate, temperate. Allegro--cheerful, gay, mirthful, merry, brisk, quick. Vivace--lively, spirited, gay. Presto--quick, nimble, ready, prompt.

Usage. Many of these terms are frequently modified by such auxiliaries as non troppo, "not too much"; assai, "quite"; molto, "very," etc., and by terms that indicate the manner of performance. Moderato and vivace are sometimes used to modify allegro and the former also to modify other words. It should be remembered that -etto and -ino are diminutive suffixes, -issimo the superlative suffix.

The use of tempo marks made its appearance at approximately the same time as that of *dynamic marks, and for the same reason--namely as a measure necessitated by the rise of independent instrumental music.

It is perhaps unfortunate that German and Austrian composers have tried to substitute German terms for the familiar Italian expressions. French and Belgian composers followed suit by employing French; later Englishmen and Americans introduced English. A moment's thought suggests that by the time Norwegian, Russian, Chinese, Hottentot, and other composers add their tongues to the list, the eventual result will be a musical Tower of Babel equivalent to possessing no terms at all! (It is indeed strange that Esperanto has never been suggested.) In addition, a casual glance at a few compositions employing German or French terms will show that there seems to be no end to them; Italian terms, on the other hand, seem to be drawn from a fairly constant and unchanging storehouse. The universality of the present system of *notation suggests that universal terminology in indicating manner of performance should be equally advantageous.

With the *dynamic indications, however, the predominance of the Italian terms remains unchallenged among composers of all nationalities.

Tempo terms cannot be reduced to metronome marks; it is misleading to set up two numerals as the limits under which a given tempo mark will fall.

See also metronome, accelerando, ritardando, ritenuto, meno mosso, più mosso.

●† tempo primo, † tempo I, † tempo I°. In the first *tempo of the composition; used after a second rate of speed has been established and there is to be a return to the first speed. Example: A composition begins andante; later there is a fast section marked allegro; then the composer wants to return to the tempo that prevailed at the beginning. He may do this by the use of tempo primo or by repeating the direction andante.

The directions tempo II and tempo III are rarely used, although obviously there are occasions when they are serviceable.

●† tempo rubato. A manner of performing in which slight variations in *tempo, tiny *ritardandos and *accelerandos, miniature *fermatas, and the like, are inserted into the music though not actually indicated by the notation and directions. The performer's taste, judgment, and above all conscience determine the extent to which it is employed.

Observers have often pointed out that all good playing and singing has a slight amount of rubato; that is, the rhythm is a bit elastic rather than rigidly mechanical; there is a certain amount of fluidity around the exact time-measurements. The sensitive performer always tends to linger ever so little at certain spots and to hurry ever so little at others.

Some musicians contend that every ritardando should have a balancing accelerando to compensate for it-- that the elapsed time of performance should square with the duration that would apply if strict tempo were maintained throughout. (This, how- ever, should probably be taken more as a guiding principle or hint than as an infallible rule.)

It is regrettable that tempo rubato has been badly misunderstood by certain persons and shamelessly abused by others. Matters have gone entirely too far when a quarter- note is made as long as a half-note, when 3-4 time sounds exactly like 4-4, when the direction tempo rubato is misinterpreted as a blanket li- cense to superimpose onto a passage any rhythm that irresponsible whim may dictate. Musicians insist that rhythmically the result should always sound the way the written time- values clearly indicate. In general, the abuse of tempo rubato is a sign

of old-fashioned training based on concepts that have long been dis- credited; yet its judicious employ- ment--in moderation--is essential to all sensitive performing.

*Tempo giusto may be regarded more or less as the antonym, though it by no means connotes mechanical or unfeeling performance.

Tempo rubato literally means "robbed time."

See also liberamente, senza misura.

● ten.   The abbreviation for tenuto.

●† tenebroso.   Dark, gloomy.

●† teneramente.   Tenderly.
Variant form: tenero.

●† tenerezza.   Tenderness.

●† tenero.   Tenderly, delicately.
Variant form: teneramente.
Pronunciation: accent first syllable.

● tenor.   (1) The highest adult male voice. Its quality is lighter, more "ringing," and less "rumbling" than the baritone's.

See example at bottom of page for range (in actual sounds).

There are several ways of writing for the tenor voice. (A) The G clef may be employed, and the notes written an octave higher than the sounds desired. This method treats the tenor voice like a *transposing instrument. (B) The G clef with an 8 under it or the double G clef may be used. Again the written notes sound

Easy   For artist

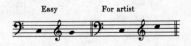

an octave lower than when the
ordinary G clef is found, but since
the two clefs just mentioned are
regarded as indicating the G below
*middle C (rather than the G above
it), nominally no transposition is
involved. (This reasoning of course
verges on the specious.) (C) The
G clef may be supplemented by a
miniature C clef made to fall on

the third space

of the staff. This reads exactly
like the preceding. (D) The C clef
may be used, placed on the third
space of the staff.

This indicates that middle C occurs
on that location; hence the actual
sounds are once more an octave
lower than those that would be heard
with an ordinary G clef. Many musicians object to this usage of the
C clef. (E) The bass clef may be
employed with the voice written at
actual pitch. Numerous *leger lines
above the staff will be necessary.
This method is customary in printing *hymns, where the tenor voice
shares a staff with the bass voice,
though it is not exclusive to hymn-
books.

The first and last of these usages
(A and E) are the only ones to enjoy
full and widespread acceptance.

The second tenor voice used to be
called the quintus.

(2) The *viola (obsolete).

(3) The *melody, thought of in
contrast to a subordinate accompaniment (obsolete).

(4) *Cantus firmus (obsolete). This
usage reminds us of the frequency
with which the borrowed melody was
entrusted to the tenor voice (usually
second tenor).

● tenor clef. See clef.

● tenor drum. An indefinite pitch
*percussion instrument, without
snares, midway in pitch between the
*snare drum and the *bass drum.
Its *tone-color somewhat resembles
that of the *tom-tom.

Italian: tambura rullante. French:

caisse roulante. German: Rührtrom-
mel, Wirbeltrommel, or Rolltrommel.

● tenor horn. A brass instrument
once popular in the *band, now practically obsolete. It has the same
range and appearance as the *baritone (2), but is of lighter build and
has a "lighter" tone-quality.

The German word Tenorhorn indicates the baritone, not the tenor horn.

● tenor tuba. A *brass instrument,
higher in pitch than the ordinary (i. e.,
bass) *tuba. There seems to be some
disagreement among musicians as to
whether it is or should be the same
thing as the *euphonium, or as the
tenor form of the *Wagner tuba, or
the small-sized tuba in B-flat.

● tenths. *Intervals consisting of an
*octave plus a third.

●† tenuto. Held for full value. Often
placed over a note, a chord, or an
entire passage to caution against any
trace of *staccato; also over a single
note as a caution against releasing
prematurely (hence generally encountered
with notes of unexpected length). In
brief, this term is purely precautionary
in nature.

Tenuto is occasionally used as a
synonym for the symbol ⌒ (the
*fermata), though the desirability is
open to question.

Abbreviation: ten.

Variant forms: tenente, tenete.

Symbol: ▬ (placed over or under
the note, preferably on the same side
as the note head, rather than on the
side of the stem).

● ternary form. A *form scheme with
the pattern: ABA. Often the composer
writes only the A and B sections and
provides for the repetition of the A by
a da capo (see D. C.). In other compositions the second A is considerably
varied; that is, the pattern would be
more accurately expressed as A^1BA^2.

The A and B sections may be in the
same or in different keys.

During the latter part of the *Baroque
Period, *arias were almost invariably
cast in ternary form; hence the synonym
aria form.

Ternary form is distinguished from first *rondo form, also ABA, by the fact that each section in ternary form is distinctly separated from the others by a decisive *cadence; often it is possible to perform either the A or the B section alone. Fine distinctions between two other ABA types, "three-part song form" and "song form with *trio (2)," are also made in treatises on *form.

Synonyms: three-part form, song form, three-part song form, aria form, tripartite form, da capo form. See also song form.

● ternary measure. Triple *meter.

●† terzetto. Same as trio (1).

●† tessitura. The general "lay" or prevailing pitches in a *melody; the region in which the majority of its tones lie.

Tessitura differs from *range in that the latter indicates the lowest and highest notes employed, while tessitura indicates the *register within which most of the tones will be found, disregarding occasional and exceptional high and low tones. It refers to the "heart" of the range.

Both of the accompanying melodies have the same range, but in the first one the tessitura is high, while in the second it is low.

Strictly speaking, this term should be applied only to vocal melodies, not instrumental, though this fine distinction is not always observed.

Plural: tessituras (English) or tessiture (Italian).

● tetrachord. A group of four tones in scalewise succession, usually totaling the interval of a perfect fourth (see intervals). A tetrachord is half of the eight tones that form a complete diatonic *scale.

●† tetro. Dark, gloomy, bleak.

● textpainting. Any musical device in which the tones appear as a direct illustration of the meaning expressed by the text. Although sometimes naive and arbitrary, the results are usually quite charming.

These illustrations may serve to clarify the term: (A) In the aria "I Know that My Redeemer Liveth" in Handel's The Messiah, the words "for now is Christ risen" are set to a series of upward-moving notes. (B) In the chorus "All We Like Sheep Have Gone Astray" from the same oratorio, the word "astray" is set to a *florid passage in which the various voices tend to move apart. (C) In the aria "Ev'ry Valley Shall Be Exalted," once more from The Messiah, the word "exalted" is treated with a bold, upward-rising sequence passage, part of

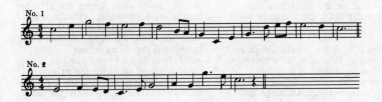

No. 1

No. 2

which is quoted in the entry
sequence. (D) In Thomas Weelkes's
*madrigal As Vesta Was Descend-
ing, the words "as two by two" are
set for only two voices; later the
words "as three by three" are assigned to three voices.

The accompanying example is
again from The Messiah: a portion
of the *recitative "Thus Saith the
Lord. "

and 16 string quartets by Beethoven,
etc.

● theme. A musical idea; the sub-
ject-matter out of which compositions
are formed. Some compositions have
only one theme; others have four or
five, or even more.

A theme may be a *melody, a
*rhythmic pattern, or a group of
*chords, but usually it contains

and I will shake _____ the heav'ns and the earth

Synonym: word painting.
See also symbolism.

● texture. This word is applied
to musical style with two entirely
different meanings.

(1) The difference between *homophonic and *polyphonic structure is
often termed a difference in "texture. " *Monophonic music (i.e., an
unaccompanied melodic line) is
sometimes classified as a third type
of "texture. "

(2) Other musicians use the term
in reference to the fulness or thinness of the sound; that is, they
speak of a thin, lean, spare "texture, " or a full, rich, resonant
"texture. "

Structure is often employed as a
synonym for the first meaning,
fabric for both, particularly the
second.

● thematic index. In addition to
the titles, the index in some collections of music also prints a
short snatch of the actual music of
each composition, normally the
opening measures. This is known
as a thematic index.

The practice is extremely valuable,
almost indispensable, in the case of
numerous compositions bearing the
same title and all by one composer,
for instance in connection with the
83 string quartets and 104 symphonies by Haydn, the 32 piano sonatas

melody, *harmony and rhythm all
united.

The first few notes of a melodic
theme (usually its most distinguishing
portion) are sometimes called the
"head" of the theme.

Synonym: subject.

● theme and variations. One of the
important and widely-used musical
*forms, wherein a theme is first
stated, then presented in a series of
more or less drastic modifications.

Assuming the composition has no
introduction, it will commence with
the statement of a theme, in orthodox
examples usually 16 or 32 measures
in length. This may be either original
or borrowed (see borrowed melodies).
The simplest are the easiest themes ·
to use, since they permit the greatest
amount of elaboration. The statement
of the theme is followed by the first
variation, wherein it is altered, usually
by the interspersing of extra notes,
which tend to be of shorter value than
those predominating in the original. In
the second variation there will be further elaboration and usually the introduction of still shorter time-values. In
general, the tendency is for each succeeding variation to be a little more
complex and to contain shorter time-
value than its predecessor, hence for
more and more notes to be intermingled
with those of the original theme; the
music seems to grow more and more
"busy. " Naturally the theme becomes

progressively disguised, though the
listener often experiences the illusion of detecting it buried under
the complicated variation web. The
art of writing variations is partially
one of making the theme increasingly less obvious, and of converting recognition to a subconscious
and intangible "memory" of it.

The number of variations depends
on the composer's ingenuity and
judgment. Usually each variation
is clearly numbered.

Although the introduction of
shorter and shorter time-values
gives the impression of increasing
rapidity, as a rule a single *tempo
actually prevails throughout. Usually
the basic pace is rather slow, for
obvious reasons, though sometimes
the final variation has a quick tempo.

In orthodox examples each variation presents a systematic and
mosaic-like working-out of a single
fundamental pattern. Only occasionally is the theme extended or
abridged during the process. All
the variations are normally in the
same key, although there is usually
at least one in the *tonic minor or
major (see minore and maggiore).
It seems almost unnecessary to
mention that more modern examples
are less orthodox, and often make
excursions to closely- or distantly-
related keys.

It will be apparent from the foregoing that variety is obtained through
multiple ways of transforming a single theme, not from balancing and
playing off two or more themes
against one another, for with very
few exceptions, only a single subject is used; variation form is essentially monothematic. (A well-
known exception is Rachmaninoff's
Rhapsody for Piano and Orchestra,
which is based on two borrowed
themes, one by Paganini, the other
the Gregorian chant Dies Irae.)

Often near the end of the composition the composer restates the
theme or attaches a *coda in the
spirit of the theme, almost as a
reminder of how far he has allowed
his imagination to soar.

In many compositions the theme
consists of two sections, both enclosed in *repeat-signs. Often every
variation is similarly cast, although
the performer may take it upon himself to omit at least some of the repeats. It is more than possible that
the composer could have intended these
repeats to be optional.

In some compositions entitled Theme
and Variations the theme remains unchanged throughout, but is *harmonized
differently on each presentation. Some
musicians recognize this is a special
type of the form; others would consider the title a near-misnomer.

From the description it might seem
that the variation technique would be
identical with the *development technique. This is by no means true.
The variation process is systematic
and mosaic-like, presenting as a rule
all of the theme on each appearance,
and is usually devoid of frequent *modulation; its cumulative effect is somewhat static. The process of development is more varied; it frequently
breaks off a fragment of the theme to
be developed separately, insisted on,
hammered home; it also often extends
the theme; modulation takes place
constantly. Where the variation process is often calm and poised, development is dramatic and sometimes
stormy.

Many examples of the theme and
variations are independent compositions,
while others appear as one of the movements (usually the slow movement) of
a *sonata, *symphony, *chamber-music work, or occasionally a *concerto
(see sonata types), also of a *suite
(2).

This form was at its height during
the *Classical Period. Its scheme
can be summarized by the formula:
$AA^1 A^2 A^3 A^4$ ... depending on the number
of variations written.

Briefly a "theme and variations" is
exactly what the term implies.

The chaconne and *passacaglia, both
described under ostinato, represent
essentially a type of variation procedure, but sufficiently different from
the form here under discussion to
warrant a separate entry. They are
essentially *polyphonic, while the theme
and variations form is characteristic
of *homophonic music.

Synonyms: variations, tema con variazioni, thème varié, and (obsolete) partita (2), divisions; for a single variation, double (3).

● theme transformation.   Same as transformation of theme.

● theorist.   A musician whose chief interest centers in the structure of music--the way compositions are organized and put together-- or in its analysis.   His function is (or should be) to systematize, codify, and explain the practice of composers.
See also rules of music.

● theory.   Broadly speaking, a systematized and rational study of the practice of composers in shaping musical works, as deduced by musical scholars.   Theory might be regarded "the grammar of music"--a glimpse into the musical workshop.   In general, theory tends to follow composers' practice, not to lead it.
The word theory, in the sense of a purely speculative abstraction concerning things which may not even exist, as the term is sometimes used in mathematics and science, is a concept foreign to music.   Musical theory and musical practice are under the best conditions one and the same thing.
In the music departments of colleges and in *conservatories, theory is used as the name of a course, or as the generic name given to a group of courses, or both.   When used as the name of a course, "theory" may consist of (A) elementary information about notation, *key-signatures, *time-signatures, terminology, etc., or (B) the foregoing plus *harmony, or (C) the afore-mentioned elementary information plus *sight-singing and *ear-training, or (D) all of these.
When used as the name of a group of subjects, it always includes the branches just mentioned, regardless of whether they are taught separately or as a single combined course. In addition it includes (A) *counterpoint, *orchestration, *form, and perhaps composition and *conducting, or (B) all of these plus history of music and music literature and appreciation, or (C) all of the foregoing plus music education (school music methods)--in other words, "theory" may be used to include everything taught in classes rather than in private lessons, everything other than *applied music.
See also rules of music.

● third.   This word has several distinct meanings in music, which must not be confused.
(1) It can refer to the third degree (mediant) of a *scale.
(2) It can refer to the third of a *triad or *seventh-chord.
(3) It can refer to the *interval of a third. (The expression double thirds is explained under double, 5.)
(4) It may possibly be used to refer to the mediant triad, or III (undesirable).
The same plurality of meanings is found with the word fifth.

● thirteenth-chord.   In its complete form, which exists only theoretically, a thirteenth-chord contains all the tones found in the *diatonic scale, redistributed as a stack of superimposed thirds (see intervals.)
Only one thirteenth-chord is in conventional use: the dominant thirteenth or V^{13}.   In actual practice the fifth, ninth, and eleventh are usually omitted, leaving the root (fundamental), third, seventh, and thirteenth, i.e., scale degree 5, 7, 4, and 3.   The thirteenth (which is the third degree of the scale) is almost invariably in the highest voice.
Other usages are considered less orthodox.
Note music diagram on next page.
See also chord, harmony, seventh-chord, ninth-chord, eleventh-chord, triad, Roman numeral.

● thirty-second note.   See time-values.

● thoroughbass.   (1) A synonym for figured bass.
(2) A synonym for harmony (2).

● three-part form, three-part song

Theoretical forms   Dominant thirteenth-chords
                           as usually employed.

form.   See ternary form; see also
song form .

● threnody.   Dirge, elegy, lament.

● through-composed.   Not having
the same music for all stanzas;
used in speaking of *songs, less
commonly of *choral compositions
and *arias.   It is not necessary that
there be different music for every
stanza; however in any case there
is never the same music for all
stanzas.

The German equivalent, durchkomponiert, is often substituted.
   Antonym: strophic.

● thumb-hole.   A hole on the
underside of certain *woodwind instruments, covered by the left
thumb.

● tie.   A curved line connecting
two notes of the same pitch, uniting
them into a single sound.   Ties are
used to make up values for which
no note exists, to make up values
of more than a measure's duration,
and to connect notes separated by
a bar-line.   See Example 1 below.

The physical appearance of the
tie and the *slur is the same: each
is a curved line.   Their function,
however, is entirely different.

When more than two notes are
tied together, each pair is joined
by a tie.   (This usage differs from
that of the slur under the same
conditions.)   See Example 2 on next
page.

When two *chords are tied together, ties must connect all the
notes, regardless how many there
are.   See Example 3 on next page.

Ex. 1

Right   Wrong

Right   Wrong

When a note affected by an *accidental is tied, it is not necessary (though it is not wrong) to repeat the accidental. See Example 4.

In writing for the piano, sometimes when melodic or arpeggio matter occurs between tied chords, crossing over them, the ties are

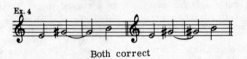

Both correct

Notes which are *enharmonically equivalent are sometimes tied, producing one sound. See Example 5.

interrupted so as not to obscure the moving notes, as shown in Example 6 on following page. It must be borne in mind that this usage is exceptional.

Ex. 6

The following notes are not tied because of the presence of the dots.

See <u>portamento</u> (2) (correctly called <u>portato</u>) and <u>staccato</u> (3).
    Synonym: <u>bind</u>.

● tierce de Picardie (French). Same as <u>Picardy third</u>.
    Plural: <u>tierces de Picardie</u>.
    Pronunciation: tyĕrs dĕ pēk-ăr-dē.

● timbales. *Timpani (kettle-drums). (French and Spanish.)
    Pronunciation: French--tă<u>n</u>-băl.
Spanish--tēm-băl-ĕs (the <u>b</u> slightly like <u>v</u>).

● timbre. *Tone-color, *tone-quality.
    Pronunciation: tĭm-bĕr, tăm-br', or t<u>ă</u>nbr'.

● timbrel. An ancient instrument resembling the modern *tambourine.

● time. This word is used in music as a synonym for (A) *rhythm (undesirable), (B) *meter, (C) length or duration ("timing") of a composition, (D) *tempo (undesirable).
    In view of the confusion that surrounds this word, some musicians urge that it never be used.

● time-signature. The two figures that appear at the beginning of a composition to indicate its *meter. They are written vertically, with the upper figure occupying the upper

half of the staff, the lower figure the lower half; that is, the middle line of the staff separates them.

They are not separated by the short straight line familiarly used in writing fractions.
    The upper figure indicates the number of beats in a *measure.
    The lower figure indicates what kind of note gets one beat. If the lower figure is 4, a quarter-note gets one beat; if it is 8 an eithth-note gets one beat, etc. The fore-going two figures are the commonest, although 2 is also frequent; however 16 is unusual, and both 1 and 32 extremely unusual.
    The two figures are called either "upper figure" and "lower figure" or "top number" and "bottom number," never "numerator" and "denominator."
    Some musicians feel the word <u>time-signature</u> is logically meaningless and substitute <u>meter-sign</u>, <u>meter-signature</u>, <u>measure-sign</u>, <u>measure-signature</u>, <u>rhythmical signature</u>, or <u>metrical signature</u>.
    The sign C is sometimes substituted for 4-4, and ¢ for 2-2, also formerly for 4-2.
    French composers sometimes omit the lower figure in 4-4, 2-2, and 3-4 time, merely placing 4, 2, or 3, respectively, in the middle of the staff--a practice which is hardly to be recommended.

To indicate quick 6-8 time, felt as two beats to a measure (a dotted-quarter-note getting a beat), some musicians have used the symbol $\mathbf{2}$ ♩. Extending from this are $\mathbf{3}$ ♩. for quick 9-8, $\mathbf{2}$ ♩. for quick 6-4, etc.

Sometimes two time-signatures appear. There are two quite distinct uses. (A) In one of these, the two time-signatures will be found to be the simple-meter and compound-meter equivalents of one another, for example 2 6, 3 9, 4 12, 4 8 4 8 4 8, or 2 6. There is neither conflict 2 4 nor contrast between the two meters. Careful study of such a passage will show that by this means the composer avoids writing many *triplets, or perhaps *sextuplets or other *irregular groupings. For a familiar example, consult the G-major prelude in Bach's The Well-Tempered Clavier, volume 1, where 4 and 24 4 16 appear simultaneously. Actually there are just four beats, with six rather than four sixteenth-notes to a beat; these could have been written as sextuplets and 24 could have been 16 dispensed with. (B) In the other use two meters alternate at regular or irregular intervals. Familiar examples will be found in Debussy's piano piece La Cathédrale Engloutie (The Submerged Cathedral), marked 3 6 some measures being in 3-2, 2 4 others in 6-4; and in the third movement of Brahms's Trio in C Minor (violin, cello, and piano), marked 3 2, in which the measures occur in 4 4, groups of three-one of 3-4 and two of 2-4.

In making reference to a time-signature in writing, all of the following forms are acceptable: 3-4, 3/4, 3/4, 3/4, three-four. 3-4 is spoken as "three-four" or "three-quarter," 6-8 as "six-eight" or "six-eighth," 2-2 as "two-two" or "two-half," and so on.

● time-values. Collective name for the various lengths (durations) of notes, particularly in reference to their mathematical inter-relation. It must be emphasized that no note has any absolute length--all lengths are entirely relative. In the values shown in the example, each type of note, considered individually, has half the value of that which precedes. Thus a whole-note equals two half-notes, four quarter-notes, or eight eighth-notes; a half-note equals two quarters or four eighths; a quarter equals two eighths, etc.

The breve (double whole-note) is not tabulated with the others; it equals two whole notes. |o| = o o

The quarter-note is invariably called "quarter-note" (or simply "quarter"), never "fourth-note."

In brief, as the names suggest, the system is based on the "multiple of 2" principle.

Eighth-notes and shorter values are sometimes written separately ♪ ♪ ♫♫ sometimes grouped together on *crossbeams. For sixteenth-notes, two crossbeams are used; for thirty-seconds, three; for sixty-fourths, four. In writing for voices, the extent of the crossbeam is synonymous with a *slur, though seldom are more than four beamed together. In writing for instruments, the grouping is done in the interests of easy reading; again more than four to a crossbeam is exceptional.

Eighths and shorter values are often mixed on a single beaming. The conventions in regard to this usage are too numerous and too complicated for discussion here. The accompanying illustration shows some typical patterns.

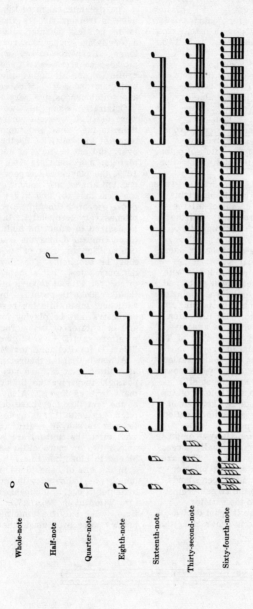

Whole-note

Half-note

Quarter-note

Eighth-note

Sixteenth-note

Thirty-second-note

Sixty-fourth-note

The forms "$\frac{1}{4}$ note," "1/8 note,"
"1/16 note," etc. for "quarter-note,"
"eighth-note," "sixteenth-note," etc.
cannot be recommended; "$\frac{1}{4}$," "1/8,"
"1/16," etc. are very poor.
For the names of the different
types of note in British nomenclature, see British terminology.
Synonyms: note-values, note-
lengths, rhythmic values.
See also note-head, stem, crossbeam, white notes, dotted notes.
For discussion of the pitch of notes,
see notation, staff, clef, leger-line.

● timpani. The kettle-drums. These
are probably the most important,
expressive, and useful of all the
*percussion instruments, and the
only definite pitch instruments of
the drum type.

A single kettle-drum has a somewhat hemispherical shape; it resembles a large copper kettle with
a strong parchment head stretched
tightly over the top. The tuning of
the drum is changed by tensing or
relaxing this head. On the older
type of timpani this was accomplished by twisting a number of T-
shaped screws placed around the
circumference; in the more modern
instruments it is done by the downward or upward movement of a
pedal attached to the bottom of the
drum, and back of it. Pedal-operated timpani are sometimes called
chromatic timpani.

A set of timpani always comprises
at least two drums--usually three,
occasionally even more. They are
of different sizes so as to produce
various pitches, the deeper sounds
being assigned to the larger drums,
the higher ones to the smaller.
The range of the timpani during the
*Classical Period is shown at A, that

for the present day at B.
The dynamic range of the instrument is tremendous; its pianissimo
is the gentlest murmur, its fortissimo
a terrifying, thunderous roar. Single
tones, alternation of two or more
pitches, short repeated groups, and
*rolls (2) are all highly effective,
both loud and soft. *Crescendos
and *diminuendos are very telling.
Originally, when only two drums
were used, it was customary to tune
them to the *tonic and *dominant
tones of the *scale. Beethoven, however, did not hesitate to use other
tunings, and since his time (1770-
1827) the player can expect to encounter almost any combination of
tones to tune to, and in the case of
pedal-operated timpani, to change the
pitches very frequently. In case it
is desired to alter the tuning of hand-
tuned timpani during the course of a
composition, a *rest of adequate length
must be supplied. The player must
not only adjust, but also test, the
pitch, yet without tapping his drums
loudly enough to be heard by the
audience; meanwhile the rest of the
orchestra may be playing fortissimo
and in a different key! The direction
to alter (say) D to E is given thus:
"Muta D (or Re) in E (or Mi)."
Although timpani theoretically sound
as written (that is, are non-transposing), they give the illusion of being
many octaves lower. Also, in spite
of the fact that they have definite
pitch, its definition is quite vague; the
listener is seldom really conscious of
what pitch the timpani are sounding,
unless two or more different tones are
placed in close contrast.
In the era of hand-tuned timpani, the
tuning was indicated with letters (or
syllables), e.g., "Timpani in D, A"
(or "Timpani in Re, La"). At one
time, when only the tonic and dominant
tunings were ever used, the timpani

were treated like a transposing instrument: the composer, after prescribing the tuning with letters, wrote the note C for the tonic tone, G for the dominant, regardless of the actual sounds. It is fortunate that this custom has long been abandoned.

Until quite recently it was common to omit *accidentals in writing for the timpani; that is, after indicating with letters that the drums should be tuned to (say) E-flat and B-flat, the composer would merely write the notes E and B, without bothering to write the flats in front of the notes. Although this custom has also disappeared, to this day the use of a *key-signature in writing for the timpani is almost unheard-of.

The player of the timpani stands while performing.

The word timpani is plural; the rarely-used singular is timpano. (Hence there is no such word as timpanies.)

Variant spelling: tympani (however, theoretically this frequently-used spelling is incorrect; timpany and tympany, though occasionally seen, are both utterly incorrect).

Synonym: kettle-drums.

Italian: timpani.   French: timbales. German: Pauken.   Spanish: timbales or tímpanos.

The player is called a timpanist (also spelled tympanist), occasionally kettle-drummer.

Pronunciation: tǐm-pă-nē.

● Tin Pan Alley. Humorous and derogatory name for the world of American "popular" music, jazz, and musical commercialism in general. There is of course no street actually called Tin Pan Alley, but the fact that the afore-mentioned elements are located either on or near Broadway in New York City has led some persons to associate this name with that thoroughfare.

● titles. The need for a composition to have a name does not loom up as pressingly in the minds of composers as of laymen. Although such terms as *symphony, *concerto,

*suite, *sonata, *trio, etc. may be regarded as "titles," they are in reality nothing more than designations of the compositions' *form, while *fugue, *barcarolle, *march, *berceuse, and all the sundry names of dances merely describe the type or style of composition. Nevertheless, plentiful examples of true titles are to be found. As a start, one can look through a list of the compositions of Debussy, although he has been accused of using titles arbitrarily. The titles of *operas and *symphonic poems are always carefully chosen; in the former category they are even re-named if there is reason to believe the original title is weak, misleading, or insufficiently provocative.

Catch-All Titles. There are a number of "titles" that are nothing more than catch-all words to which the composer can resort should his ingenuity for inventing a name fail completely; for example *prelude (5), *album leaf, *intermezzo (4), *moment musical, *impromptu, and *song without words. The same is almost as true of the terms *fantasy, *rhapsody, *overture (3), *légende, *ballade, etc.

A few composers such as Schoenberg have frankly used the "title" Piano-Piece (in German, Klavierstück).

The polyglot type of *motet (3) common during the thirteenth century and later, is a setting of several texts simultaneously and therefore often has three titles, for example En Non Diu!--Quant Voi--Eius in Oriente.

Substitutes for Titles. *Tempo indications are frequently used in titles (Adagio for Strings, Introduction and Allegro, Andante for Piano). In referring to the various movements of *symphonies, *sonatas, *concertos, etc., often the Italian tempo term is used ("adagio movement," "allegro con brio movement").

On the other hand, *opus numbers are not titles, nor substitutes for them; instead they have the function of catalogue numbers for distinguishing among a group of similarly-titled compositions.

Nicknames, Spurious Titles. Certain compositions have for a number of reasons acquired spurious names, not given or intended by their composers. When the latter has provided nothing more than a general name like Sonata, Symphony, etc. plus the name of the *key--admittedly meaningless to the non-musician--and perhaps an *opus number, some persons have with a certain amount of justification felt the need for something more concrete. Surely it is much easier for the *layman to remember such a title as "Dramatic Symphony" than "Symphony No. 2 in A Minor, op. 20."

Certain nicknames are arbitrary, foolish, misleading, or even ridiculous, yet their aid as an identification is not to be minimized, and many of them are quite well established--truly entrenched in musicians' everyday vocabularies, a good example being the so-called "Moonlight" Sonata by Beethoven.

Nicknames have been very generously applied to the more-than-100 symphonies by Haydn, stimulated by the fact that their numbering is thoroughly confused, and further aggrevated by the fact that Haydn did not use opus numbers.

A sharp distinction must be made between nicknames and official descriptive names given by the composer himself. The "Pastoral" and "Eroica" ("Heroic") Symphonies by Beethoven and the "Pathétique" ("Pathetic") Symphony by Tschaikowsky are just a few among scores of genuine, composer-given names that might be cited.

Misnamed Compositions. After allowing for the fact that numerous musical terms have changed meaning during the history of music, there remain a number of compositions whose titles were inaccurate even at the time of writing.

See also chôros.

● t-k. Direction for *double-tonguing. Triple-tonguing is indicated by t-k-t or -t-t-k.

●† toccata. A brilliant study in touch, usually for a keyboard instrument (especially organ), in free form. Some toccatas are coupled with another composition into a pair,

either as the first or second piece; others are parts of works divided into several movements; still others are purely independent.

There is of course no connection between the terms toccata and staccato. (Related English word: touch.)

● tom-tom. A simple type of drum with a single head, used by the American Indians and other primitive peoples. It is sometimes played with a stick, sometimes directly with the hands. It should not be confused with the *tam-tam, which it in no way resembles.

Synonym: Indian drum.

● tonal. Pertaining to *tonality. This word is sometimes used in contradistinction to *modal, other times to *atonal. For an additional usage see fugue.

● tonal center. Same as tonic.

● tonal imagery. The ability to hear inwardly, in the imagination, the tones represented by the musical notation one sees. Development of this skill is the chief purpose of courses in *ear-training. A high degree of facility in tonal imagery is a sign of good *musicianship.

Synonym: auditory imagery.

● tonality. (1) The quality of being in some *key (1); the musical tendency to gravitate to points of repose on certain tones rather than others; the relation of all tones to a central tone. It is the opposite of atonality, and a further description of tonality will be found under that term, for purposes of contrast.

(2) Harmonic structure built on the modern major or minor scale rather than on the church *modes.

See major and minor, major scale, minor scale, and key-signature.

● tone. (1) A single musical sound of fixed pitch. A tone is distinguished from a note in that a tone is heard, while a note is seen. A purist avoids such expressions as "I can hear the notes of the double-bass" or "That bird's call consists of two notes," though of course this matter can be carried to fussy extremes. In speaking of the simultaneous visual and auditory aspect, the term generally used is note.

(2) A synonym for *whole-step.

(3) A synonym for *tone-color or *tone-quality. We sometimes say "The oboe has a nasal tone" when "The oboe has a nasal tone-color" would be more precise.

(4) A synonym for *mode (1). Thus the "eighth tone" means the eighth (i.e., hypomixolydian) mode.

● tone-clusters. Groups of dissonant tones, usually entire scales, sounded simultaneously and with comparatively little regard for their dissonant effect. They are especially associated with the American composer Henry Cowell (1897-1965). A tone-cluster might well be described as a "chord in seconds."

When written for the piano, tone-clusters usually consist either entirely of white keys or entirely of black --occasionally a mixture. Composers sometimes use an abbreviated form of notation by writing only the highest and lowest sounds and representing the intervening notes with a straight thick line.

In playing tone-clusters on the piano, the flat palm of the hand, the elbow, the flat forearm, or even a piece of wood of a specified length are used so as to press all the keys simultaneously. The spectacular antics necessary to play tone-clusters have given some audiences a detrimental impression as to the seriousness of the compositions that contain them.

Synonym: cluster chords.

● tone-color. That property in musical tones that makes it possible to distinguish one instrument from another, or to distinguish voices from instruments; the characteristic "sound" of the various instruments and voices, without regard to pitch, duration, or loudness.

Tone-color is the result of the presence, absence, or comparative strength of the various overtones in the *harmonic series produced automatically by every instrument and voice. For example, the overtones produced by the trombone are different from those produced by the cello, some being stronger, others weaker or even totally absent; hence the trombone "sounds different" from the cello.

Variant spelling: tone-colour.

Synonyms: timbre, tone-quality (2).

Compare tone-quality (1).

See also orchestration, registration.

● tone poem. Same as symphonic poem.

● tone-quality. (1) The characteristic sound of one particular instrument or voice compared with an instrument or voice of the same kind; the element of possessing or producing a "good" tone or a "bad" one. Thus we say that a Stradivarius violin has a better tone-quality than a twenty-five dollar violin, that Heifetz gets a better tone-quality from a violin than a beginner, that Caruso's voice had a better tone-quality than the voice of a person without vocal training, etc.

(2) A synonym for tone-color (timbre).

● tone row. See twelve tone system.

● tone symbolism. See symbolism, textpainting.

● Tonette. See simple melody instruments. A trade name.

● tonguing. The use of the tongue in playing *woodwind and *brass instruments. Quick and clean *articulation of tones, good *phrasing, and sharp production of *staccato tones are all dependent on the player's tonguing technique.

See also double-tonguing. Flutter-tonguing is described under tremolo (3).

● tonic. The tone which has a feeling of finality, of being "home," of being the center around which the other tones cluster and to which they gravitate. If a melody is interrupted, even though it be totally unfamiliar, the mind will seem to imagine it continuing until it comes to rest, reaches a natural end. The tone on which it concludes is (or ought to be) the tonic. This is the first degree, or step, of the scale. It may also be considered the eighth degree, as it were--the tone an *octave above the starting-point, on which the scale naturally finishes off. We normally refer to these two as the low tonic and high (or upper) tonic. In the major mode the *syllable-name of the tonic tone is do; in minor it is la (assuming the usage customary in the United States is being employed).

The *triad built on this degree of the scale is called the tonic triad; its *Roman numeral is I.

In the *modes (1), the term final is roughly equivalent to tonic.

Synonyms: key center, home tone, key-tone, key-note, tonal center.

For tonic accent see accent.

Pronunciation: tŏn-ĭk.

● tonic minor, tonic major. Tonic minor indicates the minor *key having the same *tonic, or key center, as a given major key; tonic major indicates a major key having the same tonic as a given minor key. Thus, D minor is the tonic minor of D major, E-flat major the tonic major of E-flat minor.

It does not follow that the letter-name of the keys is invariably the same, however; one name may be the *enharmonic equivalent of the other. Thus the tonic minor of D-flat major is C-sharp minor, since there is no key of D-flat minor; F-sharp minor is the tonic minor of both F-sharp major and its enharmonic equivalent G-flat major.

Synonyms: corresponding minor (major), parallel minor (major).

Compare relative minor (major).

● Tonic Sol-fa. A system for teaching and notating vocal music,

widely used in the British Isles. It is based on the principle of movable-do *syllables, but their spelling has been thoroughly anglicized, thus: doh, ray, me, fah, soh, lah, te. In writing Tonic Sol-fa, the initial letters of these syllables, plus dashes and colons, replace the *staff and notes; the letters indicate the pitches, the colons and dashes, the duration. *Bar-lines are employed as in normal notation.

●† tornando al tempo. Same as ritornando al tempo.

●† tosto. Fast. Più tosto is a synonym for più mosso. However, this term is sometimes incorrectly used to mean almost or nearly.

● touch. The exact manner and technique of playing a keyboard instrument--especially the motion of the fingers--is called the study of touch.

● Town Hall. A concert hall in New York, used chiefly for solo recitals and chamber-music concerts. It is a favorite place for pianists and singers to use in making their *débuts.

● toy band, toy orchestra. Same as rhythm band.

● tr, tr 〰 Signs for the *trill.

● traditional music. See folk music.

●† tragico. Tragic.
Pronunciation: accent first syllable.

●† tranquillo. Quietly, peacefully.
Abbreviation: tranq.
Synonyms: calmato, quieto, placido.
Antonyms: agitato, inquieto.

● transcribe. See transcription. This is the verb form.

● transcription. (1) The arrangement or re-writing of a composition so that it may be performed by some *medium other than that for which it was originally written; for example, arranging a piano composition for orchestra, an orchestral composition for band, a

composition for voice and piano so
that it may be performed by *mixed
chorus and piano, and so on.

Transcriptions are sometimes
made by hacks, sometimes by highly
skilled musicians, and sometimes
by composers, many of whom have
transcribed their own works (e. g.
Ravel's numerous transcriptions of
his own piano pieces for orchestra).

Although purists frown on all
transcriptions, theirs is an extrem-
ist point of view.

In spite of the fact that many
transcriptions have been made with
extreme skill, there are only a
handful which surpass or are more
famous than the original form.

Synonym: arrangement.

See also piano-vocal copy, reduction.

(2) Musicologists also use the
terms transcription and transcribe
in reference to converting obsolete
forms of notation (for example,

*neumes and *tablatures) into modern
notation.   Here the word transcribe
has almost the force of decipher.

See also editor.

(3) *Electrical transcription.

● transformation of theme. A process,
chiefly associated with the *symphonic
poems of Liszt and the *music-dramas
of Wagner, wherein the character of
a *theme is made to undergo radical
change by altering its *rhythm, *dynamics, *harmonization, or *tessitura.
The transformation of theme process
can be applied to any form and any
medium; it need not be restricted to
the opera and the symphonic poem.

This evolutionary process is also
applied to *generating themes; its
presence distinguishes the generating theme from the motto theme (see
cyclic form).

The accompanying examples of
transformation of theme are from
Liszt's symphonic poem Les Préludes.

Ex. 1-A Andante maestoso

Ex. 1-B Allegro marziale animato

Ex. 2-A Andante maestoso

Ex. 2-B Tempo di marcia

Synonyms: metamorphosis of theme, theme transformation.

● transition. (1) A *modulation.

Some theorists make a distinction between transition and modulation, describing the former either as of brief duration or as of abrupt appearance (without a *pivot chord to smooth the effect).

(2) Any connecting passage of music; a bridge passage; a link passage; an episode. See also ritornello and form.

● transposing instruments. Generic name given to those instruments which do not sound the pitches that are written; the composer writes one set of notes but a different set emits from the instrument. The composer therefore does not write the sounds he actually wants, but those the performer must play.

The very existence of such a practice probably baffles the non-musician by its seeming want of logic; yet there are very good reasons why it arose and why it must be continued. The origins of this practice reach far back into the history of music, the history of the various instruments, and the technique of the various instruments, and many pages would be necessary to explain all the cases.

The convenience of this custom in one case--namely that of those instruments which transpose an octave--will be immediately apparent: the saving of many *legerlines.

LIST OF TRANSPOSING INSTRUMENTS USED IN THE ORCHESTRA AND BAND

Sounding an octave lower than written--notated an octave higher than the sounds desired:
  Double-Bass
  Contrabassoon (however Wagner and Debussy write for it at actual pitch)
  Horn in C (obsolete)
  C melody Saxophone
  Heckelphone

Sounding an octave higher than written--notated an octave lower than the sounds desired:
  Piccolo
  Celesta
  Xylophone
  Glockenspiel (Some orchestration books state that the Glockenspiel sounds two octaves higher than written, though this sometimes seems to be at variance with actual usage.)

The transposition of the two foregoing groups is very simple, not, however, those that follow.

Sounding a minor second (half-step) lower than written--notated a minor second higher than the sounds desired:
  Trumpet in B (obsolete)

Sounding a major second (whole-step) lower than written--notated a major second higher than the sounds desired:
  Clarinet in B-flat
  Bass Clarinet in B-flat when notated in "German notation" (explained in the entry bass clarinet)
  Trumpet in B-flat
  Cornet in B-flat

Flügelhorn in B-flat
Horn in B-flat alto (obsolete)
Soprano Saxophone

Sounding a minor third lower than written--notated a minor third higher than the sounds desired:
  Clarinet in A
  Bass Clarinet in A (obsolete) when notated in "German notation"
  Trumpet in A
  Cornet in A
  Oboe d'amore (however Bach writes for it at actual pitch)
  Horn in A (obsolete)

Sounding a perfect fourth lower than written--notated a perfect fourth higher than the sounds desired:
  Alto Flute
  Horn in G (obsolete)

Sounding a perfect fifth lower than written--notated a perfect fifth higher than the sounds desired:
  Horn in F
  English Horn
  Basset Horn
  Contralto Trumpet

Sounding a minor sixth lower than written--notated a minor sixth higher than the sounds desired:
  Horn in E (obsolete)

Sounding a major sixth lower than written--notated a major sixth higher than the sounds desired:
  Alto Saxophone
  Alto Clarinet
  Alto Horn (Mellophone)
  Horn in E-flat (obsolete in the orchestra, obsolescent in the band)

Sounding a minor seventh lower than written--notated a minor seventh higher than the sounds desired:
  Horn in D (obsolete)

Sounding a minor ninth (an octave plus a half-step) lower than written--notated a minor ninth higher than the sounds desired:
  Horn in B (obsolete)

Sounding a major ninth (an octave plus a whole-step) lower than written--notated a major ninth higher than the sounds desired:
  Bass Clarinet in B-flat when written in "French notation" (explained in the entry bass clarinet)

Baritone (Euphonium) when written in treble clef notation
Tenor Saxophone
Horn in B-flat basso (obsolete)

Sounding a minor tenth (an octave plus a minor third) lower than written--notated a minor tenth higher than the sounds desired:
Bass Clarinet in A (obsolete) when written in "French notation"
Horn in A basso (obsolete, rare)

Sounding an octave and a major sixth lower than written:
Baritone Saxophone

Sounding two octaves and a major second lower than written:
Bass Saxophone

Sounding a major second (whole-step) higher than written--notated a major second lower than the sounds desired:
Trumpet in D (obsolete except in the form called "little Trumpet"). (However Handel notates the Trumpet in D at actual pitch)
D Clarinet (an instrument apparently used only in Germany and Austria)

Sounding a minor third higher than written--notated a minor third lower than the sounds desired:
Trumpet in E-flat (obsolete except in the form called "little Trumpet")
Cornet in E-flat (almost obsolete)
E-flat Clarinet
Sopranino Saxophone

Sounding a major third higher than written--notated a major third lower than the sounds desired:
Trumpet in E (obsolete)

Sounding a perfect fourth higher than written--notated a perfect fourth lower than the sounds desired:
Trumpet in F (now obsolete)

Sounding a perfect fifth higher than written:
Trumpet in G (obsolete, rare)

All of the *stops on the organ except the eight-foot stops may be regarded as transposing; this is discussed under organ, though basically it is not classified as a transposing instrument.

The tenor voice, when written with the treble clef might be added to the first classification in the foregoing table, for when so written it sounds an octave lower than notated.

The foregoing list does not include a number of rare instruments, rare forms of common instruments (Horn in A-flat, Trumpet in A-flat, Horn in F-sharp, etc.), or instruments not used in the orchestra or band.

Summary in Notation. The accompanying table summarizes the workings of the various transposing instruments.

It will be observed that such expressions as "in B-flat" and "in F" refer to the actual pitch of the tone that is heard when the player sounds a written C. The transposition corresponds to the interval-relationship between C and the key in which the given instrument is pitched.

In referring to the sounds given out by transposing instruments in contrast to the written notation, the correct expression is "actual pitch," although *"concert pitch" (2) is frequently though carelessly substituted.

Non-Transposing Instruments. The following instruments do not transpose-- they are notated as they sound:
Piano
Violin
Viola
Cello (except the obsolete G clef notation once used for high notes; this is discussed in the entry cello)
Flute
Oboe
Clarinet in C (obsolete)
Bassoon
Trumpet in C
Trombone
Baritone (Euphonium) when notated with the bass clef (F clef)
Tuba
Timpani
Harp (except the *harmonics)
All of the foregoing are often called non-transposing instruments.

The term C instruments is sometimes applied to those instruments which sound as written (non-transposing) plus those which transpose an octave, either up or down.

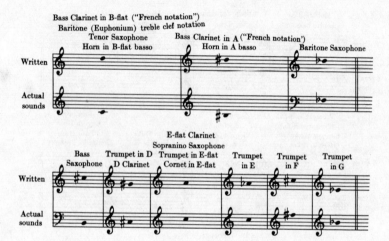

● transposition. The process of performing music in some *key (1) other than that in which it is written.   The verb form is transpose.

The accompanying shows a passage in its original form in the key of C, then written as it would sound if transposed up an augmented fourth (see intervals) to F-sharp, then written as it would sound when transposed down a major third to A-flat.

● traps.   An undesirable term sometimes used as a synonym for *percussion instruments or for *battery.

●† tratto.   Drawn out.   (Related English word: protract.)

●† trattenuto.   Held back.   Abbreviation: tratt.

●† traverso.   Transverse.   The

Players of certain orchestral instruments, especially the *horn, *trumpet, and *clarinet, must be adept at transposition because many compositions were originally written for now-obsolete forms of these instruments, such as the clarinet in C, horn in D, trumpet in F. Today's player, using a clarinet in B-flat (or possibly A), a horn in F, or a trumpet in B-flat (or possibly C), must transpose the music to bring it to the proper actual pitch. Pianists and organists sometimes find it necessary to transpose when working with solo singers and choruses, in order that the voices may find the range more comfortable.

Ability to transpose is an indication of good *musicianship.

● trap drum.   An undesirable name sometimes applied to the *snare drum.

● trap drummer.   A term often applied to the player of the very numerous *percussion instruments found in a *dance band.

*flute was once called flauto traverso or transverse flute in recognition of the fact that it is held out to the player's right side and sounded by blowing across a hole, to distinguish it from the once-popular *recorder or flûte à bec (beak flute), which is held straight out from the mouth and sounded by blowing into a whistle-type mouthpiece or fipple.   The waning of the recorder's popularity made the distinction no longer necessary.

See also German flute, English flute.

● treble.   (1) High pitches in general.
(2) A vague term for the right-hand part of a piano composition.
(3) *Soprano, especially a child soprano.   (Chiefly British.)

● treble clef.   See clef.

● treble staff.   A *staff with a treble (or G) *clef.   In music for the piano it is the upper of the two staffs bracketed together.

●† tre corde.   Release the *soft pedal; used in connection with music for the

piano. (Literally "three strings.")
It cancels una corda.

Synonym: tutte le corde.

● † tremolando.   Same as tremolo
(1, 2, 3, 4).   Literally "trembling"
or "shaking."

● tremolo.   All tremolos can be
defined as trembling or vibrating
effects produced by the rapid re-
iteration of a single tone, interval,
or chord, or by the rapidly-re-
iterated alternation of two different
tones.

Any tremolo may be done in
either of two ways: (A) It may be
made a definite number of times
per beat, carefully measured out
as groups of eighth-, sixteenth-,
or thirty-second-notes. Called the
"measured tremolo," this for all
practical purposes is an "abbreviation" to save the laborious writing-out of many short notes. (B)
The repetition may be made just
as many times as the player can
execute within the allotted time-
value of the note. This might be
termed the "indefinite" type, since
the exact number of reiterations is
not precisely indicated. To some
musicians it is the only true tremolo.

There are several distinct species
of tremolo, depending on the instrument.

(1) String Instruments, Bowed
Tremolo.   Probably the commonest
form of tremolo--the prototype for
all--is the bowed tremolo of the
string instruments.   The indicated
note is repeated very rapidly, by a
constant and quick alternation of
short *down-bows and *up-bows,
throughout its printed duration. To
secure this effect the composer inter-
sects the stem of the note with rather
thick, nearly-horizontal strokes resembling short *crossbeams.

When the bowed tremolo is to be
performed in "measured" fashion,
the composer uses one stroke to
convert the time-value into the equivalent number of eighths, two for sixteenths, three for thirty-seconds, and
so on.   It is best for him to write
out a beat or half-beat (or even a
complete measure) in the exact time-
values, then follow with the abbreviated
form, as shown in Example 1.   If
the notes in the "measured" tremolo
are to be played *staccato, dots are
placed under or over the note--as
many dots as there would be notes
if written out in full. If *portato is
wanted, the dots are grouped by a slur.
See Example 2.

When the "indefinite" type tremolo is wanted, the composer either adds the term <u>trem</u>. (abbreviation for <u>tremolo</u>) or else places a sufficient number of strokes through the stem to suggest time-values so short that no musician could possibly play the correct amount if measured out; more strokes are needed in a slow tempo than in a fast one. See Example 3.

Bowed tremolos have doubtless been abused in the composing of *operas, where all too often they accompany the villain as he creeps stealthily across the stage; yet this resource, used in moderation, can be most telling if well handled. The effect is usually quite agitated and sometimes a bit "scratchy."

(2) <u>String Instruments, Fingered</u>

Ex. 3 Allegro   Adagio   Adagio   Prestissimo

Trem.

When the "indefinite" type of tremolo is used in the orchestra--its normal habitat--some players will repeat the note more often than others, which is all to the good.

When a tremolo of either "measured" or "indefinite" type is needed for a whole-note, the little strokes are placed at the spot corresponding to that where the stem would be expected. See Example 4.

<u>Tremolo</u>. The fingered tremolo is a legato effect in which two different pitches are alternated very rapidly. Fingered tremolos are, for all practical purposes, just extended *trills. Their effect is somewhat "fluttering" and "twittering"--much smoother and less agitated than the bowed tremolo. They can be played either as "measured" tremolos or as "indefinite" ones (alternating the two

Ex. 4

When the "measured" tremolo occurs in triplets or multiples thereof, it is necessary to dot every note and to indicate the number of sounds with 3, 6, 9, 12, 24, or whatever is correct. See Example 5.

notes as rapidly as possible). A slur must always connect the two notes involved. See Example 6 on next page.

It will be observed that in writing the fingered tremolo the notation seems

Ex. 5

3   3   6   12   24   3   3   3   3   6

"Indefinite"   "Measured"

to contain twice the correct number of beats. The two notes are regarded as though they sounded simultaneously--and such is practically the effect they often give to the ear. If the passage in Example 7 were to be converted to a fingered tremolo it would be written as shown in Example 8. With

commonly with the trumpet, trombone, or tuba. These are, of course, abbreviations for repeated eighths, sixteenths, or thirty-seconds, as the case may be. Their effect is usually one of buoyant energy and exhilaration.

The unmeasured or "indefinite" type of tremolo on a single note, when performed very rapidly, is known

quarter-notes the strokes must not quite touch the stems; otherwise they will no longer be quarter-notes. With eighths, only one stroke touches the stems, with sixteenths, only two.

The intervals in the fingered tremolo are usually narrow, most frequently thirds, although wider intervals can be used by alternating between two notes on different strings.

Synonyms for fingered tremolo are legato tremolo and slurred tremolo.

(3) Wind Instruments. The repetition of single tones, as "measured" tremolos, is often used with woodwind instruments and the horn, less

as flutter-tonguing and is produced by a special technique. The effect is very odd, especially on the flute; on the muted trumpet it sounds spiteful. (See also double-tonguing.)

Tremolos of the type which alternates two pitches (i. e., legato tremolos) are possible on woodwind instruments, although best results are obtained when the interval is narrow, preferably a third. These are, again, extended trills. Even the trumpet and horn can play such passages, but on the former the effect is aggressive and noisy--even alarming; on the latter it is rather untidy.

(4) Piano. Tremolos alternating two pitches, or more than two--provided all the tones but one are com-

bined as a *chord--are possible on the piano. They are usually encountered in *transcriptions of orchestral music, for the effect, while perfectly easy, is hardly in the piano *idiom. Any interval up to and including the octave is practical. They are quite "rumbly" when set as bass octaves. See Example 9.

the stringed instruments and the voice. The rate of pulsation can be controlled by various mechanical adjustments, and on certain electronic organs it can be varied at the player's pleasure. A slight and very rapid tremulant can do much toward counteracting the mechanical effect of the organ provided the player does not employ it too often, but a slow pro-

Ex. 9

Tremolos for the piano are often carelessly written. Even the "bowed tremolo" style of notation is sometimes seen, although strictly it is unplayable on the instrument. Only in the slowest tempos can tremolos A through D in Example 10 be played exactly as written;

nounced tremulant is vulgar in the extreme. The name vibrato (5) is occasionally substituted.

(6) Voice. The word tremolo is also applied to a certain wavering in the voice, where it sounds like an exaggerated form of *vibrato. Its presence is due to faulty vocal

Ex. 10   A   B   C   D   E

otherwise all of them would be performed in the manner shown at E.

(5) Organ. The tremolo (properly tremulant) on the organ is an entirely different thing from the tremolos just discussed. It has nothing to do with the technique of playing the instrument, and its use does not involve special forms of notation. It is a mechanical device which produces a rapid pulsation in the volume of the tone. Its purpose is to simulate the *vibrato of

production.

Plural: tremolos.

Abbreviation: trem.

Variant form: tremulo.

Synonym (for meanings 1, 2, 3, 4): tremolando.

Pronunciation: trĕm-ȯ-lō.

● † tremoloso. Trembling, fluttering.

Variant form: tremuloso.

● tremulant. The correct name for the so-called tremolo (5) of the organ.

Synonym: vibrato (5).

● † tremulo, † tremuloso. Variant forms of tremolo, tremoloso.

● triad. A *chord made up of three different tones laid out as two superimposed thirds, or any of its possible ramifications.

The duplication ("doubling") of one, two or all three pitches in the *octaves above or below is not considered as the addition of new tones but as the original ones strengthened. Thus all the chords shown in Example 1 are regarded as various possible aspects of the

sharply with the lean sound of the first and second. Nevertheless musicians look upon them essentially as various possible forms of a single basic combination.

It is important to emphasize that a real triad must contain three different tones. Although the chord shown in Example 2 (at bottom of page) has three tones, there are only two different ones, for the D is duplicated. The chord is properly termed an *"open fifth, " rather than a triad.

Types. Chords are usually *"spelled"

triad CEG. Of course no person would claim that all these forms give the same aesthetic effect; the change of bass tone in particular creates a conspicuous difference (to be discussed later), and the thickness of certain chords contrasts

(i. e., named) in the closest position which they can assume. It would be impossible to place the tones CEG any closer together than shown in the first chord in Example 1.

When placed in this close position, all three notes will be on lines or all three on spaces--never a mixture.

If the chord is composed of a major third between the lowest and middle tones, and a minor third between the middle and highest (see intervals), it is called a major triad. (The distance between the lowest and highest tones will then be a perfect fifth.)

If there is a minor third below and a major third above (totaling a perfect fifth), the chord is called a minor triad.

If the chord consists of two superimposed major thirds (totaling an augmented fifth) it is called an augmented triad.

If it consists of two superimposed minor thirds (totaling a diminished fifth) it is called a diminished triad. See Example 3.

Members. The lowest of the three tones, when in close "spelling position," is called the *root or fundamental; it almost seems to generate the other tones of the triad--to be the sound out of which the entire triad grows. The middle tone is called the third; it is located at the interval of a third above the root. The highest tone is called the fifth because of its location a fifth above the root. Irrespective of where the root, third, and fifth are placed in the chord, they still retain the names used in the close ("spelling") position. These matters are illustrated in Example 5 on the following page.

Positions (Inversions). The most important tone in any chord, from the standpoint of "coloring" it and giving it character, is the one that appears in the *bass--the lowest tone.

Ex. 3

major   minor   augmented   diminished   major   minor   augmented   diminished

The table in Example 4 shows the "spelling" of all the practical major, minor, augmented, and diminished triads.

(It will be observed that chords are always "spelled" from the lowest tone upward, never from the top down.)

If the root is in the bass, the triad

Basic spelling	M ajor			Minor			Augmented			Diminished		
CEG FAC GBD	♮	♮	♮	♮	♭	♮	♮	♮	♯	♮	♭	♭
	♯	♯	♯	♯	♮	♯	♭	♭	♮	♯	♮	♮
	♭	♭	♭	♭	♭♭	♭	♯	♯	×	×	♯	♯
DFA EGB ACE	♮	♯	♮	♮	♮	♮	♮	♯	♯	♮	♮	♭
	♭	♮	♭	♯	♯	♯	♭	♮	♮	♯	♯	♮
	♯	×	♯	♭	♭	♭	♭♭	♭	♭	♭	♭	♭♭
	♭♭	♭	♭♭									
BDF	♮	♯	♯	♮	♮	♯	♮	♯	×	♮	♮	♮
	♭	♮	♮	♭	♭	♮	♭	♮	♯	♯	♯	♯
	♭♭	♭	♭				♭♭	♭	♮	♭	♭	♭

Example 4

Ex. 5

is said to be in root position or fundamental position.

If the third is in the bass, the triad is said to be in first inversion (1), or in the position of the sixth; this could be more fully expressed as six-three position. The latter expression arises from the fact that the root is located at the interval of a sixth (or its compound) above the bass tone, while the fifth is located a third (or its compound) above the bass tone.

If the fifth is in the bass, the triad is said to be in second inversion, or in six-four position, the latter because the root is a fourth (or its compound) above the bass tone and the third is a sixth (or its compound) above the bass tone.

The afore-mentioned positions are illustrated in Example 6.

Functional Aspect (Roman Numerals and Names). In addition to their intervallic structure, triads must also be considered according to the way

Ex. 6

Maj.   Aug.   Min.   Dim.   Maj.   Min.   Dim.   Aug.   Maj.   Dim.   Aug.   Min.

Root (or fundamental) position.   First inversion.   Second inversion.

they behave within a composition--
by their function. The triads that
are possible in each major and
each minor key are assigned names
and equivalent Roman numerals to
express this function. Full details
come within the scope of a course
in *harmony (2). The names and
numbers are shown in Example 7.
It must be borne in mind that it is
customary in minor keys to build
the triads from the harmonic form
of the minor scale.

dainty, exotic, or brilliant effects.
Music for the triangle is often
written on a one-line *staff.
   Italian: triangolo.   French: triangle.
German: Triangel.   Spanish: triángulo.

● trill. (1) Perhaps the most frequently-used *ornament, indicated by
the sign 𝄐 (often followed by a
wavy line) placed above the note that
is affected. It is performed by
rapidly alternating the given note with
the note just above, and is performed

Number	Name	Scale-Degrees	Type in Major	Type in Minor
I	Tonic triad	1-3-5	major	minor
II	Supertonic triad	2-4-6	minor	diminished
III	Mediant triad	3-5-7	minor	augmented
IV	Subdominant triad	4-6-1	major	minor
V	Dominant triad	5-7-2	major	major
VI	Submediant triad	6-1-3	minor	major
VII	Leading-tone triad	7-2-4	diminished	diminished

Ex. 7

   The tonic (I), subdominant (IV),
and dominant (V) triads are called
the principal or primary triads;
the others, the subordinate or secondary triads.
   The exact description of *seventh-
chords is discussed under that heading, but full details are impossible
to give in a dictionary; a harmony
textbook should be consulted.
   Synonym: common chord (2).
   See also chord, figured bass,
harmony, intervals, Roman numerals,
seventh-chord. Tones not members
of the chord with which they sound
are described under non-harmonic
tones.

● triangle. An indefinite pitch *percussion instrument, consisting of a
metal rod, bent as its name suggests,
but open at one corner. It is played
with a little metal beater; however
a rarely-employed but delightful effect can be obtained by striking the
triangle with a wooden stick.
   The tone is extremely high-pitched,
and seems to say "ting." *Rolls (2)
may be performed in one of the
corners. It is normally used for

through the entire written length of
the given note. The number of times
the two tones are repeated depends on
the *technique and taste of the performer, as well as on the length of
the note. An exact writing-out is
therefore impossible, but is more or
less as shown in Example 1 on the
next page. The effect of the trill is
often compared to the warbling of
birds.
   There are two types of trill: that
over the interval of a *whole-step
and that over a *half-step. These
are sometimes called the major trill
and minor trill, respectively. The
former occurs in Examples 1, 3, and
5; the latter in Example 4.
   In music for the voice, the employment of the trill, when indicated, is
considered optional, due to the fact
that some singers simply cannot
execute it. On the other hand, during
the *Baroque Period trills were often
interpolated into both vocal and instrumental music at points where the composer did not so indicate (though it is
more than possible that he half ex-
pected--and even approved--such an
occurrence).

Ex. 1   Written   Played (approximately)

When the trill is written over a chord or a double-note interval, only the highest note is usually understood to be affected. If both notes are to be trilled, there should be a second trill-sign, placed below the lower note. If only the lower note is to be trilled, the sign appears below the lower note only. See Example 2.

to write in the after-beat specifically, although wherever a trill without after-beat is desired, a footnote to that effect is advisable.

The notes (usually two in number) of the after-beat should be performed at the same rate of speed as the trill proper.

There is reason to believe that the symbol for the double inverted

Ex. 2

Not very clear.   Trill upper note;   Trill both   Trill lower note;   Trill all
                    sustain lower.   notes.   sustain upper.   three notes

After-Beat. It will be observed that in the first part of Example 1, at the very end of the trill there appear two notes in grace-note type, one being the tone below the trilled tone, the other the trilled tone itself. (It will be further observed that the first of these is a half-step below the trilled tone--as is almost invariable). These two are collectively called the *after-beat (1) and most trills conclude with this device. Its presence was always understood (and hence it was seldom specifically written) in earlier music. In general, trills found in works dating from the eighteenth century or earlier should end with an after-beat. In more recent times it has been customary

mordent (see mordent) has sometimes been used to indicate the trill without after-beat.

Execution. Considerable argument has arisen among musicians as to whether the trill should begin on the written note (or "principal note," as it is often called), or on the "auxiliary note," as the upper alternating (unwritten) note is called. Often it is impossible to tell which type of performance is employed. However, there is general agreement that in earlier music, trills begin on the auxiliary tone, except where the latter is the note that immediately precedes the trill; in later music it begins on the principal note, unless it is the note that immediately precedes. To eliminate any misunderstanding, some

composers place a grace-note at
the beginning of the trill as a clue
to their intention.   See Example 3.

When a trill occurs on an extremely short note it is sometimes possible
to play only three tones, the result

Ex. 3

Beginning on auxiliary note.   Beginning on principal note.

It is important to mention that
regardless of whether the tempo
is fast or slow, the trill is performed as rapidly as possible. As
stated earlier, some players will
play more notes than others.   It
is unfortunate but unavoidable that
in the first illustration of the playing of a trill (Example 1) given
above, it was necessary to write
out the execution in notes of measured value, for no other method is
possible.   The slow and measured
execution of trills, often indicated
by well-meaning editors, is invariably of a stupid and unmusical
effect.

Occasionally a performer will
commence a trill slowly, accelerate
it in the middle, and slow it down
again toward the end, but this style
of performance is open to serious
question.   Others make a practice
of playing the first pair of tones
in the trill a trifle slower than all
the others.   The employment of
this can hardly be detected, and
greater clarity in execution seems
to result.

sounding like a *triplet.   The effect
is practically the same as if an
*inverted mordent had been written.
Trills of this type are not to be
recommended to composers.

Accidentals.   When an accidental
appears over a trill-sign, it affects
the auxiliary note.   In Example 4,
the first trill is to be made with A-
flat, not A; in the second with F-
natural, not F-sharp.   A readily-
accessible example may be found in
the well-known Minuet by Paderewski,
where there is a long trill on D for
the right hand, first with E-flat,
later with E-natural; meanwhile the
left hand is playing *turns in which
some of the auxiliary tones are
modified by accidentals.

Unless an accidental appears above
the trill-sign, the auxiliary (upper)
note of the trill is always that which
the key-signature would suggest.

Ties.   There are several ways
of indicating a trill with tied notes,
some much clearer than others.
In Example 5, A suggests a fresh
attack on each note--an effect which
is of course quite feasible.

Ex. 4

Ex. 5

B almost suggests that the note is to be trilled for one measure and then sustained, untrilled, for two more. C and D both exhibit greater clarity. E is the best of all; there is no possibility of mistaking the composer's intention.

Tremolo-Type Notation. Some modern composers notate trills in the form of *tremolos. Compare the ease with which the material in Example 6 is read with Examples 1, 3, and 4; these are the very same effects in a different style of notation.

Synonym (rare): terzetto.
See groups.

(2) The middle section of a composition in *ternary (ABA) form. Here the term is a survival from the period when middle sections were customarily written for three instruments; the term has continued in use since the custom disappeared.

If the trio appears twice, alternating with the main section in the pattern ABABA, the composition is said to have a *double trio or repeated trio. If there are two different trios, alternating with the

Ex. 6

An old sign for the trill was 𝆮 (rather than 𝆯).

Synonyms: shake, occasionally gruppetto.

(2) With *percussion instruments, a rather inexact name for the *roll (2).

● trio. (1) A composition for three voices or instruments.

main section in the pattern ABACA, the composition is said to have two trios.

In a typical military march the trio occurs at the end, the design being A (principal section), B (trio). This is hardly a correct application of the term.

Of course the term middle section is often substituted for trio.

(3) A composition for *organ of
a *contrapuntal character, in which
the right hand, left hand, and pedal
all play parts quite independent of
one another, each of the three having just a single line of notes. The
two hands usually play on two different manuals.   See also trio
sonata (2).
    Plural: trios.
    Pronunciation: trḗ-ō.

● † trionfale, † trionfante. Triumphant.

● trio sonata.   (1) During the
*Baroque Period, the term trio
sonata designated a composition
for two violins (or some other
two instruments) with *figured bass
(basso continuo).   The latter was
played by *harpsichord (or piano
or organ) and *cello (or *viola da
gamba).   It will be seen that the
"trio" sonata really requires four
performers, due to the fact that
the figured bass was regarded as
a single part requiring two players.
Because of the same curious reasoning, a work nominally for four
players ("Sonata a 4") required
five, a sonata "for two" ("Sonata
a 2") required three performers,
and so on.
    The name trio sonata might well
be considered a generic term that
includes the *sonata da camera and
the *sonata da chiesa, often called
chamber sonata and church sonata,
respectively.   As the distinction
between these two became less and
less marked, the term trio sonata
became increasingly convenient.
    A work of this type does not
follow the form of the sonata (1),
nor of the trio (1) familiar in
chamber-music groups; it is not
one of the *sonata-types described
under that heading, for it was in
vogue before their advent and before
the evolution of *sonata-allegro form.
    Synonyms: sonata a 3, sonata a
tre.
    (2) The term is also used to indi-
cate works for the organ of the
*sonata da chiesa type, written con-
stantly in three "voices"--for right
hand, left hand, and pedal. Bach's
works of this type are well-known

among organists.
    See trio (3).

● tripartite form.   Same as ternary form.

● triple (verb).   Explained under
double (2).

● triple forte.   The *dynamic term
*fff is usually spoken "triple forte"
although fortissimo is sometimes
substituted.

● triple meter.   *Meter with three
beats to the *measure.   This includes not only the *time-signatures
in which the upper figure is 3, but
also those in which it is 9, since
this figure subdivides into three
groups of 3.
    Compare duple meter.
    Synonym: ternary measure.

● triple piano.   The *dynamic term
*ppp is usually spoken "triple piano"
although pianississimo is sometimes
substituted.

● triplet.   Three notes of equal
length which are performed in the
time of two of the same kind.   The
triplet is doubtless the most frequent
of *irregular groupings.
    There is a singular void in the
development of notation in that no
note has ever been invented which
is worth one-third of a beat, nor
have any notes been devised which
are worth one-third of the next value
larger.   Hence when such a division
is wanted, it is customary to resort
to a makeshift by using three notes
of the type ordinarily worth one-half
of the value to be divided, and accompanying these with a figure 3.
Thus a quarter-note is divided into
thirds by triplet eighth-notes, a
half-note by triplet quarter-notes,
an eighth-note by triplet sixteenths,
etc.   The figure 3 is often enclosed
in a bracket or *slur.   (When the
latter is used it does not necessarily
denote *legato.)   When the bracket
is used in manuscript music, it is
often broken in the middle and the
figure 3 inserted at that point.   When
a great many triplets are used in
succession, it is necessary to write

In manuscript often thus:

the 3 over the first few groups only, after which it is automatically understood.

Sometimes a rest replaces one or two of the notes. At other times a value worth two-thirds is encountered, that is, two of the values are combined into a single tone. On still other occasions one note may be dotted, another correspondingly shortened.

Triplets which divide a total value of two beats or more are sometimes called delayed triplets.

The fact that *time-values are organized on the "multiple of 2" rule makes temporary application of the "multiple of 3" principle a rather awkward affair.

Irregular groupings of two are explained under duplet, of four under quadruplet, of five under quintuplet, of six under sextuplet. Many other *irregular groupings appear occasionally.

For double triplets see sextuplets. For the notation of tremolos in triplet rhythm, see tremolo.

● triple-tonguing. Explained under double-tonguing.

● triptych. In painting, three pictures (usually on panels) that form a single unit. This term is sometimes taken into music to indicate a work divided into three movements, i.e., a three-movement *suite (2).

Compare diptych.
Pronunciation: trĭp-tĭk.

● † tristamente, † triste. Sadly.

● tritone. A term applied to either the augmented fourth or the diminished fifth (see intervals). The name is derived from the fact that this interval contains three "tones" (2) or *whole-steps.

● † trombe. *Trumpets (Italian plural).

● trombone. A medium low-pitched brass instrument, the only representative of that group that is normally played with a slide. The slide is the counterpart of the *valves in the other brass instruments; its use is described in the entry slide (1).

The tone-color of the trombone is plain, strong, severe, noble, perhaps a bit sullen. It is probably the most powerful instrument in the orchestra; yet despite its tremendous volume in fortissimo, the pianissimo is equally fine--quiet, but solid and full.

Unlike the early horn and trumpet, the trombone has always been able to play all the tones in the chromatic scale, thanks to its slide mechanism.

The Tenor Trombone. Two types of trombone are regularly used today: the tenor and the bass. The word "trombone," unmodified, is always understood to designate the tenor trombone. (Range shown on next page.) The best players can go a trifle higher than shown here.

It will be noted that the tenor trombone is the only orchestral instrument with a gap in its range. The sounds below the gap are known as pedal tones.

Tenor trombone range

Theoretically there should be seven of these, going down to low E, but even the low G shown here is not recognized by all texts on *orchestration. The pedal tones are seldom used and difficult to produce. Their sound is thick and growling, yet weak. They should be regarded as tones supplementary to the usual range.

The tenor trombone is notated, in the United States, with the bass *clef, plus the tenor clef for the very high tones. In Europe the entire range is still widely written with the tenor clef, sometimes with the alto (especially in Russia). Hence the player must be prepared to read from any of three clefs.

Other Types of Trombone. The bass trombone is usually built in F, with the following range:

and its range is a whole-step higher than shown. It is always notated with the bass clef.

Many bass trombone players use an instrument that is essentially a tenor trombone, but which is capable of being shifted a perfect fourth lower by pressing a valve installed for the purpose. Known as the tenor-bass trombone, it has a range combining that of the tenor and bass instruments, plus the pedal tones of the former. However, the low B is unplayable on many tenor-bass trombones. (See range at bottom of page.)

The contrabass trombone is rarely used. It was designed by Wagner and can descend almost as low as the *tuba. Music for the contrabass trombone is usually played on the tuba, thus destroying the color ef-

Bass trombone range

Its pedal tones are not practicable. In England it is usually built in G,

fect intended by the composer.

The alto and soprano trombones are

Tenor-bass trombone range

practically obsolete. The upper
tones of the former, often encountered in older compositions,
create considerable difficulty for
present-day players, who must
perform them on the tenor trombone. The soprano trombone had
a range about equal to that of the
*trumpet.

Nearly all scores call for three
trombones--two tenors and one
bass (in earlier works, one alto,
one tenor, and one bass).

In addition to the normal slide
trombone, there is also a valve
trombone, on which the slide is
replaced by three *valves. Its
tone-quality is inferior to that of
the usual instrument. (The latter
is often called the slide trombone
to distinguish it from the valve
trombone.)

It is interesting to note that in
the Italian language, trombone
means "big trumpet." The trombone and the trumpet, however,
are entirely distinct instruments
today, as range, mechanism, and
tone-color readily demonstrate.

Italian: trombone (plural, trom-
boni). French: trombone. German:
Posaune (plural, Posaunen). Spanish: trombón (plural, trombones).

The player is called a trombonist.

Pronunciation: trŏm-bōn or
trŏm-bōn.

●† tronca, † tronco. Cut off
abruptly, truncated.

●† troppo. Too much. It is
invariably used with non, "not,"
which is often preceded by ma,
"but." Thus: lento non troppo, not
too slow (but still indicating a
definitely slow *tempo); allegro ma
non troppo, fast but not too fast.

Synonym: tanto.

● troubadours. Minstrels active in
southern France during the twelfth
and thirteenth centuries. They were
the counterparts of the *trouvères
in northern France and the *Minnesinger in Germany. They were
often members of the aristocracy.

The songs of the troubadours,
trouvères, and Minnesinger formed

the most important body of medieval
secular music. As far as is known,
this music did not make use of
*harmony--it consisted of unharmo-
nized melodies. (Although some
musicologists are dubious about this
matter, if harmony was employed,
its nature is unknown.)

The importance of troubadour,
trouvère, and Minnesinger music is:
(A) The songs often use instrumental
introductions, interludes, and con-
clusions--rare in those days--though
apparently the instrument did not play
simultaneously with the voice. (B)
The songs are often based on the
modern *major and minor modes,
although many--probably the majority--
are based on the church *modes. (It
must be remembered that all church
music of this era used the church
modes; see Gregorian chant.) (C)
These compositions have definite
form-schemes which foreshadow much
later developments in *form. (D)
The music is known to be metrical,
being based on poetic rather than
prose texts. (However, the exact
meter is often far from clear.) (E)
The texts are in the vernacular, not
Latin--an exceptional procedure for
those times.

Normally both the words and the
music were composed by the same
individual; the typical troubadour was
a poet as well as a composer and
singer.

Variant spelling: troubador.

Pronunciation: trōō-bǎ-dōr or
trōō-bǎ-dōor.

● trouvères. Minstrels active in
northern France in the twelfth and
thirteenth centuries. They are the
counterpart of the *troubadours in
southern France and the *Minnesinger
in Germany, and like these, were
usually members of the aristocracy.

King Richard the Lion-Hearted
(1157-1199) is the best-known trouvère,
though perhaps not the most important.
The fact that he was king of England
testifies to the spread of the trouvère
movement to that country.

See also troubadours.

Pronunciation (of both singular and
plural): trōō-vâr.

● trumpet. The highest pitched brass instrument in the orchestra and band, equipped with the usual three *valves. Trumpet music is written with the treble *clef.

The *tone-color is brilliant, keen, alert, incisive, and ringing. Perhaps due to its long association with military signals (see bugle calls) or perhaps because of some inherent quality in its timbre, it seems to attract attention--to have a "sit-up-and-take-notice" quality-- even when played softly.

Most present-day orchestral trumpet players use an instrument built in B-flat which is notated a *whole-step higher than the sounds desired. A few players use the trumpet in C, which sounds as written. Range:

more often it is replaced by the *cornet.

As with the *horn, it is usually customary to employ no *key-signature in writing for the trumpet in orchestral scores; each sharp or flat is written in as needed. Many modern composers are turning their backs on this custom.

A few modern orchestral works require the little trumpet in D, notated a whole-step lower than the sounds desired. A little trumpet in E-flat is also occasionally used. In Italian and French scores, respectively, the little trumpet is designated as tromba piccola and petite trompette.

There were formerly trumpets in a number of other keys. That in D had the same transposition as the little

Written (actual sounds of C trumpet) Sounding on the B-flat trumpet

Although most B-flat trumpets are equipped with a portion of tube which can be pulled out to put the instrument in A (the actual sounds being a *half-step lower than those of the B-flat instrument, and a minor third lower than the written notes), players have become accustomed to ignoring its existence; that is, music written for the trumpet in A is *transposed and played on the B-flat or C instrument, save for the very rare occasions when range precludes this. (See transposing instruments.)

Some modern composers write nominally for the C trumpet although the range they employ proves that the B-flat instrument must actually be used. The purpose of this bit of fiction is to cut down on the number of transposing instruments appearing in the *score.

In the *band the B-flat instrument is always used, though perhaps even

trumpet of the present day, though it was a larger instrument, with a brilliant tone, while those in E-flat, E, F, and G were notated a minor third, major third, perfect fourth, and perfect fifth, respectively, lower than the sounds desired; that is, these instruments transposed upward. (The *horns in the same keys, on the other hand, transposed downward.) The brilliant-toned trumpet in F went out of use during the early years of this century. These instruments had an *overtone series built from a lower fundamental than that of the modern trumpet; the overtones were the same as those of the natural trumpet described below.

Music for these instruments is now played on the B-flat or C trumpet, and the player must transpose the notes as he plays.

Special Types of Trumpet. An instrument called the slide trumpet has been built in which a *slide, similar to that of the *trombone, replaces the valves, but it has never gained much favor.

A long, straight trumpet without any coils in the tubing is sometimes seen in paintings. Often a banner is hung from the instrument, or perhaps someone must walk ahead of the player, supporting the trumpet's bell with his shoulders. This is a primitive form of the instrument, generally known as the herald trumpet. A modern version of the herald trumpet, equipped with valves, is called the Aïda trumpet, and was designed by the composer Verdi for use in his opera of that name.

The contralto trumpet, bass trumpet, cornet, post horn, flügelhorn, and bugle should be considered distinct instruments; see separate entries. Also see Bach trumpet.

The Old Natural Trumpet. Until the application of valves to the instrument shortly before the mid-nineteenth century, composers had only the natural trumpet with which to work. Its resources were quite limited--only a little greater than those of the bugle of today; it could play only the tones in the *harmonic series. Due to the fact that the player's hand could not be placed in the bell, its possibilities were fewer than those of the *natural horn.

Natural trumpets existed in all keys from high A-flat (sounding a minor sixth higher than written) down to low A-flat (sounding a major third lower than written).

The available written tones were part of those shown in the accompanying example. The lower-pitched instruments could not play the lowest of these notes, and in some cases not even the second, while the higher-pitched group could not ascend beyond written upper G, in some cases not beyond third space C. Both B-flats and the A were too low in pitch, though the lower B-flat was pressed into service when the composer felt he simply could not dispense with it. The note between upper E and G had a pitch about midway between F and F-sharp, and by "lipping" it up or down (i.e., forcing the pitch away from its natural intonation) it could be made to do duty, more or less, sometimes for F and sometimes for F-sharp.

The reason why composers wrote a high D rather than low D for the second trumpet in such passages as on the next page is simply because the low D did not exist. The experienced musician immediately recognizes this quotation as stemming from the pre-valve era.

The fact that composers of the *Classical and early *Romantic Period were able to get any use from the trumpet at all testifies to their resourcefulness. Even then, more than one passage can be found where rests were written when the composer clearly would have liked to use notes that the instrument simply could not produce.

The trumpet used in the late seventeenth and early eighteenth centuries differed somewhat from that of the late eighteenth and early nineteenth, just discussed, for it was designed so as to make the upper tones relatively easy of production, and players cultivated this part of the range. In the

list of open tones given earlier,
it will be observed that if the sound
midway between F and F-sharp is
accepted as F, and if the remaining tones are accepted as if they
were in tune, a complete diatonic
scale is possible at the upper end
of the range. It is here that the
trumpet parts of the *Baroque
Period tend to lie; Bach's Brandenburg Concerto No. 2 is probably
the best-known of many works which
could be cited as examples. In the
later eighteenth century (Classical
Period) orchestral musicians suddenly and unaccountably lost the ability
to play these high tones. To exemplify this, one need only examine
the original trumpet parts Handel
wrote for The Messiah (he wrote
them at actual pitch) and compare
them with the extremely simplified
trumpet parts Mozart used in his
*additional accompaniment for this
work.
    The Baroque trumpet is some-
times called the clarino, clarion,

or clarin trumpet.
    Synonym (poetic, obsolete): trump.
Italian: tromba (plural, trombe).
French: trompette. German: Trom-
pete (plural, Trompeten). Spanish:
trompeta.
    See also Bach trumpet, Zink.
    The player is generally called
simply trumpet player. (The word
trumpeter tends to suggest a herald,
and there seems to be no such word
as trumpetist.)

● TTBB. First tenor, second tenor,
first bass (i.e., baritone), and
second bass. Used in designating the
voice parts in choral music.

● tuba. The lowest-pitched brass instrument. It has three to five *valves.
The *tone-color is thick and heavy, even
a little coarse and "blurty," but wonderfully full, meaty, and solid.
    The type of tuba used in the orchestra
has a bell which points upward, not forward. It is sometimes built in F, more
usually in C; that is, its *open tones are
the *overtones of one or the other of
those pitches. Range:

Skillful players can go both a little higher and lower than shown. However, the tones at the extremes of the range cannot be entrusted to players of little experience.

The tuba used in the band is built so that the tubing surrounds the player and rests on his shoulder, thus making it relatively easy to carry while marching, and the bell points forward, not upward. This type of instrument is often called the Sousaphone (after John Philip Sousa, who designed it), or helicon. It is made in two sizes, the E-flat and the double B-flat (written BB♭), with these ranges:

and the *serpent were sometimes required in orchestral scores, but the superiority of the tuba quickly drove them both from the musical scene.

Tuba is the Latin word meaning "trumpet," but the modern tuba actually bears only the slightest relation to its namesake.

Synonyms: bass tuba, bass horn (undesirable), brass bass (undesirable), bass (undesirable).

Compare Wagner tuba, tenor tuba.

The Italian, French, German, and Spanish equivalents are all tuba. (In Italian, cimbasso is sometimes substituted.) The Italian plural is tube,

Since most bands use a mixture of these two types, octaves are written when the music descends below the low A of the E-flat type; the players of the E-flat tuba understand that they should play the upper note of the octave.

A small orchestral tuba in B-flat is sometimes used. Its range is identical with that of the *baritone (2), but it has a broader and more powerful tone. Most references to the "tenor tuba," when they do not indicate the *Wagner tenor tuba, probably mean this instrument.

No matter which type of instrument is used, music for the tuba is always notated at actual pitch; it is a non-transposing instrument. Only the bass clef is used.

The tuba is one of the most modern instruments in the orchestra. It came into use about 125 years ago, at the same time that the invention of valves was freeing the horn and trumpet from their hitherto primitive stage of development. The tuba has always had valves. Before its invention the *ophicleide

the German plural, Tuben. The Italian, French, German, and Spanish equivalents of the more complete name bass tuba are, respectively, tuba bassa, tuba basse, Basstuba (often printed Baβtuba), and tuba baja.

● tubing. The coiled portion of a *brass instrument that extends from the mouthpiece to the bell is known as the tubing. It is quite intricate in some instruments. The *valves are built to work as temporary extensions of the tubing.

The tubing is coiled to keep the instrument from becoming inconveniently large.

● tubular bells. A definite pitch *percussion instrument used for bell or chime effects. Long and comparatively narrow hollow steel tubes, graduated in size, hang in a large metal frame and are struck with a short wooden hammer. The *tone-color very closely approaches that of mellow-toned church bells.

Synonyms: chimes, tubular chimes.

Italian: campane. French: cloches. German: Glocken. Spanish: campanas.

● † tumultuoso.   Vehement, agitated
tumultuous.

● tune.   (1, noun).   *Melody.
Tune is somewhat more of a colloquialism than melody, and is often
used to suggest the more obvious,
more homespun, less elegant, and
less elaborate types of melody; or
perhaps it tends to suggest the
simpler type of melody which still
remains meaningful when accompanying harmonies are removed.   In
general, however, the two words
may be considered practically interchangeable.
(2, verb) To adjust the pitch of
an instrument to a given standard
or to a given tone; to "tune up."
See also tuning.

● tuning.   (1) Adjusting an instrument to the proper *pitch.
(2) With string instruments, the
group of tones to which the several
strings are adjusted is known as
the tuning, occasionally accord or
accordatura.   Thus the tuning of
the violin is:

Any departure from the normal
tuning pattern is called *scordatura.
(3) The foregoing meaning is also
applied to the pitches to which the
*timpani are adjusted.
(4) Any of the several types of
pitch-adjustment and pitch-inter-
relation, such as *just intonation,
*equal temperament, mean-tone
tuning, Pythagorean tuning, etc.
This forms an important part of
the subject known as *acoustics.
See also 440.

● tuning-bar.   A steel bar used
to sound the pitch with which an
*orchestra or *band tunes up.   A
tuning-bar gives but a single pitch.
The bar is set in a wooden frame,
and is sounded by tapping it with
a tiny mallet or by flipping a
wooden ball secured to one end of
the frame by a flexible steel tongue.
Electronic substitutes for tuning-
bars are manufactured.
Two types of tuning-bar are in
general use.   They are built to
sound as indicated in the diagram
at the bottom of the page.
When no tuning-bar is available,
the *oboe gives the pitch.
See also stroboscope, 440.

● tuning-fork.   An implement for
sounding pitch, either for singers
or for use in tuning instruments.   It
consists of a short rod which terminates in two prongs; it resembles
a letter U mounted on the end of a
short stem.   The prongs are struck
to set the tuning-fork vibrating.
It can emit but a single tone; if
several pitches are needed, a separate tuning-fork is required for each.
The tuning-fork is one of the few
sounding bodies that are completely
without overtones (see harmonic
series); it gives off only the pure
*fundamental (2).

● "Turkish music."   A fanciful term
used in late eighteenth- and early
nineteenth-century Europe to apply to
orchestral music making prominent
use of the *triangle, *cymbals, and
wind instruments, especially the *oboe
and *piccolo.   A well-known example
of "Turkish music" may be found in
the last movement of Beethoven's
Ninth Symphony, section in B-flat
major (introduction to the tenor solo).

For orchestra
(440 vibrations)

For band
(466.2 vibrations)

The connection with the real
music of Turkey is of course largely
imaginary.

See also Oriental music.

● turn. A type of *ornament
(written ∿) in which the notes
implied by the symbol "turn"
around the principal (written) note
in the order: note just above, written note, note just below, written
note. It is often executed a little
slower than other ornaments.

In spite of its rather happy name,
there is considerable confusion about
the execution of the turn--more so
than in the case of the *trill or
*mordent.

In the performer's mind turns
should be classified into two types:
(1) the turn after the note; (2) the
turn upon the note.

(1) The turn after the note is
executed at the end of the time-

value, just before going on to the
following note. The turn character
appears to the right of the note.
The mathematical proportion of the
value that is allotted to the turn will
be greater in fast tempos than in
slow. See Example 1.

If an *accidental appears above
the turn, it affects the upper note
that is implied in the turn symbol;
if one appears below it, it affects
the lower implied note. See Example
2.

When the note affected by the
turn is followed by repetition, performance is as shown in Example
3 on the next page.

In the case of a *dotted value, it
seems generally agreed that the turn
concludes with a comparatively long
holding of the written note. See
Example 4.

(2) The turn upon the note is
executed at the beginning of the time-

Ex. 1

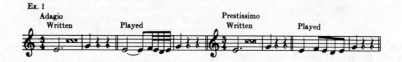

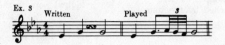

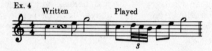

value, in which respect its behavior is reminiscent of that of the mordent. See Example 5. When the time-

little debate among musicologists relative to whether the turn should begin with the upper auxiliary note

value is short, the turn occupies the entire duration, and there is no held-out tone at the end. See Example 6. There is more than a

or with the printed note. Compare 5-A with 5-B, 6-A with 6-B. Briefly, the argument concerns whether this type of turn implies

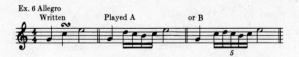

four notes or five. There is general agreement, however, that when the note affected by the turn is approached by repetition, the turn should begin on the upper auxiliary; (see Example 7) that when it is approached by the tone

still applies. See Examples 9 and 10.

The Inverted Turn. With the <u>inverted turn</u> or <u>back turn</u>, written ∿ or ⟨ the sounds "turn" around the principal note in the order: note

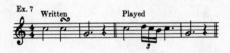

identical with the upper auxiliary, it is to commence on the given note (see Example 8).

just below, written note, note just above, written note. It can occur either on or after the note, and

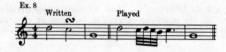

The foregoing rule about accidentals above or below the turn

there may be accidentals above or below, with effects as already de-

scribed. The uncertainty as to
the first tone, when it appears as
a turn upon the note, still remains.
See Example 11.

of an *octave plus a fifth.

● twelve tone system. A harmonic
and structural system of music,

Ex. 11

Of course no composer today
would dream of employing the symbol for the turn or inverted turn;
he would write out the effect either
in *grace-notes or in ordinary
notes.

The ambiguous term gruppetto
is sometimes substituted for turn.

●† tutte le corde. Release the
*soft pedal; used in connection with
music for the piano. (Literally
"all the strings. ")
    Synonym: tre corde.

●† tutti. (1) Literally, "all. "
Used to indicate the re-entrance
of the entire section among the
*string instruments of the *orches-
tra and the various voice-parts of
a *chorus following a passage intended for only one instrument or
voice; thus it cancels solo.
    (2) A passage in an orchestral
composition in which the entire
group plays; a passage for full
orchestra, without *rests for any
of the instruments. Obviously the
typical tutti is loud.
    (3) A passage in a *concerto,
played by the orchestra only, with
the solo instrument silent. The
number of instruments employed
may be far from a real "tutti" (2).
    (4) In the *concerto grosso, the
orchestra, in contradistinction to
the soloists or *concertino (1).
    (Related English word: total.)
    Variant forms: tutto, tutta, tutte.

● twelfths. *Intervals consisting

introduced by Arnold Schoenberg
(1874-1951) about 1923.
    In working according to this plan,
the composer takes the twelve tones
of the *chromatic scale and places
them in any sequence he believes
useful, the adopted order being known
as the tone-row. Notes may be used
only in the order in which they appear
in the tone-row, though the exact
"voice" in which each occurs, or the
exact octave, is left to the composer's
discretion, as is their length. A
tone may be repeated immediately,
but once it has been left, every one
of the remaining tones in the row
must be used before the first one
reappears. Two or more of the tones
may be sounded simultaneously--in
fact all twelve may be combined as
a chord if desired--but there must be
no actual departure from the adopted
order. However, the tone-row may
be reversed (that is, treated in retrograde motion), or *inverted, or the
retrograde form may be inverted,
always provided the entire series is
so treated. In addition, two or more
tone-rows may be used simultaneously.
    Although the avowed objective of the
plan is freedom from all previous
restrictions, many composers are opposed to the twelve tone system, main-
taining that it is far more restrictive
than any system from which the twelve
tone principle allegedly "frees" them.
However, in all fairness it must be
pointed out that the system's mecha-
ical aspects have been overstressed.
A number of modifications have become accepted, all of them in the

direction of less strictness. Exponents declare that once the composer has mastered the system, the tones naturally fall into proper place, even seem to want to occur in the adopted order.

Twelve tone music is nearly always *atonal, in fact the tone-row is normally arranged so as to produce atonality automatically. Nevertheless it is possible to slant a row toward both tonality and consonance, though this procedure is exceptional.

A sharp distinction must be made between free atonal music and twelve tone music. These terms are by no means synonymous.

Half of a tone-row is sometimes called a hexachord (2).

For many years the twelve tone system made little progress, but since the Second World War a number of composers have espoused it, including some from France, the United States, Italy and other countries; theretofore it had been associated purely with Germany and Austria. Nevertheless there is still a legion of musicians to whom the very name is anathema, and who regard it merely a desperate and effete innovation-for-innovation's-sake--an outgrowth of a decadent, bewildered, and confused European culture. They point out that much twelve tone music seems neurotic, morbid, frenetic, and overwrought--preoccupied with gruesome, abnormal, Freudian subjects that seem to exude from the innermost depths of the unconscious and subconscious. Although it is true that many of these compositions are decidedly *expressionistic, the twelve tone system nevertheless has no essential connection with any mood or any aesthetic ideal, being intrinsically a structural system, and nothing more.

Two symbols, H̅ and N̅ , have become associated with twelve tone music. The former is an abbreviation for Hauptstimme (German for "principal voice"), the latter for Nebenstimme ("subordinate voice"). These are used to distinguish prominent and semi-prominent strands of the texture from the background.

In addition to Schoenberg, other composers identified with the twelve tone system include Alban Berg (1885-1935), Anton von Webern (1883-1945)--both pupils of Schoenberg-- Ernest Křenek (1900-   ), the Frenchmen René Leibowitz (1913-   ) and Pierre Boulez (1925-   ), the Americans Wallingford Riegger (1885-1961) and Ben Weber (1916-   ), the Italian Luigi Dallapiccola (1904-   ) and others.

Both the Nazi and Soviet dictatorships condemned the twelve tone system, branding it as "degenerate" (or "cultural bolshevism") and "bourgeois decadence" respectively.

Synonyms: duodecuple (or dodecuple) scale, technique of composition with twelve tones, dodecaphony, serial technique.

● two against three. See cross rhythms (1).

● tympani. A variant spelling of timpani, frequent though questionable.

● typewriter (music). The need for a music typewriter was felt for many years before a reasonably-priced and workable one was finally placed on the market. The practical music typewriter appeared less than two decades ago.

One style of machine, which looks almost like an ordinary typewriter, prints notes of all values, including even *grace-notes and the diamond-shaped notes used for *harmonics, plus accents, accidentals, bar-lines, clefs, crossbeams, fermatas, key-signatures, leger-lines, metronome marks, rests, time-signatures, commonly-used dynamic terms such as f, mf, p, etc. Other symbols include the signs for rolled chords, for the pedal (in piano music), for up-bow and down-bow, and for the trill. It can even do an acceptable job of writing Gregorian neumes. Short ties and slurs are possible, though long ones must be added in pen and ink. In addition terms of tempo and expression and texts of vocal compositions must be added with an ordinary (preferably electric) typewriter.

Whereas the ordinary typewriter has a single shift-key, the music typewriter has many shift-positions (all made by hand) in order to place the notes and symbols properly on the staff. Their precise placement is aided by the presence of a tiny arrow placed above the point where the type strikes the paper.

The music typewriter can be used with the special transparent paper used in making *black-and-white reproductions, as well as with conventional opaque paper. It can also be used with mimeograph stencils. The paper may be already printed with staffs, or the staffs may be made with the machine.

Another style of music typewriter uses a horseshoe-shaped keyboard.

Music publishers sometimes print from a copy made on the music typewriter rather than from engraved plates.

The use of the music typewriter should not be confused with *autographing, which is done completely by hand and which is a special type of manuscript.

● Tyrolienne. A type of Austrian *folk-song or -dance in *Ländler tempo, with *yodel effects.
   Pronunciation: tĕ-rōl-yĕn.

U

● u. c. Abbreviation for una corda.

● † uguale. Equal, uniform, even.
   Variant forms: eguale, uguali.

● ukulele. A plucked string, fretted instrument strongly associated with Hawaii. Its four strings are tuned

or

The shape suggests that of a miniature guitar, except that the fingerboard is proportionately large. The instrument is made of wood, and

due to its extreme lightness may be carried about easily. It is popular among picnickers and campers, but it has no literature and cannot be taken seriously.

Since it is usually played by persons with little or no musical training, notation is effected by diagrams which are the present-day counterpart of *tablatures. Examples may be found in the sheet-music of almost any "popular" song.

The ukulele is by no means the same instrument as the *Hawaiian guitar.
   Variant spelling (questionable): ukelele.
   Synonym (colloquial): uke.
   Pronunciation: ū-kōō-lā́-lĕ or ōō-kōō-lā́-lā́.

● ultra-modern. A term once applied frequently to any music of the *Modern period that was characterized by extreme *dissonance and *cacophony. This adjective has tended to drop out of use during recent years.

● ultrasonic. Frequencies too high in pitch to be detected by the human ear are called ultrasonic or supersonic.
   See vibration.

● † umore. Humor.

● † un, † una, †uno. A, an; one.

● unaccompanied. Choral music sung without instrumental support is usually termed a cappella; consult that entry for further discussion. Except when speaking of choral music, only the word unaccompanied is usable. Thus one speaks of Bach's "compositions for unaccompanied violin," or one mentions that "Debussy's The Afternoon of a Faun opens with a short unaccompanied flute solo."

Unaccompanied does not always mean unharmonized. The Bach compositions just mentioned contain harmony, but are written for violin without piano, orchestra, or other instruments.

●† una corda. With the *soft pedal; used in connection with the piano. (Literally "one string.")

In manufacturing the piano it is customary to install three strings tuned in *unison for all the tones except the very lowest, where there is one, and the fairly low ones, where there are two. The soft pedal was originally contrived in such a way that when depressed it caused the entire set of hammers to move to the right or left so as to strike only one of the three strings, thus greatly reducing the volume. However, in all modern pianos the soft pedal actually causes the hammers to hit two of the strings, not one; hence *due corde (1) ("two strings") is a more appropriate term, though it is rarely used.

This term is canceled by tre corde (literally "three strings"), occasionally by tutte le corde ("all the strings").

Abbreviation: u. c.

● under dominant. A term occasionally substituted for subdominant.

● unessential tones. Same as nonharmonic tones.

● unison. (1) One or more tones sounding the same pitch as a given tone. The word literally means "one sound."

Unisons involving any time-value other than the whole-note are written with two stems, one turned up, the other down. Unison whole-notes

are usually written so as to overlap slightly, like the links in a chain, thus: ⟨⟩

In the passage at the bottom of the page there is a unison for soprano and alto in the first chord, while all four voices come into a unison at the end.

In orchestral compositions the direction unisoni (abbreviation unis.), or occasionally uniti, is used in the music for the string instruments to cancel the direction *divisi.

(2) The complete absence of *harmony.

(3) An unharmonized passage in which the tones are duplicated at several intervals of the octave is sometimes termed a unison passage, even though octaves are actually used.

It is absolutely incorrect to apply the term unison to a passage where all the voices or instruments have a single rhythm but are actually in harmony.

●† uniti. Variant form of unisoni; see unison.

● unprepared. Explained under prepared.

● untempered. Tuned according to

*just intonation rather than *equal temperament.

● up-beat. (1) A phrase is said to start with an up-beat if it does not begin on the first beat of the *measure.

Up-beats are most conspicious to the eye in cases where the opening of the composition appears as an incomplete portion of a measure.

and 1-1/2 beats, respectively. This rule is not always observed, however.

For all practical purposes the quotation at the bottom of the page begins with an up-beat; but since the first measure is metrically complete, nominally it does not, even though its only note is worth merely a quarter of a beat. Two complete measures are shown.

In this type of beginning, the incomplete initial measure-fragment is not counted as a measure; the expression "first measure" thus denotes the first complete measure. All of the foregoing examples contain only one measure, except the last, which contains two.

Strictly, the time consumed by the up-beat should be subtracted from the conclusion of the composition; the four examples shown at the beginning should terminate with measures containing 3-1/2, 3, 3,

Up-beats are of any length less than a complete measure. The majority consume less than half a measure; many consist of only one beat or less.

It will be apparent that an up-beat, in this meaning, is by no means the opposite of a *down-beat.

Synonyms: anacrusis, "pick-up notes" (colloquial).

(2) In conducting, an upward movement of the arm. The last *beat of a *measure is always indicated with an upward motion.

Permission granted by DURAND EDITION, Paris

● up-bow. In playing the bowed string instruments, an action wherein the player moves the *bow toward the frog (the end near where he grasps it). Perhaps it would be simpler merely to say that the player pushes the bow, or that his arm moves from right to left. (Compare down-bow.)

The symbol for up-bow is $\vee$

Up-bow is normally used in producing a *crescendo, because in its execution the player's hand constantly gets closer to the string, the resulting increase in weight automatically causing the tone to increase in volume. It is also generally employed to play *up-beats (hence the first note in a measure is rarely played up-bow). Any reasonable number of notes (depending on the length of the bow and the speed with which it is drawn) may be slurred together in an up-bow (or for that matter, in a down-bow); or a single tone may be played.

See also bow, bowing.

● Urtext (German). An edition which gives the notation exactly as the composer wrote it, shorn of all editors' markings and presumably of any misprints which have crept in and been copied from one former edition to another. Obsolete types of *clef, obsolete *ornaments, and other elements of oldstyle notation will often appear in an Urtext edition. *Slurs and *dynamic markings may be sparse, and of course *fingering is never indicated.

The literal meaning is "original text" or "source text."

Pronunciation: oor-text.

●† -uto. Italian past participle ending, equivalent to English endings -ed and -en.

Variant forms: -ato, -ito.

V

●† vagamente. Vaguely.

● valse (French). Same as waltz. Valse lente, slow waltz.

Pronunciation: väls.

● valve. On the modern *brass instruments, a device which when pressed opens an additional length of tubing, causing the pitch of the instrument to descend a given *interval below the pitch of the *open tones of the instrument. There are usually three valves. The part operated by the player's finger is usually tablet-shaped on the *horn, usually button-shaped on the remaining instruments. By using the valves singly and in combination, plus the open tones produced by varying lip-tensions, it is possible to play a *chromatic scale throughout the *range of the instrument. The valves of the horn are operated with the left hand, those of the remaining instruments with the right hand.

The valves lower the pitch by the following intervals:

Valve 1--whole-step (major second).

Valve 2--half-step (minor second).

Valve 3 (or 1 and 2 together)--minor third.

Valves 2 and 3--major third.

Valves 1 and 3--perfect fourth.

All three valves--diminished fifth (augmented fourth).

It should be observed that the valve principle is one of adding interval to interval.

The following instruments have valves: trumpet, horn, tuba, cornet, alto horn (mellophone), flügelhorn, baritone (2) (euphonium), and Wagner tuba.

On the trombone the slide has a function similar to that of the valves on the other instruments.

The bugle has neither valves nor slide.

Until the valves were invented, early in the nineteenth century, the trumpet possessed only the tones of the *harmonic series; the horn could play only these tones plus those a half-step below them, and even then the latter had an entirely different *tone-quality from the ordinary tones. (The remaining valve instruments had not yet been invented.) Hence the application of valves freed these instruments from a repertory of only a few tones, and

tremendously increased the effects
possible from the brass instruments.

The trumpet and horn without
valves are known today as the
*natural trumpet and *natural horn
(or hand horn). Gluck, Haydn,
Mozart, Beethoven, Weber, Schubert,
Mendelssohn, and even Berlioz had
nothing better at their disposal.

Synonyms: piston (1), cylinder.
See also fingering (3).

● vamp. (1) A short introductory
passage, usually two measures in
length, and normally enclosed in
*repeat signs. It is often marked
"until ready" and may be repeated
as often as desired. Vamps are
found in many "popular" (1) songs.

(2) A simple, *improvised accompaniment to a simple melody.

● variations. See theme and variations. For variations on a basso
ostinato (ground bass) of the cha-
conne-*passacaglia type, see ostinato.

Abbreviation: var.
Synonyms (obsolete): divisions,
double (3).

● † variazione, † variazioni. *Vari-
ation(s). Tema con variazioni,
*theme and variations.

● vc. Abbreviation for violoncello;
usage explained under bassi.

● † velato. Veiled.

● † veloce. Quickly. This word
is not used as a *tempo mark, but
rather to indicate a passage to be
performed faster than the material
which precedes and follows. The
relation to the English word velocity
is apparent.

● † Verismo. A type of Italian
opera of the late nineteenth and early
twentieth centuries in which the composer sought to achieve "realism."
The plots are often sordid, and both
the plot and the music quite melo-
dramatic. The Verismo movement
represents a reaction against the
almost complete lack of really dramatic passages in the earlier nineteenth century Italian operas by

Bellini, Donizetti, and others. Perhaps the most characteristic composers of the Verismo movement are
Leoncavallo and Mascagni; Giordano
and Puccini are less typical.

Verismo is the Italian word meaning "realism."

● verse. (1) A stanza; a part of a
vocal composition that corresponds
in length to one stanza of the poem.

(2) The first part of a *"popular"
(1) song; the part that precedes the
*refrain and is a balance to it.

● verse anthem. Explained under
anthem.

● † via sord. (abbreviation for via
sordino). Remove the *mute. This
is sometimes used in place of senza
sord(ino).

● † vibrante. Vibrating.

● vibraphone. A definite pitch *percussion instrument which looks like
a *marimba or a large *xylophone.
Resonators are hung vertically under
the metal bars, and with the aid of
an electric motor the tone may be
noticeably prolonged. Some instruments also have a *pedal to help sustain the tone. The player strikes the
vibraphone with two (or more) mallets
(or hammers, as they are also called),
one (sometimes two) in each hand.

The bars that produce the sounds
are laid out like a piano *keyboard,
and are graduated in size, the longest
bars giving the lowest pitches.

The vibraphone has a wavering, shimmering tone, but of a saccharine, sentimental character which quickly palls.
Few orchestral compositions use the
vibraphone; its chief habitat is the
*dance band and the living-room of the
less musical *amateurs.

Variant form: vibra-harp.

● vibration. A more or less rapid
and repeated trembling, oscillating, or
quivering.

All sound is the product of vibration.
Vibrations of steady speed produce a
musical tone; irregular (spasmodic) ones
produce noise. If the area over which
the sounding body vibrates is compara-

tively large, the sound is loud; if it is small, the sound is soft. If the rate of vibration is slow, the pitch is low (deep); if rapid, it is high. Pitch also depends on the length of the vibrating body; large instruments produce low pitches, small ones, high pitches.

The rate of speed with which vibration occurs (especially the number of times in one second) is called frequency; a single complete vibration-movement is called a cycle. Thus if the A above *middle C vibrates *440 times per second, we say that its frequency is 440, or that it produces 440 cycles per second.

The human ear is able to hear sounds that vibrate from about 16 or 20 to about 16,000 or 20,000 times per second; the exact limits vary somewhat from one individual to another. Frequencies too high in pitch to be detectable by the human ear are called supersonic or *ultrasonic.

The foregoing statement about the sound resulting from irregular vibration being termed noise should in no way be interpreted to mean that the effect is either disagreeable or loud. *Percussion instruments of indefinite pitch thus produce noise, according to the physicist's definition of that word.

See also acoustics (1), harmonic series, monochord.

● vibrato. (1) A slight wavering or oscillation in pitch which can be produced on a stringed instrument by rocking the finger very rapidly back and forth as it presses the string. It thus causes the sound to fluctuate up and down, but so slightly that only a single pitch is discerned by the listener. This effect can be obtained only on tones of fairly long duration. The fluctuations are best made downward from the true pitch.

The effect of the vibrato is one of heightened emotion; it seeks to imitate the vibrato of the voice (described below). A string tone without vibrato usually sounds artificial, nasal, dull, and unappealing, like the playing of a beginner. Of course if the vibrato is too slow or too wide (that is, if the fluctuation of pitch is so great that a wobble results), the effect becomes quite detestable.

There is no sign for its employment, as it is understood that the player will use it on every note possible. However if for some reason the composer does not want the vibrato, he can indicate this by senza vibrato or senza espressione.

A skillful double-bass player can obtain a vibrato with *pizzicato tones, due to their tendency to sound for a comparatively long time on this instrument.

(2) The vibrato of the voice is also a very slight and rapid oscillation in pitch, used to give emotional effects. When properly produced, it is completely under the singer's control. An involuntary vibrato is usually called a tremolo (6) and is a symptom of faulty voice production.

(3) Vibrato can be obtained on many of the wind instruments. That of the flute is familiar, although strictly speaking it is not a vibrato, since the pitch does not change; rather it is a rapid oscillation in volume, but the general effect is analogous to that of the true vibrato. When correctly executed it is heard only when the player wants to use it; if it occurs without his volition it is a symptom of faulty technique. The vibrato of the trombone is obtained by quickly moving the slide back and forth a little; its effect is thoroughly detestable--a vulgar player's concept of the "expressive."

(4) Same as lasciare vibrare.

(5) The name vibrato is sometimes given to the *tremulant of the *organ.

When used as a noun, the plural is spelled vibratos.

Pronunciation: vē-brä́-tō.

● Victrola. *Phonograph. A trade name; undesirable unless applied to the correct brand of instrument.

● vide. Indicates an optional *"cut,"

i. e. , a passage which if desired
may be omitted from a composition.
Usually the first syllable, vi--appears
at the point where the cut begins,
the second syllable, --de, at the
point where it ends. These locations are often emphasized by the
addition of the *symbol

● vielle. The family of bowed
string instruments which preceded
the *viols, which in turn were the
precursors of the modern violin,
viola, and cello. They were probably
at their height of popularity during
the thirteenth century.

The curved cut-in portions on the
sides of the modern instruments
were almost completely missing on
the vielles, which somewhat re-
sembled the guitar in appearance.
Their tone was harsh, nasal, reedy,
slightly like that of the modern cello.

Unfortunately the name vielle has
also been applied to the *hurdy-
gurdy.

Variant spelling: vièle.
Synonyms: guitar fiddle, medieval
fiddle.
Pronunciation: vē-ĕl.

● Viennese Period. A name often
applied to the *Classical Period,
or to that portion of it that was
dominated by composers living in
Vienna. Strictly speaking, the term
Viennese Period also includes the
early stages of the *Romantic era.

●† vigoroso. Vigorously.

● vihuela (Spanish). A once-popular
plucked (occasionally bowed) string
instrument. Although tuned like
the *lute and similar in size, it
had the shape of the guitar. Its
sound was more mellow than that
of the guitar.

Variant form: vihuela de mano.
Pronunciation: vē-wä́-lä (the v
somewhat like b).

● villanelle. A vocal composition
in the style of a rustic dance, usually
in quick 6-8 time. The word is
derived from villanella, which was
originally a type of sixteenth century
Italian folk-song, but sung in parts,

including--strange to say--parallel
fifths; it was apparently a parody on
the refined style of the *madrigal.

Variant form: villanesca (plural,
villanesche).

● viol. Name for a family of bowed
string instruments, the immediate
forerunners of the present *violin
family (i. e. , violin, viola, and
cello. The viols differed from their
modern counterparts in a number of
ways, the most conspicuous being:
(A) Many of them had five, six, or
even seven strings, rather than four.
(B) The fingerboard was equipped with
movable *frets (usually made of cloth
or gut, not metal), thus facilitating
the production of the correct pitches,
but eliminating any possibility of
*vibrato (1). Apparently some of
the best players dispensed with frets,
but in general the instruments were
intended for use by *amateurs. (C)
The *tone-color was a little less
brilliant, more sober, less "singing, "
and less pliant than that of the modern
instruments. The tone could not be
forced; thrilling *fortissimos and heavy
*sforzandos were not possible on the
viols. (D) Rather than jutting from
the fingerboard at a right angle, the
shoulders of the instrument sloped,
like those of the present-day *double-
bass. (Among the modern string instruments it most closely approaches
the viols; observe that it is sometimes called the bass viol.) (E) The
back of the instrument was often flat,
rather than rounded (again often true
of the double-bass.) (F) It is doubtful whether they could play as fast as
the present string instruments. (G)
The bow was different from that in use
with the modern instruments. (H) The
viols were usually not tucked under the
chin but were held in a downward position from the shoulder. Some were
held perpendicularly, resting on or
between the knees of the player. (I)
In general they were less versatile and
less "responsive" than the modern instruments.

During the sixteenth and seventeenth
centuries a considerable amount of
music was written for ensembles of
viols. The term consort of viols was
often applied to such a group, also

<u>chest of viols</u> since the instruments
were frequently hung in a chest when
not in use.

Perhaps the most familiar of
these instruments were the bass
*viola da gamba (or simply gamba)
and the *viola d'amore (or viole
d'amour).   The latter, however, was
a late development and hardly belongs to the viol era.

Interest in these instruments is
distinctly increasing.   Their revival
is an assurance that music written
for them may be heard in exactly
the tone-colors in which the composer conceived it.   The viols can
no longer be termed "obsolete."

Pronunciation: vĭ-ōl; some musicians use vē-ōl.

● viola.   A bowed string instrument
whose four strings are tuned

It looks almost exactly like a violin, except that it is larger--about
one-seventh again as large.

The lowest and moderately high
tones of the viola are the most distinctive in *tone-color, the former
being dark, husky, hollow, and a
bit rough, the latter tart and somewhat nasal--almost reedy.   The
sober-toned middle register is
rather easily confused with the same
sounds of the *violin.

The range of the viola is:

general, everything said in regard to
the *positions of the violin, if transposed down a perfect fifth, will apply
to the viola.

The viola is not sufficiently individualized in many people's minds;
it should never be thought of as an
"alto violin" but as something clearly
distinct among the family of string
instruments.   Its homely, unpreten-
tious tone-color often makes a welcome contrast to the feminine sound
of the violin and to the intense, cloying sound of the *cello.   The viola
excels in suggesting the antique, the
mysterious, and the roughly vigorous.

Like the violin, it is held under
the chin in playing.

Synonym (obsolete): <u>tenor</u> (2).

Italian: <u>viola</u> (plural, <u>viole</u>). French:
<u>alto</u>.   German: <u>Bratsche</u> (plural,
<u>Bratschen</u>), occasionally <u>Viola</u> (plural,
<u>Violen</u>).   Spanish: <u>viola</u>.

The player is called a <u>violist</u>.
Pronunciation: vē-ō-là (not vī-ō-là).

●† viola da braccio.   Name of a
family of *viols which were held to
the shoulder in playing.   The name
literally means "arm viol."   (Compare
<u>viola da gamba</u>.)   The viola da braccio
was the immediate ancestor of the
modern violin and viola.

(The frequently-seen spelling <u>viola
da braccia</u> is not correct.)

Plural: <u>viole da braccio</u>.

●† viola da gamba.   Name of a family
of bowed string instruments of the
*viol class which were held vertically,

The alto *clef is used for the
majority of the notes, the treble
clef for the high register

The technique is very similar to
that of the violin, and the portion
of the violin entry devoted to technique should be consulted.   In

resting on or between the knees, when
in playing position.   The name literally
means "leg viol."   (Compare <u>viola da
braccio</u>.)

To most musicians, "the" viola da
gamba means the bass member of this
family, which looks like a small *cello

(not like a *viola), and resembles the cello most closely in tone-color (though with just a touch of viola quality); however its sound is smaller, more delicate, more intimate, and less colorful than that of the cello, and its lowest tones lack the "growling" character of those of the more modern instrument.

The bass viola da gamba had six, sometimes seven strings. There were several ways of tuning the instrument of which the following was the most usual.

On the seven-string instrument the extra string was the lowest, tuned to the low A two octaves below the second string.

The bass viola da gamba was often used in place of the cello for supplying the bass line in music of the *Baroque period, in conjunction with a keyboard instrument which *realized the *figured bass symbols.

Although practically obsolete for many years, the viola da gamba is re-appearing at concerts of *Renaissance and *Baroque music.

Synonym: gamba.

Plural: viole da gamba.

The player is called a violist da gamba or (more frequently) simply gambist.

●† viola d'amore. A bowed string instrument of the *viol type, rarely seen today, but popular in the seventeenth and eighteenth centuries. Its *tone-color most closely resembles that of the present-day *viola but also somewhat suggests the *violin, though it is a bit more frail and more delicate than either.

The name curiously means "viol of love."

The viola d'amore has fourteen strings, although only seven are played on or are within reach of the bow. The other seven, called sympathetic strings (always made of metal), lie directly against the belly of the instrument, and are tuned in unison with the seven speaking strings. They vibrate with the speaking strings by *sympathetic vibration--that is, provided each is perfectly in tune with its counterpart. The sympathetic strings help to give the instrument its distinctive tone-color.

*Double-stops, especially thirds (see intervals) are very easy on the viola d'amore.

Unlike the other instruments of the viol class, it does not have a *fretted fingerboard.

The appearance of the instrument is striking because of the fourteen tuning-pegs in its long neck.

The viola d'amore is usually tuned thus:

however, tunings to the D minor triad and E-flat major triad are also sometimes employed.

Bach uses two viole d'amore as *obbligato instruments in two sections of his Passion According to St. John. Meyerbeer, Charpentier, and Puccini used the instrument in The Huguenots, Louise, and Madame Butterfly respectively. Composers of the Modern period who have shown an interest in the instrument include Hindemith and Loeffler.

Plural: viole d'amore.

French: viole d'amour (plural, violes d'amour). German: Liebesgeige (plural, Liebesgeigen) or Viola d'amore (plural, Violen d'amore).

The player is known as a violist d'amore or (better) simply as viola d'amore player.

● viole d'amour. French name for the *viola d'amore.

Pronunciation: vē-ōl dä-mōor.

● violin. A bowed string instrument with four strings tuned

The numbering is in downward order, that is, the E-string is called the "first string" and the G-string the "fourth."

In beauty of tone, dynamic range, color possibilities, and resources in general, the violin is without peer among all instruments, provided it is in the hands of a good performer.

The range of the instrument is

the least. Imitations of the Stradivarius label have been pasted into thousands of cheap instruments.

Technique. In playing the violin (as well as all the bowed string instruments) the bow is held in the right hand, while the strings are fingered with the left. The various pitches depend on the exact spot where the finger presses any string. The closer the finger gets to the

Higher sounds may be obtained by an accomplished player, and even by an ordinary player with the aid of *harmonics (1).

Music for the violin is always notated with the treble *clef.

In the orchestra there are two sections of violins, known as first violins and second violins; the instrument used is of course the same in both sections.

Valuable Violins. The peculiar shape of the violin is a requisite for giving the instrument its distinctive *tone-color. Both scientists and musicians agree that the instrument is perfect--that ever since the days of Stradivarius (1644-1737) and Guarnerius (1687-1745?) no further improvement has been (or will be) possible, although some changes in the fingerboard and bridge have been made, while the *bow has been drastically altered.

The finest violins are priced well into five figures, but there are very few of these valuable instruments in existence, and practically every one of them is already known and accounted for among dealers and musicians; hence the likelihood of discovering a genuine *"Strad" in some dusty attic is a forlorn one, to say

bridge, the higher the pitch becomes. The lowest pitch which any string can emit is that which is heard when no finger presses it--when it vibrates for its total length. (This is called an *open string.)

Performers recognize a number of *"positions" in which the left hand may be located so as to press the strings. In first position the hand is held out at the end of the fingerboard, near the tuning-pegs. In third and all higher positions it is held against the rounded portion of the body. Second position is located midway between first and third.

The tones that are possible in the first seven positions are indicated on the next page. The presence of numerous alternate methods of producing various pitches contributes much to facility in playing. It is important to mention that the index finger is numbered 1, the middle finger 2, etc. as shown in the entry fingering (2). The circumstance of a note being affected by a *sharp or *flat as a rule has no effect on which finger is used in playing; thus in first position the first (index) finger plays not only the low A on the fourth (G) string, but also A-flat and A-sharp. The left thumb is not used in playing either

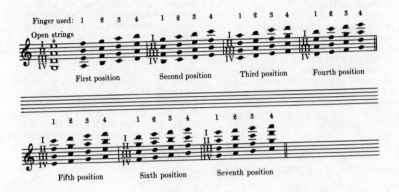

First position   Second position   Third position   Fourth position

Fifth position   Sixth position   Seventh position

the violin or the *viola, although it does find employment with the *cello and *double-bass.

Special effects possible on the violin (and other bowed string instruments) are described under the entries double-stop, pizzicato, col legno, harmonics (1), mute (1), portamento (1), glissando (1), bowing, fingering (2), sul ponticello, sul tasto, vibrato (1), tremolo (1, 2), open string, down bow, and up bow.

Synonym (colloquial): fiddle.

Italian: violino (plural violini). French: violon. German: Violine (plural Violinen) or Geige (plural Geigen). Spanish: violín (plural, violines).

The player is called a violinist. (The spelling violiniste, applied to a woman, is a bit affected.)

See also bow, fingerboard, E-string tuner.

Pronunciation: accent the last syllable, not the first.

● violin family. The *violin, *viola, and *cello are collectively termed the violin family in contradistinction to the older *viols and the still older vielles. (The *double-bass is sometimes also included, sometimes regarded as a viol.) The term is not a synonym for bowed *string instruments.

●† violino piccolo. A small-sized violin, now obsolete, which was occasionally used in the eighteenth century. It was tuned to G, C, F, and B-flat or to A, D, G, C, i. e., a minor third or perfect fourth higher than the standard violin.

Bach employs the instrument in Brandenburg Concerto No. 1.

● violin quartet. A careless and highly undesirable name sometimes used in place of *string quartet. The term is of course entirely correct when applied to an ensemble of four violins.

● violoncello. The full name of the *cello. Because the first part of the word is dropped, "purists" insist on writing the common term in the form: 'cello. It should be observed that the correct spelling of the full name is violoncello, not violincello.
Plural: violoncellos or violoncelli.
Pronunciation: vē-ō-lŏn-chĕl-ō.

●† violone. An old name for the *double-bass. This is also the name of an organ stop; see organ.

● virginal. See spinet.

● virginalist. (1) A composer of music for the *virginal.
(2) One who plays the virginal.

● virtuosity. The distinguishing qualities and skills that go to make up a *virtuoso.

● virtuoso. A brilliant performer; by extension often applied also to *conductors and others.
Plural: virtuosos or virtuosi.
Pronunciation: vŭr-tyoo-ō-sō.

●† vivace. Fast, lively. It is usually understood to be a trifle quicker than allegro, though not so fast as presto. (Related English word: vivacious.)
See tempo marks.
Synonym: vivo.

●† vivacissimo. Very lively, as lively as possible. (Superlative of *vivace.) (Rare.)

●† vivo. Same as vivace.

● vlc. Abbreviation for violoncello; usage explained under bassi.

● vocalise. (1) A vocal exercise, without words, used to develop the singer's technique to develop good

*tone-quality. It may be with or without piano accompaniment. It differs from the *solfeggio (2) in that the latter is chiefly for the purpose of developing skill in *sight-reading, and is used by all musicians, instrumentalists as well as singers. The vocalises by Giuseppe Concone (1810-1861) are widely known.
(2) A *song that has no words. It is by no means a synonym for *song without words. There are famous examples by Ravel and Rachmaninoff; A. L. Hettich edited a group by many well-known composers that was published in thirteen volumes by Leduc in Paris (1907-1931). A few songs and *arias have vocalise passages in them, for instance Grieg's Solvejg's Song, Villa-Lobos's Bachianas Brasileiras No. 5, and the castanet dance in Act II of Bizet's Carmen.
See also etude.
This word should not be confused with the verb vocalize.
Pronunciation: vō-căl-ēz.

● vocalist. A singer. Many musicians object to this word.

● vocalize. To exercise the voice, usually without words.
This verb should not be confused with the noun *vocalise.

●† voce. Voice.
Plural: voci.

● "voice." The term voice is regularly used to denote any moving or stationary line or row of notes in the fabric of music, regardless of whether it is sung or played by an instrument. The word part has the same significance when not used as a synonym for section or division. (See music diagram on next page.)
In the following bit

the upper voice consists of: quarter-rest, G, A (tied), C, B, the lower of:

5 voices in homophonic style.   3 voices in contrapuntal style.

C, F, D.   There is no voice consisting of C, G, A, F, D, C, B;
such notion is rife among some
pianists, but represents highly unmusical thinking.

Synonym: line (2).

● voice change.   See change of
voice.

● voice-leading.   The exact manner
of distributing the tones ("voices")
that appear in a succession of
*chords

In Example 1, which is for piano,
the voice-leading throughout parts

A and B is good--smooth and natural--
but in part C it is clumsy.

Both parts of Example 2, on next
page, (which is for any four voices
or instruments) contain the very
same sounds, but in part A the voice-
leading is good, while in B it is
awkward in the extreme; indeed there
is no horizontal feeling of continuous
melodic lines.

● voices.   The names for the different types of singing voice, from
highest to lowest are:

Ex. 1

Good (A&B) and bad (C) voice-leading

Ex. 2

Good (A) and bad (B) voice-leading

soprano	)	
mezzo-soprano	)	female
alto	)	voices
tenor	)	
baritone	)	male
bass	)	voices

See also alto-tenor, castrato, coloratura, countertenor, falsetto, Russian bass, treble (3), high voice, medium voice, low voice.

● † volante. Swift (literally "flying"). See also rapidamente, veloce.

● † volta. Time (in the sense of occasion or turn). Thus, when *first and second endings occur, the first may be marked prima volta, the second, seconda volta.

Plural: volte.

● volume. Comparative loudness or softness; intensity of tone.

See also dynamic marks, crescendo, diminuendo, sforzando.

● voluntary. An organ piece used to precede a church service. Most voluntaries are slow and quiet. The term has also been used as a synonym for *postlude.

Synonym: prelude (6).

● V. S.   Turn the page quickly.

Used at the bottom of pages in the *parts of instrumental works (especially band, orchestra, and chamber-music compositions) where there is very little time provided to turn. V. S. is the abbreviation for the Italian volti subito.

●† vuota.   Same as G. P.

W

● Wagner tubas.   Three different brass instruments designed by the composer Richard Wagner (1813-1883) with the intention of obtaining a new and unfamiliar *tone-color of solemn character.   They are a hybrid of the *horn and the ordinary *tuba, having the funnel-shaped (conical) mouthpiece of the former.

There are three types: tenor, bass, and contrabass.

The Wagner tenor and bass tubas have the following range:

used by Bruckner in Symphony No. 7, and may be considered "standard" notation--if there is such a thing. Observe that the tenor is here notated a major ninth above actual pitch, the bass an octave and a perfect fifth (perfect twelfth) above.

The failure of these instruments to win general acceptance is due to the fact that their tone-color is not sufficiently distinctive.   It is about halfway between that of the horn and that of the *trombone, but resembles both of them a little too much; it perhaps approximates the *baritone (2) (euphonium) most of all.   Hence we can say in all fairness that Wagner failed in his intention of introducing a new tone-color into the symphonic palette.

Synonym: Bayreuth tubas.

● waltz.   A dance in 3-4 time.   Most are of moderate speed, but slow and fast waltzes are also common.

As a rule the first beat is strongly accented, the other two appearing in

Wagner tenor tuba   Wagner bass tuba

They are intended to be used by horn-players.

The Wagner contrabass tuba is very similar to the ordinary tuba, and is entrusted to a player of that instrument.   It is written at actual pitch with the bass *clef, as a non-*transposing instrument.

Wagner wrote for five of these tubas--two tenor, two bass, and one contrabass.   He was not consistent in his method of notating the "tenor" and "bass" tubas; he sometimes wrote the former a whole-step above actual pitch, sometimes a major sixth above, while the latter was sometimes written a perfect fifth above actual pitch, other times a major ninth above.

The notations given above are those

the accompaniment as *after-beats (2).

Originating in Germany around 1800, the waltz quickly attained universal popularity, though it has become especially identified with the city of Vienna, Austria.   It has probably remained in public favor longer than any other dance in history, being still in use.

Many compositions bearing this title are of course idealizations of the style, for example Chopin's waltzes for piano.

Variant form (French): valse.

● waltz time.   3-4 time (undesirable).

● wedge. A melodic or harmonic passage in which the intervals gradually get wider; the written notes almost take the shape of a wedge. A *fugue by Bach is nicknamed the "Wedge" Fugue because of this characteristic. See also Chopin's Prelude in B-flat (op. 28, no. 21) and Mazurka in B-flat minor (op. 24, no. 4).

● "white" tone. An expression used to denote a *tone-quality of marked purity, coolness, and simplicity, somewhat ethereal in character. It by no means indicates a dull or inexpressive effect, though it strongly suggests the opposite of a rich, dark, throaty, "thrilling," or emotional color, since very little *vibrato (2, 3) is assumed.

Wedges

● wedge staccato. Staccatissimo; the extreme form of staccato that is indicated by small wedges ▲ or ▼ over or under the notes.
See staccato (2).
Synonym: dash staccato.

● whistle flute. See recorder.

● white notes. Half-notes and whole-notes (including the *dotted forms), so called because the note-head is not filled in, being therefore white. Consequently black notes are those in which the note-heads are filled in or black, namely quarter-notes and all shorter values.
In England, where the word note is often carelessly used instead of key (of the keyboard instruments), the terms white notes and black notes are often used where white keys and black keys are meant. This usage is of course undesirable.

● whole measure rest. A name sometimes used for the whole rest. See rests.

● whole-note. See time-values.

● whole-step. On the piano, a whole step may be found by starting with any key and moving to the second key distant-- that is, by skipping one key--either up or down, black or white.
A whole-step is equal to two *half-steps.
The major second (also diminished third) are both whole-step intervals. (See intervals.)
Synonyms: whole-tone, tone, step.
Compare half-step.

● whole-tone. Same as whole-step.

● whole-tone scale. A scale of six different tones, all of them a *whole-step (or whole-tone) apart. Only two whole-

The whole-tone scales

tone scales, with their *enharmonic equivalents, are possible.

Debussy was the first person to make extensive use of the whole-tone scale. Its limitations may be deduced from the fact that he nearly exhausted its possibilities.

Synonym: six tone scale (rare).

● wind instruments. The generic name applied to all instruments in which the sound is produced by air (usually the player's breath). They are normally divided into two types, *woodwind and *brass, but there are in addition a number which cannot be classified under either heading, such as the *organ, *harmonium, *accordion, *concertina, *harmonica, and (if it can be considered a "musical instrument") the *pitch-pipe.

Synonym: the winds.

● wind machine. An instrument used to imitate the rushing sound of the wind. It somewhat resembles a barrel lying on its side, with a cloth stretched around the circumference. When the player rotates the barrel by means of a handle, the cloth scrapes against the frame which holds the entire instrument. Probably the best-known composition which uses the wind machine is Richard Strauss's Don Quixote.

Though commonly classed as a percussion instrument, the wind machine does not strictly answer to the definition; and it is by no means a wind instrument. Perhaps it belongs more in the realm of sound-effects than of musical instruments.

German: Windmaschine.

● wind quintet. Flute, oboe, clarinet, horn, and bassoon. In some examples the flute alternates with piccolo or the oboe with English horn in certain parts of the composition.

The terminology woodwind quintet, although probably more frequent, is less accurate, since one of the instruments (namely the horn) is actually a brass instrument.

See also chamber music, chamber music groups.

● wireless. Radio (chiefly British).

● wire recorder. A device similar to a *tape recorder, the difference being that the recording is made on, and reproduced from, a thin steel wire rather than cellophane tape.

See also phonograph.

● wolf tones. On the bowed *string instruments there are always certain tones whose sound is not completely satisfactory; these are called wolf tones or wolf notes. There are some that are found on every instrument, others that are peculiar to the individual instrument.

● wood-block. An indefinite pitch percussion instrument. It is a hollow oblong with a slot on both of the long sides. When struck with a wooden stick its sound is very dry, hollow, high-pitched, and "clacking," seeming to say "talk." It is fastened to a chair or stand by a holder, since holding it by the hand spoils its tone.

Synonym: Chinese block.

French: bloc de bois.

● woodwind instruments. Instruments which work on the principle of the pipe with finger-holes, usually supplemented with *keys (3), are classified as woodwind instruments. Use of this generic term is purely a convention, for the instruments so classified are not necessarily made of wood nowadays, although originally that substance found exclusive employment in their manufacture.

Members of this group include the *flute, *piccolo, *oboe, *English horn, *clarinet, *bassoon, and *saxophone, and instruments related to these, plus the *recorders, *sarrusophones, *fife, *ocarina, *flageolet, penny whistle, *bagpipe, the various *simple melody instruments, etc.

The strict inaccuracy of the word woodwind is pointed up by mentioning that the saxophone is always made of metal (namely brass; yet it is seldom classified as a *brass instrument), that the flute is nowadays almost invariably metal (usually silver), that the piccolo as a rule is in a like category, while ebonite, plastic, and metal clarinets are quite common even though in the minority. Metal oboes and English horns, however, have found little acceptance, though the cheaper types are often made of plastic.

Some woodwind instruments employ a single *reed (1) (clarinet, saxophone), some a double reed (oboe, English horn, bassoon, sarrusophone), while others have no reed. The latter class divides into those instruments which have a hole mouthpiece (flute, piccolo) and those with a fipple mouthpiece (recorder).

The woodwind instruments are somewhat more individualized than the strings or brasses. *Solo passages for them are as a rule extremely effective. *Trills are well in their *idiom, being especially delightful on the flute. On the other hand, the fortissimo of the woodwinds is not very powerful; forcefulness is foreign to their character; even the piccolo stands out by reason of shrillness rather than of true volume. In addition, none but the clarinet can deliver a true *ppp. Hence it may be said that their *dynamic range is narrower than that of any of the other families of instruments.

Mechanism. All woodwind instruments have six principal fingerholes, supplemented in some cases by a *thumb-hole on the underside. These six are opened and closed by three fingers of each hand, the right hand being farther from the mouthpiece than the left. The thumb-hole, if there is one, is operated by the left hand. As the six holes are uncovered one by one the instrument's pitch rises scalewise, until only one hole remains covered (by the first finger of the left hand). A tone obtained with nothing but the thumb-hole follows on the instruments so equipped, after which still another sound is obtained by blowing into the unfingered instrument. The higher registers are obtained by *overblowing. Chromatic *inflections of the principal tones are sometimes obtained by "cross-fingerings" ("forked fingerings"), meaning the use of several holes that are not in direct order (e.g., 1-3, or 1-2-3-4-6, or 1-2-4), sometimes by using the keys with which the instrument is supplied; the latter are operated by various fingers, especially the little fingers.

With the exception of the bagpipe, no woodwind instrument can play two or more tones simultaneously.
Abbreviation: w. w.
Synonym (undesirable): the reeds.
See also orchestra.

● woodwind quartet. Usually flute, oboe, clarinet, and bassoon. See chamber music, chamber music groups.

● woodwind quintet. A rather inaccurate name for the wind quintet.

● woodwind trio. Usually flute, clarinet, and bassoon; occasionally flute, oboe, and bassoon. See chamber music, chamber music groups.

● word painting. Same as textpainting.

● work. A musical composition, especially one of an extended and ambitious character.
See also opus.

● working-out. See development; see also sonata-allegro form.

● work-song. A *folk song used while working, so as to make the task seem less drudging and--when sung by a group--to obtain synchronized effort in moving heavy objects. Water Boy and The Song of the Volga Boatmen are well-known specimens; the former originated among American Negroes, the latter among Russian barge-haulers.
Nearly all sailor *chanteys are work-songs.

● w. w. Abbreviation for *woodwinds.

X

● **xylophone.** A definite pitch *percussion instrument consisting of a graduated series of wooden bars arranged horizontally like the keys of the piano, played with two small hard hammers called *mallets. The bars are larger than those of the *glockenspiel (which are made of steel), and the tone is clattery and much harder and drier; in fact the xylophone's sustaining power is practically nil.

The instrument is best in character for music of fantastic, homorous or grotesque nature.

Range:

pecially Switzerland and the Tyrolese part of Austria. When done artistically it can be quite charming.

Variant spellings: yodle, jodel.

Z

● **zarzuela** (Spanish). A type of Spanish *opéra comique or *operetta, humorous or serious.

Pronunciation: săr-swā-lă or thăr-thwā-lă.

●† zingano, †zingaresca, † zingaro. Gypsy style.

Pronunciation: zingano and zingaro

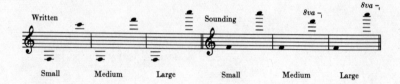

Written Sounding 8va ⌐ 8va ⌐

Small Medium Large Small Medium Large

Music for the xylophone is usually written an octave lower than the actual sounds, though occasionally at actual pitch. It will be observed that the instrument is not well standardized.

The spelling zylophone is incorrect.

Italian: silofono or xilofono. French: xylophone. German: Xylophon. Spanish: xilófono.

Pronunciation: zī-lŏ-fŏn, occasionally zĭl-ŏ-fŏn.

● **xylorimba.** An instrument which is a hybrid of *xylophone and *marimba.

Y

● **yodel.** A special style of singing, using many wide *leaps, with occasional *falsetto effects on the high tones. It is popularly cultivated in mountainous regions, es-

are accented on the first syllable.

● **Zink** (German). A practically obsolete instrument of the brass family. Actually it was never made of brass but of wood covered with leather, occasionally of ivory. The appearance of the Zink was very simple: an octagonal tube, sometimes straight, sometimes slightly bent, with fingerholes like a woodwind instrument but with the more or less cup-shaped mouthpiece of a brass instrument. It was made in three sizes. The definition "wooden trumpet" is an oversimplification.

The *tone-color might be described as the most delicate trumpet tone imaginable, with just a touch of the female voice quality. The Zink was so soft that it could balance the violin in a 1:1 proportion.

The name cornett is sometimes substituted, though the instrument is in no way similar to the modern *cornet.

The Italian name cornetto (plural, cornetti) and French cornet-à-bouquin (plural, cornets-à-bouquin. are also often taken into English.

Variant forms: Zinke (plural, Zinken), zinck.

Plural: Zinke (German) or zinks (English).

Pronunciation: tsiŋk.

● zither. A plucked string instrument popular in Germany and Austria. Two sets of strings are stretched over a shallow, hollow resonator-box of a roughly rectangular shape. The melody is played with a *plectrum on one set, which is underlaid by *frets; the accompaniment is played directly with the fingers on the other set, which is arranged in groups so as to form a limited number of *chords.

● Zopfmusik, Zopfstil (German). A derisive name applied during the middle eighteenth century to music which was stiff, formal, and correctly written, but devoid of real meaning, beauty, or originality. The literal meanings are "wig music" and "wig style. " *Kapellmeistermusik is a later name for music in a different style but equally wanting in merit.

Pronunciation: tsöpf-moo-zek, tsöpf-shtel.

● zu 2. Same as a 2.